Lecture Notes in Computer Sci

Commenced Publication in 1973
Founding and Former Series Editors:
Gerhard Goos, Juris Hartmanis, and Jan van Leeuwen

Yi Mu   Willy Susilo   Jennifer Seberry (Eds.)

Information Security and Privacy

13th Australasian Conference, ACISP 2008
Wollongong, Australia, July 7-9, 2008
Proceedings

 Springer

Volume Editors

Yi Mu
Willy Susilo
Jennifer Seberry
University of Wollongong
School of Computer Science and Software Engineering
Northfields Avenue, Wollongong, NSW 2522, Australia
E-mail: {ymu, wsusilo, jennie}@uow.edu.au

Library of Congress Control Number: Applied for

CR Subject Classification (1998): E.3, K.6.5, D.4.6, C.2, E.4, F.2.1, K.4.1

LNCS Sublibrary: SL 4 – Security and Cryptology

ISSN   0302-9743
ISBN-10   3-540-69971-6 Springer Berlin Heidelberg New York
ISBN-13   978-3-540-69971-2 Springer Berlin Heidelberg New York

Springer is a part of Springer Science+Business Media

springer.com

© Springer-Verlag Berlin Heidelberg 2008
Printed in Germany

Typesetting: Camera-ready by author, data conversion by Scientific Publishing Services, Chennai, India
Printed on acid-free paper   SPIN: 12322725   06/3180   5 4 3 2 1 0

Preface

The 13th Australasian Conference on Information Security and Privacy (ACISP 2008) was held at Wollongong, Australia, during July 7–9, 2008. The conference was sponsored by the Centre for Computer and Information Security of the University of Wollongong and the Research Network for a Secure Australia. The submission and review process was run using the iChair software, written by Thomas Baigneres and Matthieu Finiasz from EPFL, LASEC, Switzerland. We would like to thank them for letting us use their iChair software.

The conference received 111 submissions, out of which the Program Committee selected 33 papers for presentation at the conference after a rigorous review process. These papers are included in the proceedings. The accepted papers cover a range of topics in information security, including authentication, key management, public key cryptography, privacy, anonymity, secure communication, ciphers, network security, elliptic curves, hash functions, and database security. The conference proceedings contain revised versions of the selected papers. Since some of them were not checked again for correctness before publication, the authors bear full responsibility for the contents of their papers. We would like to thank the authors of all papers for submitting their papers to the conference.

In addition to the contributed papers, the program comprised three invited talks. The invited speakers were Xavier Boyen (Voltage, USA), Josef Pieprzyk (Macquarie University, Australia) and Nigel Phair (Australian High Tech Crime Centre). We would like to express our thanks to them.

As in previous years, we selected a "best student paper." To be eligible for selection, a paper has to be co-authored by a postgraduate student, whose contribution was more than 50%. The winner was Risto Hakala from Helsinki University of Technology, Finland, for the paper "Linear Distinguishing Attack on Shannon."

We would like to thank all the people who helped with the conference program and organization. In particular, we heartily thank the Program Committee and the sub-reviewers listed on the following pages for the effort and time they contributed to the review process. We would like to express our thanks to Springer for continuing to support the ACISP conference and for help in the conference proceedings production.

Finally, we would like to thank the Organizing Committee for their excellent contribution to the conference.

July 2008

Yi Mu
Willy Susilo
Jennifer Seberry

The 13th Australasian Conference on Information Security and Privacy (ACISP 2008)

Sponsored by

Centre for Computer and Information Security Research,
University of Wollongong, Australia

Research Network for a Secure Australia

General Chair

Jennifer Seberry   University of Wollongong, Australia

Program Chairs

Yi Mu   University of Wollongong, Australia
Willy Susilo   University of Wollongong, Australia

Program Committee

Michel Abdalla	ENS, Paris, France
Masayuki Abe	NTT, Japan
Colin Boyd	QUT, Australia
Feng Bao	Institute for Infocomm Research, Singapore
Lynn Batten	Deakin University, Australia
Ed Dawson	QUT, Australia
Dieter Gollmann	TU Hamburg, Germany
Aggelos Kiayias	University of Connecticut, USA
Kwangjo Kim	ICU, Korea
Tanja Lange	Technische Universiteit Eindhoven, Netherlands
Pil Joong Lee	Pohang University of Science and Technology, Korea
Benoit Libert	UCL, Belgium
Javier Lopez	University of Malaga, Spain
Chris Mitchell	RHUL, UK
Yi Mu	University of Wollongong, Australia
Kaisa Nyberg	Helsinki University of Technology, Finland
Eiji Okamoto	Tsukuba University, Japan
Josef Pieprzyk	Macquarie University, Australia
Sihan Qing	Chinese Academy of Scineces, China
Jean-Jacques Quisquater	UCL, Belgium
Rei Safavi-Naini	University of Calgary, Canada

Jennifer Seberry   University of Wollongong, Australia
Ron Steinfeld   Macquarie University, Australia
Douglas Stinson   University of Waterloo, Canada
Willy Susilo   University of Wollongong, Australia
C. Pandu Rangan   Indian Institute of Technology, India
Tsuyoshi Takagi   Future University, Japan
Vijay Varadharajan   Macquarie University, Australia
Sabrina De Capitani
   di Vimercati   University of Milan, Italy
Huaxiong Wang   Nanyang Technological University, Singapore
Duncan S. Wong   City University of Hong Kong, China
Fangguo Zhang   Sun Yat-Sen University, China
Ning Zhang   University of Manchester, UK
Jianying Zhou   Institute for Infocomm Research, Singapore

Organizing Committee

Man Ho Au   University of Wollongong, Australia
Xinyi Huang   University of Wollongong, Australia
Shams Ud Din Qazi   University of Wollongong, Australia
Mohammad Reza
   Reyhanitabar   University of Wollongong, Australia
Siamak Fayyaz
   Shahandashti   University of Wollongong, Australia
Pairat Thorncharoensri   University of Wollongong, Australia
Wei Wu   University of Wollongong, Australia
Tsz Hon Yuen   University of Wollongong, Australia

External Referees

Isaac Agudo   Reza Rezaeian Farashahi   Jang Seong Kim
Hadi Ahmadi   Gerardo Fernandez   Sun Young Kim
K. Ambika   Carmen Fernandez-Gago   Young Mok Kim
Venkat Balakrishnan   Georg Fuchsbauer   Varad Kirthane
Daniel J. Bernstein   Juan Garay   Hoi Le
Jean-Luc Beuchat   Praveen Gauravaram   Fagen Li
Peter Birkner   Juan Gonzalez   Jin Li
Billy Bob Brumley   Satoshi Hada   Vo Duc Liem
S. Chandrasekar   Risto Hakala   Peter van Liesdonk
Joo Yeon Cho   Kevin Henry   Joseph K. Liu
Sherman Chow   Matt Henricksen   Jiqiang Lu
Baudoin Collard   Jason Hinek   Mark Manulis
Alex Dent   Michael Hitchens   Krystian Matusiewicz
Dang Nguyen Duc   Qiong Huang   Antonina Mitrofanova
Sung Wook Eom   Shaoquan Jiang   Cameron McDonald

Pablo Najera
Miyako Ohkubo
Vijayakrishnan P.
Arpita Patra
Angela Piper
M.R. Reyhanitabar
Rodrigo Roman
Chun Ruan
Palash Sarkar
Sharmila Devi Selvi
Jae Woo Seo
Siamak Shahandashti
Hongsong Shi
Jong Hoon Shin
Masaaki Shirase

Igor Shparlinski
Leonie Simpson
Michal Sramka
Jerry Sui
Christophe Tartary
Ronghua Tian
Tomas Toft
Mohammed A.A. Tuhin
Udaya Kiran Tupakula
Damien Vergnaud
José Villegas
Jose L. Vivas
Yongge Wang
Baodian Wei
Kenneth Wong

Jiang Wu
Guomin Yang
Yanjiang Yang
Yeon-Hyeong Yang
Chan Yeob Yeun
Hongbo Yu
Yu Yu
Janson Zhang
Chang-An Zhao
Weiliang Zhao
Hong-Sheng Zhou
Huafei Zhu
Sebastien Zimmer

Table of Contents

New Paradigms for Password Security
(Abstract from the Keynote Lecture)

Xavier Boyen

Voltage Inc.
xb@boyen.org

For the past several decades, cryptographers have consistently provided us with stronger and more capable primitives and protocols that have found many applications in security systems in everyday life. One of the central tenets of cryptographic design is that, whereas a system's architecture ought to be public and open to scrutiny, the keys on which it depends — long, utterly random, unique strings of bits — will be perfectly preserved by their owner, and yet nominally inaccessible to foes.

This security model works well as long as one can assume the existence of an inviolate physical location or storage device to safeguard those keys. In client-server scenarios, the mere delocalization of the participants suffices to enforce a proper boundary without any further precaution. In proxy settings, one may call upon tamper-resistant "smart cards" or hardware security modules to isolate the keys adequately from most opponents.

Things break down when one can no longer assume that an external storage medium is available to store our keys, and that the only option is to remember them in our minds. The problem, of course, is a cognitive one: the human brain is ill-equipped to remember hundreds of random bits of key material for the long term without making any mistake. The secrets that our brain is keen on remembering are those of our own choosing, which for all their apparent randomness and unpredictability can certainly not be mistaken nor substituted for genuine cryptographic keys. Security from purely mental secrets requires us at the very least to compromise on key strength — this encompassing both entropy and uniformity —, and seek the best reachable security goals based not on ideal random keys but on passwords of sub-cryptographic quality.

Plain textual passwords and passphrases — or passtexts — have always been the preferred form of human-memorable secret, having the benefit of medium-independence which entails compatibility with virtually any conceivable user interface. More exotic mental secrets — passthoughts — may be based on visual or auditory recognition feedback; these are equivalent to passwords from a cryptographic perspective, but the specialized input device they require make them less practical. Secrets whose expression requires body action such as speech or ocular movements — passmoves — may also be envisaged given the proper measurement apparatus, with the proviso that the unavoidable measurement noise in the analog signal will have to be dealt with; we merely mention that errors on the post-quantization signal may be correctable using information-theoretic

Y. Mu, W. Susilo, and J. Seberry (Eds.): ACISP 2008, LNCS 5107, pp. 1–5, 2008.

cryptographic tools such as reusable and robust fuzzy extractors [1] without leaking excessive information about the secret.

Regardless of the shape of form of the secret, an important criterion for its human memorability is that its selection ultimately be left to the human who will have to remember it. Machines can assist in password selection, but should not make the final choice. Because of this, it is a near-certainty that the selected secret will not make a suitable cryptographic key, nor will it be possible to derive one from it due to lack of entropy. Hence, specialized primitives and protocols are needed that explicitly take into account those inherent weaknesses, and seek to achieve the best possible security under the circumstances.

Although password-based primitives and protocols have seen much foundational and implementational improvements during the last two decades, the general philosophy of password-based offline key derivation and online key exchange has remained essentially what it was in the early nineties. In particular, most current approaches could better handle real-life situations where the password are too weak for comfort and/or are recycled in part or in whole with multiple correspondents.

The purpose of this exposé is thus to investigate what security may indeed be attained from human-memorable passwords as they do appear in the real world — including the weak, skewed, reused, and exceedingly long-lived ones. The focus on literal passwords stems from tradition as much as convenience.

1   Halting Puzzles against Brute-Force Dictionary Attacks

Stand-alone — offline — uses of passwords mainly concern encryption and key derivation applications. The prime example of this is to encrypt the contents of a laptop so that only its owner can access it. Local authentication and device unlocking uses may also be treated as special cases of password-based encryption. At the core of these systems, one finds a Key Derivation Function (KDF), which is a one-way function taking a password and an optional public random salt as input, and producing a reproducible cryptographic key as output.

Offline applications such as those are tremendously difficult to secure with a weak password. The threat model here is the loss of the entire ciphertext and all associated hardware to an attacker, where only the password is being held back. Therefore, any opponent that simply tries out all passwords in an offline dictionary attack, e.g., by decreasing order of estimated likelihood, will eventually stumble upon the correct one and defeat the encryption. The only defense against such a threat is to slow down or deter the attacker by making the attack more daunting. There are two ways to do this: by picking an unlikely password to increase the expected number of guesses, and by making each guess more computationally demanding to verify.

One cannot really play with the choice of the password, short of encouraging the user to select a long and difficult one. Making the guesses hard to verify is possible, but only within limits, as it has the side effect of increasing the user's legitimate access latency in the same proportion. For this reason, KDFs are purposely designed to be somewhat expensive to compute, although most implementations tend to be very conservative with the amount of slowdown that they are willing to impose on users, and rarely offer the user any choice in the matter. The general trend is thus to use KDFs with a slowdown parameter (often a hash iteration count) that is conservatively chosen, once-and-for-all frozen, and publicly disclosed as part of the KDF specification or implementation. Some implementations support in-the-field adjustment of the KDF iteration count, but this parameter always remains public.

This has been and continues to be the ubiquitous way in which passwords are used for local key derivation.

In departure from this trend, we recently introduced, in [2], the notion of Halting Key Derivation Function (HKDF), which explicitly lets the user choose an arbitrary hardness parameter and emded it into the function in a cryptographically secret manner. The idea is to encourage the user to make the HKDF as difficult to compute as the delay he or she is willing to tolerate when seeking access, but conceal the value of the chosen parameter from public view, and yet not require the user to remember such value — or for that matter anything else besides the password.

The crucial element is that, on the correct password, the HKDF function will recognize that it succeeded and halt spontaneously after the intended computational delay; but on an incorrect password, it will continue indefinitely without giving any feedback until manually interrupted. The only indication given to the user that a password is incorrect will be the feeling that the key derivation is taking longer than it should. The user will naturally react by restarting the process and reentering the password more carefully without much of an afterthought. To an attacker, by contrast, this lack of feedback will disproportionately complicate the task of mounting an offline dictionary attack. The result is an effective security increase equivalent to two extra bits of password entropy, at virtually no cost to the legitimate user.

The total security gains provided by HKDFs are actually much greater than just two bits, due to a combination of factors. The main contributing factor is that legacy KDFs tend to be parameterized very conservatively, leading to exceedingly short delays ($\sim 1ms$) that are only getting shorter as computers are getting faster, raising obsolescence concerns. By contrast, HKDFs are programmed on a case-by-case basis, on the basis on actual clock times, with respect to the current state of computer performance. Even at the shorter end of HKDF delays, the "blink of an eye" ($\sim 1s$), the jump is already substantial. It will also keep up with technological progress, since a one-second-delay in ten years will entail a greater number of elementary operations than a one-second-delay today.

As discussed in [2], one should expect a fairly wide spectrum of user-selected HKDF delays to find their way in practical applications. Short delays are appropriate for frequently used day-to-day passwords with a short lifespan. Longer delays ($\sim 1m$ and more) could be used to protect longer-term backup passwords, which may need to be simpler to be memorable over a longer period. The longest delays ($\sim 1h$ and more) would be reserved for last-resort disaster-recovery passwords, never intended to be used, but that must be available and remembered if ever needed even after many years have lapsed. Such passwords would likely have to be very weak to be reliably memorable over such long periods, hence the need for very long HKDF delays to protect them from offline dictionary attacks. Notably, the same plaintext can be encrypted under different passwords using different delays, seamlessly, without any loss of security or usability.

2   Hardened Protocols toward Universal Authentication

Client-server — online — uses of passwords are primarily geared toward authentication and key exchange. Both parties share a password, and, based on it, try to establish a private authenticated channel over open communication lines. The constraints on online passwords are fairly different than in the offline case, as here the threat model typically assumes that the communicating parties are honest and try to prevent eavesdropping and impersonation by a malicious outsider (who controls the underlying communication channel).

Password-Authenticated Key Exchange (PAKE) is indeed a success story of cryptographic protocol design, as there are many protocols realizing the theoretically optimal security requirement that the only feasible attack vector be for the adversary to make online password guesses, one guess at a time, interactively with one of the honest parties — who can then detect the attack and throttle it by refusing to communicate. Secure online authentication can thus be achieved using much weaker passwords than would be thinkable in the offline case.

Extensions of this notion have been proposed for the case where the server itself may be viewed as an adversary, as is the case when the client wishes to reuse the same password with other servers. Asymmetric Password-Authenticated Key Exchange (APAKE) deals with this notion by requiring the password only on the client side; the server is instead entrusted with a derived secret that can be used to reach mutual authentication with the client, but not impersonate it to another server (in particular the password should be hard to recover from this). APAKE protocols are for this reason more desirable in practical use than PAKE, in light of the well-documented propensity of internet users to recycle the same few passwords with a broad variety of vendors. However, one concern remains, which is how difficult it actually is for a malicious server to recover its clients' passwords from the derived secrets.

The concern is that the derived secrets are typically obtained by applying a one-way function to the password w, be it a cryptographic hash $h(w)$ or a modular exponentiation g^w. Functions like these are usually very fast to compute, so even though they technically may be one way, they might be relatively easy to invert in an offline dictionary attack if the user password is not already very strong. Also, without an extra randomization step, a server can attack all of its clients' passwords for the price of one.

Since typical real-life users are probably going to continue reusing the same weak passwords with many servers regardless of whether this is considered a safe thing to do, it would be desirable to design a protocol that attempts to preserve the best possible form of online and offline password security, even under reuse of a weak password across multiple servers. The benefit from such a notion would be safe universal authentication on the internet using a single easy-to-remember password (for each user).

Ideally, one wish to combine the security of (A)PAKE against outside online attackers, with the security of HKDF against malicious servers.

To this end, we are proposing, in [3], the notion of Hardened Password-Authenticated Key Exchange (HPAKE), which offers the same security guarantees as regular asymmetric key exchange, and in addition allows the user to specify an arbitrarily expensive one-way function for the mapping from client password to server secret. This makes even relatively weak passwords infeasible to recover by malicious servers, thereby enabling the reuse of such passwords with arbitrarily many servers.

There are several difficulties with this. The first is a systemic one: the burden of computing this arbitrarily expensive one-way function should befall the client who selected it, and not the server which for scalability reasons must be able to process many authentication requests with minimal effort. The second issue is a technical one: since the one-way function is to be computed on the client side, the client must obtain the necessary inputs from the server prior to authentication. This creates a paradox, since the success of such transfer must depend on the client's knowledge of the password, but at the same time not reveal to either the client or the server whether the transfer succeeded, lets it open an avenue for offline attack to outsiders or to the server itself.

We shall discuss how these difficulties can be overcome, and how the HPAKE framework from [3] provides a plausible and practical answer to the problem of universal authentication from a single password.

3   Conclusion

The password schemes presented in this lecture have in common that they seek to provide the best possible security for the password holder, in the offline and online setting, regardless of how careless his or her use of that password may be. The only safety rule that should never be failed, is that one's password should only be seized on a local trusted HKDF or HPAKE entry device, and not shared with other less secure protocols.

References

1. Boyen, X.: Robust and Reusable Fuzzy Extractors. In: Tuyls, P., Skoric, B., Kevenaar, T. (eds.) Security with Noisy Data, Springer, Heidelberg (2007)
2. Boyen, X.: Halting Password Puzzles – hard-to-break encryption from human-memorable keys. In: SECURITY 2007, The USENIX Association (2007)
3. Boyen, X.: Hardened Password Authentication – mulitple mobile credentials from a single short secret. Manuscript (2008)

Enforcing User-Aware Browser-Based Mutual Authentication with Strong Locked Same Origin Policy

Sebastian Gajek[1], Mark Manulis[2], and Jörg Schwenk[1]

[1] Horst Görtz Institute for IT-Security, Germany
{sebastian.gajek,joerg.schwenk}@nds.rub.de
[2] UCL Crypto Group, Belgium
mark.manulis@uclouvain.be

Abstract. The standard solution for mutual authentication between human users and servers on the Internet is to execute a TLS handshake during which the server authenticates using a X.509 certificate followed by the authentication of the user either with own password or with some cookie stored within the user's browser. Unfortunately, this solution is susceptible to various impersonation attacks such as phishing as it turned out that average Internet users are unable to authenticate servers based on their certificates.

In this paper we address security of *cookie-based authentication* using the concept of *strong locked same origin* policy for browsers introduced at ACM CCS'07. We describe a cookie-based authentication protocol between human users and TLS-servers and prove its security in the extended formal model for *browser-based mutual authentication* introduced at ACM ASIACCS'08. It turns out that the small modification of the browser's security policy is sufficient to achieve provably secure cookie-based authentication protocols considering the ability of users to recognize images, video, or audio sequences.

1 Introduction

Motivation. The browser plays an indispensable function as the user's interface to access the rich world of Web based services. In order to serve the purpose of an universal client, commodity browsers have been augmented with numerous functionalities. Examples include extensions of the HTTP header to control caching and transport cookies, or the HTML markup language to enable high-level scripting and supply technologies like AJAX, AFLEX or SOAP. By contrast, much effort to amend the browser security model and provide new cryptographic services has not been spent. Since its adaption more than a decade ago [9], the Transport Layer Security (TLS) framework is the main pillar of browser-based protocols to provide Web applications with a security layer. After the protocol framework has been peer-reviewed without finding any significant vulnerabilities [25,28,24,22], it has been believed to be the holy grail for secure Web authentication. However, recent studies point out that average-skilled Internet users understand neither TLS nor its indication in commodity Web browsers at all [7,27]. Users tend to ignore browser's warnings and prefer to identify Web sites on the basis of non-technical indicators (e.g., brands, logos). This attitude provides a wrong sense of security. An adversary may fake the site and disclose the user's password (*phishing attack*).

Y. Mu, W. Susilo, and J. Seberry (Eds.): ACISP 2008, LNCS 5107, pp. 6–20, 2008.

The advent of these large-scale fraud attacks has led to several modifications in the visualization of TLS. Unfortunately, it seems to turn out that the changes do not meet their high expectations either [16].

Another line of research addresses the design of authentication protocols that provide user-awareness. The essence of user-aware protocols is to relax the assumptions on user behavior and provide secure authentication ceremonies. Recently, the authors of this paper introduced a formal security model for *browser-based mutual authentication (BBMA)* between a human user and a server where the browser is modeled as the mediator of the communication [11]. Their model is an extension of the classical model for authentication from [3] towards consideration of user-awareness within the authentication protocols on the Internet whereby user-awareness is modeled via *human perceptible authenticators (HPAs)* that are implied by natural human senses, such as recognition of images, videos, and audio sequences. In addition to the model, [11] describes a protocol called BBMA (based on the ideas of the PassMark Security Inc.'s Two-Factor-Two-Way Authentication™) which can be implemented within the standard specification of the TLS protocol. In this protocol the human user authenticates via password which is typed into an HTML form only after the successful recognition of some expected HPA sent by the server. In order to protect the disclosure of this HPA to unauthorized parties, the TLS protocol uses client (possibly self-generated) certificates which serve as a cryptographic identifier for the corresponding HPA.

Extending this line of research, we deal with user-awareness in cookie-based authentication protocols. These protocols execute a server-only authenticated TLS session, where the user authenticates through a cookie that has been previously set by the server and stored in the browser's cache. The technique has the advantage that the user is refrained from retyping the password. Further, the cookie is taken from a sufficiently large random distribution. There is no need to expect a "security defect" due to the use of low-entropy passwords. These simplifications of user authentication have led to a wide adaption of cookie-based authenticated channels in browser-based protocols and there are many protocols that build upon this technique. Unfortunately, they have been shown to be vulnerable when taking the mature browser security model into account (see Section 2 for more discussions). The crux is that the browser decides on the basis of the server's domain name whether to reveal the cookie. The adversary is feasible to steal the cookie by spoofing the domain names and there are many attacks allowing the adversary to do this (e.g., dynamic pharming, DNS rebinding [15,19].

To protect against the growing presence of these threats, Karlof et. al. propose refinements of the browser's cookie disclosure policy [23,19]. Their contribution is to augment the browser with some additional functionality which uses cryptographic mechanisms to enforce restricted access policies without relying on DNS, dubbed the *strong locked same origin (SLSO)* policy. In the context of cookie-based authentication protocols over the TLS channel, the SLSO policy enforcement means that the browser sends a cookie to the server only after the server proves the possession of a valid cryptographic identifier, namely the server's public key, i.e., the server proves the knowledge of the corresponding private key.

Contributions. In this paper we extend our model from [11] towards cookie-based authentication and consideration of the browser's SLSO policy. Using the extended model we analyze the security of the cookie-based version of BBMA from [11] re-engineered under the SLSO policy. We call the modified protocol BBMA-SLSO. It turns out that some minor changes of the browser security model to enforce the SLSO policy—which is a straightforward task compared to the large scale deployment of, say secure domain name resolution protocols (DNSSEC)—turns an insecure protocol into a provably secure one. Additionally, the use of SLSO policy allows us to eliminate the costly use of the client certificates, which are essential to prove security of BBMA. In addition to the formal security definition, BBMA-SLSO has additional advantages over previous cookie-based authentication protocols. The advantages include

1. BBMA-SLSO is *user-aware*. In order to authenticate, the server sends a HPA, which serves (i) as non-cryptographic identifier for the user to validate the server as in the physical world where identities are provided in an easily recognizable fashion and (ii) as fail-stop mechanism to hamper that she discloses private information on a faked site.
2. BBMA-SLSO fits into the standard TLS specification. There is no need to modify commodity server implementations. In fact, the necessary augmentations address browsers, more precisely their functionality to access cookies corresponding to the SLSO policy. See [23] for more details.

We remark that the enforcement of the SLSO policy is ineligible to protect against *cross-site scripting (XSS)* attacks. The anatomy of XSS attacks is to exploit weaknesses of application servers and inject malicious scripts into the communication that enable the adversary to invoke certain browser functionalities. Since the scripts are in the same security context the SLSO policy does not help. Consequently, the adversary would have access to the user's password typing, the cookie and HPA in BBMA-SLSO. Though we treat XSS attacks as (server) corruptions in our model and exclude them in the analysis, a work-around to make BBMA-SLSO resistant against the attacks is to completely isolate the named security critical information and prevent that they are accessible from the surrounding (potentially malicious) scripts. Such a feature is already available in the Internet Explorer for cookies [21]. The approach has to be extended for passwords and HPAs. Since the implementation of the SLSO policy requires the modification of the current browser's security policy anyway, we suggest to enrich this policy with the private/public tagging of elements. An element such as a password field tagged with a private value shall signal the browser that any script is prevented from access, regardless of its security context. See [10] for more details.

Organization. The remainder sections are structured as follows. We review related work in Section 2. In Section 3, we describe the formal security model for cookie-based BBMA protocols under consideration of the SLSO policy. In Section 4 we specify a concrete protocol called BBMA-SLSO using the high level description of the TLS handshake in the key transport mode and prove that it is user-aware and satisfies the defined authentication requirement. Finally, we conclude the paper in Section 5.

2 Related Work

So far, few browser-based protocols have been subject to rigorous security analysis: Kormann and Rubin [20] show that Microsoft's .NET passport, a Web-based realization of the Kerberos protocol for single sign on, is susceptible to attacks where the adversary steals the ticket granting ticket cookie. Soghoian and Jakobsson [30] investigate the SiteKey-protocol that displays a previously negotiated image in addition to password forms in order to signal that the user is connected to the benign server. The authors show the feasibility of stealing the shared secret that is stored in a cookie. Groß [12] analyzes SAML, an alternative single sign on protocol, and shows that the protocol is vulnerable to adaptive attacks where the adversary intercepts the authentication token contained in the URL. By contrast, BBMA-SLSO has formal security arguments and is provably secure in a model which takes into account the adversarial control over the network and attacks against the classical browser's security policies that reveal weak identifiers, such as cookies.

Groß et al. prove in [14] the security of WS-Federation passive Requestor Profile— a browser-based protocol for federated identity management. The proof is carried out in the browser model [13] that builds on the Reactive Simulatability framework due to Pfitzmann and Waidner [26]. The model abstracts away the TLS-protected channel through an ideal functionality that captures the same cryptographic task and presupposes ideal users who are able to identify servers based on certificates. There exists no soundness proof that TLS is simulatable and realizes such functionality, especially with respect to the relaxed user behavior assumptions. BBMA-SLSO takes explicitly into account the TLS protocol and is shown to be provably secure in the Random Oracle Model when instantiated with the widely deployed key transport cipher suite in server authentication mode.

3 Modeling BBMA with SLSO Policy

In this section we extend our security model for browser-based mutual authentication from [11] towards consideration of cookie-based authentication and the SLSO policy implemented within the browser.

3.1 Protocol Participants and Communication Model

User, Browser, Server, and their Long-Lived Keys. Let $\mathcal{U}$ denote a *human user* for whom we do not make any further assumptions except for the ability to use some naturally born senses. We assume that $\mathcal{U}$ remembers some (high-entropy) *human perceptible authenticator (HPA)* $w \in \mathcal{W}$ (e.g. an image or a video/audio sequence from some space $\mathcal{W}$) as its long-lived key $LL_{\mathcal{U}}$.

To the contrary, the *browser* $\mathcal{B}$ and the *server* $\mathcal{S}$ are modeled as PPT machines. $LL_{\mathcal{B}}$ is the browser's high-entropy long-lived key which contains $(\mathcal{S}, pk_{\mathcal{S}}, cky)$ where $\mathcal{S}$ is the identity (domain name) of the server, $pk_{\mathcal{S}} \in \{0,1\}^{p_1(\kappa)}$ its certified public key, and $cky \in \{0,1\}^{p_2(\kappa)}$ is the cookie set by $\mathcal{S}$ during the establishment of the security association with the *client* which is denoted by $\mathcal{C} = (\mathcal{U}, \mathcal{B})$. (Here and in the following,

$p_i : \mathbb{N} \to \mathbb{N}, i \in [1,5]$ is a polynomial and $\kappa \in \mathbb{N}$ the security parameter.) We assume that cky contains secret information (e.g. obfuscated or cryptographically processed password) which allows $\mathcal{S}$ to uniquely identify $\mathcal{U}$. Similarly, $LL_\mathcal{S}$ contains the private key $sk_\mathcal{S} \in \{0,1\}^{p_1(\kappa)}$ and the tuple $(\mathcal{U}, cky, w)$.

Additionally, by $\mathcal{C}$ we denote the traditional *client* given by a pair $(\mathcal{U}, \mathcal{B})$.

Communication between $\mathcal{B}$ and $\mathcal{U}$ via render-Function. Let $\lambda_i : \mathbb{N} \to \mathbb{N}, i \in [1,2]$ be two polynomials. $\mathcal{B}$ communicates to $\mathcal{U}$ through the *visualization function* render : $\mathcal{M} \times \Psi \to \mathcal{M}^*$ where $\mathcal{M} \in \{0,1\}^{\lambda_1(\kappa)}$ is the message space (space of all HTML messages) and $\Psi \in \{0,1\}^{\lambda_2(\kappa)}$ is the browser's configuration for message processing that may be altered by querying the browser's DOM model.

Modeling User-Awareness via recognize-Function. Similar to [11] we assume that $\mathcal{U}$ can recognize some previously remembered high-entropy HPA $w \in \mathcal{W}$. The recognition is handled by a boolean *human perception function* recognize : $\mathcal{M}^* \times \mathcal{W} \to \{0,1\}$ which on input a visualized message $m^* \in \mathcal{M}^*$ and w the recognize function outputs 1 if $\mathcal{U}$ recognizes w among the content of m^*; otherwise the output is 0. In this paper we assume that if m^* contains w (denoted as $m^*|w$) then recognize outputs 1, i.e., the ability of $\mathcal{U}$ to recognize w is *perfect*. On the other hand, we do *not* assume that w is the only HPA for which recognize outputs 1, i.e., we do *not* idealize $\mathcal{U}$ as there can be some set $\mathcal{W}^* \subseteq \mathcal{W}$ which contains HPAs that are *perfectly human-indistinguishable* from $\mathcal{U}$ according to the following definition.

Definition 1 (Perfect Human-Indistinguishability of HPAs). *Let $w \in \mathcal{W}$ be some given HPA. For any $m^* \in \mathcal{M}^*$ and any $w^* \in \mathcal{W}$, we say that w and w^* are perfectly human-indistinguishable, if for any human user $\mathcal{U}$*

$$\left| \Pr[\mathcal{U}.\mathtt{recognize}(m^*|w, w) = 1] - \Pr[\mathcal{U}.\mathtt{recognize}(m^*|w^*, w) = 1] \right| = 0$$

where the probabilities are computed over the choices of w^*. By $\mathcal{W}^* \subseteq \mathcal{W}$ we denote the set of all perfectly human-indistinguishable HPAs for some given $w \in \mathcal{W}$ assuming that $w \in \mathcal{W}^*$.

The main idea in designing user-aware security protocols based on HPAs is to opt for authenticators for which $\mathcal{W}^*$ is *sufficiently small* for most of the users. In this case the probability that an adversary chooses or guesses some HPA that cannot be distinguished from w by $\mathcal{U}$ can be kept low. The ideal case would be if $\mathcal{W}^*$ would consist only of w. We call w a *good* HPA if the size of the set $\mathcal{W}^*$ is sufficiently small such that the term $|\mathcal{W}^*|/|\mathcal{W}|$ which is used in our proof beside other cryptography-related terms to compute the overall probability of a successful attack is negligible.

For our protocol we assume that the HPA used by $\mathcal{U}$ in the execution of our protocol is good. We stress that in order to identify good HPAs extensive user experiments, possibly under consideration of specific statistic models, have to be conducted. We conjecture that good HPAs may be found from the personal digital images, audio and even video sequences.

Protocol Sessions and Participating Instances. Participation of $\mathcal{C} = (\mathcal{U}, \mathcal{B})$ and $\mathcal{S}$ in distinct executions of Π is modeled via *instances* $[\mathcal{C}, sid_\mathcal{C}]$ and $[\mathcal{S}, sid_\mathcal{S}]$ where $sid_\mathcal{C}, sid_\mathcal{S} \in \mathbb{N}$ are respective *session ids* and if $sid_\mathcal{C} = sid_\mathcal{S}$ then the instances are *partnered* – belong to the same session. We sometimes write $\mathcal{C}$ and $\mathcal{S}$ instead of their instances when the difference is visible from the context.

Execution Stages. Once initialized with the corresponding long-lived key an instance $[\mathcal{C}, sid_\mathcal{C}]$ or $[\mathcal{S}, sid_\mathcal{S}]$ is marked as *used* and turns into the *stand-by* stage where it waits for an invocation to execute the protocol. Upon receiving such invocation the instance turns into a *processing* stage where it proceeds according to the protocol specification until it collects enough information to decide whether the execution was successful or not, and to *terminate* then. If the execution is successful then we say that the instance *accepts* before it terminates; otherwise we say it *aborts*. The acceptance of $[\mathcal{C}, sid_\mathcal{C}]$ with $\mathcal{C} = (\mathcal{U}, \mathcal{B})$ is implied by the acceptance of $\mathcal{U}$ regardless of $\mathcal{B}$, as $\mathcal{U}$ is the ultimate endpoint of the communication and controls the browser. However, $[\mathcal{C}, sid_\mathcal{C}]$ aborts if either $\mathcal{U}$ or $\mathcal{B}$ does so.

3.2 Security Model

In the following we specify attacks and security goals for BBMA protocols from the perspective of fixed identities $\mathcal{S}$ and $(\mathcal{U}, \mathcal{B})$.

Assumptions on the Initialization. We assume that the establishment of the security association between $\mathcal{S}$ and $(\mathcal{U}, \mathcal{B})$ during which $\mathcal{B}$ receives (certified) $pk_\mathcal{S}$ and cky, and $\mathcal{S}$ receives w is *trusted*. In practice, this can be done through the execution of the very first TLS handshake in the key transport mode under the assumption that this first session is not compromised. We remark that this assumption has practical substantiation. For example, assume that the protocol should be deployed for the login access to the online banking service of some bank UFB (for User Friendly Bank). If some $\mathcal{U}$ who does not have any online banking account at UFB receives phishing emails with the invitation to access some fake website of UFB there will be no damage even if $\mathcal{U}$ accepts. However, after $\mathcal{U}$ subscribes for the corresponding online service of UFB and receives the user guide that usually includes information on the connection establishment, it is likely that $\mathcal{U}$, especially if $\mathcal{U}$ is technology-unaware and has no experience in online banking, will follow the guidelines, at least for the very first session in which the required security association through the upload of w will be established. Thus, for a successful attack the phishing email should be received by $\mathcal{U}$ in the time period between the subscription and the registration on the site.

Assumptions on the Adversary. The PPT adversary $\mathcal{A}$ controls all communication between the protocol parties. This implies:

- $\mathcal{A}$ controls the domain name resolution. This also allows $\mathcal{A}$ to mount phishing and pharming attacks. Due to the SLSO policy we assume that the adversary can establish security association $(\mathcal{S}', pk_{\mathcal{S}'}, cky')$ with the client $(\mathcal{U}, \mathcal{B})$ for any server identity $\mathcal{S}'$ as long as it can prove the knowledge of the corresponding private key

$sk_{S'}$.[1] Upon sending forged domain resolution responses, the adversary obtains access to the parts of the browser's DOM model which are not protected by the policy. Note also that since the human recognizable authenticator is not cached, it can not be accessed using the DOM model.

- $\mathcal{A}$ can issue public keys which $\mathcal{B}$ accepts. There is *no* trusted third party in the sense of a trusted CA. Hence, a certified public key in a X.509 server certificate is treated as a public key that can be identified by a unique identifier (i.e., hash value of the public key).

- $\mathcal{A}$ is unable to corrupt $\mathcal{B}$. Note that in this model we do not deal with malware[2] attacks against $\mathcal{B}$ and $\mathcal{S}$, therefore, do not consider the case where $\mathcal{A}$ reveals the ephemeral and long-lived secrets stored inside $\mathcal{B}$. In particular this implies that the adversary is not able to access the secure cookie cky unless its request is successfully verified by $\mathcal{B}$ based on the SLSO policy. By the same token we do not consider attacks resulting from the physical access of the adversary to the user's digital device running $\mathcal{B}$.

- $\mathcal{A}$ is unable to corrupt $\mathcal{S}$. Note also that in this model we do not deal with malware attacks against the server. This means that the adversary is excluded from revealing the ephemeral and long-lived secrets stored inside $\mathcal{S}$.

Adversarial Queries. $\mathcal{A}$ can participate in the actual protocol execution via the following queries:

- Execute($\mathcal{C}, \mathcal{S}$): $\mathcal{A}$ eavesdrops the execution of the new protocol session between $\mathcal{C}$ and $\mathcal{S}$ and receives its transcript.

- Invoke($\mathcal{C}, \mathcal{S}$): $\mathcal{U}$ starts the protocol execution with the new instance of $\mathcal{S}$ using the associated instance of browser $\mathcal{B}$ and $\mathcal{A}$ obtains the first protocol message returned by $\mathcal{B}$ (which is usually generated on some input received from $\mathcal{U}$, e.g., the entered URL).

- Send(P, m): In an active attack $\mathcal{A}$ can send a message to some (instance) of $P \in \{\mathcal{U}, \mathcal{B}, \mathcal{S}\}$ whereby messages addressed to $\mathcal{U}$ are implicitly handled as messages addressed to the associated browser $\mathcal{B}$ with the subsequent execution of $\mathtt{render}(m, \Psi)$ and visualization of its output to $\mathcal{U}$. $\mathcal{A}$ receives the response which P generates after having processed m according to the specification of Π (or an empty string if m is unexpected).

- RevealState($\mathcal{B}$): $\mathcal{A}$ receives information stored within the browser's state Ψ and which is not protected via the SLSO policy. Additionally, it returns $(\mathcal{S}, pk_S)$, i.e., $\mathcal{A}$ may learn which servers have security associations with the client, without learning their secure cookies.

---

[1] Assuming that the initialization process is done during the trusted TLS key transport session between $(\mathcal{U}, \mathcal{B})$ and $\mathcal{S}$, the adversary must be able to decrypt messages encrypted with $pk_{S'}$. Under the assumption that the deployed asymmetric encryption scheme is sufficiently secure the decryption operation can be seen as the required proof of possession.

[2] Consideration of malware attacks and augmentation of the proposed model with Trusted Computing functionalities to model resistance against malware attacks is surely an interesting aspect for the future work on security of browser-based protocols.

- SetCKY($\mathcal{B}, (\mathcal{S}', pk_{\mathcal{S}'}, cky')$): With this query (which is new in comparison to [11]) $\mathcal{A}$ sets up a new security association with $(\mathcal{U}, \mathcal{B})$ on behalf of some server $\mathcal{S}'$ as long as $pk_{\mathcal{S}'} \neq pk_{\mathcal{S}}$ (note that due to our assumptions that $\mathcal{A}$ controls the domain name resolution and can issue certificates that $\mathcal{B}$ will accept we explicitly allow $\mathcal{S}'$ to be equal to $\mathcal{S}$.) $\mathcal{A}$ receives the HPA $w' \in \mathcal{W}$ chosen by $\mathcal{U}$ such that it is distinguishable from w, i.e., $w' \notin \mathcal{W}^*$ according to the Definition 1.[3]

Correctness and Browser-Based Mutual Authentication. The following definition specifies the correctness requirement for BBMA protocols.

Definition 2 (Correctness). *A BBMA protocol Π is* correct *if each* Execute$(\mathcal{C}, \mathcal{S})$ *query results in two instances, $[\mathcal{C}, sid_{\mathcal{C}}]$ and $[\mathcal{S}, sid_{\mathcal{S}}]$ which are partnered ($sid_{\mathcal{C}} = sid_{\mathcal{S}}$) and accept prior to termination.*

In the following we define the main security requirement of browser-based mutual authentication between participating $\mathcal{U}$ and $\mathcal{S}$ with $\mathcal{B}$ acting as a mediator of the communication.

Definition 3 (Browser-Based Mutual Authentication). *Let Π be a correct protocol according to Definition 2 and* Game$_{\Pi}^{bbma}(\mathcal{A}, \kappa)$ *the interaction between the instances of $\mathcal{C} = (\mathcal{U}, \mathcal{B})$ and $\mathcal{S}$ with a PPT adversary $\mathcal{A}$ who is allowed to query* Execute, Invoke, Send, RevealState, *and* SetCKY. *We say that $\mathcal{A}$ wins if at some point during the interaction:*

1. *An instance $[\mathcal{C}, sid_{\mathcal{C}}]$ accepts but there is **no** partnered instance $[\mathcal{S}, sid_{\mathcal{S}}]$, **or***
2. *An instance $[\mathcal{S}, sid_{\mathcal{S}}]$ accepts but there is **no** partnered instance $[\mathcal{C}, sid_{\mathcal{C}}]$.*

The maximum probability of this event (over all adversaries running in time κ) is denoted Succ$_{\Pi}^{bbma}(\mathcal{A}, \kappa) = \overset{max}{\mathcal{A}} |\Pr[\mathcal{A} \text{ wins in Game}_{\Pi}^{bbma}(\mathcal{A}, \kappa)]|$. *We say that Π provides* browser-based mutual authentication *if this probability is a negligible function of κ.*

The first requirement ensures that $\mathcal{U}$ authenticates to the matching server $\mathcal{S}$. Since the acceptance of $[\mathcal{C}, sid_{\mathcal{C}}]$ with $\mathcal{C} = (\mathcal{U}, \mathcal{B})$ is implied by the acceptance of $\mathcal{U}$ the second requirement ensures that $\mathcal{S}$ authenticates to the matching user $\mathcal{U}$. In both cases $\mathcal{B}$ plays the role of the mediator of the communication and can be queried by $\mathcal{A}$; thus, not mentioning $\mathcal{B}$ in the above definition would be incorrect from the formal point of view.

4   User-Aware BBMA over TLS with the SLSO Policy

In this section we specify the BBMA-SLSO protocol which can be seen as the modification of the BBMA protocol from [11] towards cookie-based authentication and SLSO policy.

4.1   Building Blocks of BBMA-SLSO

TLS Protocol. The main pillar of BBMA-SLSO is the server authenticated *key transport*, where the server's identity is a cryptographic value independent from the Internet infrastructure. This complies with RSA-based ciphersuites as specified in [1]. These suites are preferentially negotiated between standard browsers and servers.

---

[3] Thus, we assume that users do not use same HPAs with different servers.

Cryptographic Primitives. BBMA-SLSO uses (well-known) cryptographic primitives that are deployed in the cryptographic key transport suites of the TLS protocol, namely:

- A *pseudo-random function* PRF : $\{0,1\}^{p_3(\kappa)} \times \{0,1\}^* \rightarrow \{0,1\}^*$. Note that TLS defines PRF with data expansion s.t. it can be used to obtain outputs of a variable length which becomes useful for the key extraction phase. We refer to [8] for the proof that the key extraction function in TLS is indeed pseudo-random. By $\mathsf{Adv}_{\mathsf{PRF}}^{prf}(\kappa)$ we denote the maximum advantage over all PPT adversaries (running within security parameter κ) in distinguishing the outputs of PRF from those of a random function better than by a random guess.
- A *symmetric encryption scheme* which provides indistinguishability under chosen plaintext attacks (IND-CPA). The symmetric encryption operation is denoted Enc and the corresponding decryption operation Dec. By $\mathsf{Adv}_{(Enc,Dec)}^{ind-cpa}(\kappa)$ we denote the maximum advantage over all PPT adversaries (running within security parameter κ) in breaking the IND-CPA property of (Enc, Dec) better than by a random guess;
- An IND-CPA secure *asymmetric encryption scheme* whose encryption operation is denoted $\mathcal{E}$ and the corresponding decryption operation $\mathcal{D}$. By $\mathsf{Adv}_{(\mathcal{E},\mathcal{D})}^{ind-cpa}(\kappa)$ we denote the maximum advantage over all PPT adversaries (running within security parameter κ) in breaking the IND-CPA property of $(\mathcal{E}, \mathcal{D})$ better than by a random guess; Note that the general case of RSA-OAEP encryption which is used in the TLS key transport mode has been proven in [29] based on the assumptions of the Random Oracle Model [4] to satisfy indistinguishability under *adaptive* chosen ciphertext attacks (IND-CCA2), which is stronger than IND-CPA. Also [18] provides such proof which is tailored specifically to the construction used in the TLS protocol. Still, we emphasize that for the security of BBMA-SLSO the weaker requirement of IND-CPA which is implied by IND-CCA2 is fully sufficient.
- A cryptographic *collision-resistant hash function* Hash : $\{0,1\}^* \rightarrow \{0,1\}^{p_4(\kappa)}$. By $\mathsf{Succ}_{\mathsf{Hash}}^{coll}(\kappa)$ we denote the maximum success probability over all PPT adversaries (running within security parameter κ) in finding a collision, i.e., a pair $(m, m') \in \{0,1\}^* \times \{0,1\}^*$ s.t. $\mathsf{Hash}(m) = \mathsf{Hash}(m')$.
- A *digital signature scheme* which provides existential unforgeability under chosen message attacks (EUF-CMA). The signing operation is denoted Sig and the corresponding verification operation Ver. By $\mathsf{Succ}_{(Sig,Ver)}^{euf-cma}(\kappa)$ we denote the maximum success probability over all PPT adversaries (running within security parameter κ) given access to the signing oracle in finding a forgery;
- The well-known *message authentication code* function HMAC which is believed to satisfy *weak unforgeability under chosen message attacks* (WUF-CMA) [2]. Here we remark that security of HMAC is not relevant for the security analysis of BBMA-SLSO. A detailed look on the protocol from the formal perspective shows that using HMAC is redundant since all HMAC values are encrypted prior to the transmission. Nevertheless, we do not omit protocol parts where HMAC is computed from our description since this is what happens in the today's execution of TLS.

SLSO Policy in BBMA-SLSO**.** During the initialization procedure which is assumed to be trusted server $\mathcal{S}$ establishes a security association with the client $(\mathcal{U}, \mathcal{B})$ using the

TLS protocol in key transport with its (certified) public key. For the successful verification of the SLSO policy in subsequent connections $\mathcal{B}$ stores pk_S and the http cookie provided by $\mathcal{S}$. This cookie contains information which allows $\mathcal{S}$ to authenticate $\mathcal{U}$. On each connection with $\mathcal{S}$, $\mathcal{B}$ has to make a decision whether to send cky or not. Following the definition of the SLSO policy in [19], $\mathcal{B}$ decides by comparing the public key used by the candidate server during that particular TLS handshake to the stored pk_S. If the keys are equal then cky is transmitted, otherwise not. However, since the browser is a very general piece of software that must be able to communicate with any http server on the Internet, we design BBMA-SLSO in such a way that it does not abort the communication if this verification fails; otherwise this would pose a lot of compatibility problems and could be seen as an impractical solution. Instead, if the verification fails, the browser will simply continue with the protocol, by sending the *empty cookie* which we consider as some constant publicly known value $\zeta \in \{0,1\}^{p_2(\kappa)}$. In this way the decision on whether the communication should be continued or not is mitigated to $\mathcal{S}$, which will normally abort the communication since otherwise $\mathcal{U}$ remains unauthenticated.

4.2   Protocol Description

In the following we describe the execution of the BBMA-SLSO protocol specified in Figure 1. Let l_1, l_2, l_3 and l_4 denote the publicly known *labels* specified in TLS for the instantiation of PRF. (We write in parenthesis the corresponding standard TLS messages.)

Initiate the Protocol. The user $\mathcal{U}$ initiates the protocol by communicating server's URL to the own browser $\mathcal{B}$. Upon resolving the corresponding address $\mathcal{B}$ chooses his own *nonce* r_C of length $p_5(\kappa)$ at random and forwards it to $\mathcal{S}$ (ClientHello). In response $\mathcal{S}$ chooses own random *nonce* r_S and a *TLS session identifier* sid of length $p_5(\kappa)$ and appends it to the own certificate $cert_S$ (ServerHello). We stress that sid chosen by $\mathcal{S}$ is not the session identifier sid_S used in our security model but a value specified in TLS.

Negotiate Key Material. $\mathcal{B}$ chooses a *pre-master secret* k_p of length $p_3(\kappa)$ at random and sends it to $\mathcal{S}$ encrypted with the received public key pk_S (ClientKeyExchange) taken from the servers certificate $Cert_S$. The pre-master secret k_p is used to derive the *master secret* k_m through a pseudo-random function PRF on input $(l_1, r_C - r_S)$ with k_p as the secret seed. This key derivation is performed based on the standard TLS pseudo-random function PRF (see [1, Sect. 5]). The master secret is then used as a secret seed for the instantiation of the pseudo-random function PRF on input $(l_2, r_C - r_S)$ to derive the *session keys* $k_1 | k_2$ used to encrypt and authenticate session messages exchanged between $\mathcal{B}$ and $\mathcal{S}$. TLS specifies the generation of six session keys: A symmetric encryption key, a MAC key, and an IV for block ciphers only (either for client and server). For simplicity, we denote k_1 as the encryption key and k_2 as the authentication key which are the same for $\mathcal{B}$ and $\mathcal{S}$. Here we remark that as shown later in our security analysis the use of different keys for encryption and authentication in TLS is redundant from the formal point of view. The reason is that each computed HMAC value is encrypted using

k_1 prior to its transmission over the network. Since the computed value $k_1|k_2$ can be seen as a single output of PRF the security of the applied encryption scheme is already sufficient to achieve symmetric authentication of the encrypted message.

Session Key Confirmation. $\mathcal{B}$ confirms the session key generation, i.e., $F_{\mathcal{C}}$ is the first message that is authenticated via HMAC computed with k_2 and encrypted via the symmetric encryption scheme computed with k_1. $F_{\mathcal{C}}$ is computed as output of PRF on input (l_3, h_1) with k_m as the secret seed; whereby h_1 denotes the hash value computed over all messages previously processed by $\mathcal{B}$ (ClientFinished). Further, $\mathcal{S}$ generates k_m and derives the session keys (k_1, k_2) in a similar way. $\mathcal{S}$ uses the own session keys (k_1, k_2) to ensure that it communicates with $\mathcal{B}$ through the verification of $F_{\mathcal{C}}$. If the verification fails, $\mathcal{S}$ aborts the protocol. Otherwise, it confirms the negotiated session parameters, using PRF on input (l_4, h_2) with k_m as secret seed; whereby h_2 denotes the hash value over the received messages. The output of PRF is first authenticated via HMAC computed with k_2 and then encrypted via the symmetric encryption scheme computed with k_1 (ServerFinished). The client $\mathcal{C}$ checks this message analogously.

Mutual Authentication between Browser and Server. The browser $\mathcal{B}$ now exploits the fact that the server $\mathcal{S}$ has been authenticated in the previous step by showing that he knows the private key associated with $pk_{\mathcal{S}}$. This value is used as a key to the credential store of the browser, and the corresponding cookie cky is retrieved and sent to the server, encrypted with k_1 together with the attached message authentication code computed using k_2.

Human Perceptible Server Authentication. The server selects the HPA w associated with cky, and sends it (encrypted with k_1 together with the attached message authentication code computed using k_2) for display to the browser. We call the message in a high-level description the HumanAuth message. $\mathcal{B}$ communicates the decrypted authenticator to $\mathcal{U}$ through execution of the render function which takes as input the authenticator w and state Ψ and outputs the visualization of w named w^*. The abstract human perception function recognize is used to model the ability of $\mathcal{U}$ to decide whether the authenticator w^* matches the original authenticator w which is shared with $\mathcal{S}$ after the initialization stage.

Before we continue with the security analysis we reemphasize the triangular model of authentication in BBMA-SLSO. When verifying $F_{\mathcal{S}}$, $\mathcal{B}$ knows the identity of $\mathcal{S}$. $\mathcal{B}$ resolves $pk_{\mathcal{S}}$ to look up for the corresponding cookie cky. If no matching triple $(\mathcal{S}, pk_{\mathcal{S}}, cky)$ exists, $\mathcal{B}$ sends an empty cookie ζ and continues with the protocol (it is now in responsibility of the server to abort); otherwise, $\mathcal{B}$ continues by sending cky confidentially to $\mathcal{S}$.

However, TLS in server authentication mode does not prevent $\mathcal{U}$ from contacting to a rogue server in order to disclose sensitive information. When verifying w^* through the execution of recognize, $\mathcal{U}$ is sure to be communicating to $\mathcal{S}$ through $\mathcal{B}$, since $\mathcal{S}$ is the only owner of w apart from $\mathcal{U}$. Upon this stage, the protocol ensures that $\mathcal{S}$ is authenticated to $\mathcal{U}$.

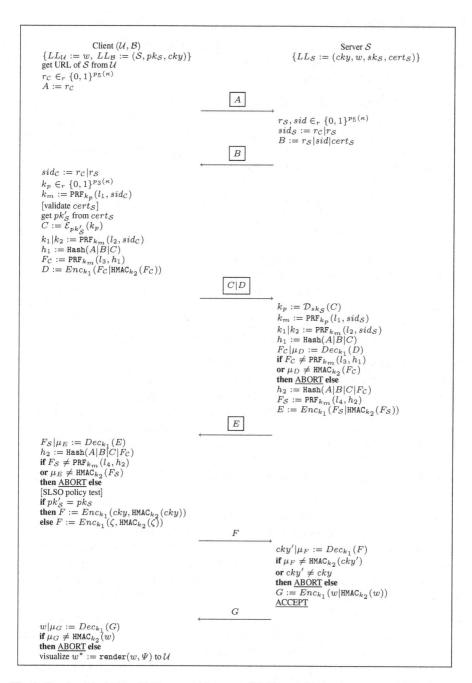

Fig. 1. Sketch of the BBMA-SLSO protocol between $(\mathcal{U}, \mathcal{B})$ and $\mathcal{S}$ based on the SLSO policy of $\mathcal{B}$. Boxed messages denote the standard TLS handshake. $\mathcal{U}$ accepts in the protocol execution only if $\mathcal{U}.\texttt{recognize}(w^*, w) = 1$.

4.3   Security Analysis

In the following we argue on the security of the proposed BBMA-SLSO protocol. We recall that the goal of the protocol is to provide mutual authentication between $\mathcal{U}$ and $\mathcal{S}$ communicating via $\mathcal{B}$ according to Definition 3.

Theorem 1 (BBMA-Security). *Let q denote the total number of executed protocol sessions during the interaction with an adversary $\mathcal{A}$ participating in $\mathsf{Game}^{bbma}_{\mathsf{BBMA-SLSO}}(\mathcal{A}, \kappa)$. If PRF is pseudo-random, Hash is collision-resistant, (Enc, Dec) and $(\mathcal{E}, \mathcal{D})$ are IND-CPA secure and $\mathcal{W}^*$ is sufficiently small, then $\mathsf{BBMA-SLSO}$ provides browser-based mutual authentication in the sense of Definition 3, and*

$$\mathsf{Succ}^{bbma}_{\mathsf{BBMA-SLSO}}(\kappa) \leq \frac{q|\mathcal{W}^*|}{|\mathcal{W}|} + \frac{3q^2}{2^{p_5(\kappa)}} + \frac{q^2}{2^{p_3(\kappa)}} + \frac{q}{2^{p_2(\kappa)}} + q\mathsf{Adv}^{ind-cpa}_{(\mathcal{E}, \mathcal{D})}(\kappa) +$$
$$4q\mathsf{Adv}^{ind-cpa}_{(Enc, Dec)}(\kappa) + 4q\mathsf{Adv}^{prf}_{\mathsf{PRF}}(\kappa) + 2q\mathsf{Succ}^{coll}_{\mathsf{Hash}}(\kappa).$$

Proof. For space limitations the proof appears in the full version of this paper. Its main idea is to simulate the execution of the protocol based on the event InjPK which occurs if $\mathcal{A}$ injects some public key certificate which does *not* contain the expected public key pk_S. In this case security of BBMA-SLSO relies on the ability of $\mathcal{U}$ to distinguish some HPA w^* chosen by $\mathcal{A}$. However, if InjPK does not occur then the security of BBMA-SLSO relies on the execution of the TLS handshake and the browser's SLSO policy.

Remark 1. Although not stated in Theorem 1 explicitly, the security proof of BBMA-SLSO based on the current TLS standard is valid in the Random Oracle Model (ROM) [4]. The reason is that the specification of TLS prescribes the use of the RSA encryption according to PKCS#1 (a.k.a. RSA-OAEP) which in turn is known to provide IND-CPA security in ROM (see [29] and [18] for the proof of the general construction and the TLS-specific construction, respectively). On the other hand, Theorem 1 assumes $(\mathcal{E}, \mathcal{D})$ to be IND-CPA secure (independent of ROM). Hence, whether BBMA-SLSO is secure under standard assumptions or not heavily relies on the assumptions underlying the security of $(\mathcal{E}, \mathcal{D})$.

Remark 2. Another look on Theorem 1 reveals that the success probability of the adversary strongly depends on the size of $\mathcal{W}^*$, i.e., the set of authenticators that are perfectly human-indistinguishable from the HPA w used in the BBMA-SLSO protocol. In fact the protocol is secure if the size of $\mathcal{W}^*$ is *sufficiently small* such that the factor $q|\mathcal{W}^*|/|\mathcal{W}|$ can be seen as negligible. This happens in case that the chosen HPA is good and is precisely what makes BBMA-SLSO user-aware.

Remark 3. As already mentioned during the description of BBMA-SLSO the HMAC construction used in the standard specification of the TLS protocol, formally, does not play any role for the security of the protocol. This is not surprisingly since every output of HMAC is encrypted using session key k_1 before being sent over the network. Since $k_1|k_2$ is treated as a single output of PRF the separation into k_1 and k_2 can be seen as redundant from the theoretical point of view. Note also that Krawczyk has proved the MAC-then-encrypt construction as secure in [22]. Though he mentions some problems in the general construction he shows that they do not apply to TLS.

5   Conclusion

Authenticating the user on the Web is an essential primitive and target to various attacks. We have introduced and analyzed a cookie-based authentication protocol BBMA-SLSO that makes very weak assumptions on user's skills and requires little modifications of the browser security model to enforce the SLSO policy in order to be provably secure. The protocol is specifically designed for security-unaware users who wish to identify Web sites through some easy-to-recognize indicators. The main assumption underlying the protocol security is that good HPAs w exist for which the size of their perfectly human-indistinguishable set W^* remains sufficiently small (for most of the users). It remains an open question, to find such HPAs. We have conjectured that good HPAs might be found among images, audio and video sequences. For example, a personal image taken during own summer vacation and extended with some additional personal text using graphic editor might be better recognizable than an image without such text. However, extensive usability experiments in this interesting research direction have still to be conducted. Nevertheless, the presented protocol is another step towards bridging the gap between protocols that are provably secure, interfaced to users who are prone to errors, and implementable within the design constraints of standard browsers.

References

1. Allen, C., Dierks, T.: The TLS Protocol — Version 1.1. Internet proposed standard RFC 4346 (2006)
2. Bellare, M., Namprempre, C.: Authenticated Encryption: Relations among Notions and Analysis of the Generic Composition Paradigm. In: Okamoto, T. (ed.) ASIACRYPT 2000. LNCS, vol. 1976, pp. 531–545. Springer, Heidelberg (2000)
3. Bellare, M., Rogaway, P.: Entity Authentication and Key Distribution. In: Stinson, D.R. (ed.) CRYPTO 1993. LNCS, vol. 773, pp. 232–249. Springer, Heidelberg (1994)
4. Bellare, M., Rogaway, P.: Random Oracles are Practical: A Paradigm for Designing Efficient Protocols. In: ACM CCS 1993, pp. 62–73. ACM Press, New York (1993)
5. Chiasson, S., van Oorschot, P.C., Biddle, R.: Graphical Password Authentication Using Cued Click Points. In: Biskup, J., López, J. (eds.) ESORICS 2007. LNCS, vol. 4734, pp. 359–374. Springer, Heidelberg (2007)
6. Dhamija, R., Tygar, J.D.: The Battle against Phishing: Dynamic Security Skins. In: SOUPS 2005, pp. 77–88. ACM Press, New York (2005)
7. Dhamija, R., Tygar, J.D., Hearst, M.A.: Why Phishing Works? In: CHI 2006, pp. 581–590. ACM Press, New York (2006)
8. Fouque, P.-A., Pointcheval, D., Zimmer, S.: HMAC is a Randomness Extractor and Applications to TLS. In: ACM ASIACCS 2008, pp. 21–32. ACM Press, New York (2008)
9. Freier, A.O., Kariton, P., Kocher, P.C.: The SSL Protocol: Version 3.0. Internet draft, Netscape Communications (1996)
10. Gajek, S., Schwenk, S.: Revising the Mature Browser Security Model. Technical Report, HGI TR-2008-004 (2008)
11. Gajek, S., Manulis, M., Sadeghi, A.-R., Schwenk, J.: Provably Secure Browser-Based User-Aware Mutual Authentication over TLS. In: ACM ASIACCS 2008, pp. 300–311. ACM Press, New York (2008)
12. Groß, T.: Security Analysis of the SAML Single Sign-on Browser/Artifact Profile. In: ACSAC 2003, pp. 298–307. IEEE CS, Los Alamitos (2003)

13. Groß, T., Pfitzmann, B., Sadeghi, A.-R.: Browser Model for Security Analysis of Browser-Based Protocols. In: di Vimercati, S.d.C., Syverson, P.F., Gollmann, D. (eds.) ESORICS 2005. LNCS, vol. 3679, pp. 489–508. Springer, Heidelberg (2005)

14. Groß, T., Pfitzmann, B., Sadeghi, A.-R.: Proving a WS-Federation Passive Requestor Profile with a Browser Model. In: SWS 2005, pp. 54–64. ACM Press, New York (2005)

15. Jackson, C., Barth, A., Bortz, A., Shao, W., Boneh, D.: Protecting Browsers from DNS Rebinding Attacks. In: CCS 2007, pp. 421–431. ACM Press, New York (2007)

16. Jackson, C., Simon, D.R., Tan, D.S., Barth, A.: An Evaluation of Extended Validation and Picture-in-Picture Phishing Attacks. In: FC 2007/USEC 2007. LNCS, vol. 4886, pp. 281–293. Springer, Heidelberg (2008)

17. Jakobsson, M., Myers, S.: Delayed Password Disclosure. IJACT 1(1), 47–59 (2008)

18. Jonsson, J., Kaliski, B.S.: On the Security of RSA Encryption in TLS. In: Yung, M. (ed.) CRYPTO 2002. LNCS, vol. 2442, pp. 127–142. Springer, Heidelberg (2002)

19. Karlof, C., Shankar, U., Tygar, J.D., Wagner, D.: Dynamic Pharming Attacks and Locked Same-Origin Policies for Web Browsers. In: ACM CCS 2007, pp. 58–71. ACM Press, New York (2007)

20. Kormann, D., Rubin, A.: Risks of the Passport Single SignOn Protocol. Computer Networks 33(1–6), 51–58 (2000)

21. Microsoft Corporation. Mitigating Cross-Site Scripting with HTTP-only Cookies (2008), http://msdn2.microsoft.com/en-us/library/ms533046.aspx

22. Krawczyk, H.: The Order of Encryption and Authentication for Protecting Communications (or: How Secure Is SSL?). In: Kilian, J. (ed.) CRYPTO 2001. LNCS, vol. 2139, pp. 310–331. Springer, Heidelberg (2001)

23. Mason, C., Baek, K.-H., Smith, S.: WSKE: Web Server Key Enabled Cookies. In: FC 2007/USEC 2007, pp. 294–306. Springer, Heidelberg (2008)

24. Mitchell, J.C., Shmatikov, V., Stern, U.: Finite-State Analysis of SSL 3.0. In: USENIX Security Symp., pp. 201–216 (1998)

25. Paulson, L.C.: Inductive Analysis of the Internet protocol TLS. ACM Trans. on Comp. and Syst. Sec. (3), 332–351 (1999)

26. Pfitzmann, B., Waidner, M.: A Model for Asynchronous Reactive Systems and its Application to Secure Message Transmission. In: IEEE S&P 2001, pp. 184–200. IEEE Computer Society Press, Los Alamitos (2001)

27. Schechter, S.E., Dhamija, R., Ozment, A., Fischer, I.: The Emperor's New Security Indicators. In: IEEE S&P 2007, pp. 51–65. IEEE Computer Society Press, Los Alamitos (2007)

28. Schneier, B., Wagner, D.: Analysis of the SSL 3.0 protocol. In: USENIX Workshop on Electronic Commerce (1996)

29. Shoup, V.: OAEP Reconsidered. Journal of Cryptology 15(4), 223–249 (2002)

30. Soghoian, C., Jakobsson, M.: A Deceit-Augmented Ma. In: The Middle Attack Against Bank of America's SiteKey Service (2007), http://paranoia.dubfire.net/2007/04/deceit-augmented-man-in-middle-attack.html

31. Suo, X., Zhu, Y., Owen, G.S.: Graphical Passwords: A Survey. In: Ann. Comp. Sec. Applic. Conf. IEEE Computer Society Press, Los Alamitos (2005)

32. W3C. Document Object Model (DOM) (2005), http://www.w3.org/DOM

Secure Biometric Authentication
with Improved Accuracy

Manuel Barbosa[2], Thierry Brouard[1],
Stéphane Cauchie[1,3], and Simão Melo de Sousa[3]

[1] Laboratoire Informatique de l'Université François Rabelais de Tours
stephane.cauchie@univ-tours.fr
[2] Departamento de Informática, Universidade do Minho
mbb@di.uminho.pt
[3] Departamento de Informática, Universidade da Beira Interior
desousa@ubi.pt

Abstract. We propose a new hybrid protocol for cryptographically
secure biometric authentication. The main advantages of the proposed
protocol over previous solutions can be summarised as follows: (1) potential for much better accuracy using different types of biometric signals,
including behavioural ones; and (2) improved user privacy, since user
identities are not transmitted at any point in the protocol execution.
The new protocol takes advantage of state-of-the-art identification classifiers, which provide not only better accuracy, but also the possibility
to perform authentication without knowing who the user claims to be.
Cryptographic security is based on the Paillier public key encryption
scheme.

Keywords: Secure Biometric Authentication, Cryptography, Classifier.

1   Introduction

Biometric techniques endow a very appealing property to authentication mechanisms : *the user is the key*, meaning there is no need to securely store secret
identification data. Presently, most applications of biometric authentication consist of closed self-contained systems, where all the stages in the authentication
process and usually all static biometric profile information underlying it, are
executed and stored in a controlled and trusted environment. This paper addresses the problem of implementing *distributed* biometric authentication systems, where data acquisition and feature recognition are performed by separate
sub-systems, which communicate over an insecure channel. This type of scenario may occur, for instance, if one intends to use biometric authentication to
access privileged resources over the Internet. Distributed biometric authentication requires hybrid protocols integrating cryptographic techniques and pattern
recognition tools. Related work in this area has produced valid solutions from
a cryptographic security point of view. However, these protocols can be seen
as rudimentary from a pattern-recognition point of view. In fact, regardless of

Y. Mu, W. Susilo, and J. Seberry (Eds.): ACISP 2008, LNCS 5107, pp. 21–36, 2008.

the security guarantees that so-called fuzzy cryptosystems provide, they present great limitations on the accuracy that can be achieved, when compared to purely biometric solutions resorting to more powerful pattern recognition techniques.

In this paper, we propose a solution which overcomes this accuracy limitation. Our contribution is a protocol offering the accuracy of state-of-the-art pattern recognition classifiers *and* strong cryptographic security. To achieve our goals we follow an approach to hybrid authentication protocols proposed by Bringer et al. [1]. In our solution we adapt and extend this approach to use a more accurate and stable set of models, or *classifiers*, which are widely used in the pattern recognition community in settings where cryptographic security aspects are not considered. Interestingly, the characteristics of these classifiers allow us, not only to achieve better accuracy, but also to improve the degree of privacy provided by the authentication system. This is possible because we move away from *authentication classifiers* and take advantage of an *identification classifier*. An identification classifier does not need to know who the user claims to be, in order to determine if she belongs to the set of valid users in the system and determine her user identifier. An additional contribution of this paper is to formalise the security models for the type of protocol introduced by Bringer et al. [1]. We show that the original protocol is actually insecure and under the original security model, although it can be easily fixed. We also extend the security model to account for eavesdroppers external to the system, and provide a security argument that our solution is secure in this extended security model.

The remaining of the paper is organized as follows. We first summarise related work in Section 2 and we introduce our notational framework for distributed biometric authentication systems in Section 3. We propose our secure biometric authentication protocol and security models in Section 4. In Section 5 we present a concrete implementation based on the *Support Vector Machine* classifier and the Paillier public key encryption scheme, including the corresponding security analysis. Finally, we discuss our contributions in Section 6.

2   Related Work

Fuzzy extractors are a solution to secure biometric authentication put forward by the cryptographic community [2]. Here, the pattern recognition component is based on error correction. A fuzzy extractor is defined by two algorithms. The generation algorithm takes a user's biometric data w and derives secret randomness r. To allow for robustness in reconstructing r, the generation algorithm also produces public data pub. On its own, pub reveals no useful information about the biometric data or the secret randomness. The reconstruction algorithm permits recovering r given a *sufficiently close* measurement w' and pub. To use a fuzzy extractor for secure remote authentication, the server would store (pub, r) during the enrolment stage. When the user wants to authenticate, the server provides the corresponding public information pub, so that it is possible reconstruct r from a fresh reading w'. The user is authenticated once the server confirms that r has been correctly reconstructed; for example, r can be used to derive a secret key.

A problem with this solution is that security is only guaranteed against eavesdroppers: the server must be authenticated and the public information transmitted reliably. Additionally, Boyen [3] later showed that, even in this scenario, it is not possible to guarantee that security is preserved if the same fuzzy extractor is used to authenticate a user with multiple servers. An adversary might put together public information and secrets leaked from some of the servers to impersonate the user in another server. The same author proposed improved security models and constructions to solve this problem. Boyen et al. [4] later addressed a different problem which arises when the channel to the server is not authenticated and an active adversary can change the value of **pub**. The original fuzzy extractor definition and security model does not ensure that such an adversary is unable to persuade the user that it is the legitimate server. The authors propose a robust fuzzy extractor that permits achieving mutual authentication over an insecure channel.

The protocol proposed by Bringer et al. [1] uses the Goldwasser-Micali encryption scheme, taking advantage of its homomorphic properties. The protocol performs biometric classification using the Hamming distance between fresh biometric readings and stored biometric profiles. User privacy protection is ensured by hiding the association between biometric data and user identities. For this to be possible one must distribute the server-side functionality: an *authentication service* knows the user's claimed identity and wants to verify it, a *database service* stores user biometric data in such a way that it cannot possibly determine to whom it belongs, and a *matching service* ensures that it is possible to authenticate users without making an association between their identity and their biometric profile. These servers are assumed to be honest-but-curious and, in particular, they are assumed to follow the protocol and not to collude to break its security.

Authentication Accuracy. In this paper we propose a protocol which improves authentication accuracy while ensuring strong cryptographic security. It is important to support our claims from a pattern recognition accuracy perspective. In the following table we present experimental results found in literature, to compare the accuracy (Equal Error Rate[1]) of advanced pattern recognition classifiers (*Classifier Error*) with that of those adopted in existing hybrid authentication protocols, or so called fuzzy cryptosystems (*Fuzzy Error*).

Biometric Data	References	Bit Length	Fuzzy Error	Classifier Error
Key stroke	[5]/[6]	12	48%	1.8%
Voice	[7]/[8]	46	20%	5%
Tactim	[9]	16	15%	1%
Signature	[10]/[11]	40	28%	5%
Face	[12]/[13]	120	5%	0.6%
Fingerprint	[14]/[15]	128	17%	8%
Iris	[16]	140	5%	5%

---

[1] Percentage of recognition errors when the biometric system is adjusted in order to obtain the same false positive and false negative rates.

Results are presented for both physiological (iris, face and fingerprint) and behavioural (key stroke, voice, tactim, signature) biometric data. From the results in the table, one can conclude that advanced classifiers consistently outperform simple distance-based (fuzzy) classification techniques. However, this is most important for behavioural biometry, where fuzzy techniques present significantly worse accuracy rates. An empirical explanation for this shortcoming is that fuzzy pattern recognition components can deal with acquisition variability but not with the user variability, which plays a major role in behavioral biometry. From a pattern recognition point of view, advanced classifiers are built on the assumption that two users may produce close measurements. Classification focuses on the boundaries between users, and some of them like the Support Vector Machine (SVM) classifier [17], can optimally minimize the error risk.

3   Biometric Systems

In this section we present a precise definition of a pattern recognition system for biometric authentication and identification, which we will later use in the definition of our hybrid authentication protocol. We take a particular type of biometric parameter $b \in \mathbb{B}$, where $\mathbb{B}$ denotes the complete set of biometric parameters. The basic tool associated with b is an adequate sensor, denoted by the application $\rho_b : \mathbb{U} \to \mathbb{V}$ where $\mathbb{U}$ is a set representing the universe of possible users and $\mathbb{V}$ represents a sensor-dependent space of biometric features (usually an n-tuple of real numbers). We will refer to the output of the sensor as a *feature*. [2]

Consider a set of users $U \subset \mathbb{U}$. The goal is to recover the pre-image of a feature $\rho_b(u)$, for $u \in U$, using prior knowledge of a users profile $w_U^* \in \mathbb{W}$, where $\mathbb{W}$ is a sensor-dependent set of possible users profiles, and an inversion function called a *classifier*. Usually a classifier is a two-stage procedure: (1) there is a pre-decision processing stage cl, which takes a feature and pre-established profile information and returns classification data such as confidence intervals, distances, etc.; and (2) a decision stage $\mathcal{D}$ which makes the final decision using an appropriate criterion, for example a pre-defined threshold, majority rules, etc. Ideally, one expects that classification satisfies

$$\forall u \in U, \mathcal{D}(cl(\rho_b(u), w_U^*)) = u$$
$$\forall u \in \mathbb{U}/U, \mathcal{D}(cl(\rho_b(u), w_U^*)) = \perp$$

At this stage a distinction must be made between *biometric authentication* and *biometric identification* systems. A system satisfying the previous predicate (or a close enough relaxation that is good enough for practical applications) for a set of users U such that $|U| > 1$ is called a biometric identification system. Systems satisfying these conditions for only a single user are called biometric

---

[2] In practice raw sensor outputs must be pre-processed using *feature extraction* before classification can be performed. To be precise, we could denote the acquisition of the raw signal by a non deterministic application a_b, and feature extraction by a deterministic application f. We would then have $\rho_b = a_b \circ f$.

authentication systems. Note that it is possible to use a biometric authentication system for identification, e.g. by trying all possible users in a database. However, depending on the biometric parameter and sensor technology, the accuracy of such a system may suffer from overlaps in user profiles. From the point of view of cryptographic protocols, this distinction is also important. In fact, all solutions we have encountered in literature assume that we are dealing with a biometric authentication system, which means that the user's claimed identity must be transmitted over the network. If we move to a biometric identification system, the authentication protocol can be implemented by transmitting only the user's biometric data. We will return to this issue in the next section.

Setting-up and operating a biometric authentication system involves two separate procedures: a set-up stage called *Enrolment*, and the actual operation stage called *Generalisation*. We now describe these in more detail.

Enrolment. This is usually split into two steps: (1) the *acquisition and feature extraction* step, and (2) the *learning* step. The first step constructs a reference set of feature values $\rho_b(u)$ ($\forall u \in U$), called a *training set*. The learning step uses the training set to construct the users' profile w_U^*.

Generalisation. This is also split in two steps: (1) the *acquisition and feature extraction* step, and (2) the *decision* step. The former consists of collecting a feature $v = \rho_b(\texttt{unknown})$ for an unknown user. The decision step uses the classifier cl and profile data w^* to determine which user is $\texttt{unknown}$. More precisely the decision check is $\{u \in U, \perp\} \leftarrow \mathcal{D}(cl(v, w_U^*))$.

In this context, we define a pattern recognition system for biometric identification Γ as follows.

Definition 1. *A pattern recognition system for biometric identification Γ is a 5-tuple $< b, U, \rho_b, \mathcal{D} \circ cl, w_U^* >$, where the tuple elements are as described above.*

Remark. We stress that the concept of profile w_U^* usually adopted within the pattern recognition community constitutes, in the context of our work, a security-critical parameter. This is because it usually reveals private user information such as a user-specific region in a sensor-dependent parameter space $\mathbb{W}$. In particular, if this information is leaked, anyone can determine whether a feature belongs to a particular user. The vulnerability detected in the protocol proposed by Bringer et al. is based on the fact that an attacker may recover a user profile from a protocol trace. This means that it can perform classification itself, even thought it would never be able to break the encryption scheme protecting the user features used in an authentication run.

4 Proposed Authentication Protocol

In this section we propose a new authentication protocol based on the approach in [1]. We take advantage of a biometric identification scheme implemented using a more powerful pattern recognition technique in the form of a multi-class classifier to achieve improved accuracy and security properties.

4.1   Participants and Their Roles

The following diagram depicts the data flow between the different participants
in our protocol.

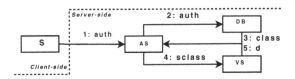

The server-side functionality is partitioned in three components to ensure that
no single entity can associate a user's identity with the biometric data being
collected during authentication. The participants in the authentication protocol
are the following:

1. The *Sensor* (*S*) is the only client-side component. Following the approach in
   [1], we assume that the sensor is capable of capturing the user's biometric
   data, extracting it into a binary string, and performing cryptographic operations such as public key encryption. We also assume a *liveness link* between
   the sensor and the server-side components, to provide confidence that the
   biometric data received on the server-side is from a present living person.
2. The *Authentication Service* (*AS*) is responsible for communicating with the
   user who wants to authenticate and organizing the entire server-side procedure. In a successful authentication the *AS* will obviously learn the user's
   identity, which means that it should learn nothing about the biometric data
   being submitted.
3. The *Database Server* (*DB*) securely stores the users' profile (w_U^*) and its
   job is to execute the pre-decision part of classification (*cl*). Since the *DB* is
   aware of privileged biometric data, it should learn nothing about the user's
   identity, or even be able to correlate or trace authentication runs from a
   given (unknown) user.
4. The *Verification Server* (*VS*) completes the authentication process by taking
   the output produced by the *DB* server and computing the final decision ($\mathcal{D}$)
   step. This implies that the *VS* possesses privileged information that allows
   it to make a final decision, and again that it should not be able to learn
   anything about the user's real identity, or even be able to correlate or trace
   authentication runs from a given (unknown) user.

4.2   Enrolment and System Set-Up

In this section we describe the procedures that must be carried out to prepare a
system using the proposed authentication protocol for normal operation. These
include the data collection procedures associated with enrolment, the construction of the static data sets assigned to each actor in the protocol, and the security
assumptions/requirements we impose on these elements.

The output of the initialisation procedure are three sets of static data (AS_{data}, DB_{data} and VS_{data}) which allow the different servers to carry out their roles:

- AS_{data} consists of a list $U = \{\text{ID}_1, \ldots, \text{ID}_{|U|}\}$ of user identities $\text{ID}_i \in \{0,1\}^*$. The index of the user in this list will be used as the application-specific user identifier $uid \in \{1 \ldots |U|\}$.
- DB_{data} consists of biometric classification data (w_U^*) for the set of valid users. This should permit computing pre-decision classification information (cl) over authentication requests, but should be totally anonymous for the DB. In particular, we require that the DB obtains information which permits performing pre-classification for the $|U|$ system users consistently with the application-specific user identifiers assigned by the AS. However, it should not receive any information about the user identities themselves.
- VS_{data} consists of information which will allow the VS to obtain a verdict from obfuscated pre-decision classification information. The need for obfuscation is justified by the apparently contradictory requirement that only the VS is capable of producing a decision verdict, but still should be unable to learn the user's real identity, or even trace requests by the same user.

We assume that some trusted authority is available to control the enrolment procedure, and ensure that the static data is assigned to the servers in a secure way: no server obtains any information concerning another server's static data, and no information is leaked to eavesdroppers external to the system.

4.3   Authentication Protocol Definition

The proposed authentication protocol is a five-tuple of probabilistic polynomial time algorithms that the different participants will execute. Each server-side participant stores corresponding static information AS_{data}, DS_{data} and VS_{data}. The algorithms are:

Participant	Algorithm
VS	$(\text{params}, k_d) \leftarrow \mathbf{Gen}(1^\kappa)$
S	$\text{auth} \leftarrow \mathbf{S}(v_{\text{ID}}, \text{params})$
DB	$\text{class} \leftarrow \mathbf{Classify}(\text{params}, \text{auth}, DB_{\text{data}})$
AS	$(\text{sclass}, \pi) \leftarrow \mathbf{Shuffle}(\text{params}, \text{class}, AS_{\text{data}})$
VS	$d \leftarrow \mathbf{Decide}(\text{sclass}, \text{params}, k_d, VS_{\text{data}})$
AS	$\text{ID}/\bot \leftarrow \mathbf{Identify}(d, \pi, AS_{\text{data}})$

1. The key generation algorithm **Gen** is executed by the VS, which stores the secret key k_d securely, and publishes a set of public parameters params.
2. On each authentication run, the sensor encrypts fresh biometric data v_{ID} from a user with identity ID using algorithm **S** and the public parameters, and produces the authentication request auth.
3. The AS receives the authentication request and passes it on to the DB for pre-decision classification. This operation is represented by algorithm **Classify** which takes also public parameters and profile information DB_{data} and returns encrypted classification information class.

4. The AS takes `class` and scrambles it in order to disassociate the decision result from previous authentication runs. This operation is represented by algorithm **Shuffle** which outputs scrambled data `sclass` and a de-scrambling key π which the AS keeps to itself.
5. The VS uses the secret key k_d and `sclass` to perform the final decision step and produces a verdict d. This operation is represented by algorithm **Decide**.
6. Finally, the AS can recover the user's real identity, or a failure symbol, from the verdict d and the de-scrambling key π using algorithm **Identify**.

The soundness condition for our protocol is that the server-side system as a whole, and the AS in particular, produces a correct decision on the user's authenticity, i.e. recognises whether a new feature belongs to a valid user, and determines the correct identity. Formally, for soundness we require that the following probability yields a value sufficiently close to one for practical use as an authentication protocol, for valid static data AS_data, DB_data and VS_data resulting from a successful enrolment procedure, and for all fresh features v_ID:

$$\Pr\left[\mathbf{Identify}(d, \pi, AS_\text{data}) = r \left| \begin{array}{l} (\text{params}, k_d) \leftarrow \mathbf{Gen}(1^\kappa) \\ \text{auth} \leftarrow \mathbf{S}(v_\text{ID}, \text{params}) \\ \text{class} \leftarrow \mathbf{Classify}(\text{params}, \text{auth}, DB_\text{data}) \\ (\text{sclass}, \pi) \leftarrow \mathbf{Shuffle}(\text{params}, \text{class}, AS_\text{data}) \\ d \leftarrow \mathbf{Decide}(\text{sclass}, \text{params}, k_d, VS_\text{data}) \end{array} \right. \right].$$

where $r = \text{ID}$ when `ID` is in the valid set of users, and $r = \perp$ otherwise.

4.4 Security Model

Intuitively, the security requirements we want to impose are the following:

- **Privacy.** None of the services (and no passive attacker observing communications) gets enough information to reconstruct an identity/feature pair. More precisely, none of the services can distinguish whether a particular measurement belongs to a particular person.
- **Untraceability.** Except for the authentication service, none of the other services (and no passive attacker observing communications) gets enough information to recognize a previously authenticated user. More precisely, the database service and the matching service cannot distinguish whether two authentication requests belong to the same person.

We assume that the servers are honest-but-curious, namely that they do not collude and follow the protocol rules, but may try to use the information they obtain to subvert the previous requirements. Formally, this translates into two security models.

Privacy: Feature Indistinguishability. The three server-side components, as well as any eavesdropper which is able to observe the message exchanges corresponding to a protocol execution, must be unable to distinguish between which of two features belongs to a particular system user. We call this requirement feature indistinguishability (fIND). We define it using the following experiment, which takes as input a parameter $\text{adv} \in \{AS, DB, VS, Eve\}$, and fresh readings v_0, from valid user $\text{ID} \in U$, and v_1 from any user.

$$\text{Exp}_{\beta}^{\text{fIND}}(\text{adv}, v_0, v_1)$$

$\quad (\text{params}, k_d) \leftarrow \textbf{Gen}(1^{\kappa})$

$\quad \text{auth} \qquad \leftarrow \textbf{S}(v_0, \text{params})$

$\quad \text{class} \qquad \leftarrow \textbf{Classify}(\text{params}, \text{auth}, DB_{\text{data}})$

$\quad (\text{sclass}, \pi) \leftarrow \textbf{Shuffle}(\text{params}, \text{class}, AS_{\text{data}})$

$\quad d \qquad\qquad \leftarrow \textbf{Decide}(\text{sclass}, k_d, SV_{\text{data}})$

$\quad r \qquad\qquad \leftarrow \textbf{Identify}(d, \pi, AS_{\text{data}})$

$\quad \text{Return} \qquad (v_{\beta}, \text{view}_{\text{adv}})$

$\text{view}_{AS} := (\text{auth}, \text{class}, \text{sclass}, \pi, d, r, AS_{\text{data}}, \text{params})$

$\text{view}_{DB} := (\text{auth}, \text{class}, DB_{\text{data}}, \text{params})$

$\text{view}_{VS} := (\text{sclass}, d, VS_{\text{data}}, k_d, \text{params})$

$\text{view}_{Eve} := (\text{auth}, \text{class}, \text{sclass}, d, \text{params})$

We require that, for all $\text{ID} \in U$ and all $\text{adv} \in \{AS, DB, VS, Eve\}$, the following distributions be computationally indistinguishable ($\equiv$):

$$\{(\text{ID}, \text{Exp}_{\beta=1}^{\text{fIND}}(\text{adv}, v_0, v_1))\} \equiv \{(\text{ID}, \text{Exp}_{\beta=0}^{\text{fIND}}(\text{adv}, v_0, v_1))\}$$

We define advantage $\text{Adv}^{\text{fIND}}(\text{adv})$ as (the absolute value of) the deviation from $1/2$ in the probability that the adversary guesses β.

Untraceability – User Indistinguishability. The back-end server-side components, DB and VS, as well as any eavesdropper which is able to observe the message exchanges corresponding to a protocol execution, must be unable to distinguish if two independent authentication runs correspond to the same system user. We call this requirement user indistinguishability (uIND). We define it using the following experiment, which takes as input a parameter $\text{adv} \in \{DB, VS, Eve\}$, and two fresh readings v_0 and v_1 corresponding to valid users uid and uid' respectively.

$$\text{Exp}_{\beta}^{\text{uIND}}(\text{adv}, v_0, v_1)$$

$\quad (\text{params}, k_d) \leftarrow \textbf{Gen}(1^{\kappa})$

$\quad \text{auth} \qquad \leftarrow \textbf{S}(v_{\beta}, \text{params})$

$\quad \text{class} \qquad \leftarrow \textbf{Classify}(\text{params}, \text{auth}, DB_{\text{data}})$

$\quad (\text{sclass}, \pi) \leftarrow \textbf{Shuffle}(\text{params}, \text{class}, AS_{\text{data}})$

$\quad d \qquad\qquad \leftarrow \textbf{Decide}(\text{sclass}, k_d, SV_{\text{data}})$

$\quad r \qquad\qquad \leftarrow \textbf{Identify}(d, \pi, AS_{\text{data}})$

$\quad \text{Return} \qquad \text{view}_{\text{adv}}$

where the different views are defined as above.

We require that, for all valid users with user identifiers uid and uid', and all $\mathtt{adv} \in \{DB, VS, Eve\}$, the following distributions be computationally indistinguishable ($\equiv$):

$$\{(uid, uid', \mathtt{Exp}^{\mathtt{uIND}}_{\beta=1}(\mathtt{adv}, v_0, v_1))\} \equiv \{(uid, uid', \mathtt{Exp}^{\mathtt{uIND}}_{\beta=0}(\mathtt{adv}, v_0, v_1))\}$$

Again, we define advantage $\mathtt{Adv}^{\mathtt{uIND}}(\mathtt{adv})$ as (the absolute value of) the deviation from $1/2$ in the probability that the adversary guesses β.

5   A Concrete Implementation

5.1   The SVM Classifier

We consider a $|U|$-class identification classifier called the Support Vector Machine (SVM) [17] and provide a short description of its operation. The basic SVM is a mono class authentication classifier[3]. Extension to U classes follows the *one-against-all* strategy: for each user $u \in U$, a mono classifier is trained using the remaining users (U/u) as the rejected class. For each user, the learning stage of the SVM determines both an outer and an inner hyperplane in a k-dimensional features space. Said hyperplanes are expressed as a linear combination of S known samples (so called support vectors $SV_{i,j} \in \mathbb{V}_{\mathtt{SVM}}, i = 1...S, j = 1...|U|$) weighted with $\alpha_{i,j} \in \mathbb{N}$ coefficients. Formally, we have

$$\mathbb{V}_{\mathtt{SVM}} = \mathbb{N}^k \text{ and } \mathbb{W}_{\mathtt{SVM}} = (\mathbb{N} \times \mathbb{V})^{S \times |U|}$$

During authentication, the SVM classifier evaluates the distance of the fresh feature v to these hyperplanes using a scalar product. To account for the fact that the user profile regions may not be linearly separable, the SVM may compute the scalar product in a higher dimension space. For this, the SVM classifier uses a kernel function $\mathbf{K}$ to project the data into the higher dimension space and compute the scalar product in this space in a single step. The advantage is that the computational cost is reduced when compared to a basic projection followed by the scalar product. The classifier function is therefore

$$cl_{\mathtt{SVM}} : \mathbb{V}_{\mathtt{SVM}} \times \mathbb{W}_{\mathtt{SVM}} \to \mathbb{N}^{|U|}$$

$$cl_{\mathtt{SVM}}(v, w^*_{|U|}) := (cl^{(1)}_{\mathtt{SVM}}(v, w^*_{|U|}), \ldots, cl^{(|U|)}_{\mathtt{SVM}}(v, w^*_{|U|}))$$

where $w^*_{|U|}$ contains $(\alpha_{i,j}, SV_{i,j})]$ for $1 \leq i \leq S$ and $1 \leq j \leq |U|$ and

$$cl^{(j)}_{\mathtt{SVM}}(v, w^*_{|U|}) := \sum_{i=1}^{S} \alpha_{i,j} \, \mathbf{K}(v, SV_{i,j}).$$

In this paper, and to simplify the presentation, we will use the particular case where $\mathbf{K}(a, b)$ refers to the scalar product between a and b in the initial space: $\mathbf{K}(a, b) = \sum_{l=1}^{k} a_l b_l$.

---

[3] A classifier used in an authentication context "Am I who I claimed to be ?".

The decision is calculated by finding the index of the maximum positive scalar contained in the vector $cl_{\text{SVM}}(v, w^*)$. If no positive scalar exists, then the reject symbol is returned ($\perp$):

$$\mathcal{D}_{\text{SVM}}(cl_{\text{SVM}}(v, w^*)) := \begin{cases} d \leftarrow \text{argmax}_{j=1}^{|U|}(cl_{\text{SVM}}^{(j)}(v, w^*)) \\ \text{If } cl_{\text{SVM}}^{(d)}(v, w^*) > 0 \\ \text{Then return } d \\ \text{Else return } \perp \end{cases}$$

5.2 Algorithm Implementations

We refer the reader to Appendix A for a description of the Paillier cryptosystem. The concrete implementations we propose for the algorithms composing our authentication protocol are the following:

- **Gen(1^κ)** $\rightarrow$ (**params**, k_d). The generation primitive simply uses the key generation algorithm for the Paillier cryptosystem to obtain (k_e, k_d), sets **params** $\leftarrow k_e$ and returns (**params**, k_d).
- **S(v)** $\rightarrow$ **auth**. This algorithm takes as input a fresh feature for an unknown user. Recall that the feature space for the SVM is $\mathbb{V}_{\text{SVM}} = \mathbb{N}^k$, but we can look at the feature as $v := (v_1, \ldots, v_k) \in \mathbb{Z}_n^k$. Encryption is carried out one component at a time and the algorithm returns:

$$\text{auth} \leftarrow (\mathcal{E}_{\text{Paillier}}(v_1, k_e), \ldots, \mathcal{E}_{\text{Paillier}}(v_k, k_e))$$

- **Classify(auth, DB_{data}, params)** $\rightarrow$ **class**. This algorithm uses the homomorphic properties of the Paillier encryption scheme to compute pre-decision SVM classification values without ever decrypting the features in **auth**. More precisely, the algorithm takes the profile data $w^*_{|U|}$ in DB_{data} and calculates for $1 \leq j \leq |U|$

$$c_j = \prod_{i=1}^{S} \overset{*}{\mathbf{K}}(\text{auth}, SV_{i,j})^{\alpha_{i,j}} = \mathcal{E}_{\text{Paillier}}(\sum_{i=1}^{S} \alpha_{i,j} \mathbf{K}(v, SV_{i,j}), \text{params})$$

where, using $[\cdot]_l$ to denote the lth component in a tuple, $\mathbf{K}^*$ is defined by

$$\overset{*}{\mathbf{K}}(\text{auth}, SV_{i,j}) := \prod_{l=1}^{k} [\text{auth}_j]_l^{[SV_{i,j}]_l}$$

To prevent the AS from performing an exhaustive search of the profile space, the DB also re-randomizes the encryptions by calculating:

$$\text{class}_j = (c_j r_j^n) \mod n^2$$

The algorithm returns $\text{class} = (\text{class}_1, \ldots, \text{class}_{|U|})$.

- **Shuffle**(class) $\rightarrow$ (sclass, π). This algorithm generates a fresh permutation $\pi : \{1, \ldots, |U|\} \rightarrow \{1, \ldots, |U|\}$, re-randomizes all the ciphertext components in class and returns the permutated re-randomized vector as sclass. More precisely, we have sclass = (sclass$_1$, ..., sclass$_{|U|}$) where

$$\texttt{sclass}_j = (\texttt{class}_{\pi(j)} r_j^n) \mod n^2$$

- **Decide**(sclass, k_d, $VS_{\texttt{data}}$) $\rightarrow$ d. This algorithm decrypts the components in sclass and performs classification as described for the SVM classifier. The result d is the index in the input vector corresponding to the largest positive scaler, or $\perp$ if no positive scalar exists.

- **Identify**(d, π, $AS_{\texttt{data}}$) $\rightarrow$ ID. For authentication runs where $d \neq \perp$, this algorithm simply finds uid such that

$$uid = \pi^{-1}(d)$$

and returns the associated identity ID. Otherwise it returns $\perp$.

5.3   Security Analysis

In the full version of the paper [18] we prove two theorems, which capture the security properties of the proposed protocol.

Theorem 1. *The proposed protocol ensures feature privacy. More precisely, any PPT adversary has negligible advantage in distinguishing the distributions associated with* $\texttt{Exp}^{\texttt{fIND}}$.

Theorem 2. *The proposed protocol ensures user untraceability. More precisely, any PPT adversary has negligible advantage in distinguishing the distributions associated with* $\texttt{Exp}^{\texttt{uIND}}$.

Remark: On the (in)security of the Bringer et al. protocol The fIND model we propose is a more formal version of *Security Requirement 2* proposed by Bringer et al. [1] for their authentication protocol. The security argument presented for this protocol describes a reduction to the semantic security of the Goldwasser-Micali cryptosystem. However, the argument fails to cover a simple attack by the AS. The attack is possible because the interaction between the AS server and the DB server does not include a re-randomization of the resulting ciphertexts. This means that it may be possible for the AS to recover the user profile data that the DB server has used in the calculations. After recovering a biometric profile, the AS server is able to determine on its own which features belong to a user, without even executing the protocol. More precisely, and referring to the notation in [1], the AS calculates $(\mathcal{E}(t_1, pk), \ldots, \mathcal{E}(t_N, pk))$, where N is the number of users, $t_j = 0$ for all indexes except $j = i$ for which $t_j = 1$, and i is the index of the user to be authenticated. The DB server receives these ciphertexts and calculates $\mathcal{E}(b_{i,k}, pk) = \prod_{j=1}^{N} \mathcal{E}(t_j, pk)^{b_{j,k}} \mod n$, for $1 \leq k \leq M$, where $(b_{i,1}, \ldots, b_{i,M})$ is the biometric profile corresponding to user i. On receiving $\mathcal{E}(b_{i,k}, pk)$, the AS can try to work out whether $b_{i,k}$ is 1 or 0. To do this, it tries to calculate $\mathcal{E}(b_{i,k}, pk)/\prod_{j \in J} \mathcal{E}(t_j, pk) \mod n$, for all subsets $J \subset \{1 \ldots N\} \setminus i$, where $\mathcal{E}(t_j, pk)$ are exactly the same as those passed originally to the DB. If in these calculations the AS obtains 1, then it knows $b_{i,k} = 0$; if it obtains $\mathcal{E}(t_i, pk)$, then it knows $b_{i,k} = 1$. The feasibility of this attack depends on the number of users N: in fact its complexity is exponential in N, which means it may be infeasible for a very large N. However, a simple patch to the protocol, preventing the attack altogether even for small N, is to ensure that the DB server re-randomises ciphertexts after applying the homomorphic transformations. We emphasise that the security reduction presented in this paper for the proposed protocol explicitly precludes this type of attack.

6   Discussion and Conclusion

We have presented a hybrid protocol for secure biometric authentication which permits adopting state-of-the art pattern recognition classifiers to improve over the authentication accuracy of existing solutions. Our protocol follows the approach of Bringer et al. [1], adopting the point of view that biometric information may be stored in public servers, as long as it is guaranteed that it remains anonymous if security is breached. To allow for the use of more powerful classification techniques, namely the SVM classifier, we use the Pailler public key encryption scheme, taking advantage of its homomorphic properties.

The main advantages of the proposed protocol over previous solutions can be summarised as follows:

- Potential for much better accuracy using different types of biometric signals, including behavioural ones.
- Improved user privacy, since user identities are not transmitted at any point in the protocol execution. This is possible because the classifiers we adopt are *identification classifiers* which do not need to know who the user claims to be in order to perform authentication and recover the user identity.

Security of the proposed protocol has been formalised in two security models: feature indistinguishability and user indistinguishability. These are extended versions of the models proposed in [1], where we also account for eavesdroppers external to the system. We provide a reduction relating the security of our authentication protocol with the security of the Paillier encryption scheme. We also describe a simple attack against the Bringer et al. protocol, and show how it can be easily repaired.

Acknowledgements. The authors would like to thank Michel Abdalla for reading and commenting on an earlier version of this paper.

References

1. Bringer, J., Chabanne, H., Izabachène, M., Pointcheval, D., Tang, Q., Zimmer, S.: An application of the goldwasser-micali cryptosystem to biometric authentication. In: Pieprzyk, J., Ghodosi, H., Dawson, E. (eds.) ACISP 2007. LNCS, vol. 4586, pp. 96–106. Springer, Heidelberg (2007)
2. Dodis, Y., Ostrovsky, R., Reyzin, L., Smith, A.: Fuzzy extractors: How to generate strong keys from biometrics and other noisy data. Cryptology ePrint Archive, Report 2003/235 (2003), http://eprint.iacr.org/
3. Boyen, X.: Reusable cryptographic fuzzy extractors. In: CCS 2004: Proceedings of the 11th ACM conference on Computer and communications security, pp. 82–91. ACM, New York (2004)
4. Boyen, X., Dodis, Y., Katz, J., Ostrovsky, R., Smith, A.: Secure remote authentication using biometric data. In: Cramer, R.J.F. (ed.) EUROCRYPT 2005. LNCS, vol. 3494, pp. 147–163. Springer, Heidelberg (2005), http://www.cs.stanford.edu/~xb/eurocrypt05b/
5. Monrose, F., Reiter, M.K., Wetzel, S.: Password hardening based on keystroke dynamics. In: CCS 1999: Proceedings of the 6th ACM conference on Computer and communications security, pp. 73–82. ACM, New York (1999)
6. Hocquet, S., Ramel, J.Y., Cardot, H.: Fusion of methods for keystroke dynamic authentication. Automatic Identification Advanced Technologies, 2005. In: Fourth IEEE Workshop, October 17–18, 2005, pp. 224–229 (2005)
7. Monrose, F., Reiter, M., Li, Q., Wetzel, S.: Cryptographic key generation from voice. In: Proceedings of IEEE Symposium on Security and Privacy, S&P 2001, pp. 202–213 (2001)
8. Yegnanarayana, B., Prasanna, S., Zachariah, J., Gupta, C.: Combining evidence from source, suprasegmental and spectral features for a fixed-text speaker verification system. IEEE Transactions on Speech and Audio Processing 13, 575–582 (2005)
9. Cauchie, S., Brouard, T., Cardot, H.: From features extraction to strong security in mobile environment: A new hybrid system. In: Meersman, R., Tari, Z., Herrero, P. (eds.) OTM 2006 Workshops. LNCS, vol. 4277, pp. 489–498. Springer, Heidelberg (2006)
10. Feng, H., Choong, W.C.: Private key generation from on-line handwritten signatures. Inf. Manag. Comput. Security 10(4), 159–164 (2002)
11. Fuentes, M., Garcia-Salicetti, S., Dorizzi, B.: On-line signature verification: Fusion of a hidden markov model and a neural network via a support vector machine. iwfhr 00, 253 (2002)
12. Goh, A., Ling, D.N.C.: Computation of cryptographic keys from face biometrics. In: Lioy, A., Mazzocchi, D. (eds.) CMS 2003. LNCS, vol. 2828, pp. 1–13. Springer, Heidelberg (2003)
13. Yan, T.T.H.: Object recognition using fractal neighbor distance: eventual convergence and recognition rates. In: Proceedings of 15th International Conference on Pattern Recognition, vol. 2, pp. 781–784 (2000)
14. Uludag, U.A.J.: Securing fingerprint template: Fuzzy vault with helper data. In: Conference on Computer Vision and Pattern Recognition Workshop, June 17-22, 2006, pp. 163–163 (2006)
15. Guo, H.: A hidden markov model fingerprint matching approach. In: Proceedings of 2005 International Conference on Machine Learning and Cybernetics, August 18-21, 2005, vol. 8, pp. 5055–5059 (2005)

16. Hao, F., Anderson, R., Daugman, J.: Combining crypto with biometrics effectively. IEEE Transactions on Computers 55(9), 1081–1088 (2006)
17. Crammer, K., Singer, Y.: On the algorithmic implementation of multiclass kernel-based vector machines. Journal of Machine Learning Research 2, 265–292 (2001)
18. Barbosa, M., Brouard, T., Cauchie, S., Sousa, S.: Secure biometric authentication with improved accuracy. Cryptology ePrint Archive (2008)
19. Paillier, P.: Public-key cryptosystems based on composite degree residuosity classes. In: Stern, J. (ed.) EUROCRYPT 1999. LNCS, vol. 1592, pp. 223–238. Springer, Heidelberg (1999)
20. Paillier, P., Pointcheval, D.: Efficient public-key cryptosystems provably secure against active adversaries. In: Lam, K.-Y., Okamoto, E., Xing, C. (eds.) ASIACRYPT 1999. LNCS, vol. 1716, pp. 165–179. Springer, Heidelberg (1999)
21. Bellare, M., Boldyreva, A., Micali, S.: Public-key encryption in a multi-user setting: Security proofs and improvements. In: Preneel, B. (ed.) EUROCRYPT 2000. LNCS, vol. 1807, pp. 259–274. Springer, Heidelberg (2000)

Appendix A: Paillier Public Key Encryption Scheme

The Paillier public key encryption scheme [19,20] can be described as follows:

- **Key generation:** $\mathcal{G}_{\texttt{Paillier}}(1^\kappa) = (k_d, k_e)$. The PPT key generation algorithm takes a security parameter 1^κ as input, and randomly generates two large prime numbers p and q, setting $n = pq$ and $\lambda = lcm(p - 1, q - 1)$. The algorithm then randomly selects $g \in \mathbb{Z}_{n^2}^*$, such that n divides the order of g. This can be ensured by checking that

$$\gcd(L(g^\lambda \mod n^2), n) = 1, \text{ where } L(u) = \frac{u - 1}{n}$$

which in turn implies that the following multiplicative inverse exists:

$$\mu = (L(g^\lambda \mod n^2))^{-1} \mod n$$

The public key is then $k_e = (n, g)$ and the secret key is $k_d = (\mu, \lambda)$.

- **Encryption:** $\mathcal{E}_{\texttt{Paillier}}(m, k_e)$. The PPT encryption algorithm takes a message $m \in \mathbb{Z}_n$ and the public key $k_e = (n, g)$, generates r uniformly at random from $\mathbb{Z}_n^*$ and outputs a ciphertext $c \in \mathbb{Z}_{n^2}$, where $c = g^m \cdot r^n \mod n^2$.
- **Decryption:** $\mathcal{D}_{\texttt{Paillier}}(c, k_d)$. The deterministic decryption algorithm takes a ciphertext c and the secret key and outputs the plaintext m, which is recovered as $m = L(c^\lambda \mod n^2) \cdot \mu \mod n$.

It has been shown [20] that, under the composite residuosity assumption, the Paillier cryptosystem provides semantic security against chosen-plaintext attacks (IND-CPA). In other words, any PPT adversary $\mathcal{A}$ has only a negligible advantage in the following game against the Paillier cryptosystem:

$$\mathrm{Exp}_{\mathtt{Paillier}}^{\mathrm{IND-CPA}}(\mathcal{A})$$

$$
\begin{aligned}
&(k_d, k_e) &&\leftarrow \mathcal{G}_{\mathtt{Paillier}}(1^\kappa)\\
&(m_0, m_1, s) &&\leftarrow \mathcal{A}_1(k_e)\\
&\beta &&\leftarrow \{0, 1\}\\
&c &&\leftarrow \mathcal{E}_{\mathtt{Paillier}}(m_\beta)\\
&\beta' &&\leftarrow \mathcal{A}_2(c, s)\\
&\text{return } \beta'
\end{aligned}
$$

where the attacker's advantage $\mathbf{Adv}_{\mathtt{Paillier}}^{\mathrm{IND-CPA}}$ is defined as:

$$\mathbf{Adv}_{\mathtt{Paillier}}^{\mathrm{IND-CPA}} = |\Pr[\mathrm{Exp}_{\mathtt{Paillier}}^{\mathrm{IND-CPA}} = 1|\beta = 1] - \Pr[\mathrm{Exp}_{\mathtt{Paillier}}^{\mathrm{IND-CPA}} = 1|\beta = 0]|$$

In our scheme we will be using the Paillier cryptosystem to encrypt biometric features represented as short sequences of integer numbers. Encryption will be component-wise, where we assume that each integer component in the feature is in a range suitable for direct encoding into the message space[4]. For this reason we require a generalisation of the IND-CPA property allowing the adversary to make a polynomial number n of queries to a Left-or-Right challenge oracle. We call this notion n-IND-CPA and emphasize that the security of the Paillier encryption scheme in this setting is implied by its semantic security [21].

We will also take advantage of the following homomorphic properties of the Paillier encryption scheme:

$$\mathcal{E}_{\mathtt{Paillier}}(a, k_e)\mathcal{E}_{\mathtt{Paillier}}(b, k_e) = \mathcal{E}_{\mathtt{Paillier}}(a + b, k_e)$$

$$\mathcal{E}_{\mathtt{Paillier}}(a, k_e)^b = \mathcal{E}_{\mathtt{Paillier}}(ab, k_e)$$

The aditive property also provides a method to re-randomize a given Paillier cryptosystem which we will use:

$$(\mathcal{E}_{\mathtt{Paillier}}(a, k_e; r') \cdot r^n) \mod n^2 = \mathcal{E}_{\mathtt{Paillier}}(a, k_e; r'r).$$

---

[4] In practice, SVM features can be represented using integers in the range -100 to 100, which can be easily encoded into $\mathbb{Z}_n$.

A Critical Analysis and Improvement of AACS Drive-Host Authentication

Jiayuan Sui and Douglas R. Stinson*

David R. Cheriton School of Computer Science
University of Waterloo
Waterloo, ON, N2L 3G1, Canada
{jsui,dstinson}@uwaterloo.ca

Abstract. This paper presents a critical analysis of the AACS drive-host authentication scheme. A few weaknesses are identified which could lead to various attacks on the scheme. In particular, we observe that the scheme is susceptible to unknown key-share and man-in-the-middle attacks. Modifications of the scheme are suggested in order to provide better security. A proof of security of the modified scheme is also presented. The modified scheme achieves better efficiency than the original scheme.

1 Introduction

Advanced Access Content System (AACS) is a content distribution system for recordable and pre-recorded media. It has been developed by eight companies: Disney, IBM, Intel, Matsushita (Panasonic), Microsoft, Sony, Toshiba, and Warner Brothers. Most notably, AACS is used to protect the next generation of high definition optical discs such as Blu-ray and HD-DVD.

To design a media protection scheme that is able to run on open platforms like PCs, designers have to make sure that the scheme is not susceptible to the "virtual device attack". A virtual device can mimic a physical hardware device in all respects, so that the CPU is tricked into believing that a device exists when actually it does not. To deploy a virtual device attack on a media system such as the DVD playback system, the attacker can build software that implements a virtual DVD drive. The content of the optical disc is moved onto the computer's hard drive as a disc image. The attacker can then play back this "DVD disc" through the virtual DVD drive on a legitimate DVD player software.

The attacker can certainly duplicate the disc image into multiple copies and disseminate them illegally, even though he never learns the content of the DVD in the clear. In order to defend against this attack, the drive has to have the ability to prove to the host (e.g. the playback software) that it is a legitimate drive. This can be done through a cryptographic authentication protocol.

The AACS drive-host authentication scheme achieves mutual authentication, which means that the drive proves to the host its legitimate identity and the

---

* Supported by the Natural Sciences and Engineering Research Council of Canada (NSERC) through the grant NSERC-RGPIN #203114-06.

Y. Mu, W. Susilo, and J. Seberry (Eds.): ACISP 2008, LNCS 5107, pp. 37–52, 2008.

host has to prove its identity to the drive. After the drive and the host complete a successful session of the protocol, a shared secret key is established between them. Therefore, AACS drive-host mutual authentication protocol is combined with a key agreement protocol. The shared secret key is then used for message authentication purposes.

1.1 Mutual Authentication Protocol and Key Agreement Protocol

In a mutual authentication protocol, the two participating entities need to prove their identities to each other. If an entity has successfully proven its identity to the other entity, the other entity is required to "accept". A session of a mutual authentication protocol is a successfully completed session if both participants have accepted by the end of the session. Mutual authentication protocols can be devised by using either symmetric or asymmetric key cryptographic primitives. Stinson [13, Chapter 9] provides some good studies on mutual authentication protocols.

After two entities have authenticated themselves to each other, most likely they will want to communicate with each other. It therefore makes sense to combine a key agreement protocol with a mutual authentication protocol, because a shared secret key provides confidentiality and/or data integrity to both communicating entities. In a key agreement protocol, both entities contribute information which is used to derive a shared secret key. A key agreement protocol most often uses asymmetric-key primitives.

A key agreement protocol is said to provide *implicit key authentication* to both entity A and entity B if A is assured that no one other than B can possibly learn the value of the shared secret key (likewise, B is assured that no one other than A can learn the value of the key). Note that this property does not necessarily mean that A is assured of B actually possessing the key nor is A assured that B can actually compute the key. A key agreement protocol with implicit key authentication is called an *authenticated key agreement* (AK) protocol.

A key agreement protocol is said to provide *implicit key confirmation* if A is assured that B can compute the secret key while no others can, and vice versa. A protocol provides *explicit key confirmation* if A is assured that B has computed the secret key and no one other than B can compute the key, and vice versa. A key agreement protocol that provides key confirmation (either implicit or explicit) to both participating entities is called an *authenticated key agreement with key confirmation* (AKC) protocol. For example, explicit key confirmation can be achieved by using the newly derived key to encrypt a known value and to send it to the other entity. In most cases, using a key agreement protocol with implicit key confirmation is sufficient. For more information on key agreement protocols, please refer to [13, Chapter 11].

1.2 Our Contributions

In this paper, we present a rigorous analysis of the AACS drive-host authentication scheme. Specifically, we identify a few weaknesses present in the scheme which could lead to various attacks. It is yet to be known whether those weaknesses will lead to piracy of multimedia content. Nevertheless, we believe that it is not desirable for such a widely-deployed system to employ a weak cryptographic protocol if it can be made secure fairly easily. We propose an improvement of the original scheme based on the well-established Station-to-Station key agreement protocol. The improved scheme provides secure mutual authentication as well as authenticated key agreement with key confirmation. We also discuss the security of the improved scheme. The improved scheme is designed with the goal of requiring little change to be made to the original scheme, so implementation of the improved scheme is straightforward. In addition, the improved scheme requires less interaction between the drive and the host, and therefore it is more efficient than the original scheme. Furthermore, our improved scheme can be easily implemented on other content distribution systems such as CSS [7] and CPPM [1] which also use weak drive-host authentication schemes.

1.3   Organization

In Section 2, we introduce the AACS drive-host authentication scheme. Our analysis of the AACS drive-host authentication scheme is presented in Section 3, where we identify several weaknesses in the scheme and provide corresponding improvements. In Section 4, we discuss the security of the improved drive-host authentication scheme, followed by a conclusion in Section 5.

2   AACS Drive-Host Authentication Scheme

When using AACS in a PC-based system where the drive and the host are separate entities, both the drive and the host are issued certificates from the AACS LA (AACS Licensing Administrator). This allows either entity to verify whether or not the other is trustworthy and in compliance with the AACS specifications. These certificates, called the *drive certificate* and *host certificate*, each contain fields stating the capabilities of the device, a unique identifier, the device's public key, and a signature from the AACS LA verifying the integrity of the certificate signed with an AACS LA private key. Both the drive and the host have the corresponding AACS LA public key for signature verification. A full description of the certificate format can be found in the AACS Introduction and Common Cryptographic Elements specification [2, Chapter 4].

   Authentication between the drive and the host occurs each time new media is placed into the drive. This is necessary because the new disc may contain updated revocation lists. Each compliant disc contains a data structure called the *media key block* (MKB), which holds the necessary information needed to derive the keys to decrypt the content. It also contains the latest *drive revocation list* (DRL) and *host revocation list* (HRL) which, respectively, contain a list of IDs of the revoked drives and a list of IDs of the revoked hosts. A drive may only communicate with a host that has not been revoked, and a host may only communicate with a drive that has not been revoked.

A detailed description of the AACS drive-host authentication scheme can be found in [2, Section 4.3]. The original scheme consists a total of twenty-nine steps. A simplified version consisting only the core steps involved in authentication and key agreement is shown in Figure 2.

After successfully completing the drive-host authentication algorithm, the drive and the host have established a shared *bus key* based on an elliptic curve Diffie-Hellman key agreement protocol [11]. It is interesting to note that while this key could be used to encrypt messages between the drive and the host, it is not actually used for this purpose. Instead, the bus key is used solely for message authentication by including a MAC for any message traveling between the drive and the host. The current AACS specifications do not require either the drive or the host to be capable of encrypting and decrypting bus messages; however there is a flag in each certificate stating whether or not an entity is capable of performing bus encryption.

3   Analysis of the AACS Drive-Host Authentication Scheme

In this section, we analyze the AACS drive-host authentication scheme. Several weaknesses are identified which could lead to various attacks, and corresponding improvements are provided to strengthen the original scheme.

Our discussion of security is based on the standard security model for authentication and key agreement schemes, which was first proposed by Bellare and Rogaway in the symmetric-key setting [4]. Blake-Wilson et al. later generalized this model into the public-key setting [6]. In the standard model, the adversary has enormous power and controls all communication between entities. The adversary can read, modify, create, delay and replay messages, and he/she can initiate new sessions at any time.

3.1   Weakness 1: Design Error

This weakness is present in the first four steps of the drive-host authentication scheme. Suppose that the DRL in the MKB is newer than the DRL stored in the host. A malicious party, Oscar, can change the MKB version number to an older one, and send the modified MKB' to the host. This modification might not be detected during the authentication procedure, because according to the specification, the host first checks the MKB version number, and if the version number is older than its DRL's, it skips over step 2, which involves verifying the signature on the DRL in the MKB.

Drive   Oscar   Host

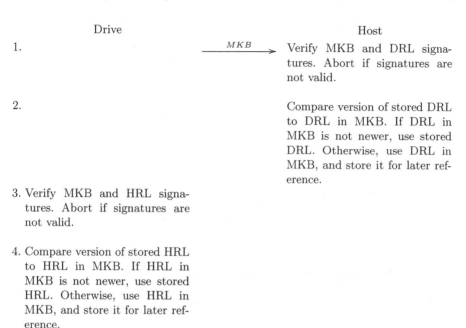

Fig. 1. Improved First Four Steps

If the drive has already been revoked, it could maliciously alter the MKB version number in order not to let the host update its DRL, so that it can keep interacting with the host.

The altered MKB might eventually be detected when the host processes the MKB during content decryption. However, it is undesirable for a revoked drive to be able to talk to the host until then.

The fix to this weakness is simple: The host should verify the MKB and DRL signatures before checking the version numbers. The same modification can be made to the drive side. Figure 1 shows the modification.

3.2 Weakness 2: Unknown Key-Share Attack

Suppose A and B are two honest participating entities trying to set up a shared secret key through a key agreement protocol, and O is an active malicious entity. An unknown key-share attack on a key agreement protocol is an attack through which O causes one of the two honest entities, say A, to believe that it shares a key with O, but it actually shares the key with the other honest entity B, and B believes that the key is shared with A. So, at the end of the protocol, O can act on behalf of B to interact with A. There are a number of papers studying unknown key-share attack and its application on a number of protocols, e.g. [3], [5], [9], [12], and [14].

We can simplify the original flow representation of the drive-host authentication scheme displayed in [2, Section 4.3] into the one shown in Figure 2 by

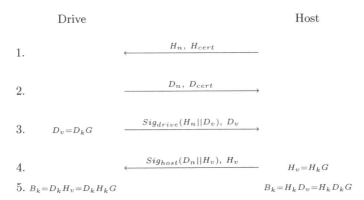

Fig. 2. Simplified AACS Drive-Host Authentication Protocol

taking into consideration only the core steps involved in authentication and key agreement. A similar flow diagram is also provided in [2, Section 4.3].

1. Host initiates a session with Drive. It sends a random nonce H_n and its certificate H_{cert} to Drive. Drive verifies the signature of the Host certificate using the AACS LA public key. If the verification fails, Drive shall abort this authentication procedure.
2. Drive replies to the Host with a random nonce D_n and its certificate D_{cert}. Host verifies the signature of the Drive certificate using the AACS LA public key. If the verification fails, Host shall abort this authentication procedure.
3. Drive generates a 160-bit random number D_k and uses it to calculate a point D_v on the elliptic curve (G is the base point of the elliptic curve). Drive then creates a signature of the concatenation of H_n and D_v. Drive sends the digital signature and D_v to Host. Host verifies the signature, and aborts the session on failure.
4. Host generates a 160-bit random number H_k and uses it to calculate a point H_v on the elliptic curve. Host then creates a signature of the concatenation of D_n and H_v. Host sends the digital signature and H_v to Drive. Drive verifies the signature, and aborts the session on failure.

On the last step, both Drive and Host calculate the shared secret bus key B_k.

An attacker, Drive$_{\text{Oscar}}$, which is also a legitimate drive, can use a parallel session to deploy an unknown key-share attack. Figure 3 shows the diagram of the attack.

The attack works in this way:

1. Host initiates a session with Drive$_{\text{Oscar}}$. It sends its random nonce H_n and certificate H_{cert} to Drive$_{\text{Oscar}}$.
2. Drive$_{\text{Oscar}}$ relays the traffic to Drive as if Host is initiating a session with Drive. Drive receives H_n and H_{cert} and verifies that H_{cert} is valid.
3. Drive sends back its random nonce D_n and certificate D_{cert} to Host, which of course get intercepted by Drive$_{\text{Oscar}}$.

4. Drive$_{\text{Oscar}}$ relays the random nonce D_n to Host, however, it does not relay the Drive's certificate. Instead, it sends its own certificate D_{O_cert} to Host. Host receives D_{O_cert} as well as D_n. It is tricked into believing that Drive$_{\text{Oscar}}$ has generated this random nonce. Host verifies Drive$_{\text{Oscar}}$'s certificate, and the verification should pass because Drive$_{\text{Oscar}}$ is a legitimate drive.

5. Following the AACS drive-host authentication protocol, Drive generates a random number D_k and calculates a point D_v on the elliptic curve. Drive then creates a signature of the concatenation of H_n and D_v. Drive sends the digital signature and D_v to Host.

6. Drive$_{\text{Oscar}}$ relays D_v to Host. However, it creates its own signature of the concatenation of H_n and D_v using its private key. It can do so because both H_n and D_v are available to it. It sends this signature instead of Drive's signature to Host. Host verifies the signature using Drive$_{\text{Oscar}}$'s public key obtained from D_{O_cert}. The verification should pass.

7. Host generates a random number H_k and calculates a point H_v on the elliptic curve. Drive then creates a signature of the concatenation of D_n and H_v. Drive sends the digital signature and H_v to Drive$_{\text{Oscar}}$.

8. Drive$_{\text{Oscar}}$ relays the traffic to Drive. Drive verifies the signature, and the verification should pass.

By the time the session is complete, Drive has accepted Host, and it can calculate the shared bus key B_k. On the other hand, Host does not accept Drive

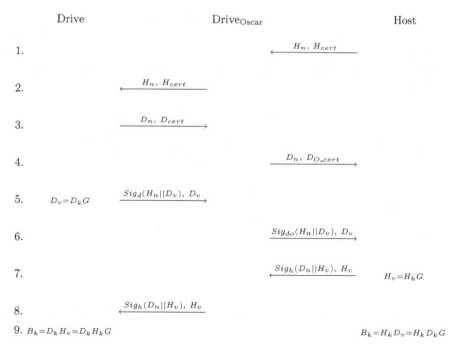

Fig. 3. Unknown Key-Share Attack on AACS Drive-Host Authentication Protocol

because it simply does not know the existence of Drive from this interaction. Instead, it has accepted Drive$_{\text{Oscar}}$. Host can also calculate the same shared bus key B_k.

Although Drive$_{\text{Oscar}}$ does not know the secret bus key B_k in the end, it has tricked Host into believing that it shares the bus key with Drive$_{\text{Oscar}}$. Host thinks that it is talking to Drive$_{\text{Oscar}}$ while actually it is interacting with Drive.

This attack could be exploited in practice. For example, suppose that Drive$_A$ is revoked. Then it can employ this attack to ask Drive$_B$, which is not revoked, to impersonate it. Since the host only sees Drive$_B$'s certificate, the authentication procedure should complete successfully. In this way, Drive$_A$ can still interact with the host after the authentication procedure. It has effectively bypassed the authentication procedure.

Such an attack is enabled due to the fact that in the last two flows Drive$_{\text{Oscar}}$ can simply copy the traffic. This problem can be fixed by including the entity IDs in the signature. (See Section 3.4).

3.3   Weakness 3: Man-in-the-Middle Attack

The adversarial goal in an attack to a mutual authentication protocol is to cause an honest participant to "accept" after a flow in which the adversary is active. To consider a mutual authentication protocol secure, it has to satisfy the following two conditions:

1. Suppose A and B are the two participants in a session of the protocol and they are both honest. Suppose also that the adversary is passive. Then A and B will both "accept".
2. If the adversary is active during a given flow of the protocol, then no honest participant will "accept" after that flow.

Figure 4 shows an attack which might not be as powerful and practical as the previous one. Nonetheless, it shows a weakness in this protocol.

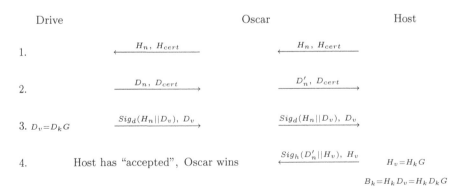

Fig. 4. A Trivial Man-In-The-Middle Attack

In this case, Oscar could be a polynomial time adversary with the ability to listen and to modify the traffic. Notice that in step 2 when Oscar relays the traffic from Drive to Host, it modifies the random nonce D_n generated by Drive into a different one D_n'. This does not make Host terminate the session. In step 3, after Host has successfully verified Drive's signature, it "accepts". This violates condition 2 mentioned above, hence the protocol should not be considered secure.

A moment of reflection regarding this attack reveals that we do not really need the two nonces "H_n" and "D_n".

3.4   Improved Scheme

Since the scheme makes use of certificates, we can improve it using a simplified *Station-to-Station* key agreement protocol (STS). STS protocol is a key agreement scheme based on Diffie-Hellman scheme that provides mutual authentication. For more information on STS protocols, please refer to [8], [13, Chapter 11], [10].

Figure 5 shows the improved drive-host authentication scheme based on STS. This modification solves both problems stated in weakness 2 and 3 (a security proof is given in the next section). In addition, it improves the efficiency of the original protocol, because the number of interactions between Drive and Host is reduced.

1. Host initiates a session with Drive. It generates a 160-bit random number H_k and uses it to calculate a point H_v on the elliptic curve. It sends the H_v and its certificate H_{cert} to Drive. Drive verifies the signature of the Host certificate using the AACS LA public key. If the verification fails, Drive shall abort this session.
2. Drive generates a 160-bit random number D_k and uses it to calculate a point D_v on the elliptic curve. Drive then creates a signature of the concatenation of the Host ID, D_v, and H_v. Drive sends the digital signature, D_v, and its certificate D_{cert} to Host. Host verifies the signature created by Drive: $ver_{drive}(ID_{host}||D_v||H_v, \text{Drive's signature}) \overset{?}{=} \text{true}$, and it also verifies the

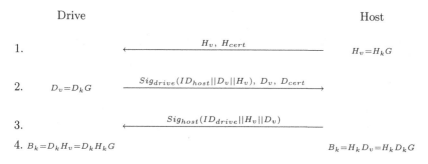

Fig. 5. Improved Scheme Based on the Station-to-Station Protocol

signature of the Drive certificate. If any of the two verifications fail, Host shall abort the session.

3. Host creates a signature of the concatenation of the Drive ID, H_v, and D_v and sends it to Drive. Drive verifies the signature: $ver_{host}(ID_{drive}||H_v||D_v,$ Host's signature) $\stackrel{?}{=}$ true, and aborts the session on failure.

At the end of the protocol, both Drive and Host are able to establish the shared secret bus key B_k. Points H_v and D_v in this protocol also play a role as random challenges.

The new protocol solves all the aforementioned problems. Since the random challenges H_n and D_n are omitted, it enables the drive and the host to perform fewer interactions, and is therefore more efficient.

Appendix A shows a flow representation of the entire improved drive-host authentication protocol.

4   Security of the Improved Drive-Host Authentication Scheme

The improved scheme protects against the unknown key-shared attack mentioned earlier.

In Figure 6, a question mark following a signature indicates that the adversary is unable to compute this signature. At step 3, the signature which Host sends to Drive$_{\mathrm{Oscar}}$ contains Drive$_{\mathrm{Oscar}}$'s ID not Drive's ID because Host believes that it is talking to Drive$_{\mathrm{Oscar}}$. Drive$_{\mathrm{Oscar}}$ cannot compute Host's signature on the string $ID_{drive}||H_v||D_v$ because he does not know Host's private signing key. As a result, unknown key-share attack is thwarted.

After step 2, Host "accepts" the authentication because it should successfully verify Drive$_{\mathrm{Oscar}}$'s signature and certificate. This does not violate the second condition of considering a mutual authentication protocol secure mentioned in Section 3.3, because Host is authenticating with Drive$_{\mathrm{Oscar}}$.

The improved scheme also protects against man-in-the-middle attack.

As shown in Figure 7, if Oscar modifies H_v, he then would not be able to produce Host's signature on $ID_{drive}||H_v'||D_v$ because he does not know Host's

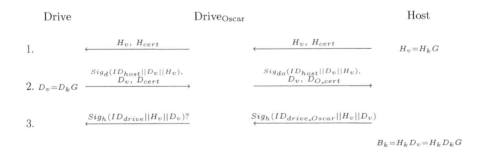

Fig. 6. Protection Against Unknown Key-Share Attack

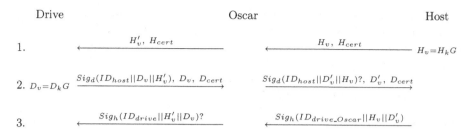

Fig. 7. Prevention of Man-In-The-Middle Attack

private signing key. Likewise, if Oscar modifies D_v, he then would not be able to produce Drive's signature on $ID_{host}||D_v'||H_v$ because he does not know Drive's private signing key.

Of course, we want to show that the improved scheme is secure against all possible attacks, not just two particular attacks. Hence, we need to show that the improved scheme is a secure mutual authentication scheme, and that it provides assurances regarding knowledge of the shared secret key. For the proof of security of our improved scheme, an informal treatment based on [13, Chapter 11] is given in the rest of this section.

4.1   Secure Mutual Authentication

A secure mutual authentication has to satisfy the two conditions described in Section 3.3. Let us first show that our improved scheme satisfies the first condition.

Since no one is modifying the traffic, if the adversary is passive and the two participants are honest they should successfully authenticate themselves to each other and both compute the shared secret key as in the Diffie-Hellman key agreement scheme. Assuming the intractability of the *Decision Diffie-Hellman* problem, the inactive adversary cannot compute the share secret key.

To prove that our improved scheme satisfies the second condition, let us assume that the adversary is active. The adversary wants to fool at least one of the two participants to "accept" after a flow in which he is active. We show that the adversary will not scceed in this way, except with a very small probability.

Definition 1. *A signature scheme is (ϵ, Q, T)-secure if the adversary cannot construct a valid signature for any new message with probability greater than ϵ, given that he has previously seen at most Q different valid signatures, and given that his computation time is limited to T.*

Definition 2. *A mutual authentication scheme is (ϵ, Q, T)-secure if the adversary cannot fool any honest participants into accepting with probability greater than ϵ, given that he has observed at most Q previous sessions between the honest participants, and given that the his computation time is at most T.*

Time T is usually chosen to be very long so that by the time the adversary successfully computes the correct result the value of the result has decreased to an insignificant level. For simplicity of notation, we omit the time parameter. Q is a specified security parameter. Depending on the application, it could be assigned with various values. The probability ϵ is usually chosen to be so small that the chance of success is negligible.

Theorem 1. *Suppose that Sig is an (ϵ, Q)-secure signature scheme, and suppose that random challenges H_v and D_v are k bits in length. Then the scheme shown in Figure 5 is a $(Q/2^{k-1} + 2\epsilon, Q)$-secure mutual authentication scheme.*

Proof. The adversary, Oscar, observes Q previous sessions of the protocol before making his attack. A successful attack by Oscar is to deceive at least one honest participant in a new session into accepting after he is active in one or more flows.

1. Oscar tries to deceive Host. In order to make Host accept, it has to receive a signature signed by Drive containing the Host ID and the random challenge H_v. There are only two ways for Oscar to acquire such a signature: either from a previously observed session or by computing it himself.

   To observe such a signature from a previous session, H_v has to be used in that session. The probability that Host has already used the challenge in a specific previous session is $1/2^k$. There are at most Q previous sessions under consideration, so the probability that H_v was used as a challenge in one of these previous sessions is at most $Q/2^k$. If this happens, Oscar can re-use Drive's signature and D_v' (which may or may not be the same as D_v) from that session to fool Host.

   To compute such a signature himself, Oscar has at most a chance of ϵ, since Sig is (ϵ, Q)-secure.

   Therefore, Oscar's probability of deceiving Host is at most $Q/2^k + \epsilon$.

2. Oscar tries to deceive Drive. This is quite similar to the case we have discussed above. In order to fool Drive, Oscar has to have a legitimate signature signed by Host. As in the previous case, the two ways for Oscar to acquire such a signature are either from a previously observed session or by computing it himself.

   To observe such a signature from a previous session, Oscar re-uses a H_v from a previous session S to send to Drive, and hopes that Drive will reply with the same D_v as in S so that he can re-use the corresponding signature. This happens with probability $1/2^k$. The best case scenario for the adversary would be that all Q previously observed sessions have the same H_v. Because if any D_v from the Q sessions is re-used by Drive, Oscar can then re-use the corresponding signature to fool Drive. Hence, Oscar has at most $Q/2^k$ probability to re-use Host's signature to deceive Drive.

   Again since Sig is (ϵ, Q)-secure, Oscar can compute such a signature with a probability of at most ϵ.

   Therefore, Oscar's probability of deceiving Drive is at most $Q/2^k + \epsilon$.

Summing up, the probability for Oscar to deceive one of Host or Drive is at most $(Q/2^k + \epsilon) + (Q/2^k + \epsilon) = Q/2^{k-1} + 2\epsilon$.

4.2   Implicit Key Confirmation

Now, let us see what we can infer about the improved scheme if Host or Drive "accepts". Firstly, suppose that Host "accepts". Because the improved scheme is a secure mutual authentication scheme, Host can be confident that it has really been communicating with Drive and that the adversary was inactive before the last flow. Assuming that Drive is honest and that it has executed the scheme according to the specifications, Host can be confident that Drive can compute the value of the secret bus key, and that no one other than Drive can compute the value of the bus key.

Let us consider in more detail why Host should believe that Drive can compute the bus key. The reason for this belief is that Host has received Drive's signature on the values H_v and D_v, so it is reasonable for Host to infer that Drive knows these two values. Now, since Drive is a honest participant and executed the scheme according to the specifications, Host can infer that Drive knows the values of D_k. Drive is able to compute the value of the bus key, provided that he knows the values of H_v and D_k. Of course, there is no guarantee to Host that Drive has actually computed the bus key at the moment when Host "accepts". We can be sure that no one else can compute the bus key because D_k is meant to be known to Drive only.

The analysis from the point of view of Drive is very similar. If Drive "accepts", then it is confident that it has really been communicating with Host, and that the bus key can be computed only by Host and no one else.

The improved scheme does not make immediate use of the new bus key, so we do not have explicit key confirmation. However, it does achieve implicit key confirmation. Moreover, it is always possible to augment any key agreement scheme with implicit key confirmation so that it achieves explicit key confirmation (the SIGMA protocol is an efficient key agreement scheme similar to STS which provides explicit key confirmation [10]), if so desired. In essence, the improved scheme provides authenticated key agreement with key confirmation.

5   Conclusion

We have described three weaknesses in the AACS drive-host authentication scheme. Specifically, the scheme is susceptible to unknown key-share attack and man-in-the-middle attack. As a goal to improve the scheme to resist all kinds of attacks, we have modified the original scheme based on a simplified Station-to-Station key agreement protocol to provide secure mutual authentication as well as authenticated key agreement with key confirmation. In addition, our modified scheme achieves better efficiency than the original scheme.

References

1. 4C Entity LLC, Content Protection For Prerecorded Media Specification, Revision 1.0 (January 2003)
2. AACS LA, Advanced Access Content System (AACS) - Introduction and Common Cryptographic Elements, Revision 0.91, February 17 (2006), http://www.aacsla.com/specifications/specs091/AACS_Spec_Common_0.91.pdf
3. Baek, J., Kim, K.: Remarks on the Unknown Key Share Attacks. IEICE Transactions on Fundamentals of Electronics, Communications and Computer Sciences E83-A(12), 2766–2769 (2000)
4. Bellare, M., Rogaway, P.: Entity Authentication and Key Distribution. In: Stinson, D.R. (ed.) CRYPTO 1993. LNCS, vol. 773, pp. 232–249. Springer, Heidelberg (1994)
5. Blake-Wilson, S., Menezes, A.: Unknown Key-Share Attacks on the Station-to-Station (STS) Protocol. In: Imai, H., Zheng, Y. (eds.) PKC 1999. LNCS, vol. 1560, pp. 154–170. Springer, Heidelberg (1999)
6. Blake-Wilson, S., Johnson, D., Menezes, A.: Key Agreement Protocols and Their Security Analysis. In: Darnell, M.J. (ed.) Cryptography and Coding 1997. LNCS, vol. 1355, pp. 30–45. Springer, Heidelberg (1997)
7. DVD Copy Control Association, CSS Procedural Specification, Version 2.9 (January 2007)
8. Diffie, W., van Oorschot, P.C., Wiener, M.J.: Authentication and Authenticated Key Exchanges. Designs, Codes and Cryptography 2(2), 107–125 (1992)
9. Kaliski Jr., B.S.: An Unknown Key-Share Attack on the MQV Key Agreement Protocol. ACM Transactions on Information and System Security 4(3), 275–288 (2001)
10. Krawczyk, H.: SIGMA: The 'SIGn-and-MAc' Approach to Authenticated Diffie-Hellman and Its Use in the IKE Protocols. In: Boneh, D. (ed.) CRYPTO 2003. LNCS, vol. 2729, pp. 400–425. Springer, Heidelberg (2003)
11. National Institute of Standards and Technology, Special Publication 800-56A, Recommendation for Pair-Wise Key Establish Schemes Using Discrete Logarithm Cryptography (March 2007)
12. Shim, K.: Unknown Key-Share Attack on Authenticated Multiple-Key Agreement Protocol. Electronics Letters 39(1), 38–39 (2003)
13. Stinson, D.R.: Cryptography Theory and Practice, Third Edition, 3rd edn. Chapman & Hall/CRC, Boca Raton (2006)
14. Zhou, H., Fan, L., Li, J.: Remarks on Unknown Key-Share Attack on Authenticated Multiple-Key Agreement Protocol. Electronics Letters 39(17), 1248–1249 (2003)

A   Improved Drive-Host Authentication Scheme

Drive   Host

1. $\xrightarrow{\quad MKB \quad}$ Verify MKB and DRL signatures. Abort if signatures are not valid.

2.

Compare version of stored DRL to DRL in MKB. If DRL in MKB is not newer, use stored DRL. Otherwise, use DRL in MKB, and store it for later reference.

3. Verify MKB and HRL signatures. Abort if signatures are not valid.

4. Compare version of stored HRL to HRL in MKB. If HRL in MKB is not newer, use stored HRL. Otherwise, use HRL in MKB, and store it for later reference.

5.

$$AGID \longrightarrow$$

6.

Generate 160-bit random number H_k.

7.

Calculate $H_v = H_k G$ where G is the base point of the elliptic curve.

8.

$$\longleftarrow H_v, Hcert$$

9. Verify host certificate type and length. Abort on failure.

10. Verify signature on host certificate. Abort on failure.

11. Check HRL and abort if Host ID is found.

12.

Request a point on the elliptic curve D_v, signature, and drive certificate.

13. Generate 160-bit random value D_k.

14. Calculate $D_v = D_k G$ where G is the base point of the elliptic curve.

15. Calculate D_{sig} as the signature of $ID_{host} \| D_v \| H_v$ using the drive's private key.

16. $\xrightarrow{\quad D_{sig},\ D_v,\ Dcert \quad}$

17.   Verify drive certificate type and length. Abort on failure.

18.   Verify signature on drive certificate. Abort on failure.

19.   Check DRL and abort if Drive ID is found.

20.   Verify D_{sig} and abort on failure.

21.   Calculate H_{sig} as the signature of $ID_{drive} \| H_v \| D_v$ using the host's private key.

22. $\xleftarrow{\quad H_{sig} \quad}$

23. Verify H_{sig} and abort on failure.

24. Calculate Bus Key B_k as the 128 least significant bits of x-coord($D_k H_v$).

25.   Calculate Bus Key B_k as the 128 least significant bits of x-coord($H_k D_v$).

Comparing the Pre- and Post-specified Peer Models for Key Agreement

Alfred Menezes and Berkant Ustaoglu

Department of Combinatorics & Optimization, University of Waterloo
{ajmeneze,bustaoglu}@uwaterloo.ca

Abstract. In the pre-specified peer model for key agreement, it is assumed that a party knows the identifier of its intended communicating peer when it commences a protocol run. On the other hand, a party in the post-specified peer model for key agreement does not know the identifier of its communicating peer at the outset, but learns the identifier during the protocol run. In this paper we compare the security assurances provided by the Canetti-Krawczyk security definitions for key agreement in the pre- and post-specified peer models. We give examples of protocols that are secure in one model but insecure in the other. We also enhance the Canetti-Krawczyk security models and definitions to encompass a class of protocols that are executable and secure in both the pre- and post-specified peer models.

1 Introduction

In 1993, Bellare and Rogaway [1] presented the first formal security model and security definition for key agreement. The model and associated definitions evolved over the years, culminating in the 2001 work of Canetti and Krawczyk [4] and its recent extension by LaMacchia, Lauter and Mityagin [13]. In all the aforementioned works, key agreement protocols are analyzed in the so-called *pre-specified peer model* wherein it is assumed that a party knows the identifier of its intended communicating peer when it commences a run of the protocol. That is, it is assumed that the exchange of identifiers, and possibly also the long-term public keys of the communicating parties, is handled by the application that invokes a run of the protocol.

In 2002, Canetti and Krawczyk [5] introduced the *post-specified peer model* wherein a party is activated to establish a session key knowing only a destination address (such as the IP address of a server) of the communicating peer, and only learns the peer's identifier during the execution of the protocol. According to [5], this scenario is common in practical settings where the peer's identifier is simply unavailable at the outset, or if one party wishes to conceal its identity from eavesdroppers or active adversaries. The IKE protocols [8,9] (see also [10]) are important examples of key agreement protocols that provide the option of identity concealment.

In the remainder of this paper we will not consider the identity concealment attribute of key agreement protocols. We will often shorten 'pre-specified peer model' to 'pre model', and 'post-specified peer model' to 'post model'.

Y. Mu, W. Susilo, and J. Seberry (Eds.): ACISP 2008, LNCS 5107, pp. 53–68, 2008.
© Springer-Verlag Berlin Heidelberg 2008

We say that a key agreement protocol designed for one of the pre or post models is *executable* in the other model if it can be run in the second model without requiring any additional message flows (and without making any fundamental changes to the protocol description). It is clear that any key agreement protocol designed for the post model is executable in the pre model. Indeed, if the peer's identifier (and long-term public key) is not needed at the start of the protocol, then the protocol can also be executed given the peer's identifier. Canetti and Krawczyk observed that the Σ_0 key agreement protocol is secure in the post model with respect to the security definition given in [5], but not secure in the pre model with respect to the security definition given in [4]. Hence, even though any protocol designed for the post model can be executed in the pre model, security in the post model of [5] does not guarantee security in the pre model of [4].

In this paper we explore the executability and security in the post model of key agreement protocols that have been designed for and analyzed in the pre model. Of course any protocol designed for the pre model can be modified for the post model by adding message flows which include the identifiers and long-term public keys of the communicating parties; however such a modification does not conform to our notion of executability because of the additional message flows. We provide an example of a key agreement protocol that is secure in the pre model but is not executable in the post model. We also observe that the HMQV protocol [11], which has been proven to be secure in the pre model, is executable in the post model (without the addition of message flows) but not secure unless additional measures are taken. These examples illustrate the essential differences between the two models, and highlight the danger of running in the post model a protocol that has only been analyzed in the pre model.

It is natural then to ask when a protocol secure in one model is executable and secure in the other model. We identify a class of *modifiable* key agreement protocols that have been designed for the pre model but can be executed with minimal modifications in the post model. This class includes many of the protocols that have been proposed in the literature including station-to-station [7], UM [19,16], MQV [15], Boyd-Mao-Paterson [2], HMQV [11], KEA+ [14], NAXOS [13], CMQV [20] and Okamoto [18]. (See [3] for an extensive list of key establishment protocols.) Such protocols have a *hybrid* description that combine the specification for the pre model and the specification of the modified protocol suitable for the post model. We develop a *combined* model and associated security definition that aims to simultaneously capture the security assurances (and more) of the extended Canetti-Krawczyk pre-specified peer model [13] and the Canetti-Krawczyk post-specified peer model [5]. The combined model has the feature that if a hybrid key agreement protocol is proven secure in that model, then its specializations are guaranteed to be secure when run in the pre and post models.

The remainder of this paper is organized as follows. In §2 we provide informal overviews of the Canetti-Krawczyk pre and post models and security definitions for key agreement. The differences between the two models are explored in §3. Protocol $\mathcal{P}$ is described in §3.1 as an example of a protocol that is secure in the pre model but not executable in the post model. In §3.2 we describe an attack on HMQV, demonstrating that the protocol is not secure in the post model. The Σ_0 protocol, which is an example of a protocol that is secure in the post model but insecure in the pre model, is revisited in §3.3. Our combined model and security definition are presented in §4. The NAXOS-C protocol is presented in §5 as an example of a protocol that is secure in the combined model.

Notation and Terminology. Let $G = \langle g \rangle$ denote a multiplicatively-written cyclic group of prime order q, and let $G^* = G \setminus \{1\}$. The *Computational Diffie-Hellman (CDH) assumption* in G is that computing $\text{CDH}(U, V) = g^{uv}$ is infeasible given $U = g^u$ and $V = g^v$ where $u, v \in_R [1, q - 1]$. The *Decisional Diffie-Hellman (DDH) assumption* in G is that distinguishing DH triples (g^a, g^b, g^{ab}) from random triples (g^a, g^b, g^c) is infeasible. The *Gap Diffie-Hellman (GDH) assumption* in G is that the CDH assumption holds even when a CDH solver is given a DDH oracle that distinguishes DH triples from random triples.

We consider Diffie-Hellman type protocols where the two communicating parties exchange static (long-term) and ephemeral (one-time) public keys. Party $\hat{A}$'s static private key is an integer $a \in_R [1, q - 1]$, and her corresponding static public key is $A = g^a$. Similarly, party $\hat{B}$ has a static key pair (b, B), and so on. A certifying authority (CA) issues certificates that binds a party's identifier to its static public key. We do not assume that the CA requires parties to prove possession of their static private keys, but we do insist that the CA verifies that static public keys belong to G^*. We restrict our attention to protocols where a party $\hat{A}$ called the *initiator* commences the protocol by selecting an ephemeral key pair and then sends the ephemeral public key (and possibly other data) to the second party. In our protocols, the ephemeral private key is either a randomly selected integer $x \in [1, q - 1]$ or a randomly selected binary string $\tilde{x}$ which is used together with the static private key to derive an integer $x \in [1, q - 1]$, and the corresponding ephemeral public key is $X = g^x$. Upon receipt of X, the *responder* $\hat{B}$ selects an ephemeral private key y or $\tilde{y}$ and sends $Y = g^y$ (and possibly other data) to $\hat{A}$. The parties may exchange some additional messages, after which they compute a session key. We use $\mathcal{I}$ and $\mathcal{R}$ to denote the constant strings "initiator" and "responder".

2 Security Definitions for Key Agreement

We provide overviews of the Canetti-Krawczyk pre- and post-specified peer models for key agreement and the associated security definitions. For full details and further explanations refer to [4] and [5].

2.1 Pre-specified Peer Model

Communications take place in a multi-party system, where the parties are identified by $\hat{A}$, $\hat{B}$, $\hat{C}$, ... At any given point in time, a party may be engaged in multiple instances of the protocol, each called a *session*. A session is created at $\hat{A}$ via a message containing at least three parameters $(\hat{A}, \hat{B}, s)$, where $\hat{A}$ is the session's *owner*, $\hat{B}$ is the intended *peer*, and s is a number that is unique among all sessions owned by $\hat{A}$. ($\hat{A}$ uses s to direct incoming messages to the appropriate session within $\hat{A}$.) Once created, a session is said to be *active* and maintains a *session state* where session-specific short-lived data such as an ephemeral private key is stored. The session processes incoming messages and produces outgoing messages. A session may *abort* without producing a session key, or may *complete* by accepting a session key and erasing its session state.

The adversary $\mathcal{M}$, modeled as a probabilistic Turing machine, controls all communications between parties as well as the activation of sessions. In order to model the possible leakage of secret information, $\mathcal{M}$ is allowed to issue the following queries to parties:

- *SessionStateReveal*: $\mathcal{M}$ learns the contents of the session state for a (not yet completed) session of its choosing. The session can no longer be activated and stops producing output.
- *Expire*: $\mathcal{M}$ directs a completed session to delete its session key.
- *SessionKeyReveal*: $\mathcal{M}$ learns the session key held by a (completed but unexpired) session of its choosing.
- *Corrupt*: $\mathcal{M}$ learns all the secret information held by a party of its choosing, including the party's static private key, all session states, and all session keys. The party can no longer be activated and stops producing output.

The adversary's goal is to distinguish a session key from a random key. Obviously the adversary should not be allowed to learn the session key by trivial means, for example by asking for the session key via a *SessionKeyReveal* query. To this end, a session $(\hat{A}, \hat{B}, s)$ is said to be *locally exposed* if $\mathcal{M}$ issued a *SessionStateReveal* or *SessionKeyReveal* query to that session, or if $\mathcal{M}$ issued a *Corrupt* query to $\hat{A}$ before the session expired (this includes the case in which $\hat{A}$ is corrupted before the session is created). Moreover, the session $(\hat{B}, \hat{A}, s)$ is defined to be *matching* to the session $(\hat{A}, \hat{B}, s)$, and $(\hat{A}, \hat{B}, s)$ is said to be *unexposed* if neither this session nor its matching session are locally exposed. Now, $\mathcal{M}$ selects a session that is completed, unexpired, and unexposed, and issues a special *Test* query to that session. ($\mathcal{M}$ is not allowed to issue the *Test* query more than once.) In response, $\mathcal{M}$ is given with equal probability either the session key held by the test session or a random key. $\mathcal{M}$ can continue to issue queries, however must ensure that the test session remains unexposed. Finally, $\mathcal{M}$ is said to win its distinguishing game (and thereby break the protocol) if it guesses correctly whether the key is random or not with success probability significantly greater than $\frac{1}{2}$. A key agreement protocol is said to be *secure* (in the pre-specified peer model) if (i) uncorrupted parties who complete matching sessions compute the same session key (except with negligible probability); and (ii) there is no adversary $\mathcal{M}$ who wins the distinguishing game.

2.2   Post-specified Peer Model

The Canetti-Krawczyk post-specified peer model and associated security definition [5] are essentially the same as in the pre model, but there are two important differences.

First, a session at $\hat{A}$ is created via a message containing (at least) three parameters $(\hat{A}, \hat{d}, s)$, where $\hat{d}$ is a *destination address* to which outgoing messages should be delivered. That is, party $\hat{A}$ does not know the identifier of its peer when it starts the session. During the course of the protocol run, $\hat{A}$ learns the (alleged) identifier $\hat{B}$ of the communicating party; this party is referred to as $\hat{A}$'s peer for that session.

Second, the definition of a matching session is different. Let $(\hat{A}, s)$ be a session that has completed with peer $\hat{B}$. Then a session $(\hat{B}, s)$ is said to be *matching* to $(\hat{A}, s)$ if either (i) $(\hat{B}, s)$ has not yet completed; or (ii) $(\hat{B}, s)$ has completed and its peer is $\hat{A}$. Condition (i) is necessary because the incomplete session $(\hat{B}, s)$ may not yet have determined its peer and hence could have been communicating with $(\hat{A}, s)$, in which case exposure of $(\hat{B}, s)$ could possibly reveal non-trivial information about the session key held by $(\hat{A}, s)$.

3   Differences between the Two Models

This section presents three examples to illustrate the differences between the Canetti-Krawczyk security definitions for key agreement in the pre- and post-specified peer models. Protocol $\mathcal{P}$ is secure in the pre model, but cannot be executed in the post model. HMQV is an example of a protocol that is secure in the pre model, and executable but not secure in the post model. The Σ_0 protocol is secure in the post model but insecure in the pre model.

3.1   Protocol $\mathcal{P}$

We present a two-pass Diffie-Hellman key agreement protocol $\mathcal{P}$. The protocol can be proven secure in the pre-specified peer model under the GDH assumption and where H and H_2 are modeled as random functions. (The reductionist security argument is elementary but tedious, and hence is omitted.) Observe that the initiator $\hat{A}$ cannot prepare the first outgoing message without knowledge of the peer's identifier $\hat{B}$ and static public key B. Hence, unless protocol $\mathcal{P}$ is modified in a fundamental way, it cannot be executed in the post-specified peer model without additional message flows to exchange identifiers and static public keys.

1. On input $(\hat{A}, \hat{B}, s)$, party $\hat{A}$ (the initiator) does the following:
   (a) Create an active session $(\hat{A}, \hat{B}, s, \mathcal{I})$.
   (b) Select an ephemeral private key $x \in_R [1, q-1]$.
   (c) Compute $X = g^x$ and $t_A = H_2(B^a, \mathcal{I}, s, \hat{A}, \hat{B}, X)$.
   (d) Send $(\hat{B}, \hat{A}, s, X, t_A)$ to $\hat{B}$.
2. Upon receiving $(\hat{B}, \hat{A}, s, X, t_A)$, party $\hat{B}$ (the responder) does the following:
   (a) Create an active session $(\hat{B}, \hat{A}, s, \mathcal{R})$.
   (b) Verify that $X \in G^*$.
   (c) Compute $\sigma_s = A^b$ and verify that $t_A = H_2(\sigma_s, \mathcal{I}, s, \hat{A}, \hat{B}, X)$.
   (d) Select an ephemeral private key $y \in_R [1, q-1]$.
   (e) Compute $Y = g^y$, $t_B = H_2(\sigma_s, \mathcal{R}, s, \hat{B}, \hat{A}, Y)$, and $k = H(X^y, X, Y)$.
   (f) Destroy y and σ_s.

(g) Send $(\hat{A}, \hat{B}, s, \mathcal{I}, Y, t_B)$ to $\hat{A}$.

(h) Complete the session $(\hat{B}, \hat{A}, s, \mathcal{R})$ and accept k as the session key.

3. Upon receiving $(\hat{A}, \hat{B}, s, \mathcal{I}, Y, t_B)$, party $\hat{A}$ checks that she owns an active session with identifier $(\hat{A}, \hat{B}, s, \mathcal{I})$. If so, then $\hat{A}$ does the following:

   (a) Verify that $Y \in G^*$.

   (b) Verify that $t_B = H_2(B^a, \mathcal{R}, s, \hat{B}, \hat{A}, Y)$.

   (c) Compute $k = H(Y^x, X, Y)$.

   (d) Destroy x.

   (e) Complete the session $(\hat{A}, \hat{B}, s, \mathcal{I})$ by accepting k as the session key.

3.2   HMQV Protocol

HMQV [11] is an efficient two-pass Diffie-Hellman key agreement protocol that has been proven to be secure in the pre-specified peer model under the CDH and KEA1 assumptions and where the hash functions employed are modeled as random functions.[1] The following informal description of the protocol omits some technical details that are not relevant to our analysis.[2]

Let $\overline{H}$ denote a hash function whose outputs are bitstrings of length l, where l is half the bitlength of the group order q. In HMQV, the initiator $\hat{A}$ sends $(\hat{B}, \hat{A}, X)$ to $\hat{B}$, who responds with $(\hat{A}, \hat{B}, Y)$. Party $\hat{A}$ computes the session key $k = H(\sigma_A)$, where $\sigma_A = (YB^e)^{x+da}$ and $d = \overline{H}(X, \hat{B})$ and $e = \overline{H}(Y, \hat{A})$. Party $\hat{B}$ computes the same session key as $k = H(\sigma_B)$, where $\sigma_B = (XA^d)^{y+eb}$.

Unlike protocol $\mathcal{P}$, HMQV is executable in the post-specified peer model. Indeed, the initiator can prepare the first message (which essentially consists of the ephemeral public key X) without knowledge of the peer's identifier $\hat{B}$ or static public key B. It is natural then to ask whether HMQV is secure in the post model. This is also important because the version of HMQV that is being considered for standardization by the P1363 working group [12] does not mandate that the protocol be executed in the pre model (i.e., there is no requirement that the communicating parties possess each other's identifiers and static public keys prior to a protocol run), and consequently the protocol may in fact be executed in the post model in applications where the responder's identifier is not available to the initiator at the beginning of the protocol run.

We describe an attack which demonstrates that HMQV (without further modification such as the addition of message flows to exchange identifiers and static public keys) is not secure in the post model. The attack makes the following plausible assumptions: (i) the group order q is a 160-bit prime and so the outputs of $\overline{H}$ have bitlength 80; (ii) the best attack on the CDH problem in G takes approximately 2^{80} steps; (iii) there are at least 2^{20} honest (i.e., uncorrupted) parties; (iv) a party can select its own identifier; and (v) the certification authority does

---

[1] The security definition used in [11] is stronger than the security definition outlined in §2.1 in the sense that the adversary is granted certain additional capabilities. For example, the adversary is allowed to register a static key pair at any time thus allowing the modeling of attacks by malicious insiders.

[2] In particular, we omit session identifiers and assume that all static and ephemeral public key are fully validated, i.e., verified as belonging to G^*.

not require parties to prove knowledge of the static private keys corresponding to their static public keys during registration.[3] The attack proceeds as follows.

1. The adversary $\mathcal{M}$ induces $\hat{A}$ to create a session with a destination address $\hat{d}$ controlled by $\mathcal{M}$. In response, $\hat{A}$ selects ephemeral key pair (x, X) and sends $(\hat{d}, \hat{A}, X)$.
2. $\mathcal{M}$ intercepts $(\hat{d}, \hat{A}, X)$ and does the following:
   (a) Compute $S = \{(\hat{C}, \overline{H}(X, \hat{C})) \mid \hat{C}$ is an honest party$\}$.
   (b) Select an identifier $\hat{M}$ (not the same as the identifier of an honest party) such that $(\hat{B}, \overline{H}(X, \hat{M})) \in S$ for some $\hat{B}$.
   (c) Select $M = B$ as $\hat{M}$'s static public key (note that $\mathcal{M}$ does not know the corresponding private key).
   (d) Send $(\hat{B}, \hat{A}, X)$ to $\hat{B}$.
3. $\mathcal{M}$ intercepts $\hat{B}$'s reply $(\hat{A}, \hat{B}, Y)$ and sends $(\hat{A}, \hat{M}, Y)$ to $\hat{A}$.

Party $\hat{A}$ computes the session key $k = H(\sigma_A)$, where $\sigma_A = (YM^e)^{x+da}$ and $d = \overline{H}(X, \hat{M})$ and $e = \overline{H}(Y, \hat{A})$. Party $\hat{B}$ computes the session key $k' = H(\sigma_B)$, where $\sigma_B = (XA^{d'})^{y+e'b}$ and $d' = \overline{H}(X, \hat{B})$ and $e' = \overline{H}(Y, \hat{A})$. Since $d' = d$, $e' = e$, and $M = B$, we have $\sigma_A = \sigma_B$ and hence $k' = k$. The problem is that while $\hat{B}$ correctly believes that k is shared with $\hat{A}$, party $\hat{A}$ mistakenly believes that k is shared with $\hat{M}$. Thus $\mathcal{M}$ has successfully launched an 'unknown key-share' or 'identity misbinding' attack on HMQV in the post model. The expected running time of the attack is about 2^{60} (for step 2b). Since most of the work has to be done online, the attack cannot be considered practical. Nevertheless it demonstrates that HMQV does not attain an 80-bit security level in the post model as it presumably does in the pre model.

The mechanisms of the attack were outlined in Remark 7.2 of [11]. However, the adversary considered in [11] operates in a different setting, namely the pre model where party $\hat{A}$ precomputes and stores her ephemeral public keys X which are then inadvertently leaked to $\mathcal{M}$ *before* $\hat{A}$ uses them in a session. Three countermeasures were proposed in [11] for foiling this attack: (i) increase the output length of $\overline{H}$ to 160 bits; (ii) include the identifiers $\hat{A}$, $\hat{B}$ in the key derivation function whereby the session key is computed as $k = H(\sigma, \hat{A}, \hat{B})$; and (iii) include random nonces (which are not precomputed and stored) in the derivation of exponents d and e, whereby the exponents are computed as $d = \overline{H}(X, \hat{B}, \nu_A)$ and $e = \overline{H}(Y, \hat{A}, \nu_B)$ where ν_A and ν_B are $\hat{A}$'s and $\hat{B}$'s nonces, respectively. Countermeasures (i) and (ii) are successful in thwarting the attack described above on HMQV in the post model. However, it can easily be seen that countermeasure (iii) does *not* prevent the attack in the post model, thus demonstrating that the two attacks are indeed different. The reason countermeasure (iii) fails is that, unlike in the pre model, the peer's identifier is not known to $\hat{A}$ when she creates the session in the post model.

---

[3] In [11] it is noted that the HMQV security proof does not depend on the CA performing any proof-of-possession checks.

3.3 Σ_0 Protocol

The Σ_0 protocol [5] is a simplified version of one of the IKE key agreement protocols. In the protocol description below, PRF is a pseudorandom function family, MAC is a message authentication code algorithm, and sig_A and sig_B are the signing algorithms for $\hat{A}$ and $\hat{B}$, respectively.

1. Party $\hat{A}$ (the initiator) selects an ephemeral key pair (x, X), initializes the session identifier to $(\hat{A}, s)$, and sends $(\hat{d}_B, \hat{d}_A, s, X)$. Here $\hat{d}_A$ and $\hat{d}_B$ are destination addresses for $\hat{A}$ and $\hat{B}$, respectively.
2. Upon receipt of $(\hat{d}_B, \hat{d}_A, s, X)$, $\hat{B}$ (the responder) selects an ephemeral key pair (y, Y), and computes $\sigma = X^y$, $k = \text{PRF}_\sigma(0)$, and $k' = \text{PRF}_\sigma(1)$. $\hat{B}$ then destroys y and σ, initializes the session identifier to $(\hat{B}, s)$, and sends $m_1 = (\hat{d}_A, \hat{B}, s, Y, \text{sig}_B(\mathcal{R}, s, X, Y), \text{MAC}_{k'}(\mathcal{R}, s, \hat{B}))$.
3. Upon receiving m_1, $\hat{A}$ computes $\sigma = Y^x$, $k = \text{PRF}_\sigma(0)$, and $k' = \text{PRF}_\sigma(1)$. $\hat{A}$ then verifies the signature and MAC tag in m_1, and sends $m_2 = (\hat{B}, \hat{A}, s, \text{sig}_A(\mathcal{I}, s, Y, X), \text{MAC}_{k'}(\mathcal{I}, s, \hat{A}))$. Finally, $\hat{A}$ accepts the session key k with peer $\hat{B}$, and erases the session state.
4. Upon receiving m_2, $\hat{B}$ verifies the signature and MAC tag in m_2, accepts the session k with peer $\hat{A}$, and erases the session state.

In [5], the Σ_0 protocol is proven secure in the post-specified peer model provided that the DDH assumption holds in G and that the PRF, MAC, and sig primitives are secure. However, the following attack described in [5] shows that Σ_0 is not secure in the pre-specified peer model.

1. Create a session $(\hat{A}, \hat{B}, s)$ at $\hat{A}$.
2. Intercept $\hat{A}$'s outgoing message $(\hat{B}, \hat{A}, s, X)$ and send $(\hat{B}, \hat{M}, s, X)$ to $\hat{B}$.
3. Intercept $\hat{B}$'s response $(\hat{M}, \hat{B}, s, Y, S_B, t_B)$, where $S_B = \text{sig}_B(\mathcal{R}, s, X, Y)$ and $t_B = \text{MAC}_{k'}(\mathcal{R}, s, \hat{B})$, and send $(\hat{A}, \hat{B}, s, Y, S_B, t_B)$ to $\hat{A}$.
4. The session $(\hat{A}, \hat{B}, s)$ at $\hat{A}$ completes and accepts k as the session key.
5. Intercept and delete $\hat{A}$'s final message, and issue a *SessionStateReveal* query to the session $(\hat{B}, \hat{M}, s)$ thus learning k and k'.
6. Issue the *Test* query to the session $(\hat{A}, \hat{B}, s)$ and use knowledge of k to win the distinguishing game.

Notice that the attack is legitimate in the pre-specified peer model since the exposed session $(\hat{B}, \hat{M}, s)$ is not matching to the test session $(\hat{A}, \hat{B}, s)$. On the other hand, such an attack is not permitted in the post-specified peer model because in step 5 of the attack the session $(\hat{B}, s)$ is still incomplete and therefore matching to the *Test* session (and thus cannot be exposed). This is all rather counterintuitive since one would expect that if a protocol is secure when the initiator does not have a priori knowledge of the peer's identifier, then it should remain secure when the peer's identifier is known at the outset.

One feature of both the pre and post models is that an exposed session does not produce any further output. In practice, however, one might desire the assurance that a particular session is secure even if the adversary learns some secret state information (such as an ephemeral private key) associated with that session or its matching session. For this reason, the security models in recent papers such as [11], [13] and [20] permit exposed sessions to continue producing output, and furthermore allow the adversary to issue a *SessionStateReveal* query (or its equivalent) to the *Test* session and its matching session (cf. §4.3). However, if the adversary $\mathcal{M}$ were equipped with these extra capabilities, then the Σ_0 protocol would be insecure in both the pre and post models since $\mathcal{M}$ could issue a *SessionStateReveal* query to $(\hat{A}, s)$ after step 1 to learn x and thereafter compute the session key. Furthermore, the Σ_0 protocol falls in the post model to the following analogue of the attack described above. The attack is a little more realistic than the attack described above in the pre model because we now assume that the *SessionStateReveal* query does not yield the session key k (which may be stored in secure memory). $\mathcal{M}$'s actions are the following:

1. Create a session $(\hat{A}, s)$ at $\hat{A}$ with peer destination address $\hat{d}_B$.
2. Intercept $\hat{A}$'s outgoing message $(\hat{d}_B, \hat{d}_A, s, X)$ and send $(\hat{d}_B, \hat{d}_M, s, X)$ to $\hat{B}$.
3. Intercept $\hat{B}$'s response $(\hat{d}_M, \hat{B}, s, Y, S_B, t_B)$, where $S_B = \text{sig}_B(\mathcal{R}, s, X, Y)$ and $t_B = \text{MAC}_{k'}(\mathcal{R}, s, \hat{B})$, and send $(\hat{d}_A, \hat{B}, s, Y, S_B, t_B)$ to $\hat{A}$.
4. Intercept $\hat{A}$'s final message and delete it. The session $(\hat{A}, s)$ completes with peer $\hat{B}$ and session key k.
5. Issue a *SessionStateReveal* query to the incomplete session $(\hat{B}, s)$ and learn the MAC key k'.
6. Compute $S_M = \text{sig}_M(\mathcal{I}, s, Y, X)$ and $t_M = \text{MAC}_{k'}(\mathcal{I}, s, \hat{M})$, and send $(\hat{B}, \hat{M}, s, S_M, t_M)$ to $\hat{B}$.

The session $(\hat{B}, s)$ completes with peer $\hat{M}$ and session key k. Thus $\mathcal{M}$ has successfully launched an unknown key-share attack on Σ_0 in the post model. The two attacks demonstrate that a protocol proven secure in the post-specified peer model of [5] may no longer be secure if exposed sessions are allowed to continue producing output.

4   Combining the Two Models

In this section we introduce the notion of a modifiable key agreement protocol — protocols designed for the pre-specified peer model but which can be adapted with minor changes to be executable in the post-specified peer model. We also introduce the notion of a hybrid key agreement protocol, which simultaneously describes a modifiable protocol and its modification suitable for the post model. We then develop a security definition that, if satisfied by a hybrid protocol, guarantees that the associated protocols are secure in the pre and post models.

4.1   Modifiable Protocols

Consider a key agreement protocol Π designed for the pre model where the first outgoing message prepared by the initiator $\hat{A}$ is of the form $(\hat{B}, \hat{A}, \text{RoundOne})$. Then Π is said to be *modifiable* if *RoundOne* can be computed before the session is created at $\hat{A}$; in particular, this means that *RoundOne* does not depend on $\hat{B}$'s identifier or static public key.

A modifiable protocol Π can be easily adapted for the post-specified peer model by incorporating identity establishment into the protocol flows. The required changes are the following. The initiator $\hat{A}$, who is activated to create a session with a destination address $\hat{d}$ (and without knowledge of the recipient's identifier or static public key), sends $(\hat{d}, \hat{A}, RoundOne)$ as her first outgoing message. Since this message contains the identifier $\hat{A}$, the responder has all the information he needs to prepare his first outgoing message as specified by Π. The responder appends his identifier to this outgoing message (if the message does not already contain the identifier). After $\hat{A}$ receives this reply, both $\hat{A}$ and the responder can proceed with Π without any further modifications. Notice that the modified protocol Π' has the same number of message flows as the original protocol Π; except for appending a public value to the first outgoing message, the remainder of the protocol remains the same.

As mentioned in §1, the class of modifiable key agreement protocols includes many of the protocols that have been proposed in the literature. However, not all key agreement protocols are modifiable; for example, protocol $\mathcal{P}$ defined in §3.1 is not modifiable. Furthermore, as demonstrated by the attack on HMQV in §3.2, security of a modifiable protocol Π in the pre model does not imply security of the modified protocol Π' in the post model.

4.2   Hybrid Protocols

Suppose that Π is a modifiable key agreement protocol, and Π' its modification suitable for the post model. The specification of Π and Π' can be combined as described below, resulting in a protocol $\tilde{\Pi}$ called a *hybrid* protocol.

We use $\tilde{A}$ to denote either an identifier $\hat{A}$ or a destination address $\hat{d}$ that can be used to send messages to some party $\hat{A}$ whose identifier is not known to the sender; note that the address $\hat{d}$ may not necessarily be under $\hat{A}$'s control. In the description of $\tilde{\Pi}$, a session is created at initiator $\hat{A}$ via a message containing $(\hat{A}, \tilde{B})$. The first outgoing message from $\hat{A}$ is $(\tilde{B}, \hat{A}, RoundOne)$. The responder $\hat{B}$ includes the identifiers $\hat{A}$ and $\hat{B}$ in his response, and the remainder of the protocol description is the same as for Π.

A hybrid protocol $\tilde{\Pi}$ can be specialized for the pre model by using an identifier $\hat{B}$ for $\tilde{B}$. Protocol $\tilde{\Pi}$ can also be specialized for the post model by using a destination address for $\tilde{B}$. An example of a hybrid protocol is given in §5.

4.3   Combined Security Model

This section describes a "combined" model and associated security definition that aims to simultaneously capture the security assurances of the pre- and post-specified peer models. That is, if a hybrid protocol $\tilde{\Pi}$ is proven secure with respect to the new definition, then its specializations Π and Π' are guaranteed to be secure when run in the pre and post models, respectively. More precisely, when run in the pre model, Π satisfies the extended Canetti-Krawczyk (eCK) definition [13] suitably enhanced to capture attacks where an adversary is able to learn ephemeral public keys of parties *before* they are actually used in a protocol session.[4] Such attacks were considered by Krawczyk [11], but were not incorporated into his security model. When run in the post model, the modified protocol Π' satisfies a strengthened version of the Canetti-Krawczyk definition from [5], suitably enhanced to offer security assurances similar to the eCK definition (including resistance to attacks where the adversary learns ephemeral private keys of the session being attacked) and to capture attacks where the adversary learns ephemeral public keys before they are actually used.

Instead of using pre-determined session numbers s to identify sessions (cf. §2.1), our session identifiers will consist of the identities of the communicating parties together with a concatenation of the messages exchanged during a protocol run. As shown in [6], this notion of session identifier yields a security model for key agreement that is at least as strong as other security models.

Notation. We assume that messages are represented as binary strings. If m is a vector then $\#m$ denotes the number of its components. We say that two vectors m_1 and m_2 are *matched*, written $m_1 \sim m_2$, if the first $t = \min\{\#m_1, \#m_2\}$ components of the vectors are pairwise equal as binary strings. We write $\hat{A} \equiv \hat{D}$ if either $\tilde{D} = \hat{A}$ or if $\tilde{D}$ is a destination address that can be used to send messages to $\hat{A}$.

Session Creation. A party $\hat{A}$ can be activated via an incoming message to create a session. The incoming message has one of the following forms: (i) $(\hat{A}, \tilde{B})$ or (ii) $(\tilde{A}, \hat{B}, In)$. If $\hat{A}$ was activated with $(\hat{A}, \tilde{B})$ then $\hat{A}$ is the session initiator; otherwise $\hat{A}$ is the session responder.

Session Initiator. If $\hat{A}$ is the session initiator then $\hat{A}$ creates a separate session state where session-specific short-lived data is stored, and prepares a reply *Out* that includes an ephemeral public key X. The session is labeled active and identified via a (temporary and incomplete) session identifier $s = (\hat{A}, \tilde{B}, \mathcal{I}, Comm)$ where *Comm* is initialized to *Out*. The outgoing message is $(\tilde{B}, \hat{A}, Out)$.

Session Responder. If $\hat{A}$ is the session responder then $\hat{A}$ creates a separate session state and prepares a reply *Out* that includes an ephemeral public key X. The session is labeled active and identified via a (temporary and incomplete) session identifier $s = (\hat{A}, \hat{B}, \mathcal{R}, Comm)$ where $Comm = (In, Out)$. The outgoing message is $(\hat{B}, \hat{A}, \mathcal{I}, In, Out)$.

Session Update. A party $\hat{A}$ can be activated to update a session via an incoming message of the form $(\hat{A}, \hat{B}, role, Comm, In)$, where $role \in \{\mathcal{I}, \mathcal{R}\}$. Upon receipt of this message, $\hat{A}$ checks that she owns an active session with identifier $s = (\hat{A}, \hat{B}, role, Comm)$ or $s = (\hat{A}, \hat{d}, role, Comm)$ where $\hat{d}$ is a destination address; except with negligible probability, $\hat{A}$ can own at most one such session. If no such session exists then the message is rejected. If a session $s = (\hat{A}, \hat{d}, role, Comm)$ or $s = (\hat{A}, \hat{B}, role, Comm)$ exists, then in the former case $\hat{A}$ updates the session

---

[4] As discussed in [11], such attacks may be possible in situations where a party pre-computes ephemeral public keys in order to improve on-line performance.

identifier to $s = (\hat{A}, \hat{B}, role, Comm)$; in either case, $\hat{A}$ updates s by appending In to $Comm$. If the protocol requires a response by $\hat{A}$, then $\hat{A}$ prepares the required response Out; the outgoing message is $(\hat{B}, \hat{A}, role, Comm, Out)$ where $role$ is $\hat{B}$'s role as perceived by $\hat{A}$, and the session identifier is updated by appending Out to $Comm$. If the protocol specifies that no further messages will be received, then the session completes and accepts a session key.

Matching Sessions. Since ephemeral public keys are selected at random on a per-session basis, session identifiers are unique except with negligible probability. Party $\hat{A}$ is said to be the owner of a session $(\hat{A}, \tilde{B}, *, *)$. For a session $(\hat{A}, \hat{B}, *, *)$ we call $\hat{B}$ the session *peer*; together $\hat{A}$ and $\hat{B}$ are referred to as the *communicating parties*. Let $s = (\hat{A}, \tilde{B}, role_A, Comm_A)$ be a session owned by $\hat{A}$, where $role_A \in \{\mathcal{I}, \mathcal{R}\}$. A session $s^* = (\hat{C}, \tilde{D}, role_C, Comm_C)$, where $role_C \in \{\mathcal{I}, \mathcal{R}\}$, is said to be *matching* to s if $\hat{C} \equiv \tilde{B}$, $\hat{A} \equiv \tilde{D}$, $role_A \neq role_C$, and $Comm_C \sim Comm_A$. It can be seen that the session s, except with negligible probability, can have more than one matching session if and only if $Comm_A$ has exactly one component, i.e., is comprised of a single outgoing message.

Aborted Sessions. A protocol may require parties to perform some checks on incoming messages. For example, a party may be required to perform some form of public key validation or verify a signature. If a party is activated to create a session with an incoming message that does not meet the protocol specifications, then that message is rejected and no session is created. If a party is activated to update an active session with an incoming message that does not meet the protocol specifications, then the party deletes all information specific to that session (including the session state and the session key if it has been computed) and *aborts* the session; such an abortion occurs before the session identifier can be updated. At any point in time a session is in exactly one of the following states: active, completed, aborted.

Adversary. The adversary $\mathcal{M}$ is modeled as a probabilistic Turing machine and controls *all* communications. In particular, this means that $\hat{A} \equiv \hat{d}$ for all parties $\hat{A}$ and all destination addresses $\hat{d}$. Parties submit outgoing messages to $\mathcal{M}$, who makes decisions about their delivery. The adversary presents parties with incoming messages via $Send$(message), thereby controlling the activation of parties. The adversary does not have immediate access to a party's private information, however in order to capture possible leakage of private information $\mathcal{M}$ is allowed to make the following queries:

- $StaticKeyReveal(\hat{A})$: $\mathcal{M}$ obtains $\hat{A}$'s static private key.
- $EphemeralKeyReveal(s)$: $\mathcal{M}$ obtains the ephemeral private key held by session s.[5] We will henceforth assume that $\mathcal{M}$ issues this query only to sessions that hold an ephemeral private key.

---

[5] The *EphemeralKeyReveal* query can be made functionally equivalent to the *SessionStateReveal* query by defining the ephemeral private key to consist of all ephemeral secret data that a session may hold.

- *SessionKeyReveal(s)*: If s has completed then $\mathcal{M}$ obtains the session key held by s. We will henceforth assume that $\mathcal{M}$ issues this query only to sessions that have completed.
- *EphemeralPublicKeyReveal($\hat{A}$)*: $\mathcal{M}$ obtains the ephemeral public key that $\hat{A}$ will use the next time a session is created within $\hat{A}$.
- *EstablishParty($\hat{A}, A$)*: This query allows $\mathcal{M}$ to register an identifier $\hat{A}$ and a static public key A on behalf of a party. The adversary totally controls that party, thus permitting the modeling of attacks by malicious insiders. Parties that were established by $\mathcal{M}$ using *EstablishParty* are called *corrupted* or *adversary controlled*. If a party is not corrupted it is said to be *honest*.

Adversary Goal. To capture the indistinguishability requirement, $\mathcal{M}$ is allowed to make a special query *Test(s)* to a 'fresh' session s. In response, $\mathcal{M}$ is given with equal probability either the session key held by s or a random key. $\mathcal{M}$ meets its goal if it guesses correctly whether the key is random or not. Note that $\mathcal{M}$ can continue interacting with the parties after issuing the *Test* query, but must ensure that the test session remains fresh throughout $\mathcal{M}$'s experiment.

Definition 1. Let s be the identifier of a completed session, owned by an honest party $\hat{A}$ with peer $\hat{B}$, who is also honest. Let s^* be the identifier of the matching session of s, if it exists. Define s to be *fresh* if none of the following conditions hold:

1. $\mathcal{M}$ issued *SessionKeyReveal(s)* or *SessionKeyReveal(s^*)* (if s^* exists).
2. s^* exists and $\mathcal{M}$ issued one of the following:
    (a) Both *StaticKeyReveal($\hat{A}$)* and *EphemeralKeyReveal(s)*.
    (b) Both *StaticKeyReveal($\hat{B}$)* and *EphemeralKeyReveal(s^*)*.
3. s^* does not exist and $\mathcal{M}$ issued one of the following:
    (a) Both *StaticKeyReveal($\hat{A}$)* and *EphemeralKeyReveal(s)*.
    (b) *StaticKeyReveal($\hat{B}$)*.

Definition 2. A key agreement protocol is *secure* if the following conditions hold:

1. If two honest parties complete matching sessions then, except with negligible probability, they both compute the same session key.
2. No polynomially bounded adversary $\mathcal{M}$ can distinguish the session key of a fresh session from a randomly chosen session key, with probability greater than $\frac{1}{2}$ plus a negligible fraction.

5   NAXOS-C Protocol

In this section we present the hybrid version of the NAXOS-C key agreement protocol, which is essentially the NAXOS protocol of [13] augmented with key confirmation. In the protocol description, λ is the security parameters, and $H : \{0,1\}^* \to \{0,1\}^\lambda \times \{0,1\}^\lambda$, $H_1 : \{0,1\}^* \to [1, q-1]$, and $H_2 : \{0,1\}^* \to \{0,1\}^\lambda$ are hash functions. NAXOS-C can be specialized to run in either the pre or the post model. Moreover, it can be proven secure in the combined model of §4.3 provided that the GDH assumption holds in G and that the hash functions H, H_1 and H_2 are modeled as random functions; a reductionist security argument can be found in the full version of this paper [17]. Hence NAXOS-C is secure in both the pre- and post-specified peer models.

The purpose of presenting the NAXOS-C protocol is to demonstrate that the security definition of §4.3 is useful (and not too restrictive) in the sense that there exist practical protocols that meet the definition under reasonable assumptions. The protocol was designed to allow a straightforward (albeit tedious) reductionist security argument, and has not been optimized. In particular, not all the inputs to the hash functions H, H_1 and H_2 may be necessary for security, and in practice H_2 would be implemented as a MAC algorithm (with secret key k').

1. Party $\hat{A}$ (the initiator) does the following:
   (a) Select an ephemeral private key $\tilde{x} \in_R \{0,1\}^\lambda$, and compute $x = H_1(a, \tilde{x})$ and $X = g^x$.
   (b) Destroy x.
   (c) Initialize the session identifier to $(\hat{A}, \tilde{B}, \mathcal{I}, X)$.
   (d) Send $(\tilde{B}, \hat{A}, X)$ to $\tilde{B}$.
2. Upon receiving $(\tilde{B}, \hat{A}, X)$, party $\hat{B}$ (the responder) does the following:
   (a) Verify that $X \in G^*$.
   (b) Select an ephemeral private key $\tilde{y} \in_R \{0,1\}^\lambda$, and compute $y = H_1(b, \tilde{y})$ and $Y = g^y$.
   (c) Compute $\sigma_1 = A^y$, $\sigma_2 = X^b$ and $\sigma_e = X^y$.
   (d) Compute $(k, k') = H(\hat{A}, \hat{B}, X, Y, \sigma_1, \sigma_2, \sigma_e)$ and $t_B = H_2(k', \mathcal{R}, \hat{B}, \hat{A}, Y, X)$.
   (e) Destroy $\tilde{y}, y, \sigma_1, \sigma_2$ and σ_e.
   (f) Initialize the session identifier to $(\hat{B}, \hat{A}, \mathcal{R}, X, Y, t_B)$.
   (g) Send $(\hat{A}, \hat{B}, X, Y, t_B)$ to $\hat{A}$.
3. Upon receiving $(\hat{A}, \hat{B}, X, Y, t_B)$, party $\hat{A}$ checks that she owns an active session with identifier $(\hat{A}, \hat{B}, \mathcal{I}, X)$. If so, then $\hat{A}$ does the following:
   (a) Verify that $Y \in G^*$.
   (b) Compute $x = H_1(a, \tilde{x})$, $\sigma_1 = Y^a$, $\sigma_2 = B^x$ and $\sigma_e = Y^x$.
   (c) Compute $(k, k') = H(\hat{A}, \hat{B}, X, Y, \sigma_1, \sigma_2, \sigma_e)$.
   (d) Destroy $\tilde{x}, x, \sigma_1, \sigma_2$ and σ_e.
   (e) Verify that $t_B = H_2(k', \mathcal{R}, \hat{B}, \hat{A}, Y, X)$.
   (f) Compute $t_A = H_2(k', \mathcal{I}, \hat{A}, \hat{B}, X, Y)$.
   (g) Destroy k'.
   (h) Send $(\hat{B}, \hat{A}, X, Y, t_B, t_A)$ to $\hat{B}$.
   (i) Update the session identifier to $(\hat{A}, \hat{B}, \mathcal{I}, X, Y, t_B, t_A)$ and complete the session by accepting k as the session key.
4. Upon receiving $(\hat{B}, \hat{A}, X, Y, t_B, t_A)$, party $\hat{B}$ checks that he owns an active session with identifier $(\hat{B}, \hat{A}, \mathcal{R}, X, Y, t_B)$. If so, then $\hat{B}$ does the following:
   (a) Verify that $t_A = H_2(k', \mathcal{I}, \hat{A}, \hat{B}, X, Y)$.
   (b) Destroy k'.
   (c) Update the session identifier to $(\hat{B}, \hat{A}, \mathcal{R}, X, Y, t_B, t_A)$ and complete the session by accepting k as the session key.

6   Conclusions

We compared the Canetti-Krawczyk pre- and post-specified peer models for key agreement, and demonstrated that security in one model does not guarantee security or even executability in the other model. We also presented a combined security model and definition that simultaneously encompasses strengthened versions of the Canetti-Krawczyk definitions. The new definition is stronger in that it permits the adversary to learn ephemeral public keys before they are used, and to learn secret information from the session being attacked. Useful directions for future research would be the development of an optimized protocol that satisfies the new security definition, perhaps modified to allow for identity concealment, and the extension of the definition to capture a wider class of key agreement protocols.

References

1. Bellare, M., Rogaway, P.: Entity authentication and key distribution. In: Stinson, D.R. (ed.) CRYPTO 1993. LNCS, vol. 773, pp. 232–249. Springer, Heidelberg (1994), http://www.cs.ucdavis.edu/~rogaway/papers/eakd-abstract.html
2. Boyd, C., Mao, W., Paterson, K.: Key agreement using statically keyed authenticators. In: Jakobsson, M., Yung, M., Zhou, J. (eds.) ACNS 2004. LNCS, vol. 3089, pp. 248–262. Springer, Heidelberg (2004)
3. Boyd, C., Mathuria, A.: Protocols for Authentication and Key Establishment. Springer, Heidelberg (2003)
4. Canetti, R., Krawczyk, H.: Analysis of key-exchange protocols and their use for building secure channels. In: Pfitzmann, B. (ed.) EUROCRYPT 2001. LNCS, vol. 2045, pp. 453–474. Springer, Heidelberg (2001), http://eprint.iacr.org/2001/040
5. Canetti, R., Krawczyk, H.: Security analysis of IKE. In: Yung, M. (ed.) CRYPTO 2002. LNCS, vol. 2442, pp. 143–161. Springer, Heidelberg (2002), http://eprint.iacr.org/2002/120
6. Choo, K., Boyd, C., Hitchcock, Y.: Examining indistinguishability-based proof models for key establishment protocols. In: Roy, B. (ed.) ASIACRYPT 2005. LNCS, vol. 3788, pp. 585–604. Springer, Heidelberg (2005)
7. Diffie, W., van Oorschot, P., Wiener, M.: Authentication and authenticated key exchanges. Designs, Codes and Cryptography 2, 107–125 (1992)
8. Harkins, D., Carrel, D.: The internet key exchange (IKE)., RFC 2409, Internet Engineering Task Force (1998)
9. Kaufman, C. (ed.): Internet key exchange (IKEv2) protocol, RFC 4306, Internet Engineering Task Force (2005)
10. Krawczyk, H.: SIGMA: The 'SIGn-and-MAc' approach to authenticated Diffie-Hellman and its use in the IKE protocols. In: Boneh, D. (ed.) CRYPTO 2003. LNCS, vol. 2729, pp. 400–425. Springer, Heidelberg (2003)
11. Krawczyk, H.: HMQV: A high-performance secure Diffie-Hellman protocol., Cryptology ePrint Archive, Report 2005/176, http://eprint.iacr.org/2005/176; In: Shoup, V. (ed.) CRYPTO 2005. LNCS, vol. 3621, pp. 546–566. Springer, Heidelberg (2005)
12. Krawczyk, H.:"HMQV in IEEE P1363", submission to the IEEE P1363 working group, July 7 (2006), http://grouper.ieee.org/groups/1363/P1363-Reaffirm/submissions/krawczyk-hmqv-spec.pdf

13. LaMacchia, B., Lauter, K., Mityagin, A.: Stronger security of authenticated key exchange. In: Susilo, W., Liu, J.K., Mu, Y. (eds.) ProvSec 2007. LNCS, vol. 4784, pp. 1–16. Springer, Heidelberg (2007)
14. Lauter, K., Mityagin, A.: Security analysis of KEA authenticated key exchange. In: Yung, M., Dodis, Y., Kiayias, A., Malkin, T.G. (eds.) PKC 2006. LNCS, vol. 3958, pp. 378–394. Springer, Heidelberg (2006)
15. Law, L., Menezes, A., Qu, M., Solinas, J., Vanstone, S.: An efficient protocol for authenticated key agreement. Designs, Codes and Cryptography 28, 119–134 (2003)
16. Menezes, A., Ustaoglu, B.: Security arguments for the UM key agreement protocol in the NIST SP 800-56A standard. In: Proceedings of ASIACCS 2008, pp. 261–270. ACM Press, New York (2008)
17. Menezes, A., Ustaoglu, B.: Comparing the pre- and post-specified peer models for key agreement, Technical Report CACR 2008-07, University of Waterloo (2008), http://www.cacr.math.uwaterloo.ca
18. Okamoto, T.: Authenticated key exchange and key encapsulation in the standard model. In: Kurosawa, K. (ed.) ASIACRYPT 2007. LNCS, vol. 4833, pp. 474–484. Springer, Heidelberg (2007)
19. SP 800-56A Special Publication 800-56A, Recommendation for Pair-Wise Key Establishment Schemes Using Discrete Logarithm Cryptography, National Institute of Standards and Technology (March 2006)
20. Ustaoglu, B.: Obtaining a secure and efficient key agreement protocol from (H)MQV and NAXOS. Designs, Codes and Cryptography 46, 329–342 (2008)

Efficient One-Round Key Exchange in the Standard Model*

Colin Boyd[1], Yvonne Cliff[1], Juan Gonzalez Nieto[1], and Kenneth G. Paterson[2]

[1] Information Security Institute,
Queensland University of Technology,
GPO Box 2434 Brisbane Qld 4001, Australia
y.cliff@isi.qut.edu.au, {c.boyd,j.gonzaleznieto}@qut.edu.au
[2] Information Security Group,
Royal Holloway University of London,
Egham, Surrey TW20 0EX, U.K.
Kenny.Paterson@rhul.ac.uk

Abstract. We consider one-round key exchange protocols secure in the standard model. The security analysis uses the powerful security model of Canetti and Krawczyk and a natural extension of it to the ID-based setting. It is shown how KEMs can be used in a generic way to obtain two different protocol designs with progressively stronger security guarantees. A detailed analysis of the performance of the protocols is included; surprisingly, when instantiated with specific KEM constructions, the resulting protocols are competitive with the best previous schemes that have proofs only in the random oracle model.

Keywords: Key exchange, standard model.

1 Introduction

There has been a recent rapid growth of interest in efficient cryptographic primitives of all kinds that carry proofs in the standard model. Avoiding the random oracle model (ROM) or generic group model is to be preferred, given the known problems with instantiating these models in practice [8]. However, the usual price to be paid for working in the standard model is a loss of efficiency.

This paper initiates the systematic study of key exchange protocols whose security can be analyzed in the standard model. Our focus here is on two-party, one-round protocols — protocols in which only two message flows are required to securely establish a key between two parties. We provide two related, yet distinct, approaches to building such protocols using KEMs [1], both in the ID-based setting and the traditional PKI-based setting. Our security proofs use the Canetti-Krawczyk model (appropriately adapted for the identity-based case), which is sufficiently powerful to allow the capture of a variety of security properties including basic session key security, key compromise impersonation resistance, and various types of forward security.

---

* See [6] for the full version of this paper.

Y. Mu, W. Susilo, and J. Seberry (Eds.): ACISP 2008, LNCS 5107, pp. 69–83, 2008.
© Springer-Verlag Berlin Heidelberg 2008

In the identity-based setting, there is no shortage of protocols with security analysis in the ROM, with Chen, Cheng and Smart [10] providing a useful survey and comparison of these. Our protocols appear to be the first explicit constructions that are proven secure in the standard model in this setting. A recent preprint [22] also considers ID-based key exchange in the standard model, but the security analysis therein is incomplete – we comment in more detail on this below. We consider the instantiation of our ID-based protocol designs with a variety of suitable concrete KEM components. These are derived from ID-based KEMs of Kiltz [14], Kiltz-Galindo [16] and Gentry [12]. By modifying these to operate in the setting of asymmetric pairings and ordinary elliptic curves, we are able to produce concrete ID-based protocols with security proven in the standard model that are only 2.5 times slower than the most efficient protocols with security established in the ROM, the comparison being made on elliptic curves with a 128-bit security level.

In the PKI setting we also obtain efficient, one round, concrete protocol designs in the standard model, which compare favorably with the protocols of Jeong, Katz and Lee [13], Krawczyk [18] and Okamoto [21] which are to our knowledge the only one-round protocols secure in the standard model. The protocols are reasonably efficient even when compared to the best ROM protocols. For example, they can be instantiated with standard model KEMs to yield protocols with a computational increase of a factor around 3 when compared with HMQV [19].

Our first protocol design is the most efficient of the two, and provides key-compromise impersonation (KCI) resistance but not forward secrecy (FS). The basic idea of our first protocol design is very simple: the two parties simply send each other a random secret value using the IB-KEM and then use a randomness extractor to derive a session key from the combined secrets. Our second protocol design is based on the first, but adds an independent Diffie-Hellman exchange to achieve forward secrecy. It also achieves KCI resistance.

1.1   Related Work

Following the development of practical schemes for identity-based encryption many other identity-based primitives have been designed; due to their practical importance, these have included many key exchange protocols. Chen et al. [10] have provided a useful survey and comparison of work to date on identity-based key exchange.

Initially all security proofs for identity-based primitives relied on the random oracle model. More recently there has been a focus on providing new identity-based encryption (IBE) and identity-based key encapsulation (IB-KEM) schemes with security proofs in the standard model. Recent and quite efficient proposals include those of Waters [23], Kiltz [14], Gentry [12] and Kiltz–Galindo [16,17].

Up until now, all proofs for identity-based key exchange protocols have continued to rely on the ROM, with the exception [22] noted. However, although Wang et al. [22] propose three protocols, a proof for only one is provided; the other two proofs supposedly use similar techniques. The protocol with a claimed proof applies a key derivation function H_2 to the shared secret, exchanged messages and identities. No properties of the key derivation function are stated or used in the proof; indeed the proof ignores the presence of H_2 altogether. However, without the key derivation function, the protocol is completely insecure, because it is based on the CPA (rather than CCA) version of Gentry's IB-KEM [12] and so has malleable messages. This malleability is easily exploited to find attacks which break the security of the protocol. The problems in the paper of Wang et al. [22] illustrate that it is not hard to devise ID-based protocols that look secure in the standard model but making the proofs work is not always so simple.

We note too that it is relatively straightforward to obtain standard-model secure key exchange protocols (in both settings) using the authenticator approach of Canetti-Krawczyk [9], by working with standard-model-secure cryptographic primitives. The resulting protocols can be quite computationally efficient, but generally require more than one round of communication. A detailed study of such protocols is deferred to our future work.

In the normal public key model, Jeong et al. [13], proposed a protocol, called TS3, which is one-round and proven secure in the standard modelTS3 is a Diffie-Hellman (DH) key exchange authenticated using a MAC keyed under the (static) DH of the long term keys of the two users. TS3 provides (weak) forward secrecy, but fails to achieve KCI resistance – a consequence of the static key used for authentication being the same for both parties. Interestingly, the ID-version of TS3, appears to be limited to be only secure in the ROM. An ID-based version of TS3 secure in the standard model would imply a non-interactive ID-based key establishment protocol also secure in the standard model, which to date is not known. Even if we had such a primitive, the protocol would still not be KCI resistant.

More recently and closely related to our work, Okamoto [21] has proposed a one-round PKI-based protocol also secure in the standard model, which provides both (weak) forward secrecy and KCI resistance. The main advantage of our protocols over Okamoto's is that ours are generic. They can be instantiated using any combination of KEMs as long as they are CCA secure. Okamoto's protocol is highly specialised and the proof does not seem to generalise easily. Additionally Okamoto's key derivation function needs a non-standard notion of pseudo-random function security. Okamoto's proof is in the extended Canetti-Krawczyk (eCK) security model proposed by [20], while our proofs are on the Canetti-Krawczyk (CK) model, with the modifications by Krawcyzk [19] to capture KCI security and weak FS. The difference between the two models is rather subtle and is discussed in the full version of this paper [6]. However, we remark now that contrary to Okamoto's statement in his paper, the eCK model is not stronger than the CK model, i.e. security in the eCK model does not imply security in the CK model. Furthermore it is arguable whether the eCK adversarial model is more realistic than the CK one.

2   Preliminaries

In this section we present standard definitions and results needed in the rest of the paper.

Definition 1 (Min-entropy). *Let $\mathcal{X}$ be a probability distribution over A. The min-entropy of $\mathcal{X}$ is the value*

$$\text{min-ent}(\mathcal{X}) = \min_{x \in A: \Pr_{\mathcal{X}}[x] \neq 0}(-log_2(\Pr_{\mathcal{X}}[x])) \tag{1}$$

(Note that if $\mathcal{X}$ has min-entropy t then for all $x \in A$, $\Pr_{\mathcal{X}}[x] \leq 2^{-t}$.)

Definition 2 (Strong randomness extractor). *A family of efficiently computable hash functions $\mathcal{H} = \{h_{\kappa} : \{0,1\}^n \to \{0,1\}^k | \kappa \in \{0,1\}^d\}$ is called a strong (m, ϵ)-randomness extractor, if for any random variable X over $\{0,1\}^n$ that has min-entropy at least m, if κ is chosen uniformly at random from $\{0,1\}^d$ and R is chosen uniformly at random from $\{0,1\}^k$, the two distributions $\langle \kappa, h_{\kappa}(X) \rangle$ and $\langle \kappa, R \rangle$ have statistical distance ϵ, that is*

$$\frac{1}{2} \sum_{x \in \{0,1\}^k} |\Pr[h_{\kappa}(X) = x] - \Pr[R = x]| = \epsilon$$

To implement the randomness extraction function, one could apply the work of Chevassut *et al.* [11] to use a pseudo-random function as a randomness extractor.

Definition 3 (Pseudorandom Function Family (PRF)). *Let $\mathcal{F} = \{f_s\}_{s \in S}$ be a family of functions for security parameter $k \in \mathbb{N}$ and with seed $s \in S = S(k)$. Let $\mathcal{C}$ be an adversary that is given oracle access to either F_s for $s \in_R K$ or a truly random function with the same domain and range as the functions in $\mathcal{F}$. $\mathcal{F}$ is said to be* pseudorandom *if $\mathcal{C}$'s advantage in distinguishing whether it has access to a random member of $\mathcal{F}$ or a truly random function is negligible in k, for all polynomial-time adversaries $\mathcal{C}$. That is,*

$$\mathbf{Adv}_{\mathcal{F},\mathcal{C}}^{\text{p-rand}}(k) = |\Pr[\mathcal{C}^{F_s(\cdot)}(1^k) = 1] - \Pr[\mathcal{C}^{\text{Rand}(\cdot)}(1^k) = 1]|$$

is negligible in k.

Functions that are proven to be pseudorandom include CBC-MAC [4] (provided the underlying block cipher is a secure pseudorandom permutation family and the input length is constant) and HMAC [2] (provided the compression function is a PRF).

Assumption 1 (Decisional Diffie-Hellman (DDH)) *Let F be a cyclic group of order p' generated by an element f. Consider the set $F^3 = F \times F \times F$ and the following two probability distributions over it:*

$$\mathcal{R}_F = \{(f^a, f^b, f^c) \text{ for } a, b, c \in_R \mathbb{Z}_{p'}\} \tag{2}$$

and

$$\mathcal{DH}_F = \{(f^a, f^b, f^{ab}) \text{ for } a, b \in_R \mathbb{Z}_{p'}\} \tag{3}$$

We say the Decisional Diffie-Hellman (DDH) Assumption holds over $F = \langle f \rangle$ if the two distributions $\mathcal{R}_F$ and $\mathcal{DH}_F$ are indistinguishable by all polynomial-time adversaries $\mathcal{D}$. More precisely, for $k = |p'|$

$$\mathbf{Adv}_{F,\mathcal{D}}^{\text{ddh}}(k) = |\Pr[\mathcal{D}(1^k, \rho) = 1 | \rho \in_R \mathcal{DH}_F] - \Pr[\mathcal{D}(1^k, \rho) = 1 | \rho \in_R \mathcal{R}_F]|$$

is negligible in k.

Definition 4 (ID-based KEM). *An IB-KEM* $\mathcal{E}$ = (*KeyGen, KeyDer,Enc, Dec*) *consists of four polynomial-time algorithms:*

- $(pk, \alpha) \in_R$ *KeyGen*(1^k), *given the security parameter* $k \in \mathbb{N}$, *returns a master public key, pk, and master secret key* α;
- $d_{id} \in_R$ *KeyDer*(pk, α, id) *generates a private key corresponding to the identity id.*
- $(C, K) \in_R$ *Enc*(pk, id) *outputs a key* $K \in_R \mathbb{K}$ *(the key space) and an encapsulation (ciphertext)* C *of the key under the identity id;*
- $K =$ *Dec*(pk, d_{id}, C) *outputs key* K *corresponding to the encapsulation* C.

Our definition of security for an identity-based key-encapsulation mechanism (IB-KEM) scheme is based upon that of Kiltz and Galindo [16].

Definition 5 (IB-KEM-CCA Security). *The security of an IB-KEM scheme* $\mathcal{E}$ = (*KeyGen, KeyDer, Enc, Dec*) *is defined using the following experiment.*

$$\textbf{\textit{Experiment} } \textbf{Exp}_{\mathcal{E},\mathcal{A}}^{\text{ib}-\text{kem}-\text{cca}}(k)$$
$$(pk, \alpha) \in_R \textit{KeyGen}(1^k)$$
$$(id^*, state) \in_R \mathcal{A}^{\mathcal{O}_{KeyDer}(\cdot), \mathcal{O}_{Dec}(\cdot,\cdot)}(\textit{find}, pk)$$
$$K_0^* \in_R \mathbb{K}$$
$$(C^*, K_1^*) \in_R \textit{Enc}(pk, id^*)$$
$$\gamma \in_R \{0, 1\}$$
$$K^* = K_\gamma^*$$
$$\gamma' \in_R \mathcal{A}^{\mathcal{O}_{KeyDer}(\cdot), \mathcal{O}_{Dec}(\cdot,\cdot)}(\textit{guess}, K^*, C^*, state)$$
$$\textit{If } \gamma \neq \gamma' \textit{ then return 0 else return 1}$$

where the oracles and advantage of $\mathcal{A}$ *are defined as follows:*

$$\mathcal{O}_{KeyDer}(id) = \textit{KeyDer}(pk, \alpha, id) \textit{ (where } id \neq id^*)$$
$$\mathcal{O}_{Dec}(id, C) = \textit{Dec}(pk, \textit{KeyDer}(pk, \alpha, id), C) \textit{ (where } id \neq id^* \textit{ or } C \neq C^*)$$

The advantage of $\mathcal{A}$ *in the above experiment is:*

$$\textbf{Adv}_{\mathcal{E},\mathcal{A}}^{\text{ib}-\text{kem}-\text{cca}}(k) = \left| 2\Pr\left[\textbf{Exp}_{\mathcal{E},\mathcal{A}}^{\text{ib}-\text{kem}-\text{cca}}(k) = 1 \right] - 1 \right| .$$

$\mathcal{E}$ *is secure against adaptively-chosen ciphertext attacks if* $\textbf{Adv}_{\mathcal{E},\mathcal{A}}^{\text{ib}-\text{kem}-\text{cca}}(k)$ *is a negligible function in k for all polynomial-time adversaries* $\mathcal{A}$.

3 Canetti-Krawczyk Model

In this section the CK approach is reviewed. Further details of the model can be found in the original papers [3,9].

In the CK model a protocol π is modeled as a collection of n programs running at different parties, $P_1, \ldots, P_n$. Each program is an interactive probabilistic polynomial-time (PPT) machine. Each invocation of π within a party is defined to be a *session*, and each party may have multiple sessions running concurrently. The communications network is controlled by an adversary $\mathcal{A}$, also a PPT machine, which schedules and mediates all sessions between the parties. When first invoked within a party, a key exchange protocol π calls an initialization function that returns any information needed for the bootstrapping of the cryptographic authentication functions. After this initialization stage, the party waits for activation. $\mathcal{A}$ may activate a party P_i in two ways:

1. By means of an establish-session(P_i, P_j, s) request, where P_j is another party with whom the key is to be established, and s is a session-id string which uniquely identifies a session between the participants.
2. By means of an *incoming message m* with a specified sender P_j.

Upon activation, the parties perform some computations, update their internal state, and may output messages together with the identities of the intended receivers. Two sessions (P_i, P_j, s) and (P_i', P_j', s') are said to be *matching sessions* if $P_i = P_j'$, $P_j = P_i'$, and $s = s'$, i.e. if their session-ids are identical and they recognised each other as their respective communicating partner for the session. In the analysis of the protocols in this paper, we define the session-id as the concatenation of the messages sent and received by the party. In addition to the activation of parties, $\mathcal{A}$ can perform the following queries:

1. corrupt(P_i). With this query $\mathcal{A}$ learns the long term key of P_i.
2. session-key(P_i, P_j, s). This query returns the session key (if any) accepted by P_i during a given session s with P_j.
3. session-state(P_i, P_j, s). This query returns all the internal state information of party P_i associated to a particular session s with P_j, but does not include the long term key of P_i.
4. session-expiration(P_i, P_j, s). This query is used for defining *forward secrecy* and erases from memory the session key on a completed session. The session is thereafter said to be expired.
5. test-session(P_i, P_j, s). To respond to this query, a random bit b is selected. If $b = 1$ then the session key is output. Otherwise, a random key is output chosen from the probability distribution of keys generated by the protocol. This query can only be issued to a session that has not been *exposed*. A session is exposed if the adversary performs any of the following actions:
   - A session-state or session-key query to this session or to the matching session, or
   - A corrupt query to either partner before the session expires at that partner.

Security is defined based on a game played by the adversary. In this game $\mathcal{A}$ interacts with the protocol. In a first phase of the game, $\mathcal{A}$ is allowed to activate sessions and perform corrupt, session-key, session-state and session-expiration queries as described above. The adversary then performs a test-session query to a party and session of its choice. The adversary is not allowed to expose the test session. $\mathcal{A}$ may then continue with its regular actions with the exception that no more test-session queries can be issued. Eventually, $\mathcal{A}$ outputs a bit b' as its guess on whether the returned value to the test-session query was the session key or a random value, then halts. $\mathcal{A}$ wins the game if $b = b'$. The definition of security follows.

Definition 6. *A key establishment protocol π is called* session key (SK-) *secure with* perfect forward secrecy (PFS) *if the following properties are satisfied for any adversary $\mathcal{A}$.*

1. *If two uncorrupted parties complete matching sessions then they both output the same key;*
2. *The probability that $\mathcal{A}$ guesses correctly the bit b is no more than $\frac{1}{2}$ plus a negligible function in the security parameter.*

We define the advantage of $\mathcal{A}$ to be

$$\mathbf{Adv}_{\mathcal{A}}^{\mathrm{sk}} = |2\Pr[b = b'] - 1|\,.$$

Hence the second requirement will be met if the advantage of $\mathcal{A}$ is negligible. Canetti and Krawczyk also provide a definition of SK-security *without PFS*. The only difference with respect to the above definition is that now the adversary is not allowed to expire sessions.

Krawczyk [19] showed that forward secrecy in the usual sense cannot be achieved in a two-pass protocol such as the ones that we consider. Therefore we restrict our concern to what Krawczyk calls *weak forward secrecy (WFS)*, in which the adversary is forbidden from taking an active part in the test session. We will also consider *partial WFS*, where we further restrict the adversary to corrupt at most one party to the test session. In the ID-based setting, WFS implies *key escrow freeness*, i.e. it protects against attacks in which the Key Generation Centre, who knows all the long term keys of all the parties, tries to (passively) eavesdrop in the communications of any two parties.

The original CK model does not consider *key compromise impersonation (KCI)* attacks, where the adversary, after compromising the long-term key of a party A, engages in a successful protocol run with A posing as a third party B, i.e. A accepts a session key in the belief that it is shared with B, when in fact is shared with the adversary. Thus in a KCI attack there is no matching session to the test session. To model KCI resistance for our protocols we modify the definition of security to allow the adversary to corrupt the owner A of the test session (A, B, s).

4   Generic 2×KEM Protocols

In this section, we present Protocols 1 and 2, two generic protocols based on the use of any CCA-secure IB-KEM. The first, Protocol 1, is the most efficient of the two, and provides KCI resistance, but does not provide forward secrecy. The basic idea of Protocol 1 is very simple: the two parties simply send each other a random secret value using the IB-KEM and then derive a session key from the combined secrets using a randomness extractor and expander. Protocol 2 adds an independent Diffie-Hellman exchange in a group generated by f to achieve (weak) forward secrecy. It also achieves KCI resistance. The description of both protocols for the PKI-based setting is the same except that the identities are substituted with the public keys of the parties.

The protocol messages and actions are symmetrical for the parties in our protocols. It is assumed that the IB-KEM is defined to output a random key if a ciphertext is not valid. Because the protocols complete in one round, the actual order in which the two parties A and B exchange their messages is irrelevant. In the descriptions provided we let A be the one party such that $id_A < id_B$, using some agreed order relation, e.g. lexicographic order.

In defining the session id s we have assumed that the randomness expander is able to accept inputs at least as long as s. If this were not the case, a collision resistant hash function can be used in order to shorten the length of the input to the expander. Our security analysis can be easily modified to accept this change.

Note that each party must check that the identity of the party in its incoming message is actually the identity of its intended partner. Furthermore, the decapsulated IB-KEM key must be securely erased in the same activation in which it is decapsulated. Thus we are making the restriction that session-state reveal queries do not return decapsulated keys. Note however that once the key is decapsulated it can be inmediately used to compute the session key, so there is no need to store decapsulated keys. This restriction is critical, otherwise the protocol can be trivially broken by the adversary, as follows. Let (A, C_A^*, B, C_B^*) be the transcript of an observed protocol run that the adversary $\mathcal{A}$ seeks to compromise. $\mathcal{A}$ initiates a new session with B by sending D, C_A^* to B, i.e. $\mathcal{A}$ pretends to be D and replays the target ciphertext C_A^*. The adversary could then issue a session-state reveal for the new session to B, thus obtaining the decryption C_A^*. Using the same strategy with A, the adversary could find out the decryption of C_B^*, which would then allow the adversary to compute the session key corresponding to the session (A, C_A^*, B, C_B^*). We emphasize that all other session state can be revealed as part of a session-state query, in particular, encapsulated keys (at the party that generated them) and DH exponentials. Despite of this, in the description of our protocols, we explicitly ask for all intermediate state to be erased once the session key is computed. It would seem artificial to specify that only the decapsulated key be deleted, when there is no need to store anything apart from the session key and the session id.

Interestingly, Protocol 2 does not require that the parties check group membership of the Diffie-Hellman exponentials Y_A and Y_B. This is because the security of the protocol does not depend on them except for proving weak forward secrecy, where the adversary is passive, in which case these values are assumed to be correctly generated. We can intuitively see that the security of Protocol 2 is independent of the Diffie-Hellman exchange when the adversary does not corrupt the owners to the test session. To do so, let us assume that the adversary is able to somehow choose the values Y_A and Y_B itself (but the rest of the protocol is

$$A \qquad\qquad\qquad\qquad\qquad\qquad B$$

$$(C_A, K'_A) \in_R \mathsf{Enc}(pk, id_B) \qquad\qquad (C_B, K'_B) \in_R \mathsf{Enc}(pk, id_A)$$

$$\xrightarrow{\quad A, C_A \quad}$$

$$\xleftarrow{\quad B, C_B \quad}$$

$$K'_B = \mathsf{Dec}(pk, d_{id_A}, C_B) \qquad\qquad K'_A = \mathsf{Dec}(pk, d_{id_B}, C_A)$$
$$K''_A = \mathsf{Exct}_\kappa(K'_A); K''_B = \mathsf{Exct}_\kappa(K'_B) \qquad K''_B = \mathsf{Exct}_\kappa(K'_B); K''_A = \mathsf{Exct}_\kappa(K'_A)$$
$$s = A||C_A||B||C_B \qquad\qquad\qquad s = A||C_A||B||C_B$$
$$K_A = \mathsf{Expd}_{K''_A}(s) \oplus \mathsf{Expd}_{K''_B}(s) \qquad K_B = \mathsf{Expd}_{K''_B}(s) \oplus \mathsf{Expd}_{K''_A}(s)$$
$$\text{Erase all state except } (K_A, s) \qquad\qquad \text{Erase all state except } (K_B, s)$$
$$\text{'Established } (A, B, s, K_A)\text{'} \qquad\qquad \text{'Established } (B, A, s, K_B)\text{'}$$

Protocol 1. Generic 2×KEM

executed by the parties normally). The session key is computed as $\mathsf{Expd}_{K''_B}(s) \oplus \mathsf{Expd}_{K''_A}(s) \oplus \mathsf{Expd}_{K''_{AB}}(s)$. The adversary effectively chooses the subkey K''_{AB}, thus the goal of the adversary is reduced to distinguishing $\mathsf{Expd}_{K''_B}(s) \oplus \mathsf{Expd}_{K''_A}(s)$ from random. This is same goal as a that of an adversary against Protocol 1, the difference being that while in Protocol 1, s is fixed for A, C_A, B, C_B, here s depends also on Y_A and Y_B. However a crucial property of Protocol 2 is that each different choice of Y_A, Y_B defines a different session id s, therefore $\mathsf{Expd}_{K''_A}(s) \oplus \mathsf{Expd}_{K''_B}(s)$ will also be pseudo-random across different sessions, even if K''_A and K''_B are fixed.

For the same reason, Protocol 2 is immune to malleability attacks where an active adversary tries to take advantage of the malleability of the Diffie-Hellman key-exchange part of the protocol. An example of such attack is as follows. A sends A, C_A, Y_A to B, who outputs B, C_B, Y_B. The adversary intercepts the latter message and changes it to B, C_B, Y_B^r where r is chosen by the adversary. Thus the key as computed by B is $K_B = \mathsf{Expd}_{K''_B}(s) \oplus \mathsf{Expd}_{K''_A}(s) \oplus \mathsf{Expd}_{K''_{AB}}(s)$, whereas A computes $K_B = \mathsf{Expd}_{K''_B}(\bar{s}) \oplus \mathsf{Expd}_{K''_A}(\bar{s}) \oplus \mathsf{Expd}_{(K''_{AB})^r}(\bar{s})$. Even though the Diffie-Hellman subkeys K''_{AB} and $(K''_{AB})^r$ are related, the two session keys are indistinguishable from random to the adversary.

In the description of both protocols we have assumed that the same public parameters are used by both parties. This is however not necessary. Each party could be using different public parameters, IB-KEMs, or even one party could be using a IB-KEM and the other a PKI-based KEM.

We are now in a position to state the security theorems for the two protocols. For both these theorems we use the following notation:

- $\{\mathsf{Expd}_K(\cdot)\}_{K \in \mathbb{U}_1} : \{0,1\}^\sigma \to \mathbb{U}_2$ is a pseudorandom function family, (as described in Definition 3),
- $\mathsf{Exct}_\kappa(\cdot) : \mathbb{K} \to \mathbb{U}_1$ is chosen uniformly at random from a strong (m, ϵ)-strong randomness extractor for appropriate m and ϵ (as described in Definition 2),
- n_{orac} is the total number of oracles (i.e. sessions) created by $\mathcal{B}$ against the protocol, and

	A		B

$$y_A \in_R \mathbb{Z}_{p'}^*; Y_A = f^{y_A} \qquad\qquad y_B \in_R \mathbb{Z}_{p'}^*; Y_B = f^{y_B}$$
$$(C_A, K_A') \in_R \mathsf{Enc}(pk, id_B) \qquad\qquad (C_B, K_B') \in_R \mathsf{Enc}(pk, id_A)$$

$$\xrightarrow{\ A, C_A, Y_A\ }$$
$$\xleftarrow{\ B, C_B, Y_B\ }$$

$$K_B' = \mathsf{Dec}(pk, d_{id_A}, C_B) \qquad\qquad K_A' = \mathsf{Dec}(pk, d_{id_B}, C_A)$$
$$K_A'' = \mathsf{Exct}_\kappa(K_A'); K_B'' = \mathsf{Exct}_\kappa(K_B') \qquad K_B'' = \mathsf{Exct}_\kappa(K_B'); K_A'' = \mathsf{Exct}_\kappa(K_A')$$
$$K_{AB}'' = \mathsf{Exct}_\kappa(Y_B^{y_A}) \qquad\qquad K_{BA}'' = \mathsf{Exct}_\kappa(Y_A^{y_B})$$
$$s = A||C_A||Y_A||B||C_B||Y_B; \qquad\qquad s = A||C_A||Y_A||B||C_B||Y_B;$$
$$K_A = \mathsf{Expd}_{K_A''}(s) \oplus \mathsf{Expd}_{K_B''}(s) \qquad K_B = \mathsf{Expd}_{K_B''}(s) \oplus \mathsf{Expd}_{K_A''}(s)$$
$$\oplus\mathsf{Expd}_{K_{AB}''}(s) \qquad\qquad \oplus\mathsf{Expd}_{K_{BA}''}(s)$$
$$\text{Erase all state except } (K_A, s) \qquad\qquad \text{Erase all state except } (K_B, s)$$

Protocol 2. Generic 2×KEM + Diffie-Hellman

– $\frac{1}{p}$ is the maximum probability that $C_1 = C_2$ where $(C_1, K_1) \in_R \mathsf{Enc}(pk, id)$ and $(C_2, K_2) \in_R \mathsf{Enc}(pk, id)$ for any identity (if $C_1 = C_2$ then $K_1 = K_2$ also since both ciphertexts decrypt to the same value).

Theorem 1. *Let $\mathcal{B}$ be any adversary against Protocol 1. Then the advantage of $\mathcal{B}$ against the SK-security (with partial WFS and KCI resistance) of Protocol 1 is:*

$$\mathbf{Adv}_\mathcal{B}^{sk}(k) \leq \frac{n_{orac}^2}{p} + 2n_{orac}\left(\mathbf{Adv}_{\mathcal{E},\mathcal{A}}^{ib-kem-cca}(k) + \epsilon + \mathbf{Adv}_{\mathcal{F},\mathcal{C}}^{p-rand}(k)\right)$$

Theorem 2. *Let $\mathcal{B}$ be any adversary against Protocol 2. Then the advantage of $\mathcal{B}$ against the SK-security (with WFS and KCI resistance) of Protocol 2 is:*

$$\mathbf{Adv}_\mathcal{B}^{sk}(k) \leq \max\left(2n_{orac}^2\mathbf{Adv}_{F,\mathcal{D}}^{ddh}(k) + 2\epsilon + 2\mathbf{Adv}_{\mathcal{F},\mathcal{C}}^{p-rand}(k)\,,\right.$$

$$\left.\frac{n_{orac}^2}{p} + 2n_{orac}\left(\mathbf{Adv}_{\mathcal{E},\mathcal{A}}^{ib-kem-cca}(k) + \epsilon + \mathbf{Adv}_{\mathcal{F},\mathcal{C}}^{p-rand}(k)\right)\right).$$

The proofs of Theorems 1 and 2 can be found in the full version of this paper [6]. We remark that, despite the simplicity of the protocols, proving their security turns out to be less simple than one might expect.

5   Protocol Comparison: ID-Based Case

We now compare Protocols 1 and 2 with that of Boyd et al. [7] (BMP) which is one of the most efficient listed by Chen et al. in their survey of protocols [10, Table 6]. Unlike our protocols, which consist of two passes and a single round and only provide implicit authentication, BMP is a three-round three-pass protocol and provides explicit authentication. Thus it may appear that BMP is not a good

Table 1. Security and efficiency comparison (IB setting)

	weak FS	KCI	Standard Model	Cost per party
Protocol 1	✗	✓	✓	56
Protocol 2	✓	✓	✓	59
BMP [7]	✓	✗	✗	23

choice to compare our protocols with. However if desired, our protocols can be modified to provide explicit authentication using the well-known key confirmation method discussed by Krawczyk [19, Section 8] at a cost of an extra pseudo-random function computation per party and the addition of a third message.

Table 1 summarises the properties of the protocols under consideration. The costs per party given in the table for Protocols 1 and 2 assume the use of Kiltz's IB-KEM. We note that the BMP protocol does not have a proof of security in the standard model, unlike Protocols 1 and 2. Protocol 2 is the only one for which we have been able to prove both weak forward security (FS) and KCI resistance in the standard model.

To compare the efficiency of the protocols we use the costs per operation provided by Chen et al. [10] for Type 3 pairings with a security parameter of 128, which are the most efficient type of pairings for security levels higher than 80 bits. The values are shown in Table 2, which also shows the costs of Kiltz, Kiltz-Galindo and Gentry IB-KEMs. These figures require 256 bits to represent an element of $\mathbb{G}_1$, 512 bits to represent an element of $\mathbb{G}_2$, and 3072 bits to represent an element of $\mathbb{G}_T$. As suggested by Chen et al., we assume that all elements of the ciphertext are checked to determine that they lie in the correct subgroup to avoid attacks such as the small subgroup attack.

All of these IB-KEMs were originally proposed to use Type 1 pairings, and so to obtain the costs we have had to convert the three IB-KEMs to work with Type 3 pairings. The modified schemes can be found in the full version of this paper [6] together with a discussion on their security and efficiency.

Table 2. Costs of IB-KEMs using Type 3 pairings

	Type 3 cost	Kiltz			Kiltz-Galindo			Gentry		
		Enc	Dec	KeyDer	Enc	Dec	KeyDer	Enc	Dec	KeyDer
$\mathbb{G}_1$ exp, multi-exp.	1, 1.5	-,1	-,1	2,-	1,1	1,1	1,-	-,1	-,-	-,-
$\mathbb{G}_2$ exp, multi-exp.	3, 4.5	1,-	1,-	1,-	1,-	2,-	1,-	-,-	-,1	-,3
$\mathbb{G}_T$ exp, multi-exp.	3, 4.5	1,-	-,-	-,-	1,-	-,-	-,-	3,1	-,1	-,-
Pairing	20	-	2	-	-	3	-	-	1	-
$\mathbb{G}_1$ subgroup check	1	-	1	-	-	2	-	-	1	-
$\mathbb{G}_2$ subgroup check	3	-	1	-	-	1	-	-	-	-
$\mathbb{G}_T$ subgroup check	4	-	-	-	-	-	-	-	3	-
Total cost		7.5	48.5	5	8.5	73.5	4	15	42	13.5
Total Enc + Dec cost		56			82			57		

In BMP each party sends only one element of $\mathbb{G}_1$ to the other, so the bandwidth is smaller than using Kiltz's IB-KEMs with Protocol 1. Each party computes one pairing and two exponentiations in $\mathbb{G}_1$, as well as a subgroup check of one element in $\mathbb{G}_1$. Therefore the total cost per party is 23 time units, as opposed to the 56 units for the Kiltz IB-KEM with Protocol 1. This means that we have achieved identity based key exchange in the standard model in less than 2.5 times the cost in the random oracle model using the size of curve given above. Given the better security guarantees of the standard model, this extra cost may be considered quite reasonable.

The efficiency of Protocol 2 will be worse than that of Protocol 1, but depending on the choice of the group $\langle f \rangle$, it may not be much worse. For example, if the DDH assumption holds in $\mathbb{G}_1$ (this will require $\mathbb{G}_1 \neq \mathbb{G}_2$ and no efficiently computable homomorphism from $\mathbb{G}_1$ to $\mathbb{G}_2$), only 3 extra time units would be required per party (e.g. for party A, one to generate Y_A, one to perform a subgroup check on Y_B, and one to find $Y_B^{y_A}$). The increase in message size would be an extra 256 bits per message.

6   Protocol Comparison: PKI-Based Case

We now consider our two generic protocols in the traditional PKI-based setting and compare them with existing protocols. Table 3 shows the computational cost of Protocol 1 and 2 when instantiated with the recently proposed KEMs of Kiltz [15] and Okamoto [21]. The efficiency of these two KEMs is shown in Table 4. The computational cost figures of both Table 3 and 4 include the cost of performing group membership tests (1 exponentiation per test) and distinguishes regular exponentiations from multi-exponentiations. However we ignore "half-exponentiations" that maybe possible when exponents are the outputs of hash functions. We stress that the shown computational costs are only rough indicative figures. The exact computational costs depend on actual choices of groups. We see that Kiltz's KEM is more efficient than Okamoto's by one regular exponentiation in the decapsulation algorithm. Kiltz's KEM security is based on the Gap Hashed Diffie-Hellman (GHDH) problem, while Okamoto's is based

Table 3. Security and efficiency comparison (PKI setting)

	weak FS	KCI	Standard Model	Cost (exp, multi-exp)
Protocol 1 - Kiltz	✗	✓	✓	3,2
Protocol 1 - Okamoto	✗	✓	✓	4,2
Protocol 2 - Kiltz	✓	✓	✓	5,2
Protocol 2 - Okamoto	✓	✓	✓	6,2
Okamoto	✓	✓	✓	4,2
Jeong-Katz-Lee	✓	✗	✓	3,-
HMQV	✓	✓	✗	4,-

Table 4. Costs of KEMs

	Enc (exp, multi-exp)	Dec (exp, multi-exp)	Security Assumption	Ciphertext (#group elements)
Kiltz	2,1	1,1	GHDH	2
Okamoto	2,1	2,1	DDH+πPRF	2

on the DDH problem and the existence of pseudo-random functions with pair-wise independent random sources (πPRF).

Table 3 also shows the costs of the protocols due to Jeong *et al.* [13] and Okamoto [21], which to our knowledge are the only one-round protocols whose security has been proven in the standard model. HMQV [19], whose security has only been shown in the random oracle model, is also included. Jeong *et al.*'s protocol is the most efficient of all of the compared protocols, but does not provide KCI resistance. Protocol 1 instantiated with Kiltz's KEM results in the cheapest protocol with KCI resistance but only provides partial FS. Of the protocols providing both weak FS and KCI resistance in the standard model, Okamoto's protocol is the cheapest by one regular exponentiation. As discussed in the full version of this paper [6], Okamoto's protocol can be seen as an instantiation of Protocol 2 with Okamoto's KEM but using a different key derivation function. We note that even though Okamoto's protocol is slightly more efficient than Protocol 2 instantiated with the currently most efficient KEM (Kiltz's KEM), Protocol 2 has the advantage of being generic. It is also possible that if a more efficient KEM is devised, then the generic Protocol 2 would be more efficient that Okamoto's. Note that Okamoto's key derivation function poses constraints on the KEM key space and hence cannot be applied generally to all KEMs.

Finally, we note that Protocol 2 is reasonably efficient when compared with HMQV. In its most optimised form (where there is no subgroup membership checking and considering short-exponents) HMQV requires around 2.2 exponentiations. We can roughly approximate 1 multi-exponentiation to 1.2 regular exponentiations [5], which makes the cost of Protocol 2-Kiltz 7.4 regular exponentiations.

7   Conclusion

We have proven secure two generic protocols that may be used with any KEM to achieve secure key exchange in the standard model, in either the ID-based setting or the normal public key setting.In addition, we provided a detailed analysis of the protocols' efficiency on Type 3 curves; this necessitated the extension of the IB-KEMs of Kiltz [14], Kiltz-Galindo [16] and Gentry [12] to use ordinary elliptic curves. We found that both our protocols take approximately 2.5 times as long as the protocol of Boyd, Mao, and Paterson [7] (which is only proven secure in the random oracle model) when both protocols are implemented on elliptic curves with a 128 bit security level. The PKI versions of our protocols also compare favourably with the existing ones of Jeong *et al.* [13] and Okamoto [21].

Protocol 2 provides more security than Jeong's protocol and the same as Okamoto's. When instantiated with Kiltz' PKI-based KEM [15] Protocol 2 is slightly less efficient than Okamoto's. However, Protocol 2 has the advantage of being generic, i.e. it can be used together with any KEM which is CCA secure and our security analysis still applies.

References

1. Abe, M., Gennaro, R., Kurosawa, K., Shoup, V.: Tag-KEM/DEM: A new framework for hybrid encryption and a new analysis of Kurosawa-Desmedt KEM. In: Cramer, R.J.F. (ed.) EUROCRYPT 2005. LNCS, vol. 3494, pp. 128–146. Springer, Heidelberg (2005)
2. Bellare, M.: New proofs for NMAC and HMAC: Security without collision-resistance. In: Dwork, C. (ed.) CRYPTO 2006. LNCS, vol. 4117, pp. 602–619. Springer, Heidelberg (2006)
3. Bellare, M., Canetti, R., Krawczyk, H.: A modular approach to the design and analysis of authentication and key exchange protocols. In: Proceedings of the thirtieth annual ACM symposium on Theory of computing, pp. 419–428. ACM Press, New York (1998)
4. Bellare, M., Kilian, J., Rogaway, P.: The security of the cipher block chaining message authentication code. Journal of Computer and System Sciences 61(3), 362–399 (2000)
5. Bernstein, D.J.: Pippenger's exponentiation algorithm (2001), http://cr.yp.to/papers.html
6. Boyd, C., Cliff, Y., Gonzalez Nieto, J.M., Paterson, K.G.: Efficient one-round key exchange in the standard model. Cryptology ePrint Archive, Report 2008/007 (2008), http://eprint.iacr.org/
7. Boyd, C., Mao, W., Paterson, K.G.: Key agreement using statically keyed authenticators. In: Jakobsson, M., Yung, M., Zhou, J. (eds.) ACNS 2004. LNCS, vol. 3089, pp. 248–262. Springer, Heidelberg (2004)
8. Canetti, R., Goldreich, O., Halevi, S.: The random oracle methodology, revisited. In: Proceedings of the 30th Annual ACM Symposium on Theory of Computing—STOC 1998, pp. 209–218. ACM Press, New York (1998)
9. Canetti, R., Krawczyk, H.: Analysis of key-exchange protocols and their use for building secure channels. In: Pfitzmann, B. (ed.) EUROCRYPT 2001. LNCS, vol. 2045, pp. 453–474. Springer, Heidelberg (2001)
10. Chen, L., Cheng, Z., Smart, N.P.: Identity-based key agreement protocols from pairings. Cryptology ePrint Archive, Report 2006/199 (2006), http://eprint.iacr.org/2006/199
11. Chevassut, O., Fouque, P.-A., Gaudry, P., Pointcheval, D.: Key derivation and randomness extraction. Cryptology ePrint Archive, Report 2005/061 (2005), http://eprint.iacr.org/2005/061
12. Gentry, C.: Practical identity-based encryption without random oracles. In: Vaudenay, S. (ed.) EUROCRYPT 2006. LNCS, vol. 4004, pp. 445–464. Springer, Heidelberg (2006)
13. Jeong, I.R., Katz, J., Lee, D.H.: One-round protocols for two-party authenticated key exchange. In: Jakobsson, M., Yung, M., Zhou, J. (eds.) ACNS 2004. LNCS, vol. 3089, pp. 220–232. Springer, Heidelberg (2004)

14. Kiltz, E.: Direct chosen-ciphertext secure identity-based encryption in the standard model with short ciphertexts. Cryptology ePrint Archive, Report 2006/122 (2006), http://eprint.iacr.org/2006/122
15. Kiltz, E.: Chosen-ciphertext secure key-encapsulation based on gap hashed diffie-hellman. In: Okamoto, T., Wang, X. (eds.) PKC 2007. LNCS, vol. 4450, pp. 282–297. Springer, Heidelberg (2007)
16. Kiltz, E., Galindo, D.: Direct chosen-ciphertext secure identity-based key encapsulation without random oracles. Cryptology ePrint Archive, Report 2006/034 (2006), http://eprint.iacr.org/2006/034
17. Kiltz, E., Galindo, D.: Direct chosen-ciphertext secure identity-based key encapsulation without random oracles. In: Batten, L.M., Safavi-Naini, R. (eds.) ACISP 2006. LNCS, vol. 4058, pp. 336–347. Springer, Heidelberg (2006)
18. Krawczyk, H.: SKEME: A Versatile Secure Key Exchange Mechanism for Internet. Proceedings of SNDSS 96, 114 (1996)
19. Krawczyk, H.: HMQV: A high-performance secure diffie-hellman protocol. In: Shoup, V. (ed.) CRYPTO 2005. LNCS, vol. 3621, pp. 546–566. Springer, Heidelberg (2005)
20. LaMacchia, B.A., Lauter, K., Mityagin, A.: Stronger security of authenticated key exchange. In: Susilo, W., Liu, J.K., Mu, Y. (eds.) ProvSec 2007. LNCS, vol. 4784, pp. 1–16. Springer, Heidelberg (2007)
21. Okamoto, T.: Authenticated key exchange and key encapsulation in the standard model. In: Kurosawa, K. (ed.) ASIACRYPT 2007. LNCS, vol. 4833, pp. 474–484. Springer, Heidelberg (2007)
22. Wang, S., Cao, Z., Choo, K.-K.R.: New identity-based authenticated key agreement protocols from pairings (without random oracles). Cryptology ePrint Archive, Report 2006/446 (2006), http://eprint.iacr.org/
23. Waters, B.: Efficient identity-based encryption without random oracles. In: Cramer, R.J.F. (ed.) EUROCRYPT 2005. LNCS, vol. 3494, pp. 114–127. Springer, Heidelberg (2005)

On the Improvement of the BDF Attack on LSBS-RSA

Hung-Min Sun[1], Mu-En Wu[1,2], Huaxiong Wang[2,3], and Jian Guo[2]

[1] Department of Computer Science,
National Tsing Hua University, Taiwan
hmsun@cs.nthu.edu.tw, mn@is.cs.nthu.edu.tw
[2] School of Physical & Mathematical Sciences,
Nanyang Technological University, Singapore
{hxwang,guojian}@ntu.edu.sg
[3] Centre for Advanced Computing - Algorithms and Cryptography
Department of Computing
Macquarie University, Australia

Abstract. An (α, β, γ)-LSBS RSA denotes an RSA system with primes sharing α least significant bits, private exponent d with β least significant bits leaked, and public exponent e with bit-length γ. Steinfeld and Zheng showed that LSBS-RSA with small e is inherently resistant to the BDF attack, but LSBS-RSA with large e is more vulnerable than standard RSA. In this paper, we improve the BDF attack on LSBS-RSA by reducing the cost of exhaustive search for k, where k is the parameter in RSA equation: $ed = k \cdot \varphi(N) + 1$. Consequently, the complexity of the BDF attacks on LSBS-RSA can be further reduced. Denote σ as the multiplicity of 2 in k. Our method gives the improvements, which depend on the two cases:

1. In the case $\gamma \leq \min\{\beta, 2\alpha\} - \sigma$, the cost of exhaustive search for k in LSBS-RSA can be simplified to searching k in polynomial time. Thus, the complexity of the BDF attack is independent of γ, but it still increases as α increases.
2. In the case $\gamma > \min\{\beta, 2\alpha\} - \sigma$, the complexity of the BDF attack on LSBS-RSA can be further reduced with increasing α or β.

More precisely, we show that an LSBS-RSA is more vulnerable under the BDF attack as $\max\{2\alpha, \beta\}$ increases proportionally with the size of N. In the last, we point out that although LSBS-RSA benefits the computational efficiency in some applications, one should be more careful in using LSBS-RSA.

Keywords: RSA, partial key exposure (PKE), the BDF attack, least significant bit (LSB), LSBS-RSA, exhaustive search.

1 Introduction

RSA [12] is the most widely used public key cryptosystem in the world. It is not only built into several operating systems, such as Microsoft, Apple, Sun, and

Y. Mu, W. Susilo, and J. Seberry (Eds.): ACISP 2008, LNCS 5107, pp. 84–97, 2008.
© Springer-Verlag Berlin Heidelberg 2008

Novell, but is also used for securing web traffic, e-mail, smart cards and IC cards. Since the encryption and decryption in RSA require taking heavy exponential multiplications modulus of N, the efficiency problem is the main disadvantage of using RSA. In order to overcome these drawbacks, many researchers have studied variants of RSA which reduce the computational costs [10], [11]. In general, the RSA encryption and decryption time are roughly proportional to the number of bits in public and secret exponents, respectively. To reduce the encryption time (or the signature-verification time), one may wish to use a small public exponent e. The smallest possible value for e is 3, however, it has been proven to be insecure against some small public exponent attacks [9]. Therefore, a more widely accepted and used public exponent is $e = 2^{16} + 1 = 65537$ or larger but far smaller than $\varphi(N)$.

In 1998, Boneh, Durfee, and Frankel [1], [2] first proposed the partial key exposure (PKE) attacks on RSA. They showed that for low public exponent RSA, given a fraction of the bits of the private exponent, an adversary can recover the entire private key and thus break the RSA. We call their methods the BDF attacks throughout this paper. More results of the partial key exposure attacks on RSA were proposed in 2003, and 2005 by Blömer & May [3], and Ernst, Jochemsz, May, & Weger [8], respectively.

In this paper, we improve the BDF attack on LSBS-RSA. An LSBS-RSA denotes an RSA system with modulus primes sharing a number of least significant bits (LSBs), i.e. $p - q = r \cdot 2^{\alpha}$ for some odd integer r, and $\alpha > 1$, where $r, \alpha \in \mathbb{N}$. This concept was first proposed by Steinfeld and Zheng [13] to improve the efficiency of a server aided RSA signature generation (SASG) [4]. In [13] and [14], Steinfeld and Zheng analyze the complexity of the BDF attack on LSBS-RSA. Their results show that low public exponent LSBS-RSA is inherently resistant to the partial key exposure attacks. That means, the BDF attacks will be less effective for LSBS-RSA with small e than for standard RSA. However, this is not true for large public exponent LSBS-RSA. LSBS-RSA with large e is more vulnerable under such attacks than standard RSA. In this paper, we give the detailed analysis to further support Steinfeld and Zheng's argument. We improve the BDF attack by reducing the cost of exhaustive search for k in LSBS-RSA, where k is the parameter in RSA equation: $ed = k \cdot \varphi(N) + 1$.

Denote σ as the multiplicity of 2 in k. Our improvements depend on the two cases: $\gamma \leq \min\{\beta, 2\alpha\} - \sigma$ and $\gamma > \min\{\beta, 2\alpha\} - \sigma$:

In the case $\gamma \leq \min\{\beta, 2\alpha\} - \sigma$, the cost of exhaustive search for k in LSBS-RSA can be simplified to searching k in polynomial time. Thus, the complexity of the BDF attack in this case can be further reduced. On the other hand, in the case $\gamma > \min\{\beta, 2\alpha\} - \sigma$, the complexity of searching k in LSBS-RSA still can be improved instead of finding k by exhaustive search totally. Thus, the BDF attack on LSBS-RSA in this case is improved as well. Furthermore, we show that an LSBS-RSA is more vulnerable under the BDF attack as $\max\{2\alpha, \beta\}$ increases proportionally with the size of N.

The remainder of this paper is organized as follows. In Section 2, we briefly review theorems and lemmas related to the BDF attack. In Section 3, we revise the BDF attack on LSBS-RSA and show the complexity analysis in Section 4. In Section 5, further discussions about the feasibility and the efficiency are proposed. Finally, we conclude this paper and give some open problems in Section 6.

2 Preliminary

2.1 RSA, LSBS-RSA and Some Notations

In standard RSA, let N $(= p \times q)$ be the product of two large primes p and q. The public exponent e and the private exponent d satisfy $e \times d \equiv 1 \pmod{\varphi(N)}$, where $\varphi(N) = (p-1) \times (q-1)$ is the Euler totient function of N. Here, N is called the RSA modulus. The public key is the pair (N, e) that is used for encryption (or signature-verification): $c \equiv m^e \pmod{N}$, where m is the message and c is the corresponding ciphertext. The private key is the pair (N, d) that enables the decryption of ciphertext (or signature-generation): $m \equiv c^d \pmod{N}$. In the key generation of RSA, we usually select two primes (about 512 bits) p and q, and then multiply them to obtain N (about 1024 bits). Next, we pick the public exponent e first, and then compute the private exponent d by $d \equiv e^{-1} \pmod{\varphi(N)}$ by Euclidean algorithm. With high probability, no matter what size of e is chosen, the size of d is as large as the size of $\varphi(N)$ almost.

Throughout this paper, we follow the notation (α, β, γ), which is also used by Steinfeld and Zheng. An (α, β, γ)-LSBS RSA is an RSA system with the following properties:

α:	α-LSBS RSA modulus: $N = pq$, where $|p - q| = r \cdot 2^\alpha$ for some odd integer r.
β:	The β least significant bits of the private exponent d are available.
γ:	The public exponent e with bit-length γ.

In addition, we use the symbols κ and λ to denote the multiplicity of 2 in k and $\varphi(N)$, respectively. Moreover, given an integer x of m bits, whose binary representation is

$$(x)_2 = (x_m, x_{m-1}, \ldots x_j, \ldots, x_i, \ldots, x_2, x_1)_2,$$

where $x_i = 0$ or 1 for $i = 1, \ldots, m$. We call x_m the most significant bit of x and x_1 the least significant bit of x. Denote "$\mathrm{LSB}_{i\text{-}j}(x)$" as the i-th to j-th least significant bits of $(x)_2$, where $i < j$. That is,

$$\mathrm{LSB}_{i\text{-}j}(x) = (x_j, \ldots, x_i)_2.$$

and "$\mathrm{LSB}_i(x)$" as the i-th least significant bit of $(x)_2$. That is,

$$\mathrm{LSB}_i(x) = x_i.$$

2.2 The BDF Attack on LSBS-RSA

Here we briefly introduce the BDF attack on LSBS-RSA. All the following theorems and lemmas can be found in [13] and [14]. The goal is to use the information of partial key to find $\mathrm{LSB}_{1\text{-}\frac{n}{4}}(p)$ or $\mathrm{LSB}_{1\text{-}\frac{n}{4}}(q)$. Then, use Coppersmith's method (see Theorem 1) to factor N.

Theorem 1. *(Coppersmith's method [5]) Let $N = pq$ be an n-bit RSA modulus. If $LSB_{1-\frac{n}{4}}(p)$ or $LSB_{1-\frac{n}{4}}(q)$ is given, then there exists an algorithm to factor N in polynomial time in n.*

We denote $T_{Cop}(n)$ as the complexity of the algorithm in Theorem 1. The improved versions of Coppersmith's method can be found in [6] and [7].

Lemma 1. *Consider the modular equation $x^2 \equiv c \pmod{2^r}$ and let $m_2(c)$ denote the multiplicity of 2 in c. That is, $c = c_{odd} \cdot 2^{m_2(c)}$, where c_{odd} is the largest odd factor of c. Then, the solutions are summarized in the following table:*

Conditions	Solution #	Solution Forms
If $r \leq m_2(c)$	$2^{\lfloor r/2 \rfloor}$	$x \equiv 0 \pmod{2^{\lceil r/2 \rceil}}$
If $r > m_2(c)$ and $m_2(c)$ is odd	0	-
If $r > m_2(c)$ and $m_2(c)$ is even, there are three subcases:		
subcase 1: $r = m_2(c) + 1$	$2^{\frac{m}{2}}$	$x \equiv 2^{\frac{m}{2}} \pmod{2^{\frac{m}{2}+1}}$
subcase 2: $r = m_2(c) + 2$ $c_{odd} \equiv 1 \pmod 4$	$2 \cdot 2^{\frac{m}{2}}$	$x \equiv \pm 2^{\frac{m}{2}} \pmod{2^{\frac{m}{2}+2}}$
subcase 3: $r \geq m_2(c) + 3$ $c_{odd} \equiv 1 \pmod 8$	$4 \cdot 2^{\frac{m}{2}}$	$x \equiv \pm s \cdot 2^{\frac{m}{2}} \pmod{2^{r-\frac{m}{2}}}$, or $x \equiv (\pm s + 2^{r-m-1}) \cdot 2^{\frac{m}{2}} \pmod{2^{r-\frac{m}{2}}}$, where $s^2 \equiv c_{odd} \pmod{2^{r-m}}$.
Otherwise	0	-

Proof. The proof can be found in Lemma 1 of [13], or [14].

Note that if there exist solutions for $x^2 \equiv c \pmod{2^r}$, then c and r must satisfy one of the conditions in the above table. Next, we show the properties of an α-LSBS RSA.

Lemma 2. *Let $N = pq$ denote an n-bit α-LSBS-RSA modulus. There exists an algorithm to compute the $LSB_{1-2\alpha}(p+q)$, $LSB_{1-\alpha}(p)$, and $LSB_{1-\alpha}(q)$ in polynomial time $O(n^2)$.*

Proof. Let $p = p_H \cdot 2^\alpha + l$ and $q = q_H \cdot 2^\alpha + l$. Thus, l is a solution to the modular quadratic congruence $x^2 \equiv N \pmod{2^\alpha}$, and it can be computed at most for 4 candidates in time polynomial in n^2. From

$$p \cdot q = N, \tag{1}$$

we may replace p and q by $p_H \cdot 2^\alpha + l$ and $q_H \cdot 2^\alpha + l$, respectively. This conducts to

$$LSB_{1-2\alpha}\left(l \cdot (p_H + q_H) \cdot 2^\alpha + l^2\right) = LSB_{1-2\alpha}(N). \tag{2}$$

Since l is an odd integer, $l^{-1} \pmod{2^{2\alpha}}$ exists. We have

$$LSB_{1-2\alpha}((p_H + q_H) \cdot 2^\alpha) = LSB_{1-2\alpha}\left(l^{-1} \cdot (N - l^2)\right). \tag{3}$$

The identity (3) shows that $\text{LSB}_{1^{\sim}\alpha}(p_H + q_H)$ can be totally computed from $l^{-1} \cdot (N - l^2)$. Thus, we have

$$\text{LSB}_{1^{\sim}2\alpha-1}\left(\tfrac{p+q}{2}\right)$$

$$= \text{LSB}_{1^{\sim}2\alpha-1}((p_H + q_H) \cdot 2^{\alpha-1} + l) \tag{4}$$

$$= \text{LSB}_{1^{\sim}\alpha}(p_H + q_H) \parallel \text{LSB}_\alpha\left((p_H + q_H) \cdot 2^{\alpha-1} + l\right) \parallel \text{LSB}_{1^{\sim}\alpha-1}(l).$$

where "$\parallel$" denotes the concatenation. Therefore, we get

$$\text{LSB}_{1^{\sim}2\alpha}(p + q) = \text{LSB}_{1^{\sim}2\alpha-1}\left(\tfrac{p+q}{2}\right) \parallel 0,$$

which completes the proof.

In the following we show the result of the BDF attack on LSBS-RSA, which is called the generalized BDF attack.

Theorem 2. (Generalized BDF Attack, [13], [14]) Let $N = pq$ denote an n-bit α-LSBS RSA modulus, d is a private exponent, and e is a public exponent with bit-length γ. Given $d_0 = \text{LSB}_{1^{\sim}\beta}(d)$, the Generalized BDF attack factors N within the following time complexity:

$$\text{If } \beta < 2(\alpha - 1) + \gamma, \text{ then } T_{BDF}(n) = O\left(\gamma 2^\gamma \cdot \lceil 2^{\frac{n}{4} - \frac{\beta}{2}} \rceil \cdot T'_{Cop}(n)\right);$$

$$\text{If } \beta \geq 2(\alpha - 1) + \gamma, \text{ then } T_{BDF}(n) = O\left(\gamma 2^\gamma \cdot \lceil 2^{\frac{n}{4} + \alpha - \beta} \rceil \cdot T'_{Cop}(n)\right), \tag{5}$$

where $T'_{Cop}(n) = T_{Cop}(n) + O(n^2)$, which is the complexity of Coppersmith's method plus the $O(n^2)$ for the other computations.

Note that in the case $\beta \geq 2(\alpha - 1) + \gamma$, $T_{BDF}(n)$ increases as α increases, which shows Steinfeld and Zheng's argument: low public exponent LSBS-RSA is inherently resistant to the BDF attack. In addition, as can be seen in (5), $T_{BDF}(n)$ decreases as β increases. We divide the process of the BDF attack on LSBS-RSA into three parts:

1. Exhaustive search the parameter k in RSA equation: $ed = k \cdot \varphi(N) + 1$, where $1 < k < e$.
2. With the information of k, compute $\text{LSB}_{1^{\sim}\frac{n}{4}}(p)$ by solving the quadratic modular equation.
3. Once $\text{LSB}_{1^{\sim}\frac{n}{4}}(p)$ is known, use Coppersmith's method to factor N.

Since $k < e$ and $2^{\gamma-1} \leq e < 2^\gamma$, the step 1 requires the time complexity $O(\gamma 2^\gamma)$ to exhaustive search for k. The step 2 requires the time complexity $O\left(2^{\frac{n}{4} - \frac{\beta}{2}}\right)$ or $O(2^{\frac{n}{4} + \alpha - \beta})$, depends on the relations between α, β, and γ. The step 3 requires the cost $T'_{Cop}(n)$, which is the complexity of Coppersmith's method plus $O(n^2)$.

3   The Revised BDF Attack on LSBS-RSA

In this section we show the revised BDF attack on LSBS-RSA. The main improvement is to reduce the cost of searching k in LSBS-RSA. Thus, the complexity in the step 1, which is $O\left(\gamma 2^{\gamma}\right)$, can be further reduced. Before that, we show the process of recovering $\mathrm{LSB}_{1 \sim \frac{n}{4}}(p)$ by solving the quadratic modular equation, and then use Coppersmith's method to factor N.

3.1   The Process of the BDF Attack

From the RSA equation we have

$$ed - 1 - k\left(N + 1 - p - \tfrac{N}{p}\right) = 0.$$

Multiplying p modulo 2^{β} yields the following modular equation with root p:

$$kx^2 + (ed_0 - k(N+1) - 1)x + kN \equiv 0 \pmod{2^{\beta}}, \tag{6}$$

where $d_0 = \mathrm{LSB}_{1 \sim \beta}(d)$ is known to the attacker.

Suppose $k = k_{odd} \cdot 2^{\kappa}$, where k_{odd} is the largest odd factor of k, and κ denotes the multiplicity of 2 in k. Eliminating the leading coefficient of (6) yields

$$x^2 + \left(k_{odd}^{-1} \cdot \tfrac{ed_0 - 1}{2^{\kappa}} - (N+1)\right)x + N \equiv 0 \pmod{2^{\beta - \kappa}}, \tag{7}$$

where k_{odd}^{-1} denotes the inverse of k_{odd} in $\mathbb{Z}_{2^{\beta - \kappa}}^{*}$. Consequently, (7) is reduced to

$$\left(x + \tfrac{b(k)}{2}\right)^2 \equiv c(k) \pmod{2^{\beta - \kappa}}, \tag{8}$$

where

$$b(k) = k_{odd}^{-1} \cdot \tfrac{ed_0 - 1}{2^{\kappa}} - (N+1), \text{ and}$$

$$c(k) = \left(\tfrac{b(k)}{2}\right)^2 - N.$$

Now, we solve the modular equation (8) by applying Lemma 1. Since

$$b(k) = k_{odd}^{-1} \cdot \tfrac{ed_0 - 1}{2^{\kappa}} - (N+1)$$

$$\equiv k_{odd}^{-1} \cdot \tfrac{k((N+1)-(p+q))}{2^{\kappa}} - (N+1) \pmod{2^{\beta - \kappa}}$$

$$\equiv -(p+q) \pmod{2^{\beta - \kappa}},$$

we get

$$c(k) = \left(\tfrac{b(k)}{2}\right)^2 - N \pmod{2^{\beta - \kappa}}$$

$$\equiv \left(\tfrac{p+q}{2}\right)^2 - N \pmod{2^{\beta - \kappa}}$$

$$\equiv \left(\tfrac{p-q}{2}\right)^2 \pmod{2^{\beta - \kappa}}.$$

Moreover, since N is an α-LSBS RSA modulus, we may write $p - q = r \cdot 2^{\alpha}$ for some odd integer r, which shows the multiplicity of 2 in $\left(\frac{p-q}{2}\right)^2$ is $2(\alpha - 1)$. Consequently, according to Lemma 1, the number of the solutions of (8) depends on the two cases: $\beta - \kappa \le 2(\alpha - 1)$ and $\beta - \kappa > 2(\alpha - 1)$.

In the case $\beta - \kappa \le 2(\alpha - 1)$, there are $2^{\lfloor \frac{\beta - \kappa}{2} \rfloor}$ solutions of the form

$$x + \frac{b(k)}{2} \equiv 0 \ (\mathrm{mod} \ 2^{\lceil \frac{\beta - \kappa}{2} \rceil})$$

for the modular equation (8). Thus, the $\lceil \frac{\beta - \kappa}{2} \rceil$ least significant bits of the root, i.e., p, are known to the attacker, which is the same as $\mathrm{LSB}_{1 - \lceil \frac{\beta - \kappa}{2} \rceil}\left(-\frac{b(k)}{2}\right)$. Since $\mathrm{LSB}_{1 - \frac{n}{4}}(p)$ (or $\mathrm{LSB}_{1 - \frac{n}{4}}(q)$) is the minimum requirement to apply Coppersmith's method, the remaining unknown part of p is $\mathrm{LSB}_{(\lceil \frac{\beta - \kappa}{2} \rceil + 1) - \frac{n}{4}}(p)$. Therefore, in this case the search for the parameter k with the cost $2^{\frac{n}{4} - \lceil \frac{\beta - \kappa}{2} \rceil}$ is required. We simplify the cost to $O\left(2^{\frac{\kappa}{2}} \cdot 2^{\frac{n}{4} - \frac{\beta}{2}}\right)$.

In the case $\beta - \kappa > 2(\alpha - 1)$, three subcases are discussed below according to Lemma 1:

Subcase 1: If $\beta - \kappa = 2(\alpha - 1) + 1$, there are $2^{\alpha - 1}$ solutions of the form

$$x + \frac{b(k)}{2} \equiv 2^{\alpha - 1} \ (\mathrm{mod} \ 2^{\alpha}).$$

Subcase 2: If $\beta - \kappa = 2(\alpha - 1) + 2$, and $(\alpha - 1)_{odd} \equiv 1 \ (\mathrm{mod} \ 4)$, there are $2 \cdot 2^{\alpha - 1}$ solutions of the form

$$x + \frac{b(k)}{2} \equiv \pm 2^{\alpha - 1} \ (\mathrm{mod} \ 2^{\alpha + 1}).$$

Subcase 3: If $\beta - \kappa \ge 2(\alpha - 1) + 3$, and $(\alpha - 1)_{odd} \equiv 1 \ (\mathrm{mod} \ 8)$, there are $4 \cdot 2^{\alpha - 1}$ solutions of the form

$$x + \frac{b(k)}{2} \equiv (\pm s) \cdot 2^{\alpha - 1} \ (\mathrm{mod} \ 2^{(\beta - \kappa) - (\alpha - 1)}), \ \mathrm{or}$$

$$x + \frac{b(k)}{2} \equiv \left(\pm s + 2^{(\beta - \kappa) - 2(\alpha - 1) - 1}\right) \cdot 2^{\alpha - 1} \ (\mathrm{mod} \ 2^{(\beta - \kappa) - (\alpha - 1)}).$$

Note that s is any solution to $s^2 \equiv (\alpha - 1)_{odd} \ (\mathrm{mod} \ 2^{(\beta - \kappa) - 2(\alpha - 1)})$, where $(\alpha - 1)_{odd}$ is the largest odd factor of $\alpha - 1$.

In the subcase 1, $\mathrm{LSB}_{1 - \alpha}(p)$ is known to the attacker. In order to apply Coppersmith's method, the remaining unknown part of p is $\mathrm{LSB}_{(\alpha + 1) - \frac{n}{4}}(p)$. Thus, in this case it requires the search with cost $2^{\frac{n}{4} - \alpha}$.

In the subcase 2, $\mathrm{LSB}_{1 - \alpha + 1}(p)$ is known to the attacker. In order to apply Coppersmith's method, the remaining unknown part of p is $\mathrm{LSB}_{(\alpha + 2) - \frac{n}{4}}(p)$. We simplify the cost to $O\left(2^{\frac{n}{4} - \alpha}\right)$.

In the subcase 3, $\mathrm{LSB}_{1 - (\beta - \kappa) - (\alpha - 1)}(p)$ is known to the attacker. In order to apply Coppersmith's method, the remaining unknown part of p is $\mathrm{LSB}_{(\beta - \kappa - \alpha) - \frac{n}{4}}(p)$. Thus, in this case it requires the search with cost $2^{\frac{n}{4} - ((\beta - \kappa) - (\alpha - 1))}$. We simplify the cost to $O\left(2^{\kappa} \cdot 2^{\left(\frac{n}{4}-\beta\right)+\alpha}\right)$. As a result, the complexity of the BDF attack on (α, β, γ)-LSBS RSA is concluded as follows.

If $\beta \leq 2(\alpha - 1) + \kappa$, then

$$T_{BDF}(n) = O\left(|K_c| \cdot (2^{\frac{\kappa}{2}} \cdot 2^{\frac{n}{4}-\frac{\beta}{2}}) \cdot T'_{Cop}(n)\right); \tag{9}$$

If $\beta = 2(\alpha - 1) + \kappa + 1$, or $\beta = 2(\alpha - 1) + \kappa + 2$, then

$$T_{BDF}(n) = O\left(|K_c| \cdot (2^{\frac{n}{4}-\alpha}) \cdot T'_{Cop}(n)\right); \tag{10}$$

If $\beta \geq 2(\alpha - 1) + \kappa + 3$, then

$$T_{BDF}(n) = O\left(|K_c| \cdot (2^{\kappa} \cdot 2^{\left(\frac{n}{4}-\beta\right)+\alpha}) \cdot T'_{Cop}(n)\right), \tag{11}$$

where $|K_c|$ denotes the number of candidates of k, which is required to test by exhaustive search. Next, we show how to reduce the size of K_c in LSBS-RSA.

3.2 Searching k in LSBS-RSA

We consider the following lemma:

Lemma 3. *Consider the three positive integers A, B, and C, where $C = A \times B$. If $LSB_{1^{\sim}m}(A)$ and $LSB_{1^{\sim}m}(C)$ are given, we can compute $LSB_{1^{\sim}m-m_2(A)}(B)$ in polynomial time in m, where $m_2(A)$ denotes the multiplicity of 2 in A.*

Proof. Suppose that $A = A_1 \cdot 2^m + A_2$ and $B = B_1 \cdot 2^m + B_2$, where $A_2 = LSB_{1^{\sim}m}(A)$ and $B_2 = LSB_{1^{\sim}m}(B)$, respectively. We may write $A_2 = A \pmod{2^m}$ and $B_2 = B \pmod{2^m}$. Since

$$A \times B = (A_1 B_1) \cdot 2^{2m} + (A_1 B_2 + A_2 B_1) \cdot 2^m + A_2 B_2 = C,$$

we have

$$C \pmod{2^m} \equiv A_2 B_2 \pmod{2^m}. \tag{12}$$

Denote $A_2 = a_2 \cdot 2^{m_2(A_2)}$, where $m_2(A_2)$ denotes the multiplicity of 2 in A_2. Since $C = A \times B$, we may set $C = c \cdot 2^{m_2(A_2)}$. Consequently, simplifying (12) yields

$$a_2 \times B_2 \pmod{2^{m-m_2(A_2)}} = c \pmod{2^{m-m_2(A_2)}},$$

which implies

$$B_2 \pmod{2^{m-m_2(A_2)}} = a_2^{-1} \times c \pmod{2^{m-m_2(A_2)}},$$

where a_2^{-1} denotes the inverse of a_2 in $\mathbb{Z}^*_{2^{m-m_2(A_2)}}$. Note that $m_2(A_2)$ is smaller than or equal to $m_2(A)$, but the case "$m_2(A_2) = m_2(A)$" happens with probability $1 - \frac{1}{2^m}$, which is close to 1 if m is not too small. Thus, in our case we may assume that $m_2(A_2) = m_2(A)$ and get

$$LSB_{1^{\sim}m-m_2(A)}(B) = a_2^{-1} \times c \pmod{2^{m-m_2(A)}}, \tag{13}$$

which completes the proof.

Moreover, if $B \leq 2^{m-m_2(A)}$, then B can be completely determined immediately. Following corollary shows our method for searching k in LSBS-RSA

Corollary 1. *In (α, β, γ)-LSBS RSA, $LSB_{1^- \min\{\beta,2\alpha\}-\sigma}(k)$ can be computed in polynomial time in n, where σ denotes the multiplicity of 2 in $\varphi(N)$.*

Proof. From RSA equation we have $ed - 1 = k \cdot \varphi(N)$. Since $d_0 = LSB_{1^-\beta}(d)$ is known, we can compute $LSB_{1^-\beta}(ed - 1)$. In addition, $LSB_{1^-2\alpha}(p + q)$ can be computed efficiently according to Lemma 2, and thus $LSB_{1^-2\alpha}(\varphi(N))$ can be derived to the attacker immediately. Now, setting $C = ed - 1$, $A = \varphi(N)$, and $B = k$ in Lemma 3, we get the result:

$$LSB_{1^- \min\{\beta,2\alpha\}-\sigma}(k) = (ed_0 - 1) \cdot \varphi^{-1}(\bmod\ 2^{\min\{\beta,2\alpha\}-\sigma}), \qquad (14)$$

which completes the proof.

Note that we have $k < e \approx 2^\gamma$ due to the process of RSA-key generation. Hence, if the public exponent e is small enough such that $\gamma \leq \min\{\beta, 2\alpha\} - \sigma$, then k can be completely determined immediately in polynomial time in n. On the other hand, if the public exponent e satisfying $\gamma > \min\{\beta, 2\alpha\} - \sigma$, Corollary 1 implies that finding k requires exhaustive search with cost $2^{\gamma-(\min\{\beta,2\alpha\}-\sigma)}$. Therefore, the size of K_c can be set to $\max\{1, 2^{\gamma-(\min\{\beta,2\alpha\}-\sigma)}\}$. Apply $|K_c|$ to the revised BDF attack, the corresponding complexity analysis is shown in the next section.

4   The Complexity Analysis

According to Corollary 1, the complexity of the BDF attack on LSBS-RSA is discussed in the two cases: small public exponent and large public exponent.

4.1   LSBS-RSA with Small Public Exponent e ($\gamma \leq \min\{\beta, 2\alpha\} - \sigma$)

In LSBS-RSA with small e satisfying $\gamma \leq \min\{\beta, 2\alpha\} - \sigma$, according to Corollary 1, the parameter k can be computed immediately. Hence, the term $|K_c|$ in (9), (10), and (11) can be replaced by $T_k(n)$, where $T_k(n)$ denotes the complexity of computing k from (14), which is polynomial time in n.

4.2   LSBS-RSA with Large Public Exponent e ($\gamma > \min\{\beta, 2\alpha\} - \sigma$)

For large public exponent e, i.e., $\min\{\beta, 2\alpha\} - \sigma < \gamma$, we may set $|K_c| = 2^{\gamma-(\min\{\beta,2\alpha\}-\sigma)}$. Thus, the complexity of searching k in this case depends on the two cases: $\beta < 2\alpha$, and $2\alpha \leq \beta$.

In the Case $\beta < 2\alpha$. First we consider the case $\beta < 2\alpha$. According to Corollary 1, $LSB_{1^-\beta-\sigma}(k)$ is known to the attacker. Thus, finding the unknown part of k requires exhaustive search with the cost $2^{\gamma-(\beta-\sigma)}$. After replacing $|K_c|$ in (9), (10), and (11) by $2^{\gamma-(\beta-\sigma)}$, we get the following results:

In the case $\beta < 2\alpha$ and $\beta \leq 2(\alpha - 1) + \kappa$, we have

$$T_{BDF}(n) = O\left(2^{\gamma-(\beta-\sigma)} \cdot 2^{\frac{\kappa}{2}+\frac{n}{4}-\frac{\beta}{2}} \cdot T'_{Cop}(n)\right)$$
$$= O\left(2^{\frac{\kappa}{2}+\sigma} \cdot 2^{(\frac{n}{4}+\gamma)-\frac{3\beta}{2}} \cdot T'_{Cop}(n)\right).$$

In the case $\beta < 2\alpha$ and $\beta = 2(\alpha - 1) + \kappa + 1$, we get $2\alpha + \kappa - 1 < 2\alpha$, which implies $\kappa \leq 0$. Since κ denotes the multiplicity of 2 in k, we get $\kappa = 0$, which conducts to $\beta = 2\alpha - 1$. Thus,

$$T_{BDF}(n) = O\left(2^{\gamma-(\beta-\sigma)} \cdot (2^{\frac{n}{4}-\alpha}) \cdot T'_{Cop}(n)\right)$$
$$= O\left(2^{\sigma} \cdot 2^{(\frac{n}{4}+\gamma)-(\alpha+\beta)} \cdot T'_{Cop}(n)\right).$$

In the case $\beta < 2\alpha$ and $\beta = 2(\alpha - 1) + \kappa + 2$, we get $2\alpha + \kappa < 2\alpha$, which implies $\kappa \leq -1$. This is a contradiction for any non-negative integer κ. The same result for the case $\beta < 2\alpha$ and $\beta \geq 2(\alpha - 1) + \kappa + 3$, we get $2\alpha + \kappa + 1 \leq \beta < 2\alpha$. It implies that $\kappa \leq -2$, which is also a contradiction.

In the Case $2\alpha \leq \beta$. Secondly, we consider the case $2\alpha \leq \beta$. According to Corollary 1, $\text{LSB}_{1\text{-}2\alpha-\sigma}(k)$ is known to the attacker. Thus, finding the unknown part of k requires the exhaustive search with the cost $2^{\gamma-(2\alpha-\sigma)}$. Replacing $|K_c|$ by $2^{\gamma-(2\alpha-\sigma)}$ in (9), (10), and (11), we get the following results:

In the case $2\alpha \leq \beta$ and $\beta \leq 2(\alpha - 1) + \kappa$, we have

$$T_{BDF}(n) = O\left(2^{\gamma-(2\alpha-\sigma)} \cdot 2^{\frac{\kappa}{2}+\frac{n}{4}-\frac{\beta}{2}} \cdot T'_{Cop}(n)\right)$$
$$= O\left(2^{\frac{\kappa}{2}+\sigma} \cdot 2^{(\frac{n}{4}+\gamma)-(2\alpha+\frac{\beta}{2})} \cdot T'_{Cop}(n)\right).$$

In the case $2\alpha \leq \beta$ and $\beta = 2(\alpha - 1) + \kappa + 1$, we have

$$T_{BDF}(n) = O\left(2^{\gamma-(2\alpha-\sigma)} \cdot (2^{\frac{n}{4}-\alpha}) \cdot T'_{Cop}(n)\right)$$
$$= O\left(2^{\sigma} \cdot 2^{(\frac{n}{4}+\gamma)-3\alpha} \cdot T'_{Cop}(n)\right).$$

The same result above in the case $2\alpha \leq \beta$ and $\beta = 2(\alpha - 1) + \kappa + 2$, and thus we ignore it.

In the case $2\alpha \leq \beta$ and $\beta \geq 2(\alpha - 1) + \kappa + 3$, we have

$$T_{BDF}(n) = O\left(2^{\gamma-(2\alpha-\sigma)} \cdot 2^{\kappa+\frac{n}{4}+\alpha-\beta} \cdot T'_{Cop}(n)\right)$$
$$= O\left(2^{\kappa+\sigma} \cdot 2^{(\frac{n}{4}+\gamma)-(\alpha+\beta)} \cdot T'_{Cop}(n)\right).$$

4.3   Summary of the Revised BDF Attack on LSBS-RSA

We give the summary for the complexity of the revised BDF attack on LSBS-RSA. We just count in the complexity of the exponent, but eliminate the complexity of polynomial time. In addition, σ and κ are both small constants with high probability, and thus we can ignore them in the "Big O" notation.

Table 1. The Summary of the BDF Attack on LSBS-RSA with Small Public Exponent

Condition	$T_{BDF}(n)$
$\beta \leq 2(\alpha - 1) + \kappa$	$O\left(T_k(n) \cdot 2^{\frac{n}{4} - \frac{\beta}{2}} \cdot T'_{Cop}(n)\right)$
$\beta = 2\alpha + \kappa$,or $\beta = 2\alpha + \kappa - 1$	$O\left(T_k(n) \cdot (2^{\frac{n}{4} - \alpha}) \cdot T'_{Cop}(n)\right)$
$\beta \geq 2\alpha + \kappa + 1$	$O\left(T_k(n) \cdot 2^{\frac{n}{4} + \alpha - \beta} \cdot T'_{Cop}(n)\right)$

Table 2. The Summary of the BDF Attack on LSBS-RSA with Large Public Exponent

Condition I	Condition II	$T_{BDF}(n)$
$\beta < 2\alpha$	$\beta \leq 2(\alpha - 1) + \kappa$	$O\left(2^{(\frac{n}{4} + \gamma) - \frac{3\beta}{2}} \cdot T'_{Cop}(n)\right)$
$\beta < 2\alpha$	$\beta = 2\alpha - 1$ and $\kappa = 0$	$O\left(2^{(\frac{n}{4} + \gamma) - (\alpha + \beta)} \cdot T'_{Cop}(n)\right)$
$2\alpha \leq \beta$	$\beta \leq 2(\alpha - 1) + \kappa$	$O\left(2^{(\frac{n}{4} + \gamma) - (2\alpha + \frac{\beta}{2})} \cdot T'_{Cop}(n)\right)$
$2\alpha \leq \beta$	$\beta = 2\alpha + \kappa$, or $\beta = 2\alpha + \kappa - 1$	$O\left(2^{(\frac{n}{4} + \gamma) - 3\alpha} \cdot T'_{Cop}(n)\right)$
$2\alpha \leq \beta$	$\beta \geq 2\alpha + \kappa + 1$	$O\left(2^{(\frac{n}{4} + \gamma) - (\alpha + \beta)} \cdot T'_{Cop}(n)\right)$

Table 1 shows the complexity of the revised BDF attack on LSBS-RSA when $\gamma \leq \min\{\beta, 2\alpha\} - \sigma$.

As can be seen in Table 1, γ is independent to the complexity of BDF attack on LSBS-RSA. However, in case of $\beta \geq 2\alpha + \kappa + 1$, $T_{BDF}(n)$ increases as α increases, which is further supporting Steinfeld and Zheng's argument [14]: Low public exponent LSBS-RSA is inherently resistant to the partial key exposure attack.

Moreover, if we set $\chi_{\max} = \max\{2\alpha, \beta\}$ and $\chi_{\min} = \min\{2\alpha, \beta\}$, then all the complexities in the exponential cost are in the interval:

$$\left[\frac{n}{4} - \frac{1}{2}\chi_{\max}, \frac{n}{4} - \frac{1}{2}\chi_{\min}\right].$$

Therefore, we conclude that the complexity of the revised BDF attack on (α, β, γ)-LSBS RSA with small e is in the range

$$O\left(T_k(n) \cdot 2^{\frac{n}{4} - \frac{1}{2}\chi_{\max}} \cdot T'_{Cop}(n)\right) \leq T_{BDF}(n) \leq O\left(T_k(n) \cdot 2^{\frac{n}{4} - \frac{1}{2}\chi_{\min}} \cdot T'_{Cop}(n)\right). \quad (15)$$

Table 2 shows the complexity of the revised BDF attack on LSBS-RSA when $\min\{\beta, 2\alpha\} - \sigma < \gamma$. As shown in the table, the complexity of the revised BDF attack is independent to α in the case $\beta < 2\alpha$ and $\beta \leq 2(\alpha - 1) + \kappa$. In the other cases, the complexity decrease as α and β increase.

All the complexities in exponential cost are in the interval:

$$\left[(\tfrac{n}{4} + \gamma) - \tfrac{3}{2}\chi_{\max}, (\tfrac{n}{4} + \gamma) - \tfrac{3}{2}\chi_{\min}\right].$$

Therefore, we conclude that the complexity of the revised BDF attack on (α, β, γ)-LSBS RSA with large e is in the range

$$O\left(2^{(\frac{n}{4}+\gamma)-\frac{3}{2}\chi_{\max}} \cdot T'_{Cop}(n)\right) \leq T_{BDF}(n) \leq O\left(2^{(\frac{n}{4}+\gamma)-\frac{3}{2}\chi_{\min}} \cdot T'_{Cop}(n)\right). \qquad (16)$$

From (15) and (16), we know that an LSBS-RSA is more vulnerable under the BDF attack as $\chi_{\max} = \max\{2\alpha, \beta\}$ increases proportionally with the size of N.

5   Further Discussions

5.1   The Relation between (α, β, γ) and $(\alpha, 0, \gamma)$-LSBS RSA

The following result shows that for $\beta \leq 2\alpha$ and small difference of γ and β, to break (α, β, γ)-LSBS RSA is as hard as to break $(\alpha, 0, \gamma)$-LSBS RSA.

Theorem 3. *(Revised Theorem 4 in [14]) In (α, β, γ)-LSBS RSA, given (N, e, d_0), suppose an algorithm A can factor N in time $T_A(n)$, where $d_0 = LSB_{1\text{-}\beta}(d)$ and $\beta \leq 2\alpha$. Then, there exists a factoring algorithm F for $(\alpha, 0, \gamma)$-LSBS RSA, that given (N, e), factors N in time $T_F(n)$, where*

$$T_F(n) = O\left(2^{\gamma-\beta} \cdot \left(T_A(n) + n^2\right)\right).$$

Proof. The proof is almost the same as the proof of the theorem 4 in [14]. The difference is that the cost for exhaustive search for k is reduced to $O\left(2^{\gamma-\beta}\right)$ rather than $O(2^\gamma)$. Thus, for each candidate $k_c \in K_c$, we may compute

$$d_0 = e^{-1}\left[1 + k_c(N+1-s_0)\right] \pmod{2^{2\alpha}}, \qquad (17)$$

where $s_0 \equiv p + q \pmod{2^{2\alpha}}$ is available according to Lemma 2. Consequently, $d_0 = LSB_{1\text{-}2\alpha}(d)$ consists of the 2α least significant bits of d, which also consists of $LSB_{1\text{-}\beta}(d)$. Applying (N, e, d_0) to the input of A succeeds to factor N in time

$$O\left(2^{\gamma-\beta} \cdot \left(T_A(n) + n^2\right)\right),$$

which denotes the complexity of $T_F(n)$.

Note that (17) also implies that $LSB_{1\text{-}2\alpha}(d)$ is leaked in $(\alpha, 0, \gamma)$-LSBS RSA if the cost of $2^{\gamma-\beta}$ is feasible under current computational capability. Therefore, for $\beta \leq 2\alpha$ and $\gamma - \beta < E_s$, where E_s denotes the bit number of the feasible exhaustive search, Theorem 3 also shows the hardness of breaking (α, β, γ)-LSBS RSA is equivalent to that of $(\alpha, 0, \gamma)$-LSBS RSA.

5.2   Feasibility and Further Reducing the Cost of Searching k

Under the current computational capability, we may set $E_s = 64$, which means the exhaustive search for $O\left(2^{64}\right)$ is feasible. According to our result, The revised BDF attack on LSBS-RSA with small e , *i.e.*, $\gamma \leq \min\{\beta, 2\alpha\} - \sigma$, is feasible if

$$\frac{n}{4} - \frac{1}{2}\chi_{\min} \leq 64.$$

For LSBS-RSA with large e, *i.e.*, $\gamma > \min\{\beta, 2\alpha\} - \sigma$, the attack is feasible if

$$(\tfrac{n}{4} + \gamma) - \tfrac{3}{2}\chi_{\min} \leq 64.$$

We should point out that our method for finding k is still a kind of brute method. In fact, we can estimate the value of k before the exhaustive search. Denote the estimation of φ to be $\varphi_E := N + 1 - 2\lceil\sqrt{N}\rceil$. Compute $\widetilde{k}$ and $\widetilde{d}$ by using Euclidean algorithm such that $e\widetilde{d} = \widetilde{k}(N + 1 - 2N) + 1$, where $0 < \widetilde{k} < e$ and $0 < \widetilde{d} < \varphi_E$. Then, searching k from $\widetilde{k}$ with the fixed part of least significant bits will further reduce the cost.

6   Conclusion and Future Work

In this paper we improve the BDF attack on LSBS-RSA. With our improvement, the complexity of the BDF attack is further reduced with less cost for exhaustive search. More precisely, we show that the lower bound of exponential cost in the BDF attack increases with decreasing $\max\{2\alpha, \beta\}$, and the upper bound of exponential cost in the BDF attack decreases with increasing $\min\{2\alpha, \beta\}$. Our result is further supporting the claim in [14]: Low public exponent LSBS-RSA is resistant to partial key exposure attacks but large public exponent LSBS-RSA is vulnerable under the attacks.

To further reduce the complexity of the BDF attack, we may focus on improving the efficiency of Coppersmith's method, such as [6], [7]. Moreover, an open question has been mentioned for many times: whether the information of the $\frac{n}{4}$ least significant bits of p (or q) is the minimum requirement to factor N in polynomial time? Moreover, to further extend the partial key exposure attack on LSBS-RSA, the lattice technique should be considered to analyze.

LSBS-RSA is beneficial to computational efficiency of server-aided signature generation, such as [4]. However, we believe that an RSA system with modulus primes sharing a large number of bits also raises the risk in the security [15], [16]. It is a trade-off between the efficiency and the security level. Thus, one should be more careful in using such RSA variants.

Acknowledgement

The authors would like to thank Ron Steinfeld for his helpful discussion and anonymous reviewers for their valuable comments. This work was supported in part by the National Science Council, Taiwan, under Contract NSC 96-2628-E-007-025-MY3 and NSC 096-2917-I-007-022, the Ministry of Education of Singapore under grant T206B2204, and the Australian Research Council under ARC Discovery Project DP0665035.

References

1. Boneh, D., Durfee, G., Frankel, Y.: An Attacks on RSA Given a Small Fraction of the Private Key Bits. In: Ohta, K., Pei, D. (eds.) ASIACRYPT 1998. LNCS, vol. 1514, pp. 25–34. Springer, Heidelberg (1998)

2. Boneh, D., Durfee, G., Frankel, Y.: Exposing an RSA Privae Key Given a Small Fraction of its Bits. Full version of the work from Asiacrypt 1998 (1998), http://crypto.stanford.edu/~dabo/abstracts/bits_of_d.html
3. Blömer, J., May, A.: New Partial Key Exposure Attacks on RSA. In: Boneh, D. (ed.) CRYPTO 2003. LNCS, vol. 2729, pp. 27–43. Springer, Heidelberg (2003)
4. Bellare, M., Rogaway, P.: The exact security of digital signatures: How to sign with RSA and Rabin. In: Maurer, U.M. (ed.) EUROCRYPT 1996. LNCS, vol. 1070, pp. 399–416. Springer, Heidelberg (1996)
5. Coppersmith, D.: Finding a Small Root of a Bivariate Integer Equation; Factoring with High Bits Known. In: Maurer, U.M. (ed.) EUROCRYPT 1996. LNCS, vol. 1070, pp. 178–189. Springer, Heidelberg (1996)
6. Coron, J.-S.: Finding Small Roots of Bivariate Integer Polynomial Equations Revisited. In: Cachin, C., Camenisch, J.L. (eds.) EUROCRYPT 2004. LNCS, vol. 3027, pp. 492–505. Springer, Heidelberg (2004)
7. Coron, J.-S.: Finding Small Roots of Bivariate Integer Polynomial Equations: A Direct Approach. In: Menezes, A. (ed.) CRYPTO 2007. LNCS, vol. 4622, pp. 379–394. Springer, Heidelberg (2007)
8. Ernst, M., Jochemsz, E., May, A., de Weger, B.: Partial Key Exposure Attacks on RSA up to Full Size Exponents. In: Cramer, R.J.F. (ed.) EUROCRYPT 2005. LNCS, vol. 3494, pp. 371–386. Springer, Heidelberg (2005)
9. Hastad, J.: Solving simultaneous modular equations of low degree. SIAM J. of Computing 17, 336–341 (1988)
10. Sun, H.-M., Yang, W.-C., Laih, C.-S.: On the design of RSA with short secret exponent. In: Lam, K.-Y., Okamoto, E., Xing, C. (eds.) ASIACRYPT 1999. LNCS, vol. 1716, pp. 150–164. Springer, Heidelberg (1999)
11. Sun, H.-M., Yang, C.-T.: RSA with balanced short exponents and its application to entity authentication. In: Vaudenay, S. (ed.) PKC 2005. LNCS, vol. 3386, pp. 199–215. Springer, Heidelberg (2005)
12. Rivest, R., Shamir, A., Aldeman, L.: A Method for Obtaining Digital Signatures and Public-Key Cryptosystems. Communications of the ACM 21(2), 120–126 (1978)
13. Steinfeld, R., Zheng, Y.: An Advantage of Low-Exponent RSA with Modulus Primes Sharing Least Significant Bits. In: Naccache, D. (ed.) CT-RSA 2001. LNCS, vol. 2020, pp. 52–62. Springer, Heidelberg (2001)
14. Steinfeld, R., Zheng, Y.: On the Security of RSA with Primes Sharing Least-Significant Bits. Appl. Algebra Eng. Commun. Comput. 15,3(4), 179–200 (2004)
15. de Weger, B.: Cryptanalysis of RSA with small prime difference. Applicable Algebra in Engineering, Communication and Computing 13, 17–28 (2002)
16. Zhao, Y.-D., Qi, W.-F.: Small Private-Exponent Attack on RSA with Primes Sharing Bits. In: Garay, J.A., Lenstra, A.K., Mambo, M., Peralta, R. (eds.) ISC 2007. LNCS, vol. 4779, pp. 221–229. Springer, Heidelberg (2007)

Public-Key Cryptosystems with Primitive Power Roots of Unity

Takato Hirano*, Koichiro Wada, and Keisuke Tanaka

Department of Mathematical and Computing Sciences, Tokyo Institute of
Technology. W8-55, 2-12-1 Ookayama, Meguro-ku, Tokyo 152-8552, Japan
{hirano6, wada4, keisuke}@is.titech.ac.jp

Abstract. We first consider a variant of the Schmidt-Samoa–Takagi encryption scheme without losing additively homomorphic properties. We show that this variant is secure in the sense of IND-CPA under the decisional composite residuosity assumption, and of OW-CPA under the assumption on the hardness of factoring $n = p^2q$. Second, we introduce new cryptographic properties "affine" and "pre-image restriction", which are closely related to homomorphism. Intuitively, "affine" is a tuple of functions which have a special homomorphic property, and "pre-image restriction" is a function which can restrict the receiver to having information on the encrypted message. Then, we propose an encryption scheme with primitive power roots of unity in $(\mathbb{Z}/n^{s+1})^{\times}$. We show that our scheme has the above cryptographic properties.

Keywords: Paillier encryption scheme, factoring assumption, homomorphism, power roots of unity.

1 Introduction

Background. Homomorphism is one of the most useful cryptographic properties, and has been well-studied. For groups G and H, a function $f : G \to H$ is (group) homomorphism if for $g, g' \in G$, $f(g) \circ_H f(g') = f(g \circ_G g')$, where $\circ_G$ and $\circ_H$ are the group operations G and H, respectively. In mathematical points of view, this property means that f preserves the group structure of G. In cryptographic points of view, we can make a meaningful ciphertext from ciphertexts without knowing the hidden messages or the secret key. This property is useful to many cryptographic applications such as electronic voting, electronic cash, and so on.

We call f a multiplicative homomorphism if $\circ_G$ is the multiplication "$\times$". There exist many encryption schemes with multiplicatively homomorphic properties, for example, the RSA encryption scheme [7], the ElGamal encryption scheme [3]. We call f an additive homomorphism if $\circ_G$ is the addition "$+$". There also exist many encryption schemes with additively homomorphic properties, for example, the Goldwasser-Micali encryption scheme [4], the Paillier

---

* Supported in part by Global COE: Computationism as a Foundation for the Sciences of Tokyo Institute of Technology.

Y. Mu, W. Susilo, and J. Seberry (Eds.): ACISP 2008, LNCS 5107, pp. 98–112, 2008.

encryption scheme [5]. In particular, the Paillier encryption scheme has interesting structure and many mathematical advantages. Many variants of his scheme have been proposed.

Our Contribution. In this paper, we first formalize the notion of a general homomorphic property as follows: Let $f_1, f_2, \ldots, f_k, f$ be functions, and $*, g$ polynomial-time computable operations. For $m_1, m_2, \ldots, m_k$, we have $f_1(m_1) * f_2(m_2) * \cdots * f_k(m_k) = f(g(m_1, m_2, \ldots, m_k))$.

These functions do not always have common domain or common range. A multiplicative homomorphism can be expressed by $f_1 = f_2 = \cdots = f_k = f$ and $g(m_1, m_2, \ldots, m_k) = m_1 \times m_2 \times \cdots \times m_k$, and an additive homomorphism $f_1 = f_2 = \cdots = f_k = f$ and $g(m_1, m_2, \ldots, m_k) = m_1 + m_2 + \cdots + m_k$. With this formalization, we consider two properties. A tuple $(\{f_1, f_2, \ldots, f_k\}, f)$ of functions is called "affine with $x_1, x_2, \ldots, x_k$" if $f_1(m_1) * f_2(m_2) * \cdots * f_k(m_k) = f(x_1 m_1 + x_2 m_2 + \cdots + x_k m_k)$, that is, $g(m_1, m_2, \ldots, m_k) = x_1 m_1 + x_2 m_2 + \cdots + x_k m_k$. An additive homomorphism can be considered as a special case that $f_1 = f_2 = \cdots = f_k = f$ and g is addition and $x_1 = x_2 = \cdots = x_k = 1$. A tuple $(\{f_1, f_2, \ldots, f_k\}, f)$ of functions is called "pre-image restriction with modulo n" if $m = m_1 = m_2 = \cdots = m_k$ and $f_1(m) * f_2(m) * \cdots * f_k(m) = f(m \bmod n)$, that is, $g(m, m, \ldots, m) = m \bmod n$.

In this paper, we first consider a variant of the Schmidt-Samoa–Takagi encryption scheme [8] without losing additively homomorphic properties, described as $\mathcal{E}(r, m) = r^{n^s}(1 + n^t)^m \bmod n^{s+1}$, where $m \in \mathbb{Z}/(n^{s-t+1}/p)$ is a message and $r \in (\mathbb{Z}/n)^\times$ is a random number. We show that this variant is secure in the sense of IND-CPA under the decisional composite residuosity assumption, and of OW-CPA under the assumption on the hardness of factoring $n = p^2 q$.

Then, by extending our variant, we propose an encryption scheme with primitive power roots of unity in $(\mathbb{Z}/n^{s+1})^\times$. We show that this extended scheme has, in addition to the additively homomorphic property, the above properties. We also show that our extended scheme is secure in the sense of IND-CPA under the decisional composite residuosity assumption, and of OW-CPA under the assumption on the hardness of factoring $p^2 q$. In order to show that our scheme works, we analyze several properties on primitive power roots of unity in $(\mathbb{Z}/n)^\times$, and give an algorithm which finds them efficiently. Furthermore, we discuss a relation between factoring n and knowing primitive power roots of unity.

Related Works. In 1998, Okamoto and Uchiyama proposed a public-key encryption scheme which employs the modulus $n = p^2 q$. Their scheme is secure in the sense of OW-CPA under the assumption on the hardness of factoring $n = p^2 q$, and of IND-CPA under the p-subgroup assumption. In addition, the scheme has an additively homomorphic property.

In 1999, Paillier proposed a public-key encryption scheme, which has an additively homomorphic property [5]. He showed that the encryption scheme is secure in the sense of IND-CPA under the decisional composite residuosity assumption. However, it is not known whether the one-wayness is reduced to the problem of the hardness of factoring $n = pq$. In addition to IND-CPA, Paillier and Pointcheval proposed its variant by using a conversion technique, which has the indistinguishability against the chosen ciphertext attack (IND-CCA2) in the random oracle model under the decisional composite residuosity assumption [6].

Damgård and Jurik proposed a variant of the Paillier encryption scheme where the ciphertext space $(\mathbb{Z}/n^2)^\times$ is extended to $(\mathbb{Z}/n^{s+1})^\times$ [1]. Thereby, it can handle efficiently messages of arbitrary length in their scheme, although the public key and the secret key are fixed. The security of their variant is similar to that of the Paillier encryption scheme and it is not known whether the one-wayness is reduced to the problem of the hardness of factoring $n = pq$. Their scheme can be applied to threshold cryptosystem and zero-knowledge protocols. Then, they constructed an electronic voting scheme by using these protocols and their threshold variant [2].

Schmidt-Samoa and Takagi proposed another variant which employs modulus $n = p^2q$ instead of $n = pq$ [8], where p and q are primes with the same length. Their scheme is secure in the sense of not only IND-CPA under the decisional composite residuosity assumption, but also OW-CPA under the assumption on the hardness of factoring $n = p^2q$. They constructed trapdoor hash families based on the problem of factoring $n = p^2q$, by applying the encryption scheme. These hash families are suitable for on-line/off-line or chameleon signatures schemes.

Organization. The organization of this paper is as follows. In Section 2, we give some definitions. In Section 3, we review the Schmidt-Samoa–Takagi encryption scheme, and propose its variant. In Section 4, we describe new cryptographic properties and a construction of primitive power roots of unity in $(\mathbb{Z}/n^{s+1})^\times$. Then, we extend our variant with primitive power roots of unity. In Section 5, we discuss a relation between factoring n and knowing of primitive power roots of unity.

2   Preliminaries

We denote $\{0, 1, \ldots, n-1\}$ by $\mathbb{Z}/n$, and its reduced residue class group by $(\mathbb{Z}/n)^\times$, namely, $(\mathbb{Z}/n)^\times = \{x \in \mathbb{Z}/n | \gcd(x, n) = 1\}$. For $g \in (\mathbb{Z}/n)^\times$, $\mathrm{ord}_n\, g$ is defined as the smallest positive integer e such that $g^e \equiv 1 \pmod{n}$.

We denote the probability distribution on set X by $x \leftarrow X$ and the uniform distribution by $x \xleftarrow{u} X$.

We denote the set of positive real numbers by $\mathbb{R}^+$. We say that a function $\varepsilon : \mathbb{N} \to \mathbb{R}^+$ is negligible if and only if for every polynomial p, there exists $k_0 \in \mathbb{N}$ such that for all $k \geq k_0$, $\varepsilon(k) < \frac{1}{p(k)}$.

We review the definitions of public-key encryption schemes, of the one-wayness against the chosen plaintext attack (OW-CPA), and of the indistinguishability against the chosen plaintext attack (IND-CPA).

Definition 1. *A public-key encryption scheme $\Pi = (\mathcal{K}, \mathcal{E}, \mathcal{D})$ consists of the following three algorithms:*

Key Generation $\mathcal{K}(1^k)$: *The key generation algorithm $\mathcal{K}$ is a randomized algorithm that takes a security parameter k and returns a pair (pk, sk) of keys, a public key and a matching secret key.*

Encryption $\mathcal{E}(pk, r, m)$**:** *The encryption algorithm* $\mathcal{E}$ *is a randomized algorithm that takes the public key pk, a randomness r, and a plaintext m and returns a ciphertext c.*

Decryption $\mathcal{D}(sk, c)$**:** *The decryption algorithm* $\mathcal{D}$ *is a deterministic algorithm that takes the secret key sk and a ciphertext c and returns the corresponding plaintext m or a special symbol* $\perp$ *to indicate that the ciphertext is invalid.*

Definition 2. *(OW-CPA) Let* $\Pi = (\mathcal{K}, \mathcal{E}, \mathcal{D})$ *be a public-key encryption scheme and* $\mathcal{A}$ *an adversary. We define an advantage of* $\mathcal{A}$ *via*

$$\mathbf{Adv}_{\Pi, \mathcal{A}}^{\text{ow-cpa}}(k) = \Pr[(pk, sk) \leftarrow \mathcal{K}(1^k); c \leftarrow \mathcal{E}(pk, r, m) : \mathcal{A}(pk, c) = m].$$

We say that Π *is secure in the sense of OW-CPA if* $\mathbf{Adv}_{\Pi, \mathcal{A}}^{\text{ow-cpa}}(k)$ *is negligible in k, for any polynomial-time adversary* $\mathcal{A}$.

Definition 3. *(IND-CPA) Let* $\Pi = (\mathcal{K}, \mathcal{E}, \mathcal{D})$ *be a public-key encryption scheme and* $\mathcal{A} = (\mathcal{A}_1, \mathcal{A}_2)$ *an adversary. We define the advantage of* $\mathcal{A}$ *via*

$$\mathbf{Adv}_{\Pi, \mathcal{A}}^{\text{ind-cpa}}(k) = |2 \Pr[(pk, sk) \leftarrow \mathcal{K}(1^k); m_0, m_1, state \leftarrow \mathcal{A}_1(pk);$$
$$b \xleftarrow{u} \{0, 1\}; c \leftarrow \mathcal{E}(pk, r, m_b) : \mathcal{A}_2(m_0, m_1, c, state) = b] - 1|.$$

We say that Π *is secure in the sense of IND-CPA if* $\mathbf{Adv}_{\Pi, \mathcal{A}}^{\text{ind-cpa}}(k)$ *is negligible in k, for any polynomial-time adversary* $\mathcal{A}$.

3   A Variant of the Schmidt-Samoa–Takagi Encryption Scheme

In [5], Paillier proposed the public-key encryption scheme with the additively homomorphic property which can be applied many cryptographic applications. Several variants of the Paillier encryption scheme have been studied. In this section, we review the Schmidt-Samoa–Takagi encryption scheme which is a variant of the Paillier encryption scheme [8], and study a variant of this encryption scheme without losing homomorphic properties. Furthermore, we show that the security of our variant is the same as that of the Schmidt-Samoa–Takagi encryption scheme.

3.1   The Schmidt-Samoa–Takagi Encryption Scheme

We review the Schmidt-Samoa–Takagi encryption scheme [8]. Let $n = p^2 q$, where p and q are primes with same length. The Schmidt-Samoa–Takagi function f is as follows:

$$(\mathbb{Z}/n)^{\times} \times \mathbb{Z}/n \longrightarrow (\mathbb{Z}/n^2)^{\times}$$
$$(r, m) \longmapsto r^n(1 + mn) \bmod n^2,$$

where m is a message and r is a random number. Then, we obtain the following properties on f:

- f is additively homomorphic in m.
- $f(r, m) = f(r + ipq, m - (r^{-1} \bmod n)ipq)$ for $i \in \{1, 2, \ldots, p\}$, that is, f is a p-to-1 function.
- The restriction $f_r = f|_{(\mathbb{Z}/pq)^\times \times \mathbb{Z}/n}$ on r is 1-to-1. Then it has a group homomorphism with respect to the group operation $\circ_r : (r_1, m_1) \circ_r (r_2, m_2) = (r_1 r_2 \bmod pq, m_1 + m_2 + r_{pq}^{-1} lpq \bmod n)$, where $r_{pq} = r_1 r_2 \bmod pq$ and $l \in \{1, 2, \ldots, p\}$ such that $r_1 r_2 = r_{pq} + lpq \bmod n$.
- The restriction $f_m = f|_{(\mathbb{Z}/n)^\times \times \mathbb{Z}/pq}$ on m is 1-to-1. Then it has a group homomorphism with respect to the group operation $\circ_m : (r_1, m_1) \circ_m (r_2, m_2) = (r_1 r_2 - lpq \bmod n, m_1 + m_2 \bmod pq)$, where $m_{pq} = m_1 + m_2 \bmod pq$ and $l \in \{1, 2, \ldots, p\}$ such that $m_1 + m_2 = m_{pq} - r_{pq}^{-1} lpq \bmod n$.
- The scheme (whose encryption function $\mathcal{E}$ is f_m) is secure in the sense of OW-CPA under the assumption of the hardness of factoring $n = p^2 q$.
- The scheme (whose encryption function $\mathcal{E}$ is f_m) is secure in the sense of IND-CPA under the decisional composite residuosity assumption.

The decisional composite residuosity assumption is the assumption that there is no polynomial-time algorithm which solves "the decisional composite residuosity problem" with non-negligible advantage.

Definition 4. *(The Decisional Composite Residuosity Problem) Let n be a randomly chosen k-bit $p^2 q$ modulus. For a probabilistic polynomial-time algorithm $\mathcal{A}$, we define the following probabilities:*

$$P_{Random} = \Pr[x \leftarrow (\mathbb{Z}/n^2)^\times : \mathcal{A}(x) = 1]$$

and

$$P_{Residue} = \Pr[x \leftarrow (\mathbb{Z}/n)^\times : \mathcal{A}(x^n \bmod n^2) = 1].$$

Then, we denote an advantage of $\mathcal{A}$ by

$$\mathbf{Adv}_{\mathcal{A}}^{DCR}(k) = |P_{Random} - P_{Residue}|.$$

In this paper, we use the above definition by replacing $(\mathbb{Z}/n^2)^\times$ and $x^n \bmod n^2$ with $(\mathbb{Z}/n^{s+1})^\times$ and $x^{n^s} \bmod n^{s+1}$, respectively.

3.2 Our Encryption Scheme

We consider a variant of the Schmidt-Samoa–Takagi encryption scheme by using the idea of Damgård and Jurik [1]. Let $n = p^2 q$, where p and q are primes with same length. In addition, we introduce new parameters $s, t \in \mathbb{N}$ such that $s \geq t$ to the Schmidt-Samoa–Takagi function. Then, we define a function f as follows:

$$
\begin{aligned}
(\mathbb{Z}/n)^\times \times \mathbb{Z}/n^s &\longrightarrow (\mathbb{Z}/n^{s+1})^\times \\
(r, m) &\longmapsto r^{n^s}(1 + n^t)^m \bmod n^{s+1},
\end{aligned}
$$

where m is a message and r is a random number. We note that our function coincides with the Schmidt-Samoa–Takagi function if $s = t = 1$. Obviously, our function is an additive homomorphism in m. We show that f is an $(n^{t-1}p)$-to-1 function.

Lemma 5. *Let $s, t \in \mathbb{N}$ such that $t < s < p, q$. Then,*

1. $1 + an^s \equiv (1 + n^t)^{an^{s-t}} \pmod{n^{s+1}}$ *for* $a \in (\mathbb{Z}/n^{s+1})^{\times}$.
2. $\mathrm{ord}_{n^{s+1}} (1 + n^t) = n^{s-t+1}$, *that is,* $\langle 1 + n^t \rangle \simeq \mathbb{Z}/n^{s-t+1}$.

Proof. 1. $(1 + n^t)^{an^{s-t}} = 1 + an^s + n^{s+1}(\frac{an^{t-1}(an^{s-t}-1)}{2} + \cdots) \equiv 1 + an^s$
$\pmod{n^{s+1}}$.

2. Let $x = \mathrm{ord}_{n^{s+1}} (1 + n^t)$, that is, $(1 + n^t)^x \equiv 1 \bmod n^{s+1}$. Meanwhile $(1 + n^t)^{n^{s-t+1}} = 1 + n^{s+1}(1 + \cdots) \equiv 1 \pmod{n^{s+1}}$. Hence, $x \mid n^{s-t+1}$. We set $x = p^e q^{e'}$ such that $e \leq 2(s - t + 1), e' \leq s - t + 1$. We consider the equation $(1 + n^t)^x = \sum_{i=0}^{x} \binom{x}{i} n^{it}$. Let $\delta \in \mathbb{N}$ such that $\delta t < s + 1 \leq (\delta + 1)t$. Clearly, $\delta < s + 1 \leq p, q$ from $t \geq 1$. Then $(1 + n^t)^x = \sum_{i=0}^{x} \binom{x}{i} n^{it} \equiv \sum_{i=0}^{\delta} \binom{x}{i} n^{it} \pmod{n^{s+1}}$. It follows that $\sum_{i=1}^{\delta} \binom{x}{i} n^{it} \equiv 0 \pmod{n^{s+1}}$ by the definition of x. In particular, $\sum_{i=1}^{\delta} \binom{x}{i} n^{(i-1)t} \equiv 0 \pmod{n^{s-t+1}}$, that is, $n^{s-t+1} \mid \sum_{i=1}^{\delta} \binom{x}{i} n^{(i-1)t}$. For $i \leq \delta$, $\gcd(i!, p) = \gcd(i!, q) = 1$ from $\delta < p, q$. Hence, we obtain $x \mid \binom{x}{i}$ by $x = p^e q^{e'}$. Now, we assume $x < n^{s-t+1}$ and show a contradiction. Let $y = \sum_{i=1}^{\delta} \binom{x}{i} n^{(i-1)t}$. Since $n^{s-t+1} \mid y$, $x \mid y$, and $x \mid n^{s-t+1}$, it holds $\frac{n^{s-t+1}}{x} \mid \frac{y}{x} = 1 + n^t(\binom{x}{2} + \cdots)$. Then, we see that $p \mid 1$ or $q \mid 1$ since $p \mid \frac{n^{s-t+1}}{x} \mid \frac{y}{x}$ or $q \mid \frac{n^{s-t+1}}{x} \mid \frac{y}{x}$, and obtain a contradiction. □

By Lemma 5, we have the following theorem and corollary.

Theorem 6. $f(r, m) = f(r + ipq, m - (r^{-1} \bmod n^s)in^{s-t}pq + jn^{s-t+1})$ *for* $i \in \{1, 2, \ldots, p\}$ *and* $j \in \{1, 2, \ldots, n^{t-1}\}$, *that is,* f *is an* $(n^{t-1}p)$-to-1 *function.*

Proof. The following congruence relation means that over $(\mathbb{Z}/n^{s+1})^{\times}$. r^{-1} means $r^{-1} \bmod n^s$.

$$f(r + ipq, m - n^{s-t}r^{-1}ipq + jn^{s-t+1}) \equiv (r + ipq)^{n^s}(1 + n^t)^{m - n^{s-t}r^{-1}ipq + jn^{s-t+1}}$$
$$\equiv r^{n^s}(1 + n^s r^{-1}ipq)(1 + n^t)^{m - n^{s-t}r^{-1}ipq}$$
$$\equiv r^{n^s}(1 + n^t)^{n^{s-t}r^{-1}ipq + m - n^{s-t}r^{-1}ipq}$$
$$\equiv r^{n^s}(1 + n^t)^m$$
$$\equiv f(r, m).$$

Hence, we see that $f(r, m) = f(r + ipq, m - (r^{-1} \bmod n^s)n^{s-t}ipq + jn^{s-t+1})$. Therefore, f is an $(n^{t-1}p)$-to-1 function. □

Corollary 7. *(of Theorem 6)*

1. *The restriction* $f_r = f|_{(\mathbb{Z}/pq)^{\times} \times \mathbb{Z}/n^{s-t+1}}$ *on* r *is 1-to-1. Then* f_r *holds the following equation :* $f_r(r_1, m_1)f_r(r_2, m_2) = f_r(r_1 r_2 \bmod pq, m_1 + m_2 + (r_{pq}^{-1} \bmod n^s)ln^{s-t}pq \bmod n^{s-t+1})$, *where* $r_{pq} = r_1 r_2 \bmod pq$ *and* $l \in \{1, 2, \ldots, p\}$ *such that* $r_1 r_2 = r_{pq} + lpq \bmod n$.
2. *The restriction* $f_m = f|_{(\mathbb{Z}/n)^{\times} \times \mathbb{Z}/(n^{s+t-1}/p)}$ *on* m *is 1-to-1. Then* f_m *holds the following equation :* $f_m(r_1, m_1)f_m(r_2, m_2) = f_m(r_1 r_2 - lpq \bmod n, m_1 + m_2 \bmod (n^{s-t+1}/p))$, *where* $m_{pq} = m_1 + m_2 \bmod (n^{s-t+1}/p)$ *and* $l \in \{1, 2, \ldots, p\}$ *such that* $m_1 + m_2 = m_{pq} - (r_{pq}^{-1} \bmod n^s)ln^{s-t}pq \bmod n^{s-t+1}$.

We also show properties of f, which can help us to compute f^{-1}.

Lemma 8. *For $x, y \in (\mathbb{Z}/n)^\times$ and $s \geq 1$, $x^{n^s} \equiv y^{n^s} \pmod{n}$ if and only if $x \equiv y \pmod{pq}$.*

Corollary 9. *(of Lemma 8) $\{x \in (\mathbb{Z}/n)^\times \mid x \equiv y^{n^s} \pmod{n}, y \in (\mathbb{Z}/n)^\times\}$ is a subgroup of $(\mathbb{Z}/n)^\times$ whose order is $(p-1)(q-1)$. Especially, the subgroup is equivalent to $\{x^{n^s} \bmod n \mid x \in (\mathbb{Z}/pq)^\times\}$.*

Our encryption scheme is described as follows. We refer the detail description of the decryption algorithm to the full paper.

Key Generation: Given a security parameter k, choose at random a modulus $n = p^2 q$ of k bits, where p, q have same length with $t < s < p, q$. Compute $d \equiv n^{-s} \pmod{(p-1)(q-1)}$ and $l \in \mathbb{Z}$ such that $2^l < pq < 2^{l+1}$. Then, the public key is $pk = (n, l)$ and the secret key is $sk = (p, q, d)$.

Encryption: To encrypt a message $m \in \mathbb{Z}/(n^{s-t+1}/p)$, choose $r \in (\mathbb{Z}/n)^\times$ at random and compute $\mathcal{E}(r, m)$, where $\mathcal{E} = f_m$, that is,

$$\mathcal{E}(r, m) = r^{n^s}(1 + n^t)^m \bmod n^{s+1}.$$

Decryption: To decrypt a ciphertext c, compute $r = c^d \bmod pq$, and $y = c(r^{-1})^{n^s} \bmod n^{s+1}$. Then, by using Algorithm **XDJ**, we obtain a message $m \in \mathbb{Z}/(n^{s-t+1}/p)$ by

$$\mathcal{D}(c) = \mathbf{XDJ}(s, t, n, y, 1) \bmod (n^{s-t+1}/p).$$

Algorithm 10. *Let $L_{n^t}(x) = \frac{x-1}{n^t}$. The following algorithm takes $y \in (\mathbb{Z}/n^{s+1})^\times$, $a \in (\mathbb{Z}/n^{s+1})^\times$, and $s, t \in \mathbb{N}$ such that $t \leq s$, and computes $x \in \mathbb{Z}/n^{s-t+1}$ such that $y = (1 + an^t)^x \bmod n^{s+1}$:*

$$
\begin{aligned}
&\mathbf{XDJ}(s, t, n, y, a) \\
&\quad x := 0 \\
&\quad \delta := \lceil \tfrac{s}{t} \rceil - 1 \\
&\quad \mathbf{for}\ (i := 1\ \mathbf{to}\ \delta) \\
&\quad\quad t_1 := (a^{-1} \bmod n^{(i+1)t}) \times L_{n^t}(y \bmod n^{(i+1)t}) \bmod n^{it} \\
&\quad\quad t_2 := x \\
&\quad\quad \mathbf{for}\ (j := 2\ \mathbf{to}\ i) \\
&\quad\quad\quad x := x - 1 \\
&\quad\quad\quad t_2 := t_2 \times x \bmod n^{it} \\
&\quad\quad\quad t_1 := t_1 - \frac{t_2 \times (an^t)^{j-1}}{j!} \bmod n^{it} \\
&\quad\quad x := t_1 \\
&\quad \mathbf{return}\ x \bmod n^{s-t+1}
\end{aligned}
$$

We note that Algorithm **XDJ** coincides with that by Damgård and Jurik when $t = a = 1$, and works for any $n \in \mathbb{N}$.

We give the following theorem on the security for our scheme.

Theorem 11. *We have the following properties on $\mathcal{E}$.*

1. *Our scheme is secure in the sense of OW-CPA under the assumption of the hardness of factoring $n = p^2 q$.*
2. *Our scheme is secure in the sense of IND-CPA under the decisional composite residuosity assumption by replacing $(\mathbb{Z}/n^2)^{\times}$ and $x^n \bmod n^2$ with $(\mathbb{Z}/n^{s+1})^{\times}$ and $x^{n^s} \bmod n^{s+1}$, respectively.*

Proof. 1. We assume that there exists an adversary $\mathcal{A}$ that on input a random ciphertext $c = \mathcal{E}_m(r, m) = r^{n^s}(1 + n^t)^m \bmod n^{s+1}$, outputs $m \in \mathbb{Z}/(n^{s-t+1}/p)$ with non-negligible probability ϵ, that is, $\mathbf{Adv}_{\Pi, \mathcal{A}}^{ow-cpa}(k) = \epsilon$. Then we will construct a probabilistic polynomial-time algorithm $\mathcal{B}$ which factors n by using this adversary $\mathcal{A}$.

$\mathcal{B}$ chooses $r' \in (\mathbb{Z}/n)^{\times}$ and $m' \in \mathbb{Z}/n^{s-t+1}$. Then with probability $1 - 1/p$, $\mathcal{B}$ obtains $m' > n^{s-t+1}/p$. $\mathcal{B}$ computes $c' = (r')^{n^s}(1 + n^t)^{m'} \bmod n^{s+1}$. The distribution of c' is exactly the same as the distribution of the valid ciphertexts. $\mathcal{B}$ runs $\mathcal{A}$ on c'. Since $\mathcal{E}(r, m) = \mathcal{E}(r + ipq, m - (r^{-1} \bmod n)n^{s-t}ipq + jn^{s-t+1})$, $\mathcal{A}(c')$ outputs $M = m' - ((r')^{-1} \bmod n^s)n^{s-t}ipq \bmod n^{s-t+1} \in \mathbb{Z}/(n^{s-t+1}/p)$ with probability ϵ. From $m' - M = ((r')^{-1} \bmod n^s)n^{s-t}ipq$ (i.e. $(m' - M)/n^{s-t} = ((r')^{-1} \bmod n^s)ipq)$, $r' \in (\mathbb{Z}/n)^{\times}$ and $0 \leq i < p$, we obtain $\gcd((m' - M)/n^{s-t}, n) = pq$. Hence, $\mathcal{B}$ can factor $n = p^2 q$ with non-negligible probability $(1 - 1/p)\epsilon$.

2. We will construct a probabilistic polynomial-time algorithm $\mathcal{D}$ such that breaks the decisional composite residuosity assumption by using the adversary $\mathcal{A} = (\mathcal{A}_1, \mathcal{A}_2)$ against IND-CPA with the advantage $\mathbf{Adv}_{\Pi, \mathcal{A}}^{ind-cpa}(k) = \epsilon$. Let x be an instance of the decisional composite residuosity problem. $\mathcal{A}_1$ outputs $(m_0, m_1, state)$, where $m_0, m_1 \in \mathbb{Z}/(n^{s-t+1}/p)$. Next $\mathcal{D}$ chooses a random bit $b \in \{0, 1\}$, computes $c = x(1 + n^t)^{m_b} \bmod n^{s+1}$, and runs $\mathcal{A}_2$ on (m_0, m_1, c). If x is an n^s-th residue, then c is a valid ciphertext, otherwise c is a random element of $(\mathbb{Z}/n^{s+1})^{\times}$. Therefore, let $\mathcal{D}$ outputs 1 if $\mathcal{A}_2(m_0, m_1, c) = b$, or 0 otherwise. Hence, we can obtain that $\mathbf{Adv}_{\mathcal{D}}^{DCR}(k)$ equals non-negligible advantage $\epsilon/2$. $\square$

4 Constructions Based on Primitive Power Roots of Unity

In this section, we first introduce new cryptographic properties related to the homomorphic property. Second, we describe some facts on primitive power roots of 1, and apply them to our encryption function. Then, we propose an extended encryption scheme which has the new cryptographic properties.

4.1 New Cryptographic Properties

In this section, we formalize the notion of a general homomorphic property as follows: Let $f_1, f_2, \ldots, f_k, f$ be functions, and $*, g$ polynomial-time computable operations. For $m_1, m_2, \ldots, m_k$, we have $f_1(m_1) * f_2(m_2) * \cdots * f_k(m_k) =$

$f(g(m_1, m_2, \ldots, m_k))$. These functions do not always have common domain or common range. For example, a multiplicative homomorphism can be expressed by $f_1 = f_2 = \cdots = f_k = f$ and $g(a_1, a_2, \ldots, a_k) = a_1 \times a_2 \times \cdots \times a_k$. With this formalization, we consider two properties. A tuple $(\{f_1, f_2, \ldots, f_k\}, f)$ of functions is called "affine with $x_1, x_2, \ldots, x_k$" if $f_1(m_1) * f_2(m_2) * \cdots * f_k(m_k) = f(x_1 m_1 + x_2 m_2 + \cdots + x_k m_k)$, that is, $g(m_1, m_2, \ldots, m_k) = x_1 m_1 + x_2 m_2 + \cdots + x_k m_k$. An additive homomorphism can be considered as the special case. A tuple of $(\{f_1, f_2, \ldots, f_k\}, f)$ of functions is called "pre-image restriction with modulo n" if $m = m_1 = m_2 = \cdots = m_k$ and $f_1(m) * f_2(m) * \cdots * f_k(m) = f(m \bmod n)$, that is, $g(m, m, \ldots, m) = m \bmod n$.

Definition 12. *(Affine) A tuple $(\{f_1, f_2, \ldots, f_k\}, f)$ of functions has the property of affine with $x_1, x_2, \ldots, x_k$ if for $m_1, m_2, \ldots, m_k$, $f_1(m_1) * f_2(m_2) * \cdots * f_k(m_k) = f(x_1 m_1 + x_2 m_2 + \cdots + x_k m_k)$.*

Definition 13. *(Pre-Image Restriction) A tuple of functions $(\{f_1, f_2, \ldots, f_k\}, f)$ has the property of pre-image restriction with modulo n if for m, $f_1(m) * f_2(m) * \cdots * f_k(m) = f(m \bmod n)$.*

4.2 Our Extended Function

In order to extend our function f in Section 3.2, we introduce primitive power roots of 1 in $(\mathbb{Z}/n^{s+1})^\times$ to f.

First, we give some facts on primitive power roots of 1 in $(\mathbb{Z}/n^{s+1})^\times$.

Lemma 14. *For $\ell \in \mathbb{N}$, let p be an odd prime such that $\ell \mid p - 1$. Then, there exist $\varphi(\ell)$ primitive ℓ-th roots of 1 in $(\mathbb{Z}/p)^\times$, where φ is the Euler phi-function, and we can compute them efficiently if we know prime factors of $p - 1$.*

Before we prove this lemma, we describe a fact for primitive ℓ-th roots of 1 in $(\mathbb{Z}/p)^\times$.

Fact 15. *We can identify the existence of primitive ℓ-th roots of 1 in $(\mathbb{Z}/p)^\times$ with that of a subgroup $\mathbb{G}$ of $(\mathbb{Z}/p)^\times$ whose order is ℓ. This means that, if we find an element $g \in (\mathbb{Z}/p)^\times$ with order ℓ, then g is a primitive ℓ-th root of 1 in $(\mathbb{Z}/p)^\times$ since $g^i \not\equiv 1 \pmod{p}$ for $1 \leq i \leq \ell - 1$.*

Proof. (Lemma 14) Since $(\mathbb{Z}/p)^\times$ is a cyclic group, there exists a generator $g \in (\mathbb{Z}/p)^\times$. In particular, we find g efficiently if we know prime factors $p - 1$. Then, $\mathrm{ord}_p\, g^{(p-1)/\ell} = \ell$ since $\ell \mid \mathrm{ord}_p\, g = p - 1$. Therefore, $g^{(p-1)/\ell}$ is a primitive ℓ-th root of 1. Now, let g_ℓ be $g^{(p-1)/\ell}$. We define a subgroup $\mathbb{G}$ of $(\mathbb{Z}/p)^\times$ as $\{g_\ell, g_\ell^2, \ldots, g_\ell^\ell\}$. Then, for any $g' \in \mathbb{G}$, $(g')^\ell \equiv 1 \pmod{p}$. We note that any subgroups of cyclic groups are also cyclic. In addition, for subgroups $\mathbb{G}, \mathbb{G}'$ of a cyclic group, it holds $\mathbb{G} = \mathbb{G}'$ if $|\mathbb{G}| = |\mathbb{G}'|$. Therefore, the number of primitive ℓ-th roots of 1 in $(\mathbb{Z}/p)^\times$ is $\varphi(\ell)$. □

Now, we apply primitive ℓ-th roots of 1 in $(\mathbb{Z}/p)^\times$ to those in $(\mathbb{Z}/n^{s+1})^\times$ by using the Chinese Remainder Theorem, where $n = p^2 q$ and $s \in \mathbb{N}$ such that $s < p, q$. Then, we give the following important lemma (see e.g. [9, Section 6.5]).

Lemma 16. *Let p, q be distinct odd primes, and e, e' positive integers.*

1. $(\mathbb{Z}/p^e)^\times$ *is a cyclic group. In particular,* $|(\mathbb{Z}/p^e)^\times| = p^{e-1}(p-1)$.
2. *For a group* $(\mathbb{Z}/p^e q^{e'})^\times$, $\max_{g \in (\mathbb{Z}/p^e q^{e'})^\times}\{\mathrm{ord}_{p^e q^{e'}} g\} = \mathrm{lcm}(|(\mathbb{Z}/p^e)^\times|,$
   $|(\mathbb{Z}/q^{e'})^\times|) = \mathrm{lcm}(p^{e-1}(p-1), q^{e'-1}(q-1))$.

We can compute efficiently a generator g of $(\mathbb{Z}/p^{2s+2})^\times$ using the Hensel lifting if we know prime factors of $p-1$, due to Lemma 16. Similarly, we can compute a generator h of $(\mathbb{Z}/q^{s+1})^\times$ efficiently. Then, from g and h, we can find an element $w \in (\mathbb{Z}/n^{s+1})^\times$ such that $\mathrm{ord}_{n^{s+1}} w = \mathrm{lcm}(p^{2s+1}(p-1), q^s(q-1))$, by using the Chinese Remainder Theorem. Now, let $p - 1 = \ell p'$, $q - 1 = \ell q'$, and $\gcd(p-1, q-1) = \ell$, where $p', q' \in \mathbb{N}$. Let $w_\ell = w^{(\mathrm{ord}_{n^{s+1}} w)/\ell} \bmod n^{s+1}$, w_ℓ is a primitive ℓ-th root of 1 in $(\mathbb{Z}/n^{s+1})^\times$ since $\mathrm{ord}_{n^{s+1}} w = p^{2s+1}q^s p' q' \ell$. Thus, we can compute a primitive ℓ-th root of 1 efficiently.

Remark 17. *If* $\gcd(\ell, (p-1)(q-1)) = 1$, *we see that there exists no primitive ℓ-th root of 1. In the RSA encryption scheme [7], the encryption function* $f(X) = X^e \bmod n$, *where the exponent e is relatively prime to* $\varphi(n) = (p-1)(q-1)$, *is a permutation on* $(\mathbb{Z}/n)^\times$. *Therefore, it holds also on* $(\mathbb{Z}/p)^\times$ *and* $(\mathbb{Z}/q)^\times$ *by the Chinese Remainder Theorem. Hence, for all* $x \in (\mathbb{Z}/n)^\times$, *there exists only one e-th root, that is, the e-th root of 1 is 1 in* $(\mathbb{Z}/n)^\times$.

In many cryptographic settings depending on the hardness of factoring n, the product of two strong primes are recommended (we note that $p \in \mathbb{N}$ is a strong prime if p is prime and $p = 2p' + 1$, where p' is also prime). It is well-known that strong primes have resistance against factoring attacks which depend on the structure of primes, such as the $p-1$ method and the elliptic curve method. However, since ℓ is limited to 2 or p' for a strong prime p, there are only g_2, $g_{p'}$ in $(\mathbb{Z}/p)^\times$ as primitive ℓ-th roots of 1. Hence, we consider to use the following primes with many power roots of 1 in $(\mathbb{Z}/p)^\times$, and can resist against factoring attacks above.

Definition 18. *(Semi ℓ-Smooth Primes) For $\ell \in 2\mathbb{N}$, a prime $p \in \mathbb{N}$ is semi ℓ-smooth if $p = \ell p' + 1$, where p' is prime.*

In our extended function and scheme, we require that ℓ is constant and much smaller than p'. However, we do not know whether the number of the primes above is infinite, as well as that of strong primes. Nevertheless, we assume that there exist infinite number of semi ℓ-smooth primes for any $\ell \in \mathbb{N}$. Henceforth in this paper, we assume that p and q are semi ℓ-smooth prime.

For $i \in \{1, 2, \ldots, \ell\}$, we define an extended function f_i with a primitive ℓ-th root of 1 in $(\mathbb{Z}/n^{s+1})^\times$ as follows:

$$f_i : (\mathbb{Z}/n)^\times \times \mathbb{Z}/n^s \longrightarrow (\mathbb{Z}/n^{s+1})^\times$$
$$(r, m) \longmapsto r^{n^s}(1 - w_\ell^i n)^m \bmod n^{s+1},$$

where m is a message, r is a random number, and w_ℓ is a primitive ℓ-th root of 1. We note that our extended function is similar to the Schmidt-Samoa–Takagi function if $s = 1$ and $i = \ell$, since $w_\ell^\ell \equiv 1 \pmod{n^{s+1}}$. Obviously, our function is additive homomorphism in m. We give the following property on f_i.

Corollary 19. *(of Lemma 5) Let $s \in \mathbb{N}$ and $a \in (\mathbb{Z}/n^{s+1})^\times$. Then, $\mathrm{ord}_{n^{s+1}}(1 + an) = n^s$, that is, $\langle 1 + an \rangle \simeq \mathbb{Z}/n^s$.*

That is, we see that $\mathrm{ord}_{n^{s+1}}(1 - w_\ell^i n) = n^s$ since w_ℓ^i is relatively prime to n for any i. Therefore, for any i, we obtain the properties similar to Theorem 6 and Corollary 7.

Theorem 20. *For any $i \in \{1, 2, \ldots, \ell\}$,*

1. *$f_i(r, m) = f_i(r + jpq, m - (r^{-1} \bmod n^s)jpq)$ for $j \in \{1, 2, \ldots, p\}$, that is, f_i is a p-to-1 function.*
2. *The restriction $f_{i,r} = f_i|_{(\mathbb{Z}/pq)^\times \times \mathbb{Z}/n^s}$ on r is 1-to-1. Then $f_{i,r}$ holds the following equation : $f_{i,r}(r_1, m_1)f_{i,r}(r_2, m_2) = f_{i,r}(r_1 r_2 \bmod pq, m_1 + m_2 + (r_{pq}^{-1} \bmod n^s)lpq \bmod n^s)$, where $r_{pq} = r_1 r_2 \bmod pq$ and $l \in \{1, 2, \ldots, p\}$ such that $r_1 r_2 = r_{pq} + lpq \bmod n$.*
3. *The restriction $f_{i,m} = f_i|_{(\mathbb{Z}/n)^\times \times \mathbb{Z}/(n^s/p)}$ on m is 1-to-1. Then $f_{i,m}$ holds the following equation : $f_{i,m}(r_1, m_1)f_{i,m}(r_2, m_2) = f_{i,m}(r_1 r_2 - lpq \bmod n, m_1 + m_2 \bmod (n^s/p))$, where $m_{pq} = m_1 + m_2 \bmod (n^s/p)$ and $l \in \{1, 2, \ldots, p\}$ such that $m_1 + m_2 = m_{pq} - (r_{pq}^{-1} \bmod n^s)lpq \bmod n^{s-t+1}$.*

4.3   Our Extended Scheme

We propose a concrete scheme based on our extended function f_i. We describe our extended encryption scheme as follows:

Key Generation: Given a security parameter k, choose at random a modulus $n = p^2 q$ of k bits, where p, q are semi ℓ-smooth prime such that $p \nmid q - 1$ and $q \nmid p - 1$ with the same length, and $\ell < s < p, q$. Compute $d \equiv n^{-s} \pmod{(p-1)(q-1)}$, $l \in \mathbb{Z}$ such that $2^l < pq < 2^{l+1}$ and a primitive ℓ-th root w_ℓ of 1 as above. Then, the public key is $pk = (n, l, w_\ell)$ and the secret key is $sk = (p, q, d)$.

Encryption: To encrypt a message $m \in \mathbb{Z}/(n^s/p)$, choose $i \in \{1, 2, \ldots, \ell\}$ and $r_i \in (\mathbb{Z}/n)^\times$ at random, and compute $\mathcal{E}_i(r_i, m)$, where $\mathcal{E}_i = f_{i,m}$, that is,

$$c_i = \mathcal{E}_i(r_i, m) = r_i^{n^s}(1 - w_\ell^i n)^m \bmod n^{s+1}.$$

Then, the ciphertext is (c_i, i).

Decryption: To decrypt c_i, compute $r = c_i^d \bmod pq$ and $y = c_i(r^{-1})^{n^s} \bmod n^{s+1}$. Then, by using Algorithm **XDJ**, we obtain a message $m \in \mathbb{Z}/(n^s/p)$ by

$$\mathcal{D}((c_i, i)) = \mathbf{XDJ}(s, 1, n, y, -w_\ell^i) \bmod (n^s/p).$$

Obviously, $\mathcal{E}_i$ has the additively homomorphic property, for any i.

Now, we can prove the following security proofs, in a similar fashion of Theorem 11.

Theorem 21. *For any $i \in \{1, 2, \ldots, \ell\}$, our extended scheme is secure in the sense of OW-CPA under the assumption on the hardness of factoring $n = p^2 q$, and of IND-CPA under the decisional composite residuosity assumption by replacing $(\mathbb{Z}/n^2)^\times$ and $x^n \bmod n^2$ with $(\mathbb{Z}/n^{s+1})^\times$ and $x^{n^s} \bmod n^{s+1}$, respectively.*

In addition to the security proof, our extended scheme satisfies new crypto-graphic properties "affine" and "pre-image restriction". Let $\mathcal{E}^{(t)}(m) = \mathcal{E}^{(t)}(r, m) = r^{n^s}(1 - n^t)^m \bmod n^{s+1}$. This is similar to our original function.

Theorem 22. *For the functions $\mathcal{E}_1, \mathcal{E}_2, \ldots, \mathcal{E}_\ell$, we have the following properties:*

1. *For all $i, j, k \in \{1, 2, \ldots, \ell\}$, there exist $x_{i,k}$ and $x_{i,j}$ such that $(\{\mathcal{E}_i, \mathcal{E}_j\}, \mathcal{E}_k)$ is an affine tuple with $x_{i,k}$ and $x_{j,k}$, that is, for all $m_1, m_2 \in \mathbb{Z}/(n^s/p)$, $\mathcal{E}_i(m_1)\mathcal{E}_j(m_2) = \mathcal{E}_k(x_{i,k}m_1 + x_{j,k}m_2)$, where $x_{a,b} \in \mathbb{Z}/n^s$ such that $1 - w_\ell^a n \equiv (1 - w_\ell^b n)^{x_{a,b}} \pmod{n^{s+1}}$. In particular, we can compute $x_{i,k}$ and $x_{j,k}$, efficiently.*
2. *For all $t \in \mathbb{N}$ such that $t \mid \ell$, $(\{\mathcal{E}_\delta, \mathcal{E}_{2\delta} \ldots \mathcal{E}_{t\delta}\}, \mathcal{E}^{(t)})$ is a pre-image restriction tuple, where $\delta = \ell/t$, that is, for all $m \in \mathbb{Z}/n^s$, $\mathcal{E}_\delta(m)\mathcal{E}_{2\delta}(m)\cdots\mathcal{E}_{t\delta}(m) = \mathcal{E}^{(t)}(m \bmod n^{s-t+1})$. In particular, $\mathcal{E}_\delta(m)\mathcal{E}_{2\delta}(m)\cdots\mathcal{E}_{t\delta}(m) = \mathcal{E}^{(t)}(m)$.*

Proof. 1. By using Algorithm **XDJ**, we compute $x_{a,b}$ such that $1 - w_\ell^a n \equiv (1 - w_\ell^b n)^{x_{a,b}} \pmod{n^{s+1}}$ as follows, that is, $x_{a,b} = \mathbf{XDJ}(s, 1, n, 1 - w_\ell^a n, -w_\ell^b) \bmod n^s$. Hence, we can compute $x_{a,b}$ efficiently. In particular, $x_{a,a} = 1$. Then,

$$\mathcal{E}_i(m_1)\mathcal{E}_j(m_2) = r_1^{n^s}(1 - w_\ell^i n)^{m_1} r_2^{n^s}(1 - w_\ell^j n)^{m_2} \bmod n^{s+1}$$
$$= (r_1 r_2)^{n^s}(1 - w_\ell^k n)^{x_{i,k}m_1 + x_{j,k}m_2} \bmod n^{s+1}$$
$$= \mathcal{E}_k(x_{i,k}m_1 + x_{j,k}m_2).$$

2. For $t \in \mathbb{N}$ such that $t \mid \ell$, we have

$$\prod_{i=1}^{t} \mathcal{E}_{i\delta}(m) = \prod_{i=1}^{t} r_{i\delta}^{n^s}(1 - w_\ell^{i\delta} n)^m \bmod n^{s+1}$$
$$= r^{n^s}\left(\prod_{i=1}^{t}(1 - w_\ell^{i\delta} n)\right)^m \bmod n^{s+1},$$

where $r = r_{1\delta} r_{2\delta} \cdots r_{t\delta}$. Since w_ℓ is a primitive ℓ-th root of 1, $w_\ell^\delta, w_\ell^{2\delta}, \ldots, w_\ell^{t\delta}$ are distinct t-th roots of 1. Hence, $(1 - w_\ell^\delta n)(1 - w_\ell^{2\delta} n)\cdots(1 - w_\ell^{t\delta} n) = 1 - n^t$. Therefore, $r^{n^s}\left(\prod_{i=1}^{t}(1 - w_\ell^{i\delta} n)\right)^m = r^{n^s}(1 - n^t)^m \bmod n^{s+1}$. From $\mathrm{ord}_{n^{s+1}}(1 - n^t) = n^{s-t+1}$, we obtain $(1 - n^t)^m \equiv (1 - n^t)^{m \bmod n^{s-t+1}} \pmod{n^{s+1}}$. Then, we have

$$\prod_{i=1}^{t} \mathcal{E}_{i\delta}(m) = r^{n^s}(1 - n^t)^m \bmod n^{s+1}$$
$$= r^{n^s}(1 - n^t)^{m \bmod n^{s-t+1}} \bmod n^{s+1}$$
$$= \mathcal{E}^{(t)}(m \bmod n^{s-t+1}).$$

$\square$

We have proposed an extended scheme based on the Schmidt-Samoa–Takagi encryption scheme with primitive ℓ-th root of 1. We can also construct a scheme from the Damgård and Jurik encryption scheme [1] instead of their scheme, although we do not know whether the one-wayness is reduced to the problem of factoring $n = pq$.

5   Properties on Primitive Power Roots of Unity

In this section, we discuss a relation between factoring n and knowing of a primitive ℓ-th root of 1 in $(\mathbb{Z}/n^{s+1})^\times$, where $n = p^2q$ and p, q are semi ℓ-smooth prime. For the sake of simplicity, we consider primitive ℓ-th roots of 1 in $(\mathbb{Z}/n)^\times$ since $w_\ell \bmod n$ is also a primitive ℓ-th root of 1 in $(\mathbb{Z}/n)^\times$, where w_ℓ is a primitive ℓ-th root of 1 in $(\mathbb{Z}/n^{s+1})^\times$. We note that the following argument can be applied to the case of n^{s+1} or $n = pq$.

First, by using $w_\ell = w_2$, we describe a well-known relation between factoring n and knowing square roots. Second, we generalize the argument for ℓ.

5.1   Square Roots

We consider the case of square roots, that is, $\ell = 2$. Let x and y be elements of $(\mathbb{Z}/n)^\times$ such that $y \equiv x^2 \pmod{n}$. We identify x with $(x_p, x_q) = (x \bmod p^2, x \bmod q)$ from $(\mathbb{Z}/n)^\times \simeq (\mathbb{Z}/p^2)^\times \times (\mathbb{Z}/q)^\times$. Then, for a variable X, all of the solutions to the equation $y \equiv X^2 \pmod{n}$ satisfy the following equations:

$$
\begin{aligned}
x = x_1 &= (x \bmod p^2, x \bmod q) &= (x_p, x_q), \\
x_2 &= (-x \bmod p^2, -x \bmod q) &= (-x_p, -x_q), \\
x_3 &= (x \bmod p^2, -x \bmod q) &= (x_p, -x_q), \\
x_4 &= (-x \bmod p^2, x \bmod q) &= (-x_p, x_q).
\end{aligned}
$$

Obviously, $x_i^2 \equiv y \pmod{n}$ for $i = 1, 2, 3, 4$. In particular, $x_1 \equiv -x_2 \pmod{n}$ and $x_3 \equiv -x_4 \pmod{n}$.

On the other hand, we have that a primitive square root in $(\mathbb{Z}/n)^\times$ of 1 is $w_2 = -1 \equiv n - 1 \pmod{n}$, and identified w_2 with $(w_2 \bmod p^2, w_2 \bmod q) = (g_2, h_2) = (-1, -1)$, where $g_2 \equiv -1 \pmod{p^2}$ is a primitive square root of 1 in $(\mathbb{Z}/p^2)^\times$, and $h_2 \equiv -1 \pmod{q}$ is also that in $(\mathbb{Z}/q)^\times$. Then, we can interpret x_i $(i = 1, 2, 3, 4)$ as follows:

$$
\begin{aligned}
x = x_1 &= (x \bmod p^2, x \bmod q) &= (x_p, x_q), \\
x_2 &= (w_2 x \bmod p^2, w_2 x \bmod q) &= (g_2 x_p, h_2 x_q), \\
x_3 &= (x \bmod p^2, w_2 x \bmod q) &= (x_p, h_2 x_q), \\
x_4 &= (w_2 x \bmod p^2, x \bmod q) &= (g_2 x_p, x_q).
\end{aligned}
$$

Similarly, $x_1 \equiv w_2 x_2 \pmod{n}$ and $x_3 \equiv w_2 x_4 \pmod{n}$.

As is well-known, given $y \in (\mathbb{Z}/n)^\times$, finding a "random" square root of it is equivalent to factoring n. This means that if we have a pair (x_i, x_j) such that $x_i \not\equiv w_2^e x_j \pmod{n}$ for $e = 1, 2$, then we obtain prime factors p and q of n from

$\gcd(x_i - w_2^e x_j, n)$. For example, for x_1, x_3 as above, it holds $x_1 \not\equiv w_2^e x_3$ ($e = 1, 2$), therefore we obtain $\gcd(x_1 - x_3, n) = p^2$ since $x_1 - x_3 = (x_p - x_p, x_q - h_2 x_q) = (0, x_q(1-h_2))$. That is, $x_1 - x_3 \equiv 0 \pmod{p^2}$ and $\not\equiv 0 \pmod{q}$. Conversely, if we only have pairs (x_i, x_j) such that $x_i \equiv w_2^e x_j \pmod{n}$, it is hard to factor n. This situation is similar to the following case. We choose $x \in (\mathbb{Z}/n)^\times$ at random, and compute $y = x^2 \bmod n$. Since anyone knows that one of primitive square roots of 1 is -1 in any fields or rings, we have $(x, w_2 x)$ such that $x^2 \equiv (w_2 x)^2 \pmod{n}$ and $x \equiv w_2^2 x \pmod{n}$, as a pair of square roots of y in $(\mathbb{Z}/n)^\times$. However, it is hard to find non-trivial square roots of 1 without knowing prime factors p, q of n, due to the factoring assumption. That is, it is hard to factor n even if we have information on $w_2 = -1$ or $\ell = 2$. In addition, we note that, given $y \in (\mathbb{Z}/n)^\times$, randomly finding a square root of y is equivalent to randomly finding a square root of 1, since $x_i/x_j \not\equiv w_2^e \pmod{n}$ is also a ℓ-th root of 1 if $x_i^2 \equiv x_j^2 \pmod{n}$ and $x_i \not\equiv w_2^e x_j \pmod{n}$ for $e = 1, 2$.

5.2 Power Roots

We describe the case that $\ell \mid p - 1$ and $\ell \mid q - 1$ for each $\ell \neq p', q'$. This can be considered as a generalization of $\ell = 2$.

In our extended scheme, we first find generators g and h of $(\mathbb{Z}/p^2)^\times$ and $(\mathbb{Z}/q)^\times$, respectively, with prime factors of $p-1$ and $q-1$. Second, we compute g_ℓ and h_ℓ, which are primitive ℓ-th roots of 1 in $(\mathbb{Z}/p^2)^\times$ and $(\mathbb{Z}/q)^\times$, respectively, by using g and h. Then, we construct w_ℓ from g_ℓ and h_ℓ, by applying the Chinese Remainder Theorem.

For $1 \leq e \leq \ell$, w_ℓ^e satisfy the following equations:

$$w_\ell = (w_\ell \bmod p^2, w_\ell \bmod q) = (g_\ell, h_\ell),$$
$$w_\ell^2 = (w_\ell^2 \bmod p^2, w_\ell^2 \bmod q) = (g_\ell^2, h_\ell^2),$$
$$\vdots$$
$$(1 =) w_\ell^\ell = (1 \bmod p^2, 1 \bmod q) = (1, 1).$$

We also see that the following $z_{\ell,1}, z_{\ell,2}, \ldots, z_{\ell,\ell-1}$ are also ℓ-th roots of 1 in $(\mathbb{Z}/n)^\times$, which are different from w_ℓ^e:

$$z_{\ell,1} = (1 \bmod p^2, w_\ell \bmod q) = (1, h_\ell),$$
$$z_{\ell,2} = (1 \bmod p^2, w_\ell^2 \bmod q) = (1, h_\ell^2),$$
$$\vdots$$
$$z_{\ell,\ell-1} = (1 \bmod p^2, w_\ell^{\ell-1} \bmod q) = (1, h_\ell^{\ell-1}).$$

It follows that for $1 \leq i \leq \ell - 1$ and $1 \leq e \leq \ell$, $w_\ell^e z_{\ell,i} \bmod n$ are also ℓ-th roots of 1 in $(\mathbb{Z}/n)^\times$. It holds $w_\ell^e z_{\ell,i} \not\equiv z_{\ell,j} \pmod{n}$ for $i \neq j$ and $1 \leq e \leq \ell$. Therefore, the number of ℓ-th roots of 1 is ℓ^2 (In particular, there exist $\varphi(\ell^2)$ primitive ℓ-th roots of 1).

Now, we can see that it is easy to factor n by using w_ℓ and one of $z_{\ell,i}$ above, since $(w_\ell^e)^\ell \equiv z_{\ell,i}^\ell \equiv 1 \pmod{n}$ and $w_\ell^e \not\equiv z_{\ell,i} \pmod{n}$ for $1 \leq e \leq \ell$. Hence, we must not give other primitive ℓ-th roots of 1 publicly. Conversely, we regard the problem of finding other ℓ-th roots which are not the power of w_ℓ as a hard problem.

Furthermore, we must construct w_ℓ from g_ℓ and h_ℓ, otherwise, for some $1 \leq e \leq \ell - 1$, there exists the following (primitive) ℓ-th root y_ℓ of 1: $y_\ell^e \equiv 1 \pmod{p^2}$ and $y_\ell^e \not\equiv 1 \pmod{q}$ or $y_\ell^e \not\equiv 1 \pmod{p^2}$ and $y_\ell^e \equiv 1 \pmod{q}$. In other words, this situation is equivalent to the case when a non-primitive ℓ-th root in $(\mathbb{Z}/p^2)^\times$ or that in $(\mathbb{Z}/q)^\times$ instead of g_ℓ or h_ℓ, respectively, is used for constructing w_ℓ. Hence, it is easy to factor n, that is, we must compute w_ℓ with g_ℓ and h_ℓ.

Thus, we can see that it is hard to factor n even if we give a primitive power roots of 1 publicly. This situation is similar to that of strong primes. That is, if w_ℓ or ℓ can help for factoring n, then $w_2 = -1$ or $\ell = 2$ must.

References

1. Damgård, I., Jurik, M.: A Generalisation, a Simplification and Some Applications of Paillier's Probabilistic Public-Key System. In: Kim, K.-c. (ed.) PKC 2001. LNCS, vol. 1992, pp. 119–136. Springer, Heidelberg (2001)
2. Damgård, I., Jurik, M.: A Length-Flexible Threshold Cryptosystem with Applications. In: Safavi-Naini, R., Seberry, J. (eds.) ACISP 2003. LNCS, vol. 2727, pp. 350–364. Springer, Heidelberg (2003)
3. ElGamal, T.: A Public Key Cryptosystem and a Signature Scheme Based on Discrete Logarithms. IEEE Transactions on information Theory 31(4), 469–472 (1985)
4. Goldwasser, S., Micali, S.: Probabilistic Encryption & How to Play Mental Poker Keeping Secret All Partial Information. In: STOC 1982: Proceedings of the fourteenth annual ACM symposium on Theory of computing, pp. 365–377 (1982)
5. Paillier, P.: Public-Key Cryptosystems Based on Composite Degree Residuosity Classes. In: Stern, J. (ed.) EUROCRYPT 1999. LNCS, vol. 1592, pp. 223–238. Springer, Heidelberg (1999)
6. Paillier, P., Pointcheval, D.: Efficient Public-Key Cryptosystems Provably Secure against Active Adversaries. In: Lam, K.-Y., Okamoto, E., Xing, C. (eds.) ASIACRYPT 1999. LNCS, vol. 1716, pp. 165–179. Springer, Heidelberg (1999)
7. Rivest, R.L., Shamir, A., Adleman, L.: A Method for Obtaining Digital Signatures and Public-key Cryptosystems. Communications of the ACM 21(2), 120–126 (1978)
8. Schmidt-Samoa, K., Takagi, T.: Paillier's Cryptosystem Modulo $p^2 q$ and Its Applications to Trapdoor Commitment Schemes. In: Dawson, E., Vaudenay, S. (eds.) Mycrypt 2005. LNCS, vol. 3715, pp. 296–313. Springer, Heidelberg (2005)
9. Shoup, V.: A Computational Introduction to Number Theory and Algebra. Cambridge University Press, Cambridge (2005), http://www.shoup.net/ntb/ntb-v2_1.pdf

Relationship between Two Approaches for Defining the Standard Model PA-ness

Isamu Teranishi[1] and Wakaha Ogata[2]

[1] NEC Corporation.
1753, Shimonumabe, Nakahara-Ku, Kawasaki, Kanagawa, 211-0011, Japan
teranisi@ah.jp.nec.com
[2] Tokyo Institute of Technology.
2-12-1 Ookayama, Meguro-Ku Tokyo, 152-8550, Japan
wakaha@mot.titech.ac.jp

Abstract. There are two approaches to define Plaintext Awareness (PA). The first one is a classical approach to define the PA security and is used to define the PA security of the random oracle model. This approach enables us to define the PA-ness simply, but no one know whether we can define the standard model PA security based on this approach. In contrast, the second approach is a current approach to define the PA security. It enables us to define the standard model PA security formally, but it is more elaborate than the overwhelming-based approach. In this paper, we aim to clarify relations between the two approaches. We define the standard model PA security based on the first approach. Then we show that, under a very weak condition, it is equivalent to the known definition of the standard model PA security based on the second approach.

Keywords: Plaintext Awareness, Standard Model.

1 Introduction

1.1 Background

The *Plaintext Awareness (PA)* [BR94, BDPR98, HLM03, BP04, D06, TO06, BD07] is one of the most fundamental notion about a Public-Key Encryption scheme (PKE). Intuitively, we say that a PKE is PA secure, if it satisfies the following property: whenever an adversary generates a ciphertext, the adversary "knows" the corresponding plaintext.

The PA notion is important, because the PA-ness together with the IND-CPA security implies the IND-CCA2 security [BR94, BDPR98, BP04]. This means that we can use the PA security when we show the IND-CCA2 security. Moreover, it can bring some insight or an alternative perspective on the design of existing PKE with IND-CCA2 security, as said by Bellare and Palacio [BP04].

Although the intuitive definition mentioned above is quite simple, it is elaborate task to define the PA notion formally. Therefore, many definitions of the PA security are there. Mainly, there are two approaches to defining PA security,

Y. Mu, W. Susilo, and J. Seberry (Eds.): ACISP 2008, LNCS 5107, pp. 113–127, 2008.
© Springer-Verlag Berlin Heidelberg 2008

which we will call "overwhelming-based approach" and "indistinguishability-based approach."

The *overwhelming-based approach* is a classical approach to define the PA security and is used to define the PA security [BR94, BDPR98] of the random oracle model. This approach enables us to define the PA-ness simply, but no one know whether we can define the standard model PA security based on this approach. In contrast, the *indistinguishability-based approach* is a current approach to define the PA security. It enables us to define the standard model PA security formally [BP04], but it is more elaborate than the overwhelming-based approach.

Reviewing Two Approaches. Both the overwhelming-based approach and the indistinguishability-based approach are defined by using an adversary and an extractor. However, the details of two approaches are quite different. In the case of the overwhelming-based approach, the adversary outputs one ciphertext and the extractor extracts the corresponding plaintext from the ciphertext. We say that a PKE is PA secure, if there exists an extractor which succeeds the extraction with overwhelming probability.

In contrast, the indistinguishability-based approach defines the PA security through the indistinguishability of two worlds. In the first and second worlds, an adversary can polynomially many times access to the decryption oracle and the extractor respectively. We say that a PKE is *perfectly/statistically/computationally PA secure*, if these two worlds are perfectly/statistically/computationally indistinguishable for the adversary.

1.2   Our Contributions

Motivation. In order to see the motivation of our work, we review the intuition behind the PA-ness. Recall that the intuition behind the PA-ness is "$\mathcal{A}$ knows the decrypted plaintext M," and this intuition is realized by the existence of an extractor $\mathcal{K}$ which can extract M.

In the definition of the standard model PA-ness [BP04], an extractor $\mathcal{K}$ requires to extract polynomially many plaintexts $M_1, \ldots, M_n$. This means that the standard model PA-ness [BP04] requires that "$\mathcal{A}$ knows all of $M_1, \ldots, M_n$."

However, our intuition suggests that "$\mathcal{A}$ knows all of $M_1, \ldots, M_n$" holds if and only if all of the following facts holds: "$\mathcal{A}$ knows M_1,"..., and "$\mathcal{A}$ knows M_n." Therefore, the extractor $\mathcal{K}$ should be "decomposed" into the extractors $\mathcal{K}_1, \ldots, \mathcal{K}_n$. Here $\mathcal{K}_i$ is an extractor which can extract M_i.

We would like to know whether this intuition is true or not. Recall that the overwhelming-based PA-ness requires an extractor to extract only one plaintext. Therefore, if the above intuition is true, the extractor $\mathcal{K}$ for the standard model PA-ness of [BP04] can "decompose" into the extractors $\mathcal{K}_1, \ldots, \mathcal{K}_n$ of the overwhelming-based PA security. So, the above motivation can rephrase as follows: "Can we define the standard model PA-ness by using the overwhelming-based methodology?"

Two Approaches are Almost Equivalent. In this paper, we define *OverWhelming-Based PA security (OWB-PA) in the standard model* and study the relationship between the OWB-PA security and the indistinguishability-based PA security [BP04]. In particular, we show that the extractor $\mathcal{K}$ for statistical PA-ness, which extracts $M_1, \ldots, M_n$ can be constructed from the extractor $\mathcal{K}_1, \ldots, \mathcal{K}_n$ of the OWB-PA security. Here $\mathcal{K}_i$ is an extractor which extracts M_i.

A naive definition of the OWB-PA security is obtained by "directly standard modelizing" the overwhelming-based PA security [BR94, BDPR98] of the random oracle model. However, we can show that the naive OWB-PA security seems to be equivalent to none of the perfect/statistical/computational PA security [BP04]. Therefore, we somewhat modify the definition of the OWB-PA security, assume a very weak condition on a PKE and show that this (modified) OWB-PA security is equivalent to the statistical PA-security under this condition.

The modification we use is allowing an adversary to access the decryption oracle, and giving an auxiliary input to the adversary. Our condition for a PKE is about secret keys. Recall that, in some PKE such as the Cramer-Shoup scheme [CS98], one public key has two or more corresponding secret keys. Our condition, named sk-*non-redundancy*, is as follows: "If two secret keys sk_1 and sk_2 correspond to the same public key, $\mathsf{Dec}_{\mathsf{sk}_1}(C) = \mathsf{Dec}_{\mathsf{sk}_2}(C)$ holds for any ciphertext C." Clearly, this condition is satisfied for any honestly generated ciphertext $C = \mathsf{Enc}_{\mathsf{pk}}(M)$, because $\mathsf{Dec}_{\mathsf{sk}_1}(C) = \mathsf{Dec}_{\mathsf{sk}_2}(C) = M$ holds. The heart of the sk-non-redundancy is that $\mathsf{Dec}_{\mathsf{sk}_1}(C) = \mathsf{Dec}_{\mathsf{sk}_2}(C)$ holds even for maliciously generated ciphertext C. We can say that our sk-non-redundancy condition is very weak, because all known PKEs satisfy this condition.

Significance. One of the most significant point of our result is that it shows the "independence" of knowledge extractions. Recall that our result shows that the extractor $\mathcal{K}$ for the statistical PA-ness can be "decomposed" into the extractor $\mathcal{K}_1, \ldots, \mathcal{K}_n$ of the OWB-PA security. Here $\mathcal{K}$ is an extractor which extracts all $M_1, \ldots, M_n$ from decryption queries $C_1, \ldots, C_n$ of an adversary and $\mathcal{K}_i$ is an extractor which extracts M_i from C_i. Since $\mathcal{K}_i$ can extract M_i independent from other $\mathcal{K}_j$, this means that the knowledge extractions of M_i and M_j are "independent" from each other.

This independence is non-trivial fact from the folloing reason. Recall that the definition of the statistical PA-ness requires that $(M_1, \ldots, M_n) \simeq (\mathsf{Dec}_{\mathsf{sk}}(C_1), \ldots, \mathsf{Dec}_{\mathsf{sk}}(C_n))$ holds. Here "$\simeq$" denote the statistical indistinguishability.

However, the statistical indistinguishability $(X_1, \ldots, X_n) \simeq (Y_1, \ldots, Y_n)$ may not hold even if $X_1 \simeq Y_1, \ldots, X_n \simeq Y_n$ holds, where X_i and Y_i are random variables. (In fact, $(X_1, \ldots, X_n) \simeq (Y_1, \ldots, Y_n)$ hold only if the distribution of $X_1, \ldots, X_n$ are independent from each other.) Recall that an adversary of the statistical PA-ness can output $\{C_i\}_i$ such that the distribution of C_i is *not* independent from that of other C_j. Therefore, if $\mathcal{K}$ extracts $M_i \simeq \mathsf{Dec}_{\mathsf{sk}}(C_i)$ one by one, $(M_1, \ldots, M_n) \simeq (\mathsf{Dec}_{\mathsf{sk}}(C_1), \ldots, \mathsf{Dec}_{\mathsf{sk}}(C_n))$ may not holds.

Our result is non-trivial because it shows that $(M_1, \ldots, M_n) \simeq (\mathsf{Dec}_{\mathsf{sk}}(C_1), \ldots, \mathsf{Dec}_{\mathsf{sk}}(C_n))$ always holds even if $\mathcal{K}$ extracts $M_i \simeq \mathsf{Dec}_{\mathsf{sk}}(C_i)$ one by one by using the extractor K_i of the OWB-PA-ness. That is, our result shows that the "independence" of knowledge extraction holds even if the distributions of C_1, ..., C_n are dependent.

More Detailed Studies about the Equivalence. As mentioned before, we show that the OWB-PA security was equivalent to the statistical PA security [BP04] only if a PKE is sk-non-redundant. However, we also consider a slightly modified version of the PA security [BP04] (named sk-*PA security*), where a distinguisher is provided with the secret key. Then we show that the OWB-PA security is equivalent to the sk-statistical PA security, even if a PKE is not sk-non-redundant.

In the statistical case, we can say that the difference between the sk-PA security and the original PA security is quite small, because we can show that these two notions are equivalent for a sk-non-redundant PKE and all known PKEs are sk-non-redundant.

However, the definition of the computational PA security dramatically changes if a distinguisher is provided with the secret key. In fact, we can prove that the sk-computational PA security is equivalent to the sk-statistical PA security, although the original computational PA security is strictly weaker than the original statistical PA security [TO06, TO08].

We can say that the above result show what the difference between the computational PA security and the statistical PA is. That is, we can say that the only difference between the computational PA security and the statistical PA security is in the knowledge of sk.

Computational PA-ness. We finally note about the computational PA-ness. One may think that our result can be generalized to the case of the computational PA-ness. That is, one may think that the computational PA-ness is equivalent to the "computational OWB-PA-ness." Here the computational OWB-PA-ness is a variant of the OWB-PA-ness such that an extractor requires to extract a plaintext only from one ciphertext and the extracted plaintext is only required to be computationally indistinguishable from the decrypted plaintext.

However, Bellare and Palacio [BP04] already showed that such computational OWB-PA-ness was strictly weaker than the computational PA-ness. (They used the term "PA0-ness" for the computational OWB-PA-ness.)

2   Standard Model PA-ness

We review the definition of the standard model PA-ness, which was given by Bellare and Palacio [BP04] and was given through indistinguishability-based methodology. From a technical reason, we slightly change the definition of [BP04]. That is,

- we give an auxiliary input to an adversary.

We will see in Subsection 4.2 why we need this modification.

Definition 1 (Standard Model PA-ness[BP04]). Let $\Pi = (\mathsf{Gen}, \mathsf{Enc}, \mathsf{Dec})$ be a PKE. Let $\mathcal{A}$, $\mathcal{K}$, $\mathcal{P}$ be polytime machines, which are respectively called *adversary*, *extractor*, and *plaintext creator*.

$-\mathsf{PA}^{\mathsf{Dec}}_{\Pi,\mathcal{A},\mathsf{Enco}\mathcal{P}}(\lambda,z)-$	$-\mathsf{PA}^{\mathcal{K}}_{\Pi,\mathcal{A},\mathsf{Enco}\mathcal{P}}(\lambda,z)-$
Take random tapes R and μ for $\mathcal{A}$ and $\mathcal{P}$.	Take random tapes R, μ, and ρ for $\mathcal{A}$, $\mathcal{P}$, $\mathcal{K}$.
$(\mathsf{pk},\mathsf{sk})\leftarrow\mathsf{Gen}(1^{\lambda})$.	$(\mathsf{pk},\mathsf{sk})\leftarrow\mathsf{Gen}(1^{\lambda})$.
	Initialize the list EList to ε.
	Initialize the state $\mathsf{St}_{\mathcal{K}}$ of $\mathcal{K}$ to ε.
Run $\mathcal{A}(\mathsf{pk},z;R)$ until it halts:	Run $\mathcal{A}(\mathsf{pk},z;R)$ until it halts:
If $\mathcal{A}$ makes an encryption query (enc,Q)	If $\mathcal{A}$ makes an encryption query (enc,Q)
$C\leftarrow\mathsf{Enc}_{\mathsf{pk}}\circ\mathcal{P}(Q;\mu)$.	$C\leftarrow\mathsf{Enc}_{\mathsf{pk}}\circ\mathcal{P}(Q;\mu)$, $\mathsf{EList}\leftarrow\mathsf{EList}\|C$.
Send C to $\mathcal{A}$ as the reply.	Send C to $\mathcal{A}$ as the reply.
If $\mathcal{A}$ makes a decryption query (dec,Q)	If $\mathcal{A}$ makes a decryption query (dec,Q)
$M\leftarrow\mathsf{Dec}_{\mathsf{sk}}(Q)$.	$(M,\mathsf{St}_{\mathcal{K}})\leftarrow\mathcal{K}(\mathsf{pk},z,Q,R,\mathsf{EList},\mathsf{St}_{\mathcal{K}};\rho)$.
Send M to $\mathcal{A}$ as the reply.	Send M to $\mathcal{A}$ as the reply.
Return an output T of $\mathcal{A}$.	Return an output T of $\mathcal{A}$.

Fig. 1. Experiments for the Standard Model PA-ness of Bellare-Palacio [BP04]

For a plaintext creator $\mathcal{P}$, let $\mathsf{St}_{\mathcal{P}}$ and μ denote the state of $\mathcal{P}$ and the random tape of $\mathcal{P}$ respectively. The state $\mathsf{St}_{\mathcal{P}}$ is initialized to the null string ε. We let $\mathsf{Enc}_{\mathsf{pk}}\circ\mathcal{P}(Q;\mu)$ denote the algorithm which executes the following procedures: $(M,\mathsf{St}_{\mathcal{P}})\leftarrow\mathcal{P}(Q,\mathsf{St}_{\mathcal{P}};\mu)$, $C\leftarrow\mathsf{Enc}_{\mathsf{pk}}(M)$, and output C.

For a security parameter λ, a polynomial poly, and an auxiliary input $z\in\{0,1\}^{\mathsf{poly}(\lambda)}$ of $\mathcal{A}$, we define two experiments $\mathsf{PA}^{\mathsf{Dec}}_{\Pi,\mathcal{A},\mathsf{Enco}\mathcal{P}}(\lambda,z)$ and $\mathsf{PA}^{\mathcal{K}}_{\Pi,\mathcal{A},\mathsf{Enco}\mathcal{P}}(\lambda,z)$, shown in Fig. 1. For a distinguisher $\mathcal{D}$, we set

$$P_{\mathcal{A},\mathsf{poly},\mathcal{K},\mathcal{P},\mathcal{D}}(\lambda)=\max_{z\in\{0,1\}^{\mathsf{poly}(\lambda)}}|\Pr[\mathcal{D}(\mathsf{PA}^{\mathsf{Dec}}_{\Pi,\mathcal{A},\mathsf{Enco}\mathcal{P}}(\lambda,z))=1]-\Pr[\mathcal{D}(\mathsf{PA}^{\mathcal{K}}_{\Pi,\mathcal{A},\mathsf{Enco}\mathcal{P}}(\lambda,z))=1]|.$$

We say that a PKE Π is *perfectly, statistically,* or *computationally PA secure (with auxiliary input)* if it satisfies the following property 1, 2, or 3 respectively.

1. $^{\forall}\mathcal{A}^{\forall}\mathsf{poly}^{\exists}\mathcal{K}^{\forall}\mathcal{P}^{\forall}\mathcal{D}$ (superpolytime distinguisher)$^{\forall}\lambda:P_{\mathcal{A},\mathsf{poly},\mathcal{K},\mathcal{P},\mathcal{D}}(\lambda)=0$.
2. $^{\forall}\mathcal{A}^{\forall}\mathsf{poly}^{\exists}\mathcal{K}^{\forall}\mathcal{P}^{\forall}\mathcal{D}$ (superpolytime distinguisher)   : $P_{\mathcal{A},\mathsf{poly},\mathcal{K},\mathcal{P},\mathcal{D}}(\lambda)$ is negligible for λ.
3. $^{\forall}\mathcal{A}^{\forall}\mathsf{poly}^{\exists}\mathcal{K}^{\forall}\mathcal{P}^{\forall}\mathcal{D}$ (polytime   distinguisher)   : $P_{\mathcal{A},\mathsf{poly},\mathcal{K},\mathcal{P},\mathcal{D}}(\lambda)$ is negligible for λ.

We say that $\mathcal{K}$ is *successful* for $\mathcal{A}$ if it satisfies the above relation for any $\mathcal{P}$ and any $\mathcal{D}$.

We stress that $(\mathsf{pk},\mathsf{sk})$ *is chosen after z is determined.* This fact is important. In fact, if the auxiliary input z depends on $(\mathsf{pk},\mathsf{sk})$, the definition of the PA-ness become meaningless. If we allow z to depend on $(\mathsf{pk},\mathsf{sk})$, z can be equal to some ciphertext $z=\mathsf{Enc}_{\mathsf{pk}}(M)$. Then $\mathcal{A}$ can obtain an auxiliary input $z=\mathsf{Enc}_{\mathsf{pk}}(M)$ "without knowing" the plaintext M. Then clearly, no extractor can obtain M, if $\mathsf{Enc}_{\mathsf{pk}}$ is oneway. Therefore, no non-trivial scheme satisfies the PA-ness.

Take random tapes R and ρ for $\mathcal{A}$ and $\mathcal{K}$.
$(\mathsf{pk}, \mathsf{sk}) \leftarrow \mathsf{Gen}^{\mathsf{Hash}}(1^\lambda)$.
$C_0 \leftarrow \mathcal{A}^{\mathsf{Hash}, \mathsf{Enc}_{\mathsf{pk}}^{\mathsf{Hash}}}(\mathsf{pk}; R)$.
EList $\leftarrow$ (The list of all answers from the oracle $\mathsf{Enc}_{\mathsf{pk}}^{\mathsf{Hash}}$).
HList $\leftarrow$ (The list of all pairs of hash queries of $\mathcal{A}$ and the corresponding answers).
$M_0 \leftarrow \mathcal{K}(\mathsf{pk}, C_0, \mathsf{EList}, \mathsf{HList}; \rho)$.
If $M_0 = \mathsf{Dec}_{\mathsf{sk}}^{\mathsf{Hash}}(C_0)$ return 1. Otherwise return 0.

Fig. 2. Experiment used to define the random oracle PA security [BDPR98]

3   Definition of Overwhelming-Based Standard Model PA

3.1   Definition

We review the definition of the random oracle PA-ness [BR94, BDPR98], because the random oracle PA-ness is given through the overwhelming-based approach.

Definition 2 (Overwhelming-Based PA Security in the Random Oracle Model [BR94, BDPR98]). Let $\Pi = (\mathsf{Gen}^{\mathsf{Hash}}, \mathsf{Enc}^{\mathsf{Hash}}, \mathsf{Dec}^{\mathsf{Hash}})$ be a PKE which uses a hash function Hash. Let $\mathcal{A}$ and $\mathcal{K}$ be polytime machines, which are respectively called *adversary* and *extractor*. For a security parameter λ, we define an experiment $\mathsf{OWB\text{-}PA}_{\Pi,\mathcal{A},\mathcal{K},\mathsf{Enc}}^{\mathsf{RO}}(\lambda)$ as in Fig.2. In this experiment, C_0 must not be an element of EList.

We say that Π is *OverWhelming-Based PA secure (OWB-PA) in the random oracle model*, if Π satisfies the following property:

$$\exists \mathcal{K}^\forall \mathcal{A} : \Pr[\mathsf{OWB\text{-}PA}_{\Pi,\mathcal{A},\mathcal{K},\mathsf{Enc}}^{\mathsf{RO}}(\lambda) \neq 1] \text{ is negligible for } \lambda.$$

We give an overwhelming-based standard model PA-ness by modifying the above definition in the following ways:

1. We "directly standard modelize" Definition 2. That is,
   (a) We remove the random oracle.
   (b) We allow a non-black-box extractor.
   (c) We add a plaintext creator $\mathcal{P}$.
2. We give an auxiliary input to $\mathcal{A}$.
3. We allow an adversary to access the decryption oracle.

As mentioned in [BP04], the modifications (a), (b), and (c) are definitely required when we define the standard model PA-ness. The modification 2 and 3 are required in order to show the equivalence between the OWB-PA-ness and the indistinguishability-based statistical PA-ness. See Subsection 4.2 for the details.

Definition 3 (OverWhelming-Based PA security (OWB-PA) in the Standard Model). We take $\Pi = (\mathsf{Gen}, \mathsf{Enc}, \mathsf{Dec})$, $\mathcal{A}$, $\mathcal{K}$, $\mathcal{P}$, λ, and poly, as in Definition 1. We let define $\mathsf{Enc}_{\mathsf{pk}} \circ \mathcal{P}$ as in the Definition 1. For an auxiliary

---

—OWB-PA$_{\Pi,\mathcal{A},\mathcal{K},\mathsf{Enco}\mathcal{P}}(\lambda, z)$—

Take random tapes R, ρ, and μ for $\mathcal{A}$, $\mathcal{K}$, and $\mathcal{P}$.
$(\mathsf{pk}, \mathsf{sk}) \leftarrow \mathsf{Gen}(1^\lambda)$.
$C_0 \leftarrow \mathcal{A}^{\mathsf{Enc}_{\mathsf{pk}}\circ\mathcal{P}(\cdot;\mu),\mathsf{Dec}_{\mathsf{sk}}}(\mathsf{pk}, z; R)$
EList $\leftarrow$(The list of all answers from the oracle $\mathsf{Enc}_{\mathsf{pk}}$).
DList $\leftarrow$(The list of all answers from the oracle $\mathsf{Dec}_{\mathsf{sk}}$).
$M_0 \leftarrow \mathcal{K}(\mathsf{pk}, z, C_0, R, \mathsf{EList}, \mathsf{DList}; \rho)$.
If $M_0 = \mathsf{Dec}_{\mathsf{sk}}(C_0)$, return 1. Otherwise return 0.

Fig. 3. Experiment used to define the Definition of OWB-PA security

input $z \in \{0,1\}^{\mathsf{poly}(\lambda)}$ of $\mathcal{A}$, we define an experiment OWB-PA$_{\Pi,\mathcal{A},\mathcal{K},\mathsf{Enco}\mathcal{P}}(\lambda, z)$ as in Fig.3. In this experiment, C_0 must not be an element of EList.

We say that Π satisfies *OverWhelming-Based PA security (OWB-PA) in the standard model*, if it satisfies the following property:

$$^\forall\mathcal{A}^\forall\mathsf{poly}^\exists\mathcal{K}^\forall\mathcal{P} : \max_{z\in\{0,1\}^{\mathsf{poly}(\lambda)}} \Pr[\mathsf{OWB\text{-}PA}_{\Pi,\mathcal{A},\mathcal{K},\mathsf{Enco}\mathcal{P}}(\lambda, z) \neq 1] \text{ is negligible for } \lambda.$$

We say that $\mathcal{K}$ is *successful* for $\mathcal{A}$ if it satisfies the above property for any $\mathcal{P}$.

3.2   The Decryption Oracle Strengthens the Definition

At first glance, the modification 3 of Subsection 3.1 seems to be meaningless, because (1) the OWB-PA security (with or without the modification 3) means that "an adversary $\mathcal{A}$ knows a plaintext corresponding to the ciphertext generated by $\mathcal{A}$," (2) in particular, "an adversary knows the plaintext M_i corresponding to the i-th decryption query C_i," (3) therefore, an adversary can obtain M_i without accessing the decryption oracle.

However, the above discussion is not true. Recall that the intuition "an adversary $\mathcal{A}$ knows a plaintext" is realized by using a polytime extractor. Therefore, "an adversary knows the plaintext M_i corresponding to the i-th decryption query C_i" means that "there exists a polytime extractor $\mathcal{K}_i$ which can extract M_i from C_i." The problem is in the dependency of $\mathcal{K}_i$ on i. Suppose that $\mathcal{A}$ makes decryption query λ times, where λ is the security parameter. Since $\mathcal{K}_i$ depends on i, the number of steps T_i of $\mathcal{K}_i$ also depends on i. Therefore, it is possible that $T_i = 2^i p_i(\lambda)$ holds for some polynomial p_i.

For each fixed i, the number of steps $T_i = 2^i p_i(\lambda)$ of $\mathcal{K}_i$ is polynomial of the security parameter λ. Therefore, each $\mathcal{K}_i$ is a polytime machine. However, $\mathcal{A}$ needs superpolytime if $\mathcal{A}$ executes all of $\mathcal{K}_1, \ldots, \mathcal{K}_\lambda$. Therefore, if $\mathcal{A}$ cannot access the decryption oracle, $\mathcal{A}$ needs superpolytime in order to obtain all of $M_1, \ldots, M_\lambda$. This means that the polytime adversary $\mathcal{A}$ cannot obtain all of $M_1, \ldots, M_\lambda$. Therefore, we can say that the decryption oracle is meaningful. Note that Bellare and Palacio [BP04] use similar discussions in other context.

4 OWB-PA Security Implies Statistical PA

4.1 Result

In this section, we prove that the OWB-PA-ness implies the statistical PA-ness:

Theorem 4 (OWB-PA ⇒ Statistical PA). *Let Π be a PKE satisfying the OWB-PA security. Then Π satisfies the statistical PA security.*

We here give the idea behind the proof. The formal proof will be depicted in the full paper.

Proof. (idea) Let Π be an OWB-PA secure PKE, $\mathcal{A}_0$ be an adversary for the statistical PA-ness of Π and n_0 be the number of decryption queries of $\mathcal{A}_0$. Bellow, z is an auxiliary input of $\mathcal{A}_0$ and $(\mathsf{pk}, \mathsf{sk})$ is a public key/secret key pair.

1. We construct an adversary $\mathcal{B}_0$ of the OWB-PA security such that, on input $(\mathsf{pk}, 1^i \| z)$, $\mathcal{B}_0$ outputs the i-th decryption query of $\mathcal{A}_0(\mathsf{pk}, z)$. The description of $\mathcal{B}_0(\mathsf{pk}, z')$ is as follows:
   - $\mathcal{B}_0$ parses z' as $1^i \| z$. (If z' is not this type, $\mathcal{B}_0$ outputs $\bot$ and terminates.)
   - $\mathcal{B}_0$ executes $\mathcal{A}_0(\mathsf{pk}, z)$ if $i \leq n_0$. (Otherwise, $\mathcal{B}_0$ outputs $\bot$ and terminates.)
   - If $\mathcal{A}$ makes encryption queries $\mathcal{B}_0$ answers them by passing the queries to the encryption oracle of $\mathcal{B}_0$.
   - If $\mathcal{A}$ makes the j-th decryption query C_j for $j < i$, $\mathcal{B}_0$ answers them by passing the query to the decryption oracle of $\mathcal{B}_0$.
   - If $\mathcal{A}$ makes the i-th decryption query C_i, $\mathcal{B}_0$ outputs it and terminates.
2. From the OWB-PA security of Π, there exists an extractor $\mathcal{L}_0$ for $\mathcal{B}_0$.
3. We let $\mathcal{K}_0(\mathsf{pk}, 1^i \| z, C_i, R, \mathsf{EList}, \mathsf{St}; \rho)$ be the algorithm which executes $\mathcal{L}_0(\mathsf{pk}, 1^i \| z, C_i, R, \mathsf{EList}, \mathsf{St}; \rho)$, obtains an output M_i of $\mathcal{L}_0$, and outputs M_i.

Since $\mathcal{K}_0(\mathsf{pk}, 1^i \| z, C_i, R, \mathsf{EList}, \mathsf{St}; \rho)$ executes the extractor $\mathcal{L}_0(\mathsf{pk}, 1^i \| z, C_i, R, \mathsf{EList}, \mathsf{St}; \rho)$ for $\mathcal{B}_0(\mathsf{pk}, 1^i \| z)$, and since $\mathcal{B}_0$ outputs the i-th decryption query of $\mathcal{A}_0(\mathsf{pk}, 1^i \| z)$, the outputs M_i of $\mathcal{K}_0$ is equal to $\mathsf{Dec}_{\mathsf{sk}}(C_i)$ with overwhelming probability.

We show that the number T of steps of $\mathcal{K}_0(\mathsf{pk}, 1^i \| z, C_i, R, \mathsf{EList}, \mathsf{St}; \rho)$ is bounded by some polynomial, which is independent from i. Note that the independency from i is quite important. If T depends on i, $T = 2^i p_i(\lambda)$ can hold for some polynomial $p_i(\lambda)$. This means that T become superpolynomial $T = 2^\lambda p_\lambda(\lambda)$ when $\mathcal{K}_0$ extracts a plaintext from λ-th decryption query of $\mathcal{A}$.

Since $\mathcal{K}_0(\mathsf{pk}, 1^i \| z, C_i, R, \mathsf{EList}, \mathsf{St}; \rho) = \mathcal{L}_0(\mathsf{pk}, 1^i \| z, C_i, R, \mathsf{EList}, \mathsf{St}; \rho)$, we have to show the following facts in order to show that $\mathcal{K}_0$ is a polytime machine:

- The description of $\mathcal{L}_0$ is independent from i.
- The length of the input $(\mathsf{pk}, 1^i \| z, C_i, R, \mathsf{EList}, \mathsf{St}; \rho)$ of $\mathcal{L}_0$ is bounded by some polynomial, which is independent from i.

We can prove that the description of $\mathcal{L}_0$ is independent from i, because the $\mathcal{L}_0$ depends only on $\mathcal{B}_0$ and because the description of $\mathcal{B}_0$ is independent from i. We next prove that the length of the input $(\mathsf{pk}, 1^i\|z, C_i, R, \mathsf{EList}, \mathsf{St}, \rho)$ is bounded by some polynomial, which is independent from i. Recall that i is the number of decryption queries of $\mathcal{A}$. Since $\mathcal{A}$ is a polytime machine, this means that i is bounded by the polynomial n_0 which is independent from i. Here n_0 is the number of steps of $\mathcal{A}$. This means that the length of 1^i is bounded by the polynomial n_0 which is independent from i. Moreover, from the definition of the statistical PA-ness, the length of z is bounded by some polynomial $\mathsf{poly}(\lambda)$, which is independent from i. The lengths of other inputs are clearly bounded by a polynomial which is independent from i.   □

4.2   Why Are the Modified Definitions Required?

When we define the (standard model) OWB-PA-ness, we modify the random oracle OWB-PA-ness in two ways. That is, we give an auxiliary input to an adversary and allows an adversary to access the decryption oracle. Similarly, we slightly modify the original definition of the statistical PA-ness [BP04] and give an auxiliary input to an adversary for it.

We think that these modifications are quite important to show Theorem 4. In this subsection, we see why these modifications are required.

Effect of Auxiliary Inputs: In the proof of Subsection 4.1, we use an adversary $\mathcal{B}_0$ such that, by giving an auxiliary input $1^i\|z$, $\mathcal{B}_0$ outputs the i-th decryption query C_i of $\mathcal{A}_0$. Therefore, if we do not give adversaries to auxiliary inputs, we cannot use the proof of Subsection 4.1.

One way to "prove" Theorem 4 without using auxiliary inputs is to construct adversary $\mathcal{B}_i$ which depends on i. That is, we "prove" Theorem 4 as follows. Here $\mathcal{A}_0$ is an adversary for the statistical PA security. We would like to construct an extractor for $\mathcal{A}_0$.

- For each i, we construct an adversary $\mathcal{B}_i$ for the OWB-PA security, such that $\mathcal{B}_i$ outputs the i-th decryption query C_i of $\mathcal{A}_0$. (Contrary to the previous $\mathcal{B}_0$, each i is coded in the program of $\mathcal{B}_i$. Therefore, $\mathcal{B}_i$ does not require an auxiliary input $1^i\|z$.)
- From the OWB-PA-ness of the PKE Π, there exists extractor $\mathcal{L}_i$ for each $\mathcal{B}_i$.
- We construct an extractor $\mathcal{K}_0$ for $\mathcal{A}_0$ such that $\mathcal{K}_0$ uses $\mathcal{L}_i$ in order to extract a plaintext from C_i.

The failure of the above "proof" is that the above $\mathcal{K}_0$ may be superpolytime machine. The reason is as follows. In the above "proof," we construct $\mathcal{B}_i$ which depends on i. Hence, the extractor $\mathcal{L}_i$ of $\mathcal{B}_i$ depends on i also. Therefore, the number T_i of steps of $\mathcal{L}_i$ can depend on i. Therefore, it is possible that $T_i = 2^i p_i(\lambda)$ holds for some polynomial p_i.

For each fixed i, the number of steps $T_i = 2^i p_i(\lambda)$ of $\mathcal{L}_i$ is polynomial of the security parameter λ. Therefore, $\mathcal{L}_i$ is a polytime extractor of $\mathcal{B}_i$ for the OWB-PA security. However, $\mathcal{K}_0$ becomes a superpolynomial extractor, because $\mathcal{K}_0$ uses all of $\mathcal{L}_1, \ldots, \mathcal{L}_{n_0}$ and therefore requires steps more than $2^{n_0} p_{n_0}(\lambda)$. Here n_0 is the number of steps of $\mathcal{A}_0$ and therefore is a polynomial of λ.

Effect of the Decryption Oracle: In the proof of Subsection 4.1, we use an adversary $\mathcal{B}_0$ which accesses the decryption oracle. Therefore, if we do not allow an adversary to access the decryption oracle, we cannot use the proof of Subsection 4.1.

One way to to "prove" Theorem 4 without using the decryption oracle is to construct adversaries and their extractors recursively. That is, we seem to "prove" Theorem 4 as follows. Here $\mathcal{A}_0$ is an adversary for the statistical PA security. We would like to construct an extractor for $\mathcal{A}_0$.

- For each i, we construct an adversary $\mathcal{B}_i$ for the OWB-PA-ness and its extractor $\mathcal{L}_i$ recursively:
  - We define $\mathcal{B}_i$ as follows: $\mathcal{B}_i$ executes $\mathcal{A}_0$ and answers the j-th decryption query C_j of $\mathcal{A}_0$ by using $\mathcal{L}_j$ for $j < i$, and outputs i-th decryption query C_i of $\mathcal{A}_0$.
  - We set $\mathcal{L}_i$ to an extractor of $\mathcal{B}_i$ for the OWB-PA-ness.
- We construct an extractor $\mathcal{K}_0$ for $\mathcal{A}_0$ such that $\mathcal{K}_0$ uses $\mathcal{L}_i$ in order to extract a plaintext from C_i.

The failure of the above "proof" is that the above $\mathcal{K}_0$ may be superpolytime machine. The reason is similar to that for an auxiliary input. In the above "proof," $\mathcal{B}_i$ and $\mathcal{L}_i$ depends on i also. Therefore, it is possible that the number T_i of steps of $\mathcal{L}_i$ satisfies $T_i = 2^i p_i(\lambda)$ for some polynomial p_i.

For each fixed i, the number of steps $T_i = 2^i p_i(\lambda)$ of $\mathcal{L}_i$ is polynomial of the security parameter λ. Therefore, $\mathcal{L}_i$ is a polytime extractor of $\mathcal{B}_i$ for the OWB-PA security. However, $\mathcal{K}_0$ becomes a superpolynomial extractor, because $\mathcal{K}_0$ uses all of $\mathcal{L}_1, \ldots, \mathcal{L}_{n_0}$ and therefore requires steps more than $2^{n_0} p_{n_0}(\lambda)$. Here n_0 is the number of steps of $\mathcal{A}_0$ and therefore is a polynomial of λ.

5   The Statistical PA Is Equivalent to the OWB-PA Security, under Very Weak Condition

We already showed that the OWB-PA security implied the statistical PA security of Section 2. In this section, we show that the converse holds under very weak condition.

5.1   Equivalency under Very Weak Condition

We first give the condition (named sk-*non-redundancy*), under which the OWB-PA security is equivalent to the statistical PA security. Recall that each public key pk of a some PKE, such as the Cramer-Shoup scheme [CS98, CS01], has many corresponding secret keys. (Here we say that a public key pk *corresponds* to sk, if there exists a random tape ν satisfying $(\mathsf{pk}, \mathsf{sk}) = \mathsf{Gen}(1^\lambda; \nu)$.) Intuitively, the sk-non-redundancy is the condition which ensures that $\mathsf{Dec}_{\mathsf{sk}_1}(C) = \mathsf{Dec}_{\mathsf{sk}_2}(C)$ holds

$$\boxed{\begin{array}{l}
\text{—Gen}'(1^\lambda)\text{—} \\
(\mathsf{pk}, \mathsf{sk}) \leftarrow \mathsf{Gen}(1^\lambda) \\
R \leftarrow (\lambda\text{-bit random bit string}). \\
\mathsf{pk}' \leftarrow \mathsf{pk}, \ \mathsf{sk}' \leftarrow \mathsf{sk} \| R. \\
\text{Output } (\mathsf{pk}', \mathsf{sk}'). \\
\hline
\text{—Enc}'_{\mathsf{pk}'}(M)\text{—} \\
C \leftarrow \mathsf{Enc}_{\mathsf{pk}}(M), \ C' \leftarrow 0 \| C. \text{ Output } C'. \\
\hline
\text{—Dec}'_{\mathsf{sk}'}(C')\text{—} \\
\text{Parse } C' \text{ as } b \| C. \\
\text{If } b = 0, \text{ output } \mathsf{Dec}_{\mathsf{sk}}(C). \\
\text{Otherwise, output } R.
\end{array}}$$

Fig. 4. A Scheme Π' which is not sk-non-redundant

with overwhelming probability for any secret keys sk_1 and sk_2 corresponding to the same public key pk. Clearly, this condition is satisfied for any honestly generated ciphertext $C = \mathsf{Enc}_{\mathsf{pk}}(M)$, because $\mathsf{Dec}_{\mathsf{sk}_1}(C) = \mathsf{Dec}_{\mathsf{sk}_2}(C) = M$ holds. The heart of the sk-non-redundancy is that $\mathsf{Dec}_{\mathsf{sk}_1}(C) = \mathsf{Dec}_{\mathsf{sk}_2}(C)$ holds even for maliciously generated ciphertext C.

We can say that our sk-non-redundancy condition is very weak, because all known PKEs satisfy this condition. However, we can give an artificial example $\Pi' = (\mathsf{Gen}', \mathsf{Enc}', \mathsf{Dec}')$ of Fig.4 such that Π' is not sk-non-redundant. Here $\Pi = (\mathsf{Gen}, \mathsf{Enc}, \mathsf{Dec})$ is an arbitrary PKE. Since $\mathsf{sk}' = \mathsf{sk} \| R$ holds and since $\mathsf{Dec}_{\mathsf{sk}'}(1 \| C)$ is equal to R, the output $\mathsf{Dec}_{\mathsf{sk}'}(1 \| C)$ varies depending on a secret key sk', even if the corresponding public key pk' does not vary. Note that Bellare and Palacio [BP04] used a similar scheme in other context.

We now formalize the sk-non-redundancy. Recall that the sk-non-redundancy means that $\mathsf{Dec}_{\mathsf{sk}_1}(C) = \mathsf{Dec}_{\mathsf{sk}_1}(C)$ holds for any secret keys sk_1 and sk_2 corresponding to the same public key pk. In other words, $\mathsf{Dec}_{\mathsf{sk}}(C)$ depends only on pk and C, and therefore does not depend on sk. If $\mathsf{Dec}_{\mathsf{sk}}(C)$ is determined from pk and C, we can define a (superpolytime) function $\overline{\mathsf{Dec}}$ satisfying $\overline{\mathsf{Dec}}_{\mathsf{pk}}(C) = \mathsf{Dec}_{\mathsf{sk}}(C)$.

Definition 5. Let $\Pi = (\mathsf{Gen}, \mathsf{Enc}, \mathsf{Dec})$ be a PKE. We say that Π satisfies sk-*non-redundancy* if there exists a *superpolytime* deterministic function $\overline{\mathsf{Dec}}$ such that

$$\max_{\substack{C \in \{0,1\}^* \\ \mathsf{pk}_0 \in \{0,1\}^*}} \Pr[(\mathsf{pk}, \mathsf{sk}) \leftarrow \mathsf{Gen}(1^\lambda) : \mathsf{Dec}_{\mathsf{sk}}(C) \neq \overline{\mathsf{Dec}}_{\mathsf{pk}_0}(C) \mid \mathsf{pk} = \mathsf{pk}_0] \text{ is negligible for } \lambda.$$

We next give our main result:

Theorem 6 (OWB-PA = Statistical PA under sk-non-redundancy). *Let Π be a* sk-*non-redundant PKE. Then Π is statistically PA secure if and only if OWB-PA secure.*

The "only-if" part of the above theorem has already been shown in Theorem 4. We give the idea behind the proof of the "if"-part. The formal proof will be described in the full paper.

Proof. (idea) Let Π be a PKE which is sk-non-redundant and is statistically PA secure. Let $\mathcal{A}_0$ be an adversary for the OWB-PA security, $(\mathsf{pk}, \mathsf{sk})$ be a public key/secret key pair and z is an auxiliary input for $\mathcal{A}_0$. We construct an adversary $\mathcal{B}_0$ for the statistical PA security as follows. $\mathcal{B}_0(\mathsf{pk}, z)$ executes $\mathcal{A}_0(\mathsf{pk}, z)$. If $\mathcal{A}_0$ makes a decryption query, $\mathcal{B}_0$ answers it by passing it to the decryption oracle. $\mathcal{A}_0$ finally outputs a ciphertext C_0 and terminates. Then $\mathcal{B}_0$ makes decryption query C_0, obtains answer M_0 to the query, outputs (pk, C_0, M_0), and terminates. From the assumption, there is an extractor $\mathcal{K}_0$ for $\mathcal{B}_0$ of the statistical PA security.

We construct a superpolytime distinguisher $\mathcal{D}_0$ which tries to distinguish an output of $\mathsf{PA}^{\mathsf{Dec}}_{\Pi, \mathcal{B}_0, \mathsf{Enc} \circ \mathcal{P}_0}(\lambda, z)$ and that of $\mathsf{PA}^{\mathcal{K}_0}_{\Pi, \mathcal{B}_0, \mathsf{Enc} \circ \mathcal{P}_0}(\lambda, z)$, where $\mathcal{P}_0$ is a plaintext creator. $\mathcal{D}_0(\mathsf{pk}, C_0)$ computes (one of) a secret key sk' corresponding to pk by using superpolytime. Then $\mathcal{D}_0$ outputs 1 or 0, depending on whether $M_0 = \mathsf{Dec}_{\mathsf{sk}'}(C_0)$ holds or not.

In $\mathsf{PA}^{\mathsf{Dec}}_{\Pi, \mathcal{B}_0, \mathsf{Enc} \circ \mathcal{P}_0}(\lambda, z)$, the decryption oracle sends the answer $\mathsf{Dec}_{\mathsf{sk}}(C_0)$ to $\mathcal{A}_0$. From the sk-non-redundancy, $\mathsf{Dec}_{\mathsf{sk}'}(C_0) = \mathsf{Dec}_{\mathsf{sk}}(C_0)$ holds with overwhelming probability. Therefore, $\mathcal{D}_0$ outputs 1 if (pk, C_0, M_0) is an output of $\mathsf{PA}^{\mathsf{Dec}}_{\Pi, \mathcal{B}_0, \mathsf{Enc} \circ \mathcal{P}_0}(\lambda, z)$. This means that even if (pk, C_0, M_0) is an output of $\mathsf{PA}^{\mathcal{K}_0}_{\Pi, \mathcal{B}_0, \mathsf{Enc} \circ \mathcal{P}_0}(\lambda, z)$, $\mathcal{D}_0$ outputs 1 with overwhelming probability. That is, an output of $\mathcal{K}_0$ is equal to $\mathsf{Dec}_{\mathsf{sk}}(C_0)$ with overwhelming probability. This means that $\mathcal{K}_0$ can use an extractor for $\mathcal{A}_0$ of the OWB-PA security. Since $\mathcal{A}_0$ is an arbitrary adversary for the OWB-PA security, this means that Π is OWB-PA secure. $\square$

5.2   Effect of sk-non-Redundancy

The sk-non-redundancy is important to show Theorem 6. In fact, we can show that the OWB-PA security does not imply the statistical PA security, if we suppose no assumption for the PKE:

Theorem 7 (Perfect, Statistical and Computational PA $\not\Rightarrow$ OWB-PA).
Suppose the existence of a perfectly (resp. statistically, computationally) PA secure PKE in the standard model. Then there exists a PKE which is not OWB-PA secure but is perfectly (resp. statistically, computationally) PA secure in the sence of Section 2.

Proof. (idea) We only show the theorem for the case of the statistical PA security. We can show the theorem for other cases quite similarly.

Let $\Pi = (\mathsf{Gen}, \mathsf{Enc}, \mathsf{Dec})$ be a PKE which is statistically PA secure. By using Π, we construct another PKE $\Pi' = (\mathsf{Gen}', \mathsf{Enc}', \mathsf{Dec}')$ as in Fig.4. We show that Π' is not OWB-PA secure. Let $\mathcal{A}$ be an adversary which outputs $C' = 1 \| \mathsf{Enc}_{\mathsf{pk}'}(0)$. Then an extractor $\mathcal{K}$ for $\mathcal{A}$ has to output $R = \mathsf{Dec}_{\mathsf{sk}'}(C')$. However, $\mathcal{K}$ succeeds in outputting R with only negligible probability, because the distribution of R is independent from the view of $\mathcal{K}$. This means that Π' is not OWB-PA secure.

We next show that Π' is statistically PA secure. Let $\mathcal{A}$ be an adversary for Π'. We can recognize $\mathcal{A}$ as adversary for Π. Since Π is statistical PA secure, there exists an extractor $\mathcal{K}$ of $\mathcal{A}$ for Π. We construct an extractor $\mathcal{K}'$ of $\mathcal{A}$ for Π' as follows. $\mathcal{K}'$ selects R' randomly and fixed it. If $\mathcal{K}'$ is provided with a ciphertext $C' = 0\|C$ for some C, $\mathcal{K}'$ executes $\mathcal{K}$ by giving C, obtains the output M of $\mathcal{K}$, and sends M back to $\mathcal{A}$. If $\mathcal{K}'$ is provided with a ciphertext $C' = 1\|C$ for some C, $\mathcal{K}'$ sends R' back to $\mathcal{A}$.

We see that $\mathcal{K}'$ is a successful extractor. Since $\mathcal{K}$ is a successful extractor, if $C' = 0\|C$ holds, $\mathcal{K}'$ obviously succeeds in simulating the decryption oracle with overwhelming probability. Since the distribution of R is independent from the view of $\mathcal{A}$, $\mathcal{A}$ cannot distinguish R and R'. Therefore, even if $C' = 1\|C$ holds, $\mathcal{K}'$ succeeds in simulating the decryption oracle with overwhelming probability. $\square$

6   The sk-PA Security

We showed that the OWB-PA security was equivalent to the statistical PA security [BP04] only if a PKE was sk-non-redundant. In this section, we consider a slightly modified version of the PA security [BP04] (named sk-*PA security*), where a distinguisher is provided with the secret key. Then we see that the OWB-PA security is equivalent to the sk-statistical PA security, even if a PKE is not sk-non-redundant. The formal definition of the sk-PA security will depicted in the full paper. Note that Fujisaki [F06] also considered a variant of a PA-ness where a distinguisher is provided with the secret key.

The modification that we give the secret key to a distinguisher is quite small, in the case of statistical PA security. In fact, since a distinguisher $\mathcal{D}$ of the statistical PA security is a superpolytime machine, $\mathcal{D}$ can compute a secret key corresponding to the public key pk by using superpolytime. However, there may be many secret keys corresponding to pk as mentioned in Subsection 5.1, and $\mathcal{D}$ cannot know which one is true sk. Therefore, we can say that the only advantage of the sk-statistical PA security is that the distinguisher can know which one is sk.

If a PKE is sk-non-redundant, $\mathsf{Dec}_{\mathsf{sk}}(C) = \mathsf{Dec}_{\mathsf{sk}'}(C)$ holds for any sk and sk$'$ corresponding to the same public key pk. Therefore, the sk-statistical PA security is not advantageous to the statistical PA security, in this case. Hence, we can show the following theorem. The proof will be described in the full paper.

Theorem 8 (statistical PA = sk-statistical PA, under sk-non-redundancy). *Suppose that a PKE Π satisfies the* sk-*non-redundancy. Then Π satisfies the statistical PA security if and only if it satisfies the* sk-*statistical PA security.*

We now give our result.

Theorem 9 (OWB-PA = sk-statistical PA = sk-computational PA). *The following properties are equivalent:*

- *the OWB-PA security.*
- *the* sk-*statistical PA security.*
- *the* sk-*computational PA security.*

We can prove the above theorem in a similar way to that of Theorem 4. The proof will be described in the full paper. Note that we can generalize Theorem 9 into the case of the perfect PA security, if we allow an extractor to output fail with negligible probability.

One of the most surprising fact of the above theorem is that the sk-statistical PA security is equivalent to the sk-computational PA security. This fact is impressed because the statistical PA security is strictly stronger than the computational PA security [TO06, TO08]. Therefore we can say that the only difference between the statistical PA security and the computational PA security is in the knowledge of sk.

We can also define more stronger variant of PA security, named the *View-PA security*, such that a distinguisher is given the views of all entities. Above, "the views of all entities" means the key generation algorithm Gen, an adversary $\mathcal{A}$, a plaintext creator $\mathcal{P}$, and the encryption oracle $\mathsf{Enc}_{\mathsf{pk}}(\cdot)$. Then it is also equivalent to the OWB-PA security. We will describe the proof in the full paper.

Theorem 10 (OWB-PA = View-statistical PA = View-computational PA).
The following properties are equivalent:

- *the OWB-PA security.*
- *the View-statistical PA security.*
- *the View-computational PA security.*

7 Conclusion

There were two approaches to define the PA-ness, the indistinguishability-based approach and the overwhelming-based approach. The current definition [BP04] of the PA-ness was given by using the indistinguishability-based approach.

In this paper, we defined an alternative definition of the (standard model) PA-ness, OWB-PA security, based on the overwhelming-approach. Basically, this notion was given by "standard modelizing" the random oracle model PA-ness [BR94, BDPR98]. However, we essentially changed the definition in one point, that is, we allowed an adversary to access the decryption oracle.

We then showed that our OWB-PA security was equivalent to the statistical PA security of [BP04], under a very weak condition, the sk-non-redundancy. We also gave a new definition of the PA-ness, named sk-PA-ness, and showed that the OWB-PA security was equivalent to the sk-statistical PA-ness, even if a PKE was not sk-non-redundant.

References

[BDPR98]   Bellare, M., Desai, A., Pointcheval, D., Rogaway, P.: Relations Among Notions of Security for Public-Key Encryption Schemes. In: Krawczyk, H. (ed.) CRYPTO 1998. LNCS, vol. 1462, pp. 26–45. Springer, Heidelberg (1998)

[BP04]   Bellare, M., Palacio, A.: Towards plaintext-aware public-key encryption without random oracles. In: Lee, P.J. (ed.) ASIACRYPT 2004. LNCS, vol. 3329, pp. 48–62. Springer, Heidelberg (2004)

[BR94]   Bellare, M., Rogaway, P.: Optimal Asymmetric Encryption. In: De Santis, A. (ed.) EUROCRYPT 1994. LNCS, vol. 950, pp. 92–111. Springer, Heidelberg (1995)

[BD07]   Birkett, J., Dent, A.W.: Relations Among Notions of Plaintext Awareness. PKC 2008, 47–64 (2007) eprint 2007/291

[CS98]   Cramer, R., Shoup, V.: A Practical Public Key Cryptosystem Provably Secure Against Adaptive Chosen Ciphertext Attack. In: Krawczyk, H. (ed.) CRYPTO 1998. LNCS, vol. 1462, pp. 13–25. Springer, Heidelberg (1998)

[CS01]   Cramer, R., Shoup, V.: Design and Analysis of Practical Public-Key Encryption Schemes (2001)

[D91]   Damgård, I.: Towards practical public key systems secure against chosen ciphertext attacks. In: Feigenbaum, J. (ed.) CRYPTO 1991. LNCS, vol. 576, pp. 445–456. Springer, Heidelberg (1992)

[D06]   Dent, A.W.: Cramer-Shoup is Plaintext-Aware in the Standard Model. In: Vaudenay, S. (ed.) EUROCRYPT 2006. LNCS, vol. 4004. Springer, Heidelberg (2006)

[F06]   Fujisaki, E.: Plaintext Simulatability. IEICE Transactions 89-A(1), 55–65 (2006)

[FO99]   Fujisaki, E., Okamoto, T.: How to Enhance the Security of Public-Key Encryption at Minimum Cost. In: Imai, H., Zheng, Y. (eds.) PKC 1999. LNCS, vol. 1560, pp. 53–68. Springer, Heidelberg (1999)

[HT06]   Hayashi, R., Tanaka, K.: PA in the Two-Key Setting and a Generic Conversion for Encryption with Anonymity. In: Batten, L.M., Safavi-Naini, R. (eds.) ACISP 2006. LNCS, vol. 4058, pp. 271–282. Springer, Heidelberg (2006)

[HLM03]   Herzog, J., Liskov, M., Micali, S.: Plaintext Awareness via Key Registration. In: Boneh, D. (ed.) CRYPTO 2003. LNCS, vol. 2729, pp. 548–564. Springer, Heidelberg (2003)

[S01]   Shoup, V.: OAEP Reconsidered. In: Kilian, J. (ed.) CRYPTO 2001. LNCS, vol. 2139, pp. 223–249. Springer, Heidelberg (2001)

[TO06]   Teranishi, I., Ogata, W.: Relationship between Standard Model Plaintext Awareness and Message Hiding. In: Lai, X., Chen, K. (eds.) ASIACRYPT 2006. LNCS, vol. 4284, pp. 226–240. Springer, Heidelberg (2006)

[TO08]   Teranishi, I., Ogata, W.: The full paper of [TO06]. IEICE Transactions 91-A(1), 244–261 (2008)

Distributed Verification of Mixing - Local Forking Proofs Model[*]

Jacek Cichoń, Marek Klonowski, and Mirosław Kutyłowski

Institute of Mathematics and Computer Science, Wrocław University of Technology
Jacek.Cichon@pwr.wroc.pl, Marek.Klonowski@pwr.wroc.pl,
Marek.Klonowski@pwr.wroc.pl

Abstract. One of generic techniques to achieve anonymity is to process messages through a batch of cryptographic mixes. In order to guarantee proper execution verifiable mixes are constructed: each mix provides a proof of correctness together with its output. However, if a mix is working on a huge number of messages at a time, the proof itself is huge since it concerns processing all messages. So in practice only a few verifiers would download the proofs and in turn we would have to trust what they are saying.

We consider a different model in which there are many verifiers, but each of them is going to download only a limited number of bits in order to check the mixes. Distributed character of the process ensures effectiveness even if many verifiers are dishonest and do not report irregularities found.

We concern a fully distributed and intuitive verification scheme which we call *local forking proofs*. For each intermediate ciphertext a verifier may ask for a proof that its re-encrypted version is in the output of the mix concerned. The proof shows that the re-encrypted version is within some subset of k ciphertexts from the output of the mix, and it can be performed with strong zero-knowledge or algebraic methods. They should work efficiently concerning communication complexity, if k is a relatively small constant.

There are many issues concerning stochastic properties of local forking proofs. In this paper we examine just one: we estimate quite precisely how many mixes are required so that if a local proof is provided for each message, then a plaintext hidden in an input message can appear on any position of the final output set.

Keywords: mix, anonymity, distributed system.

1 Introduction

Anonymity and hiding origin of the messages and electronic documents becomes today one of the crucial issues for e-society. This is one of the major issues for applications such like electronic voting. Providing privacy in the sense that in sensitive cases the origin of a message should be unrevealed unless it is necessary for some explicit reason, becomes one of the most challenging questions in computer security.

[*] Partially supported by Polish Ministry of Science and Higher Education, grant N N206 1842 33.

Y. Mu, W. Susilo, and J. Seberry (Eds.): ACISP 2008, LNCS 5107, pp. 128–140, 2008.
© Springer-Verlag Berlin Heidelberg 2008

MIXes. D. Chaum [4] introduced concept of a MIX, which is a basic primitive for systems providing anonymity. A MIX takes a number of encrypted messages, say $E(m_1)$, ..., $E(m_n)$, processes them in some way (for instance decrypts or re-encrypts them) and posts the result in a random order π:

$$E'(m_{\pi(1)}), E'(m_{\pi(2)}), \ldots, E'(m_{\pi(n)}) .$$

It should be guaranteed that nobody (except for the mix concerned) can link these input and the output messages. For the rest of this paper we shall assume that cryptographic methods used are strong enough to guarantee this. We also assume that the system is used in a sound way - for instance, we cannot distinguish ciphertexts of m_i by inspecting their lengths.

In order to achieve anonymity a set of messages is processed by a cascade of independent MIXes: the output of MIX i becomes the input for MIX $i+1$. The output of the last MIX in a cascade becomes the output of the system. As long as at least one of the MIXes is honest and does not reveal its permutation used, the link between the input to the system and its output cannot be established.

Problems. A single honest mix in a cascade ensures unlinkability between the input and the output of the mix cascade. However, for some applications it is crucial to ensure that none of the original plaintext messages gets removed and replaced by a ciphertext of another message, or becomes modified. Of course, if at least one of the MIXes is dishonest, then the final output might be corrupted.

For applications like anonymous access to WWW pages, this leads to some degradation of service, only. However, it is critical for e-voting schemes that employ MIX servers for processing encrypted ballots. Even worse situation occurs in case of auction schemes - a single message injected at a late stage may change the outcome of the whole procedure (which is practically not the case for large scale voting).

Verifiable MIXes. In order to enforce an honest execution of a mixing protocol, each MIX has to be controlled in some way so that:

- With a reasonable probability a dishonest MIX will be caught even if a single plaintext message gets modified,
- The verification procedure does not endanger unlinkability.

These goals can be reached. However, the following issues have been concerned:

(a) Reducing conceptual complexity of the verification scheme so that it can be easily understood and trusted at least by a skilled non-specialist,
(b) Reducing computational effort of the prover and of the verifier: since usually the arithmetic operations such as exponentiations take most of computation time, their number should be minimized,
(c) Reducing communication cost of the prover and the verifier, i.e. reducing the total volume of the messages exchanges as well as the number of communication rounds.

For instance, it was pointed by some authors that the tricky scheme from [20] might be too complicated to reach general acceptance. For (b), computational complexity of verification process has been considered in many papers. Many schemes with a linear number of exponentiations have been designed, differing by the constants standing in front of n: $12n$ in case of [20], $10n$ in case of [7,15], $8n$ in case of [11], and about $6n$ in case of [22]. Computational efficiency can improve even more, if we perform some computations in an offline phase [1].

Communication overhead in the number of bits has been considered, too. For instance, according to [9], the method from [7] has communication cost $6388n$ bits, the method from [11] has communication cost $2528n$ bits, while [9] requires $1344n$ bits. A higher number of bits is required when we admit long messages [8] (see also [12]).

In order to improve efficiency, Peng *et al.* [21] propose to reorganize the process of mixing so that at each stage the ciphertexts mixed are divided into groups and the re-encrypting and shuffling process proceeds in groups. This approach results in a lower communication complexity, however only a small fraction of permutations can be reached in this way.

A different approach called *randomized partial checking* (RPC) is presented in [14]. The idea is that after getting the final results a MIX is asked to reveal values of permutation π used for a random set of $n/2$ arguments. Moreover, the MIX has to show that the ciphertexts $E(m_i)$ and $E'(m_{\pi(i)})$ contain the same plaintext for each i such that $\pi(i)$ becomes revealed. (In fact, the connections to be revealed must be chosen with care so that no path of length higher than 2 gets disclosed.)

Revealing part of the connections might be psychologically unacceptable for two reasons: first, an average person might claim that it is still possible that the results are incorrect, since we had bad luck and the fraud has not been detected. The second problem is that a person with mathematical experience (see e.g. [11]) might ask himself what is effect of revealing the connections in a stochastic sense – does it change substantially conditional probabilities of potential permutations of messages? However, there are strong mathematical arguments that security of the scheme remains intact [10].

Distributed versus Non-distributed Verifiability. With a few exceptions the protocols concerned so far in the literature consider verification as a process performed by a verifier having similar computational resources as a mix. Moreover, the proof concerns the whole batch of ciphertexts. Consequently, the volume of verification data is linear in the number n of ciphertexts mixed.

For certain applications mixing might concern a huge amount of data. For instance, it may be the case for e-voting protocols where the ballots are processed by a single cascade of mixes. With more than 100.000 voters and communication complexity of more than $1000n$ bits, we get about 100Mbits communication volume to check one mix. Since the number of mixes should be at least the number of participating parties (say 20), the communication volume could be something like 2Gbits. Assuming that a voter communicates with a 1Mbit/sec. link, the communication would take 2000 seconds ≈ 33 minutes. It is sound to assume that almost no citizen would use this checking possibility and would have to trust some agent. This is not a good solution since one of the major goals of advanced e-voting procedures is to provide transparency in absence of *any* trusted third party.

Due to the reasons mentioned, in certain situations it would be helpful to design a verification method having the following properties:

1. Checking process is performed by a large number of independent verifiers,
2. Computational and communication complexity for each of the verifiers is negligible,
3. Probability that no verifier catches a dishonest mixer on a fraud is small,
4. Collective knowledge of all verifiers should not enable to break anonymity.

Additionally, we should assume that some limited number of participants of the protocol can be corrupted by the mix(es) so that negative verification results will not be shown in case of a fraud. Hence, it may occur that the centralized protocols concerned in the literature fail, since the verification process requires fetching long data and so the number of verifiers will be small. On the other hand, a fully decentralized setting has the advantage that it is impossible to corrupt all members of a crowd of verifiers.

2 k-Local Forking Proofs

Assume that for set of ciphertexts $C_1, \ldots, C_n$, a MIX gave an output $C'_1, \ldots, C'_n$ using a (hidden) permutation Π (that is, C_i and $C'_{\Pi(i)}$ correspond to the same plaintext, for each i). Honesty of the mix is checked by the following protocol:

Initialization: for each $i \leq n$, the prover determines a random set S_i of cardinality $k+1$ such that $\Pi(i) \in S_i$, (that is, $\Pi(i)$ is the only non-random element of S_i, the remaining k elements are chosen uniformly at random).
Challenge: a verifier may challenge the prover with an arbitrary $i \leq n$,
Response: the prover presents a proof that one of the ciphertexts C'_j for $j \in S_i$ corresponds to the same plaintext as C_i.

Note that the initialization is performed for all verifiers, so if two different verifiers challenge the same i, they get an answer concerning the same set S_i. We do not specify here what kind of proof is delivered in the response phase. Obviously, if every i gets challenged and the prover responds correctly, then in the shuffled batch there is every plaintext contained in $C_1, \ldots, C_n$. Hence, if the plaintexts are unique, correctness of shuffling of the mix is assured.

A verifier may challenge any of the mixes of the cascade, may be more than once. It depends only on the computation time and bandwidth that one wishes to devote for checking. Since k is assumed to be a small constant, this means a negligible effort for each check as long as relatively efficient proof methods are used.

Models for Analysis. There is a number of questions concerning the framework of local proofs. Certainly, data obtained by verifiers leak some information on permutations used by a mix. The problem is how does it influence unlinkability of the whole process. The example of RPC shows that unlinkability property might be preserved [10].

We may consider diverse models concerning verification process. For instance, we may assume that each single user may fetch only a limited number of local proofs, and that only a fraction of users will forward the data obtained to a given adversary willing to break anonymity. In this case only a fraction of verification data can be gathered in one place. So we have a situation that resembles RPC – only a limited number of links becomes revealed. However, unlike for RPC, we cannot put any restrictions on which local proofs can be gathered together. The verifiers may even work adaptively to increase their chances to break anonymity. On the other hand, for a given message its re-encrypted version after leaving the current mix is not shown - all we know is that it is contained in a set of k messages. The second more pessimistic model to concern is that all information obtained by the verifiers might be gathered by some party.

Unlinkability Goals. Let Π denote a random variable such that for $i \leq n$ (n is the number of messages) $\Pi(i)$ is the position of the ith plaintext in the output of a mix cascade concerned. Let $\mathcal{D}$ denote the probability distribution corresponding to Π. For a reasonable system of mixes we may assume that $\mathcal{D}$ is a uniform distribution. However, based on the information from local proofs, the adversary may (at least theoretically) compute conditional probability distribution $\mathcal{D}'$ of Π. There is a number of questions that might be asked about $\mathcal{D}'$:

1. What is the distance between distributions $\mathcal{D}$ and $\mathcal{D}'$ (e.g. concerning L_1 norm or information theoretic distance ([3,23])),
2. What is the maximum value of $\mathcal{D}'$.

An answer of the first question provides very strong anonymity estimates. However, results of this kind are quite rare and hard to get. An answer to the second question gives an idea how immune the system is against brute force and guessing attacks.

   We can also confine ourselves to a single message and probability distribution of its position in the final batch, without local proofs ($\mathcal{S}$) and with them ($\mathcal{S}'$). Since $\mathcal{S}$ should be uniform we are are concerned about

1. The distance between distributions $\mathcal{S}$ and $\mathcal{S}'$ with respect to a given norm,
2. The maximum value of $\mathcal{S}'$,
3. Support of $\mathcal{S}'$, i.e. the set of positions where the probability is positive i.e. the *anonymity set* of the message concerned.

While a good bound for question 1 is highly desirable, a small bound for question 2 already says that there are no relatively likely positions. Getting a big anonymity set is important to eliminate impossible positions and in this way enable linking all final messages to the message concerned. This property might be all one needs for many procedures in a court of law. For further discussion concerning anonymity measures see [5,6].

   One difficulty for performing mathematical analysis of forking proofs is that distributions $\mathcal{D}'$ and $\mathcal{S}'$ depend very much on the sets S_i chosen by each mix and that apparently there are some bad choices for these sets. So the final results may only be stated in the form *"With a high probability, distribution ..."*

   One should also notice that there is a major difference between considering $\mathcal{S}'$ and $\mathcal{D}'$. For $k = 2$, local forking proofs behave quite poorly with respect to $\mathcal{D}'$, while for $k = 3$ the situation is much better. Such a phase transition does not occur if we consider the final position of a single message.

   There are many scenarios corresponding to many different practical situations, but due to available space we have to concentrate ourselves on one model. For the rest of the paper we assume that all local proofs can be gathered by an adversary; second, we are interested in anonymity set rather than the maximum probability or distance to uniform distribution.

Main Result. Our goal is to find a precise estimation of the number of mixes such that with local forking proofs we reach the maximal possible size of anonymity sets.

Theorem 1. *Consider a cascade of T MIX-servers processing n messages. Consider verification data for each position and each MIX created according k-local forking proofs strategy. Then, the size of anonymity set of particular message entering the MIX-cascade is equal to n with probability greater than* $1 - 1/n$, *if* $T > T_0$, *where*

$$
T_0 = \left(0.8 + \frac{4.4}{k}\right) \log n + 1.7 \frac{\log\left(\frac{16}{k}\log n\right)}{\log\left(1 + \frac{k}{3}\right)} + \frac{\log(n/2)}{\log(1 + \frac{k}{4})}
$$
$$
+ \sqrt{2.7 \frac{\log\left(\frac{16}{k}\log n\right)}{\log\left(1 + \frac{k}{3}\right)} \log n + 0.65 \log^2 n}.
$$

Up to a constant, this is the optimal result since to obtain anonymity set equal to n we need $T \geq \lceil \log_k(n) \rceil$. The crucial message of Theorem 1 is that the sufficient number of MIXes in a cascade is not much higher than in the trivial lower bound.

3   Mathematical Modeling

Anonymity Metrics. Even if *anonymity* or *unlinkability* have their well established intuitive meaning, it is unclear how to measure anonymity level in a uniform mathematical way. For the rest of this paper we focus on definition from [16] that catches idea introduced in [17]. Let us suppose that we have n encrypted, enumerated messages. Then the ciphertexts are processed by the system of MIXes. As an output we get another n enumerated ciphertexts. The mixing process is modeled by a random variable – a permutation Π. So $\Pi(i) = j$ menas that the i-th message in the first MIX after processing is placed on the j-th position in the output of the last MIX. Then anonymity of the i-th input object inp_i can be measured by

$$
S(\mathrm{inp}_i) = |\{1 \leq j \leq n : \Pr[\Pi(i) = j] > 0\}|,
$$

where probability is conditioned on the knowledge available for an observer.

The value is $S(\mathrm{inp}_i)$ called the size of *anonymity set* of the input inp_i.

Infection Process. Let us consider following infection process: we have n distinguishable objects. The process consists of steps $t = 1, 2, \ldots$. Each object is either infected or not. Initially, exactly one object is infected. At each step, every infected object chooses k distinct objects, uniformly at random. Then it infects these objects (if they are not infected yet).

We are interested how many steps are required so that with a high probability every object gets infected, where probability is considered over the choices made by the infected objects during each step.

Of course, the process of infection models the possible destinations of a message given the information revealed by Local Forking Proofs. The infected nodes correspond to those ciphertexts that can keep the plaintexts of the message considered with a non-zero probability.

Infection Process in Details. While it is quite obvious that eventually all objects get infected and the time required is $O(\log n)$, for n equal to the total number of objects, determining precisely the time necessary to infect all object is of big practical importance. Namely, it determines the number of mixes in a cascade as a function of the parameter n. Note that since we are interested in some relatively small values of k, the constant factor may easily dominate the term $\log n$.

Consider now the number of infected objects. At the beginning we have 1 infected object, then exactly k objects, but starting from the third step, the number of infected objects becomes uncertain. It is hard to say how many new objects become infected at each step. Of course it is strongly correlated with the number of objects already infected. More precisely, probability that a particular infected object infects a new object is decreasing with the number of already infected objects. At the end, a majority consisting of infected objects tries to „hit" a few non-infected remainders. On the other hand, growing number of infected elements obviously increases the chance of being infected for the object not infected yet.

Technical Result. Spirit of infection process seems to be similar to the well-known *epidemic processes* (see for example [2]). However, we are not aware of any analysis for the particular model considered here. We prove the following technical theorem:

Theorem 1. *Let $N(t)$ be a random variable denoting the number of infected objects after step t of the infection process. Let T be the random variable equal to the index of the first step such that all n objects are infected: $T = \min\{t \in \mathbf{N} | N(t) = n\}$. Then $\Pr(T < T_0) > 1 - \frac{1}{n}$ for T_0 given by Theorem 1.*

3.1 Mathematical Preliminaries

Consider a sequence of n independent (Bernoulli) trials, where each trial succeeds with probability p and fails with probability $1 - p$. The number of successes has binomial distribution denoted here by $Bi(n, p)$. Obviously, $E[Bi(n, p)] = pn$. Let us recall the following well known bound (see [13] (Theorem 2.1, Corollary 2.4):

Lemma 1. *Let the random variable X has binomial distribution with parameters n and p, i.e. $X \sim Bi(n, p)$. Then for any $t > 0$:*

$$\Pr(X \leq E(X) - t) \leq \exp\left(-\frac{2t^2}{n}\right) .$$

In particular, for any $1 > \varepsilon > 0$:

$$\Pr(X \leq (1 - \varepsilon)E(X)) \leq \exp\left(-\frac{2(\varepsilon E(X))^2}{n}\right) .$$

Now we would like to ask a related question. We have to find a number of trials n^* such that the number of successes X within n^* trials is equal or greater than r with probability higher than ϱ.

Fact 1. *Let us consider the series of Bernoulli's trials with success probability p. It is enough to try*

$$n^* = \left\lceil \frac{4pr + \log \varrho^{-1} + \sqrt{8pr \log \varrho^{-1} + (\log \varrho^{-1})^2}}{4p^2} \right\rceil$$

times in order to have at least r successes with probability ϱ.

This fact is implied directly by the Lemma 1. Indeed, let us note that expected number of successes is equal to $n^* \cdot p$. So, using Lemma 1 one can easily see that

$$\Pr\left[X < k\right] = \Pr\left[X < n^*p - (n^*p - k)\right] < \exp\left(-\frac{2(n^*p - k)^2}{n^*}\right) =$$

$$\exp\left(-\frac{2\left(\frac{\log \varrho^{-1} + \sqrt{8pk \log \varrho^{-1} + (\log \varrho^{-1})^2}}{4p}\right)^2}{\frac{4pk + \log \varrho^{-1} + \sqrt{8pk \log \varrho^{-1} + (\log \varrho^{-1})^2}}{4p^2}}\right) = \exp(-\log \varrho^{-1}) = \varrho.$$

We say that the random variable X is stochastically dominated by the random variable Y if for each $t \in \mathbf{R}$,

$$\Pr\left[X > t\right] \le \Pr\left[Y > t\right].$$

Stochastic dominance is useful when some weak dependencies occur. An example of such case is following fact:

Fact 2 (see [18]). *Let $X_1, X_2, \ldots, X_n$ be a sequence of random variables in an arbitrary domain, and let $Y_1, Y_2, \ldots, Y_n$ be a sequence of binary random variables with the property that $Y_i = Y_i(X_1, X_2, \ldots, X_i)$. If*

$$\Pr[Y_i = 1 | X_1, X_2, \ldots, X_{i-1}] \le p$$

then sum of $Y_i's$ is stochastically dominated by the binomial distribution:

$$\Pr\left[\sum_{i=1}^{n} Y_i > k\right] \le \Pr[Bi(n, p) > k].$$

Similarly, if $\Pr[Y_i = 1 | X_1, X_2, \ldots, X_{i-1}] \ge p$, then $\sum_{i=1}^{n} Y_i$ stochastically dominates $Bi(n, p)$.

Recall also the following version of Azuma's inequality (for a proof see [18]).

Lemma 2. *Let $X = (X_1, X_2, \ldots, X_n)$ be a vector of independent random variables with X_i taking values in a set A_i for each i. Suppose that a real-valued function f defined on $A_1 \times A_2 \times \ldots \times A_n$ satisfies:*

$$|f(x) - f(x')| \le c_i$$

if the vectors x and x' differ only on the ith coordinate. Let $E(f(X)) = \mu$. Then for any $d \geq 0$,

$$\Pr\left[f(X) \leq \mu - d\right] \leq \exp(-2d^2 / \textstyle\sum_{i=1}^{n}(c_i)^2) \ .$$

Lemma 2 can be very useful when we consider a process which is determined by a set of independent experiments and each experiment has a limited in advance influence on the overall process result.

Finally, let us consider the following randomized process. We have n bins. At each time we choose uniformly at random exactly one bin and we put a ball inside the bin chosen. Let $T_c(n)$ denote the number of balls thrown so that we get at least one ball in each bin for the first time. Of course, $T_c(n)$ is a random variable.

Lemma 3. $\Pr(T_c(n) > \beta n \log n) < n^{1-\beta}$ for any $\beta > 1$.

Lemma 3 is a version of the well-known coupon collector's problem. This particular version can be found in [19]. Let us note that one can find a better asymptotic estimation for coupon's collector problem. However this version is fairly enough for our purposes.

3.2   Proof of the Main Result

Overview. Since from a practical point of view it is very important to have possibly small constants, we split the infection process into three conceptual phases: beginning of the process (small number of infected elements, high probability of infecting), stabilization („middle part" with a significant number of already infected elements and fairly large probability of successful infection) and the end (with a few non-infected elements difficult to be chosen).

Let us define three random variables

$$\begin{aligned}
T_1 &= \max\{i \mid N(i) \leq 8\log n^2 \ , \text{ if } N(1) = k\} \ , \\
T_2 &= \max\{i \mid N(i) \leq n/2 \ , \text{ if } N(0) = \lceil 8\log n^2\rceil\} \ , \\
T_3 &= \min\{i \mid N(i) = n \ , \text{ if } N(0) = \lceil n/2\rceil\} \ .
\end{aligned}$$

In other words, the random variables T_1, T_2, T_3 denote the number of steps necessary to go from 0 to $\lfloor 8\log n^2\rfloor$ infected objects, from $\lceil 8\log n^2\rceil$ to $\lfloor n/2\rfloor$ infected objects and from $\lceil n/2\rceil$ to n infected objects, respectively.

Probabilistic Analysis of the Process. Throughout this analysis assume that $k \geq 2$ and $n \geq 128$. Let us consider the expected number of infected objects after step $t + 1$ conditioned by the value of $N(t)$.

Fact 3

$$E(N(t+1)|N(t)) = N(t) + (n - N_t)\left(1 - \left(1 - \tfrac{k}{n-1}\right)^{N_t}\right)$$

The formula above follows from following observation: in the consecutive step already infected items stays infected, and each of $n - N(t)$ not infected items become infected iff it is not the case that every infected item chooses different items to infect.

Bounding T_1. In this point we start with exactly k infected items, i.e. $N(1) = k$, and we look for the first T_1 such that $N(T_1 + 1) \geq 8 \log n^2$. Let us represent the number of infected objects in step $t + 1$ step as:

$$N(t + 1) = N(t) + \Delta(N(t)) .$$

Let us now think about the random variable $\Delta(N(t))$ in terms of balls and bins. Each of $N(t)$ infected objects throws k balls trying to hit $n - N(t)$ empty bins. It is easy to observe that at each moment at least $n - kN(t)$ balls are empty. Using Lemma 2 we can see that the number of bins filled during step $t + 1$ stochastically dominates $Bi(kN(t), 1 - kN(t)/n)$. It is easy see that each ball is placed in an empty bin with probability greater than $1 - kN(t)/n$, independently on the previous placements.

By Lemma 1 we get:

$$\Pr\left[N(t + 1) < (1 + k/3)N(t)\right] <$$
$$\Pr\left[N(t + 1) < N(t) + \tfrac{1}{2}N(t)k\left(1 - \tfrac{8 \log n^2}{n}\right)\right] <$$
$$\exp\left(-\tfrac{k^2}{2}\left(1 - \tfrac{8 \log n^2}{n}\right)^2\right) < 1/e$$

for all values considered here (that is, $k < N(t + 1) < 8 \log n^2$) and n considered in our analysis.

If the condition $N(t + 1) > (1 + k/3)N(t)$ is fulfilled, then we say that step $t + 1$ is *successful*. Note that it is enough to have $\lceil \log(\tfrac{16}{k} \log n) / \log(1 + \tfrac{k}{3}) \rceil$ successful rounds to obtain at least $8 \log n^2$ infected elements. However, not all rounds have to be successful. So T_1 is stochastically dominated by the number of steps necessary to get an appropriate number of successful steps. Let us note that we can consider each step as a separate and independent experiment with probability of success at least $1 - 1/e$. Using Fact 1, we can easily prove that after

$$\frac{\frac{4\left(\frac{e-1}{e}\right)\log\left(\frac{16}{k}\log n\right)}{\log\left(1+\frac{k}{3}\right)} + 1.2 \log n + \sqrt{9.6\frac{e-1}{e}\frac{\log\left(\frac{16}{k}\log n\right)}{\log\left(1+\frac{k}{3}\right)}\log n + 1.44(\log n)^2}}{4\left(\frac{e-1}{e}\right)^2}$$

steps, we have the required number of successful steps with probability greater than $1 - 1/n^{1.2}$.

As we noted before, it is sufficient for finishing the first phase of the process. Using simple calculations and facts that

$$9.6\frac{e-1}{e} < 6.05 \quad \text{and} \quad 4\left(\frac{e-1}{e}\right)^2 > 1.5$$

we get:

$$\Pr\left[T_1 > 0.8 \log n + 1.7\frac{\log\left(\frac{16}{k}\log n\right)}{\log\left(1 + \frac{k}{3}\right)} + \sqrt{2.7\frac{\log\left(\frac{16}{k}\log n\right)}{\log\left(1 + \frac{k}{3}\right)}\log n + 0.65(\log n)^2}\right] < 1/n^{1.2} .$$

Bounding T_2. It is easy to see that if $8 \log n^2 \leq N(t+1) \leq n/2$, then

$$E(N(t+1)|N(t)) > \left(1 + \tfrac{k}{2}\right) N(t) \ .$$

Indeed, each infected object chooses k objects. Since each choice infects new object with probability proportional to the fraction of non-infected objects (greater than $1/2$), so expected number of newly infected elements must be greater than $k/2 \cdot N(t)$. For this reason, by Theorem 2 we get immediately:

$$\Pr\left(N(t+1) \leq \left(1 + \tfrac{k}{4}\right) N(t)\right) \leq \exp\left(-2 \left(\tfrac{k}{4} N(t)\right)^2 / N(t) k^2\right) = \exp(-N(t)/8) \ .$$

Since $8 \log n^2 < N(t)$, one can easily see that

$$\Pr\left[N(t+T) < \left(1 + \tfrac{k}{4}\right)^T N(t)\right] < T \exp(-8 \log n^2 / 8)$$

as long as $8 \log n^2 \leq N(t) \leq N(t+T) \leq n/2$. This implies that:

$$\Pr\left[T_2 > \frac{\log(n/2)}{\log(1 + \tfrac{k}{4})}\right] < \frac{\log(n/2)}{\log(1 + \tfrac{k}{4})} \frac{1}{n^2} \ .$$

Estimating T_3. In this case we start with at least $\lceil n/2 \rceil$ infected objects. At each time, each infected chooses k distinct objects in order to infect them. First of all let us look at the process $N(t)$ in terms of balls and bins. Again, let us assume that each object is represented by a bin. Each infected object throws independently k balls to distinct bins. So the number of balls is equal to the number of infected items multiplied by the number of balls k. All objects become infected when each bin contains at least one ball. Note that we assumed that we have at least $n/2$ already infected objects at the beginning. So, it is easy to see that T_3 is statistically dominated by $\left\lceil \frac{2T_c(n)}{nk} \right\rceil$. Now by applying Lemma 3 to these considerations, we easily obtain the following bound on T_3:

$$\Pr\left[T_3 \geq \frac{4.4}{k} \log(n)\right] > \Pr\left[T_c(n) \geq 2.2 n \log(n)\right] \leq \frac{1}{n^{1.2}} \ .$$

Bounding parameter T. Let

$$S = 0.8 \log n + 1.7 \frac{\log\left(\tfrac{16}{k} \log n\right)}{\log\left(1 + \tfrac{k}{3}\right)} + \sqrt{2.7 \frac{\log\left(\tfrac{16}{k} \log n\right)}{\log\left(1 + \tfrac{k}{3}\right)} \log n + 0.65 \log n}$$
$$+ \frac{\log(n/2)}{\log(1 + \tfrac{k}{4})} + \frac{4.4}{k} \log(n).$$

Using estimations of T_1, T_2 and T_3 obtained before we get:

$$\Pr\left[T > S\right] \le$$

$$< \Pr\left[T_1 > 0.8\log n + 1.7\frac{\log\left(\frac{16}{k}\log n\right)}{\log\left(1 + \frac{k}{3}\right)} + \sqrt{2.7\frac{\log\left(\frac{16}{k}\log n\right)}{\log\left(1 + \frac{k}{3}\right)}\log n + 0.65\log n}\right] +$$

$$+ \Pr\left[T_2 > \frac{\log(n/2)}{\log(1 + \frac{k}{4})}\right] + \Pr\left[T_3 > \frac{4.4}{k}\log(n)\right] <$$

$$< \frac{1}{n^{1.2}} + \frac{\log(n/2)}{\log(1 + \frac{k}{4})}\frac{1}{n^2} + \frac{1}{n^{1.2}} < \frac{1}{n}$$

This completes the proof of the Theorem 1. $\square$

Examples. For and $k = 2$ and $k = 6$ we get, respectively:

$$T_{k=2} < 6.3\ln n + 3.4\ln(8\ln n) + 2.3\sqrt{\ln(8\ln n)\ln n}$$

and

$$T_{k=6} < 3.45\ln n + 1.55\ln(2.7\ln n) + 1.8\sqrt{\ln(2.7\ln n)\ln n}$$

Let us also note that from practical point of view, it does not make sense to use too big forking parameter k. Increasing k always accelerates the process, but we gain decreases with k.

Acknowledgements. Authors would like to thank anonymous reviewers for their valuable comments.

References

1. Adida, B., Wikström, D.: Offline/Online Mixing. In: Arge, L., Cachin, C., Jurdziński, T., Tarlecki, A. (eds.) ICALP 2007. LNCS, vol. 4596, pp. 484–495. Springer, Heidelberg (2007)
2. Athreya, K.B., Ney, P.E.: Branching Processes. Springer, Heidelberg (1972)
3. Berman, R., Fiat, A., Ta-Shma, A.: Provable Unlinkability Against Traffic Analysis. In: Juels, A. (ed.) FC 2004. LNCS, vol. 3110, pp. 266–280. Springer, Heidelberg (2004)
4. Chaum, D.: Untraceable Electronic Mail, Return Addresses, and Digital Pseudonyms. CACM 24(2), 84–88 (1981)
5. Danezis, G., Serjantov, A.: Towards an Information Theoretic Metric for Anonymity. In: Dingledine, R., Syverson, P.F. (eds.) PET 2002. LNCS, vol. 2482, pp. 41–53. Springer, Heidelberg (2003)
6. Diaz, C., Seys, S., Claessens, J., Preneel, B.: Towards measuring anonymity Metric for Anonymity. In: Dingledine, R., Syverson, P.F. (eds.) PET 2002. LNCS, vol. 2482, pp. 41–53. Springer, Heidelberg (2003)
7. Furukawa, J., Sako, K.: An Efficient Scheme for Proving a Shuffle. In: Kilian, J. (ed.) CRYPTO 2001. LNCS, vol. 2139, pp. 368–387. Springer, Heidelberg (2001)
8. Furukawa, J., Sako, K.: An Efficient Publicly Verifiable Mix-Net for Long Inputs. In: Di Crescenzo, G., Rubin, A. (eds.) FC 2006. LNCS, vol. 4107, pp. 111–125. Springer, Heidelberg (2006)

9. Furukawa, J.: Efficient, Verifiable Shuffle Decryption and Its Requirement of Unlinkability. In: Bao, F., Deng, R., Zhou, J. (eds.) PKC 2004. LNCS, vol. 2947, pp. 319–332. Springer, Heidelberg (2004)
10. Gomułkiewicz, M., Klonowski, M., Kutyłowski, M.: Rapid Mixing and Security of Chaum's Visual Electronic Voting. In: Snekkenes, E., Gollmann, D. (eds.) ESORICS 2003. LNCS, vol. 2808, pp. 132–145. Springer, Heidelberg (2003)
11. Groth, J.: A Verifiable Secret Shuffle of Homomorphic Encryptions. In: Desmedt, Y.G. (ed.) PKC 2003. LNCS, vol. 2567, pp. 145–160. Springer, Heidelberg (2002)
12. Groth, J., Lu, S.: Verifiable Shuffle of Large Size Ciphertexts. In: Okamoto, T., Wang, X. (eds.) PKC 2007. LNCS, vol. 4450, pp. 377–392. Springer, Heidelberg (2007)
13. Janson, S., Łuczak, T., Ruciński, A.: Random Graphs. John Wiley & Sons, Chichester (2002)
14. Jakobsson, M., Juels, A., Rivest, R.L.: Making Mix Nets Robust For Electronic Voting By Randomized Partial Checking. In: USENIX Security Symposium, pp. 339–353 (2002)
15. Nguyen, L., Safavi-Naini, R., Kurosawa, K.: Verifiable Shuffles: A Formal Model and a Paillier-Based Efficient Construction with Provable Security. In: Jakobsson, M., Yung, M., Zhou, J. (eds.) ACNS 2004. LNCS, vol. 3089, pp. 61–75. Springer, Heidelberg (2004)
16. Kesdogan, D., Egner, J., Büschkes, R.: Stop-and-Go-MIXes Providing Probabilistic Anonymity in an Open System. In: Aucsmith, D. (ed.) IH 1998. LNCS, vol. 1525, pp. 83–98. Springer, Heidelberg (1998)
17. Köhntopp, M., Pfitzmann, A.: Anonymity, Unobservability, and Pseudonymity: A Proposal for Terminology. In: Federrath, H. (ed.) Designing Privacy Enhancing Technologies. LNCS, vol. 2009, pp. 1–9. Springer, Heidelberg (2001)
18. McDiarmid, C.: On the method of bounded differences. Surveys in Combinatorics. Cambridge University Press, Cambridge (1989)
19. Mitzenmacher, M., Upfal, E.: Probability and computation. Cambridge University Press, Cambridge (2005)
20. Neff, A.: Verifiable mixing(shuffling) of El-Gamal pairs (2004), http://www.votehere.net/documentation/vhti
21. Peng, K., Boyd, C., Dawson, E., Viswanathan, K.: A Correct, Private and Efficient Mix Network. In: Bao, F., Deng, R., Zhou, J. (eds.) PKC 2004. LNCS, vol. 2947, pp. 439–454. Springer, Heidelberg (2004)
22. Peng, K., Boyd, C., Ed Dawson, E.: Simple and Efficient Shuffling with Provable Correctness and ZK Privacy. In: Shoup, V. (ed.) CRYPTO 2005. LNCS, vol. 3621, pp. 188–204. Springer, Heidelberg (2005)
23. Rackoff, C., Simon, D.R.: Cryptographic Defense Against Traffic Analysis. In: STOC, vol. 25, pp. 672–681.

Fully-Simulatable Oblivious Set Transfer

Huafei Zhu

C&S Department, I^2R, Singapore
huafei@i2r.a-star.edu.sg

Abstract. In this paper, a new notion which we call oblivious set transfer is introduced and formalized. An oblivious set transfer in essence, is an extension of the notions of oblivious bit transfer and oblivious string transfer protocols. The security of oblivious set transfer protocols is defined in the real/ideal world simulation paradigm. We show that oblivious set transfer protocols that are provably secure in the full simulation model can be efficiently implemented assuming the existence of semantically secure encryption schemes, perfectly hiding commitments and perfectly binding commitments.

Keywords: Oblivious set transfer, perfectly hiding commitment, perfectly binding commitment, real/ideal world simulation paradigm.

1 Introduction

The oblivious transfer introduced by Rabin [17], and extended by Even, Goldreich and Lempel [6] and Brassard, Crépeau and Robert [2] is one of the most basic and widely used protocol primitives in cryptography. The concept of oblivious transfer protocol stands at the center of the fundamental results on secure two-party and multi-party computation showing that any efficient functionality can be securely computed ([18] and [11]). Due to its general importance, the task of constructing efficient oblivious transfer protocols has attracted much interest. The state-of-the-art of security definitions of oblivious transfer protocols are defined in the following three models:

- In the semi-honest model, an adversary follows the protocol specification but tries to learn more than allowed by examining the protocol transcript. It is possible to construct efficient oblivious transfer protocols from trapdoor permutations [6] and homomorphic encryptions ([1] and [12]).
- The notion of semi-simulatable model first introduced and formalized by Naor and Pinkas [14], considers malicious senders and receivers, but handles their security separately. Receiver security is defined by requiring that the sender's view of the protocol when the receiver chooses index σ_0 is indistinguishable from a view of protocol when the receiver's chooses σ_1. Sender security follows the real/ideal world paradigm and guarantees that any malicious receiver in the real world can be mapped to a receiver in an idealized game in which the oblivious transfer protocol is implemented by a trusted third party.

Y. Mu, W. Susilo, and J. Seberry (Eds.): ACISP 2008, LNCS 5107, pp. 141–154, 2008.

- The notion of fully-simulatable model was introduced and formalized by Camenisch, Neven and Shelat [3]. In the full simulation model, the security employs the real/ideal world paradigm for both receiver and the sender. The difficulty in obtaining secure oblivious transfer protocols in this model is the strict security requirement of simulation based definition.

The implementations of efficient oblivious transfer protocols that reach full simulation level of security are of great interest. One possibility is to use the protocol compiler of Goldreich, Micali and Wigderson (GMW compiler [11]) to transform oblivious protocols for semi-honest adversaries into protocols that are secure in the presence of malicious adversaries. Here an essential tool is the result that all NP languages possess zero-knowledge proofs. That is, each party is required to prove in zero-knowledge that each message he sends is what he should have sent being honest, given his private input, his random choice and the messages he received so far. If a malicious party frustrated at not being able to send messages according to a different program, decide to stop, his input and random bits will be reconstructed by the community who will compute his messages when necessary, without skewing the probability distribution of the final outcome.

1.1   The State-of-the-Art

Very recently, two fully simulatable oblivious transfer protocols without using the generic GMW compiler are reported in the literature:

- Camenisch, Neven and Shelat [3] proposed two interesting implementations of oblivious string transfer protocols. The first protocol is constructed from any unique blind signature scheme in the random oracle model. The second construction is based on the q-power decisional Diffie-Hellman assumptions. As noted by Green and Hohenberger [10], the dynamic assumptions of their scheme seem significantly stronger than well established primitives such as the Diffie-Hellman decisional problem and quadratic residuosity assumptions. Thus, a well-motivated problem is to find efficient, fully simulatable oblivious transfer schemes under weaker complexity assumptions.
- Green and Hohenberger [10] proposed alternative implementation of oblivious string transfer protocols based on the Decisional Bilinear Diffie-Hellman assumption. Zero-knowledge proof must be used in Green and Hohenberger' protocol otherwise, it seems difficult to show their protocol is fully-simulatable as the ideal sender would have to form the N cipher-texts before learning the messages that K of them must decrypt to. The security of their scheme is based on the Decisional Bilinear Diffie-Hellman assumption that seems a less well-established primitive.

Since the protocols described above are all based on less well-established primitives, a well-motivated problem is thus to find efficient yet fully simulatable oblivious transfer schemes under standard complexity assumptions.

Lindell's oblivious bit transfer protocol [13]: Lindell has presented the first efficient implementation of fully-simulatable oblivious bit transfer protocols under the decisional Diffie-Hellman problem, the Nth residuosity and quadratic residuosity assumptions as well as the assumption of that homomorphic encryption exists. All protocols are nice since they are provably secure in the presence of malicious adversaries under the real/ideal model model simulation paradigm without using general zero-knowledge proofs under standard complexity assumptions. The idea behind Lindell's construction is that it makes use of the cut-and-choose technique so that each party is not required to prove in zero-knowledge and allows a simulator to rewind the malicious party so that an expected polynomial time simulator under the standard cryptographic primitives can be defined.

Lindell's protocol works by the receiver generating a tuple (g^a, g^b, g^c, g^d) with the following property: if the receiver's input is 0, then $c = ab$ and d is random, and if the receiver's input equals 1, then $d = ab$ and c is random. The sender receives this tuple and carries out a manipulation that randomizes the tuple so that if $c = ab$ then the result of the manipulation on (g^a, g^b, g^c) is still a Decisional Diffie-Hellman tuple and the result of the manipulation on (g^a, g^b, g^d) yields a completely random tuple. The sender then derives a secret key from the multiplication of each of (g^a, g^b, g^c) and (g^a, g^b, g^d), and sends information that enables the receiver to derive the same secret key from the Decisional Diffie-Hellman tupel while the key from the non-Decisional Diffie-Hellman remains completely random. The design mechanism allows one to implement 1-out-2 oblivious bit transfer protocols. We however do not know how to extend Lindell's scheme to the multi-bit (i.e., oblivious string transfer protocols) case. As a result, the construction of oblivious string transfer protocols in the full simulation paradigm remains a challenge task in the research community.

1.2   Our Results

In this paper, we introduce and formalize a new notion which we call oblivious set transfer. An oblivious set transfer is a natural extension of the notions of oblivious bit transfer and oblivious string transfer. If a set consists of two bits then the definition of our protocols coincides with the definition of standard oblivious bit transfer protocols. If a set consists of k indices, then our definition coincides with the standard definition of oblivious string transfer protocols (see the definition of oblivious set transfer in Section 2 for more details). We then present an efficient implementation of oblivious set transfer protocols that are secure in the presence of malicious adversaries in the real/ideal world simulation paradigm. That is, assuming that Paillier's encryption scheme is semantically secure and assuming that COM_h is a perfectly hiding commitment and COM_b is a perfectly binding commitment, the oblivious set transfer protocol described in this paper is secure in the full simulation model.

The idea behind of our construction is that a receiver encodes a set of strings to an L-adic that will be retrieved at the end of execution of the oblivious set transfer protocol, and then runs with the sender a two-party computation of an encrypted linear function $E(\alpha x + y)$, where x and y are two random strings used to hide the exact message α whereas E is an additively homomorphic encryption (say, Paillier encryption scheme) used by the sender. It follows that if the receiver obtains an decryption of the encrypted linear message, then the set of desired messages can be retrieved.

2   Definitions

The oblivious set transfer functionality in this paper is an extension of [13], i.e., the oblivious set transfer functionality is formally defined as a function f with two inputs and one output. The first input is an n-tuple message $\overline{m}=(m_1,\cdots,m_n)$, and the second input is an index set $S=\{i_1,\cdots,i_k\}$, where $k \leq n$. The output is a subset $\{m_{i_1},\cdots,m_{i_k}\}$ of the n-tuple message. Party 1, also known as the sender, inputs $(m_1,\cdots,m_n)$ and receives no output. In contrast, Party 2, also known as the receiver, inputs the set of indices $\{i_1,\cdots,i_k\}$ and receives $M_S=\{m_{i_1},\cdots,m_{i_k}\}$. Formally, we write $f(\overline{m},S)=(\perp,m_S)$.

Adversarial behavior: In this paper, we consider malicious adversaries who may arbitrarily deviate from the specified protocol. We however, consider the static corruption model, where one of the parties is adversarial while the other is honest, and this is fixed before the execution begins.

Execution in the real world model. In the real world, a malicious party may follow an arbitrary feasible strategy. Let π be a two-party protocol, and let $\overline{M}=(M_1,M_2)$ be a pair of non-uniform probabilistic polynomial time machines. We assume that such a pair is admissible meaning that for at least one $i \in \{1,2\}$ we have M_i is honest. The joint execution of π under $\overline{M}$ in the real model on inputs $\overline{m}=(m_1,\cdots,m_n)$ and $S=\{i_1,\cdots,i_k\}$, denoted by $\mathrm{REAL}_{\pi,\overline{M}}(\overline{m},S)$, is defined as the output of pair of M_1 and M_2 resulting from the protocol interaction.

Execution in the ideal world model. An ideal oblivious set transfer proceeds as follows:

- Inputs: Party 1 obtains an input pair $\overline{m}=(m_1,\cdots,m_n)$ with $|m_i|=|m_j|$, and Party 2 obtains an input $S=\{i_1,\cdots,i_k\}$, where $1 \leq k \leq n$.
- Send inputs to trusted party: An honest party always sends its inputs to the trust party without any modification. A malicious party may either abort, in which case it sends $\perp$ to the trust party, or sends some other input to the trusted party.
- If the trusted party receives $\perp$ from one of the parties, then it sends $\perp$ to both parties and halts. Otherwise, upon receiving some $(m_1',\cdots,m_n')$ from Party 1 and $\{i_1',\cdots,i_k'\}$ from Party 2, the trusted party sends $\{m_{i_1'}',\cdots,m_{i_k'}'\}$ to Party 2 and halts.
- An honest party always outputs the message it has obtained from the trusted party. A malicious party may output an arbitrary function of its initial input and the message obtained from the trusted party.

By f we denote the oblivious set transfer functionality and let $\overline{M}=(M_1,M_2)$ be a pair of non-uniform probabilistic expected polynomial-time machines which is admissible. Then the joint execution of f under $\overline{M}$ in the ideal world model, denoted by $\text{IDEAL}_{f,\overline{M}}(\overline{m}, S)$, is defined as the output pair of M_1 and M_2 from the above ideal execution.

Definition 1. *Let f denote the functionality of oblivious set transfer protocol and let π be a two-party protocol. Protocol π is said to be a secure oblivious set transfer protocol if for every pair of admissible non-uniform probabilistic polynomial-time machines $\overline{A}=(A_1, A_2)$ for the real world model, there exists a pair of admissible non-uniform probabilistic expected polynomial-time time machines $\overline{B}=(B_1, B_2)$ for the ideal world, such that for every n-tuple message $\overline{m}=(m_1, \cdots, m_n)$ of the same length, and for every indices subset $S=\{i_1, \cdots, i_k\}$, where $k \leq n$, $\text{IDEAL}_{f,\overline{B}}(l, \overline{m}, S) \approx \text{REAL}_{l,\pi,\overline{M}}(\overline{m}, S)$, where l is a security parameter.*

3 Building Blocks

3.1 Paillier's Additively Homomorphic Encryptions

Paillier investigated a novel computational problem called the composite residuosity class problem (CRS), and its applications to public key cryptography in [16].

Decisional composite residuosity class problems: Let $N = pq$, where p and q are two large safe prime numbers. A number z is said to be a N-th residue modulo N^2, if there exists a number $y \in Z^*_{N^2}$ such that $z = y^N \mod N^2$. The decisional composite residuosity class problem states the following thing: given $z \in_r Z^*_{N^2}$ deciding whether z is N-th residue or non N-th residue. The decisional composite residuosity class assumption means that there exists no polynomial time distinguisher for N-th residues modulo N^2.

Paillier's encryption scheme: the public key is a k-bit RSA modulus $N=pq$, where p, q are two large safe primes with length k. The plain-text space is Z_N and the cipher-text space is $Z^*_{N^2}$. To encrypt a message $m \in Z_N$, one chooses $r \in Z^*_N$ uniformly at random and computes the cipher-text as $E_{PK}(m, r) = g^m r^N \mod N^2$, where $g = (1 + N)$ has order N in $Z^*_{N^2}$. The private key is (p, q). It is straightforward to verify that given $c = (1 + N)^m r^N \mod N^2$, and the trapdoor information (p, q), one can first compute $c_1 = c \mod N$, and then compute r from the equation $r = c_1^{N^{-1} \mod \phi(N)} \mod N$; Finally, one can compute m from the equation $cr^{-N} \mod N^2 = 1 + mN$. The encryption function is homomorphic, i.e., $E_{PK}(m_1, r_1) \times E_{PK}(m_2, r_2) \mod N^2 = E_{PK}(m_1 + m_2 \mod N, r_1 \times r_2 \mod N)$. Paillier's scheme is semantically secure if the decisional composite residuosity class problem is hard.

3.2 Perfectly Hiding Commitment Schemes and Perfectly Binding Commitment Schemes

Loosely speaking, a commitment is an efficient two-phase two-party protocol through which one party, called the sender, can commit itself to a value so the following two conflicting requirements are satisfied:

- Secrecy (hiding): at the end of commit phase, the other party, called the receiver, does not gain any computational knowledge of the sender's value. This requirement has to be satisfied even if the receiver tries to cheat;
- Non-ambiguity (binding): given a transcript of the interaction in the commit phase, there exists at most one value which the receiver may accept as a legal opening of the commitment. This requirement has to be satisfied even if the sender tires to cheat.

Definition 2. *A perfectly hiding (and computationally binding/computationally non-ambiguity) commitment scheme is a triple of efficient algorithms (KG, COM, VER) satisfying the following properties:*

- *Correctness: for all security parameter k and input α,*

$$Prob[pk \leftarrow KG(1^k), (c, d) \leftarrow COM(pk, \alpha) : VER(pk, \alpha, c, d) = TRUE] = 1$$

- *Perfectly hiding: for all k, and all inputs α and β the following distributions are identical:*

$$< pk \leftarrow KG(1^k); (c, d) \leftarrow COM(pk, \alpha) : (pk, c) >$$

and

$$< pk \leftarrow KG(1^k); (c, d) \leftarrow COM(pk, \beta) : (pk, c) >$$

- *Computationally binding/computationally non-ambiguity: for all k, and for any probabilistic polynomial time cheating sender C^*:*

$$Prob[pk \leftarrow KG(1^k), (c, d_1, d_2, \alpha_1, \alpha_2) \leftarrow C^* :$$

$$VER(pk, c, d_1, \alpha_1) = VER(pk, c, d_2, \alpha_2) = TRUE \wedge \alpha_1 \neq \alpha_2] < v(k)$$

where $v(k)$ is a negligible function.

Remark 1. Pedersen's commitment scheme [15] is a perfectly hiding (and computationally binding/computationally non-ambiguity) protocol.

Definition 3. *A perfectly binding/perfectly non-ambiguity (and computationally hiding) commitment scheme is a triple of efficient algorithms (KG, COM, VER) satisfying the following properties:*

- *Correctness: for all security parameter k and input α and ,*

$$Prob[pk \leftarrow KG(1^k), (c, d) \leftarrow COM(pk, \alpha) : VER(pk, \alpha, c, d) = TRUE] = 1$$

- *Computationally hiding: for all k, and all inputs α and β the following distributions are computationally indistinguishable:*

$$< pk \leftarrow KG(1^k); (c, d) \leftarrow COM(pk, \alpha) : (pk, c) >$$

and

$$< pk \leftarrow KG(1^k); (c, d) \leftarrow COM(pk, \beta) : (pk, c) >$$

– *Perfectly binding/non-ambiguity: for all k, and for any C^*:*

$$Prob[pk \leftarrow KG(1^k), (c, d_1, d_2, \alpha_1, \alpha_2) \leftarrow C^* :$$

$$VER(pk, c, d_1, \alpha_1) = VER(pk, c, d_2, \alpha_2) = TRUE \wedge \alpha_1 \neq \alpha_2] = 0$$

Remark 2. Paillier's public-key encryption scheme is an example of perfectly binding/non-ambiguity (and computationally hiding) commitment scheme.

4 Oblivious Set Transfer

4.1 Description of Oblivious Set Transfer Protocol

Common reference string: The sender, Party 1 has an instance of Paillier's encryption scheme denoted by (pk, sk), Party 2, a receiver obtains pk (including the description of encryption algorithm E and the description algorithm D) but knows nothing about sk at all.

Both parties also have a description of the specified common reference string: a description of perfectly hiding and computationally binding commitment (COM_h) and a description of a perfectly binding and computationally hiding commitment (COM_b). The description of COM_h is denoted by m_H; The description of COM_h is denoted by m_B.

Input: The sender has an input pair $\overline{m} = (m_0, \cdots, m_{n-1})$ with $m_i \in \{0, 1\}^\iota$, and the receiver has an input $S = \{\sigma_1, \cdots, \sigma_k\} \subseteq \{0, \cdots, n-1\}$, where $0 \leq \sigma_i \leq n-1$.

The protocol

– Step 1: For $i=0$ to $n-1$, the sender computes $c_i = E(m_i, r_{m_i})$, where E is Paillier's encryption algorithm.

   Let L be an upper bound of m_i $(0 \leq i \leq n-1)$ such that $m_0 L^0 + m_1 L + \cdots + m_{n-1} L^{n-1} < N$ (this assumption can be relaxed if Damgård-Jurik encryption scheme is applied [5]).

   By m_L, we denote $m_0 L^0 + m_1 L + \cdots + m_{n-1} L^{n-1}$. Obviously, given m_L, $(m_0, \cdots, m_{n-1})$ can be uniquely retrieved.

– Step 2: For $j=1$ to t where $t = \binom{n}{k}$, the receiver computes $K_1, \cdots, K_t$, where $K_j = E(m_{j_1})^{L^{j_1}} \cdots E(m_{j_k})^{L^{j_k}}$. The receiver further performs the following computations, where s is a security parameter:

   (2.1) for $j=1$ to t

   (2.2) for $i = 1$ to s,

   (2.3) chooses $(\alpha_j^i, \beta_j^i) \in_R Z_N^* \times Z_N^*$,

   (2.4) computes $K_j^{\alpha_j^i} E(1)^{\beta_j^i}$. By $L(i, j)$, we denote $K_j^{\alpha_j^i} E(1)^{\beta_j^i}$;

   (2.5) commits $L(i, j)$ using the perfectly hiding and computationally binding commitment (COM_h) which is denoted by $COM_h(L(i, j))$

   (2.6) finally, the receiver **randomly reorders all computed commitments** $(COM_h(L(i, j)), 0 \leq i \leq s, 0 \leq j \leq t)$ to get a random commitment-table:

$$\begin{pmatrix} c_{1,1} & \cdots & c_{1,t} \\ \cdots & \cdots & \cdots \\ c_{s,1} & \cdots & c_{s,t} \end{pmatrix}$$

- Step 3: Coin tossing:

  (3.1) the sender P_1 chooses a random $R_1 \in_R \{0,1\}^{st}$ and sends $\text{COM}_h(R_1)$ to P_2;

  (3.2) the receiver P_2 chooses a random $R_2 \in_R \{0,1\}^{st}$ and sends $\text{COM}_b(R_2)$ to P_1;

  (3.3) P_1 sends the de-commitment of $\text{COM}_h(R_1)$ to P_2;

  (3.4) P_2 sends the de-commitment of $\text{COM}_b(R_2)$ to P_1;

  (3.5) P_1 and P_2 set $r = R_1 \oplus R_2$. Denote $r = (r_{1,1}, \cdots, r_{1,t}), \cdots, (r_{s,1}, \cdots, r_{s,t})$.

- Step 4: If all commitments of the chooser's indies are located at $r_{i,j} = 1$, then P_2 outputs $\perp$, otherwise, it continues the following process (notice that the probability that P_2 outputs $\perp$ is $(1/2)^s$ that is negligible in the function of the security parameter s). That is, for every $1 \leq i \leq s$ and $1 \leq j \leq t$ for which $r_{i,j} = 1$, P_2 sends the de-commitment of $c_{i,j}$. Namely, if $c_{i,j} = \text{COM}_h(L(i',j'))$, then P_2 sends the following strings to P_1

  (4.1) $L(i',j')$ and its random string $l_{i',j'}$ used to generate $c_{i,j}$;

  (4.2) $K_{j'}$ and $(\alpha_{j'}^{i'}, \beta_{j'}^{i'})$;

  (4.3) $(c_{j'_1}, L^{j'_1}), \cdots, (c_{j'_k}, L^{j'_k})$;

- Step 5: P_1 tests the validity of the following equations

  (5.1) $(L(i',j'), l_{i',j'})$ is a valid de-commitment to $c_{i,j}$;

  (5.2) $L(i',j') = K_{j'}^{\alpha_{j'}^{i'}} E(1)^{\beta_{j'}^{i'}}$;

  (5.3) $K_{j'} = c_{j'_1}^{L^{j'_1}} \cdots c_{j'_k}^{L^{j'_k}}$.

  If any of the checks fails, P_1 halts and outputs $\perp$. Otherwise, P_1 continues the following process with P_2.

- Step 6: P_2 chooses (i'^*, j'^*) such that $r_{i'^*, j'^*} = 0$ and $L_{(i^*, j^*)}$ be an randomized encryption of L-adic of P_2's indices with auxiliary strings $\alpha_{j^*}^{i^*}$ and $\beta_{j^*}^{i^*}$. P_2 now sends a de-commitment of $c_{i'^*, j'^*}$ to P_1 (i.e., sends $L(i^*, j^*)$ to P_1 such that $\text{COM}_h(L(i^*, j^*), l_{i^*, j^*}) = c_{i'^*, j'^*}$.

- Step 7: P_1 checks the validity of the de-commitment. P_1 sends the decryption of $L(i^*, j^*)$ to P_2 if the de-commitment is correct, otherwise output $\perp$;

- Step 8: P_2 recovers $(m_{\sigma_1}, \cdots, m_{\sigma_k})$ from the plain-text $[(m_{\sigma_1}L^{\sigma_1} + \cdots + m_{\sigma_k}L^{\sigma_k}) \times \alpha_{j^*}^{i^*} + \beta_{j^*}^{i^*}] \bmod N$ with auxiliary strings $\alpha_{j^*}^{i^*}$ and $\beta_{j^*}^{i^*}$.

In case that P_1 and P_2 are honest participants, then one can verify that the scheme works with overwhelming probability $1-(1/2)^s$.

4.2 The Proof of Security

Expected polynomial-time simulator for coin-tossing protocol: we first show that the coin-tossing protocol employed in the oblivious set transfer protocol is simulatable in the expected polynomial time. If we are able to show the existence of such simulator, then we are able to extract a malicious party's input to the trusted party within expected polynomial-time and thus we are able to show that our protocol is secure in the real/ideal world simulation paradigm.

Coin-tossing protocol

Common Input: A perfectly hiding and computationally binding commitment (COM$_h$). The description of COM$_h$ is denoted by m_h; A perfectly binding and computationally hiding commitment (COM$_b$). The description of COM$_h$ is denoted by m_b;

Auxiliary Input to two parties: Auxiliary input to one party Alice (A) is r_A, and auxiliary input to another party Bob (B) is r_B.

On input $inp_A = (m_h, m_b, r_A)$ and input $inp_B = (m_h, m_b, r_B)$, A and B proceed the following steps:

- A sends $c_A = \text{COM}_h(s_A, r_{s_A})$ to B;
- B sends $c_B = \text{COM}_b(s_B, r_{s_B})$ to B;
- A sends the de-commitment (s_A, r_{s_A}) of c_A to B;
- B sends the de-commitment (s_B, r_{s_B}) of c_B to A;
- shared coin toss is $s_A \oplus s_B$ which is denoted by s (i.e, $s = s_A \oplus s_B$).

If A is corrupted, then we will show that there exists an expected polynomial-time simulator sim_A. The simulator starts by selecting and fixing a random type r_A and m_h and then feeds (r_A, m_h) to sim_A. The simulator sim_A proceeds in two steps:

- (S1) Extracting committed value: The simulator generates c_A and sends it to B; The simulator then generates a random commitment to a dummy value c'_B (say a commitment to 1) and feeds it to A. In case A replies by revealing correctly de-commitment, denoted by (s_A, r_{s_A}), the simulator records the value and proceeds the next step; In case the reply of A is not a valid revealing of the commitment c_A, the simulator halts and outputs current view of A.
- (S2) Generating real commitment: Let (s_A, r_{s_A}) denotes de-commitment recorded in Step (S1). The simulator now rewinds A from scratch with the same random type r_A and the same message m_h and generates c_B $= \text{COM}_h(s_B, r_{s_B})$ such that $s = s_A \oplus s_B$, where s is a random string. The simulator feeds c_B and (s_B, r_{s_B}) to A.

Let $q(k)$ denote the probability that program A, on input m_h, m_b and r_A, correctly reveals the commitment made in Step(S1) after receiving random commitment to a dummy value; Let $p(k)$ denote the probability that program A, on input m_h, m_b and r_A, correctly reveals the commitment made in Step(S1) after receiving a genuine commitment; We stress that the difference between $q(k)$ and $p(k)$ is negligible, otherwise one can derives contradiction to the computational secrecy of A. It follows that the expected number of times that Step(S2) is invoked when running simulator is $q(k) \times 1/p(k)$. Unfortunately, even though, $p(k)$ and $q(k)$ are at most polynomially far away from each, the value $q(k) \times 1/p(k)$ may not necessary be polynomial. Thus, the expected running-time of sim_A is not necessary polynomial. We now make use of well studied technique (say, [4], [8] and [7]) to solve this problem.

A modified simulator $\widetilde{sim}_A$.

- (S1) Extracting committed value: The simulator then generates a random commitment to a dummy value c'_B and feeds it to A. The simulator generates c_A and sends it to B; In case A replies by revealing correctly de-commitment, denoted by (s_A, r_{s_A}), the simulator records the value and proceeds the next step; In case the reply of A is not a valid revealing of the commitment c_A, the simulator halts and outputs current view of A.
- (S1.5) Approximating $q(k)$: If the simulator does not halt in Step(S1) then the simulator needs to approximate $q(k)$ so that an expected polynomial-time simulator can be constructed. Let $n(k)$ be a polynomial, and let X_i be a random variable such that $X_i = 1$ if the i-th revealed commitment is correct, and $X_i = 0$, otherwise. Running Step(S1) $n(k)$ times. The output of $n(k)$ repeatedly sampling is $\frac{\sum_{i=1}^{n(k)} X_i}{n(k)}$ which is denoted by $\widetilde{q}(k)$.
- (S2) Generating real commitment: Repeat the performance of Step(S2) $\frac{t(k)}{\widetilde{q}(k)}$ times. If none of these executions yield a correct reveal of A, the simulator outputs a special symbol indicating time-out; If A ever reveals a correct opening of the commitment that is different from the one recorded in Step(S1), the simulator halts outputting a special symbol indicating ambiguity.

This ends the description of $\widetilde{sim}_A$. One can easily verified that the modified simulator has expected running time bounded by $\widetilde{q}(k) \times \frac{t(k)}{\widetilde{q}(k)} = t(k)$. Furthermore, $\widetilde{sim}_A$ has the following nice features as well.

Lemma 1. $\widetilde{q}(k)$ is within a constant factor of $q(k)$ with overwhelmingly high probability

Proof. Let X_i be a random variable such that $X_i = 1$ if the i-th revealed commitment is correct, and $X_i = 0$, otherwise. By applying Chernoff bound, we know that

$$Prob(|\frac{\sum_{i=1}^{n(k)} X_i}{n(k)} - q(k)| > \delta) < 2e^{-n\frac{\delta^2}{2p(1-p)}} \le 2e^{-n\frac{\delta^2}{4}}$$

It follows that $\widetilde{q}(k)$ is within a constant factor of $q(k)$ with overwhelmingly high probability $1 - e^{-n\frac{\delta^2}{4}}$, where δ is any constant smaller than $q(1 - q)$.

Lemma 2. *The probability that the event time-out happens is negligible.*

Proof. Let $u(k)$ be the probability that $\widetilde{sim}_A$ outputs a special time-out symbol. Then,

$$u(k) = Prob(\frac{q(k)}{\widetilde{q}(k)} = \Theta(1))(1 - p(k))^{\frac{t(k)}{\widetilde{q}(k)}} + Prob(\frac{q(k)}{\widetilde{q}(k)} \neq \Theta(1))(1 - p(k))^{\frac{t(k)}{\widetilde{q}(k)}}$$

$$< q(k)(1 - p(k))^{\frac{t(k)}{q(k)}} + 2e^{-n\frac{\delta^2}{4}}$$

Since the difference between $p(k)$ and $q(k)$ are negligible, by applying the standard truncated technique, we know that $u(k)$ is negligible in k.

Lemma 3. *The probability that the event ambiguity happens is negligible.*

Proof. Let $v(k)$ be the probability that $\widetilde{sim}_A$ outputs a special ambiguity symbol. Assume by the contradiction that the ambiguity symbol is output with probability at least $Q(k)$ for a polynomial $Q(\cdot)$, and an infinite sequence of committed values. By running Step(S2) more than $2t(k)Q(k)$, it follows that $\widetilde{sim}_A$ outputs an ambiguity symbol with probability at least $\frac{1}{2Q(k)}$. As a result, when $\widetilde{sim}_A$ invokes A at the moment then the event ambiguity happens with the probability at least $\frac{1}{2Q(k)}$. This contradicts the assumption of non-ambiguity of B's commitment scheme.

Combining the above lemmas, we have the following statement immediately. That is,

Corollary 1. *The output distribution of simulator $\widetilde{sim}_A$ differs from the output distribution of simulator sim_A is at most negligible.*

Proof. Notice that the output distribution of simulator $\widetilde{sim}_A$ differs from the output distribution of simulator sim_A in two types of executions: time-out and ambiguity. Due to the above lemmas, we know that the output distribution of simulator $\widetilde{sim}_A$ differs from the output distribution of simulator sim_A is at most negligible.

Lemma 4. *Assuming that COM_h is a perfect hiding and computational binding commitment and COM_b is a perfectly binding and computationally hiding commitment, then the shared coin tossing protocol is secure against malicious adversary A. Furthermore, the simulator sim_A runs in expected polynomial time.*

Proof. According to the description of simulator, one can verify that the modified simulator has expected running time bounded by $\widetilde{q}(k) \times \frac{t(k)}{\widetilde{q}(k)} = t(k)$. The rest of this work is to show the view of A is computationally indistinguishable from that generated by sim_A. Since the simulator then generates a random commitment to a dummy value c'_B (say a commitment to 1) and feeds it to A, and the commitment that generates the dummy value is perfectly biding and computationally hiding, it follows that the view of A is computationally indistinguishable from that generated by sim_A.

Using the same technique, we can show that

Lemma 5. *Assuming that COM_h is a perfect hiding and computational binding commitment and COM_b is a perfectly binding and computationally hiding commitment, then the shared coin tossing protocol is secure against malicious adversary B. Furthermore, the simulator sim_B runs in expected polynomial time.*

Expected polynomial time simulator for oblivious set transfer protocol: We now show that the proposed scheme is fully simulatable in the real/ideal world paradigm by considering the following two cases:

Case 1 – P_1 is corrupted. Let A_1 be a non-uniform probabilistic polynomial time real adversary that controls P_1. We construct a non-uniform probabilistic expected polynomial time ideal model adversary/simulator S_1. The task of S_1 now is to extract the input messages that P_1 hands to the trusted party with the help of auxiliary information of (pk, sk) of Paillier's encryption scheme.

- S_1 chooses $r \in \{0,1\}^{st}$ uniformly at random;
- S_1 receives $(c_0, \cdots, c_{n-1})$ from A_1, generates $K_1, \cdots, K_t$ and constructs a garble table according to Step 2;
- S_1 receives a commitment c_h from A_2, chooses $R_2 \in \{0,1\}^{st}$ uniformly at random and sends $c_b = \mathrm{COM}_b(R_2)$ to A_1. If A_1 does not send a valid de-commitment to c_h, then S_1 simulates P_2 aborting. Otherwise, if A_1 sends a valid de-commitment to c_h, S_1 sets $R_2' = R_1 \oplus r$, rewinds A_1 and hands c_b' $=\mathrm{COM}_b(R_2')$;
- For every $1 \leq i \leq s$ and $1 \leq j \leq t$ for which $r_{i,j} = 1$, S_1 sends the decommitments according to Step 4 in the protocol; Namely, if $c_{i,j} = \mathrm{COM}_h(L(i',j'))$, then P_2 sends the following strings to P_1
  $L(i',j')$ and its random string $l_{i',j'}$ used to generate $c_{i,j}$;
  $K_{j'}$ and $(\alpha_{j'}^{i'}, \beta_{j'}^{i'})$;
  $(c_{j_1'}, L^{j_1'}), \cdots, (c_{j_k'}, L^{j_k'})$;
- A_1 tests the validity of the received strings, according to Step 5, namely
  $(L(i',j'), l_{i',j'})$ is a valid de-commitment to $c_{i,j}$;
  $L(i',j') = K_{j'}^{\alpha_{j'}^{i'}} E(1)^{\beta_{j'}^{i'}}$;
  $K_{j'} = c_{j_1'}^{L^{j_1'}} \cdots c_{j_k'}^{L^{j_k'}}$.
- S_1 receives a de-commitment $L(i^*, j^*)$ and obtains $m_{j_1^*}, \cdots, m_{j_k^*}$ according to Step 7.
- The output of S_1 is $m_{j_1^*}, \cdots, m_{j_k^*}$.

The simulator now runs the above procedure $(n - k)$ times (again the running time is within expected polynomial time), it follows that S_1 is able to extract all messages $\{m_0, \cdots, m_{n-1}\}$ with overwhelming probability. Given $\{m_0, \cdots, m_{n-1}\}$, S_1 runs with the honest party P_2 by simply handing the input messages to the trusted party (the input of P_2 is chosen uniformly at random by the trusted third party on behalf of P_2). As a result, the view of simulation when S_1 runs with P_2 in the ideal world is computationally indistinguishable from the view of real oblivious set transfer protocol when A_1 runs with P_2 in the real world.

Case 2 – P_2 is corrupted. Let A_2 be a non-uniform probabilistic polynomial time real adversary that controls P_2. We construct a non-uniform probabilistic expected polynomial time ideal model adversary/simulator S_2. The task of S_2 now is to extract the input set that P_2 hands to the trusted party with the help of auxiliary information of (pk, sk) of Paillier's encryption scheme.

Step S1: S_2 generates n dummy encryptions $c_0, \cdots, c_{n-1}$ and sends these dummy encryptions to A_2;
Step S2: S_2 is given a garble table

$$\begin{pmatrix} c_{1,1} \cdots c_{1,t} \\ \cdots \cdots \cdots \\ c_{s,1} \cdots c_{s,t} \end{pmatrix}$$

Step S3: S_2 runs coin-tossing protocol with A_2, the resulting shared string is denoted by $r = (r_{1,1}, \cdots, r_{1,t}), \cdots, (r_{s,1}, \cdots, r_{s,t})$;

Step S4: For every $1 \le i \le s$ and $1 \le j \le t$ for which $r_{i,j} = 1$, S_2 receives the de-commitment $c_{i,j}$; Namely, if $c_{i,j} = \mathrm{COM}_h(L(i', j'))$, then S_2 receives the following strings:

- $L(i', j')$ and its random string $l_{i',j'}$ used to generate $c_{i,j}$;
- $K_{j'}$ and $(\alpha_{j'}^{i'}, \beta_{j'}^{i'})$;
- $(c_{j_1'}, L^{j_1'}), \cdots, (c_{j_k'}, L^{j_k'})$;

S_2 tests the validity of the received strings, according to Step 5, namely

- $(L(i', j'), l_{i',j'})$ is a valid de-commitment to $c_{i,j}$;
- $L(i', j') = K_{j'}{}^{\alpha_{j'}^{i'}} E(1)^{\beta_{j'}^{i'}}$;
- $K_{j'} = c_{j_1'}{}^{L^{j_1'}} \cdots c_{j_k'}{}^{L^{j_k'}}$.

Step S5: S_2 receives a query message (i^*, j^*) such that $r_{i^*,j^*} = 0$ and the de-commitment of c_{i^*,j^*} (i.e., S_2 also receives $L(i^*, j^*)$ and its random string used to commit c_{i^*,j^*}).

Step S6: S_2 now rewinds A_2 at the Step S3 by running the coin-tossing protocol with A_2. The resulted string is denoted by $r' = (r'_{1,1}, \cdots, r'_{1,t}), \cdots, (r'_{s,1}, \cdots, r'_{s,t})$.

The existence of two random strings such $r_{i^*,j^*} = 0$ but $r'_{i^*,j^*} = 1$ is guaranteed since S_2 can rewind the simulator of the coin-tossing protocol and the running time of such a simulator is within expected polynomial time. It follows that the simulator S_2 obtains the input message $\sigma = \pi_i(j)_1, \cdots, \pi_i(j)_k$ of A_2 within expected polynomial time. Given σ, S_2 runs with the honest party P_1 by simply handing the input messages to the trusted party (the input of P_1 is chosen uniformly at random by the trusted third party on behalf of P_1). As a result, the view of simulation when S_2 runs with P_1 in the ideal world is computationally indistinguishable from the view of real oblivious set transfer protocol when A_2 runs with P_1 in the real world.

Combining the above results, we have the following main statement immediately

Theorem 1. *Assuming that Paillier's encryption scheme is semantically secure and assuming that COM_h is a perfectly hiding commitment and COM_b is a perfectly binding commitment. Then the oblivious set transfer protocol described above is secure in the full simulation model.*

5   Conclusion

We have introduced and formalized the notion of oblivious set transfer, an nat-ural extension of the notion of oblivious bit transfer and the notion of oblivious string transfer. The security of oblivious set transfer is defined in the real/ideal world simulation paradigm. We have proposed an feasible implementation of oblivious set transfer protocol in the presence of malicious adversaries in the simulation paradigm.

References

1. Aiello, W., Ishai, Y., Reingold, O.: Priced Oblivious Transfer: How to Sell Digital Goods. In: Pfitzmann, B. (ed.) EUROCRYPT 2001. LNCS, vol. 2045, pp. 119–135. Springer, Heidelberg (2001)
2. Brassard, G., Crépeau, C., Robert, J.-M.: All-or-Nothing Disclosure of Secrets. In: Odlyzko, A.M. (ed.) CRYPTO 1986. LNCS, vol. 263, pp. 234–238. Springer, Heidelberg (1987)
3. Camenisch, J., Neven, G., Shelat, A.: Simulatable Adaptive Oblivious Transfer. In: Naor, M. (ed.) EUROCRYPT 2007. LNCS, vol. 4515, pp. 573–590. Springer, Heidelberg (2007)
4. Canetti, R., Even, G., Goldreich, O.: Lower Bounds for Sampling Algorithms for Estimating the Average. Inf. Process. Lett. 53(1), 17–25 (1995)
5. Damgård, I., Jurik, M.: A Generalisation, a Simplification and Some Applications of Paillier's Probabilistic Public-Key System. In: Proceedings of the 4th International Workshop on Practice and Theory in Public Key Cryptography, pp. 119–136 (2001)
6. Even, S., Goldreich, O., Lempel, A.: A Randomized Protocol for Signing Contracts. Commun. ACM 28(6), 637–647 (1985)
7. Decatur, S.E., Goldreich, O., Ron, D.: Computational Sample Complexity. SIAM J. Comput. 29(3), 854–879 (1999)
8. Goldreich, O., Kahan, A.: How to Construct Constant-Round Zero-Knowledge Proof Systems for NP. J. Cryptology 9(3), 167–190 (1996)
9. Goldreich, O., Micali, S., Wigderson, A.: How to Play any Mental Game or A Completeness Theorem for Protocols with Honest Majority STOC, pp. 218–229 (1987)
10. Green,, Hohenberger,: Green and Hohenberger: Blind identity-based encryption and simulatable oblivious transfer. In: Kurosawa, K. (ed.) ASIACRYPT 2007. LNCS, vol. 4833, pp. 265–282. Springer, Heidelberg (2007)
11. Goldreich, O., Micali, S., Wigderson, A.: How to Play any Mental Game or A Completeness Theorem for Protocols with Honest Majority STOC 1987, pp. 218–229 (1987)
12. Kushilevitz, E., Ostrovsky, R.: Replication is NOT Needed: SINGLE Database, Computationally-Private Information Retrieval. In: FOCS 1997, pp. 364–373 (1997)
13. Lindell, Y.: Efficient Fully-Simulatable Oblivious Transfer. In: CTRSA 2008 (2008)
14. Naor, M., Pinkas, B.: Computationally Secure Oblivious Transfer. J. Cryptology 18(1), 1–35 (2005)
15. Pedersen, T.P.: Non-Interactive and Information-Theoretic Secure Verifiable Secret Sharing. In: Feigenbaum, J. (ed.) CRYPTO 1991. LNCS, vol. 576, pp. 129–140. Springer, Heidelberg (1992)
16. Paillier, P.: Public-Key Cryptosystems Based on Composite Degree Residuosity Classes. In: Stern, J. (ed.) EUROCRYPT 1999. LNCS, vol. 1592, pp. 223–238. Springer, Heidelberg (1999)
17. Rabin, M.O.: How to exchange secrets by oblivious transfer. Technical Report TR-81, Aiken Computation Laboratory, Harvard University (1981)
18. A.C.-C. Yao.: Protocols for Secure Computations (Extended Abstract). In: FOCS 1982, pp. 160-164 (1982)

Efficient Disjointness Tests for Private Datasets

Qingsong Ye[1], Huaxiong Wang[1,2], Josef Pieprzyk[1], and Xian-Mo Zhang[1]

[1] Centre for Advanced Computing – Algorithms and Cryptography
Department of Computing, Macquarie University, NSW 2109, Australia
{qingsong,hwang,josef,xianmo}@ics.mq.edu.au
[2] Division of Mathematical Sciences
School of Physical and Mathematical Sciences
Nanyang Technological University, Singapore

Abstract. We present efficient protocols for private set disjointness tests. We start from an intuition of our protocols that applies Sylvester matrices. Unfortunately, this simple construction is insecure as it reveals information about the cardinality of the intersection. More specifically, it discloses its lower bound. By using the Lagrange interpolation we provide a protocol for the honest-but-curious case without revealing any additional information. Finally, we describe a protocol that is secure against malicious adversaries. The protocol applies a verification test to detect misbehaving participants. Both protocols require $O(1)$ rounds of communication. Our protocols are more efficient than the previous protocols in terms of communication and computation overhead. Unlike previous protocols whose security relies on computational assumptions, our protocols provide information theoretic security. To our knowledge, our protocols are first ones that have been designed without a generic secure function evaluation. More importantly, they are the most efficient protocols for private disjointness tests for the malicious adversary case.

Keywords: Private Set Disjointness, Private Matching, Secure Multi-Party Computation.

1 Introduction

Suppose two parties, Alice and Bob, each has a private dataset of some items denoted by A and B, respectively. Alice wishes to learn whether these two sets are disjoint, that is, whether $A \cap B = \emptyset$ or not. In doing so, Alice does not want to reveal any information about her set A to Bob, who, in turn, does not wish to reveal any information about his set B, other than whether $A \cap B = \emptyset$ or not. This is called a *private disjointness test* [1].

A private disjointness test is a useful primitive in various online service applications. For example, Bob is a club owner offering a special-status membership called "Super Fun" and Alice would like to know whether she is eligible for membership. Alice has a smart card issued by the state authority containing her resident address, her age band (assuming that 0 for age $0-9$, 1 for the age $11-19$, 2 for the age $20-29$ and so on), her membership status, etc. Bob determines whether Alice is eligible for the special-status membership based on Alice's attribute information. For example, Bob may require that at least one of the following three conditions holds: (1) Alice lives in the same suburb as Bob; (2) Alice's age band is 5; (3) Alice is the member of Good Credit Union.

Y. Mu, W. Susilo, and J. Seberry (Eds.): ACISP 2008, LNCS 5107, pp. 155–169, 2008.

Bob considers the detail of his policy to be commercial secret and does not want to reveal it to others. Alice is interested in this membership and would like to go forward; however, she wants to reveal as little information about her as possible. On the other hand, Bob wants Alice to know only whether she is eligible for the membership, but nothing else.

There are several protocols to tackle this problem, such as Freedman, Nissim and Pinkas (FNP) [2], Hohenberger and Weis (HW) [3] and Kiayias and Mitrofanova (KM) [1]. The KM protocols have either high round complexity or high communication complexity, while the FNP and HW protocols leak the information about the intersection cardinality. Moreover, both FNP and KM protocols require random oracles and costly sub-protocols that have to be secure in the presence of a malicious adversaries. The HW protocol only considers the malicious Bob and assumes the honest Alice in order to make the protocol efficient. This paper provides efficient protocols for private disjointness tests. The protocols are unconditionally secure against malicious adversaries.

Related Work. Freedman, Nissim and Pinkas (FNP) [2] proposed a protocol for the private computation of set disjointness. The protocol is based on the representation of datasets as roots of a polynomial and applies oblivious polynomial evaluation techniques [4]. The protocol simply lets Alice represent her dataset $A = \{a_1, \ldots, a_m\}$ over a field as a polynomial $\mathcal{F}(y) = \prod_{a_i \in A} (y - a_i) = \sum_{i=0}^{m} \alpha_i y^i$ in that field. Alice then encrypts coefficients of $\mathcal{F}$ with a homomorphic cryptosystem such as Paillier's [5]. Thus, given encrypted coefficients of $\mathcal{F}$, Bob first evaluates $\mathcal{F}(b_i)$ for each elements $b_i \in B$, and then returns encrypted $\gamma \mathcal{F}(b_i)$ where γ is a random non-zero value picked by Bob. Note that any $b_i \in A$ if and only if $\mathcal{F}(b_i) = 0$, which not only indicates the disjointness status but also reveals the information of the intersection cardinality.

The FNP construction leads to a very efficient protocol assuming honest-but-curious adversaries. This construction heavily influences two other related works of Kiayias and Mitrofanova [1] and of Hohenberger and Weis [3]. To cope with malicious adversaries, the FNP protocol employs random oracle and invokes expensive sub-protocols.

Hohenberger and Weis [3] have taken a similar approach to the one given in [2] and designed a protocol using an oblivious polynomial evaluation. The security proof relies on the difficulty of discrete logarithm. Assume $\mathbb{G}$ is a group with the composite order $n = pq$ where $p < q$ are primes. Let g, u be random generators of $\mathbb{G}$ and $h = u^q$. As in the FNP protocol, Alice represents her dataset A by the polynomial $\mathcal{F}(y) = \sum_{i=0}^{|A|} \alpha_i y^i \in \mathbb{Z}_q[y]$, chooses a random polynomial $R(x) = \sum_{i=0}^{|A|} r_i x^i \in \mathbb{Z}_p[x]$ and publishes n and commitments of $\mathcal{F}(y)$, $g^{\alpha_i} h^{r_i}$ for $i \in [0, \ldots, |A|]$. For each $b_j \in B$ selected in random order, Bob obliviously evaluates $v_j = g^{\mathcal{F}(b_j)} h^{R(b_j)}$ and sends $w_j = v_j^{\gamma_j}$ to Alice, where γ_j is a non-zero value randomly picked from $\mathbb{Z}_n^*$. Note that if $b_j \in A$, then $g^{\gamma_j \mathcal{F}(b_j)}$ will have order p. Since h has order p, Alice concludes $A \cap B \neq \emptyset$ if $w_j^p = 1$ with overwhelming probability.

The protocol is efficient and secure without using the random oracle. The security, however, is proven under the assumption that Alice is honest (but Bob can be malicious). If both Alice and Bob are malicious, then the cost of the protocol is the same as in the FNP protocol. Moreover, their security properties are the same as of the FNP protocol and allow Alice to discover the intersection cardinality. In our membership example, if Alice knows the intersection cardinality, she may learn some extra information about Bob's business policy which is against Bob's will.

Kiayias and Mitrofanova [1] provided three protocols for private set disjointness tests. The first protocol assumed that the domain is relatively small, which is not relevant to our work. Our work is related to their second and third protocols, denoted by KM$-$2 and KM$-$3, respectively. KM$-$2 uses a new primitive called *superposed encryption* based on Pedersen commitments [6]. Superposed encryption is closely related to a homomorphic ElGamal variant first used in voting schemes by Cramer et.al. [7]. In the KM$-$2 protocol, Bob returns to Alice a single ciphertext of $\gamma |A \cap B|$, where γ is a random non-zero value. This protocol needs $|B|$ rounds of communication between two parties. The total communication cost is $|A| \cdot |B|$ if the adversary is honest but curious, but increases by a quadratic factor if either party behaves maliciously. To reduce the high round complexity in KM$-$2, the authors presented the KM$-$3 protocol that uses a multivariate polynomial so the task can be done in a single round. The price to be paid is a high communication cost $\Theta\left(\binom{|A| + |B|}{|B|}\right)$ for the honest-but-curious case. The disadvantage of those two protocols is obvious. It is unlikely for causal clients to use such online services which require either extensive network communication or numerous interactions.

Kissner and Song [8] presented FNP-inspired schemes for various private set operations such as set intersection, set union, threshold cardinality of the set intersection, and multiplicity tests. The problem of secure computation of the subset relation of two private datasets is a variant of the private set intersection problem where the intersection content is one party's whole dataset. This operation can be computed by extending the FNP protocol. The applications of the subset relation were discussed in [9, 10]. Protocols for private equality tests are a special case of the private disjointness tests, where each party has a single element in the dataset. These protocols were proposed in [11, 4, 12]. The distributed case of private equality tests and various private set operations were considered in [13, 14].

Secure determinant computation by multiple parties is discussed in [15]. The secure shares computation and distribution of a matrix are based on the Lagrange interpolation. Using similar technique, Mohassel and Franklin [16] proposed a multi-party computation protocol to securely test whether two shared polynomials are coprime. Their construction applies Sylvester matrices [17] construction.

Our Results: We present two disjointness test protocols. Each protocol takes $O(1)$ rounds. The second protocol that provides verifiability, is secure against malicious adversaries, and the parties learn nothing more than the desired result. In our construction, we build two polynomials g and h whose roots are representing the datasets A and B of the two parties, respectively. The polynomials are next used to form a Sylvester matrix. The determinant of the matrix tells us whether g and h share any root and therefore allows us to ascertain if the intersection of the datasets is empty or not.

We first give an intuition of our protocols that applies a Sylvester matrix directly. However, this simple construction is not secure as Alice can learn the intersection cardinality by computing the rank of the matrix. Note, this is allowed in [2, 3].

To reduce the amount of information leaking about the intersection of sets, we can modify the simple construction as the following. We let two parties cooperate to multiply the Sylvester matrix and its transpose. In such a way that Alice still knows whether the determinant of the related Sylvester matrix is zero. Consequently, this improved version reveals the lower bound of the intersection cardinality only.

To achieve no information leaks apart from the fact that whether $A \cap B = \emptyset$ or not, we utilize a secure determinant evaluation scheme in a multi-party computation setting developed by Cramer and Damgard [15]. In this protocol, Bob randomly picks $|A| + |B| + 1$ distinct indexes and forwards them to Alice along with the shares of his dataset. Alice then constructs the corresponding $|A| + |B| + 1$ shares of the masked Sylvester matrix associated with g and h. Using the Lagrange interpolation, Alice is able to test if the determinant of the masked Sylvester matrix is zero or not. This approach requires $O((|A| + |B|)^2)$ communication cost and $O((|A| + |B|)^{3.697})$ field operations.

We then further employ a verification test to detect misbehaving participants. The test is going to double the communication cost.

The advantage of our solution is that our protocols are conceptually simple. Comparing to the previous work, our protocols are very efficient. In particular, our solution can deal with malicious Bob and malicious Alice at same time. Unlike the previous solutions, our schemes provide unconditional security. Our approach is of a great advantage, where the communication facilities are in a short supply and consequently, protocols with small number of rounds are preferred. Our protocols do not leak any information apart from whether $A \cap B = \emptyset$ or not.

Our paper is organized as follows. In Section 2, we introduce the notations, Sylvester matriices and some techniques that will be used in this paper. In Section 3, we discuss the adversary model and define the problem in hand. A general description of a simple and insecure protocol that is based on Sylvester matrices is presented in Section 4. In Section 5, we show our main protocols for the private disjointness test of two datasets based on the Sylvester matrix construction and demonstrate its security. We also analyze the efficiency of our protocols in this section. Finally, we give concluding remarks in Section 6.

2 Preliminaries

Throughout this paper, let $GL_n(K) \subset K^{n,n}$ denote the group of $n \times n$ non-singular matrices over an arbitrary finite field K. We assume that the number of elements in the field $q = |K|$ is much larger than the dimension n.

2.1 Sylvester Matrix

Given two polynomials $g(x) = \sum_{i=0}^{m} \alpha_i x^i \in \mathbb{Z}_q[x]$ and $h(x) = \sum_{i=0}^{n} \beta_i x^i \in \mathbb{Z}_q[x]$ of degrees m and n, respectively. The Sylvester matrix S associated with g and h is then the $(m + n) \times (m + n)$ matrix obtained as follows:

- The first row is: $(\alpha_m, \alpha_{m-1}, \ldots, \alpha_0, 0, \ldots, 0)$.
- The next row is obtained from the previous one by shifting it one position (column) to the right and putting zero in the first position.

- This process is repeated $n - 2$ times.
- The $(n + 1)^{\text{th}}$ row is $(\beta_n, \beta_{n-1}, \ldots, \beta_0, 0, \ldots, 0)$.
- Next $m - 1$ rows are created in the same way as for the first row. The only difference is the number of rows.

For example, the Sylvester matrix S associated with g and h for $m = 4$ and $n = 3$ is:

$$S = \begin{pmatrix} \alpha_4 & \alpha_3 & \alpha_2 & \alpha_1 & \alpha_0 & 0 & 0 \\ 0 & \alpha_4 & \alpha_3 & \alpha_2 & \alpha_1 & \alpha_0 & 0 \\ 0 & 0 & \alpha_4 & \alpha_3 & \alpha_2 & \alpha_1 & \alpha_0 \\ \beta_3 & \beta_2 & \beta_1 & \beta_0 & 0 & 0 & 0 \\ 0 & \beta_3 & \beta_2 & \beta_1 & \beta_0 & 0 & 0 \\ 0 & 0 & \beta_3 & \beta_2 & \beta_1 & \beta_0 & 0 \\ 0 & 0 & 0 & \beta_3 & \beta_2 & \beta_1 & \beta_0 \end{pmatrix} .$$

Thus, the determinant of the associated Sylvester matrix is defined by the two associated polynomials g and h. Consequently, two polynomials do not share a common root if and only if the determinant of the Sylvester matrix is non-zero value. If the determinant of the Sylvester matrix is zero, then the rank of the Sylvester matrix determines the degree of the greatest common divisor of g and h. That is:

$$\deg(\gcd(g, h)) = m + n - \text{rank}(S).$$

2.2 Building Blocks

In general, any secret sharing scheme can be used in our protocol. Since there are only two parties involved in our protocol, we assume that (2-out-of-2)-Shamir secret sharing is used. The computations in this paper are carried out over a finite field K. The two parties are Alice and Bob. We frequently use the following building blocks from [18] and [15].

Secure Inversion of Shared Field Elements and Matrices is a protocol that accepts a list of shares of an invertible field element or matrix as its input and generates a list of shares of the inverse. We denote this secure computation of shares of the inverse by $[x^{-1}]_i = [x]_i^{-1}$, and $[M^{-1}]_i = [M]_i^{-1}$ respectively for an element x and a matrix M, where $[x^{-1}]_i$'s are shares of the inverse, $[x]_i^{-1}$'s are the inverse of shares, and $i \in \{A, B\}$ in our protocol. In our protocols, we slightly modify the original protocol to let only one party compute such inverses as the following.

Input: Shares $[x]_A, [x]_B$ of the element x.
Output: Shares $[x^{-1}]_A, [x^{-1}]_B$ of the inverse element x^{-1}.
Protocol:

1. Compute shares $[\rho]_A, [\rho]_B$ of an element $\rho \in K$ that is random and non-zero,
2. Compute $[\sigma]_A = [\rho]_A \cdot [x]_A$ and $[\sigma]_B = [\rho]_B \cdot [x]_B$,
3. Calculate σ from the shares $[\sigma]_A$ and $[\sigma]_B$,
4. Find $[x^{-1}]_A = \sigma^{-1} \cdot [\rho]_A$ and $[x^{-1}]_B = \sigma^{-1} \cdot [\rho]_B$.

Note that the other party i, who receives the pair $[x]_i$ and $[x^{-1}]_i$, cannot find any information about x. This is also true for the matrix M. For simplicity, we denote

$[\sigma]_i = [\rho]_i \cdot [x]_i$ in Step 2. Actually, the computation of $[\sigma]_i$ is not simple and we need to employ an appropriate sub-protocol such as the one presented in Section 1.1 of [18]. Although the secure computation of $[\sigma]_i$ is not required in this protocol, but it is necessary in the next protocols where the appropriate sub-protocol is applied. A constant-round sub-protocol between Alice and Bob might be also needed if a secure computation of $[\sigma]_i$ is expected.

Secure Multiplication of Shared Field Elements is a protocol that produces a share of the product of two shared field elements $[x \cdot y]_A, [x \cdot y]_B$ of x and y. The protocol can be successfully run if all shares are invertible. It proceeds according to the following steps:

Input: Alice and Bob hold their shares of two elements x and y, i.e. Alice has $[x]_A, [y]_A$ and Bob owns $[x]_B$ and $[y]_B$.

Output: Alice gets the shares $[x \cdot y]_A, [x \cdot y]_B$.

Protocol:

1. Alice
   (a) generates shares $[\rho_1]_A, [\rho_1]_B$ of ρ_1, and $[\rho_2]_A, [\rho_2]_B$ of ρ_2 independently at random from all non-zero values.
   (b) computes $[\sigma_1]_A = [x]_A \cdot [\rho_1]_A$, and $[\sigma_2]_A = [\rho_1]_A^{-1} \cdot [y]_A \cdot [\rho_2]_A$,
   (c) sends $[\rho_1]_B, [\rho_2]_B, [\rho_1]_B^{-1}, [\sigma_1]_A, [\sigma_2]_A$ to Bob.
2. Bob
   (a) computes $[\sigma_1]_B = [x]_B \cdot [\rho_1]_B$, and $[\sigma_2]_B = [\rho_1]_B^{-1} \cdot [y]_B \cdot [\rho_2]_B$,
   (b) constructs σ_1, σ_2 from computed shares,
   (c) sends $(\sigma_1 \cdot \sigma_2)$ to Alice.
3. Alice computes $[x \cdot y]_A = \sigma_1 \cdot \sigma_2 \cdot [\rho_2]_A^{-1}$ and $[x \cdot y]_B = \sigma_1 \cdot \sigma_2 \cdot [\rho_2]_B^{-1}$.

Note that only Alice could compute $[x \cdot y]_A$ and $[x \cdot y]_B$. Consequently, Alice learns the result of $x \cdot y$. This is allowed in our protocol. The security requirement of our protocol is that Alice learns $x \cdot y$ without knowing the value of x and/or y.

In general, if one of the inputs is zero, then Ben-Or and Cleve showed in [19] how to modify the protocol given above.

Secure Shared Matrix Multiplication is a protocol that securely generates shares $[M \cdot M']_A, [M \cdot M']_B$ for Alice and Bob respectively, from shares $[M]_A, [M]_B$ of a matrix M, and $[M']_A, [M']_B$ of M', where $[M]_A, [M']_A$ are held by Alice and $[M]_B, [M']_B$ are possessed by Bob. This protocol works in an obvious way following the previous *Secure Multiplication of Shared Field Elements* protocol.

Secure Determinant Evaluation *(SDE)* computes the determinant of a matrix $M \in K^{n,n}$ from a list of related non-singular matrices. Let $z_0, \ldots, z_n$ are distinct and random integers selected from K. We simplify the technique of secure determinant evaluation in the multiparty computation model introduced by Cramer and Damgard [15], and we use the following equation

$$\det(M) = (-1)^n \cdot \sum_{i=0}^{n} \left(\left(\prod_{\substack{0 \leq j \leq n \\ j \neq i}} \frac{z_j}{z_i - z_j} \right) \cdot \det(z_i I_{m+n} - M) \right),$$

where I_n denotes the $n \times n$ identity matrix. For each $z_i \in K$, it holds that $(z_i I_n - M) \in GL_n(K)$ if and only if z_i is not an eigenvalue of M. Since M has at most n eigenvalues, each matrix $z_i I_n - M$ is invertible, when z_i is randomly and independently chosen, except with the probability at most $\frac{n}{q}$.

3 Model and Definition

This section formally defines our verifiable disjointness test of two private datasets. Our construction can be described as follows. Let Alice $\mathcal{P}_A$ and Bob $\mathcal{P}_B$ be two probabilistic polynomial time interactive Turing machines. Let $A = \{a_1, \ldots, a_m\}$, $B = \{b_1, \ldots, b_n\}$ be datasets owned by $\mathcal{P}_A$ and $\mathcal{P}_B$, respectively. We assume that the set cardinalities $|A|$ and $|B|$ are not secret. The private disjointness test checks whether $A \cap B = \emptyset$ or not. For sets $A, B \subset K$, define the disjointness predicate $\mathcal{D}(A, B) = (A \cap B = \emptyset)$, that is, $\mathcal{D}(A, B)$ will have value 1 if and only if A and B are disjoint otherwise, the predicate is equal zero. The interaction between $\mathcal{P}_A$ and $\mathcal{P}_B$ yields a result that is known to $\mathcal{P}_A$ only.

In our model, an adversary can be misbehaving Bob, misbehaving Alice or both. In particular, we cannot hope to avoid parties that (i) refuse to participate in the protocol, (ii) substitute a correct input by an arbitrary value, and (iii) abort the protocol any time. In our work, we do not address these issues. The way that security is dealt in this case is by comparing the player's views with respect to an "ideal" protocol implementation, using a trusted third party. The reader is referred to [20] for a more complete discussion.

Definition 1. (Private Disjointness Testing) *Two probabilistic polynomial time interactive Turing machines, $\mathcal{P}_A$ and $\mathcal{P}_B$, define a Private Disjointness Testing protocol if the following conditions hold:*

Completeness. *If both parties are honest, the protocol works and $\mathcal{P}_A$ learns the disjointness predicate, that is whether $A \cap B = \emptyset$.*

Soundness. *For an unknown $\mathcal{P}_A$'s set $A \subset K$, the probability that $\mathcal{P}_B$ will convince $\mathcal{P}_A$ to accept $A \cap B \neq \emptyset$ is negligible.*

Security. *Assume that the size of both datasets are public. With an overwhelming probability, $\mathcal{P}_A$ does not get any extra information about $\mathcal{P}_B$'s dataset beyond the knowledge of the disjointness predicate. $\mathcal{P}_B$ learns nothing about $\mathcal{P}_A$'s set.*

Informally, completeness means that a correct execution between two honest parties will return the correct value of the disjointness predicate to $\mathcal{P}_A$. The soundness implies that on an unknown input set $A \subset K$ for $\mathcal{P}_B$, $\mathcal{P}_A$ has no chance of obtaining a non-zero result when interacting with any malicious Bob $\mathcal{P}_B^*$. That is, unless $\mathcal{P}_B^*$ actually knows a value in $\mathcal{P}_A$'s set, $\mathcal{P}_A$ will not be fooled into thinking otherwise. As pointed out in [3], both FNP and KM protocols are not sound according to this definition. In those schemes, $\mathcal{P}_A$ will believe that there is an intersection if it receives the value zero encrypted under a public-key. $\mathcal{P}_B^*$ could trivially violate the soundness property by encrypting a zero value itself.

In a verifiable protocol, $\mathcal{P}_A$'s privacy requires that no malicious Bob $\mathcal{P}_B^*$ can learn anything about the set A beyond $|A|$ from an interaction with $\mathcal{P}_A$. Using the same argument for a malicious Alice $\mathcal{P}_A^*$, $\mathcal{P}_B$'s privacy ensures that $\mathcal{P}_A^*$ does not learn anything about B beyond the set cardinality.

4   Intuition of Set Disjointness Test from Sylvester Matrix Construction

Our solution is based on the Sylvester matrix construction. To test if $\mathcal{P}_A$'s dataset $A = \{a_1, \ldots, a_m\}$ and $\mathcal{P}_B$'s dataset $B = \{b_1, \ldots, b_n\}$ are disjoint, we represent two datasets as two polynomials $g(x) = \prod_{a_i \in A}(x - a_i) = \sum_{i=0}^{m} \alpha_i x^i$ and $h(x) = \prod_{b_j \in B}(x - b_j) = \sum_{j=0}^{n} \beta_j x^j$, respectively. As in Section 2.1, we can build a Sylvester matrix S from the polynomials g and h. Then, the determinant of S indicates whether A and B are disjoint.

In order to protect datasets privacy, we can let $\mathcal{P}_A$ send encrypted g to $\mathcal{P}_B$ by using a public-key homomorphic cryptosystem, such as Paillier's [5], where the encrypted g is denoted as the encryption of g's coefficients with $\mathcal{P}_A$'s public key. $\mathcal{P}_B$ then constructs the Sylvester matrix based on the polynomial h and encrypted polynomial g. To protect the privacy of the polynomial h, $\mathcal{P}_B$ randomly selects $R_1 \in GL_{m+n}(K)$ and obliviously computes $R_1 \cdot S$ by using the homomorphic properties of the encryption applied. After receiving the cryptogram of $R_1 \cdot S$, $\mathcal{P}_A$ decrypts it and is able to compute $\det(R_1 \cdot S)$. In such a way, $\mathcal{P}_A$ learns $\det(R_1 \cdot S) = 0$ if and only if $\det(S) = 0$ without leaking any information about the polynomial g and gaining no other information apart from the disjointness of two datasets.

However, if we apply this idea directly to construct a protocol, then $\mathcal{P}_A$ can learn the intersection cardinality. This is because $\mathrm{rank}(R_1 \cdot S) = \mathrm{rank}(S)$. Thus, $\deg(\gcd(g, h)) = \deg(g) + \deg(h) - \mathrm{rank}((R_1 \cdot S))$ which reveals $|A \cap B|$. However, with slightly bigger communication cost, we could let $\mathcal{P}_A$ learn only the lower bound of the intersection by securely computing $\det(S^T \cdot S)$. It is easy to see that $\mathcal{P}_A$ is still able to determine whether $\det(S)$ is zero or not from the computation. The fact is that $\mathrm{rank}(S^T \cdot S) \leq \mathrm{rank}(S)$. Denote $S = \begin{pmatrix} M_B \\ M_A \end{pmatrix}$, then,

$$S^T \cdot S = M_A^T \cdot M_A + M_B^T \cdot M_B$$

where $M_A^T \cdot M_A$ and $M_B^T \cdot M_B$ can be computed independently by $\mathcal{P}_A$ and $\mathcal{P}_B$. The secure computation of $\det(S^T \cdot S)$ works in the same way as the one discussed above.

5   Private Disjointness Test

In this section, we propose a solution to test the disjointness without releasing any extra information beyond $|A|$ and $|B|$. Our private computation is based on the Sylvester matrix construction and the technique of secure determinant evaluation in the multi-party computation model introduced by Cramer and Damgard [15]. Let polynomials g and h represents the datasets A and B.

5.1   Protocol without Bob-Verifiability

To secure construct a Sylvester matrix S from the polynomials g and h, and accordingly evaluate if $\det(S) = 0$, we employ the SDE technique. We form a list of $(\deg(g) + \deg(h) + 1)$ shares of S held by two parties in a certain way to let one party to compute $\det(S)$ without knowing the $\operatorname{rank}(S)$. The protocol runs according to the following steps.

Input: $\mathcal{P}_A$ and $\mathcal{P}_B$ hold the datasets A and B, respectively.
Output: $\mathcal{P}_A$ learns if $A \cap B = \emptyset$.
Protocol Π_1

1. $\mathcal{P}_A$ constructs the polynomial g from the dataset A, computes shares $[g]_A, [g]_B$ of g, and sends $[g]_B$ to $\mathcal{P}_B$.
2. $\mathcal{P}_B$
   (a) constructs the polynomial h from the dataset B, computes shares $[h]_A, [h]_B$ of h, and forms an $m \times (m + n)$ half Sylvester matrix $[M_B]_B$ related to $[h]_B$ as

$$\begin{pmatrix} [\beta_n]_B & [\beta_{n-1}]_B & \cdots & [\beta_0]_B & 0 & 0 & \cdots & 0 & 0 & 0 \\ 0 & [\beta_n]_B & \cdots & [\beta_1]_B & [\beta_0]_B & 0 & \cdots & 0 & 0 & 0 \\ \vdots & \vdots & \ddots & \vdots & \vdots & \vdots & \ddots & \vdots & \vdots & \vdots \\ 0 & 0 & \cdots & [\beta_n]_B & [\beta_{n-1}]_B & [\beta_{n-2}]_B & \cdots & [\beta_0]_B & 0 & 0 \\ \vdots & \vdots & \ddots & \vdots & \vdots & \vdots & \ddots & \vdots & \vdots & \vdots \\ 0 & 0 & \cdots & 0 & 0 & [\beta_n]_B & \cdots & [\beta_2]_B & [\beta_1]_B & [\beta_0]_B \end{pmatrix},$$

   (b) generates shares $[R]_A, [R]_B$ for a random matrix $R \in GL_{m+n}(K)$ in a certain way that both $[R]_A$ and $[R]_B$ are invertible (the reader is refered to [15] for more information). Let $d = \det(R)$,
   (c) forms an $n \times (m + n)$ half Sylvester matrix $[M_A]_B$ from received $[g]_B$ as in Step $2(a)$,
   (d) randomly selects distinct non-zero $z_0, \ldots, z_{m+n}$ from the field K, and assigns $[z_i]_A = [z_i]_B$ for each z_i,
   (e) sends $[h]_A, [R]_A, d^{-1}, [z_0]_A, \ldots, [z_{m+n}]_A$ to $\mathcal{P}_A$.
3. $\mathcal{P}_B$ assists $\mathcal{P}_A$ in computing $[S_i']_A = [R]_A \cdot ([z_i]_A \cdot I_{m+n} - \begin{pmatrix} [M_B]_A \\ [M_A]_A \end{pmatrix})$,

   $[S_i']_B = [R]_B \cdot ([z_i]_B \cdot I_{m+n} - \begin{pmatrix} [M_B]_B \\ [M_A]_B \end{pmatrix})$ separately as in Sect. 2.2, where the
   matrices $[M_A]_A, [M_B]_A$ are constructed by $\mathcal{P}_A$ in the same way as $[M_A]_B, [M_B]_B$.
4. $\mathcal{P}_A$
   (a) computes S_i' from shares $[S_i']_A, [S_i']_B$ and further computes $\det(z_i \cdot I_{m+n} - \begin{pmatrix} M_B \\ M_A \end{pmatrix}) = \det(S_i') \cdot d^{-1}$, where $S_i' = R \cdot (z_i \cdot I_{m+n} - \begin{pmatrix} M_B \\ M_A \end{pmatrix})$,

(b) concludes $A \cap B \neq \emptyset$ if and only if

$$
\sum_{i=0}^{m+n} \left(\left(\prod_{\substack{0 \le j \le m+n \\ j \neq i}} \frac{z_j}{z_i - z_j} \right) \cdot \det(z_i \cdot I_{m+n} - \begin{pmatrix} M_B \\ M_A \end{pmatrix}) \right) = 0.
$$

Theorem 1. *The construction of Protocol Π_1 is correct and secure with no other information revealed beyond $|A|$ and $|B|$ if both parties follow the protocol faithfully.*

Poof. The soundness proof is irrelevant to this protocol based on Definition 1, since $\mathcal{P}_B$ is honest-but-curious and follows the protocol faithfully.

Completeness. The completeness of this protocol is clear. This is ensured by the Sylvester matrix construction. $\det(\begin{pmatrix} M_B \\ M_A \end{pmatrix}) = 0$ if and only if related polynomials g and h share common root(s), in other word $A \cap B \neq \emptyset$. The correct computation of $\det(\begin{pmatrix} M_B \\ M_A \end{pmatrix})$ from related $m + n + 1$ matrices is provided by Cramel and Damgard's SDE scheme. The associated shares construction and computation are guaranteed by the Shamir secret sharing scheme.

Security. The privacy of $\mathcal{P}_A$'s g is unconditional. It is guaranteed by the perfectness of Shamir secret sharing, since $\mathcal{P}_B$ only knows partial share of g owned by $\mathcal{P}_A$.

$\mathcal{P}_B$'s security ensures that $\mathcal{P}_A$ given $S'_i = R \cdot (z_i \cdot I_{m+n} - \begin{pmatrix} M_B \\ M_A \end{pmatrix})$ cannot learn anything about B beyond $|B|$.

The proof of $\mathcal{P}_B$'s security is that an honest-but-curious $\mathcal{P}_A^*$ is not able to glean any information about B from the result of $R \cdot (z_i \cdot I_{m+n} - \begin{pmatrix} M_B \\ M_A \end{pmatrix})$ with unknown matrices R and M_B, where $R \in GL_{m+n}(K)$ is random, M_B is an $m \times (m + n)$ matrix with a half Sylvester matrix form. $\mathcal{P}_A^*$ can launch an attack on M_B with

$$
S'_i = R \cdot (z_i \cdot I_{m+n} - \begin{pmatrix} M_B \\ M_A \end{pmatrix}) \tag{1}
$$

Denote $\begin{pmatrix} \hat{M}_B \\ \hat{M}_A \end{pmatrix} = (z_i \cdot I_{m+n} - \begin{pmatrix} M_B \\ M_A \end{pmatrix})$ where M_B and $\hat{M}_B$ are same size. $\mathcal{P}_A^*$ knows S'_i and $\hat{M}_A$, and tries to find out the matrix $\hat{M}_B$ (really just one row of the entry, the polynomial h). Note that $\begin{pmatrix} \hat{M}_B \\ \hat{M}_A \end{pmatrix}$ is non-singular, and $R \in GL_{m+n}(K)$. Therefore, S'_i must be non-singular. By only knowing $\hat{M}_A$ and with no knowledge about h, $\mathcal{P}_A^*$ can search possible candidate polynomial, which can assure $\begin{pmatrix} \hat{M}_B \\ \hat{M}_A \end{pmatrix}$ be non-singular (in other words, can satisfy Equation 1).

Non-singular $\begin{pmatrix} \hat{M}_B \\ \hat{M}_A \end{pmatrix}$ means that $\det \begin{pmatrix} \hat{M}_B \\ \hat{M}_A \end{pmatrix} \neq 0$. Let $\det \begin{pmatrix} \hat{M}_B \\ \hat{M}_A \end{pmatrix}$ $= f(\beta_0, \beta_1 \ldots, \beta_n)$ where f is a polynomial with $n + 1$ unknowns. For any β_j by fixing $\beta_i, 0 \leq i \leq n$ and $i \neq j$, $\deg(f) = n$ and there are at most n solutions for $f(\ldots, \beta_j, \ldots) = 0$. We know that there are q possible selections for β_j in the field. Therefore, there must exists at least $q - n$ possible choices for β_j, such that $f(\ldots, \beta_j, \ldots) \neq 0$. Since the polynomial f has $n + 1$ unknowns, the total possible candidates for $\hat{M}_B$ are $(q - n)^{n+1}$. If q is large enough, $\mathcal{P}_A^*$ only has a negligible probability to guess h correctly.

5.2 Verifiable Disjointness Test Protocol

In order to deal with a malicious $\mathcal{P}_B$, $\mathcal{P}_A$ needs to verify whether the matrix M_B associated with the shared polynomial h has the full rank as he claims to prevent the malicious $\mathcal{P}_B$ inserting one row zeros or two dependent rows in the matrix. In the following, we show how to modify our previous protocol to gain security against malicious $\mathcal{P}_B$ with a verification test. Assume that $\deg(h)$ is known by $\mathcal{P}_A$. Otherwise, $\mathcal{P}_B$ needs to send a single value $\deg(h)$ to $\mathcal{P}_A$ at the beginning of the protocol. Suppose that $\mathcal{P}_A$ has a private and random permutation function π, which permutes each of $m + n$ tuples.

Input: $\mathcal{P}_A$ and $\mathcal{P}_B$ hold the datasets A and B, respectively.
Output: $\mathcal{P}_A$ learns if $A \cap B = \emptyset$.
Protocol Π_2

1. $\mathcal{P}_A$
   (a) constructs the polynomial g from the dataset A, and computes n pairs of shares $\{([g]_{1_A}, [g]_{1_B}), \ldots, ([g]_{(m+n)_A}, [g]_{(m+n)_B})\}$, where the combination of two shares in any pair can find g,
   (b) sets an constant polynomial $g' = 1$, and computes n pairs of shares as in previous step, so she gets $\{([g']_{1_A}, [g']_{1_B}), \ldots, ([g']_{(m+n)_A}, [g']_{(m+n)_B})\}$,
   (c) obtains $\{(e_{1_{\pi_1(1)}}, e_{1_{\pi_1(2)}}), \ldots, (e_{(m+n)_{\pi_{m+n}(1)}}, e_{(m+n)_{\pi_{m+n}(2)}})\}$ by performing $\pi\{(e_{1_1}, e_{1_2}), \ldots, (e_{(m+n)_1}, e_{(m+n)_2})\}$, where $\{(e_{1_1}, e_{1_2}), \ldots, (e_{(m+n)_1}, e_{(m+n)_2})\} = \{([g]_{1_B}, [g']_{1_B}), \ldots, ([g]_{(m+n)_B}, [g']_{(m+n)_B})\}$,
   (d) sends $\{(e_{1_{\pi_1(1)}}, e_{1_{\pi_1(2)}}), \ldots, (e_{(m+n)_{\pi_{m+n}(1)}}, e_{(m+n)_{\pi_{m+n}(2)}})\}$ to $\mathcal{P}_B$;
2. For each pair $(e_{i_{\pi_j(1)}}, e_{i_{\pi_j(2)}})$, the protocol runs step 2 and 3 of Protocol Π_1 parallel with the same parameters and computes

$$[S_i']_{\pi_j(1)_A} = [R]_A \cdot ([z_i]_A \cdot I_{m+n} - \begin{pmatrix} [M_B]_A \\ [M_A]_{i_{\pi_j(1)_A}} \end{pmatrix})$$

$$[S_i']_{\pi_j(1)_B} = [R]_B \cdot ([z_i]_B \cdot I_{m+n} - \begin{pmatrix} [M_B]_B \\ [M_A]_{i_{\pi_j(1)_B}} \end{pmatrix})$$

$$[S_i']_{\pi_j(2)_A} = [R]_A \cdot ([z_i]_A \cdot I_{m+n} - \begin{pmatrix} [M_B]_A \\ [M_A]_{i_{\pi_j(2)_A}} \end{pmatrix})$$

$$[S'_i]_{\pi_j(2)_B} = [R]_B \cdot ([z_i]_B \cdot I_{m+n} - \left(\begin{matrix} [M_B]_B \\ [M_A]_{i_{\pi_j(2)_B}} \end{matrix}\right))$$

where $[M_A]_{i_{\pi_j(1)}}, [M_A]_{i_{\pi_j(2)}}$ are constructed from $[g]_i$ and $[g']_i$ with the order determined by the permutation π_j, which is unknown to $\mathcal{P}_B$.

3. $\mathcal{P}_A$

(a) computes $S'_{i_{\pi_j(1)}}$ from shares $[S'_i]_{\pi_j(1)_A}, [S'_i]_{\pi_j(1)_B}$, and $S'_{i_{\pi_j(2)}}$ from shares $[S'_i]_{\pi_j(2)_A}, [S'_i]_{\pi_j(2)_B}$,

(b) obtains $\{(S'_{1_1}, S'_{1_2}), \ldots, (S'_{(m+n)_1}, S'_{(m+n)_2})\}$ by performing $\pi^{-1}\{(S'_{1_{\pi_1(1)}}, S'_{1_{\pi_1(2)}}), \ldots, (S'_{(m+n)_{\pi_{m+n}(1)}}, S'_{(m+n)_{\pi_{m+n}(2)}})\}$

(c) computes $f_{i_1} = \det(S'_{i_1})$ and $f_{i_2} = \det(S'_{i_2})$ for $i \in \{0, \ldots, m+n\}$ as in Protocol Π_1,

(d) computes $\det(z_i \cdot I_{m+n} - \left(\begin{matrix} M_B \\ M'_A \end{matrix}\right)) = f_{i_2} \cdot d^{-1}$ for $i \in \{0, \ldots, m+n\}$, where M'_A denotes a half Sylvester matrix constructed from the polynomial g',

(e) halts if

$$(-1)^{m+n} \cdot \sum_{i=0}^{m+n} \left(\left(\prod_{\substack{0 \le j \le m+n \\ j \ne i}} \frac{z_j}{z_i - z_j}\right) \cdot \det(z_i \cdot I_{m+n} - \left(\begin{matrix} M_B \\ M'_A \end{matrix}\right))\right) \ne 1.$$

(f) computes $\det(z_i \cdot I_{m+n} - \left(\begin{matrix} M_B \\ M_A \end{matrix}\right)) = f_{i_1} \cdot d^{-1}$ for $i \in \{0, \ldots, m+n\}$,

(g) concludes $A \cap B \ne \emptyset$ if and only if

$$\sum_{i=0}^{m+n} \left(\left(\prod_{\substack{0 \le j \le m+n \\ j \ne i}} \frac{z_j}{z_i - z_j}\right) \cdot \det(z_i \cdot I_{m+n} - \left(\begin{matrix} M_B \\ M_A \end{matrix}\right))\right) = 0.$$

Theorem 2. *The construction of the Protocol Π_2 is complete and sound against a malicious adversaries. With overwhelming probability, a malicious $\mathcal{P}_B^*$ will be caught. In other word, unless $\mathcal{P}_B^*$ actually knows a value in $\mathcal{P}_A$'s set, $\mathcal{P}_A$ will not be fooled into thinking otherwise. The security of both $\mathcal{P}_A$ and $\mathcal{P}_B$ is also protected based on the shares of each polynomial are randomly selected from field, and the* Secure Determinant Evaluation.

Proof. The correctness proof is the same as for the Protocol Π_1. The only difference is that we use $m+n$ pairs of shares $[g]_{i_A}, [g]_{i_B}$ for g. The reason for doing this is to ensure the soundness of this protocol, and will be discussed shortly. The security proof is the similar as the one in the Protocol Π_1. An adversary does not gain any extra information. This is because of the perfectness of Shamir secret sharing and the SDE we used.

Soundness. In the given soundness definition, $\mathcal{P}_B^*$ is operating with an unknown dataset $A \subset K$. From our construction, $\mathcal{P}_B$ does not know anything about A beyond a share of A and $\mathcal{P}_A$ knows a share of B. $\mathcal{P}_A$ will only accept $A \cap B \ne \emptyset$ when $\det(\left(\begin{matrix} M_B \\ M_A \end{matrix}\right)) = 0$.

Note that $[g]_{i_A}$ is sent along with $[g']_{i_A}$ for $i \in \{1, \ldots, m+n\}$. In the setting, $[g]_{i_A} \neq [g]_{j_A}$ and $[g']_{i'_A} \neq [g']_{j'_A}$ for $i \neq j$ and $i' \neq j'$. With the randomness of $[g]_{i_A}$'s and $[g']_{i_A}$'s, $\mathcal{P}_{\mathcal{B}}^*$ could deliberately set $\mathrm{rank}(M_B) < n$. This way $\mathcal{P}_{\mathcal{A}}$ will accept $A \cap B \neq \emptyset$ since $\det\left(\begin{pmatrix} M_B \\ M_A \end{pmatrix}\right) = 0$. The only way for letting $\mathrm{rank}(M_B) < n$ is to set h be a zero polynomial in our setting. But this will be challenged by our verification test, which $\mathcal{P}_{\mathcal{A}}$ only accepts h when

$$(-1)^{m+n} \cdot \sum_{i=0}^{m+n} \left(\left(\prod_{\substack{0 \leq j \leq m+n \\ j \neq i}} \frac{z_j}{z_i - z_j} \right) \cdot \det(z_i \cdot I_{m+n} - \begin{pmatrix} M_B \\ M'_A \end{pmatrix}) \right) = 1.$$

The malicious Bob $\mathcal{P}_{\mathcal{B}}^*$ can find the shares $[h]_A, [h']_B, [h]_B$ for the polynomial h, such that h can be reconstructed through the shares $[h]_A$ and $[h]_B$, but the combination of $[h]_A$ and $[h']_B$ corresponds to a zero polynomial. $\mathcal{P}_{\mathcal{B}}^*$ can then use $[h]_B$ for the verification test and $[h']_B$ for disjointness test if he can guess which one of $(e_{i_{\pi(1)}}, e_{i_{\pi(2)}})$ corresponds to $[g']_{i_A}$. But the chance $\mathcal{P}_{\mathcal{B}}^*$ guesses correctly in each pair is $\frac{1}{2}$. Thus, the chance $\mathcal{P}_{\mathcal{B}}^*$ can guess correctly for all $m+n$ pairs is $\frac{1}{2^{m+n}}$. If m and n are reasonable sizes, $\mathcal{P}_{\mathcal{B}}^*$ will be caught with an overwhelming probability.

5.3 Computation and Communication Complexity

Two protocols proposed in this paper are very simple and require only $O(1)$ rounds of communication. The communication cost is in terms of number of $\lceil \log_2 q \rceil$ bits that are transmitted. The computation cost is measured in number of field operations. In our calculation, the complexity of matrix multiplication is $O((m+n)^{2.375})$ [21]; the complexity of determinant computation is $O((m+n)^{2.697})$ [22].

The communication complexity of the Protocol Π_1 is $O((m+n)^2)$. The protocol requires $2(m+n)$ matrix multiplication, and $m+n$ determinant computations. The overall computation complexity is $O((m+n)^{3.697})$ field operations.

There is slightly more commnication cost for Protocol Π_2, but complexity is still $O((m+n)^2)$. The computation cost is only double the cost of the Protocol Π_1.

6 Conclusion

We proposed protocols for private disjointness tests that are based on the polynomial representation of datasets and Sylvester matrix construction. We first introduced the structure of Sylvester matrices and the intuition of our protocols that applies Sylvester matrices. To avoid revealing the intersection cardinality by directly applying Sylvester matrices, we provided a protocol to test the set disjointness without revealing any additional information in the honest-but-curious case. Finally, we described a protocol to against malicious adversaries by applying a verification test.

The protocols constructed in this paper are more efficient than previous protocols with respect to communication and computation complexity. They are all $O(1)$ rounds, and do not require the parties to compute exponentiations or any other kind of public key operations. Our protocols also provide information theoretic security, and do not rely on any computational assumption.

Acknowledgment

The authors are grateful to the anonymous reviewers for their comments to improve the quality of this paper. We also like to thank C. Pandu Rangan for some helpful discussions. This work was supported by the Australian Research Council under ARC Discovery Projects DP0558773, DP0665035 and DP0663452. Qingsong Ye's work was funded by an iMURS scholarship provided by Macquarie University. The research of Huaxiong Wang is partially supported by the Ministry of Education of Singapore under grant T206B2204.

References

[1] Kiayias, A., Mitrofanova, A.: Testing disjointness and private datasets. In: S. Patrick, A., Yung, M. (eds.) FC 2005. LNCS, vol. 3570, pp. 109–124. Springer, Heidelberg (2005)

[2] Freedman, M.J., Nissim, K., Pinkas, B.: Efficient private matching and set intersection. In: Cachin, C., Camenisch, J.L. (eds.) EUROCRYPT 2004. LNCS, vol. 3027, pp. 1–9. Springer, Heidelberg (2004)

[3] Hohenberger, S., Weis, S.A.: Honest-verifier private disjointness testing without random oracles. In: Danezis, G., Golle, P. (eds.) PET 2006. LNCS, vol. 4258, pp. 277–294. Springer, Heidelberg (2006)

[4] Naor, M., Pinkas, B.: Oblivious transfer and polynomial evaluation. In: 31st annual ACM Symposium on Theory of Computing (STOC 1999), Atlanta, Georgia, May 1999, pp. 245–254 (1999)

[5] Paillier, P.: Public-key cryptosystems based on composite degree residuosity classes. In: Stern, J. (ed.) EUROCRYPT 1999. LNCS, vol. 1592, pp. 223–238. Springer, Heidelberg (1999)

[6] Pedersen, T.P.: Non-interactive and information-theoretic secure verifiable secret sharing. In: Feigenbaum, J. (ed.) CRYPTO 1991. LNCS, vol. 576, pp. 129–140. Springer, Heidelberg (1992)

[7] Cramer, R., Gennaro, R., Schoenmakers, B.: A secure and optimally efficient multi-authority election scheme. In: Fumy, W. (ed.) EUROCRYPT 1997. LNCS, vol. 1233, pp. 103–118. Springer, Heidelberg (1997)

[8] Kissner, L., Song, D.: Privacy-preserving set operaitons. In: Shoup, V. (ed.) CRYPTO 2005. LNCS, vol. 3621, pp. 241–257. Springer, Heidelberg (2005)

[9] Laur, S., Lipmaa, H., Mielikainen, T.: Private itemset support counting. In: Qing, S., Mao, W., López, J., Wang, G. (eds.) ICICS 2005. LNCS, vol. 3783, pp. 97–111. Springer, Heidelberg (2005)

[10] Kiayias, A., Mitrofanova, A.: Syntax-driven private evaluation of quantified membership queries. In: Zhou, J., Yung, M., Bao, F. (eds.) ACNS 2006. LNCS, vol. 3989, pp. 470–485. Springer, Heidelberg (2006)

[11] Fagin, R., Naor, M., Winkler, P.: Comparing information without leaking it. Communications of the ACM 39(5), 77–85 (1996)

[12] Lipmaa, H.: Verifiable homomorphic oblivious transfer and private equality test. In: Laih, C.-S. (ed.) ASIACRYPT 2003. LNCS, vol. 2894, pp. 416–433. Springer, Heidelberg (2003)

[13] Ye, Q., Wang, H., Tartary, C.: Privacy-preserving distributed set intersection. In: The 2nd Workshop on Advances in Information Security (conjuncted with ARES 2008), Barcelona, Spain, March 2008, pp. 1332–1339. IEEE Computer Society Press, Los Alamitos (2008)

[14] Ye, Q., Wang, H., Pieprzyk, J.: Distributed private matching and set operations. In: ISPEC 2008, April 2008. LNCS, vol. 4991, pp. 347–360. Springer, Heidelberg (2008)

[15] Cramer, R., Damgard, I.: Secure distributed linear algebra in a constant number of rounds. In: Kilian, J. (ed.) CRYPTO 2001. LNCS, vol. 2139, pp. 119–136. Springer, Heidelberg (2001)

[16] Mohassel, P., Franklin, M.: Efficient polynomial operations in the shared-coefficients setting. In: Yung, M., Dodis, Y., Kiayias, A., Malkin, T.G. (eds.) PKC 2006. LNCS, vol. 3958, pp. 44–57. Springer, Heidelberg (2006)

[17] von zur Gathen, J., Gerhard, J.: Modern Computer Algebra. Cambridge University Press, Cambridge (2003)

[18] Bar-Ilan, J., Beaver, D.: Non-cryptographic fault-tolerant computing in a constant number of rounds of interaction. In: 8th ACM Annual Symposium on Principles of Distributed Computing (PODC 1989), pp. 201–209. ACM Press, New York (1989)

[19] Ben-Or, M., Cleve, R.: Computing algebraic formulas using a constant number of registers. In: 20th annual ACM Symposium on Theory of Computing (STOC 1988), pp. 254–257. ACM Press, New York (1988)

[20] Goldreich, O.: The Foundations of Cryptography, vol. 2. Cambridge University Press, Cambridge (2004)

[21] Coppersmith, D., Winograd, S.: Matrix multiplication via arithmetic progressions. Journal of Symbolic Computing 9, 251–280 (1990)

[22] Kaltofen, E., Villard, G.: On the complexity of computing determinants. Computational Complexity 13(3-4), 91–130 (2005)

Efficient Perfectly Reliable and Secure Message Transmission Tolerating Mobile Adversary

Arpita Patra, Ashish Choudhary*, Madhu Vaidyanathan,
and C. Pandu Rangan**

Dept of Computer Science and Engineering
IIT Madras, Chennai India 600036
arpita@cse.iitm.ernet.in, ashishc@cse.iitm.ernet.in,
madhu@cse.iitm.ernet.in, rangan@iitm.ernet.in

Abstract. In this paper, we study the problem of *Perfectly Reliable Message Transmission* (PRMT) and *Perfectly Secure Message Transmission* (PSMT) between two nodes **S** and **R** in an undirected synchronous network, a part of which is under the influence of an *all powerful mobile Byzantine* adversary. We design a *three* phase *bit optimal* PSMT protocol tolerating mobile adversary, whose communication complexity matches the existing lower bound on the communication complexity of any multi phase PSMT protocol, tolerating mobile adversary. This significantly reduces the phase complexity of the existing $O(t)$ phase bit optimal PSMT protocol tolerating mobile adversary, where t denotes the number of nodes corrupted by the mobile adversary. Furthermore, we design a three phase *bit optimal* PRMT protocol which achieves reliability with *constant factor* overhead against a mobile adversary. These are the *first* ever constant phase *bit optimal* PRMT and PSMT protocols against mobile Byzantine adversary. We also characterize PSMT protocols in *directed* networks tolerating mobile adversary. Finally, we derive tight bound on the number of rounds required to achieve reliable communication from **S** to **R** tolerating a mobile adversary with arbitrary roaming speed[1]. Finally, we show how our constant phase PRMT and PSMT protocols can be adapted to design *round optimal* and *bit optimal* PRMT and PSMT protocols, provided the network is given as collection of vertex disjoint paths.

Keywords: Information Theoretic Security, Mobile Adversary.

---

* Work Supported by Project No. CSE/05-06/076/DITX/CPAN on Protocols for Secure Communication and Computation Sponsored by Department of Information Technology, Government of India.
** Work Supported by Project No. CSE/05-06/076/DITX/CPAN on Protocols for Secure Communication and Computation Sponsored by Department of Information Technology, Government of India.
[1] By roaming speed we mean the speed with which the adversary changes the set of corrupted node.

1   Introduction

Consider the following problem: a sender **S** and a receiver **R**, who want to "talk" to each other via an underlying communication network that they do not trust. Note that if **S** and **R** are connected directly via a private and authenticated link (like in the generic solutions for secure multiparty computation [3, 7, 15, 19]), secure communication is trivially guaranteed. However, in reality, it is not economical to directly connect *every* two players in the network. The sender's distrust in the underlying communication network is modeled by a virtual entity called the *adversary* that has *unbounded computing power* and can corrupt some of the players (nodes) in the network. In spite of the presence of such an adversary in the network, **S** wishes to send a message m chosen from a finite field $\mathbb{F}$, reliably to **R**, in a *guaranteed manner*. This problem is called *perfectly reliable message transmission* (PRMT). The problem of *perfectly secure message transmission* (PSMT) has an additional constraint that the adversary should get *no* information about m. Security against such an adversary with unbounded computational power is called *information theoretic or perfect security*.

The problem of PRMT and PSMT was introduced and studied by Dolev et.al [5], who assumed that the adversary can corrupt any t nodes in the network and that the adversary is *static* Byzantine, i.e., a player once corrupted remains so subsequently. More recent efforts using the same (static) adversarial model for the problem of PSMT include [4, 10, 14, 16, 17]. However, as first noticed in [12], the static model implicitly assumes that the number of dishonest players in the network is independent of the protocol's execution time. This is usually not true in practice. Furthermore, since a corrupted player could be corrected given sufficient time, [12] proposed the mobile adversary model wherein the adversary could move around the network whilst still corrupting up to t players at any given instant. Subsequently, extensive research efforts on tolerating mobile adversaries have resulted in what is well-known as *proactive security* [2, 6, 8, 9].

Existing Results: It is known that for the existence of any r-phase [2] $(r \geq 2)$ PRMT/PSMT protocol, $n \geq 2t + 1$ vertex disjoint paths (also called as wires) between **S** and **R** is necessary and sufficient to tolerate a t-active static adversary [5]. Also, as reported in [17], any r phase $(r \geq 2)$ PSMT protocol has a communication complexity of $\Omega\left(\frac{n\ell}{n-2t}\right)$ field elements, to securely send ℓ field elements against a t-active static adversary. While for PSMT we have a proven lower bound for communication complexity, for PRMT it can be as small as $\Omega(l)$ for communicating message of ℓ field elements. The authors of [14] have designed a three phase PRMT protocol which satisfies the above defined bound and sends a message containing ℓ field elements by communicating $O(\ell)$ field elements. Such a protocol is called *bit-optimal* PRMT protocol. In addition, the authors [14] also reported a three phase PSMT protocol, whose communication complexity is $O\left(\frac{n\ell}{n-2t}\right)$ (asymptotically touching the lower bound specified for multiphase

---

[2] A phase is a send from **S** to **R** or vice-versa.

PSMT) and hence it is *bit optimal* against a static adversary. Designing a two phase PSMT protocol against a t-active static adversary, whose communication complexity is $O\left(\frac{n\ell}{n-2t}\right)$ has been an outstanding open problem [1] and recently it is solved by Kurosawa et.al in [11].

Unlike *static adversary*, a t-active *mobile adversary* can corrupt different set of t wires during different phases of the protocol. Thus, a wire once corrupted, may not remain corrupted in subsequent phases. Intuitively, it is more difficult to tolerate a t-active *mobile adversary* in comparison to a t-active *static adversary*. However, in [18], it is shown that $n \geq 2t + 1$ wires between **S** and **R** is necessary and sufficient for the possibility of any r-phase ($r \geq 2$) PRMT/PSMT protocol against a t-active mobile adversary. Thus mobility of adversary *does not* affects its tolerability. In [17], the communication complexity of any r-phase ($r \geq 2$) PSMT protocol is stated to be $\Omega\left(\frac{n\ell}{n-2t}\right)$, where ℓ is the message to be sent securely against a t-active mobile adversary. The authors of the same paper has also designed a $O(t)$ phase PSMT protocol satisfying the bound.

Our Contribution, Its Motivation and Significance: The following are the main contribution of this paper: **(a)** A *bit-optimal* three phase PRMT protocol, which sends a message of ℓ field elements by communicating $O(\ell)$ field elements and thus achieves reliability with *constant factor* overhead in three phases even in the presence of mobile adversary. **(b)** A *bit-optimal* three phase PSMT protocol satisfying the bound for communication complexity proved in [17]. Both these protocols uses a *novel* technique, very different from the techniques adapted in the three phase *bit-optimal* PRMT and PSMT protocol proposed in [14] tolerating a static adversary. We also give the *first ever* characterization of PSMT protocols in *directed* networks tolerating mobile adversary.

All existing PRMT and PSMT protocols abstract the underlying network as vertex disjoint paths, called *wires*, between **S** and **R**, thus neglecting the intermediate nodes in these paths. However, we show that such an abstraction gives an incorrect estimation on the communication complexity and round complexity of PRMT and PSMT protocols, in many practical scenarios. Hence, it is essential to consider all the intermediate nodes in each wire for the design and analysis of PRMT and PSMT protocols. Also, considering the intermediate nodes/details of each wire motivates to use more finer notion of *round* [3] in comparison to phase. Accordingly, the behavior of *mobile adversary* is re-defined to allow the adversary to corrupt any set of t nodes after every $\rho \geq 1$ rounds, where ρ is called the roaming speed of the adversary. In this work, our contribution also encompasses: **(c)** Computation of a tight bound on the minimum number of rounds r_{min}, required for the existence of any PRMT protocol tolerating mobile adversary, with roaming speed of $\rho = 1$. **(d)** The same for an adversary with arbitrary roaming speed $\rho \geq 2$. **(e)** Finally, adaptation of our constant *phase* PRMT and PSMT protocols into round optimal and communication optimal PRMT and PSMT protocols in a given network, provided the network is given as a collection of disjoint paths.

---

[3] A round is a send from one node to its neighbor.

As mentioned earlier, abstraction of network as wires leads to incorrect estimation on communication and round complexity of protocols. But still wired abstraction eases deriving lower bounds on communication complexity and finding out the connectivity requirement for PRMT/PSMT problem and also simplifies the analysis of protocols. That is why we have designed phase-based protocols for PRMT and PSMT and later adapted them to work in terms of rounds.

2 Proactive PRMT and PSMT in Terms of Phases

Network Settings and Computational Model: Recall that a phase is a send from **S** to **R** or vice-versa. While designing protocols in terms of phases, following the approach of [5], we abstract the network as a collection of vertex disjoint paths called wires between **S** and **R**, neglecting the intermediate nodes in these paths. A t-active mobile adversary can corrupt different set of t wires during different phases of the protocol. Hence a wire w, which is corrupted in some phase, may not remain corrupted during subsequent phases and can behave honestly. Also by corrupting a wire w during a particular phase, adversary does not get any information which was transmitted over w in earlier phase(s) (unless w was corrupted in earlier phase(s) also). We assume that **S** and **R** are connected by $n \geq 2t+1$ bi-directional wires $w_1, w_2, \ldots w_n$, which is necessary and sufficient for PRMT/PSMT protocols against a t-active mobile adversary [17]. In our protocols, all computation are done from a finite field $\mathbb{F}$ of prime order, with $|\mathbb{F}| > n$. Any information which is sent over all the n wires is said to be "broadcast". If $x \in \mathbb{F}$ is "broadcast" over $n > 2t$ wires, then it will be always recovered correctly at the receiving end by taking the majority.

Extracting Randomness [17]: Let **S** and **R** agree on an n-tuple $x = [x_1, x_2, \ldots x_n] \in \mathbb{F}^n$, such that the adversary knows $n - f$ components of x, but has no information about other f components of x. However, **S** and **R** do not know which values are known to the adversary. But they want to agree on a sequence of f elements $y_1, y_2, \ldots y_f \in \mathbb{F}$ such that $y_1, y_2, \ldots y_f$ is information theoretically secure. This is achieved by algorithm **EXTRAND**$_{n,f}(x)$ proposed in [17].

Algorithm EXTRAND$_{n,f}(x)$. Let V be a $n \times f$ Vandermonde matrix with elements from $\mathbb{F}$ and is known publicly. **S** and **R** locally compute $[y_1 \ y_2 \ \ldots \ y_f] = [x_1 \ x_2 \ \ldots \ x_n]V$.

Communicating Conflict Graph: Consider the following scenario: **S** and **R** are connected by $n = 2t + 1$ wires. **S** selects at random n polynomials $p_i(x)$, $1 \leq i \leq n$ over $\mathbb{F}$, each of degree t. Next through wire $w_i, 1 \leq i \leq n$, **S** sends to **R** the polynomial $p_i(x)$ and for each j, $1 \leq j \leq n$, the value of $p_j(\alpha_i)$ denoted by r_{ji}, where α_i's are arbitrary distinct publicly specified members of $\mathbb{F}$.

Let **R** receives polynomial $p_i'(x)$ and the values r_{ji}' along w_i. **R** tries to find as many faults as he can find that occurred in the previous phase and communicates his findings reliably to **S**. Towards this, **R** constructs a directed graph called conflict graph $H = (\mathcal{W}, E)$, where $\mathcal{W} = \{w_1, w_2, \ldots, w_n\}$ and arc $(w_i, w_j) \in E$ if

$r'_{ij} \neq p'_i(\alpha_j)$. There can be $\Theta(n^2)$ arcs in the conflict graph. For each $(w_i, w_j) \in E$, $\mathbf{R}$ adds a four tuple $\{w_i, w_j, p'_i(\alpha_j), r'_{ij}\}$ to a list X. $\mathbf{R}$ then broadcasts X to $\mathbf{S}$. $\mathbf{S}$ reliably receives X. For each $\{w_i, w_j, p'_i(\alpha_j), r'_{ij}\} \in X$, $\mathbf{S}$ verifies $r'_{ij} \overset{?}{=} r_{ij}$ and $p'_i(\alpha_j) \overset{?}{=} p_i(\alpha_j)$. Depending upon the outcome of the test, $\mathbf{S}$ concludes that either $\mathbf{R}$ has received incorrect r'_{ij} over wire w_j or incorrect $p'_i(x)$ over wire w_i (or both) and accordingly adds w_i or w_j (or both) to a list L_{fault}. $\mathbf{S}$ then broadcasts L_{fault} to $\mathbf{R}$. Now we can say the following:

Theorem 1. *If w_i delivers $p'_i(x) \neq p_i(x)$ to $\mathbf{R}$, then $\mathbf{S}$ will know this from X. Moreover, $\mathbf{S}$ will be able to reliably send this information to $\mathbf{R}$.*

Proof. As $p'_i(x)$ and $p_i(x)$ are of degree t, they can intersect at most at t points. So there exist at least one honest wire, say w_j, such that $r_{ij} = r'_{ij}$ and $p'_i(\alpha_j) \neq r'_{ij}$. So w_j will contradict w_i and the arc (w_i, w_j) will be present in the conflict graph and hence the four tuple $\{\alpha_i, \alpha_j, p'_i(\alpha_j), r'_{ij}\}$ will be present in the list X. Since X is broadcast over $2t+1$ wires, $\mathbf{S}$ will correctly receive X and eventually knows that w_i has delivered incorrect polynomial, adds w_i to L_{fault} and then reliably sends L_{fault} to $\mathbf{R}$ by broadcasting. □

Theorem 2. *The communication complexity of broadcasting the list X is $O(n^3)$.*

Remark 1. An efficient way of sending the conflict graph (which contains $O(n^2)$ edges) by communicating $O(n^2)$ field elements, against static adversary was introduced in [17] and subsequently used in [14]. The method deals with finding maximum matching of conflict graph and a few notions from coding theory. However, the same technique will not work against mobile adversary, as it can choose to corrupt different set of t wires in different phases. So only way of reliably sending the conflict graph against mobile adversary is by broadcasting.

2.1   Proactive PRMT with Constant Factor Overhead

We propose a three phase PRMT protocol **PRMT_Optimal** which sends a message containing $n(t+1)^2 = \Omega(n^3)$ field elements by communicating $O(n^3)$ field elements against a t-active mobile Byzantine adversary, where $\mathbf{S}$ and $\mathbf{R}$ are connected by $n = 2t+1$ wires. Thus, **PRMT_Optimal** achieves reliability with constant factor overhead in constant phases and thus is *bit-optimal*. In [14], a three phase *bit-optimal* PRMT protocol had been presented against a static adversary which sends $\Omega(n^2)$ field elements by communicating $O(n^2)$. Thus, extra adversarial power of *mobility* does not hinder achieving *bit-optimality* in the same number of phases (three) except that the optimality is achieved for larger message size!! Before describing the protocol, we describe a technique used in our protocol which we call as **Union Technique**.

Union Technique: Recall the same scenario described in previous section. During first phase $\mathbf{R}$ receives n polynomials $p'_i(x), 1 \leq i \leq n$, each of degree t and n values corresponding to each polynomial denoted by r'_{ij}. Let B denote the set of n polynomials and their n values as received by $\mathbf{R}$. Using B, $\mathbf{R}$ can construct a conflict graph. In our protocol **PRMT_Optimal**, instead of a single set B, $\mathbf{R}$

Table 1. Data Flow over n wires in **Phase I** of **PRMT_Optimal**

Wire	B_1	$\ldots$	B_k	$\ldots$	B_n
w_1	$P_{11}(x)\ r_{11,1}, r_{12,1}, \ldots r_{1n,1}$	$\ldots$	$P_{k1}(x)\ r_{k1,1}, r_{k2,1}, \ldots r_{kn,1}$	$\ldots$	$P_{n1}(x)\ r_{n1,1}, r_{n2,1}, \ldots r_{nn,1}$
w_2	$P_{12}(x)\ r_{11,2}, r_{12,2}, \ldots r_{1n,2}$	$\ldots$	$P_{k2}(x)\ r_{k1,2}, r_{k2,2}, \ldots r_{kn,2}$	$\ldots$	$P_{n2}(x)\ r_{n1,2}, r_{n2,2}, \ldots r_{nn,2}$
$\ldots$	$\ldots$	$\ldots$	$\ldots$	$\ldots$	$\ldots$
w_i	$P_{1i}(x)\ r_{11,i}, r_{12,i}, \ldots r_{1n,i}$	$\ldots$	$P_{ki}(x)\ r_{k1,i}, r_{k2,i}, \ldots r_{kn,i}$	$\ldots$	$P_{ni}(x)\ r_{n1,i}, r_{n2,i}, \ldots r_{nn,i}$
$\ldots$	$\ldots$	$\ldots$	$\ldots$	$\ldots$	$\ldots$
w_n	$P_{1n}(x)\ r_{11,n}, r_{12,n}, \ldots r_{1n,n}$	$\ldots$	$P_{kn}(x)\ r_{k1,n}, r_{k2,n}, \ldots r_{kn,n}$	$\ldots$	$P_{nn}(x)\ r_{n1,n}, r_{n2,n}, \ldots r_{nn,n}$

receives n such sets denoted as $B_k, 1 \leq k \leq n$, where B_k contains n polynomials $p'_{ki}(x), 1 \leq i \leq n$ and n values for each $p'_{ki}(x)$ denoted by $r'_{ki,j}, 1 \leq j \leq n$. The flow of information over n wires during **Phase I** is given in Table 1.

R then constructs conflict graph H_k using the set B_k. For each H_k, we can say the following from Theorem 1: if during **Phase I**, **R** receives a corrupted polynomial $p'_{ki}(x) \neq p_{ki}(x)$ over w_i, then there exist at least one directed arc (w_i, w_j) in H_k, where w_j is an honest wire. If **R** broadcasts all conflict graphs, then from Theorem 1, both **S** and **R** would come to know the identity of all faulty wires w_i over which **R** has received at least one faulty $p'_{ki}(x), 1 \leq k \leq n$ during **Phase I**. However, from Theorem 2, broadcasting all of them requires communicating $O(n^4)$ field elements. So we now introduce a method of combining n conflict graphs into a single directed conflict graph H. By broadcasting H to **S**, **R** can ensure that **S** will be able to identify all w_i's over which **R** has received at least one faulty polynomial $p'_{ki}(x)$. The combined directed conflict graph $H = (V, E)$ will have vertices and edges as follows: $V = \{w_1, w_2, \ldots, w_n\}$ and $E = \{(w_i, w_j)\}$ where arc $(w_i, w_j) \in E$ if (w_i, w_j) occurs in at least one $H_k, 1 \leq k \leq n$. Since an arc (w_i, w_j) can occur in multiple H_k's, **R** considers (w_i, w_j) from the minimum indexed H_γ among all such H_k's, keeping a note that (w_i, w_j) is added from H_γ. For each $(w_i, w_j) \in E$, **R** adds a five tuple $\{w_i, w_j, \gamma, p'_{\gamma i}(\alpha_j), r'_{\gamma i,j}\}$ to a list X, provided (w_i, w_j) is taken from H_γ. It is easy to see that there can be $\Theta(n^2)$ edges in H and hence $\Theta(n^2)$ tuples in X. In the next theorem, we prove that **S** can identify all faulty wires over which **R** received at least one faulty polynomial after receiving X.

Theorem 3. *In* **Union Technique**, *if* **R** *broadcasts* X *to* **S**, *then* **S** *identifies all faulty wires* w_i *over which* **R** *has received at least one* $p'_{ki}(x) \neq p_{ki}(x)$.

Proof. Similar to the proof of Theorem 1 and hence is omitted due to space constraint. For complete proof, see [13]. □

Now we are well-equipped to understand **Protocol PRMT_Optimal**, given in Table 2. Intuitively, the protocols works as follows: **S** selects n bivariate polynomials whose coefficients are the message to be sent. **S** then generates n sets B_k, $1 \leq k \leq n$ from n bivariate polynomials and communicates them to **R** in **Phase I**. On receiving n B_k's, **R** first constructs n conflict graphs H_k's and then combine all of them to a single graph H and broadcast H to **S** in **Phase II**. In **Phase III**, **S** identifies all faulty wires (which delivered incorrect polynomials during **Phase I**) from the knowledge of H and sends their identity to **R**. Finally,

Table 2. PRMT_Optimal: A three phase proactive bit optimal PRMT protocol

---

Let the sequence of $n(t+1)^2$ field elements that **S** wishes to transmit be denoted by $m_{k,ij}$, $0 \leq i, j \leq t$ and $1 \leq k \leq n$.

Phase I: (S to R)

• **S** defines n bivariate polynomials $q_k(x, y), 1 \leq k \leq n$ over $\mathbb{F}$, where $q_k(x, y) = \sum_{i=0, j=0}^{i=t, j=t} m_{k,ij} x^i y^j$. **S** evaluates $q_k(x, y)$ at n publicly known distinct values $\alpha_1, \alpha_2, \ldots, \alpha_n$ to get polynomials $p_{ki}(x), 1 \leq k \leq n, 1 \leq i \leq n$, each of degree t, where $p_{ki}(x) = q_k(x, \alpha_i)$. **S** then sends values to **R** over wire $w_i, 1 \leq i \leq n$ as shown in Table 1.

Phase II (R to S)

• Let **R** receives over wire $w_i, 1 \leq i \leq n$ the polynomials $p'_{ki}(x)$ and the values $r'_{kj,i}, 1 \leq k, j \leq n$. For $1 \leq k \leq n$, **R** considers the polynomials $p'_{k1}(x), p'_{k2}(x), \ldots, p'_{kn}(x)$ and the values $r'_{kj,i}, 1 \leq j, i \leq n$ and constructs the conflict graph H_k, where $(w_i, w_j) \in H_k$ if $p'_{ki}(\alpha_j) \neq r'_{ki,j}$. **R** combines $H_k, 1 \leq k \leq n$ into a single conflict graph H using **Union Technique** and forms the corresponding list of five tuples X and broadcasts X to **S**.

Phase III (S to R)

• **S** reliably receives the list X. **S** then creates a list L_{fault} which is initialized to $\emptyset$. For each tuple $\{w_i, w_j, k, p'_{ki}(\alpha_j), r'_{ki,j}\} \in X$, **S** locally verifies $r'_{ki,j} \stackrel{?}{=} r_{ki,j}$ and $p'_{ki}(\alpha_j) \stackrel{?}{=} p_{ki}(\alpha_j)$. Depending upon the output of the verification, **S** concludes that w_i or w_j or both are faulty and adds to L_{fault}. **S** finally broadcasts the list L_{fault} to **R** and terminates the protocol.

Message Recovery by R.

• **R** reliably receives L_{fault} and identifies all w_i over which it had received at least one faulty polynomial during **Phase I** (see Theorem 4). **R** neglects all the polynomials received over $w_i \in L_{fault}$,. Using the remaining (at least) $t + 1$ p'_{ki}'s, $1 \leq k \leq n$, **R** correctly recovers the polynomials $q_k(x, y)$'s, $1 \leq k \leq n$ and hence the message.

R recovers the message by reconstructing all the n bivariate polynomials using the identity of the faulty wires communicated by **S**.

Theorem 4. PRMT_Optimal *correctly delivers the message to* **R**.

Proof: In **PRMT_Optimal**, to recover m, **R** should be able to interpolate each bivariate polynomial $q_k(x, y), 1 \leq k \leq n$. Since each $q_k(x, y)$ is of degree t in both x and y, **R** requires $t + 1$ correct $q_k(x, \alpha_i) = p_{ki}(x)$'s to recover $q_k(x, y)$. Since among n wires at most t can be corrupted, **R** will receive at least $t + 1$ correct $p_{ki}(x)$'s. Now **R** wants to know the identity of $t + 1$ correct $p_{ki}(x)$'s. During **Phase II**, **R** constructs n conflict graph $H_k, 1 \leq k \leq n$ and combine them into a single conflict graph H using **Union Technique**, forms X and broadcasts it to **S**. Now from the working of the protocol and Theorem 3, from list L_{fault}, **R** identifies all faulty wires over which it has received at least one faulty polynomial during **Phase I** and neglects such wires. **R** will now have at least $t + 1$ correct $p_{ki}(x)$ for each $1 \leq k \leq n$, using which **R** recovers each $q_k(x, y)$ and hence m. $\square$

Theorem 5. *The communication complexity of* **PRMT_Optimal** *is* $O(n^3)$.

Proof: Follows from the protocol and hence is omitted due to space constraint. For complete proof, see [13]. □

2.2   Constant Phase Bit Optimal Proactive PSMT Protocol

We now present a three phase proactive PSMT protocol **PSMT_Optimal**, given in Table 3. The protocol securely sends $n(t+1) = \Omega(n^2)$ field elements by communicating $O(n^3)$ field elements, where $n = 2t + 1$. This matches the existing lower bound on the communication complexity of multi phase proactive PSMT protocol, as proved in [17]. It also significantly reduces the $O(t)$ phase communication optimal proactive PSMT protocol given in [17].

Theorem 6. **PSMT_Optimal** *correctly delivers the message to* **R** *by communicating* $O(n^3)$ *field elements..*

Proof: For complete proof, see [13]. □

Theorem 7. *In* **PSMT_Optimal***, any mobile adversary* $\mathcal{A}$*, controlling at most* t *wires will get no information about the message* m.

Proof: Without loss of generality, assume during **Phase I**, $\mathcal{A}$ controls $w_1, w_2, \ldots, w_t$. Thus $\mathcal{A}$ knows the constant terms of the polynomials $p_{ki}(x), 1 \leq k \leq n, 1 \leq i \leq t$ and t points on remaining polynomials $p_{kj}, t+1 \leq j \leq n$. Since the degree of each $p_{kj}, t+1 \leq j \leq n$ is t, $\mathcal{A}$ lacks one point for each of these polynomials implying information theoretic security for the constant terms of these polynomials. From Theorem 6, during **Phase III**, **S** will be able to identify all the faulty wires over which **R** had received at least one faulty polynomial during **Phase I**. **S** adds all such wires to L_{fault} and neglects them. **S** is left with $n - |L_{fault}|$ wires, out of which at most $t - |L_{fault}|$ wires were passively listened by the adversary. So **S** forms the vector x which is the list of constant terms of all the polynomials which were delivered correctly to **R** during **Phase I**. Since, there are $t + 1$ honest (not controlled by adversary) wires, **S** generates a one time pad of length $n(t+1)$ from x by executing **EXTRAND**. The proof now follows from the correctness of the **EXTRAND** algorithm. Note that during **Phase II**, the list X broadcast by **R**, reveals no new information to $\mathcal{A}$. Suppose $\{w_i, w_j, k, p'_{ki}(\alpha_j), r'_{ki,j}\} \in X$. Then either w_i or w_j or both had been corrupted by $\mathcal{A}$ during **Phase I**. So $\mathcal{A}$ already knows $r_{ki,j} = p_{ki}(\alpha_j)$. Thus X reveals no new information to $\mathcal{A}$. □

Optimality of PSMT_Optimal: In [17], it is shown that any three phase proactive PSMT protocol which securely sends $n(t+1) = \Omega(n^2)$ field elements, need to communicate $\Omega(n^3)$ field elements. Since, the communication complexity of **PSMT_Optimal** is $O(n^3)$, it is asymptotically optimal.

2.3   Proactive PSMT in Directed Networks

In [4], the authors have studied PSMT in directed networks in the presence of a static adversary, where the network is abstracted in the form of directed wires,

Table 3. PSMT_Optimal: A Three Phase Optimal Proactive PSMT Protocol

---

Let the sequence of $n(t+1)$ field elements that **S** wishes to transmit securely be denoted by $m_i, 1 \leq i \leq n(t+1)$.

Phase I: S to R
• **S** selects n^2 random polynomials $p_{ki}(x), 1 \leq k, i \leq n$ over $\mathbb{F}$ each of degree t. Over $w_i, 1 \leq i \leq n$, **S** sends the values to **R**, as shown in Table 1.

Phase II (R to S)
• Let **R** receives over $w_i, 1 \leq i \leq n$ the polynomials $p'_{ki}(x)$ and the values $r'_{kj,i}, 1 \leq k, j \leq n$. Then similar to **PRMT_Optimal** protocol, **R** constructs the conflict graphs $H_1, H_2, \ldots, H_n$ and combine them to a single conflict graph H using **Union Technique**, forms the list of five tuples X and broadcasts X to **S**.

Phase III (S to R)
• Similar to the **PRMT_Optimal** protocol, **S** correctly receives X and identifies all faulty wires w_i over which **R** must have received at least one faulty polynomial during **Phase I**. **S** adds all such wires L_{fault}. **S** neglects all $w_i \in L_{fault}$.

• **S** is left with $(n - |L_{fault}|)$ wires after neglecting all the faulty wires in the previous step. **S** then forms a vector x of length $(n - |L_{fault}|) * n$ which is the concatenation of the constant terms of all the polynomials $p_{ki}(x), 1 \leq k \leq n$ such that $w_i \notin L_{fault}$.

• **S** computes a pad y of length $n(t+1)$ by executing **EXTRAND**$_{n(n-|L_{fault}|), n(t+1)}(x)$. **S** computes $c = y \oplus m$, broadcasts L_{fault}, c to **R** and terminates.

Message Recovery by R.
• **R** reliably receives the list L_{fault} and identifies all the wires w_i over which it has received at least one faulty polynomial during **Phase I** (see Theorem 6) and neglects such w_i's. **R** then generates the pad y of length $n(t+1)$ following the same procedure as done by **S** and finally recovers the message m by computing $m = c \oplus y$.

---

directed either from **S** to **R** or vice-versa. Modeling the underlying network in the form of a directed graph is important in many practical scenarios. For instance, a base-station may communicate to even a far-off hand-held device but the other way round is not possible. Hence the digraph model is practically well-motivated. We now characterize proactive PSMT in directed networks.

Theorem 8. *Let $G = (V, E)$ be a directed network, where **S**, **R** $\in V$. Then a r-phase ($r \geq 2$) proactive PSMT protocol between **S** and **R** against a t-active adversary is possible iff G is $(2t+1)$-(**S**, **R**) and $(2t+1)$-(**R**, **S**) connected.*

Proof: **Sufficiency:** Let G be $(2t+1)$-(**S**, **R**) and $(2t+1)$-(**R**, **S**) connected. So there exists $2t+1$ directed wires from **S** to **R** and vice-versa. It is easy to see that protocol **PSMT_Optimal** can be correctly and securely executed over G.

Necessity: Since any proactive PSMT protocol should communicate the message reliably, **S** and **R** should be $2t+1$ connected in forward direction which is necessary for PRMT [5]. Similarly, we can show that $2t+1$ wires are necessary from **R** to **S**. If not, then since the adversary is mobile and can corrupt different set of t wires, it will fail any reliable communication from **R** to **S**, thus making any communication from **R** to **S** is useless. This reduces any multiphase protocol to a single phase protocol where **S** has to securely send a message over $(2t+1)$ wires tolerating a t-active Byzantine adversary, which is impossible from the results of [5]. Hence the theorem holds.   □

3   Proactive PRMT and PSMT in Terms of Rounds

Till previous section, we focussed on the design of *bit-optimal phase-based* PRMT (PSMT) protocols on a network abstracted in terms of wires. The merits of working in such a model are as follows: (i) It eases deriving the connectivity requirement for the possibility of PRMT/PSMT protocols and also deriving lower bounds for the communication complexity for protocols. (ii) It simplifies the analysis of any protocol designed on such model. But this model has its own demerits which are brought to the fore by the following example.

Consider the network on $(2t + 8)$ vertices given in Figure 1. Suppose the network in Figure 1 is abstracted as a collection of $(2t + 2)$ wires, under the control of a t-active mobile adversary. From [17], there exist an *optimal* single phase PRMT protocol with communication complexity of $O(n\ell)$ to send ℓ field elements, where n is the number of wires from **S** to **R** (which in this case is $2t + 2$). Now suppose that the protocol execution take place in a sequence of rounds, where at the beginning of each round, each node send messages to their neighbors. Thus, the messages sent by a player in round k reaches its neighbor at the beginning of round $k + 1$. Then the so called single phase "optimal"

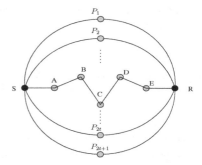

Fig. 1. A $(2t+2)$-(**S**,**R**)-connected Network

protocol of [17] runs in *six* rounds (which is the length of the longest path), with a communication complexity of $O(n)$ times the message size. Now the question is whether there exists a 6-round PRMT protocol in the network of Figure 1 with a better communication complexity. The answer is yes! Consider the following protocol: **S** and **R** run the 3-phase **PRMT_Optimal** protocol using the wires $P_1, P_2, \ldots, P_{2t+1}$, neglecting the path of length six (The longest path takes 6 rounds! While all other paths delivers message in two rounds). Thus while the single phase protocol has a complexity of $O(n\ell)$, the 3-phase protocol has a communication complexity of $O(\ell)$. Thus in Figure 1, an $O(\ell)$ 6-round protocol is possible. However, the information regarding the *length* of each of the paths (wires) in the actual network is completely lost in the wired abstraction. Thus wired abstraction causes an over estimation in the round complexity and communication complexity of protocols in the original network. We thus redefine our network model and adversary settings.

Round Based Network and Adversary Settings: As shown in previous example, it is necessary to use more fine-grained and stronger model, namely graph based one (in comparison to collection of wires) for designing and analyzing *optimal* PRMT and PSMT protocols. So we consider a graph with internal details in the following way. Let H be an undirected graph under the control of a t-active mobile adversary. From [18], H should be $(2t+1)$-$(\mathbf{S}, \mathbf{R})$ connected which is necessary and sufficient for PRMT and PSMT. Let G be the subgraph of H induced by the $2t+1$ vertex disjoint paths. If there are more than $2t+1$ vertex disjoint paths in H, then G will also contain these paths. In the following sections, we work on G to derive tight lower bound on round complexity for reliable communication and design protocols on G.

The system is synchronous and the protocol is executed in a sequence of rounds wherein in each round, a player can perform some local computation, send new messages to his out-neighbors, receive the messages sent in previous round by his in-neighbor, in that order. The distrust in the network is modeled by a mobile Byzantine adversary. The behavior of *mobile adversary* is re-defined to allow it to corrupt any set of t nodes after every $\rho \geq 1$ rounds, where ρ is called the roaming speed of the adversary. We first consider the worst case where $\rho = 1$, and later on, we will consider any arbitrary value of ρ. More formally before the beginning of round k, the adversary can corrupt any subset $\mathcal{P}_{corrupt}$ consisting of t players. Then the adversary has access to the messages sent to the players in $\mathcal{P}_{corrupt}$ in round $k-1$ and can alter the behavior of the players in $\mathcal{P}_{corrupt}$ arbitrarily in the round k. However by corrupting a player P in a round k the adversary does not obtain information about the messages to and from the node P in all the previous rounds, i.e., the protocol can choose to delete some information from the (honest) node at the end of a round, to make sure that the information is not available to the adversary even if he corrupts the node at a later round. We now define transmission graph, which is used in our protocols.

Transmission Graph [18]: In the case of mobile adversary, where the adversary can corrupt different set of nodes at different times, a graph representation of the network is inadequate. However since the protocol itself discretizes time in terms of rounds, it is sufficient to model the system at each round rather than each time instant. Hence, in [18], the author have introduced the concept of transmission graph $\mathcal{G}^d$ to study the execution of a protocol that has run d rounds. In the transmission graph $\mathcal{G}^d$, each node P is represented by a set of nodes $\{P_0, P_1, P_2 \ldots P_d\}$. The node P_r corresponds to the node P at round r. For any two neighboring nodes P and Q and any $1 \leq r \leq d$, a message sent by P to Q in round $r-1$ is available to Q only at round r. Hence there is an edge in $\mathcal{G}^d$ connecting the node P_{r-1} to the node Q_r for all $1 \leq r \leq d$. Note that the transmission graph is a directed graph, because of the directed nature of time. So the edges between the nodes at consecutive time steps are always oriented towards increasing time. We now give the formal definition.

Definition 1. *Given a graph $G = (V, E)$ and a positive integer d, the transmission Graph $\mathcal{G}^d$ is a directed graph defined as follows*

– *Nodes of $\mathcal{G}^d$ belong to $V \times \{0 \ldots d\}$ where the node $(P, r) \in V \times \{0 \ldots d\}$ is denoted by P_r.*
– *The edge set of $\mathcal{G}^d$ is $E^d = E_1 \cup E_2$ where, $E_1 = \{(P_{a_{r-1}}, P_{b_r}) \,|\, (P_a, P_b) \in E$ and $1 \leq r \leq d\}$ and $E_2 = \{(P_{a_{r-1}}, P_{a_r}) | P_a \in V$ and $1 \leq r \leq d\}$.*

Let $\mathcal{P}^r$ denote the set of nodes corresponding to nodes at round r, $\mathcal{P}^r = \{P_{a_r} \,|\, P_a \in V\}$. Let $\mathcal{ADV}_{mobile}$ be a threshold mobile adversary acting on a network G that can corrupt any t nodes in a single round. Consider an execution Γ of a d-round protocol on G. Suppose $\mathcal{ADV}_{mobile}$ corrupts a set of nodes $Adv_r = \{P_1, P_2, \ldots P_t\}$ in round r in G, then the same effect is obtained by corrupting the nodes $Adv^r = \{P_{1_r}, P_{2_r}, \ldots P_{t_r}\}$ in $\mathcal{G}^d$. Hence the effect of $\mathcal{ADV}_{mobile}$ on execution Γ can be simulated by a static general adversary who corrupts $\bigcup_{r=1}^{d} Adv^r$ on $\mathcal{G}^d$. More formally, we have the following lemma:

Lemma 1. *Mobile adversary $\mathcal{ADV}_{mobile}$ acting on the original graph G for d rounds can be simulated by a static adversary given by the adversary structure $\mathcal{ADV}^d_{static} = \{Adv^1 \cup Adv^2 \cup Adv^3 \ldots \cup Adv^d | Adv^r \in \Pi_t(\mathcal{P}^r), 1 \leq r \leq d\}$ on $\mathcal{G}^d$, where $\Pi_t(\mathcal{P}^r)$ denotes set of all subsets of cardinality t of the set $\mathcal{P}^r$.*

Example 1. Consider the network shown in Figure 2: The network is 3-(**S**,**R**)-connected and hence at most one mobile adversary ($t = 1$) can be tolerated by any PRMT (PSMT) protocol. Consider $\mathcal{G}^4$, where the adversary structure $\mathcal{ADV}^4_{static} = \{Adv^1 \cup Adv^2 \cup Adv^3 \cup Adv^4\}$, where each $Adv^r \in \Pi_1(\mathcal{P}^r), 1 \leq r \leq 4$ and $\Pi_1(\mathcal{P}^r)$ denotes the set of all subsets of cardinality 1 of the set $\mathcal{P}^r$. For example, $\{H_1, E_2, B_3, A_4\}$ is an element of $\mathcal{ADV}^4_{static}$ in $\mathcal{G}^4$, which denotes an adversarial strategy where in the original network, the adversary corrupts the nodes H, E, B and A during first, second, third and fourth round respectively.

In order to find the minimum number of rounds for reliable communication, we slightly modify the definition of transmission graph as follows:

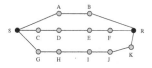

Definition 2. *Given a graph G and an integer $d >$ 0 the modified Transmission Graph G^d is the graph $\mathcal{G}^d$ along with two additional nodes $\mathbf{S}, \mathbf{R}$. $\mathbf{S}$ is connected to all $\mathbf{S}_r, 0 \leq r \leq d$ and each $\mathbf{R}_r, 0 \leq r \leq d$*

Fig. 2. Graph G

is connected to $\mathbf{R}$. Further the edges between $(\mathbf{S}_{r-1}, \mathbf{S}_r)$ and $(\mathbf{R}_{r-1}, \mathbf{R}_r)$ for $1 \leq r \leq d$ are removed.

Definition 3. *Two paths Γ_1 and Γ_2 between the nodes $\mathbf{S}$ and $\mathbf{R}$ in the modified transmission graph G^d are said to be securely disjoint if the only common nodes between the two paths are $\mathbf{S}_a$ and $\mathbf{R}_b$ for some value of a and b. That is, $\Gamma_1 \cap \Gamma_2 \subset \{\mathbf{S}_0, \mathbf{S}_1, \mathbf{S}_2 \ldots \mathbf{S}_d\} \cup \{\mathbf{R}_0, \mathbf{R}_1, \mathbf{R}_2 \ldots \mathbf{R}_d\}$.*

Definition 4. *Given a path $\Gamma = \{\mathbf{S}, P_1, P_2 \ldots P_z, \mathbf{R}\}$ from $\mathbf{S}$ to $\mathbf{R}$ in the underlying graph G, the space-time path Γ^i in graph G^d is defined as $\Gamma^i = \{\mathbf{S}, \mathbf{S}_i, P_{1_{i+1}}, P_{2_{i+2}}, \ldots P_{z_{i+z}}, \mathbf{R}_{i+z+1}, \mathbf{R}\}, \quad 0 \leq i \leq d - z - 1$.*

Example 2. Consider the path $\Gamma = \{\mathbf{S}, A, B, \mathbf{R}\}$ in Figure 2. Now in G^5, there are three space time paths corresponding to the path Γ, namely $\Gamma^0 = \{\mathbf{S}, \mathbf{S}_0, A_1, B_2, \mathbf{R}_3, \mathbf{R}\}$, $\Gamma^1 = \{\mathbf{S}, \mathbf{S}_1, A_2, B_3, \mathbf{R}_4, \mathbf{R}\}$ and $\Gamma^2 = \{\mathbf{S}, \mathbf{S}_2, A_3, B_4, \mathbf{R}_5, \mathbf{R}\}$. The space time path Γ^0 can be interpreted as $\mathbf{S}$ communicating to A in the 0th round, A communicating to B in the first round, B communicating to $\mathbf{R}$ in the second round which is received by $\mathbf{R}$ in the third round. Note that in G^5, there are only three space time paths corresponding to the path Γ in G. In general, let G be a graph and Γ be a path between $\mathbf{S}$ and $\mathbf{R}$ containing z nodes (i.e., the path length is $z + 1$). Then in the transmission graph $G^d, d > z$, there will be $d - z$ space time paths corresponding to the path Γ, namely $\Gamma^i, 0 \leq i \leq d - z - 1$.

Lemma 2 ([18]). *For any path Γ of length z from $\mathbf{S}$ to $\mathbf{R}$ in G, the paths $\Gamma^i, 0 \leq i \leq d - z$ are pairwise securely disjoint. Further, for any two vertex disjoint paths Γ_1, Γ_2 and for any i, j the paths Γ_1^i and Γ_2^j are securely disjoint.*

3.1   Computing Minimum Number of Rounds for PRMT with $\rho = 1$

In [18], the authors have computed the minimum number of rounds d for reliable communication from $\mathbf{S}$ to $\mathbf{R}$ which is $d > (2t + 1)N$ (see Lemma 4.1 of [18]), where $\mathbf{S}$ and $\mathbf{R}$ are connected by $2t + 1$ paths and N is the total number of nodes in the given network. However, we show that the bound in [18] is not tight. So, we derive tight bound on the minimum number of rounds, denoted by r_{min} required for reliable communication from $\mathbf{S}$ to $\mathbf{R}$. Consider a graph G where $\mathbf{S}$ and $\mathbf{R}$ are connected by $2t+1$ vertex disjoint paths $\{\Gamma_1, \Gamma_2, \ldots, \Gamma_{2t+1}\}$. Without loss of generality, assume that the paths are arranged in ascending order of path length. Let N_i denotes the number of nodes in $\Gamma_i, 1 \leq i \leq 2t + 1$. Then in G^d, there will be $d - N_i$ space time paths corresponding to $\Gamma_i, 1 \leq i \leq 2t + 1$ in G, provided $d - N_i > 0$. If $d - N_i \leq 0$ then there will be no space time path corresponding to Γ_i in G^d. Assuming that each of the term $d - N_i$ is positive, the total number of the space time paths in G^d is $\sum_{i=1}^{i=2t+1}(d - N_i)$. From Lemma 2, all these paths are securely disjoint. Now if any reliable protocol is executed on the original graph G for d rounds, then the adversary can make corruption only up to $(d - 1)$ rounds because in any reliable protocol, which is executed for d rounds, $\mathbf{R}$ will receive information from its neighboring nodes in round d, which they sent to $\mathbf{R}$ in round $d - 1$ and terminates the protocol. So even if adversary corrupts some node in round d, it will not effect the protocol, because the protocol will terminate in the dth round itself. Note that if at least one node in a space time path in G^d is corrupted, it implies that the entire space time path is corrupted because the corrupted data introduced by the corrupted node will be forwarded by other nodes of the path in subsequent rounds. In general, since the adversary can corrupt at most t nodes in each round of any reliable protocol, it can corrupt at most $t(d - 1)$ nodes in G^d which can be in worst case distributed on $t(d - 1)$ secure disjoint paths and hence each element in $\mathcal{ADV}_{static}^d$ is of maximum cardinality $t(d - 1)$. We now state the following theorem.

Theorem 9. *Let G be an undirected network where $\mathbf{S}$ and $\mathbf{R}$ are connected by $2t+1$ vertex disjoint paths $\Gamma_1, \Gamma_2, \ldots, \Gamma_{2t+1}$ with N_i nodes in $\Gamma_i, 1 \leq i \leq 2t+1$. Let $\mathcal{ADV}_{mobile}$ be a mobile adversary corrupting any set (probably different) of t nodes in each round. Then the minimum number of rounds required for reliable communication is r_{min} iff $r_{min} \geq N - 2t + 1$ where $N = \sum_{i=1}^{i=2t+1} N_i$.*

Proof. **Necessity**: Let r_{min} be the minimum number of rounds required for reliable communication in G. Then as explained above, any mobile adversary $\mathcal{ADV}_{mobile}$ can be simulated by a static adversary structure $\mathcal{ADV}_{static}^{r_{min}}$ where each element of it is of cardinality $t(r_{min} - 1)$. Also in $G^{r_{min}}$, there will be $\sum_{i=1}^{i=2t+1}(r_{min} - N_i)$ securely disjoint paths between $\mathbf{S}$ and $\mathbf{R}$ out of which at most $t(r_{min} - 1)$ can be under the control of the adversary. Now it is known from [10], that reliable communication between $\mathbf{S}$ and $\mathbf{R}$ in a network in the presence of a static adversary given by an adversary structure is possible iff removal of of any two adversarial sets from the adversary structure does not disconnect $\mathbf{S}$ and $\mathbf{R}$. It implies that reliable communication in G under the presence of $\mathcal{ADV}_{mobile}$ is possible in r_{min} rounds if $\sum_{i=1}^{i=2t+1}(r_{min} - N_i) \geq 2t(r_{min} - 1) + 1$. Solving this we get $r_{min} \geq N - 2t + 1$ where $N = \sum_{i=1}^{i=2t+1} N_i$.

Sufficiency: Suppose $r_{min} \geq N - 2t + 1$ where $N = \sum_{i=1}^{i=2t+1} N_i$. Then in $G^{r_{min}}$ there are $2t(r_{min} - 1) + 1$ securely disjoint paths from $\mathbf{S}$ to $\mathbf{R}$, out of which at most $t(r_{min} - 1)$ can be under the control of the adversary $\mathcal{ADV}_{static}^{r_{min}}$. Let us denote these paths by $w_1, w_2, \ldots, w_{2q+1}$, where $q = t(r_{min} - 1)$. We now describe a reliable protocol **REL** on the graph $G^{r_{min}}$ and show how it can be executed on the real network G to reliably send m.

Protocol REL: Round-Optimal Reliable Message transmission of message m.

- The sender $\mathbf{S}$ sends the message m along all the paths w_i, $1 \leq i \leq 2q + 1$.
- All nodes P_{a_b} along a path w_i just forward the message to the next node along w_i.
- $\mathbf{R}$ on receiving the values along all the paths takes the majority as m.

REL can be emulated on G in the following way: if a node P_{1_b} and $P_{2_{b+1}}$ are consecutive nodes in $G^{r_{min}}$ along some path w_i, where w_i is the space time path corresponding to some physical path $\Gamma_j, 1 \leq j \leq 2t + 1$, then P_1 on receiving m' (possibly changed m) along the path Γ_j at the beginning of round b forward it to the node P_2 at the end of round b which is received by P_2 in round $b + 1$. The protocol has a communication complexity of $O((2t(r_{min} - 1)|m|)$ and this is polynomial in N. The correctness of the protocol is obvious. $\square$

3.2   Proactive PRMT and PSMT Protocols in Terms of Rounds

From Theorem 9, in $G^{r_{min}}$ there will be $2t(r_{min} - 1) + 1$ securely disjoint paths out of which at most $t(r_{min} - 1)$ can be corrupted. However each of these paths are temporal and hence can be used at most once. We now present the modified version of three phase protocol **PRMT_Optimal**, called **PRMT_Round**, as

Table 4. PRMT_Round: A $3r_{min}$ Round Proactive PRMT Protocol

Let the sequence of $n(q+1)^2$ field elements that **S** wishes to transmit be denoted by $m_{k,ij}, 0 \leq i,j \leq q$ and $1 \leq k \leq n$.

First r_{min} rounds: (S to R) executed over space time paths $\Gamma_i^{(1)}, 1 \leq i \leq 2q+1$

- Using the $m_{k,ij}$ values, **S** defines n bivariate polynomials $q_k(x,y), 1 \leq k \leq n$, where $q_k(x,y) = \sum_{i=0,j=0}^{i=q,j=q} m_{k,ij} x^i y^j$. **S** evaluates each $q_k(x,y)$ at n publicly known distinct values $\alpha_1, \alpha_2, \ldots, \alpha_n$ to obtain total n^2 polynomials $p_{ki}(x), 1 \leq k \leq n, 1 \leq i \leq n$ over $\mathbb{F}$, each of degree q where $p_{ki}(x) = q_k(x, \alpha_i)$. Over space time paths $\Gamma_i^{(1)}, 1 \leq i \leq 2q+1$, **S** sends $p_{ki}(x), 1 \leq k \leq n$ and the values $p_{kj}(\alpha_i)$, denoted by $r_{kj,i}$, for $1 \leq k, j \leq n$.

Second r_{min} rounds: (R to S) executed over space time paths $\Gamma_i^{(2)}, 1 \leq i \leq 2q+1$

- Let **R** receives over space time path $\Gamma_i^{(1)}, 1 \leq i \leq n$ the polynomials $p'_{ki}(x)$ and the values $r'_{kj,i}, 1 \leq k, j \leq n$. **R** considers the polynomials $p'_{k1}(x), p'_{k2}(x), \ldots, p'_{kn}(x)$ and the values $r'_{kj,i}, 1 \leq j, i \leq n$ and constructs the conflict graph $H_k, 1 \leq k \leq n$. **R** then combines $H_k, 1 \leq k \leq n$ into a single directed conflict graph H using **Union Technique** and forms the corresponding list of five tuples X and reliably sends X to **S** by executing **REL** protocol over the space time paths $\Gamma_i^{(2)}, 1 \leq i \leq 2q+1$.

Last r_{min} rounds: S to R executed over space time paths $\Gamma_i^{(3)}, 1 \leq i \leq 2q+1$

- **S** reliably receives the list X and identifies all faulty space time paths $\Gamma_i^{(1)}$ over which **R** has received at least one faulty polynomial $p'_{ki}(x), 1 \leq k \leq n$ during first r_{min} rounds. **S** adds all such paths to a list L_{fault}. Note that $|L_{fault}| \leq q$. **S** then reliably sends L_{fault} to **R** by executing **REL** protocol over the space time paths $\Gamma_i^{(3)}, 1 \leq i \leq 2q+1$.

Message Recovery by R.

- **R** reliably receives L_{fault} and identifies all space time path $\Gamma_i^{(1)}$ over which it has received at least one faulty polynomial during first r_{min} rounds (proof is similar to Theorem 4) and neglects those space time paths. Using the remaining (at least) $q+1$ p'_{ki}'s, $1 \leq k \leq n$, **R** correctly recovers the bivariate polynomials $q_k(x,y)$'s, $1 \leq k \leq n$ and hence the message.

shown in Table 4, tolerating a mobile adversary who can corrupt any t nodes in every round. **PRMT_Round** is executed for $3r_{min}$ rounds on G where G is the original network consisting $2t+1$ vertex disjoint paths between **S** and **R**. The first phase of **PRMT_Optimal** is executed in the first r_{min} rounds from **S** to **R**, the second phase of **PRMT_Optimal** is executed in the next r_{min} rounds from **R** to **S** and finally the third phase in the last r_{min} rounds from **S** to **R**. This can be visualized as executing a $3r_{min}$ round protocol on $G^{3r_{min}}$, where first r_{min} rounds are executed from **S** to **R**, next r_{min} rounds from **R** to **S** and finally last r_{min} rounds from **S** to **R**. Let $q = t(r_{min} - 1)$ and $n = 2q+1$. We refer to the nodes corresponding to the first r_{min} rounds from **S** to **R** as the first half denoted by $\Gamma_i^{(1)}, 1 \leq i \leq 2q+1$, the nodes in the next r_{min} rounds from **R** to **S** as second half denoted by $\Gamma_i^{(2)}, 1 \leq i \leq 2q+1$ and the nodes in the last r_{min} rounds from **S** to **R** as third half denoted by $\Gamma_i^{(3)}, 1 \leq i \leq 2q+1$. From Theorem 9, $r_{min} = N - 2t + 1$. The protocol is same as **PRMT_Optimal** except that degree of each bi-variate polynomial is q. Moreover, **Phase** $i, 1 \leq i \leq 3$

is executed in r_{min} rounds on $\Gamma_j^{(i)}, 1 \leq j \leq 2q + 1$. **PRMT_Round** can be simulated on G following the explanation provided earlier for **REL** protocol. Note that Theorem 4 and Theorem 5 will hold for **PRMT_Round** with q in the place of t. The protocol reliably sends $n(q + 1)^2 = \Omega(n^3)$ field elements by communicating $O(n^3)$ field elements in $3r_{min}$ rounds.

Computing r_{min} for Arbitrary Roaming Speed: We now consider a mobile adversary with roaming speed $\rho > 1$ and compute the minimum number of rounds r_{min}^ρ, required for reliable communication from **S** to **R**, against a t-active mobile adversary, corrupting t nodes after every ρ rounds. Note that a mobile adversary with roaming speed one is the strongest adversary.

Theorem 10. *Let G be a $(2t + 1)$-(**S**, **R**) connected undirected network under the influence of a t-active mobile adversary with roaming speed of $\rho > 1$. Then the minimum number of rounds r_{min}^ρ required for reliable communication is given by $r_{min}^\rho = min\ \{r, r_{min}^{\rho-1}\}$ where r is the minimum value satisfying $\sum_{i=1}^{i=2t+1} \lceil \frac{r-N_i}{\rho} \rceil \geq 2 \lceil \frac{r-1}{\rho} \rceil * t + 1$.*

Proof: For complete proof see [13]. □

References

1. Agarwal, S., Cramer, R., Haan, R.d.: Asymptotically optimal two-round perfectly secure message transmission. In: Dwork, C. (ed.) CRYPTO 2006. LNCS, vol. 4117, pp. 394–408. Springer, Heidelberg (2006)
2. Backes, M., Cachin, C., Strobl, R.: Proactive secure message transmission in asynchronous networks. In: Proc. of PODC 2003, pp. 223–232 (2003)
3. Ben-Or, M., Goldwasser, S., Wigderson, A.: Completeness theorems for non-cryptographic fault-tolerant distributed computation. In: Proc. of 20th ACM STOC, pp. 1–10 (1988)
4. Desmedt, Y., Wang, Y.: Perfectly secure message transmission revisited. In: Knudsen, L.R. (ed.) EUROCRYPT 2002. LNCS, vol. 2332, pp. 502–517. Springer, Heidelberg (2002)
5. Dolev, D., Dwork, C., Waarts, O., Yung, M.: Perfectly secure message transmission. JACM 40(1), 17–47 (1993)
6. Frankel, Y., Gemmell, P., MacKenzie, P.D., Yung, M.: Proactive RSA. In: Kaliski Jr., B.S. (ed.) CRYPTO 1997. LNCS, vol. 1294, pp. 440–452. Springer, Heidelberg (1997)
7. Goldreich, O., Micali, S., Wigderson, A.: How to play any mental game. In: Proc. of 19th ACM STOC, pp. 218–229 (1987)
8. Herzberg, A., Jakobson, M., Jarecki, S., Krawczyk, H., Yung, M.: Proactive Public Key and Signature Systems. In: Proceedings of 4th Conference on Computer and Communications Security, pp. 100–110 (1997)
9. Herzberg, A., Jarecki, S., Krawczyk, H., Yung, M.: Proactive Secret Sharing, or: How to Cope with Perpetual Leakage. In: Coppersmith, D. (ed.) CRYPTO 1995. LNCS, vol. 963, pp. 339–352. Springer, Heidelberg (1995)
10. Kumar, M.V.N.A., Goundan, P.R., Srinathan, K., Rangan, C.P.: On perfectly secure communication over arbitrary networks. In: Proc. of PODC 2002, pp. 193–202 (2002)

11. Kurosawa, K., Suzuki, K.: Truly efficient 2-round perfectly secure message transmission scheme. In: Proc. of EUROCRYPT, pp. 324–340 (2008)
12. Ostrovsky, R., Yung, M.: How to withstand mobile virus attacks. In: Proc. of 10th PODC, pp. 51–61. ACM Press, New York (1991)
13. Patra, A., Choudhary, A., Gayatri, M., Pandu Rangan, C.: Efficient perfectly reliable and secure communication tolerating mobile adversary. Cryptology ePrint Archive, Report 2008/086 (2008)
14. Patra, A., Choudhary, A., Srinathan, K., Rangan, C.P.: Constant phase bit optimal protocols for perfectly reliable and secure message transmission. In: Barua, R., Lange, T. (eds.) INDOCRYPT 2006. LNCS, vol. 4329, pp. 221–235. Springer, Heidelberg (2006)
15. Rabin, T., Ben-Or, M.: Verifiable secret sharing and multiparty protocols with honest majority. In: Proc. of 21st ACM STOC, pp. 73–85 (1989)
16. Sayeed, H., Abu-Amara, H.: Efficient perfectly secure message transmission in synchronous networks. Information and Computation 126(1), 53–61 (1996)
17. Srinathan, K., Narayanan, A., Rangan, C.P.: Optimal perfectly secure message transmission. In: Franklin, M. (ed.) CRYPTO 2004. LNCS, vol. 3152, pp. 545–561. Springer, Heidelberg (2004)
18. Srinathan, K., Raghavendra, P., Rangan, C.P.: On proactive perfectly secure message transmission. In: Pieprzyk, J., Ghodosi, H., Dawson, E. (eds.) ACISP 2007. LNCS, vol. 4586, pp. 461–473. Springer, Heidelberg (2007)
19. Yao, A.C.: Protocols for secure computations. In: Proc. of 23rd IEEE FOCS, pp. 160–164 (1982)

Methods for Linear and Differential Cryptanalysis of Elastic Block Ciphers

Debra L. Cook[1], Moti Yung[2], and Angelos D. Keromytis[3]

[1] Bell Labs, New Providence, NJ, USA
dcook@cs.columbia.edu[*]
[2] Google, Inc. and Department of Computer Science, Columbia University, New York, NY, USA
moti@cs.columbia.edu
[3] Department of Computer Science, Columbia University, New York, NY, USA
angelos@cs.columbia.edu

Abstract. The elastic block cipher design employs the round function of a given, b-bit block cipher in a black box fashion, embedding it in a network structure to construct a family of ciphers in a uniform manner. The family is parameterized by block size, for any size between b and $2b$. The design assures that the overall workload for encryption is proportional to the block size. When considering the approach taken in elastic block ciphers, the question arises as to whether cryptanalysis results, including methods of analysis and bounds on security, for the original fixed-sized cipher are lost or, since original components of the cipher are used, whether previous analysis can be applied or reused in some manner.

With this question in mind, we analyze elastic block ciphers and consider the security against two basic types of attacks, linear and differential cryptanalysis. We show how they can be related to the corresponding security of the fixed-length version of the cipher. Concretely, we develop techniques that take advantage of relationships between the structure of the elastic network and the original version of the cipher, independently of the cipher.

This approach demonstrates how one can build upon existing components to allow cryptanalysis within an extended structure (a topic which may be of general interest outside of elastic block ciphers). We show that any linear attack on an elastic block cipher can be converted efficiently into a linear attack on the fixed-length version of the cipher by converting the equations used to attack the elastic version to equations for the fixed-length version. We extend the result to any algebraic attack. We then define a general method for deriving the differential characteristic bound of an elastic block cipher using the differential bound on a single round of the fixed-length version of the cipher. The structure of elastic block ciphers allows us to use a state transition method to compute differentials for the elastic version from differentials of the round function of the original cipher.

Keywords: security analysis, linear cryptanalysis, differential cryptanalysis.

1 Introduction

Elastic block ciphers were designed to convert existing fixed-length block ciphers into variable-length block ciphers in an efficient manner. Furthermore, the design allows

---

[*] This work was performed primarily while the author was at Columbia University.

Y. Mu, W. Susilo, and J. Seberry (Eds.): ACISP 2008, LNCS 5107, pp. 187–202, 2008.
© Springer-Verlag Berlin Heidelberg 2008

certain properties of the fixed-length cipher to remain intact in the elastic version, creating a well-defined relationship between the security of the elastic and fixed-length versions [3,4]. Exploiting existing ciphers' components in the design of new ciphers is not uncommon. In the elastic block cipher case, since the cipher attempts to cover a large range of block sizes, a specific design for each size was traded against a general design methodology. Naturally, in a general design, as opposed to an optimized design for a specific block size, one may lose the ability to provide tight security bounds, but security analysis is required nevertheless. A natural approach when building upon existing components is to reuse the security properties of the building blocks. Thus, our work is concerned with how the security of an elastic block cipher relates to the security of the fixed-length version.

In more detail, we view elastic block ciphers as a category of block ciphers with (somewhat generic) design rules, and we consider how to evaluate their security against the two most basic types of cryptanalysis: linear [6] and differential cryptanalysis [1]. The elastic design is a generic approach that inserts the round function from an existing block cipher into a network structure (the elastic network). Therefore, new methods are needed to perform our analysis that are derived from the structure of the elastic network. Since the approach taken in forming elastic block ciphers is non-traditional in the sense that it does not focus on optimizing the design for a specific block size, one may dismiss the entire idea and stick to usual designs of ciphers of fixed size; however, we believe that the idea of having a substitution-permutation network that is size-flexible (*i.e.*, the elastic network) and is somewhat generic is an interesting subject that deserves investigation. This work is a step in this direction.

Concretely, we first prove that any linear attack on an elastic block cipher can be converted in polynomial time and memory into a linear attack on the fixed-length version of the cipher. This is done by showing how to convert the equations for such an attack on the elastic version to an attack on the fixed-length version. Therefore, if the fixed-length version is immune to linear cryptanalysis, the elastic version is also immune. We extend the result to any algebraic attack. We then define a general method for deriving the differential characteristic bound of an elastic block cipher from the differential bound on a round of the fixed-length version. We summarize our application of the method to elastic versions of AES [9] and MISTY1 [7].

The remainder of the paper is organized as follows. In Section 2, we briefly review the construction of elastic block ciphers. In Section 3, we prove that a linear attack, or more generally any algebraic attack, on an elastic block cipher implies that such an attack exists on the fixed-length version of the block cipher. In Section 4, we define our method for deriving differential bounds on an elastic block cipher. Section 5 concludes the paper.

2   Elastic Block Cipher Review

2.1   Overview

We briefly review the method presented by Cook, *et. al,* for creating elastic block ciphers [3]. The method converts the encryption and decryption functions of existing

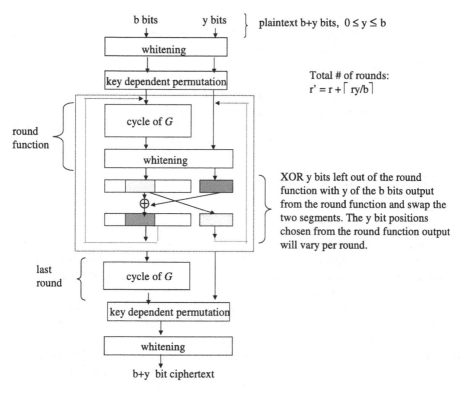

Fig. 1. Elastic Block Cipher Structure [3]

block ciphers to accept blocks of size b to $2b$ bits, where b is the block size of the original block cipher. The general structure of an elastic block cipher is shown in Figure 1. An elastic version of a block cipher is created by inserting the cycle of the original fixed-length block cipher into the network structure to form the round function of the elastic version. In each round the leftmost b bits are processed by the round function and the rightmost y bits are omitted from the round function. Afterwards, the rightmost y bits are XORed with a subset of the leftmost b bits and the results swapped. This swapping of bits may be omitted after the last round. The elastic version also includes initial and end of round whitening, and an initial and final key dependent permutation. The number of expanded-key bits required varies based on the block size and the original block cipher. The key schedule of the original cipher is replaced with a generic key schedule that generates as many expanded-key bits as needed. In theory, the expanded key bits can take on any value and we view the expanded key bits in this manner in our analysis. For actual implementations, a stream cipher was suggested as one option for the key schedule [3].

We use the following notation:

– G denotes any existing fixed-length block cipher.
– r denotes the number of cycles in G, where a cycle in G is the point at which all b bits of the block have been processed by the round function of G. For example, if

G is a Feistel network, a cycle is the sequence of applying the round function of G to the left and right halves of the b-bit block. In AES, the round function is a cycle.

- b denotes the block length of the input to G in bits.
- y is an integer in the range $[0, b]$.
- G' denotes the elastic version of G with a $(b + y)$-bit input for any valid value of y.
- r' denotes the number of rounds in G'. $r' = r + \lceil \frac{ry}{b} \rceil$.
- The round function of G' will refer to one entire cycle of G.
- The swap step will refer the step in which the rightmost y bits are XORed with a subset of the leftmost b bits and the results swapped.

3   Linear Cryptanalysis

We consider linear attacks and algebraic attacks on elastic block ciphers in general. We prove that any practical linear or algebraic attack on an elastic block cipher, G', can be converted into a polynomial time related attack on the original cipher, G, independently of the specific block cipher used for G. We take advantage of the elastic block cipher structure to define a linear relationship, if one exists, across r rounds of G' in terms of any linear relationship in a cycle of G.

Linear cryptanalysis involves finding equations relating plaintext, ciphertext and key (usually expanded-key) bits via XORs that hold with probability $\frac{1}{2} + \alpha$ for non-negligible α. Without loss of generality, we assume the equations are in the form such that $0 < \alpha \leq \frac{1}{2}$, and that the equations involve the expanded-key bits. We omit the initial and final key-dependent permutations in the elastic block cipher construction when performing our analysis in order to focus on the core structure of elastic block ciphers. The two permutations do not impact any relationship that exists across the rounds of G'.

We show that a linear relationship across r rounds of G' implies such a relationship across r cycles of G. If any such linear relationship holds with a probability such that fewer than $2^{(b-1)}$ (plaintext, ciphertext) pairs are required for an attack, then G is subject to a linear attack that requires fewer plaintexts, on average, than an exhaustive search over all plaintexts. Whether or not using the equations is computationally feasible depends on number of (plaintext, ciphertext) pairs and the number of equations that must be computed. If at least $2^{(b-1)}$ plaintext, ciphertext pairs are required for an attack on r rounds of G', then either the attack is infeasible on r rounds of G' from a practical perspective or G is subject to a brute force attack in practice. Note that we are dealing with an attack on only r rounds of G' and the probability of a linear relationship holding across $r' = r + \lceil \frac{ry}{b} \rceil$ rounds of G' will be less than that for r rounds. More specifically, if the attack on G' involves a maximum correlation between plaintext, ciphertext and key bits which occurs with probability $\leq 2^{-b}$ on r rounds (thus requiring in practice $\geq 2^b$ plaintexts), then an attack on $2r$ rounds involves a maximum correlation that occurs with probability $\leq 2^{-2b}$ and requires $> 2^{2b}$ plaintexts. In this case, G' is practically secure against a linear attack when $\lceil \frac{ry}{b} \rceil = r$. A direct implication of our result is that if G' is subject to an attack using any algebraic equations, as opposed to just linear equations, then so is G.

Theorem 1. *Given a block cipher G with a block size of b bits and r cycles, and its elastic version G' with a block size of $b + y$ bits for $0 \leq y \leq b$, if G' is subject to a* *linear attack on r rounds then either G is subject to a linear attack or the resources exist to perform an exhaustive search on G over all plaintexts, assuming the key schedules of G and G′ do not produce message-dependent expanded keys, meaning any expanded-key bits depend only on the key and do not vary based on the plaintext or ciphertext input to the cipher.*

Proof. We first note that if the linear attack on r rounds of G' requires at least 2^b (plaintext, ciphertext) pairs then either the attack is computationally infeasible or G is insecure independent of the attack (since the attacker has the resources to encrypt 2^b plaintexts). Therefore, it can be assumed that the attack on G' requires $< 2^b$ (plaintext, ciphertext) pairs. The assumption that the expanded key bits do not depend on the input to the cipher (the plaintext or ciphertext) is true of block ciphers used in practice and of elastic block ciphers. The theorem is proved by showing how a linear attack on G' can be converted into an attack in G. With no further assumptions about the key schedules, the result is an attack that finds an expanded key for G that produces the $(plaintext, ciphertext)$ pairs consistent with G, but which may or may not adhere to the key schedule of G. If the expanded key is inconsistent with the key schedule of G, this itself indicates another weakness in G because it means there is some expanded key that is not produced by the key schedule of G but which produces the same $(plaintext, ciphertext)$ pairs that G would produce when using some key generated by G's key schedule (*i.e.* the attack finds an equivalent key). If the following three assumptions are placed on the expanded key bits of G', then the attack on G will find a key consistent with the key schedule of G:

- The rightmost y bits of each whitening step in G' can take on any value and are independent of any other expanded-key bits.
- Any expanded-key bits used in the round function of the first r consecutive rounds of G' can take on the same values as the expanded-key bits used in the cycles of G.
- If G contains initial and end of cycle whitening, any expanded-key bits used for the leftmost b bits of each whitening step in the first r consecutive rounds of G' can take on the same values as the corresponding whitening bits in G.

To understand how a linear relationship (if one exists) between the plaintext, ciphertext and expanded-key bits is determined for G', we first consider how a linear relationship is derived for a block cipher structured as a series of rounds with block length b and then add the impact of the whitening and swap step to these relationships. We number the rounds from 1 to r. We will refer to any initial whitening step that occurs prior to the first round as round 0 and the round function of round 0 is just the initial whitening. The relationship between the output of the jth round/cycle and the input to the $(j+1)^{st}$ round/cycle is depicted in Figure 2 for both G and G'.

We use the following notation for describing the relationships across the rounds of G':

- Two bits, $x1$ and $x2$, cancel each other in an equation means $x1 \oplus x2 = 0$ with probability 1.
- Let u_{ji} denote the ith bit of the input to the round function in round j, $1 \leq i \leq b$, $0 \leq j \leq r$.
- Let v_{ji} denote the ith bit of the output from the round function in round j, $1 \leq i \leq b$, $0 \leq j \leq r$.

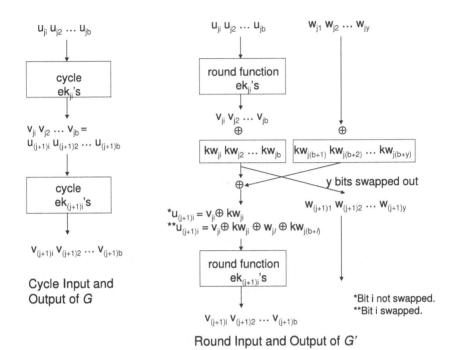

Fig. 2. Linear Relationship Between Round j's Output and Round $(j + 1)$'s Input

- Let n_j denote the number of expanded-key bits used in the round function in round j, $0 \leq j \leq r$. This does not include any end of round whitening added to form G', but does include the end of round whitening if it is part of the cycle of G (as is the case with AES). If G does not contain initial whitening, the round function in round 0 is the identity function and $n_0 = 0$.
- Let ek_{ji} denote the ith expanded-key bit in the round function in round j, $1 \leq i \leq n_j$.
- Let $L_j([u_{j1}, ...u_{jb}] \oplus [v_{j1}, ...v_{jb}] \oplus [ek_{j1}, ...ek_{jn_j}])$ denote the set of linear equations (if any) relating the input, output and round key bits with non-negligible probability for the round function in round j, $0 \leq j \leq r$. We will abbreviate this as L_j. An equation in L_j holds with probability $\frac{1}{2} + \alpha$ for some non-negligible α such that $0 < \alpha \leq \frac{1}{2}$. For example, if $u_{12} \oplus v_{13} \oplus ek_{15} = 0$ with probability 0.75, this equation will be in L_1. Any equation which reflects a negative relationship, meaning the equation holds with probability $\frac{1}{2} - \alpha$, is rewritten as an equation holding with probability $\frac{1}{2} + \alpha$.
- Without loss of generality, the equations in L_j are in reduced form; for example, $u_{j2} \oplus u_{j2} \oplus u_{j2} = 1$ will be reduced to $u_{j2} = 1$.
- Internal variables will refer to the set of u_{ji} for $1 \leq j \leq r$ and v_{ji} for $0 \leq j \leq r-1$, with $1 \leq i \leq b$. i.e., any variable corresponding to an input bit for rounds 1 to r or to an output bit of rounds 0 (initial whitening step) to $r - 1$.

A linear relationship across consecutive rounds is obtained by combining the linear equations for each of the rounds, with v_{ji} becoming $u_{(j+1)i}$. A linear relationship exists that involves only plaintext, ciphertext and expanded-key bits if the intermediate round inputs and outputs (the internal variables) cancel when combining the per round equations, leaving equation(s) involving only u_{0i}'s, v_{ri}'s and expanded-key bits. For example, if in G with two cycles: $u_{11} \oplus v_{12} = ek_{11}$ and $u_{22} \oplus v_{26} = ek_{23}$. Then, since $v_{12} = u_{22}$, $u_{11} \oplus ek_{11} \oplus v_{26} = ek_{23}$.

We now consider how the steps between the rounds in G' impact the linear relationships across the rounds.

- Let Y denote the rightmost y bits of the data block for a $(b + y)$-bit data block.
- Let Γ' refer to the set of the equations used in a linear attack on r rounds of G' formed from combining the L_j's for the individual rounds along with the end of round whitening and swap steps.
- Let Γ refer to a set of linear equations for G formed from equations in Γ'.
- Let kw_{ji} denote the ith key bit used for the whitening step added in round j when constructing G', $1 \leq i \leq b + y$ and $1 \leq j \leq r$. $kw_{ji} = 0$ for $1 \leq i \leq b$ if the cycle of G includes end of cycle whitening and $kw_{0i} = 0$ for $1 \leq i \leq b$ if G contains initial whitening because G' does not add whitening to the b bits when it is already present.
- Let w_{jl} denote the lth bit of the Y portion of the data, for $1 \leq l \leq y$ and $2 \leq j \leq r$. $w_{jl} = v_{(j-1)h} \oplus kw_{(j-1)h}$ where $1 \leq h \leq b$ and h is the bit position swapped with bit position l in the previous swap. When $j = 1$, $w_{1l} = w_{0l} \oplus kw_{0(b+l)}$, the initial input bit XORed with the initial whitening applied.

With the addition of the whitening and swap steps, the input to the round function is now defined as:

- $u_{(j+1)i} = v_{ji} \oplus kw_{ji}$ when v_{ji} is not involved in the swap step.
- $u_{(j+1)i} = v_{ji} \oplus kw_{ji} \oplus w_{jl} \oplus kw_{j(b+l)}$ when v_{ji} is involved in the swap step. When $j \geq 2$, this can be written as $u_{(j+1)i} = v_{ji} \oplus kw_{ji} \oplus v_{(j-1)h} \oplus kw_{(j-1)h} \oplus kw_{j(b+l)}$.

Notice that the steps between applications of the round function in G' maintain a linear relationship between the output of one round and the input of the next round.

If the key schedule of G' produces whitening bits which are created independently of the key bits used within the round function (to the extent that the key bits are pseudo-random), and of the round function's input and output, these whitening bits will cancel with any v_{ji}, u_{j+1} and/or ek_{ji} with probability $\frac{1}{2} + e$ for negligible e (*i.e.*, there is no discernable relationship between these whitening bits and any of the plaintext, ciphertext and expanded-key bits used internal to the round function by definition of the key schedule). Thus, the kw_{ji}'s added when forming G' will not increase the probability of a linear relationship between plaintext bits, ciphertext bits and expanded-key bits used in the round function. If a key schedule is used for G' that does not guarantee independence amongst the kw_{ji}'s and that results in cancellation among some kw_{ji}'s, this is merely cancelling variables that are not present in the linear equations for the round function and thus will not simplify the equations or increase the probability that an equation holds across r applications of the round function.

Now we assume a set of equations, Γ', exist for G' that contains no internal variables and show how to convert them to a set of equations for G. Given the sets, L_j's, of linear equations for the round function in G', these same sets of equations hold for G because the elastic version does not alter the cycle of G. These equations are combined across cycles as was done for the rounds of G', except to form the input to one cycle from the output of the previous cycle, the impact of the swap step and any whitening added when forming G' is removed as follows:

- Set kw_{ji} to 0 for $0 \leq j \leq r$ and $1 \leq i \leq b$ so these whitening bits are omitted from the resulting equations. This removes any initial and end of round whitening that was added to the leftmost b bits when forming G'. Recall that if G had initial and end of cycle whitening, it was treated as part of the round function of G and additional whitening on the leftmost b bits in each round was not added when forming G' (i.e. kw_{ji} was already 0 in the equations for G' for $0 \leq j \leq r$ and $1 \leq i \leq b$).
- Set $kw_{0(b+l)} = 0$ and $kw_{1(b+l)} = 0$ for $1 \leq l \leq y$. This sets the rightmost y bits of the initial whitening and of the end of round whitening in the first round to 0. By using plaintexts that have the rightmost y bits set to 0, this results in the rightmost y bits in the first round having no impact on the equations.
- Set $kw_{j(b+l)}$ to $v_{(j-1)h}$ for $2 \leq j \leq r - 1$ and $1 \leq l \leq y$, where h is the index in the leftmost b bits corresponding to the bit position swapped with the lth bit of the rightmost y bits. This removes the impact of the swap steps by having the rightmost y bits of whitening in each round cancel with the y bits omitted from each round. These settings are needed only on rounds 2 through $r - 1$. The output of the rth round function is the ciphertext so the swap step is not applicable after the rth round. Per the previous item, the rightmost y bits in the first round can be set to have no impact on the equations. Each such setting can add an internal variable, $v_{(j-1)h}$, which now equals u_{jh}, to the equations.

These settings result in each input bit to the $(j + 1)^{st}$ round function being of the form $u_{(j+1)i} = v_{ji}$ and the impact of any added end of round whitening and the swap step being removed. The equations will combine to form a set of equations, Γ from the equations in Γ' with any kw_{ji}'s which appear in Γ' removed and with at most $(r - 2)y$ internal variables added to the equations. Before explaining how these variables can be accommodated, we first state a few additional notes on the resulting equations. The equations in Γ may contain up to y extra plaintext bits and up to y extra ciphertext bits beyond the b-bit block size of G since G' processes $b + y$ bit blocks. The attacker can set these extraneous y plaintext bits to any value (the whitening bits were set in the conversion based on these plaintext bits being set to 0) and the extra y ciphertext bits are identical to y of the bits output from the next to last round function. For any equation $Eq' \in \Gamma'$ that holds with probability $\frac{1}{2} + \alpha$, the corresponding equation, $Eq \in \Gamma$, formed by removing the $kw'_{ji}s$ from Eq' will also hold with probability $\frac{1}{2} + \alpha$. Furthermore, only variables representing whitening bits not present in G are deleted when converting Γ' to Γ and no equations are added or removed. An equation will not disappear when removing kw_{ji} variables because that would imply the equation did not involve plaintext and/or ciphertext bits.

We now address the presence of the internal variables in Γ. Since it was assumed Γ' consists entirely of equations involving only plaintext, ciphertext and expanded-key bits, the removal of the swap step can introduce up to y internal variables, $(v_{ji'}s)$, per round (cycle) into the equations. The removal of the swap step impacts $r - 2$ rounds (cycles), resulting in a maximum of $(r - 2)y$ internal variables in the equations in Γ.

If equations in Γ' corresponding to some $y > 0$ are converted directly into equations for the original cipher ($y = 0$), this results in at most $2^{(r-2)y}$ possible values to try for the internal variables. However, it is possible to make the number of such values to test linear in y instead of exponential in y. Instead of converting the attack on G' directly to an attack on G, repeatedly decrease y one bit at a time (decrease the block size of G') converting the attack on G' with a $b + n$ bit block size to an attack on G' with a $b + n - 1$ bit block size, for $n = y, y - 1, ...1$. When Γ' is converted into a set of equations for the cipher corresponding to a $b + y - 1$ blocksize, there are at most $r - 2$ internal values, one for each of rounds 2 to $r - 1$, and therefore at most 2^{r-2} possible combinations of values for the internal values. Let Γ'_{b+y-1} denote this set of equations. Using (plaintext,ciphertext) pairs with a $b + y - 1$ bit block size, solve the equations, setting the $r - 2$ internal variables in the equations to the specific values that result in a solution consistent with the (plaintext, ciphertext) pairs. In the worst case, all possible combinations of values for the interal variables must be tested in the equations, resulting in at most $2^{(r-2)}$ combinations to test. Then repeat the process, decreasing the block size one bit at a time. In each iteration, there are at most $r - 2$ internal variables whose values need to be determined.

More formally, given G' with a block size of $b + y$ bits, where $0 \leq y \leq b$ and the set of linear equations Γ' used to attack r consecutive rounds of G':

- Let G'_{b+n} refer to an elastic version of G with a $(b + n)$- bit block size, where $0 \leq n \leq y$.
- Let Γ^*_{b+n} refer to the set of linear equations for r consecutive rounds of G'_{b+n} with at most $r - 2$ internal variables present in the equations.
- Let Γ'_{b+n} refer Γ^*_{b+n} with the values of the internal variables determined. This is a set of linear equations involving only plaintext, ciphertext and expanded key bits for r rounds of G'_{b+n}.
- Let A_{b+n} refer to the attack on G'_{b+n} using Γ'_{b+n}.

Convert the attack on G' to an attack on G as follows:

$$n = y$$
$$\Gamma'_{b+n} = \Gamma'$$
while ($n > 0$) {
      convert Γ'_{b+n} to Γ^*_{b+n-1}
      Using (plaintext,ciphertext) pairs for G'_{b+n-1}, solve for any
      internal variables in Γ^*_{b+n-1} to obtain Γ'_{b+n-1}.
      $n \leftarrow n - 1$
}

The set of equations, Γ, used to attack G will be Γ'_b. This results in at most $\sum_1^y 2^{(r-2)} = y2^{(r-2)}$ possible combinations of the internal variables to try as opposed to $\leq 2^{(r-2)y}$ combinations. Since r is constant (and small in practice) and y is bounded by b, which is constant, the amount of work in converting the attack on G' to an attack on G is polynomial in the time to attack G', specifically, the work is bounded by a constant times the time to attack G'. For example, in AES with a 128-bit key, $b = 128$ and $r = 10$, thus $y \leq 128$ and $y(2^{(r-2)}) \leq 128 * 256 = 32768$. The amount of memory required is linear in the amount of memory required to attack G'. In the worst case, a separate amount of memory is required when forming each Γ'_{b+n}. Thus, a linear attack on a r-round version of G' that requires less than 2^b (plaintext, ciphertext) pairs implies a linear attack exists on G.

Theorem 1 can be applied to algebraic equations in general. An algebraic attack on a block cipher G is defined in the same manner as the linear attack with the modification that the equations can involve any algebraic operations, not just XORs.

Lemma 1. *Given a block cipher G with a block size of b bits and r cycle, and its elastic version G' with a block size of $b + y$ bits for $0 \leq y \leq b$, if G' is subject to an algebraic attack on r rounds then either G is subject to an algebraic attack or the resources exist to perform an exhaustive search on G over all plaintexts.*

Proof. The proof follows directly from the proof to Theorem 1 by removing the qualification in Theorem 1's proof that the equations in the L_j sets are linear. Now Γ' and Γ contain algebraic equations instead of only linear equations. Γ is formed from Γ' exactly as before (the conversion adds only XORs of variables to the equations). Therefore, if an algebraic attack exists on r rounds of G' then an attack exists on G.

4 Differential Cryptanalysis

4.1 Overview

We consider how the conversion of a block cipher to its elastic form impacts differential cryptanalysis. We define a general method for bounding the probability a differential characteristic occurs in the elastic version of a cipher when given the bound for a single round of the original cipher. We have illustrated the method on elastic versions of AES and MISTY1 in [2]. We use the symbol Δ to refer to the XOR of two bit strings. The sequence of Δ inputs and outputs of the rounds of a block cipher is a differential characteristic. Specifically, let $(P1, C1)$ and $(P2, C2)$ be two (plaintext, ciphertext) pairs for a block cipher with r rounds. $\Delta P = P1 \oplus P2$ and $\Delta C = C1 \oplus C2$. Let λ_{ij} refer to the delta input to round j and let λ_{oj} refer to the delta output of round j. $\lambda_{i1} = \Delta P$. $\lambda_{or} = \Delta C$. Let pr_j be the probability λ_{oj} occurs given λ_{ij}. Let $\Omega = (\lambda_{i1}, \lambda_{o1}, \lambda_{i2}, \lambda_{o2}...\lambda_{ir}, \lambda_{or})$. The probability Ω ocurrs is $\prod_{j=1}^{j=r} pr_j$. If the block size is b bits, it is sufficient to show that no differential characteristic occurs with probability $\leq 2^{-b}$ in order to prove a cipher is immune to differential cryptanalysis (because this implies $\geq 2^b$ (plaintext, ciphertext pairs) are required for the attack).

The variable block size and the swap step in elastic block ciphers significantly increase the number of cases to explore when determining the probability of a differential characteristic compared to that of the fixed-length version of a block cipher. This is the reason why we had to find a new approach to modelling the differentials instead of using an existing approach, such as the differential trails approach used on AES [5]. Furthermore, the structure of elastic block ciphers allows analysis performed on the fixed-length version to be partially reused when evaluating the elastic version.

The method we use to bound the probabilities of differential characteristics for an elastic block cipher involves defining states representing which bytes in the differential input to a round have a non-zero delta and tracking what sequences of states the cipher can potentially pass through over a number of rounds. Using this method and differential bounds for the round function of the original cipher, we can derive an upper bound on differential characteristics for the elastic version of a cipher. We exclude the initial and final key-dependent mixing steps from our analysis in order to focus on the core structure and these permutations will only reduce the probability of any specific differential characteristic occurring.

4.2 General Observation

The first observation we make regarding differential cryptanalysis of elastic block ciphers is that, unlike linear cryptanalysis where the equations for the elastic version, G', of a block cipher can be converted directly into equations for the original cipher G, a differential characteristic for G' cannot be converted directly into a differential characteristic for G except for one special case.

We use the following notation when describing a differential characteristic of an elastic block cipher.

- ΔY_i is the XOR of two y-bit segments for round i.
- ΔBin_i is the XOR of two b-bit segments input to the round function in round i.
- $\Delta Bout_i$ is the XOR of two b-bit segments output from the round function in round i.
- A b-bit value formed from the XOR of a b-bit value and a y-bit value, where $y \leq b$, refers to the b-bit result when the y bits are XORed with a subset of y bits of the b bits and the remaining $b - y$ bits are unchanged.
- Forming ΔY_{i+1} from $\Delta Bout_i$ refers to setting ΔY_i to the y bits from $\Delta Bout_i$ that are in the bit positions involved in the swap step after round i.
- ΔY, ΔBin and $\Delta Bout$ without a subscript of i refers to a specific delta independently of the round.

In the elastic version of a cipher, ΔBin_{i+1} is determined by $\Delta Bout_i$ and ΔY_i. If $\Delta Y_i \neq 0$ then $\Delta Bin_{i+1} \neq \Delta Bout_i$; whereas, $\Delta Bin_{i+1} = \Delta Bout_i$ in the original block cipher. This is shown in Figure 3. Therefore, a sequence of deltas ocurring across multiple rounds in the elastic version will not hold across the original version unless $\Delta Y_i = 0$ for r sequential rounds.

Now we consider the special case where r consecutive ΔY_i's are 0.

Lemma 2. *If a differential characteristic occurs in the elastic version, G', of a block cipher that contains r consecutive rounds with $\Delta Y_i = 0$ and this characteristic can be used to attack G', then it can be used to attack G.*

Proof. Let Ω' be the characteristic corresponding to the ΔBin_i values and $\Delta Bout_i$ values for the r consecutive rounds each with $\Delta Y_i = 0$. Ω' is also a characteristic for the r rounds of G. Ω' must hold with probability $> 2^{-b-y}$ to be used in an attack on G'. If Ω' holds with probability $2^{-\alpha} > 2^{-b}$, then it can be used to attack G directly, provided the probability is large enough that it is computationally feasible to encrypt $O(2^{\alpha})$ plaintexts.

If it holds with probability $2^{-\alpha}$ such that $2^{-b} > 2^{-\alpha} > 2^{-b-y}$, it can be used to attack G as follows: Using an r round version of G' and (plaintext, ciphertext) pairs consistent

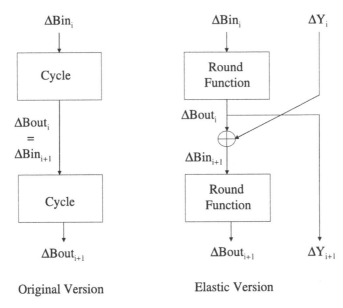

Fig. 3. Differential in Original and Elastic Versions of a Cipher

with the delta input and delta output of Ω' by setting the leftmost b bits to be consistent with Ω' and the rightmost y bits to have a Δ of 0. Then apply the attack on G' to find the round keys for the r rounds and use these as the keys for the r cycles of G.

However, if this later case where $2^{-b} > 2^{-\alpha} > 2^{-b-y}$ is computationally feasible, it implies it is computationally feasible to encrypt 2^b plaintexts with G. Thus G is insecure because given a ciphertext, C, an attacker can ask for all 2^b plaintexts be encrypted with the same key (which is unknown) used to generate C and see which plaintext produces C. As an estimate of the probability of r consecutive rounds having $\Delta Y = 0$, consider what happens if the y bits left out of each round in G' take on any of the possible 2^y values with equal probability. Then, ignoring the differential for the b-bit portions of each round's input and output, a case where $\Delta Y_i = 0$ for r consecutive rounds may be found for small values of y and r. If each ΔY_i occurs with probability 2^{-y}, then the probability that $\Delta Y_i = 0$ in r consecutive rounds is 2^{-yr}. For example, in MISTY1, $r = 4$ (MISTY1 contains four cycles and a cycle is used as the round function in the elastic version). When $y = 1$, the probability of r consecutive ΔY's being zero is $\frac{1}{16}$.

4.3   State Transition Method

We now consider how to evaluate any elastic block cipher's immunity or susceptibility to differential cryptanalysis by using the bound from a single cycle of the fixed-length version of the cipher.

Theorem 2. *The differential probabilities from the cycle of a fixed-length block cipher G can be used to bound the probability that a differential characteristic occurs in its elastic version G'.*

The general method we use is the tracking of states through the rounds of an elastic block cipher. We devise a method for categorizing the impact of the swapping of bits between rounds on the differentials entering a round. We combine the impact of the swap step with the upper bound on the probability a differential characteristic occurs in a single application of the round function (from available analysis on G) to determine an upper bound the probability of a differential characteristic across multiple rounds in G'. By obtaining a bound, x, on the probability across n rounds in G', the probability across r' rounds can be bounded by $x^{\lfloor \frac{r'}{n} \rfloor}$.

In the case where the round function of G is a cycle, such as in AES, we view the $(b + y)$-bit data block entering a round of G' as a b-bit segment and a y-bit segment. Three main states are defined:

$(\Delta Bin = 0$ and $\Delta Y \neq 0), (\Delta Bin \neq 0$ and $\Delta Y = 0), (\Delta Bin \neq 0$ and $\Delta Y \neq 0)$

The state in which $\Delta Bin = 0$ and $\Delta Yin = 0$ is not of interest because, given a non-zero delta input to the cipher, a delta of zero across all $b + y$ bits cannot occur. Within a main state, the number of bytes for which the delta is non-zero are counted. For example, if the input to the third round has a ΔBin that is 1 in the 2nd and 18th bit positions and is zero in all other bits, then there are two bytes with non-zero deltas in ΔBin. Tracking of states between rounds involves determining what $\Delta Bin || \Delta Y$ can result for the $(i + 1)^{st}$ round based on the delta in the ith round. For example, if $\Delta Bin = 0$ and $\Delta Y \neq 0$ in the input to round i, then $\Delta Bin \neq 0$ and $\Delta Y = 0$ in round $i + 1$. This is because the delta output of the ith round function will be zero, then the non-zero ΔY will be swapped into the b-bit portion input to the $(i + 1)^{st}$ round and a delta of zero will be swapped out to form the ΔY for the $(i + 1)^{st}$ round.

When the original cipher is a Feistel network (or is a Feistel network with additional steps as in the case of MISTY1), the ΔBin portion is viewed as a left half (ΔLin) and right half (ΔRin). The main states are the seven combinations of $\Delta L, \Delta R$ and ΔY being $= 0$ or $\neq 0$ with at least one being $\neq 0$.

Using the states, an upper bound (which is not necessarily a tight upper bound) can be determined for the probability of a differential characteristic for r' rounds of G'. The probability of a differential characteristic occurring for a single application of the round function of G and the possible ΔB or $\Delta L || \Delta R$ values entering the round function in each round are used to bound the probability for a round of G'. The possible ΔB or $\Delta L || \Delta R$ and ΔY values in a round determine the possible input states to the next round of G'.

4.4 Examples

We applied the state transition method to the elastic versions of AES and MISTY1 described in [3]. The process and results are described in [2]. We briefly state the results of the work here. Elastic AES is an example in which the input to each round is viewed in the form of $\Delta Bin || \Delta Y$. AES is a 128-bit block cipher with 10 rounds. The number of rounds, r', in the elastic version is $10 + \lceil \frac{10y}{128} \rceil$. Elastic MISTY1 is an example in which the input to each round is viewed in the form of $\Delta L || \Delta R || \Delta Y$. MISTY1 is a 64-bit block cipher involving four cycles of a Feistel network. $r' = 4 + \lceil \frac{4y}{64} \rceil$ in the elastic version of MISTY1.

We analyzed the elastic versions without the initial and final key dependent permutations to simplify the model since these permutations will only decrease the probability that a specific differential characteristic occurs. Our analysis is independent of the key schedule.[1] The swap step is performed by selecting y consecutive bits from the round function's output to XOR and swap with the y bits left out of the round function. In the implementation of elastic AES, the starting position of the y bits selected rotates to the right one byte each round. In elastic MISTY1, the starting position alternates between the left and right halves of the b bit segment in addition to rotating to the right within the half block each round.

When analyzing the state transitions for both elastic AES and elastic MISTY1, we are concerned with how many byte positions have non-zero deltas. Therefore, we only need to consider each block size where Y contains an integer number of bytes. The case for $y = 8x$ where x is an integer such that $1 \leq x \leq \frac{b}{8}$ covers the cases of y such that $8(x - 1) < y \leq 8x$. For example, the lower bound on a differential characteristic occurring for the case of $y = 8$ is also the lower bound for values of y in the range of 1 to 7 because this range of y influences exactly one byte in b-bit portion during each of the swap steps.

In order to analyze the state transitions in elastic AES, we created a program that tracks how many bytes contain a non-zero differential characteristic in each round and determines the possible next states. The number of bytes with a non-zero delta in the b-bit portion in a single round bounds the probability that a differential characteristic holds through that round. A lower bound on the differential probability for a single round of AES is $\leq 2^{-exp}$ where $exp = 6 * |\Delta Bin|$. The multiplication by 6 is due to the fact that the probability a specific difference in two one-byte inputs to AES's S-Box produces a specific difference in the two outputs of the S-Box is 2^{-6} or 2^{-7}, depending on the exact byte values ([5] pages 205-206). For block sizes of 17, 18 ... to 32 bytes, the model was run through three rounds for all possible input states. A lose lower bound for all r' rounds was then calculated by viewing the r' rounds as 3 round segments plus 0 to 2 additional rounds, depending on the exact value of r'. Sequences producing a three round bound which did not exclude the possibility of a differential attack were traced through subsequent rounds, with the number of rounds depending on the exact size of y and the probability produced after each round. The results from our analysis show that the probability of a differential characteristic occurring is $\leq 2^{-128-y}$. Therefore, a differential attack is impossible.

Our analysis of elastic AES is general in terms of block size but only considers a single method for selecting the bits to swap (described previously) after each round as opposed to all possible ways of selecting y bits from 128 bits. In [4] it was proven that an elastic version of a cipher is immune to any practical key-recovery attack if the original cipher is immune to the attack regardless of the specific bit positions chosen for the swap steps. Differential cryptanalysis is covered by this result. The state transition method can be applied to any choice of bits to swap, but it is computationally infeasible to include in one model all $2^{y(r'-1)}$ possible ways of selecting the bits to swap in the first $r' - 1$ rounds (recall that the swap step adds no value after the last round and thus can be omitted from round r').

---

[1] In the constructions from [3], the stream cipher RC4 was used for the key schedule.

MISTY1 uses two functions, referred to as $F0$ and FL, as building blocks along with a Feistel network. $F0$ is the round function in the Feistel network. In each cycle of the Feistel network, FL is applied to one half of the data and FL^{-1} is applied to the other half. An upper bound of 2^{-56} on the probability a differential characteristic occurs was derived for 4 cycles of the 64-bit version [8] by using a bound of 2^{-14} per cycle due entirely to the bound from the $F0$ function. Using a manual analysis of state transitions and only the bound for the $F0$ function, we derive an upper bound on the elastic version of MISTY1 of $2^{-14(r'-1)}$, where r' is the number of rounds (cycles of MISTY1) in the elastic version. This bound is not tight and does not by itself eliminate the possibility of a differential attack (either in MISTY1 or the elastic version). However, the state transition analysis does reduce the number of state sequences that need to be investigated to tighten the bound over r' rounds. The bound of $2^{-14(r'-1)}$ also allows the potential contribution needed from the initial and final key-dependent mixing steps in preventing differential attacks to be determined.

5   Conclusions

We showed how to convert a linear, or more generally any algebraic, attack on an elastic block cipher into such an attack on the fixed-length version of the block cipher to prove that if the fixed-length version is immune to such an attack then so is the elastic version. This was accomplished by proving that any set of linear or algebraic equations used in an attack on the elastic version can be converted in polynomial time and memory into equations for the fixed-length version. We also devised a method for bounding the probability of a differential characteristic on the elastic version of a block cipher using the differential bounds for the cycle of the fixed-length version of the cipher. When performing differential cryptanalysis on an elastic block cipher, the differential bound for the round function is the bound from the cycle of the original version of the cipher. The swapping of bits between rounds in the elastic version impacts the sequence of differentials entering the series of rounds by altering the output of the ith application of the round function before it is input to the $(i + 1)^{st}$ application of the round function. The bound for the round function and the impact of the swap step can be combined to bound the probability a differential characteristic occurs in the elastic version of a block cipher. This is accomplished by defining states representing whether or not there is a non-zero differential in the b-bit portion and/or y-bit portion of the round's input, then determining what states may potentially occur as input to each round. The possible state sequences in the elastic version of the cipher are combined with the probabilities a differential characteristic occurs in one cycle of the original cipher to bound the probability of a differential characteristic across all rounds of the elastic version of the cipher.

Acknowledgments

This work was partially supported by NSF Grants ITR CNS-04-26623 and CPA CCF-05-41093. Any opinions, findings, and conclusions or recommendations expressed in this material are those of the authors and do not necessarily reflect the views of the NSF or the U.S Government.

References

1. Biham, E., Shamir, A.: Differential Cryptanalysis of the Data Encryption Standard. Springer, New York (1993)
2. Cook, D.: Elastic Block Ciphers, Ph.D. Thesis, Columbia University (2006)
3. Cook, D., Yung, M., Keromytis, A.: Elastic Block Ciphers: The Basic Design. In: Proceedings of ASIACCS, pp. 350–355. ACM, New York (2007)
4. Cook, D., Yung, M., Keromytis, A.: The Security of Elastic Block Ciphers Against Key-Recovery Attacks. In: Garay, J.A., Lenstra, A.K., Mambo, M., Peralta, R. (eds.) ISC 2007. LNCS, vol. 4779, pp. 89–103. Springer, Heidelberg (2007)
5. Daemen, J., Rijmen, V.: The Design of Rijndael: AES the Advanced Encryption Standard. Springer, Berlin (2002)
6. Matsui, M.: Linear Cryptanalysis Method for DES Cipher. In: Helleseth, T. (ed.) EURO-CRYPT 1993. LNCS, vol. 0765, pp. 386–397. Springer, Heidelberg (1994)
7. Matsui, M.: New Block Encryption Algorithm MISTY. In: Biham, E. (ed.) FSE 1997. LNCS, vol. 1267, pp. 54–68. Springer, Heidelberg (1997)
8. Matsui, M.: New Structure of Block Ciphers with Provable Security Against Differential and Linear Cryptanalysis. In: Gollmann, D. (ed.) FSE 1996. LNCS, vol. 1039, pp. 205–218. Springer, Heidelberg (1996)
9. NIST, FIPS 197 Advanced Encryption Standard (AES) (2001)

Multidimensional Linear Cryptanalysis of Reduced Round Serpent

Miia Hermelin[1], Joo Yeon Cho[1], and Kaisa Nyberg[1,2]

[1] Helsinki University of Technology
[2] Nokia Research Center, Finland

Abstract. Various authors have previously presented different approaches how to exploit multiple linear approximations to enhance linear cryptanalysis. In this paper we present a new truly multidimensional approach to generalise Matsui's Algorithm 1. We derive the statistical framework for it and show how to calculate multidimensional probability distributions based on correlations of one-dimensional linear approximations. The main advantage is that the assumption about statistical independence of linear approximations can be removed. Then we apply these new techniques to four rounds of the block cipher Serpent and show that the multidimensional approach is more effective in recovering key bits correctly than the previous methods that use a multiple of one-dimensional linear approximations.

1 Introduction

Linear cryptanalysis introduced by Matsui in [1] has become one of the most important cryptanalysis methods for symmetric ciphers. Matsui analysed the DES block cipher using a linear approximation of the known data bits, which holds with a large correlation independently of the key, and presented two ways of exploiting this property: Algorithm 1 which determines one bit from the secret key and Algorithm 2 which recovers a part of the last (or first) round key bits. Originally, only one approximative linear relation was used. In [2], two approximations were used to reduce the amount of data needed for the attack. This idea was developed further by Kaliski and Robshaw in [3], and later by Biryukov, et al., in [4], where the goal was to use several linear approximations simultaneously in order to recover more key bits with equal amount of data. In both [3] and [4] the fundamental assumption was that the approximations are statistically independent. This assumption is hard to verify in practice. The main contribution of this paper is to remove this assumption.

In [5], Baignères, et al., analysed the statistical properties of multidimensional linear approximations without the assumption of statistical independence. They proved that by using multiple approximations, less data is needed to have the same level of test as with only one approximation. However, their target system was a block cipher, which was assumed to have a Markovian property [6]. Consequently, no practical way of building the probability distributions for the purposes of Matsui's Algorithm 1 can be found.

In [7] Englund and Maximov calculated directly the multidimensional probability distribution needed for the distinguisher. However, their calculations become infeasible

Y. Mu, W. Susilo, and J. Seberry (Eds.): ACISP 2008, LNCS 5107, pp. 203–215, 2008.

for systems with word-size of 64 or more. In this paper, it will be shown how one-dimensional linear approximations can be combined to determine the multidimensional linear approximation and the corresponding probability distribution. The method can be applied to both stream and block ciphers of any word size.

The goal of this paper is to present a key recovery attack by generalising Algorithm 1 to the multidimensional case. This algorithm will be compared with the method suggested by Biryukov, et al., in [4] and the experimental results presented in [8].

The structure of this paper is as follows: In Sect. 2 the notation and the theoretical basics needed in this paper are given. Section 3 starts with showing how linear one-dimensional approximations can be used to make multidimensional linear approximations. Using the results of [5] it is then shown that it is advantageous to use multiple approximations instead of just one. The rest of the Sect. 3 shows how to generalise Matsui's Algorithm 1. Section 4 shows how the method can be applied to the block cipher Serpent. The results will also be compared to those presented in [8], where Biryukov's method was applied to Serpent. Finally, Sect. 5 draws conclusions.

2   Probability Distribution of a Boolean Function

We will denote the space of n-dimensional binary vectors by V_n. The inner product is defined for $a = (a^1, \ldots, a^n), b = (b^1, \ldots, b^n) \in V_n$ as $a \cdot b = a^1 b^1 + \cdots + a^n b^n$, where $+$ is sum modulo 2.

A function $f : V_n \to V_1$ is called a Boolean function. A function $f : V_n \to V_m$ with $f = (f_1, \ldots, f_m)$, where f_i are Boolean functions is called a vector Boolean function of dimension m. A linear Boolean function from $V_n \to V_m$ is represented by an $m \times n$ binary matrix U. The m rows of U are denoted by $u_1, \ldots, u_m$, where each u_i is a binary vector of length n.

A random variable (r.v.) is denoted by boldface, capital letters, e.g., $\mathbf{X}, \mathbf{Y}, \mathbf{Z}, \ldots$. The abbreviation i.i.d. will mean independent and identically distributed.

Let $\mathbf{Y}$ be a r.v. in V_m, and denote by $p_\eta = \Pr(\mathbf{Y} = \eta)$. Then the probability distribution (p.d.) of $\mathbf{Y}$ is the vector $p = (p_0, \ldots, p_{2^m-1})$. Let $f : V_n \to V_m$ be a vector Boolean function, and let $\mathbf{X}$ be a r.v. in V_n with the 2^n-dimensional uniform distribution vector $\theta_n = 2^{-n}(1, \ldots, 1)$. Then we associate with f a r.v. $\mathbf{Y} = f(\mathbf{X})$ in V_m with a probability distribution $p(f) = (p_0(f), \ldots, p_{2^m-1}(f))$, where $\Pr(f(\mathbf{X}) = \eta) = p_\eta(f), \eta \in V_m$. This p.d. is called the probability distribution of f and is denoted by $p(f)$. We may also abbreviate $p_\eta(f)$ by p_η if the function is clear from the context. Two Boolean functions f and g are called statistically independent if the associated r.v.'s are statistically independent.

The correlation between a binary r.v. $\mathbf{X}$ and zero is defined as $\Pr(\mathbf{X} = 0) - \Pr(\mathbf{X} = 1)$. The correlation of a Boolean function $g : V_n \to V_1$ to zero shall be referred to as the correlation (of g) and is defined as

$$2^{-n} (\#\{\xi \mid g(\xi) = 0\} - \#\{\xi \mid g(\xi) = 1\}) = 2\Pr(g(\mathbf{X}) = 0) - 1,$$

where $\mathbf{X}$ is uniformly distributed.

Capacity was defined by Biryukov in [4] where they showed that it was inversely proportional to the data complexity of their distinguishing attack. We will now generalise the definition.

Definition 1. *Let* $p = (p_0, \ldots, p_M)$ *and* $q = (q_0, \ldots, q_M)$ *be two p.d.'s. Their (mutual) capacity is then*

$$C(p, q) = \sum_{\eta=0}^{M} \frac{(p_\eta - q_\eta)^2}{q_\eta}. \tag{1}$$

If $M = 2^m - 1$ *and* $q = \theta_m$ *is uniform then* $C(p, \theta_m) = 2^m \|p - \theta_m\|_2^2$ *will be called the capacity of* p *and we will denote it by* $C(p)$. *It can also be called the Squared Euclidean Imbalance [5].*

In the next section, we will see that the generalised capacity will be inversely proportional to the data complexity of a multidimensional linear distinguisher.

3   Multidimensional Approximation of Boolean Functions

3.1   From One-Dimensional Probability Distributions to Multiple Dimensions

Let $f : V_\ell \rightarrow V_n$ be a vector Boolean function and binary vectors $w_i \in V_n$ and $u_i \in V_\ell$, $i = 1, 2, \ldots, m$ be linear masks such that the paired masks (u_i, w_i) are linearly independent. Let us define functions g_i by

$$g_i(\xi) := w_i \cdot f(\xi) + u_i \cdot \xi, \tag{2}$$

and assume g_i's have correlations ρ_i, $i = 1, 2, \ldots, m$. We will call these correlations the base-correlations, and the corresponding linear approximations of f the base-approximations. We want to find the p.d. of the m-dimensional linear expression

$$g(\xi) := W f(\xi) + U \xi,$$

where $W = (w_1, \ldots, w_m)$, $U = (u_1, \ldots, u_m)$ and $g = (g_1, \ldots, g_m)$. Let the p.d. of g be p. Assume that we have the correlations $\rho(a)$ of all the linear mappings $a \cdot g$ of g, $a \in V_m$. If $e_i = (0 \ldots 010 \ldots 0)$ with 1 at the ith position, then $\rho(e_i) = \rho_i$, $i = 1, \ldots, m$. We will call the correlations $\rho(a), a \neq e_i$ the combined correlations of f and the corresponding approximations the combined approximations. Recall the following lemma from [9].

Lemma 1. *Let* $g = (g_1, \ldots, g_m) : V_n \rightarrow V_m$ *be a vector-valued Boolean function and* p *it's p.d. Then*

$$2^n p_\eta = 2^{-m} \sum_{a \in V_m} \sum_{\xi \in V_n} (-1)^{a \cdot (g(\xi) + \eta)}.$$

The correlations $\rho(a)$ can be written as

$$\rho(a) = 2^{-n} \sum_{\xi \in V_n} (-1)^{a \cdot g(\xi)}.$$

Using this and Lemma 1 we get the following corollary that connects p and the one-dimensional correlations $\rho(a)$:

Corollary 1. *Let $g : V_n \to V_m$ be a Boolean function with p.d. p and one-dimensional correlations $\rho(a)$ of $a \cdot g$. Then*

$$p_\eta = 2^{-m} \sum_{a \in V_m} (-1)^{a \cdot \eta} \rho(a).$$

The following corollary is obtained using Parseval's theorem. An equivalent form of it can be found in [5], where the proof was based on the inverse Walsh-Hadamard transform of the deviations ϵ_η from the uniform distribution, $\epsilon_\eta = p_\eta - 2^m$.

Corollary 2. *Let g be the Boolean function defined as previously with p.d. p. Then*

$$C(p) = 2^m \sum_\eta \epsilon_\eta^2 = \sum_{a \neq 0} \rho(a)^2.$$

We will need this equality in the next section where we study how linear distinguishing is done in multiple dimensions.

3.2   One vs. Multidimensional Linear Distinguishers

In this section we will present the general statistical framework of multidimensional approximation.

The theory of hypothesis testing can be found for example in [10]. Here we will restrict to the most essential parts of the theory. Assume we have two p.d's p and q, $q \neq p$ and consider two hypotheses: H_0 states that the experimental data $\mathbf{z}^N$ of N words is derived from p and H_1 states that $\mathbf{z}^N$ is derived from q.

In the one-dimensional case, we have a linear approximation such as (2). Let ρ be the correlation of the approximation. The number of bits N_1 needed to distinguish $\mathbf{z}^N$ from a random sequence is λ/ρ^2, where λ depends on the level and the power of the test. It was already noted in [1] that the data complexity N_1 is proportional to $1/\rho^2$. For proof, see [11]. Note that the bias used in [1] is the correlation divided by two.

The data complexity of the attack in [4] using multiple linear approximations, was shown to be proportional to $N_{\text{s.i.}}$, where

$$N_{\text{s.i.}} = \frac{1}{\sum_{i=1}^{m} \rho_i^2} = \frac{1}{\bar{c}^2}, \tag{3}$$

and $\bar{c}^2$ is the capacity as defined in [4]. This means a significant improvement in data complexity, but relies on the assumption that the base approximations are statistically independent.

Let us next study the case of multiple approximations without the assumption of statistical independence. The log-likelihood ratio (LLR) is defined as follows:

$$l(\mathbf{z}^N) = \sum_{\eta=0}^{M} N(\eta) \log \frac{p_\eta}{q_\eta}, \tag{4}$$

where p and q are defined as in Definition 1 and $N(\eta)$ is the experimental frequency of the value η in $\mathbf{z}^N$. The LLR was used as the distinguisher in [5] to proof the following theorem.

Theorem 1. *Let us have a hypothesis testing problem with H_0 stating that the data $\mathbf{z}^N$ is drawn i.i.d. from p.d. p and H_1 stating that the data is drawn from $q \neq p$. Assume that the p.d.'s are close to each other:*

$$|q_\eta - p_\eta| \ll q_\eta, \text{ for all } \eta. \tag{5}$$

Then the amount of data needed for distinguishing the hypotheses is proportional to

$$N = \frac{\lambda}{C(p,q)}, \tag{6}$$

where λ depends on the level and the power of the test.

If we want to distinguish a distribution of some data related to a cipher from that of a truly random source we will use the previous hypothesis test with q as the ciphers p.d. and p as the uniform distribution. Using (2) we will see that $N_{\text{s.i.}}$ given by (3) is actually greater than the true amount of data needed for $m \leq n$ linear approximations, since by using Corollary 2, the latter is proportional to

$$N_m = \frac{\lambda}{C(q)} = \frac{\lambda}{\sum_{a \neq 0} \rho(a)^2}.$$

In an "optimal case" we can make an m-dimensional approximation where all the correlations $\rho(a)$ are (in absolute) value equal to the maximal one-dimensional correlations. If N_1 is the data requirement for one approximation, then $N_m = N_1/(2^m - 1)$. On the other hand, if only a single one-dimensional approximation has a large correlation, then $N_m \approx N_1$ and it is not useful to use multiple approximations.

In [5] Markovian block ciphers were analysed using multidimensional distinguishers on the probability distributions related to the Markovian transition probabilities averaged over the keys. Hence, their main goal was to improve the efficiency of Algorithm 2. Next, we will generalise Matsui's Algorithm 1 to the multidimensional case. In the practical experiments we use Corollary 1 to determine the related multidimensional probability distributions from the correlations of the one-dimensional linear approximations.

3.3 Key Recovery Attack

We will show how to find m key bits of the key K using a multidimensional version of Algorithm 1. Let $\mathbf{X}$ be a uniformly distributed r.v. and $\mathbf{Y} = f(\mathbf{X})$, where $(\mathbf{X}, \mathbf{Y})$ is a plaintext-ciphertext pair. We consider the r.v.

$$U\mathbf{X} \oplus W\mathbf{Y} \oplus VK, \tag{7}$$

with a fixed unknown key K, and use p to denote the r.v.'s p.d. Here $U = (u_1, \ldots, u_m)$, $W = (w_1, \ldots, w_m)$ and $V = (v_1, \ldots, v_m)$ are some maskmatrices. This approximation can be generated from linearly independent one-dimensional approximations with correlations $\rho_1, \ldots, \rho_m$ using Corollary 1 (assuming that we are also given the combined correlations). The linear mapping V divides the key space to equivalence classes

$k = VK \in \mathcal{Z}$. The bits $k_i = v_i \cdot K$ are called the parity bits. For each k the expected p.d. p^k of $\mathbf{Z}^k = U\mathbf{X} \oplus W\mathbf{Y}$ for the distribution originating from the empirical data will be some permutation of p determined by the key (class) k. For the purposes of this study, we assume that all the keys give distinct permutations such that $p^k \neq p^j$, if $k \neq j$.

Biryukov's attack introduced in [4] uses $m' \geq m$ linear approximations to select the correct key class from $\mathcal{Z}$. It has three phases: distillation, analysis and search phases. They can be described as follows:

1. **Distillation phase.** Obtain N plaintext-ciphertext pairs (x_t, y_t) and calculate the empirical correlation vector $\hat{\mathbf{c}} = (\hat{\rho}_1, \ldots, \hat{\rho}_{m'})$.
2. **Analysis phase.** For each key class k, give the key a rank d_k and make a sorted list of the keys with smallest d_k at the top of the list.
3. **Search phase.** Run through the list and try all keys contained in the equivalence classes until the correct key is found.

The statistic used is $d_k = \|\hat{\mathbf{c}} - \mathbf{c}_k\|_2$, where $\mathbf{c}_k = ((-1)^{k_1}\rho_1, \ldots, (-1)^{k_{m'}}\rho_{m'})$, a vector consisting of the theoretical correlations and the parity bits of k. In addition a measure "gain" was defined to analyze the success of the method taking into account the time complexity of the search phase.

The purpose of our multidimensional approach is to improve the distillation phase in theory and in practice. In order to compare the distillation phase of Biryukov's and our multidimensional method, we discuss a plain multiple linear cryptanalysis method (the plain method), which is similar to the Biryukov's method but without the grading of the key candidates. We measure the success of the plain method and our method using the probability P_{OK}, which is the probability that the right key is at the top of the list. We assume that the plain method uses m linearly and statistical independent linear approximations and recovers m bits of the key based on the deviations d_k. Let q be the experimental p.d. constructed from the data. Our method uses the m base approximations, $2^m - m - 1$ combined approximations and the Kullback-Leibler distance between q and p^k. The Kullback-Leibler distance is used in measuring the difference between p.d.'s. It can be seen to be related to the LLR:

Definition 2. *The relative entropy or the Kullback-Leibler distance between two distributions $p = (p_0, \ldots, p_M)$ and $q = (q_0, \ldots, q_M)$ is defined as*

$$D(q\|p) = \sum_{\eta=0}^{M} q_\eta \log \frac{q_\eta}{p_\eta}. \tag{8}$$

Then, in the analysis phase, instead of a grading problem we face the following multiple hypothesis testing problem.

Theorem 2. *Let us have an $|\mathcal{Z}|$-ary hypothesis problem, with $|\mathcal{Z}|$ hypotheses H_k stating that the data originates from p^k, where $k \in \mathcal{Z}$ corresponds to the key. The hypothesis for which the Kullback-Leibler distance $D(q\|p^k)$ is smallest is selected. Given some success probability P_{OK}, the lower bound N_{key} for the amount of data needed to give the smallest value of the statistic when the correct key is used, is given by*

$$N_{key} \approx \frac{4 \log_2 |\mathcal{Z}|}{\min_{j \neq 0} C(p^0, p^j)}. \tag{9}$$

Proof. For each key k we must distinguish p^k from p^j, for all $j \neq k$. Using Proposition 3 in [5], the probability that we choose j when k is true is

$$\Pr(H_j|H_k) = \Phi\left(-\sqrt{N_{kj}C(p^k, p^j)/2}\right),$$

where Φ is the distribution function of the normed normal distribution. Let the probability of successfully distinguishing H_k from all the other hypotheses be P_{OK}. Then $P_{OK} = \prod_{j \neq i}(1 - \Pr(H_j|H_k))$. Assume $N_{kj}C(p^k, p^j) \gg 1$ for all $j \neq k$. Then

$$P_{OK} \approx \exp\left(-\frac{1}{\sqrt{2\pi}} \sum_{j \neq k} e^{-N_{kj}C(p^k, p^j)/4}\right). \tag{10}$$

Let $N_k = \max_j N_{kj}$. Since we have to collect the amount of N_k for at least one test with k we can use the same amount for all the tests. On the other hand, let us define $c_k = \min_j C(p^k, p^j)$. Replacing the capacities with c_k, N_k must be increased to get the required success probability. We get a lower bound for N_k by solving N_k from (10)

$$N_k \approx \frac{4 \log_2 |\mathcal{Z}| - 4 \ln(\sqrt{2\pi} \ln P_{OK})}{c_k}.$$

Since we do not know which k is the right key, we have to choose $N = \max_k N_k$ to be able to find the right key. Since p^j's are each others' permutations, we have $C(p^k, p^j) = C(p^0, p^{k+j})$. But then $c_k = \min_{s \neq 0} C(p^0, p^s) = c_0$ which is independent of k and (9) follows.   □

Note that we need the assumption that $p^i \neq p^j$ to ensure that $\min_j C(p^0, p^j) \neq 0$. In [5] a similar formula was derived for the purposes of Algorithm 2 to distinguish the distribution related to the correct key from the, presumably uniform, distribution related to a wrong key. Formula (9) gives an estimate how much data is needed to reliably determine which of the $|\mathcal{Z}|$ distributions gives the best fit with the empirical data. Exactly the same calculations can be done to the Biryukov's statistic with the help of proof of Theorem 1 in [4]. Then the data complexity of the plain attack is proportional to N_{plain} which is given by the formula

$$N_{plain} = \frac{8 \log_2 |\mathcal{Z}|}{\min_{j,k \, j \neq k} \|\mathbf{c}_k - \mathbf{c}_j\|_2} = \frac{2 \log_2 |\mathcal{Z}|}{\min_j \rho_j^2}.$$

Since the denominator in N_{key} is usually much larger than in N_{plain}, we have $N_{plain} > N_{key}$. Especially, if the combined correlations are large, the advantage is significant.

The data, time and memory complexities of distillation and analysis phases have been given in Table 1. The main difference in the complexities between our method and the plain method is due to the fact that our method uses the full m-dimensional distributions and needs to compute 2^m empirical values from the data, while the plain method determines only the m entries of the empirical correlation vector $\hat{c}$.

The main improvements introduced by Biryukov, et al., in [4] is the implementation of the key ranking procedure and its statistical treatment using the concepts of capacity

Table 1. Complexities of Algorithm 1 for plain, Biryukov's and our multidimensional method

	Distillation			Analysis		
	Plain	Biryukov	Our method	Plain	Biryukov	Our method
Data	$O(N_{plain})$	$O(N_{s.i.})$	$O(N_{key})$	-	-	-
Time	$O(mN_{plain})$	$O(m'N_{s.i.})$	$O(2^m N_{key})$	$O(m\lvert\mathcal{Z}\rvert)$	$O(m'\lvert\mathcal{Z}\rvert)$	$O(2^m\lvert\mathcal{Z}\rvert)$
Memory	$O(m)$	$O(m')$	$O(2^m)$	$O(\lvert\mathcal{Z}\rvert)$	$O(\lvert\mathcal{Z}\rvert)$	$O(\lvert\mathcal{Z}\rvert)$

and gain which helps to reduce the lower bound of the data complexity to $N_{s.i.}$. For additional improvement of the practical performance of their method, Biryukov, et al., extend the base set of the m linearly (and presumably also statistically) independent approximations with combined approximations. This extension was justified in [4] by informal arguments and assuming that the linear approximations also in the extended set are statistically independent. Statistical independence of linear approximations is difficult to verify in practice. One method would be to evaluate experimentally the correlations of all linear combinations of the approximations and use Piling-Up Lemma [1] to check for statistical independence. In practical applications of the method of Biryukov, et al., in [4] and [8], statistical independence was not verified. Let us denote by m' the number of approximations used, where $m \le m' < 2^m$. The resulting complexities are given in Table 1. Selection of m is always a trade-off between complexity and maximising the capacity. Typical values for m and m' are, for example, $m = 10$ and $m' = 86$ in [4] and $m = 10$ and $m' = 64$ in [8]. Also often $\lvert\mathcal{Z}\rvert = 2^m$.

In the next section we will compare Biryukov's method and our method in practice using small experiments on the four-round Serpent. The same "test-bed" was previously used by Collard, et al., in [8] to carry out experiments of Biryukov's method. When comparing our results with their results we can see that similar advantage in practical performance can be achieved using our method and the Biryukov's with $m' > m$, compared to the plain method with just m approximations. In addition, our method has a few important advantages over the Biryukov's. We provide sound theoretical justification for using combined approximations. More importantly, no assumption about statistical independence of the approximations is needed.

4   Multidimensional Linear Attack on 4-Round Serpent

Serpent [12] is one of the block ciphers proposed to the Advanced Encryption Standard (AES) competition. It was selected to be among the five finalists [13]. The best known linear approximation of 9-round Serpent was reported by Biham et al. in FSE 2001 [14]. Recently, experimental results on multiple linear cryptanalysis of 4-round Serpent were presented by Collard, et al., in [8]. In this section, we will apply the multidimensional linear attack to the reduced round Serpent and compare our results to the previous attacks presented in [8].

4.1   Multidimensional Linear Attack on 4-Round Serpent

In [8], authors used maximum $m' = 64$ linear approximations to perform Matsui's Algorithm 1 type -attack on 4-round Serpent. The detailed description of approximations

Table 2. Input and output masks used for the multidimensional linear attack

	index	mask = (MSB, ..., LSB)
input mask	u_0	(0x70000000, 0x00000000, 0x00000000, 0x07000900)
	u_1	(0x70000000, 0x00000000, 0x00000000, 0x07000B00)
	u_2	(0x70000000, 0x00000000, 0x00000000, 0x0B000900)
	u_3	(0xB0000000, 0x00000000, 0x00000000, 0x07000900)
	u_4	(0x70000000, 0x00000000, 0x00000000, 0x07000500)
	u_5	(0x70000000, 0x00000000, 0x00000000, 0x07000600)
	u_6	(0x70000000, 0x00000000, 0x00000000, 0x07000C00)
	u_7	(0x70000000, 0x00000000, 0x00000000, 0x01000900)
	u_8	(0x70000000, 0x00000000, 0x00000000, 0x0A000900)
	u_9	(0xB0000000, 0x00000000, 0x00000000, 0x03000B00)
output mask	w	(0x00007000, 0x03000000, 0x00000000, 0x00000000)

can be found in [15]. Those 64 linear approximations used in the attack are not linearly independent. Hence, strictly speaking, the attack in [8] is not consistent with the technique in [4] which assumes that multiple approximations are statistically independent. On the other hand, our attack does not require such a statistical assumption. One can exploit as many approximations with non-negligible correlations as possible for recovering the targeted key bits without such restriction.

In experiments, we chose a 4-round linear trail (from S_4 to S_7) that was used in [8]. We picked up $m = 10$ linearly independent approximations $L_0, ..., L_9$ which can be used to recover 10 bits of the first round key. [1] The input and output masks of the approximations used in our attack are listed in Table 2.

Let us denote L_i as follows:

$$u_i \cdot P + w \cdot C = v_i \cdot K \quad i = 0, ..., 9 \tag{11}$$

where u_i, w and v_i stand for the input mask, output mask and the key mask, respectively and P, C and K represent the plaintext, ciphertext and the key, respectively. Note that the output mask w is identical for all the approximations since this experiment targets the first round key, not the last one.

Let $Q = \text{span}\{L_0, ..., L_9\}$ such that Q is a set of approximations generated by the 10 base approximations L_i. Then, $|Q| = 2^{10} - 1$. Note that the 64 linear approximations used in [8] form a subset of Q.

Our experiments were performed in two ways: In the first experiment, we used all the linear approximations of the set Q. Among $2^{10} - 1$ linear approximations of the Q, we found that 200 of them held with non-negligible correlations, as listed in Table 3. The correlations of the approximations were calculated by the Piling-up lemma [1]. We note that their real correlations can be different from calculated ones due to the effect of correlations of other linear trails using the same input and output masks. However, we assume that the theoretical correlations of the approximations are close to the calculated correlations.

---

[1] We can find maximum 12 linear appr. to recover 12 bits of the first round key from this linear trail. However, we targeted only 10 bits of the key for direct comparison of the performance between the Biryukov's attack and multidimensional attack.

Table 3. Correlations of approximations

correlation	# of approximations	
	64 appr.	10 base appr., 200 non-negligible
2^{-11}	8	8
2^{-12}	56	64
2^{-13}	0	128

In the second experiment, we generated from $L_0, ..., L_9$ the 64 linear approximations which were the same as those used in [8] and used them in our method while approximating the rest of the combined correlations to be zero. In this manner we get a rougher approximation of the full 10-dimensional p.d. than with using 200 approximations. The purpose of this experiment was to compare the performance of the Biryukov's attack to that of our attack when the same approximations are exploited in both attacks.

For comparison, we applied both the Biryukov's and our method to the 4-Round Serpent and measured their gains by experiment so that we could compare our method with the results in [8]. It was already noted in [8] that the plain method (using m approximations) gives poorer results than the Biryukov's method (using $m' > m$ approximations). No explanation was given to this heuristics in [4] or [8]. Following the theory of the previous sections this heuristic can be justified: Increasing m' makes the Biryukov's method approximate the real multidimensional method. However, since the LLR is the optimal statistic, the Biryukov's method cannot perform better than our method even when $m' = 2^m - 1$.

According to Lemma 1 in [4], the key class k is determined by searching for the minimum Euclidean distance $\|\hat{\mathbf{c}} - \mathbf{c}_k\|_2$, where $\hat{\mathbf{c}} = (\hat{\rho}_1, ..., \hat{\rho}_{10})$ is the estimated correlation of ten approximations. On the other hand, in our attack, we measure the empirical probability distributions q of multiple approximations and determine the key class k by searching for the minimum Kullback-Leibler distance $D(q\|p^k)$, where p^k is some permutation of the theoretical probability distribution p. The p.d. p is computed by Corollary 1 using theoretical correlations of one-dimensional approximations. The p.d. q could be calculated in the same way by using the experimental correlations but in this work it was constructed directly using 2^m counters.

We performed the experiments repeatedly 100 times and obtained the average gain of each method. We used a different 128-bit key that was randomly selected each time. The results are displayed in Fig. 1. For comparison, the gain γ of the attack was measured using the formula which was introduced in [4] as follows

$$\gamma = -\log_2 \frac{2 \cdot M - 1}{2^{10}}$$

In Fig. 1, the multidimensional attack using 10 linearly independent approximations with full span (200 non-negligible approximations) reaches the full gain at around 2^{22} texts. Compared to this result, Biryukov's attack shows that the gain of the attack is saturated with around 2^{23} texts. Hence, this experiment shows that our method requires less data to get the same accuracy as Biryukov's method. The plain method with $m = 10$ approximations would give even weaker results not reaching the maximum gain until with about 2^{26} texts, see Fig. 5 of [8].

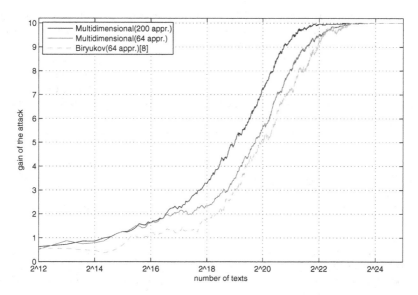

Fig. 1. Comparison of the gain of the different attacks using multiple linear approximations

5 Conclusions

In this paper we investigated a few different approaches presented in recent years on linear cryptanalysis using multiple approximations. We used the statistical theory presented in [5] and developed a new multidimensional cryptanalysis attack. For this purpose, we also showed how to construct multidimensional linear approximations from one-dimensional approximations. The main advantage of the new method is that the assumption on statistical independence of the linear approximations can be removed.

We also applied our method to the 4-round version of block cipher Serpent that was studied in [8] using Biryukov's method [4]. We studied the cases of 10 linear approximations, showed how to make multidimensional approximations from them and measured the success of recovering 10 key parity bits.

We also saw in Table 3 examples where the combined approximations had correlations of the same magnitude as the base approximations. This demonstrates that the assumption about statistical independence between the base approximations needed in Biryukov's method used in [8] does not hold. The theoretical framework presented in this paper removes the need of this assumption.

References

1. Matsui, M.: Linear cryptanalysis method for DES cipher. In: Helleseth, T. (ed.) EURO-CRYPT 1993. LNCS, vol. 765, pp. 386–397. Springer, New York (1994)
2. Matsui, M.: The First Experimental Cryptanalysis of the Data Encryption Standard. In: Desmedt, Y.G. (ed.) CRYPTO 1994. LNCS, vol. 839, pp. 1–11. Springer, Heidelberg (1994)

3. Burton, S., Kaliski, J., Robshaw, M.J.B.: Linear Cryptanalysis Using Multiple Approximations. In: Desmedt, Y.G. (ed.) CRYPTO 1994. LNCS, vol. 839, pp. 26–39. Springer, Heidelberg (1994)
4. Biryukov, A., Canniére, C.D., Quisquater, M.: On Multiple Linear Approximations. In:
Franklin, M. (ed.) CRYPTO 2004. LNCS, vol. 3152, pp. 1–22. Springer, Heidelberg (2004)
5. Baignères, T., Junod, P., Vaudenay, S.: How Far Can We Go Beyond Linear Cryptanalysis?
In: Lee, P.J. (ed.) ASIACRYPT 2004. LNCS, vol. 3329, pp. 432–450. Springer, Heidelberg
(2004)
6. Wagner, D.: Towards a unifying view of block cipher cryptanalysis. In: Roy, B., Meier, W.
(eds.) FSE 2004. LNCS, vol. 3017, pp. 16–33. Springer, Heidelberg (2004)
7. Englund, H., Maximov, A.: Attack the Dragon. In: Maitra, S., Veni Madhavan, C.E., Venkatesan, R. (eds.) INDOCRYPT 2005. LNCS, vol. 3797, pp. 130–142. Springer, Heidelberg
(2005)
8. Collard, B., Standaert, F.X., Quisquater, J.J.: Experiments on the Multiple Linear Cryptanalysis of Reduced Round Serpent. In: Proceedings of FSE 2008. LNCS, Springer, Heidelberg
(to appear, 2008)
9. Nyberg, K., Hermelin, M.: Multidimensional Walsh Transform and a Characterization of
Bent Functions. In: Tor Helleseth, P.V.K., Ytrehus, O. (eds.) Proceedings of the 2007 IEEE
Information Theory Workshop on Information Theory for Wireless Networks, pp. 83–86.
IEEE, Los Alamitos (2007)
10. Cover, T.M., Thomas, J.A.: Elements of Information Theory, 2nd edn. Series in Telecommu-
nications and Signal Processing. Wiley-Interscience, Chichester (2006)
11. Junod, P.: On the Complexity of Matsui's Attack. In: Vaudenay, S., Youssef, A.M. (eds.) SAC
2001. LNCS, vol. 2259, pp. 199–211. Springer, Heidelberg (2001)
12. Anderson, R., Biham, E., Knudsen, L.: Serpent: A Proposal for the Advanced Encryption
Standard. In: First Advanced Encryption Standard (AES) conference (1998)
13. NIST: A request for Candidate Algorithm Nominations for the Advanced Encryption Standard AES (1997), http://csrc.nist.gov/archive/aes/index2.html
14. Biham, E., Dunkelman, O., Keller, N.: Linear Cryptanalysis of Reduced Round Serpent. In:
Matsui, M. (ed.) FSE 2001. LNCS, vol. 2355, pp. 16–27. Springer, Heidelberg (2002)
15. Collard, B., Standaert, F., Quisquater, J. (2008),
http://www.dice.ucl.ac.be/fstandae/PUBLIS/50b.zip

A   Brief Description of Serpent Algorithm

We use the notation of [12]. Each intermediate value of round i is denoted by $\hat{B}_i$ (a
128-bit value). Each $\hat{B}_i$ is treated as four 32-bit words X_0, X_1, X_2, X_3 where bit j of X_i is
bit $4*i+j$ of the $\hat{B}_i$. Serpent has a set of eight 4-bit to 4-bit S Boxes $S_0, \ldots, S_7$ and a
128-bit to 128-bit linear transformation LT. Each round function R_i uses a single S-box
32 times in parallel.

Serpent ciphering algorithm is formally described as follows.

$$\hat{B}_0 = P \quad \hat{B_{i+1}} = R_i(\hat{B}_i) \quad C = B_{32},$$

where

$$R_i(X) = LT(\hat{S}_i(X \oplus \hat{K}_i)), \quad i = 0, \ldots, 30$$
$$R_i(X) = \hat{S}_i(X \oplus \hat{K}_i) \oplus \hat{K}_{32}, \quad i = 31.$$

The linear transformation LT is described as follows.

$$X_0, X_1, X_2, X_3 = S_i(B_i \oplus K_i)$$
$$X_0 = X_0 \lll 12$$
$$X_2 = X_2 \lll 3$$
$$X_1 = X_1 \oplus X_0 \oplus X_2$$
$$X_3 = X_3 \oplus X_2 \oplus (X_0 \lll 3)$$
$$X_1 = X_1 \lll 1$$
$$X_3 = X_3 \lll 7$$
$$X_0 = X_0 \oplus X_1 \oplus X_3$$
$$X_2 = X_2 \oplus X_3 \oplus (X_1 \lll 7)$$
$$X_0 = X_0 \lll 5$$
$$X_2 = X_2 \lll 22$$
$$B_{i+1} = X_0, X_1, X_2, X_3$$

The detailed description of Serpent can be found in [12].

Cryptanalysis of Reduced-Round SMS4 Block Cipher

Lei Zhang[1,2], Wentao Zhang[1], and Wenling Wu[1]

[1] State Key Laboratory of Information Security,
Institute of Software, Chinese Academy of Sciences, Beijing 100190, P.R. China
{zhanglei1015,wwl}@is.iscas.ac.cn,
zhangwt06@yahoo.com
[2] State Key Laboratory of Information Security,
Graduate University of Chinese Academy of Sciences, Beijing 100049, P.R. China

Abstract. SMS4 is a 128-bit block cipher used in the WAPI standard. WAPI is the Chinese national standard for securing Wireless LANs. Since the specification of SMS4 was not released until January 2006, there have been only a few papers analyzing this cipher. In this paper, firstly we present a kind of 5-round iterative differential characteristic of SMS4 whose probability is about 2^{-42}. Then based on this kind of iterative differential characteristic, we present a rectangle attack on 16-round SMS4 and a differential attack on 21-round SMS4. As far as we know, these are the best cryptanalytic results on SMS4.

Keywords: SMS4, Block cipher, Differential characteristic, Rectangle attack, Differential cryptanalysis.

1 Introduction

SMS4 is the underlying block cipher used in the WAPI (WLAN Authentication and Privacy Infrastructure) standard to protect WLAN products. The WAPI standard is a Chinese national standard for securing Wireless LANs, and it was also submitted to the ISO trying to be adopted as an international standard. Although it was rejected by the ISO in favor of IEEE 802.11i, the WAPI standard is still officially mandated in China. Considering that the rejection of WAPI by ISO was partially because of the uncertainties regarding the security of the undisclosed block cipher, the specification of SMS4 [1] was declassified by Chinese government in January 2006. The publication of SMS4 is supposed to encourage the cryptanalysts to evaluate its strength against all kinds of cryptanalytic attacks and gain security evidence.

SMS4 employs a 32-round unbalanced Feistel network structure, and both of its block size and key size are 128 bits. Since its publication, there have been only a few cryptanalytic results. First of all, a differential fault analysis of SMS4 was presented in [13]. Later in 2007, Liu et al [9] investigated the origin of the S-Box employed by the cipher and presented an integral attack on 13-round SMS4. In [7], Ji and Hu analyzed the structure of SMS4 from a viewpoint of algebra, and

Y. Mu, W. Susilo, and J. Seberry (Eds.): ACISP 2008, LNCS 5107, pp. 216–229, 2008.

estimated the complexity of solving the equation system. Moreover, in [10] Lu presented a rectangle attack on 14-round SMS4 and an impossible differential attack on 16-round SMS4, which are the best cryptanalytic results on SMS4 in the open literature.

Differential attack [2,3] is one of the most effective approaches in analyzing a cipher. A good cipher must provide enough security against known attacks before it is widely accepted by public. In [1] the specification of SMS4 was published without security analysis. Thus in this paper we try to search for good differential characteristics with high probabilities, and evaluate the security of SMS4 against differential-type attack. Amongst our results, we first present a kind of 5-round iterative differential characteristic of SMS4 whose average probability is 2^{-42}. Then based on a 14-round rectangle distinguisher constructed by the 5-round iterative differential, we mount a rectangle attack on 16-round SMS4. This is a better result than the rectangle attack in [10]. Furthermore, by iterating the 5-round iterative differential three and a half times, we can obtain an 18-round differential characteristic with a probability of 2^{-126}. Then we present a differential attack on 21-round SMS4, which is the best cryptanalytic result on SMS4 so far. However, our attack still can not endanger the full 32-round SMS4 since the round number has provided a sufficient safety margin.

The rest of the paper is organized as follows. Section 2 provides a description of SMS4. In Section 3, we introduce a kind of 5-round iterative differential characteristics of SMS4. Then in Sections 4 and 5, a rectangle attack on 16-round SMS4 and a differential attack on 21-round SMS4 are presented respectively. Finally, Section 6 summarizes this paper.

2   Description of SMS4

SMS4 is a block cipher with a 128-bit block size and a 128-bit key size. The overall structure of SMS4 is 32-round unbalanced Feistel network. Since the encryption procedure and the decryption procedure of SMS4 are identical except that the round subkeys are used in the reverse order, we will just describe the encryption procedure in the followings.

2.1   Notation

First of all, we introduce the following notations used throughout this paper.
- Z_2^{32} denotes the set of 32-bit words, and Z_2^8 denotes the set of 8-bit bytes;
- $Sbox(\cdot)$ is the 8×8 bijective S-Box used in the round function F;
- $\lll i$: left rotation by i bits;
- $(X_i, X_{i+1}, X_{i+2}, X_{i+3}) \in (Z_2^{32})^4$ denotes the input of the i-th round, and RK_i is the corresponding 32-bit subkey in round i $(0 \leq i \leq 31)$;
- $Prob_F(\alpha \rightarrow \beta)$: the probability that the output difference of the function F is β when the input difference is α (F can be omitted when the context is clear);
- We call a S-Box active if the input difference of it is nonzero; Otherwise, if the input difference is zero ,we call it a passive S-Box.

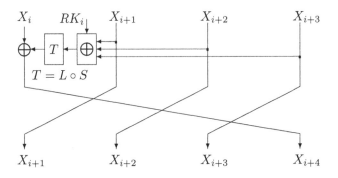

Fig. 1. The i-th round of SMS4

2.2   Encryption Procedure of SMS4

Let $(X_0, X_1, X_2, X_3) \in (Z_2^{32})^4$ and $(Y_0, Y_1, Y_2, Y_3) \in (Z_2^{32})^4$ denote the 128-bit plaintext P and the 128-bit ciphertext C respectively. The round subkeys are $RK_i \in Z_2^{32}$, $(i = 0, 1, 2, \ldots 31)$. Note that the first round is referred as Round 0. Then the encryption procedure of SMS4 is as follows:

$$X_{i+4} = F(X_i, X_{i+1}, X_{i+2}, X_{i+3}, RK_i) = X_i \oplus T(X_{i+1} \oplus X_{i+2} \oplus X_{i+3} \oplus RK_i),$$

for $i = 0, 1, \ldots, 31$. In the end, the 128-bit ciphertext is generated by applying the switch transformation R to the output of Round 31:

$$(Y_0, Y_1, Y_2, Y_3) = R(X_{32}, X_{33}, X_{34}, X_{35}) = (X_{35}, X_{34}, X_{33}, X_{32}).$$

Specifically, the i-th round of SMS4 can be expressed as follows:

$$(X_i, X_{i+1}, X_{i+2}, X_{i+3}) \xrightarrow{F} (X_{i+1}, X_{i+2}, X_{i+3}, X_{i+4}),$$

and the round function $F(X_i, X_{i+1}, X_{i+2}, X_{i+3}, RK_i)$ is defined as:

$$X_{i+4} = X_i \oplus T(X_{i+1} \oplus X_{i+2} \oplus X_{i+3} \oplus RK_i),$$

where the transformation T is composed of a non-linear transformation S and a linear diffusion function L, namely $T(\cdot) = L(S(\cdot))$.

The non-linear transformation S applies the same 8×8 S-Box four times in parallel to an 32-bit input. Let $A = (a_0, a_1, a_2, a_3) \in (Z_2^8)^4$ denotes the input of transformation S, and $B = (b_0, b_1, b_2, b_3) \in (Z_2^8)^4$ denotes the corresponding output. Then the transformation S is defined as follows:

$$(b_0, b_1, b_2, b_3) = S(A) = (Sbox(a_0), Sbox(a_1), Sbox(a_2), Sbox(a_3)).$$

The diffusion transformation L is a simple linear function whose input is the output of transformation S. Let $B \in Z_2^{32}$ and $C \in Z_2^{32}$ denote the input and output of L respectively. Then the linear function L is defined as follows.

$$C = L(B) = B \oplus (B \lll 2) \oplus (B \lll 10) \oplus (B \lll 18) \oplus (B \lll 24).$$

Fig. 1 depicts one round of the encryption procedure of SMS4. We omit the key scheduling algorithm of SMS4 as it is not involved in our analysis, and interested readers can refer to [1] and [10] for details.

3   5-Round Iterative Differential Characteristic of SMS4

In this section, we present a kind of 5-round iterative differential characteristic of SMS4 whose average probability is about 2^{-42}. Our later analysis are mainly based on this new-found iterative differential. Fig. 2 illustrates the trace of the 5-round iterative differential characteristic in detail.

Let $\alpha \in Z_2^{32} \backslash \{0\}$ denotes a 32-bit nonzero difference, and we choose the input difference of Round i as $(\alpha, \alpha, \alpha, 0)$. Then the input difference of transformation T in Round i equals to 0 $(= \alpha \oplus \alpha \oplus 0)$; thus the output difference of T also equals to 0. Therefore, the output difference of the i-th round is $(\alpha, \alpha, 0, \alpha)$ with probability 1. Next in Round $(i+1)$, the input and output difference of T are both 0; hence the output difference of the $(i+1)$-th round is $(\alpha, 0, \alpha, \alpha)$ with probability 1. Similarly, after passing through the $(i+2)$-th round, the output difference of Round $(i+2)$ is $(0, \alpha, \alpha, \alpha)$ with probability 1. In the $(i+3)$-th round, the input difference of T equals to α. Then after applying transformation T, the probability that the output difference is also α is denoted as $Prob_T (\alpha \rightarrow \alpha)$. Therefore, the output difference of Round $(i+3)$ is $(\alpha, \alpha, \alpha, \alpha)$ with probability $Prob_T (\alpha \rightarrow \alpha)$. Similar analysis can be applied to the $(i+4)$-th round, and the input difference of Round $(i+4)$ can be transformed into the output difference $(\alpha, \alpha, \alpha, 0)$ with probability $Prob_T (\alpha \rightarrow \alpha)$. Therefore, we have obtained the following 5-round iterative differential characteristic whose probability is $(Prob_T (\alpha \rightarrow \alpha))^2$.

$$(\alpha, \alpha, \alpha, 0) \xrightarrow{5R} (\alpha, \alpha, \alpha, 0), \quad p = (Prob_T (\alpha \rightarrow \alpha))^2 . \tag{1}$$

The subsequent problem would be how to select the value of α to make the probability $(Prob_T (\alpha \rightarrow \alpha))^2$ as high as possible. First of all, we introduce the following two properties of SMS4 which are important to our analysis.

Property 1. *For the S-Box of SMS4, there exist 127 possible output differences for any nonzero input difference, of which 1 output difference occurs with probability 2^{-6}, and each of the other 126 output differences occurs with probability 2^{-7}.*

Definition 1. *(Branch number) Let $W(\cdot)$ denote the byte weight function, namely the number of nonzero bytes. The branch number of a linear transformation $L : Z_2^{32} \rightarrow Z_2^{32}$ is:*

$$\min_{a \neq 0, a \in Z_2^{32}} (W(a) + W(L(a))).$$

Property 2. *The branch number of the linear transformation L in the round function of SMS4 is 5.*

Property 1 and 2 can be verified by computer programs easily. Moreover, according to Property 1, we can see that the difference distribution table of the SMS4's S-Box is similar to that of AES.

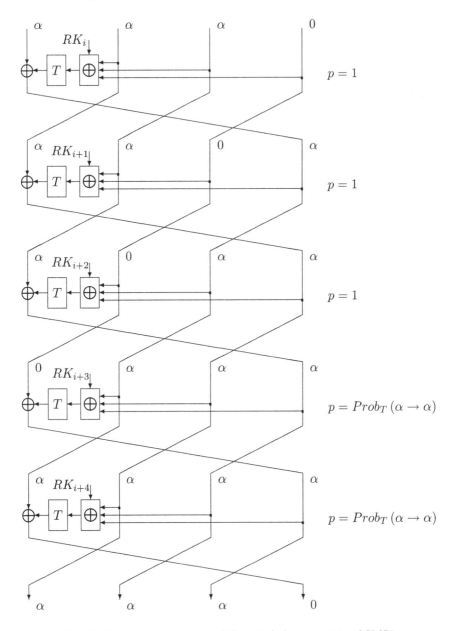

Fig. 2. The 5-round iterative differential characteristic of SMS4

In order to make the probability of the above iterative differential as high as possible, we need to make the number of active S-Boxes in the non-linear layer as low as possible. Considering that in the above differential both the input and output difference of T are α and the branch number of L is 5 according to Property 2, we can know that α has at least 3 active bytes. Therefore, the probability of the above iterative differential is maximized when α has only three active bytes. For simplicity, we can fix the passive byte as byte 0, and α is expressed as $(0, a_1, a_2, a_3)$, where $a_1, a_2, a_3 \in Z_2^8 \setminus \{0\}$. Furthermore, since the input difference of transformation S is α and the corresponding output difference is $L^{-1}(\alpha)$, the first byte of $L^{-1}(\alpha)$ must be zero, namely $L^{-1}(\alpha) = (0, b_1, b_2, b_3)$, where $b_1, b_2, b_3 \in Z_2^8 \setminus \{0\}$. After testing all the possible values of $\alpha = (0, a_1, a_2, a_3)$ by programs, there remain about 2^{16} candidates satisfying that only the first byte of $L^{-1}(\alpha)$ is zero.

For all the 2^{16} remaining candidates of α, the probability $Prob_T(\alpha \to \alpha)$ can be computed as follows.

$$Prob_{Sbox}(a_1 \to b_1) \times Prob_{Sbox}(a_2 \to b_2) \times Prob_{Sbox}(a_3 \to b_3).$$

According to Property 1, for any nonzero input difference, there are only 127 possible output differences. Therefore, $Prob_T(\alpha \to \alpha)$ is not equal to 0 for only about $2^{13}(= 2^{16} \times (1/2)^3)$ possible values of α. Our experimental results verify the theoretical estimations well, and in practice we get 7905 $(\approx 2^{12.95})$ possible values of α. Moreover, according to Property 1, only one of the 127 possible output difference occurs with probability 2^{-6}, and each of the other 126 output differences occurs with probability 2^{-7}. Thus for most of the 2^{13} possible values of α (with a probability of $(126/127)^3$), $Prob_T(\alpha \to \alpha)$ equals to $(2^{-7})^3$. Although for a few possible α, $Prob_T(\alpha \to \alpha)$ may have higher probability such as 2^{-20} and 2^{-19}. Therefore, in most cases of the 2^{13} possible α, the probability of the above 5-round iterative differential characteristics is 2^{-42}. Note that for a few α, the 5-round iterative differentials may have higher probability.

To sum up, the average probability of the 5-round iterative differential characteristic $(\alpha, \alpha, \alpha, 0) \xrightarrow{5R} (\alpha, \alpha, \alpha, 0)$ is about 2^{-42}, and there are about 2^{13} possible values of α when we fix the first byte of α as passive byte. Similar analysis can be applied to the cases when we fix the other byte as passive byte, and our testing programs get just the same results.

In the end, we give an example of the 5-round iterative differential. Choose $\alpha = 00\, e5\, ed\, ec$ (in hexadecimal), then we have $L^{-1}(\alpha) = 00\, 01\, 0c\, 34$. According to the difference distribution table of the S-Box, we have the following equations:

$$Prob_{Sbox}(e5 \to 01) = Prob_{Sbox}(ed \to 0c) = Prob_{Sbox}(ec \to 34) = 2^{-7}.$$

Thus the probability that both of the input and output difference of T are α is $Prob_T(00\, e5\, ed\, ec \to 00\, e5\, ed\, ec) = 2^{-21}$. Therefore, we get the following 5-round iterative differential characteristic of SMS4:

$$(00e5edec, 00e5edec, 00e5edec, 0) \xrightarrow{5R} (00e5edec, 00e5edec, 00e5edec, 0)$$

whose probability is 2^{-42}.

4   Rectangle Attack on 16-Round SMS4

The rectangle attack [4,5,6,11] is an improved chosen plaintext variant of the boomerang attack [8,12]. The key idea is to encrypt many plaintext pairs (P_1, P_2)

and (P_3, P_4) with input difference λ to look for quartets that conform to the rectangle distinguisher, namely $C_1 \oplus C_3 = C_2 \oplus C_4 = \delta$. First of all, a block cipher is treated as a cascade of two sub-ciphers $E = E^1 \circ E^0$, such that for E^0 there exists a differential $\lambda \to \beta$ with probability p, and for E^1 there exists a differential $\gamma \to \delta$ with probability q. Thus the probability of the rectangle distinguisher is $p^2 2^{-n} q^2$. Then by using all possible β's and γ's simultaneously, we can get a rectangle distinguisher with probability $2^{-n} (\hat{p}\hat{q})^2$, where $\hat{p} = \sqrt{\sum_{\beta} \mathrm{Pr}^2 [\lambda \to \beta]}$

and $\hat{q} = \sqrt{\sum_{\gamma} \mathrm{Pr}^2 [\gamma \to \delta]}$. Finally, by guessing subkeys of the first or the last several rounds , the rectangle distinguisher can be used for a key recovery attack.

4.1   The 14-Round Rectangle Distinguisher

In this subsection, we construct a 14-round rectangle distinguisher based on the 5-round iterative differential characteristic described in Section 3. This distinguisher can be used to mount a rectangle attack on SMS4 reduced to 16 rounds.

According to the analysis in Section 3, although for most of the 2^{13} possible values of α the probabilities of the 5-round iterative differential are 2^{-42}, there are still some α which can lead to differentials with higher probabilities. By searching through all the possible values, we choose $\alpha = 00\ c3\ 02\ 90$ which maximizes the probability of the 5-round iterative differential, and the probability of one round $Prob_T(\alpha \to \alpha)$ is computed as follows.

$Prob\,(c3 \to 90) \times Prob\,(02 \to 81) \times Prob\,(90 \to 45) = 2^{-7} \times 2^{-6} \times 2^{-6} = 2^{-19}$

Therefore, we have obtained a 5-round iterative differential with probability 2^{-38} which is higher than the average probability.

Based on this specific 5-round iterative differential, we can construct a 14-round rectangle distinguisher, and the differentials used for E^0 (Rounds 0-8) and E^1 (Rounds 9-13) are as follows.

−The following 9-round differentials are used for E^0: $(\Delta, \Delta, \Delta, 0) \to (\Delta, \Delta, \Delta, \beta)$, where $\Delta = 00\ c3\ 02\ 90$ and β has 127^3 possible values. It is constructed by iterating the above 5-round differential one and a half times, and then extending one more round in the end. Note that a half 5-round iterative differential means the first three rounds whose probabilities are all equal to 1. See Table 1 for details of the first differential, and the difference in the table means the input difference to the corresponding round.
−The following 5-round differentials are used for E^1: $(\gamma, \Psi, \Psi, \Psi) \to (\Psi, \Psi, \Psi, \delta)$, where $\Psi = 00\ 00\ 00\ 02$, $\delta = 83\ 06\ 06\ 85$ and γ has 127 possible values. It is composed of a half 5-round differential and two extended rounds before and after it. See Table 2 for details of the second differential.

For the first differential, there are 127^3 possible output differences β. According to Property 1, the probabilities of p_{β} are distributed as follows: one β has probability 2^{-18}, $3 \cdot 126$ have probability 2^{-19}, $3 \cdot 126^2$ have probability 2^{-20}, and 126^3 have probability 2^{-21}. As we use all these differentials simultaneously, the probability of the first differential is $\hat{p} = \sqrt{\sum_{\beta} \mathrm{Pr}^2 [(\Delta, \Delta, \Delta, 0) \to (\Delta, \Delta, \Delta, \beta)]} \approx$

Table 1. The first differential used for E^0

Round(i)	$\Delta X_i \Delta X_{i+1} \Delta X_{i+2} \Delta X_{i+3}$	Prob.
0	$(\Delta, \Delta, \Delta, 0)$	/
1	$(\Delta, \Delta, 0, \Delta)$	1
2	$(\Delta, 0, \Delta, \Delta)$	1
3	$(0, \Delta, \Delta, \Delta)$	1
4	$(\Delta, \Delta, \Delta, \Delta)$	2^{-19}
5	$(\Delta, \Delta, \Delta, 0)$	2^{-19}
6	$(\Delta, \Delta, 0, \Delta)$	1
7	$(\Delta, 0, \Delta, \Delta)$	1
8	$(0, \Delta, \Delta, \Delta)$	1
output	$(\Delta, \Delta, \Delta, \beta)$	p_β

Table 2. The second differential used for E^1

Round(i)	$\Delta X_i \Delta X_{i+1} \Delta X_{i+2} \Delta X_{i+3}$	Prob.
9	$(\gamma, \Psi, \Psi, \Psi)$	/
10	$(\Psi, \Psi, \Psi, 0)$	p_γ
11	$(\Psi, \Psi, 0, \Psi)$	1
12	$(\Psi, 0, \Psi, \Psi)$	1
13	$(0, \Psi, \Psi, \Psi)$	1
output	$(\Psi, \Psi, \Psi, \delta)$	2^{-6}

$2^{-48.47}$. Similar analysis can be applied to the second differential, and the total probability of the second differential is $\hat{q} = \sqrt{\sum_{\gamma} \text{Pr}^2 \left[(\gamma, \Psi, \Psi, \Psi) \to (\Psi, \Psi, \Psi, \delta) \right]} \approx$ $2^{-9.55}$. Therefore, the probability of the 14-round rectangle distinguisher is about $2^{-128} \cdot (2^{-48.47})^2 \cdot (2^{-9.55})^2 \approx 2^{-244.04}$. As for a random permutation, the probability that a quartet satisfies the distinguisher is $(2^{-128})^2 = 2^{-256} < 2^{-244.04}$, this 14-round rectangle distinguisher can be used to mount a key recovery attack.

4.2 Rectangle Attack Procedure

We set the 14-round rectangle distinguisher at Rounds $0 \sim 13$, and by guessing subkeys of the following two rounds we can mount a rectangle attack on SMS4 reduced to 16 rounds (Round $0 \sim 15$). Since the last switch transformation R has no effect to our attack, we will omit it in the later analysis. The rectangle attack procedure is as follows.

1. Choose $N = 2^{124}$ pairs of plaintexts (P_i, P_i^*), where $P_i^* = P_i \oplus (\Delta, \Delta, \Delta, 0)$. Denote the corresponding ciphertext pairs as (C_i, C_i^*), and the k-th $(0 \leq k \leq 3)$ word of C_i and C_i^* are denoted as $C_{i,k}$ and $C_{i,k}^*$ respectively. Then these pairs can generate about $N^2/2 = 2^{247}$ candidate quartets (C_i, C_i^*, C_j, C_j^*), for $1 \leq i < j \leq 2^{124}$.

2. For each candidate quartet (C_i, C_i^*, C_j, C_j^*), check if the first two words of $C_i \oplus C_j$ and $C_i^* \oplus C_j^*$ are equal to (Ψ, δ). If this is not the case, discard the quartet. After this test there remains about $2^{247} \cdot 2^{-64} \cdot 2^{-64} = 2^{119}$ quartets.

3. For all the remaining quartets, compute $C_{i,0} \oplus C_{i,1} \oplus C_{i,2}$ and $C_{j,0} \oplus C_{j,1} \oplus C_{j,2}$, which are the inputs of T in Round 15 for C_i and C_j respectively. Then insert the quartets into a hash table indexed by the 64-bit computed values. About $2^{119} \cdot 2^{-64} = 2^{55}$ collisions are expected for each index.

4. For every guess of the 32-bit subkey RK_{15} in Round 15, do as follows:

   (a) For each 64-bit index, compute the output of transformation T in Round 15, namely $T(C_{i,0} \oplus C_{i,1} \oplus C_{i,2} \oplus RK_{15})$ and $T(C_{j,0} \oplus C_{j,1} \oplus C_{j,2} \oplus RK_{15})$. Then for each quartet (C_i, C_i^*, C_j, C_j^*) that collides on the same index, decrypt Round 15 for C_i and C_j. Check if the first word of their output difference of Round 14 is equal to Ψ, and discard the unsatisfied quartets. After this test there remains about $2^{55} \cdot 2^{-32} \cdot 2^{64} = 2^{87}$ quartets.

   (b) Next insert all the remaining quartets into a hash table indexed by the 64-bit value $C_{i,0}^* \oplus C_{i,1}^* \oplus C_{i,2}^*$ and $C_{j,0}^* \oplus C_{j,1}^* \oplus C_{j,2}^*$. This will cause about $2^{87} \cdot 2^{-64} = 2^{23}$ collisions for each index. Using the guessed value of subkey RK_{15}, decrypt the 15-th round for C_i^* and C_j^*. Check if the first word of their output difference of Round 14 is equal to Ψ. If this is not the case, discard the quartet. After this test there remains about $2^{23} \cdot 2^{-32} \cdot 2^{64} = 2^{55}$ quartets.

   (c) For all the remaining quartets, try all the 2^{32} possible values of subkey RK_{14}, and decrypt the 14-th round for C_i and C_j. Check if the first word of their output difference of Round 13 is equal to Ψ. If this is not the case, discard the quartet. Then decrypt Round 14 and do the similar check for C_i^* and C_j^*, and discard the unsatisfied quartets. If 6 or more quartets pass all the tests, output the corresponding guessed subkey as correct RK_{15} and RK_{14}. Otherwise, return to Step 4 and repeat.

4.3   Analysis of the Attack

After the tests in Step 4-(c), for the wrong key guesses, the expected remaining quartet is about $2^{55} \cdot 2^{-64} = 2^{-9}$. However, for the correct key guess, it is expected that there remain about $2^{247} \cdot 2^{-244.04} \approx 8$ right quartets after all the tests. Thus the probability that a wrong subkey guess is output in Step 4-(c) is about $2^{-63.5}$, which is computed approximately by the following Poisson distribution: $X \sim Poi(\lambda = 2^{-9})$, $\Pr[X \geq 6] \approx 2^{-63.5}$. Hence the number of wrong subkey outputs is rather small, and it can be removed easily by one encryption check. For the correct key guess, the probability that 6 or more quartets pass all the tests is approximately 0.81, which is computed by the Poisson distribution $X \sim Poi(\lambda = 8)$, $\Pr[X \geq 6] \approx 0.81$. Therefore, the success probability of the rectangle attack on 16-round SMS4 is about 81%.

The attack requires 2^{125} chosen plaintexts in all, and the time complexity can be estimated as follows. Compared to the decryptions in Step 4, the computations in Steps 2 and 3 take relatively small time and thus can be omitted. For Steps 4-(a) and (b) the time complexities are both about $2^{32} \cdot 2^{64} = 2^{96}$ one round encryption. In Step 4-(c) the total number of guessed subkey bits are 64-bit, and there remains 2^{55} quartets for the first check and 2^{23} quartets for the second check; thus the time complexity of Step 4-(c) is about $2^{64} \cdot 2^{55} \cdot 2 + 2^{64} \cdot 2^{23} \cdot 2 \approx 2^{120}$ one round encryption. Therefore, the total time complexity of the attack is about $2^{120}/16 = 2^{116}$ 16-round encryption. The remaining 64-bit unknown subkeys can be obtained by other technique such as exhaustive search.

We stress that our rectangle attack on 16-round SMS4 is just a simple and standard attack, and we have not adopted any skills such as plaintext structures and divide-and-conquer technique. Therefore, we believe that by utilizing these techniques significant improvements can be made to our attack.

5   Differential Cryptanalysis on 21-Round SMS4

In this section, we construct an 18-round differential characteristic by iterating the 5-round iterative differential described in Section 3 three and a half times, and its probability is about $(2^{-42})^3 = 2^{-126}$. The 18-round differential (Rounds $0 \sim 17$) can be expressed as follows.

$$(\alpha, \alpha, \alpha, 0) \xrightarrow{5R} (\alpha, \alpha, \alpha, 0) \xrightarrow{5R} (\alpha, \alpha, \alpha, 0) \xrightarrow{5R} (\alpha, \alpha, \alpha, 0) \xrightarrow{3R} (0, \alpha, \alpha, \alpha).$$

Then by guessing subkeys of the following three rounds we can mount a differential attack on SMS4 reduced to 21 rounds.

According to the analysis in Section 3, there are about 2^{13} possible values of α when we fix the first byte as passive byte. In later analysis, we denote the set of all the 2^{13} possible α as $Diff = \{((0, u, v, w), (0, u, v, w), (0, u, v, w), (0, 0, 0, 0))\}$. Therefore, when the difference of a plaintext pair belongs to $Diff$, with a average probability of 2^{-126} the output difference of them after Round 17 is expected to be $((0, 0, 0, 0), (0, u, v, w), (0, u, v, w), (0, u, v, w))$.

5.1   Attack Procedure

We set the 18-round differential at Rounds $0 \sim 17$, and choose the differences of the plaintext pairs as $(\alpha, \alpha, \alpha, 0) \in Diff$, where $\alpha = (0, u, v, w)$. Then the output differences of Round 17 for the right pairs are expected to be $(0, \alpha, \alpha, \alpha)$, and the output differences of the following three rounds are supposed to be $(\alpha, \alpha, \alpha, *)$, $(\alpha, \alpha, *, *)$ and $(\alpha, *, *, *)$, where $*$ denotes an unknown word. The differential attack on 21-round SMS4 (Rounds $0 \sim 20$) is described as follows.

1. Select m structures of 2^{72} plaintexts each, where in each structure the 56 bits of bytes $0, 4, 8, 12, 13, 14, 15$ are fixed, and all the other 72 bits take all the possible values. Then each structure generates about $(2^{72})^2/2 = 2^{143}$ plaintext pairs with difference $((0, *, *, *), (0, *, *, *), (0, *, *, *), (0, 0, 0, 0))$, and m structures can propose about $m \cdot 2^{143}$ plaintext pairs in all.
2. For each plaintext pair, check if the difference of the plaintext pair belongs to set $Diff$. If this is not the case, discard the pair. After this test, about $m \cdot 2^{143} \cdot (2^{13}/2^{72}) = m \cdot 2^{84}$ plaintext pairs are expected to remain.

3. For each remaining pair (P_i, P_j), compute the plaintext difference and denote it as $((0, u, v, w), (0, u, v, w), (0, u, v, w), (0, 0, 0, 0))$. Then compute the difference of the corresponding ciphertext pair (C_i, C_j), and check if the first word of the ciphertext difference equals to $(0, u, v, w)$. If this is not the case, discard the pair. After this test there remains $m \cdot 2^{84} \cdot 2^{-32} = m \cdot 2^{52}$ pairs.
4. For every guess of the 32-bit subkey RK_{20} in Round 20, do as follows:
   (a) For all the remaining pairs, partially decrypt the 20-th round: $X_{20} = X_{24} \oplus T(X_{21} \oplus X_{22} \oplus X_{23} \oplus RK_{20})$. Check if the first word of the output difference of Round 19 equals to $(0, u, v, w)$, and discard the unsatisfied pairs. After this test, there remains $m \cdot 2^{52} \cdot 2^{-32} = m \cdot 2^{20}$ pairs.
   (b) For every guess of the 32-bit subkey RK_{19}, decrypt the 19-th round for the remaining pairs: $X_{19} = X_{23} \oplus T(X_{20} \oplus X_{21} \oplus X_{22} \oplus RK_{19})$. Check if the first word of the output difference of Round 18 equals to $(0, u, v, w)$, and if this is not the case discard the pair. After this test, for every guess of RK_{20} and RK_{19}, there remains about $m \cdot 2^{20} \cdot 2^{-32} = m \cdot 2^{-12}$ pairs.
   (c) Try all the 2^{32} possible values of subkey RK_{18}, and decrypt Round 18 for the remaining pairs: $X_{18} = X_{22} \oplus T(X_{19} \oplus X_{20} \oplus X_{21} \oplus RK_{18})$. Check if the first word of the output difference of Round 17 equals to 0. If this is not the case, discard the pair. After this test, for every guess of RK_{20}, RK_{19} and RK_{18}, there remains about $m \cdot 2^{-12} \cdot 2^{-32} = m \cdot 2^{-44}$ pairs.
5. Output the 96-bit subkey guess RK_{20}, RK_{19} and RK_{18} as the correct subkey, if it has maximal number of remaining pairs after Step 4-(c).

5.2   Analysis of the Attack

As the average probability of the 18-round differential is 2^{-126}, it is expected that there remains about $m \cdot 2^{84} \cdot 2^{-126} = m \cdot 2^{-42}$ right pairs for the correct key. However, for the wrong subkey guesses, the expected number of remaining pairs after Step 4-(c) is about $m \cdot 2^{84} \cdot 2^{-128} = m \cdot 2^{-44}$. In later analysis, we exploit the concept of "signal-to-noise ratio" introduced by Biham and Shamir in [3] to choose appropriate value of m to make the differential attack succeed.

The signal-to-noise ratio is defined as the proportion of the probability of the right key being suggested by a right pair to the probability of a random key being suggested by a random pair with the initial difference. According to [3], the signal-to-noise ratio can be computed by the following formula:

$$S/N = \frac{2^k \times p}{\alpha \times \beta}$$

where k is the number of guessed key bits, p is the probability of the differential characteristic, α is the average number of keys suggested by a counted pair, and β is the ratio of the counted pairs to all pairs (both counted and discarded).

In the above attack, we have guessed 96-bit subkeys and the probability of the differential characteristic is 2^{-126}. For every test in Step 4, there are 2^{32}

possible key guesses and a counted pair needs to satisfy a 32-bit condition; thus $\alpha = 1$. In Step 3, a 32-bit condition is used to discard the pairs, thus $\beta = 2^{-32}$. Therefore, the signal-to-noise ratio of the above attack is $2^{96} \cdot 2^{-126}/2^{-32} = 4$. According to the suggestions of Biham and Shamir in [3], about $20 \sim 40$ right pairs are needed to mount a successful differential attack when $S/N = 2$, and less right pairs are needed when $S/N > 2$. Hence, in our attack we can choose $m = 2^{46}$, and the expected number of right pairs is about $2^{46} \cdot 2^{-42} = 16$.

Therefore, the attack requires $2^{46} \cdot 2^{72} = 2^{118}$ chosen plaintexts in all. Since Steps 1 to 3 take relatively small time which can be omitted, the time complexity of the attack is dominated by Step 4-(a). The time complexity of this step is about $2 \cdot 2^{52} \cdot 2^{46} \cdot 2^{32} = 2^{131}$ one round encryption. Thus the total time complexity of the attack on 21-round SMS4 is about $2^{131}/21 \approx 2^{126.6}$ 21-round encryptions.

6   Conclusion

In this paper, firstly we present a kind of 5-round iterative differential characteristic whose average probability is 2^{-42}. Then based on this 5-round iterative differential, we construct a 14-round rectangle distinguisher and mount a rectangle attack on 16-round SMS4 with 2^{125} chosen plaintexts and 2^{116} encryptions. Moreover, by iterating the 5-round differential characteristic three and a half times we can obtain an 18-round differential characteristic, and a differential attack is applicable to 21-round SMS4 whose complexities are 2^{118} chosen plaintexts and $2^{126.6}$ encryptions. As far as we know, our differential attack on 21-round SMS4 is the best cryptanalytic result on SMS4. Table 3 summarizes our results along with the previously known attacks on SMS4.

Table 3. Summary of our results and the previously known results on SMS4

# of rounds	Attack type	Data Complexity	Time Complexity	Source
13	Integral Attack	2^{16}	2^{114}	[9]
14	Rectangle Attack	$2^{121.82}$	$2^{116.66}$	[10]
16	Rectangle Attack	2^{125}	2^{116}	This paper
16	Impossible Differential	2^{105}	2^{107}	[10]
21	Differential Cryptanalysis	2^{118}	$2^{126.6}$	This paper

Although our differential attack can reach up to 21 rounds of SMS4, it still can not endanger the full 32-round SMS4 since the round number has provided enough safety margin. We hope our results can be helpful in evaluating the security of SMS4 against differential-type attacks, and we look forward to further work in evaluating SMS4 against other kinds of cryptanalytic attacks.

Acknowledgments. This work is supported by the National High-Tech Research and Development 863 Plan of China (No.2007AA01Z470), the National Natural Science Foundation of China (No.90604036), and the National Grand Fundamental Research 973 Program of China (No.2004CB318004). Moreover, the authors are very grateful to the anonymous referees for their comments and editorial suggestions.

References

1. Specification of SMS4, Block Cipher for WLAN Products – SMS4 (in Chinese), http://www.oscca.gov.cn/UpFile/200621016423197990.pdf
2. Biham, E., Shamir, A.: Differential Cryptanalysis of DES-like Cryptosystem (extended abstract). In: Menezes, A., Vanstone, S.A. (eds.) CRYPTO 1990. LNCS, vol. 537, pp. 2–21. Springer, Heidelberg (1991)
3. Biham, E., Shamir, A.: Differential Cryptanalysis of the Data Encryption Standard. Springer, Heidelberg (1993)
4. Biham, E., Dunkelman, O., Keller, N.: The Rectangle Attack - Rectangling the Serpent. In: Pfitzmann, B. (ed.) EUROCRYPT 2001. LNCS, vol. 2045, pp. 340–357. Springer, Heidelberg (2001)
5. Biham, E., Dunkelman, O., Keller, N.: Related-Key Boomerang and Rectangle Attacks. In: Cramer, R.J.F. (ed.) EUROCRYPT 2005. LNCS, vol. 3494, pp. 507–525. Springer, Heidelberg (2005)
6. Biham, E., Dunkelman, O., Keller, N.: A Related-Key Rectangle Attack on the Full KASUMI. In: Roy, B. (ed.) ASIACRYPT 2005. LNCS, vol. 3788, pp. 443–461. Springer, Heidelberg (2005)
7. Ji, W., Hu, L.: New Description of SMS4 by an Embedding over $GF(2^8)$. In: Srinathan, K., Pandu Rangan, C., Yung, M. (eds.) Indocrypt 2007. LNCS, vol. 4859, pp. 238–251. Springer, Heidelberg (2007)
8. Kelsey, J., Kohno, T., Schneier, B.: Amplified Boomerang Attacks against Reduced-Round MARS and Serpent. In: Schneier, B. (ed.) FSE 2000. LNCS, vol. 1978, pp. 75–93. Springer, Heidelberg (2001)
9. Liu, F., Ji, W., Hu, L., Ding, J., Lv, S., Pyshkin, A., Weinmann, R.P.: Analysis of the SMS4 Block Cipher. In: Pieprzyk, J., Ghodosi, H., Dawson, E. (eds.) ACISP 2007. LNCS, vol. 4586, pp. 158–170. Springer, Heidelberg (2007)
10. Lu, J.: Attacking Reduced-Round Versions of the SMS4 Block Cipher in the Chinese WAPI Standard. In: Qing, S., Imai, H., Wang, G. (eds.) ICICS 2007. LNCS, vol. 4861, pp. 306–318. Springer, Heidelberg (2007)
11. Lu, J., Kim, J., Keller, N., Dunkelman, O.: Differential and Rectangle Attacks on Reduced-Round SHACAL-1. In: Barua, R., Lange, T. (eds.) INDOCRYPT 2006. LNCS, vol. 4329, pp. 17–31. Springer, Heidelberg (2006)
12. Wagner, D.: The Boomerang Attack. In: Knudsen, L.R. (ed.) FSE 1999. LNCS, vol. 1636, pp. 156–170. Springer, Heidelberg (1999)
13. Zhang, L., Wu, W.: Differential Fault Analysis on SMS4 (in Chinese). Chinese Journal of Computers 29(9), 1596–1602 (2006)

Appendix A: The S-Box of SMS4

	0x0	0x1	0x2	0x3	0x4	0x5	0x6	0x7	0x8	0x9	0xa	0xb	0xc	0xd	0xe	0xf
0x0	d6	90	e9	fe	cc	e1	3d	b7	16	b6	14	c2	28	fb	2c	05
0x1	2b	67	9a	76	2a	be	04	c3	aa	44	13	26	49	86	06	99
0x2	9c	42	50	f4	91	ef	98	7a	33	54	0b	43	ed	cf	ac	62
0x3	e4	b3	1c	a9	c9	08	e8	95	80	df	94	fa	75	8f	3f	a6
0x4	47	07	a7	fc	f3	73	17	ba	83	59	3c	19	e6	85	4f	a8
0x5	68	6b	81	b2	71	64	da	8b	f8	eb	0f	4b	70	56	9d	35
0x6	1e	24	0e	5e	63	58	d1	a2	25	22	7c	3b	01	21	78	87
0x7	d4	00	46	57	9f	d3	27	52	4c	36	02	e7	a0	c4	c8	9e
0x8	ea	bf	8a	d2	40	c7	38	b5	a3	f7	f2	ce	f9	61	15	a1
0x9	e0	ae	5d	a4	9b	34	1a	55	ad	93	32	30	f5	8c	b1	e3
0xa	1d	f6	e2	2e	82	66	ca	60	c0	29	23	ab	0d	53	4e	6f
0xb	d5	db	37	45	de	fd	8e	2f	03	ff	6a	72	6d	6c	5b	51
0xc	8d	1b	af	92	bb	dd	bc	7f	11	d9	5c	41	1f	10	5a	d8
0xd	0a	c1	31	88	a5	cd	7b	bd	2d	74	d0	12	b8	e5	b4	b0
0xe	89	69	97	4a	0c	96	77	7e	65	b9	f1	09	c5	6e	c6	84
0xf	18	f0	7d	ec	3a	dc	4d	20	79	ee	5f	3e	d7	cb	39	48

On the Unprovable Security of 2-Key XCBC

Peng Wang[1], Dengguo Feng[2], Wenling Wu[2], and Liting Zhang[2]

[1] State Key Laboratory of Information Security
Graduate University of Chinese Academy of Sciences, Beijing 100049, China
`wp@is.ac.cn`
[2] State Key Laboratory of Information Security
Institution of Software of Chinese Academy of Sciences, Beijing 100080, China
`{feng,wwl,zhangliting}@is.iscas.ac.cn`

Abstract. There has been extensive research focusing on improving CBC-MAC to operate on variable length messages with less keys and less blockcipher invocations. After Black and Rogaway's XCBC, Moriai and Imai proposed 2-Key XCBC, which replaced the third key of XCBC with its first key. Moriai and Imai "proved" that 2-Key XCBC is secure if the underling blockcipher is a pseudorandom permutation (PRP). Our research shows that it is not the case. The security of 2-Key XCBC can not be proved under the solo assumption of PRP, even if it is a RPR-RK secure against some related-key attack. We construct a special PRP (PRP-RK) to show that the main lemma in [14] is not true and 2-Key XCBC using this PRP (PRP-RK) is totally insecure.

Keywords. Blockcipher, Blockcipher mode of operation, Message authentication code, Provable security, Related-key attack.

1 Introduction

CBC-MAC [8] is the most commonly used message authentication code (MAC) based on a blockcipher. Let $E : \mathcal{K} \times \{0,1\}^n \to \{0,1\}^n$ be the underling blockcipher and let $M = M_1 \cdots M_m$ be a string we want to MAC, where $|M_1| = \cdots = |M_m| = n$. Then $\text{CBC-MAC}_K(M)$, the CBC-MAC of M under the key K, is T_m, where

$$T_i = E_K(M_i \oplus T_{i-1}) \text{ for } i = 1, \ldots, m \text{ and } T_0 = 0^n.$$

If the underling blockcipher is a pseudorandom permutation (PRP), then CBC-MAC is secure [1] in the sense of reduction-based cryptography. Unfortunately this provable security result only holds for fixed length messages and for variable length messages CBC-MAC is not secure. For example, if the CBC-MAC of a one-block message M is $T = \text{CBC-MAC}_K(M) = E_K(M)$, the CBC-MAC of the two-block message $M||(M \oplus T)$ is once again T.

To overcome this drawback, several variants of CBC-MAC such as EMAC, XCBC, TMAC and OMAC, have been proposed which are probably secure for variable length messages.

Y. Mu, W. Susilo, and J. Seberry (Eds.): ACISP 2008, LNCS 5107, pp. 230–238, 2008.
© Springer-Verlag Berlin Heidelberg 2008

EMAC [6,15] encrypt CBC-MAC by E again with a new key:

$$\text{EMAC}_{K_1,K_2}(M) = E_{K_2}(\text{CBC-MAC}_{K_1}(M)).$$

In order to operate on arbitrary length messages, some padding method must be used. For example, we append the minimal bit string 10^i to the message M to make the length a multiple of n. However, when $|M|$ is already a multiple of n, we must append an entirely extra block 10^{n-1}. That will waste a blockcipher invocation. Furthermore, because K_1 and K_2 are both keys fed to E, EMAC need two blockcipher key setups.

Black and Rogaway proposed XCBC [4] to solved the above problems. They treated different messages using different keys according to whether or not the length of the message is a multiple of n, shaved off one blockcipher invocation, and avoided keying E by multiple keys. XCBC has three keys (K_1, K_2, K_3), where $K_1 \in \mathcal{K}$ which is fed to E and $K_2, K_3 \in \{0,1\}^n$ which are XORed with the last message block. When $|M|$ is a multiple of n, XCBC does the same as CBC-MAC, except for XORing K_2 before encrypting the last block. When $|M|$ is not a multiple of n, XCBC firstly appends some 10^i to make it a multiple of n, and then does the same as CBC-MAC, except for XORing K_3 before encrypting the last block.

Kurosawa and Iwata then proposed TMAC [13] which has two keys. They replaced (K_2, K_3) in XCBC with $(K_2 \cdot u, K_2)$ where u is some non-zero constant and $\cdot$ is the multiplication in some finite field. Finally, Iwata and Kurosawa proposed OMAC [10] which has only one key. They replaced (K_2, K_3) in XCBC with $(L \cdot u, L \cdot u^2)$ (in OMAC1) or with $(L \cdot u, L \cdot u^{-1})$ (in OMAC2) where $L = E_K(0^n)$ and u is some non-zero constant. CMAC [7] which was adopted by NIST as the recommendation for MAC is just OMAC1.

Moriai and Imai proposed 2-Key XCBC [14,9] right after XCBC. Their purpose was the same as TMAC and OMAC – minimum size of key. They replaced K_3 in XCBC with K_1. So 2-Key XCBC is just XCBC with keys (K_1, K_2, K_1). Moriai and Imai "proved" that 2-Key XCBC is secure using the main lemma that $(E_K(\cdot), E_K(K \oplus \cdot))$ is indistinguishable from a pair of independent uniform random permutations (URPs), if E is an PRP.

Unfortunately, it is not the case. We notice that when the message M is not of a multiple of n, 2-Key XCBC only takes one key K_1 which is both keying E and XORed with the last padded message block. For example when $|M| = n-1$, the 2-Key CBC is

$$\text{2-Key XCBC}_{K_1,K_2}(M) = E_{K_1}(K_1 \oplus M\|1).$$

Furuya and Sakurai studied 2-Key XCBC from the attacking point of view [9]. They instantiated the underling blockcipher with practical ones such as DESX, AES, etc., and pointed out that it is very dangerous to XOR the key of the blockcipher to the message (they called it raw-key masking [9]). For example, when E is AES, the XORing of the key removes the key to the first round of AES, because they are identical, resulting in one less round AES.

1.1 Our Contributions

We study 2-Key XCBC from the provable-security point of view. We show that the proof for 2-key XCBC MAC is not correct. We give a PRP (technically, a PRP-RK) for which the 2-key XCBC MAC is easily forgeable. We therefore conclude that the 2-key XCBC MAC construction is not secure.

We construct a special PRP G such that $G_K(K \oplus 0^{n-1}1) = K$ for any key $K \in \{0,1\}^n$, from a PRP $E : \{0,1\}^n \times \{0,1\}^n \to \{0,1\}$. This construction is similar to the one used in [3]. We prove that if E is a PRP, G is also a PRP, and furthermore if E is a PRP-RK, G is also a PRP-RK for some related-key attack.

This construction implies that the main lemma in [14] does not hold. Because when one query $0^{n-1}1$ to the right oracle of $(G_K(\cdot), G_K(K \oplus \cdot))$ reveals the key K, using this information we can easily distinguish $(G_K(\cdot), G_K(K \oplus \cdot))$ from a pair of independent uniform random permutations.

This construction also implies that the underling blockcipher being a PRP (even if PRP-RK) is not enough for providing the security of 2-Key XCBC. If the underling blockcipher 2-Key XCBC is G, one query 0^{n-1} also reveals the key K_1, which enables us forge any message being of a multiple of n.

1.2 Related Work

It's dangerous to encrypt the key of scheme together with the plaintext. In [5] Black, Rogaway and Shrimpton called it key-dependent message (KDM) encryption. They also defined a general KDM security model and showed that KDM security can be achieved within the random-oracle model.

The security proof is always a subtle thing, for it is error-prone and difficult to check. Iwata and Kurosawa found some mistakes in the previous security proofs and showed that the encryption algorithm and MAC in 3GPP and a variant of OMAC are not provably secure under the assumption that the underling blockcipher is only a PRP [11,12]. But the algorithms in 3GPP are secure if the underling blockcipher is a PRP-RK secure against a certain class of related-key attacks.

2 Preliminaries

Notations. We write $s \xleftarrow{\$} S$ to denote choosing a random element s from a set S by uniform distribution. An *adversary* is a (randomized) algorithm with access to one or more oracles which are written as superscripts. We write the adversary A with oracle $\mathcal{O}$ outputing a bit b as $A^{\mathcal{O}} \Rightarrow b$. $\mathbf{Adv}_{SSS}^{GGG}(A)$ denotes the advantage of A attacking a scheme "SSS" with a goal of "GGG".

Blockcipher, PRP and PRP-RK. A blockcipher is a function $E : \mathcal{K} \times \{0,1\}^n \to \{0,1\}^n$, where $E_K(\cdot) = E(K, \cdot)$ is permutation for any key $K\mathcal{K}$. Let

Perm(n) be the set of all permutations on $\{0,1\}^n$. In the reduction-based cryptography, we usually treat a secure blockcipher as a *pseudorandom permutation* (PRP). A blockcipher is a PRP, if it is indistinguishable from a *uniform random permutation* (URP). More specifically, if the advantage

$$\mathbf{Adv}_E^{\mathrm{prp}}(A) = \Pr[K \xleftarrow{\$} \mathcal{K} : A^{E_K(\cdot)} \Rightarrow 1] - \Pr[\pi \xleftarrow{\$} \mathrm{Perm}(n) : A^{\pi(\cdot)} \Rightarrow 1]$$

is negligible for any A with reasonable resources, then E is said to be a *pseudorandom permutation* (PRP), or a secure blockcipher, or secure against chosen plaintext attack.

The notion of PRP-RK was introduced in [2], to model blockciphers secure against some related-key attacks. In this model, the adversary not only can choose plaintext but also can change the underling key using a set of related-key-deriving (RKD) functions. The RKD set depicts the adversaries' abilities for deriving related keys. We denote the RKD set as $\varPhi$. Without loss of generality, we assume that any function in $\varPhi$ is a permutation on $\mathcal{K}$. Let $\mathrm{Perm}(\mathcal{K}, n)$ be the set of all blockciphers with domain $\{0,1\}^n$ and key space $\mathcal{K}$, thus $\widetilde{\pi} \xleftarrow{\$} \mathrm{Perm}(\mathcal{K}, n)$ denotes selecting a random blockcipher, or in other words, for any $K \in \mathcal{K}$, $\widetilde{\pi}_K(\cdot)$ is a uniform random permutation (URP). Let $RK(\phi, K) = \phi(K)$, for any $\phi \in \varPhi$. A blockcipher is $\varPhi$-PRP-RK secure, if the advantage

$$\mathbf{Adv}_E^{\varPhi\text{-prp-rk}}(A) = \Pr[K \xleftarrow{\$} \mathcal{K} : A^{E_{RK(\cdot, K)}(\cdot)} \Rightarrow 1]$$
$$- \Pr[K \xleftarrow{\$} \mathcal{K}; \widetilde{\pi} \xleftarrow{\$} \mathrm{Perm}(\mathcal{K}, n) : A^{\widetilde{\pi}_{RK(\cdot, K)}(\cdot)} \Rightarrow 1]$$

is negligible for any A with reasonable resources.

MAC and Unforgeability. A MAC is function $\mathrm{MAC} : \mathcal{K} \times \mathcal{M} \to \{0,1\}^t$, which takes a key $K \in \mathcal{K}$ and a message $M \in \mathcal{M}$ to return a t-bit tag $T \in \{0,1\}^t$. We write $\mathrm{MAC}(K, \cdot)$ as $\mathrm{MAC}_K(\cdot)$ and say that an adversary $A^{\mathrm{MAC}_K(\cdot)}$ forges if it outputs (M, T) such that $T = \mathrm{MAC}_K(M)$ and A never ask query M to its oracle before. A MAC is secure if the advantage

$$\mathbf{Adv}_{\mathrm{MAC}}^{\mathrm{uf}}(A) = \Pr[K \xleftarrow{\$} \mathcal{K} : A^{\mathrm{MAC}_K(\cdot)} \text{ forges}].$$

is negligible for any A with reasonable resources. The MAC is also said to be unforgeable, or unpredictable.

XCBC and 2-Key XCBC. Let $E : \mathcal{K} \times \{0,1\}^n \to \{0,1\}^n$ be the underling blockcipher, XCBC is the following algorithm:

The only difference between XCBC and 2-Key XCBC is that in the later $K_3 = K_1$. Figure 1 illustrates XCBC and 2-Key XCBC for a message of three blocks.

Algorithm XCBC$[E]_{K_1,K_2,K_3}(M)$:
$T_0 \leftarrow 0^n$
Let $M = M_1 \cdots M_m$, where $|M_i| = n$ for $1 \le i \le m-1$ and $1 \le |M_m| \le n$
for $i = 1$ **to** $m-1$ **do**
$\quad T_i \leftarrow E_{K_1}(M_i \oplus T_{i-1})$
if $|M_m| = n$ **then** $T \leftarrow E_K(M_m \oplus K_2)$
if $|M_m| < n$ **then** $T \leftarrow E_K(M_m 10^{n-1-|M_m|} \oplus K_3)$

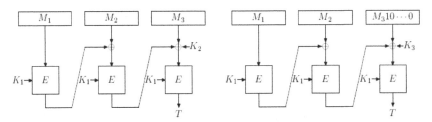

Fig. 1. XCBC and 2-Key XCBC for a message of three blocks. $K_3 = K_1$ in 2-Key XCBC. On the left is the case where $|M|$ is a multiple of n. While on the right is the case where it is not.

3   Construction of a Special PRP

In this section we construct a special PRP $G : \{0,1\}^n \times \{0,1\}^n \to \{0,1\}^n$ with following property:

$$G_K(K \oplus 0^{n-1}1) = K, \tag{1}$$

for any key $K \in \{0,1\}^n$.

We start from a PRP $E : \{0,1\}^n \times \{0,1\}^n \to \{0,1\}^n$, and define G as follows:

$$G_K(M) = \begin{cases} K & \text{if } M = K \oplus 0^{n-1}1, \\ E_K(K \oplus 0^{n-1}1) & \text{if } M = E_K^{-1}(K), \\ E_K(M) & \text{else.} \end{cases}$$

Theorem 1. *If E is a PRP, then G is a PRP. More specifically, G and E are indistinguishable. For any adversary A with q queries trying to distinguish G and E, there is an adversary B with no more than $(q+1)$ queries such that*

$$\Pr[A^G \Rightarrow 1] - \Pr[A^E \Rightarrow 1] \le 2q\mathbf{Adv}_E^{\text{prp}}(B) + \frac{2q}{2^n - q}.$$

Furthermore, B runs in approximately the same time as A.

Proof. Suppose that A makes q queries $x_i, i = 1, \ldots, q$ and the corresponding answers are $y_1, \ldots, y_q$. We describe the attacking procedure of A as the interaction with games. Game 1 illustrates how G answers A's queries.

11	$bad \leftarrow$ **false**	Game 1 and Game 2
12	when the query is x:	
13	if $x = K \oplus 0^{n-1}1$, $bad \leftarrow$ **true** , return K	
14	if $x = E_K^{-1}(K)$, $bad \leftarrow$ **true** , return $E_K(K \oplus 0^{n-1}1)$	
15	**return** $E_K(x)$	

31	$bad \leftarrow$ **false**	Game 3
32	when the query is x:	
33	if $K = x \oplus 0^{n-1}1$, $bad \leftarrow$ **true**	
34	if $K = E_K(x)$, $bad \leftarrow$ **true**	
35	**return** $E_K(x)$	

Fig. 2. Game 1, Game 2 and Game 3. Game 2 is obtained by omitting the boxed statements

Game 2 is obtained by omitting the boxed statements. Obviously Game 2 illustrates how E answers A's queries. In Game 1, each boxed statement is executed if and only if the flag bad is set to be true. Therefore we have

$$\Pr[A^G \Rightarrow 1] - \Pr[A^E \Rightarrow 1] = \Pr[A^{\text{Game 1}} \Rightarrow 1] - \Pr[A^{\text{Game 2}} \Rightarrow 1]$$
$$\leq \Pr[A^{\text{Game 2}} \text{ sets } bad]. \tag{2}$$

Notice that in the Game 2 line 14 $x = E_K^{-1}(K)$ is equivalent to $K = E_K(x)$. We recompose Game 2 into Game 3 and we have

$$\Pr[A^{\text{Game 2}} \text{ sets } bad] = \Pr[A^{\text{Game 3}} \text{ sets } bad]. \tag{3}$$

$A^{\text{Game 3}}$ set bad if and only if during the queries to $E_K(\cdot)$ the key K appears in $\{x_i \oplus 0^{n-1}1 : i = 1, \ldots, q\}$ or in $\{y_i : i = 1, \ldots, q\}$. If E is a PRP, this probability is very small. We construct a new algorithm B making use of A, trying to distinguish E from a uniformly random permutation. B randomly chooses a string in $\{x_i \oplus 0^{n-1}1 : i = 1, \ldots, q\} \cup \{y_i : i = 1, \ldots, q\}$, and takes it as the key of E. The detail is following:

Algorithm $B^{\mathcal{O}}$:
$(t, b) \xleftarrow{\$} \{1, \ldots, q\} \times \{0, 1\}$
run $A^{\mathcal{O}}$
  when A asks the tth query x_t and gets y_t
   if $b = 0, K \leftarrow x_t \oplus 0^{n-1}1$
   if $b = 1, K \leftarrow y_t$
  choose x which is not in $\{x_i : i = 1, \ldots, t\}$
  $d \leftarrow E_K(x)$
  query x and get d'
  if $d = d'$ then **return** 1
  else **return** 0

Obviously, $\Pr[K \xleftarrow{\$} \{0,1\}^n : B^{G_K(\cdot)} \Rightarrow 1] \geq \frac{1}{2q}\Pr[A^{\text{Game 3}} \text{ sets } bad]$ and $\Pr[\pi \xleftarrow{\$} \text{Perm}(n) : B^{\pi(\cdot)} \Rightarrow 1] \leq \frac{1}{2^n-q}$, so $\mathbf{Adv}_E^{\text{prp}}(B) \geq \frac{1}{2q}\Pr[A^{\text{Game 3}} \text{ sets } bad] - \frac{1}{2^n-q}$,

$$\Pr[A^{\text{Game 3}} \text{ sets } bad] \leq 2q\mathbf{Adv}_E^{\text{prp}}(B) + \frac{2q}{2^n-q}. \tag{4}$$

Combining (2), (3) and (4), we get

$$\Pr[A^G \Rightarrow 1] - \Pr[A^E \Rightarrow 1] \leq 2q\mathbf{Adv}_E^{\text{prp}}(B) + \frac{2q}{2^n-q}. \tag{5}$$

$\square$

It is easy to modify the above proof slightly to get the following theorem.

Theorem 2. *If E is Φ-PRP-RK secure, and Φ is set of permutations, then G is Φ-PRP-RK secure. More specifically, for any adversary A with q queries trying to distinguish G and E, there is an adversary B with no more than $(q+1)$ queries such that*

$$\Pr[A^G \Rightarrow 1] - \Pr[A^E \Rightarrow 1] \leq 2q\mathbf{Adv}_E^{\Phi\text{-prp-rk}}(B) + \frac{2q}{2^n-q}.$$

Furthermore, B runs in approximately the same time as A.

4 Unprovable Security of 2-Key XCBC

$(G_K(\cdot), G_K(K \oplus \cdot))$ **is distinguishable from** $(\pi_1(\cdot), \pi_2(\cdot))$. The main lemma in [14] states that if E is a PRP, $(E_K(\cdot), E_K(K \oplus \cdot))$ is indistinguishable from $(\pi_1(\cdot), \pi_2(\cdot))$, where π_1 and π_2 are two independent URPs. This lemma is the base for their security proof. But it is not the case, because $(G_K(\cdot), G_K(K \oplus \cdot))$ is distinguishable from $(\pi_1(\cdot), \pi_2(\cdot))$. We firstly query $0^{n-1}1$ to the right oracle, if it is $G_K(K \oplus \cdot)$, we get the key K. This information enable us almost totally distinguish $(G_K(\cdot), G_K(K\oplus\cdot))$ from $(\pi_1(\cdot), \pi_2(\cdot))$. The detailed algorithm is the following:

> **Algorithm** $D^{\mathcal{O}_1(\cdot),\mathcal{O}_2(\cdot)}$:
> query $0^{n-1}1$ **to** $\mathcal{O}_2(\cdot)$ and get K'
> $C \leftarrow G_{K'}(1^n)$
> query 1^n **to** $\mathcal{O}_1(\cdot)$ and get C'
> **if** $C = C'$, **return** 1
> **else return** 0

We can see that $\Pr[D^{(G_K(\cdot),G_K(K\oplus\cdot))} \Rightarrow 1] = 1$ and $\Pr[D^{(\pi_1(\cdot),\pi_2(\cdot))} \Rightarrow 1] = \frac{1}{2^n}$, so the advantage is $1 - \frac{1}{2^n}$.

2-Key-XCBC[G] is Not a Secure MAC. If the underling blockcipher 2-Key XCBC is G, one query 0^{n-1} also reveals the key K_1, which enables us to forge any message with length of a multiple of n. The detailed algorithm is the following:

> **Algorithm** $F^{\text{2-Key-XCBC}[G](\cdot)}$:
> query 0^{n-1} **to** $2-\text{Key}-\text{XCBC}[G](\cdot)$ and get K'
> $T \leftarrow G_{K'}(K' \oplus 0^{n-2}10)$
> **return** $(0^{n-2}, T)$

We notice that $K' = \text{2-Key-XCBC}[G](0^{n-1}) = G_{K_1}(K_1 \oplus 0^{n-1}1) = K_1$, so 2-Key-XCBC$[G](0^{n-2}) = G_{K_1}(K_1 \oplus 0^{n-2}10) = G_{K'}(K' \oplus 0^{n-2}10) = T$ and

$$\mathbf{Adv}^{\text{uf}}_{\text{2-Key-XCBC}[G]}(F) = 1.$$

Acknowledgment

The authors would like to thank the anonymous referees for their many valuable comments. This research is supported by the National Natural Science Foundation Of China (No. 60673083, 90604036), the National Grand Fundamental Research 973 Program of China (No.2007CB311202) and the National High-Tech Research and Development Program of China (No.2007AA01Z470).

References

1. Bellare, M., Kilian, J., Rogaway, P.: The security of cipher block chaining. In: Desmedt, Y.G. (ed.) CRYPTO 1994. LNCS, vol. 839, pp. 341–358. Springer, Heidelberg (1994)
2. Bellare, M., Kohno, T.: A theoretical treatment of related-key attacks: RKA-PRPs, RKA-PRFs, and applications. In: Biham, E. (ed.) EUROCRYPT 2003. LNCS, vol. 2656, pp. 491–506. Springer, Heidelberg (2003)
3. Black, J.: The ideal-cipher model, revisited: An uninstantiable blockcipher-based hash function. In: Robshaw, M.J.B. (ed.) FSE 2006. LNCS, vol. 4047, pp. 328–340. Springer, Heidelberg (2006)
4. Black, J., Rogaway, P.: CBC MACs for arbitrary-length messages: The three-key constructions. In: Bellare, M. (ed.) CRYPTO 2000. LNCS, vol. 1880, pp. 197–215. Springer, Heidelberg (2000)
5. Black, J., Rogaway, P., Shrimpton, T.: Encryption-scheme security in the presence of key-dependent messages. In: Nyberg, K., Heys, H. (eds.) SAC 2002. LNCS, vol. 2595, pp. 62–75. Springer, Heidelberg (2003)
6. Bosselaers, A., Preneel, B. (eds.): RIPE 1992. LNCS, vol. 1007. Springer, Heidelberg (1995)
7. Dworkin, M.: Recommendation for block cipher modes of operation: The CMAC mode for authentication. NIST Special Publication 800-38B (2005),
   http://csrc.nist.gov/publications/nistpubs/800-38B/SP_800-38B.pdf
8. FIPS-133. Federal information processing standards publication (FIPS 133). computer data authentication (1985)

9. Furuya, S., Sakurai, K.: Risks with raw-key maksing - the security evaluations of 2-Key XCBC. In: Deng, R.H., Qing, S., Bao, F., Zhou, J. (eds.) ICICS 2002. LNCS, vol. 2513, pp. 327–341. Springer, Heidelberg (2002)
10. Iwata, T., Kurosawa, K.: OMAC: One-key CBC MAC. In: Johansson, T. (ed.) FSE 2003. LNCS, vol. 2887, pp. 129–153. Springer, Heidelberg (2003)
11. Iwata, T., Kurosawa, K.: On the correctness of security proofs for the 3GPP confidentiality and integrity algorithms. In: Paterson, K.G. (ed.) Cryptography and Coding 2003. LNCS, vol. 2898, pp. 306–318. Springer, Heidelberg (2003)
12. Iwata, T., Kurosawa, K.: On the security of a new variant of OMAC. In: Lim, J., Lee, D. (eds.) ICISC 2003. LNCS, vol. 2971, pp. 67–78. Springer, Heidelberg (2004)
13. Kurosawa, K., Iwata, T.: TMAC: Two-key CBC MAC. In: Joye, M. (ed.) CT-RSA 2003. LNCS, vol. 2612, pp. 33–49. Springer, Heidelberg (2003)
14. Moriai, S., Imai, H.: 2-Key XCBC: the CBC MAC for arbitrary-length messages by the two-key construction. In: The 2002 Symposium on Cryptography and Information Security, SCIS (2002) (in Japanese)
15. Petrank, E., Rackoff, C.: CBC MAC for real-time data sources. Journal of Cryptology 13(3), 315–338 (2000)

Looking Back at a New Hash Function

Olivier Billet[1], Matthew J.B. Robshaw[1], Yannick Seurin[1], and Yiqun Lisa Yin[2]

[1] Orange Labs, Issy les Moulineaux, France
{forename.surname}@orange-ftgroup.com
[2] Independent Security Consultant
yiqun@alum.mit.edu

Abstract. We present two (related) dedicated hash functions that deliberately borrow heavily from the block ciphers that appeared in the final stages of the AES process. We explore the computational trade-off between the key schedule and encryption in a block cipher-based hash function and we illustrate our approach with a 256-bit hash function that has a hashing rate equivalent to the encryption rate of AES-128. The design extends naturally to a 512-bit hash function.

1 Introduction

After recent cryptanalytic advances [37,38] the need for new hash functions has become acute. In response NIST has made a call for proposals [28] for the development of a new *Advanced Hash Standard (SHA-3)*. However most commentators would probably agree that the field of hash functions has, until recently, been somewhat neglected and that the current knowledge of hash function design is somewhat fragmented. So difficult are the starting conditions for the development of the AHS that it is not always straightforward to exactly articulate the properties we want from a hash function. Even worse, there is little agreement on even the basic features for a successful hash function design.

By way of contrast, if we were to turn the clock back to the start of the AES process, at that time we already had five years of block cipher theory and design *after* the development of linear cryptanalysis [20] and ten years *after* the development of differential cryptanalysis [8]. And while all the AES submissions were very different, their designs had evolved from several years of research experience gained during the mid-1990s.

In this paper we propose two new (related) dedicated hash functions DASH-256 and DASH-512. Whilst they are, in principle, suitable for submission to the NIST hash function development process, this is not our intention. Instead we prefer to see the paper as research-oriented and our work is prompted by the following questions:

1. How close can we stay to AES proposals in the design of a hash function?
2. Can we use an unusual key schedule design to our advantage?

Y. Mu, W. Susilo, and J. Seberry (Eds.): ACISP 2008, LNCS 5107, pp. 239–253, 2008.
© Springer-Verlag Berlin Heidelberg 2008

2   Background, Goals, and Design Criteria

We informally recapitulate some of the classical goals for a hash function. A cryptographic hash function H takes an input of variable size and returns a hash value of fixed length while satisfying the properties of preimage resistance, second preimage resistance, and collision resistance [21]. For a secure hash function that gives an n-bit output, compromising these properties should require 2^n, 2^n, and $2^{n/2}$ operations respectively. A more thorough set of hash function requirements for the SHA-3 development process is available at [28].

The pioneering work of Merkle and Damgård [14,22] showed how to construct a collision-free hash function from a *compression function* that has a fixed-length input. This input consists of a *chaining variable* and a message extract while the new value of the chaining variable is produced as output. The chaining variable will be denoted by v_i and the message extract will be denoted by m_i. Thus, at iteration i of the Merkle-Damgård construction, we compute $v_{i+1} = $ COMPRESS(m_i, v_i). The advantages and disadvantages of the Merkle-Damgård approach are, by now, well-established. On the positive side are its simplicity and the proof of security that (loosely speaking) relates the collision-resistance of the hash function to that of the compression function. On the negative side are cryptanalytic results that take advantage of the chaining that is used in a repeated application of the compression function [15,16,18,19]. These results help provide a greater understanding of the Merkle-Damgård approach, particularly when hashing exceptionally long messages.

Design Decisions

Our design philosophy for DASH-256 (and DASH-512) can be summarised as: *keep it simple and use established techniques*. In practise this resulted in the following:

1. We base the hash function around the use of a compression function and the Merkle-Damgård paradigm [14,22]. To avoid some structural deficiencies we use the HAIFA model [7] for formatting the inputs.
2. For the compression function we use a block cipher and *Davies-Meyer* [29].
3. We revisit the AES process and appeal to the vast pool of results [25] to design a block cipher at the heart of the compression function.
4. We push the parameters of a block cipher key schedule so as to better understand the range of options for a practical hash function design.

By way of background, we now consider each issue in turn.

Using Merkle-Damgård and Davies-Meyer

While there have been proposals for alternatives to Merkle-Damgård, *e.g.* the *sponge construction* [6], we focus on the body of work that considers adjustments to Merkle-Damgård, such as those of Coron *et al* [13], Biham and Dunkelman [7], and Rivest [34]. These proposals share the property that Merkle-Damgård is used almost as is, but that additional inputs are included at each iteration of the compression function. They vary in the form of inputs and the resultant loss of efficiency, but recent work [2] has shown that the more efficient proposal by Rivest [34] does not seem to provide the additional security intended. With this in mind we use the HAsh Iterative FrAmework [7], or HAIFA model.

For the compression function itself we use a block cipher in Davies-Meyer mode. This is a mode for which there is a proof-of-security, $i.e.$ the security of Davies-Meyer can be reduced to that of the underlying block cipher. If we denote encryption of a plaintext p under a key k by $\text{ENC}_k(p)$ then the output of the Davies-Meyer mode is given by $\text{ENC}_k(p) \oplus p$. When used as a compression function, for which the chaining variable input is denoted v_i and the message input is denoted m, the next value of the chaining variable output from the compression function is given by $v_{i+1} = \text{ENC}_m(v_i) \oplus v_i$. We note that there are some unusual properties of Davies-Meyer. For instance it is easy to find fixed points for this construction. By choosing $v_i = \text{ENC}_m^{-1}(0)$ we have that $\text{COMPRESS}(m, v_i) = v_i$ since $\text{ENC}_m(v_i) \oplus v_i = v_i$. However the HAIFA model helps to mitigate the effect of these, as well as countering other recent cryptanalytic work on long-message attacks [15,16,18]. By contrast the Davies-Meyer mode has one major advantage over other single block cipher constructions [11]. Note that for the Davies-Meyer transformation $\text{ENC}_m(v_i) \oplus v_i$ the block size is given by $|v_i|$ and the key size by $|m|$. For the AES these are restricted to 128 bits and $128/192/256$ bits respectively. However our design allows the block size to vary between 256 and 512 bits while the "key" length is eight times larger; this permits larger message inputs on each iteration and a more competitive throughput. And for block cipher designs there is no better place to look than the AES process [25].

Revisiting the AES Process

Returning to the AES process with the benefit of hindsight is an interesting experience. We are not the first to do so: the designers of PRESENT [12] used the AES finalist Serpent [9] as a starting point for the development of their ultra-compact block cipher. We therefore hope to be able to make similarly advantageous observations by considering two other finalists: Rijndael ($i.e.$ the AES [24]) and RC6 [32]. Rijndael is now very well known. Like Rijndael, RC6 was a simple proposal that offered good software performance on modern processors [3]. However the 32-bit squaring operation didn't scale quite as well to 8-bit processors or hardware implementations. However, of particular interest to us here is the key schedule for RC6. While it is computationally heavy, it allows very long keys. This is ideal for a hashing application as was observed by the RC6 designers during the AES process [33].

So the block cipher that lies at the heart of DASH-256 and DASH-512 will use a topology that is similar to RC6 and CLEFIA [36] along with a key schedule that is almost identical to that used in RC5 and RC6. However we will make changes to some of the operations used to improve scalability and to reduce the potential exposure to side-channel analysis in MAC-applications [27].

Block Ciphers and Key Schedules

The performance of a block cipher is dependent on the cost of both the encryption routine and key setup. For bulk encryption the cost of a single key setup is amortized over the entire encryption session. However, when used as the basis for a hash function, the cost of the key schedule becomes a significant factor. Most modern ciphers, including the AES, tend to have a lightweight key schedule. In this paper, we want to explore what happens when we put more work into the key schedule. Given the importance of key schedule performance for hashing, at first sight this appears to be the wrong direction. Indeed for constructions where the message and chaining value must be the same size, such as Mateas-Meyer-Oseas [21] and Miyaguchi-Preneel [21] (which is used in Whirlpool [5]) this would be the case. However, the Davies-Meyer construction allows us to take a very large message block as "key" and provided there is sufficient mixing of the key there is no reason why a good performance profile cannot be attained.

3   The Specification of DASH-256 and DASH-512

Both DASH-256 and DASH-512 are built around a dedicated block cipher which we will name $\mathcal{A}_{256}$ and $\mathcal{A}_{512}$ respectively. For ease of exposition we will concentrate on DASH-256 and $\mathcal{A}_{256}$ and describe the cipher in terms of an encryption routine and a key schedule. The necessary changes for DASH-512 are given in Section 3.4.

3.1   The Encryption Routine for $\mathcal{A}_{256}$

One encryption round (out of the 30 required) is illustrated in Figure 1. Each strand represents a 64-bit word and the key schedule, see Section 3.2, generates 64 subkeys of which two are used as pre-whitening for strands B and D, 60 are used during the encryption process (two in each round), and two are used as post-whitening on strands A and C before output. The data-dependent rotations and multiplication in RC6 have been replaced in $\mathcal{A}_{256}$ with a confusion/diffusion operation closely inspired by the AES. The mixing operation M_{64} is the natural restriction of the AES diffusion layer to two columns, see Figure 2, and uses the S-boxes and AES MDS transformation directly. This allows us to combine the scalability of RC5 and RC6 with the AES diffusion operations.[1] However, AES diffusion is somewhat structured so the one-bit and eight-bit rotations help to break some alignments and avoid some trivial linear approximations.

3.2   The Key Schedule for $\mathcal{A}_{256}$

By using a key schedule that is close to that used in RC5 and RC6 we aim to leverage its long-standing in the literature and the opportunities for analysis during the AES process. We also take advantage of the fact that it allows long key inputs. The original key schedule can be found in either of [30,32] though

---

[1] Naturally other MDS transformations [17] and S-boxes may offer other advantages.

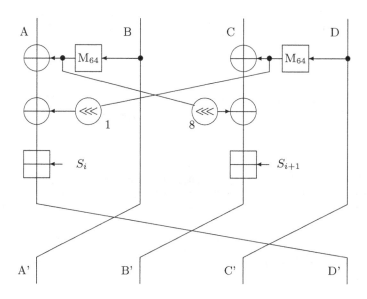

Fig. 1. One round of the encryption routine for $\mathcal{A}_{256}$ with the 256-bit input $(A\|B\|C\|D)$ being transformed into the 256-bit output $(A'\|B'\|C'\|D')$

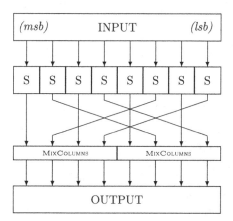

Fig. 2. The mixing operation M_{64} that is used in $\mathcal{A}_{256}$. Note that the S-boxes and MDS transformations are those specified in the AES.

we follow the example set in the encryption routine and replace the single data-dependent rotation in the key schedule with the AES-inspired diffusion operation M_{64}. This is illustrated in Figure 3. The input to be hashed at an iteration of the compression function (after HAIFA formatting) will be 256 bytes long and loaded into an array of 32 words of 64 bits $L[0], \ldots, L[31]$. From this we generate 64 words of 64 bits which are stored in an array $S[0, ..., 63]$ and used as subkeys during encryption.

$$S[0] = P_{64}$$
$$\textbf{for } i = 1 \textbf{ to } 63 \textbf{ do } S[i] = S[i-1] + Q_{64}$$

$$A = B = i = j = 0$$
$$\textbf{for } s = 1 \textbf{ to } (3 \times 64) \textbf{ do}$$
$$\{$$
$$\quad A = S[i] = (S[i] + A + B) \lll 3$$
$$\quad B = L[j] = (L[j] + A + B) \oplus \mathrm{M}_{64}(A+B)$$
$$\quad i = (i+1) \bmod 64$$
$$\quad j = (j+1) \bmod 32$$
$$\}$$

Fig. 3. The key schedule for $\mathcal{A}_{256}$. The input is represented as an array $L[\cdot]$ of 32 64-bit words and the output is a set $S[\cdot]$ of 64 64-bit subkeys. The constants $P_{64} = \texttt{0xB7E151628AED2A6B}$ and $Q_{64} = \texttt{0x9E3779B97F4A7C15}$ are those used in RC5 and RC6.

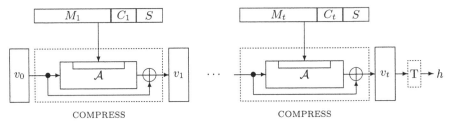

Fig. 4. The chained iteration of the compression function. In the HAIFA model, the initial value v_0 is computed from an IV (Section 3.3) which we choose to be $\texttt{0x FEDCBA9876543210} \,\|\, \texttt{0123456789ABCDEF} \,\|\, \texttt{FDB97531ECA86420} \,\|\, \texttt{02468ACE13579BDF}$

3.3   The Full Specification of DASH-256

We restrict ourselves to the case of DASH-256 and since we follow the HAIFA construction there are three inputs to the hash function; a message $\mathcal{M}$ of length n bits with $n < 2^{64}$, a salt value S of 64 bits, and the length d of the hash output or message digest. Internally, we use a 64-bit counter that takes a value denoted C_i at iteration i of the compression function. The counter stores the value—in little-endian notation—of the number of bits of $\mathcal{M}$ that have been hashed so far.

To deal with incomplete blocks we pad $\mathcal{M}$ to give a related message $\mathcal{M}'$. The input to the compression function x_i is of the form $[M_i\|C_i\|S]$ with $|C_i| = |S| = 64$ and so we generate a padded message $\mathcal{M}'$ that is of length $t \times 1920$ bits where t is the smallest integer for which $t \times 1920 > n + 73$, the strange number being explained by what follows: padding is always applied and appends a single '1' bit and as many '0' bits as needed so as to leave room for nine bits that are set[2] to the binary representation of the hash output length d and a further 64 bits

---

[2] This is required in the HAIFA model.

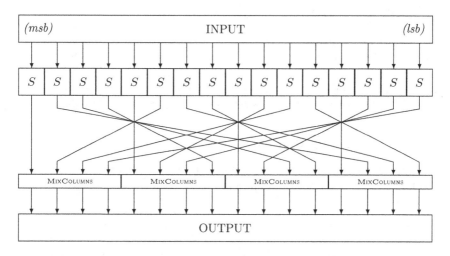

Fig. 5. The mixing operation M_{128} that is used in $\mathcal{A}_{512}$. Note that this is exactly the diffusion layer specified in the AES.

that are reserved for the binary representation of n. The resultant $\mathcal{M}'$ is then divided into t blocks $M_1, \ldots, M_t$, with each M_i being of length 240 bytes.

At each iteration of the compression function there are two inputs; the current value of the chaining variable v_i which is a 256-bit input and the 2048-bit $x_i = [M_i||C_i||S]$ that is being processed and we have $v_i = \text{COMPRESS}(x_i, v_{i-1})$ for $1 \le i \le t$. The initial value v_0 is computed as $v_0 = \text{COMPRESS}(d||\text{IV}||0)$ for a master IV, as required in HAIFA, and the output is given by the value v_t. A hash value of any shorter length, such as 224 bits, can be derived by truncation from the left, *i.e.* we use the rightmost bits. This is indicated by T in Figure 4 and would, of course, require that the representation of d in the padding and computation of v_0 be changed accordingly.

3.4 The Specification of DASH-512

The essential difference between DASH-256 and DASH-512 is that the first operates on 64-bit words while the second operates on 128-bit words. This is a direct benefit of the elegant scalability designed into RC5 [30]. All-but-one of the operations in DASH-256 scale obviously between the versions, the one exception being the M_{64} function. However for DASH-512 we use M_{128} which is a 128-bit permutation that is *identical* to one round of the AES without the key addition. This is illustrated in Figure 5. All other parts of the algorithm, illustrated in Figures 1, 3, and 4, scale in the obvious way and any 64-bit word operation is replaced by a 128-bit word operation. In Figure 3 the equivalent constants P_{128} and Q_{128} can be defined as described in [30] for $\mathcal{A}_{512}$. Future analysis will reveal the appropriate number of rounds for $\mathcal{A}_{512}$ while padding will follow the HAIFA model and this can also be used to compute a 384-bit hash value by truncation.

4   Security Analysis

The security of DASH-256 and DASH-512 can be split into a consideration of the underlying block cipher and then of the compression function and chaining mode. The latter concerns are handled by the results of Damgård [14], Merkle [22], Black *et al* [11], and Biham and Dunkelman [7] so for reasons of space we concentrate on the cipher within the compression function and particularly on $\mathcal{A}_{256}$.

4.1   The Encryption Routine in the Component $\mathcal{A}_{256}$

Many cryptanalytic tools for block ciphers can be used against hash function so we consider these classical techniques first.

Differential Cryptanalysis. We can easily identify a lower bound on the number of active S-boxes for a differential in $\mathcal{A}_{256}$ (and $\mathcal{A}_{512}$) when the expanded message words $S[\cdot]$ are the same for both pairs in a differential. The situation where the expanded message words might induce a difference is considered in the case of *local collisions* below.

   Without loss of generality, we can suppose that we have a non-zero exclusive-or difference in strand A. This will pass across a single round of $\mathcal{A}_{256}$ and $\mathcal{A}_{512}$ trivially. However it must induce a, for $1 \leq a \leq 8$, active S-boxes in the following round which, in turn, induce more active S-boxes in the rounds that follow. To establish a lower bound on the number of active S-boxes we can appeal to the properties of the MDS operation in M_{64} and M_{128} and observe that over two adjacent active rounds there must be at least five active S-boxes. Thus over any three rounds of $\mathcal{A}_{256}$ and $\mathcal{A}_{512}$—for which there is no difference in the expanded message words—there will be at least five active S-boxes. This gives a differential probability of less than 2^{-30}. Since there are 30 rounds to $\mathcal{A}_{256}$ this leads to a simple upper bound of 2^{-300} over the full encryption routine.

   This basic analysis is crude in two significant ways. First, on the positive side for the algorithm, it *significantly* under-estimates the number of active S-boxes. Second, on the negative side, this crude analysis doesn't immediately capture situations where the array $S[\cdot]$ might be used to introduce a difference. However analysis of the key schedule, see Section 4.2, and of *local collisions* later in this section suggest that more complex differential phenomena are highly unlikely and while more sophisticated analysis is underway, we expect this to confirm the difficulty of applying differential techniques.

Linear Cryptanalysis. The fixed rotations during encryption with $\mathcal{A}_{256}$ (and $\mathcal{A}_{512}$), see Figure 1, are intended to hinder the evolution of linear approximations. Note that without the fixed rotations it would be straightforward to identify linear approximations that held with probability 1 across infinitely many rounds. In particular, if we were to use Γ_i to denote the single-bit parity mask with a single one in position i, then we would have the following linear approximation for a single round of $\mathcal{A}_{256}$ with no rotations:

$$(\Gamma_0, 0, \Gamma_0, 0) \xrightarrow{\text{ONE ROUND (NO ROTATIONS)}} (0, \Gamma_0, 0, \Gamma_0).$$

This would hold with probability 1, *i.e.* with the maximum bias of $\frac{1}{2}$.

However the simple fixed rotations prevent such simple linear approximations from developing. We note that there is an interesting effect if we were to remove, or to change into exclusive-or, the operation used to introduce the expanded message words $S[\cdot]$. Let us call such a round a *linearised-round* and for this linearised variant of $\mathcal{A}_{256}$ we will consider the parity mask consisting of *all* bits, *i.e.* a mask of $\Gamma_p = \text{0xFFFFFFFFFFFFFFFF}$. Then we would have that:

$$(\Gamma_p, 0, \Gamma_p, 0) \xrightarrow{\text{ONE LINEARISED ROUND}} (0, \Gamma_p, 0, \Gamma_p)$$

with probability 1. Thus the *linearised* version of $\mathcal{A}_{256}$ (and $\mathcal{A}_{512}$) would be vulnerable to this kind of analysis, a common enough situation when ciphers are modified to facilitate analysis. However, with integer addition and an effective key schedule such parity relations are quickly destroyed.

Three-Round Local Collisions. Here we consider a typical *disturbance correction* strategy and how it might be used against $\mathcal{A}_{256}$. We consider the following perturbative-corrective pattern for a three-round local collision and the linearised version of $\mathcal{A}_{256}$, *i.e.* where the expanded message words $S[i]$ are introduced using exclusive-or. Consider the follow three rounds of expanded message

$$(\Delta S[i], 0, \Delta S[i+2], \Delta S[i+3], 0, \Delta S[i]),$$

where $\Delta S[i]$ is a low-weight perturbative vector, and $\Delta S[i+2]$ and $\Delta S[i+3]$ are deduced from the best differential of the AES S-box, *i.e.*

$$\Delta S[i+2] = (\Delta S'[i]) \lll 1 \quad \text{and} \quad \Delta S[i+3] = \Delta S'[i]$$

where $\Delta S'[i]$ is such that $\text{Pr}_C[\text{M}_{64}(C \oplus \Delta S[i]) \oplus \text{M}_{64}(C) = \Delta S'[i]]$ is maximal. The maximal differential probability of the AES S-box is 2^{-6}, hence whatever $\Delta S[i]$ and $\Delta S'[i]$, the probability of such a local collision for the linearised variant of $\mathcal{A}_{256}$ is upper bounded by 2^{-12}.

If we now return to the real $\mathcal{A}_{256}$ where the words $S[i]$ are mixed through modular addition, we can make the following analysis. For each difference bit in A and B, A + C and B + C differ only in the same bits as A and B with probability upper bounded by 2^{-r}, where r is the number of different bits, with the exception of the *most significant bit (MSB)*, in A and B. There are four additions to take into account, one for each non-zero input expanded message word. Due to the MDS property in M_{64} and M_{128}, one must have $\text{Hwt}(\Delta S[i]) + \text{Hwt}(\Delta S[i+2]) \geq 5$ as well as $\text{Hwt}(\Delta S[i]) + \text{Hwt}(\Delta S[i+3]) \geq 5$ where we use Hwt to denote the Hamming weight.

This means that there are at least six active bits across integer addition that are not in the most significant position. Hence the probability of such a local collision is upper bounded by $2^{-12} \times 2^{-6} = 2^{-18}$. To do better than the birthday attack, an attack on $\mathcal{A}_{256}$ would need an expanded message difference that combines seven or less such local collisions. However this would imply that the remaining 64-bit words in $S[\cdot]$ are identical for the two messages and there is a vanishingly small chance that an attacker can manipulate message inputs so as to give two arrays $S[\cdot]$ with the required values.

4.2   The Key Schedule in the Component $\mathcal{A}_{256}$

By choice the key schedule for $\mathcal{A}_{256}$ is closely related to that used in RC5 and RC6. In moving to the key schedule in $\mathcal{A}_{256}$ and $\mathcal{A}_{512}$ we have added some non-linearity via a series of AES S-boxes. While experiments have shown an improved avalanche of change as a result, this does not exclude some dedicated analysis.

The Attack of Saarinen on RC6. During the first round of the AES process, Saarinen made some interesting observations about the RC6 key schedule when very long keys were used [35]. Let us assume that we choose a key length so that the arrays $L[\cdot]$ and $S[\cdot]$ are of equal length.[3] The important feature of the key expansion, see Figure 3, is that state information is carried between the two arrays by two words A and B. If we take two keys that are nearly equal except for the last few words then, on the first pass through, only the last few words of the $L[\cdot]$ and $S[\cdot]$ arrays will change. If the cryptanalyst is lucky, or if we can find a high probability differential of the right form, the difference in the values of A and B at the start of the second pass will be zero. When this happens, no change is carried into the second pass and only the last few words of the $L[\cdot]$ and $S[\cdot]$ arrays will have a non-zero difference.

Moving on, if we are lucky (since we cannot rely on a differential of sufficiently high probability) the difference in the values of A and B at the start of the third pass will be zero. If this happens then, on the third and final pass through the arrays, only the later words in $S[\cdot]$ will change. Saarinen [35] was therefore able to demonstrate ciphertexts generated by related keys that had an average Hamming distance between them of 4.2 bits. This was later extended [23] to demonstrate the existence of equivalent keys for this particular instance.

Two features are important for this attack. First, being able to identify a short cancelling differential for the first pass. Second, the number of times we pass through the $L[\cdot]$ array. In the case of RC6 with 128-bit blocks and 1308-bit keys (the case looked at by Saarinen) we start the $L[\cdot]$ array three times. For the first pass the difference in A and B is zero (by definition). For the second pass it is zero by construction of the differential, and for the third pass we can use the birthday paradox to find a pair of messages that generate a zero-difference in A and B from a pool of 2^{32} possibilities.

In the case of $\mathcal{A}_{256}$ and $\mathcal{A}_{512}$, however, the $S[\cdot]$ array will always be twice the size of the $L[\cdot]$ array. Thus we will pass through the $L[\cdot]$ array six times. The conditions we need on A and B at the start of each pass is a condition on

---

[3] This is the simplest case, but variants exist for different array sizes.

128 or 256 bits respectively. The first time it is trivially satisfied and we might pessimistically assume that it can be satisfied with probability one the second time.[4] Then there remain three times for which the condition on A and B must hold by chance before we process the $S[\cdot]$ array for the final time. Thus we have a condition on 3×128 bits (3×256 resp.) which we expect to see fulfilled from a pool of 2^{192} messages (2^{384} resp.) using the birthday paradox. However this is worse than brute-force.

In fact the conditions to avoid the attack of Saarinen can be generalised and we need to pass through the $L[\cdot]$ array at least four times and the $S[\cdot]$ array at least three times. This is what we accomplish in DASH-256 and DASH-512. Interestingly, in [33] the RC6 designers propose a 1024-bit key length when using RC6, which is based on 32-bit words, for the most efficient hashing configuration. This also satisfies our general requirement.

On the Potential for Collisions in the Expansion. Consider two different inputs M_i and M_i' to an iteration of the compression function. These will be used to initialise the $L[\cdot]$ array and after the expansion phase will give the final values to the $S[\cdot]$ array. Clearly, if we derive the same $S[\cdot]$ array from different inputs then we trivially have a collision over one iteration of the compression function. However provided there is sufficient mixing of the $L[\cdot]$ and $S[\cdot]$ arrays, there are no known weak or equivalent key phenomena for RC5 or RC6 and a brute-force attack seems to pose a far greater concern. Of course this isn't the full picture. Even arrays that are identical only part of the time, or in the earlier words, can still be useful to the cryptanalyst. However, assuming sufficiently thorough mixing of the values in the $S[\cdot]$ array, collisions in the chaining variable would seem to be easier to find than pairs of messages where five or more words in $S[\cdot]$ are identical. Given 30 rounds, it is highly unlikely an exploitable weaknesses will occur by chance.

The Oneway-ness of the Key Schedule. The key schedule expands the message-related input into a set of 64 subkeys. This is done in a complicated way and it has been noted by various commentators that this delivers a certain amount of *one-wayness* [30,35]. So even if attacks on the encryption process leak information about the subkeys $S[\cdot]$ it would be very hard to relate this information to the input M_i at the ith iteration of the compression function. Yet it is information about the input M_i that is needed to compromise either the compression function or the resultant hash function.

The Role of the Key Schedule. It is well-known that many hash function designs are built around a dedicated block cipher. In such cases there is some message mixing, *i.e.* a key schedule, and some state processing, *i.e.* an encryption routine. In MD5 [31] the message-mixing involves message block repetition while in SHA-1 [26] "key expansion" is a little more involved. However it remains simple and without a strong "encryption" process it is somewhat vulnerable.

---

[4] This would require a sophisticated differential through several AES S-boxes.

By contrast, in $\mathcal{A}_{256}$ and $\mathcal{A}_{512}$ we might view the key schedule as a complex non-linear message expansion. This idea of "expansion" as a form of pre-processing appears in [1] and has been used in other hash functions [10]. Given such an expansion phase, we can then view the "encryption" as a complicated way of distilling information into the 256-bit (or 512-bit) output. But is it better to have more work done in the "expansion" or in the "distillation"? When looked at in this way, traditional hash functions of the MD-family have a computationally lightweight (almost trivial) expansion phase and compensate for this with a heavier mixing phase. For DASH-256 and DASH-512 this is reversed and we have a computationally heavy expansion paired with a lighter (though strong) distillation phase. We believe that this approach is worth exploring and could be better suited to the hashing environment where an attacker has *complete* control over the inputs to the compression function. For compression functions based on block ciphers, a simple key schedule will place a significant burden on the encryption routine.

5   Performance

Assessing the performance of a cryptographic algorithm is tricky and often incomplete. When we look at the operations in DASH-256 it is likely that most software implementations will use table look-ups for the S-box operation and that this will be the dominant operation. For DASH-256 there are $30 \times 2 \times 8 = 480$ table look-ups during encryption and $192 \times 8 = 1536$ during key expansion giving a total of 2016. Since 240 bytes are processed per compression function iteration we have 8.4 look-ups per byte. In comparison encryption with the AES-128 requires $10 \times 16 = 160$ look-ups for encryption but only 16 bytes of plaintext are encrypted giving an encryption cost of 10 look-ups per byte. Thus we might expect the bulk processing performance of DASH-256 to be comparable to the bulk encryption rate of AES-128. This seems to be a very natural target since they both offer the same 128-bit security. We can compare results from Wei Dai (see [39] for details) with our first-cut optimised version of DASH-256 where the key expansion (*exp.*) and processing time (*pro.*) are separated out.[5] The results compare well to some other recent hash function proposals [4].

platform	clock (GHz)	AES-128 (cycles/byte)	SHA-256 (cycles/byte)	DASH-256 (cycles/byte)		
[39] Opteron	2.4	15.9	21.5	-		
				exp.	*pro.*	*total*
Opteron	2.2	-	-	14.4	3.1	17.5

Unfortunately the performance of DASH-256 suffers on 32-bit machines. On the P4, for example, a first-cut implementation runs at half the speed of AES-128 and we see that even basic operations over 64-bit words can exact a heavy price.

---

[5] Note that *pro.* is not the encryption rate. If we used DASH-256 for encryption then we would need 480 table look-ups to encrypt 32 bytes giving a rate of 15 look-ups/byte.

6   Conclusions

We have presented two, closely-related, dedicated hash functions. In contrast to some other recent hash function proposals we have stayed close to known constructions and deliberately looked back at the AES process to use techniques that were analysed and discussed there. At the same time we have explored the role of a computationally-heavy key schedule which allows us to hash a large amount of message at each iteration. We believe that an appropriate balance between security and speed can be achieved in this way and we encourage others to explore the advantages and disadvantages of this approach.

Independently of the success of DASH-256, we can see several directions in which to take this work. Certainly we believe that some variants of DASH-256 may offer room for improvement. For instance, while the key schedule in DASH-256 has many interesting attributes, we feel that the design is too complex. And while its long standing is a good sign, it would be more satisfying to say something concrete about the security offered when such very long keys (messages) are being used. The state size of DASH-256 is large, though so is that of some other hash function proposals, and we note that there would be an overhead when hashing short inputs. The most significant downside, however, is that DASH-256 is oriented to 64-bit operations. Instead we feel (with hindsight) that a new design geared towards 32-bit operations would be a better starting point.

We believe that these are all interesting avenues to explore, as is the more general question of the role of the key schedule when a block cipher is used as the basis for a hash function. With this in mind, we hope that the simplicity of our proposal will promote new and independent analysis of DASH-256/512 in particular and hash functions in general; something that we strongly encourage.

References

1. Aiello, W., Haber, S., Venkatesan, R.: New Constructions for Secure Hash Functions. In: Vaudenay, S. (ed.) FSE 1998. LNCS, vol. 1372, pp. 150–167. Springer, Heidelberg (1998)
2. Andreeva, E., Bouillaguet, C., Fouque, P.-A., Hoch, J., Kelsey, J., Shamir, A., Zimmer, S.: Second Preimage Attacks on Dithered Hash Functions. In: Smart, N. (ed.) Proceedings of Eurocrypt 2008. LNCS, vol. 4965, pp. 270–288. Springer, Heidelberg (2008)
3. Aoki, K., Lipmaa, H.: Fast Implementations of AES Candidates, http://csrc.nist.gov
4. Aumasson, J.P., Meier, W., Phan, R.: The Hash Function Family LAKE. In: Nyberg, K. (ed.) Proceedings of FSE 2008 (to appear, 2008)
5. Baretto, P., Rijmen, V.: The Whirlpool Hashing Function, paginas.terra.com.br/informatica/paulobarreto/WhirlpoolPage.html
6. Bertoni, G., Daemen, J., Peeters, M., van Assche, G.: Sponge Functions. In: ECRYPT Hash Workshop, May 24-25 (2007), www.ecrypt.eu.org
7. Biham, E., Dunkelman, O.: A Framework for Iterative Hash Functions - HAIFA. In: Second NIST Cryptographic Hash Workshop, August 24-25 (2006), csrc.nist.gov/groups/ST/hash/

8. Biham, E., Shamir, A.: Differential Cryptanalysis of the Data Encryption Standard. Springer, Heidelberg (1993)
9. Anderson, R., Knudsen, L.R., Biham, E.: Serpent: A New Block Cipher Proposal. In: Vaudenay, S. (ed.) FSE 1998. LNCS, vol. 1372, pp. 222–238. Springer, Heidelberg (1998)
10. Billet, O., Robshaw, M.J.B., Peyrin, T.: On Building Hash Functions from Mutivariate Quadratic Equations. In: Pieprzyk, J., Ghodosi, H., Dawson, E. (eds.) ACISP 2007. LNCS, vol. 4586, pp. 82–95. Springer, Heidelberg (2007)
11. Black, J., Rogaway, P., Shrimpton, T.: Black-Box Analysis of the Block-Cipher-Based Hash-Function Constructions from PGV. In: Yung, M. (ed.) CRYPTO 2002. LNCS, vol. 2442, pp. 320–335. Springer, Heidelberg (2002)
12. Bogdanov, A., Knudsen, L.R., Leander, G., Paar, C., Poschmann, A., Robshaw, M.J.B., Seurin, Y., Vikkelsoe, C.: Present: An Ultra-Lightweight Block Cipher. In: Paillier, P., Verbauwhede, I. (eds.) Proceedings of CHES 2007. LNCS, vol. 4727, pp. 450–466. Springer, Heidelberg (2007)
13. Coron, J.-S., Dodis, Y., Malinaud, C., Puniya, P.: Merkle-Damgård Revisited: How to Construct a Hash Functio. In: Shoup, V. (ed.) CRYPTO 2005. LNCS, vol. 3621, pp. 430–448. Springer, Heidelberg (2005)
14. Damgård, I.: A Design Principle for Hash Functions. In: Brassard, G. (ed.) Advances in Cryptology – CRYPTO 1989. LNCS, vol. 435, pp. 416–427. Springer, Heidelberg (1989)
15. Dean, R.D.: Formal Aspects of Mobile Code Security. PhD thesis. Princeton University (1999)
16. Joux, A.: Multicollisions in Iterated Hash Functions. Application to Cascaded Constructions. In: Franklin, M. (ed.) CRYPTO 2004. LNCS, vol. 3152, pp. 306–316. Springer, Heidelberg (2004)
17. Junod, P., Vaudenay, S.: Perfect Diffusion Primitives for Block Ciphers—Building Efficient MDS Matrices. In: Handschuh, H., Hasan, M.A. (eds.) SAC 2004. LNCS, vol. 3357, pp. 84–98. Springer, Heidelberg (2004)
18. Kelsey, J., Schneier, B.: Second Preimages on n-Bit Hash Functions for Much Less than 2^n Work. In: Cramer, R.J.F. (ed.) EUROCRYPT 2005. LNCS, vol. 3494, pp. 474–490. Springer, Heidelberg (2005)
19. Kelsey, J., Kohno, T.: Herding Hash Functions and the Nostradamus Attack. In: Vaudenay, S. (ed.) EUROCRYPT 2006. LNCS, vol. 4004, pp. 183–200. Springer, Heidelberg (2006)
20. Matsui, M.: Linear Cryptanalysis Method for DES Cipher. In: Helleseth, T. (ed.) EUROCRYPT 1993. LNCS, vol. 765, pp. 386–397. Springer, Heidelberg (1994)
21. Menezes, A.J., Vanstone, S.A., Van Oorschot, P.C.: Handbook of Applied Cryptography. CRC Press, Inc., Boca Raton (1996)
22. Merkle, R.C.: One Way Hash Functions and DES. In: Brassard, G. (ed.) Advances in Cryptology – CRYPTO 1989. LNCS, vol. 435, pp. 428–446. Springer, Heidelberg (1989)
23. Mizuno, H., Kuwakado, H., Tanaka, H.: Equivalent keys in RC6-32/20/176. IEICE Transactions on Fundamentals of Electronics, Communications, and Computer Sciences E84-A(10), 2474–2481
24. National Institute of Standards and Technology. FIPS 197: Advanced Encryption Standard (November 2001), `csrc.nist.gov`
25. National Institute of Standards and Technology. AES Archive, `csrc.nist.gov`
26. National Institute of Standards and Technology. FIPS 180-2: Secure Hash Standard (August 2002), `csrc.nist.gov`

27. National Institute of Standards and Technology. FIPS 198: The Keyed-Hash Message Authentication Code (HMAC) (March 2002), csrc.nist.gov

28. National Institute of Standards and Technology. Announcing Request for Candidate Algorithm Nominations for a New Cryptographic Hash Algorithm (SHA-3) Family, csrc.nist.gov

29. Preneel, B.: Analysis and design of cryptographic hash functions. PhD thesis, Katholieke Universiteit Leuven (1993)

30. Rivest, R.L.: The RC5 Encryption Algorithm. In: Preneel, B. (ed.) Proceedings of FSE 1994. LNCS, vol. 1008, pp. 363–366. Springer, Heidelberg (1994)

31. Rivest, R.L.: RFC 1321: The MD5 Message-Digest Algorithm (April 1992), www.ietf.org/rfc/rfc1321.txt

32. Rivest, R.L., Robshaw, M.J.B., Sydney, R., Yin, Y.L.: The Block Cipher RC6, csrc.nist.gov

33. Rivest, R.L., Robshaw, M.J.B., Yin, Y.L.: The Case for RC6 as the AES, csrc.nist.gov

34. Rivest, R.L.: Abelian Square-Free Dithering for Iterated Hash Functions. In: First NIST Cryptographic Hash Workshop, October 31 - November 1 (2005), csrc.nist.gov/groups/ST/hash/

35. Saarinen, M.-J.O.: A Note Regarding the Hash Function Use of MARS and RC6, csrc.nist.gov

36. Shirai, T., Shibutani, K., Akishita, T., Moriai, S., Iwata, T.: The 128-bit Block Cipher CLEFIA. In: Biryukov, A. (ed.) FSE 2007. LNCS, vol. 4593, pp. 181–195. Springer, Heidelberg (2007)

37. Wang, X., Yu, H.: How to Break MD5 and Other Hash Functions. In: Cramer, R.J.F. (ed.) EUROCRYPT 2005. LNCS, vol. 3494, pp. 19–35. Springer, Heidelberg (2005)

38. Wang, X., Yin, Y.L., Yu, H.: Finding Collisions in the Full SHA-1. In: Shoup, V. (ed.) CRYPTO 2005. LNCS, vol. 3621, pp. 17–36. Springer, Heidelberg (2005)

39. Dai, W.: Crypto++ 5.5 Benchmarks, http://www.cryptopp.com/benchmarks.html

Non-linear Reduced Round Attacks against SHA-2 Hash Family

Somitra Kumar Sanadhya* and Palash Sarkar

Applied Statistics Unit,
Indian Statistical Institute,
203, B.T. Road, Kolkata,
India 700108
somitra_r@isical.ac.in, palash@isical.ac.in

Abstract. Most of the attacks against (reduced) SHA-2 family in literature have used local collisions which are valid for linearized version of SHA-2 hash functions. Recently, at FSE '08, an attack against reduced round SHA-256 was presented by Nikolić and Biryukov which used a local collision which is valid for the actual SHA-256 function. It is a 9-step local collision which starts by introducing a modular difference of 1 in the two messages. It succeeds with probability roughly 1/3. We build on the work of Nikolić and Biryukov and provide a generalized nonlinear local collision which accepts an arbitrary initial message difference. This local collision succeeds with probability 1. Using this local collision we present attacks against 18-step SHA-256 and 18-step SHA-512 with arbitrary initial difference. Both of these attacks succeed with probability 1. We then present special cases of our local collision and show two different differential paths for attacking 20-step SHA-256 and 20-step SHA-512. One of these paths is the same as presented by Nikolić and Biryukov while the other one is a new differential path. Messages following both these differential paths can be found with probability 1. This improves on the previous result where the success probability of 20-step attack was 1/3. Finally, we present two differential paths for 21-step collisions for SHA-256 and SHA-512, one of which is a new path. The success probabilities of these paths for SHA-256 are roughly 2^{-15} and 2^{-17} which improve on the 21-step attack having probability 2^{-19} reported earlier. We show examples of message pairs following all the presented differential paths for up to 21-step collisions in SHA-256. We also show first real examples of colliding message pairs for up to 20-step reduced SHA-512.

1   Introduction

Cryptanalysis of hash functions has been an area of intense interest to the research community since past decade and a half. Many hash functions were broken in this time, most notable among them are MD5 [13], SHA-0 [14] and theoretical

---

* This author is supported by the Ministry of Information Technology, Govt. of India.

Y. Mu, W. Susilo, and J. Seberry (Eds.): ACISP 2008, LNCS 5107, pp. 254–266, 2008.

break of SHA-1 [12]. This has directed the attention of the cryptology community to the SHA-2 family of hash functions.

Known Results for the SHA-2 Family: Gilbert and Handschuh (GH) [2] were the first to study local collisions in the SHA-2 family. They reported a 9-step local collision for linearized version of SHA-256 and estimated the probability of the differential path to be 2^{-66}. This probability estimate was later improved by Hawkes et al. [3]. Sanadhya and Sarkar [7] presented 16 new 9-step local collisions for SHA-2 family of hash functions. All these local collisions are also for the linearized version of SHA-256. The message expansion of SHA-256 was studied by Mendel et al. [4], who reported a colliding message pair for 18-step SHA-256 which was recently corrected in [5]. They used the linearized local collision from [2] in their work. Mendel et al. [4] also improved the probability estimate of the Gilbert-Handschuh local collision to values similar to those obtained in [3]. In [8], an algorithm for generating 18-step SHA-256 collisions was developed using one of the local collisions from [7] and many colliding message pairs for 18-step SHA-256 were obtained.

Recently, Nikolić and Biryukov [6] presented a new local collision which uses modular differences instead of the XOR differences. Since this local collision is for the actual SHA-256 (and not its linearized version), its probability is much higher than the linearized local collisions presented earlier. For the first time in the literature, the authors in [6] worked directly with modular differences for SHA-256. Using this local collision they obtained 20-step and 21-step collisions for SHA-256 with probabilities $1/3$ and $1/2^{19}$ respectively.

Our Contributions: We build on the work of Nikolić and Biryukov [6] and present a generalized non-linear local collision which accepts an arbitrary initial message difference. In [6], sufficient conditions for the differential path are determined and a particular local collision is obtained. We work with exact solutions of conditions imposed by the differential path and obtain general solutions of these conditions. Since we work with exact solutions of the conditions, our local collision is deterministic i.e. it holds with probability 1. Using this local collision, we obtain collisions for 18-step SHA-256 and 18-step SHA-512 with an arbitrary initial message difference. These attacks succeed with probability 1.

Then we show special instances of our generalized local collision which are suitable for finding collisions for 20-step SHA-256 and 20-step SHA-512. We present two such instances. One of these instances is a new local collision which can be realized in two different ways. The other one is the same as that presented by Nikolić and Biryukov for obtaining 20-step collision in [6]. However, unlike in [6], our 20-step attacks succeed with probability 1.

Finally, we use 20-step collisions to obtain 21-step collisions for SHA-256 as in [6]. There the probability for 21-step SHA-256 collisions is experimentally estimated to be about 2^{-19}. We improve the efficiency of the probabilistic search used in this case and obtain 21-step collisions for SHA-256 with estimated experimental probability of 2^{-15}. This is also the first time that actual collisions for SHA-512 reduced up to 20 steps are presented.

2   Notation

In this paper we use the following notation:

- $m_i \in \{0, 1\}^n$, $W_i \in \{0, 1\}^n$, $W_i' \in \{0, 1\}^n$ for any i. The word size n is 32 for SHA-256 and 64 for SHA-512.
- The colliding message pair: $\{m_0, m_1, \ldots m_{15}\}$ and $\{m_0', m_1', \ldots m_{15}'\}$.
- The expanded message pair: $\{W_0, W_1, W_2, \ldots W_{r-1}\}$ and $\{W_0', W_1', W_2', \ldots W_{r-1}'\}$. The number of steps r is 64 for SHA-256 and 80 for SHA-512.
- The internal registers for the two message pairs in step i: $\{a_i, \ldots, h_i\}$ and $\{a_i', \ldots, h_i'\}$.
- $\text{ROTR}^k(x)$: Right rotation of an n-bit quantity x by k bits.
- $\text{SHR}^k(x)$: Right shift of an n-bit quantity x by k bits.
- $\oplus$: bitwise XOR.
- $+$: addition modulo 2^n.
- $-$: subtraction modulo 2^n.
- $\delta X = X' - X$ where X is an n-bit quantity.
- $\delta\Sigma_1(e_i) = \Sigma_1(e_i') - \Sigma_1(e_i)$.
- $\delta\Sigma_0(a_i) = \Sigma_0(a_i') - \Sigma_0(a_i)$.
- $\delta f_{MAJ}^i(x, y, z)$: Output difference of the f_{MAJ} function in step i when its inputs differ by x, y and z. That is, $\delta f_{MAJ}^i(x, y, z) = f_{MAJ}(a_i + x, b_i + y, c_i + z) - f_{MAJ}(a_i, b_i, c_i)$.
- $\delta f_{IF}^i(x, y, z)$: Output difference of the f_{IF} function in step i when its inputs differ by x, y and z. That is, $\delta f_{IF}^i(x, y, z) = f_{IF}(e_i + x, f_i + y, g_i + z) - f_{IF}(e_i, f_i, g_i)$.

3   Collision Attacks Against the SHA-2 Hash Family

The SHA-2 hash function was standardized by NIST in 2002. Eight registers are used in the evaluation of SHA-2. The initial value in the registers is specified by an $8 \times n$ bit IV, n=32 for SHA-256 and 64 for SHA-512. In Step i, the 8 registers are updated from $(a_{i-1}, b_{i-1}, c_{i-1}, d_{i-1}, e_{i-1}, f_{i-1}, g_{i-1}, h_{i-1})$ to $(a_i, b_i, c_i, d_i, e_i, f_i, g_i, h_i)$ according to the following equations:

$$\left. \begin{aligned} a_i &= \Sigma_0(a_{i-1}) + f_{MAJ}(a_{i-1}, b_{i-1}, c_{i-1}) + \Sigma_1(e_{i-1}) \\ &\quad + f_{IF}(e_{i-1}, f_{i-1}, g_{i-1}) + h_{i-1} + K_i + W_i \\ b_i &= a_{i-1} \\ c_i &= b_{i-1} \\ d_i &= c_{i-1} \\ e_i &= d_{i-1} + \Sigma_1(e_{i-1}) + f_{IF}(e_{i-1}, f_{i-1}, g_{i-1}) \\ &\quad + h_{i-1} + K_i + W_i \\ f_i &= e_{i-1} \\ g_i &= f_{i-1} \\ h_i &= g_{i-1} \end{aligned} \right\} \quad (1)$$

The f_{IF} and the f_{MAJ} are three variable bitwise boolean functions *If* and *Majority* respectively. For detailed information on the function Σ_0, Σ_1 and the message expansion of SHA-2 family, see [11].

The aim of collision attacks against hash functions is to obtain two different messages which produce the same digest under that hash function. The hash functions use one word of the message in each step and process the message for multiple steps. Typically, an attacker introduces a small difference in one word of the message. Using the terminology from [1], this initial difference is called the "perturbation message difference". Next few message words are chosen to differ in such a manner that all the introduced differences cancel themselves with high probability. These later message word differences are called "correction differences".

Only the first 16 words are free in the SHA-2 design, with the rest of the message words being defined by the "message expansion". In a local collision, a differential path for small number of steps is considered in which the message expansion is ignored. We present our new nonlinear local collision next.

4   A General Class of Nonlinear Local Collisions

Table 1 shows the general structure of a 9-step local collision for SHA-2 family. The perturbation message difference is taken to be x and other message differences are later computed. In Table 1, the registers $(a_{i-1}, \ldots, h_{i-1})$ and W_i are inputs to Step i of the hash evaluation and this step outputs the registers $(a_i, \ldots, h_i)$.

Table 1. A 9-step nonlinear local collision for SHA-256

Step i	δW_i	δa_i	δb_i	δc_i	δd_i	δe_i	δf_i	δg_i	δh_i
$i-1$	0	0	0	0	0	0	0	0	0
i	x	x	0	0	0	x	0	0	0
$i+1$	δW_{i+1}	0	x	0	0	y	x	0	0
$i+2$	δW_{i+2}	0	0	x	0	z	y	x	0
$i+3$	δW_{i+3}	0	0	0	x	0	z	y	x
$i+4$	δW_{i+4}	0	0	0	0	x	0	z	y
$i+5$	δW_{i+5}	0	0	0	0	0	x	0	z
$i+6$	δW_{i+6}	0	0	0	0	0	0	x	0
$i+7$	δW_{i+7}	0	0	0	0	0	0	0	x
$i+8$	δW_{i+8}	0	0	0	0	0	0	0	0

4.1   Obtaining a Local Collision

In Step i of SHA-2, only the registers a_i and e_i are computed. Rest of the registers are copies of the old ones. Therefore we focus on these two register evaluations only. From (1), we get:

$$\delta e_i = \delta \Sigma_1(e_{i-1}) + \delta f_{IF}(\delta e_{i-1}, \delta f_{i-1}, \delta g_{i-1}) + \delta d_{i-1} + \delta h_{i-1} + \delta W_i, \qquad (2)$$

$$\delta a_i = \delta \Sigma_0(a_{i-1}) + \delta f_{MAJ}(\delta a_{i-1}, \delta b_{i-1}, \delta c_{i-1}) + \delta \Sigma_1(e_{i-1}) +$$
$$\delta f_{IF}(\delta e_{i-1}, \delta f_{i-1}, \delta g_{i-1}) + \delta h_{i-1} + \delta W_i,$$
$$= \delta \Sigma_0(a_{i-1}) + \delta f_{MAJ}(\delta a_{i-1}, \delta b_{i-1}, \delta c_{i-1}) + \delta e_i - \delta d_{i-1}. \qquad (3)$$

Table 2. Message word differences for the local collision of Table 1

1	$y = -\delta\Sigma_0(a_i) - \delta f^i_{MAJ}(x,0,0)$	2	$z = -\delta f^{i+1}_{MAJ}(0,x,0)$
3	$\delta W_i = x$	4	$\delta W_{i+1} = y - \delta f^i_{IF}(x,0,0) - \delta\Sigma_1(e_i)$
4	$\delta W_{i+2} = z - \delta f^{i+1}_{IF}(y,x,0) - \delta\Sigma_1(e_{i+1})$	5	$\delta W_{i+3} = -\delta f^{i+2}_{IF}(z,y,x) - \delta\Sigma_1(e_{i+2})$
6	$\delta W_{i+4} = -x - \delta f^{i+3}_{IF}(0,z,y)$	7	$\delta W_{i+5} = -y - \delta f^{i+4}_{IF}(x,0,z)$ $-\delta\Sigma_1(e_{i+4})$
8	$\delta W_{i+6} = -z - \delta f^{i+5}_{IF}(0,x,0)$	9	$\delta W_{i+7} = -y - \delta f^{i+6}_{IF}(0,0,x)$
10	$\delta W_{i+8} = -x$	11	$\delta f^{i+2}_{MAJ}(0,0,x) = 0$

The differential path of Table 1 defines the message word differences as shown in Table 2. The derivation of these differences can be done by techniques similar to [6]. For details on this derivation, refer to [9].

To obtain the 9-step local collision as in Table 1, we first select the perturbation message difference δW_i as a randomly generated 32-bit (or 64-bit) quantity x. The differences δW_j for $j \in \{(i+1),\ldots,(i+8)\}$ are defined as in Table 2. In addition, we need to choose W_{i+2} such that $a_{i+2} = a_{i+1}$ to ensure the success of condition 11 in Table 2. Rest of the message words could be any randomly chosen 32-bit (or 64-bit) words. This local collision holds with probability 1, since all the steps are deterministic and feasible. For details, see [9].

5   Extending a Single Local Collision to Obtain 18-Step Collisions

In this section we briefly explain how to obtain 18-step collisions using the local collision shown in this paper. We discuss three different types of differential paths depending on the value of the differential z used in δe_{i+2} to δh_{i+5} in Table 1. These values of z are $-1, 0$ and 1.

For all the different cases, we choose to span the 9-step local collision from Step 3 to Step 11. The message differentials δW_i for $i \in \{3, 4, \ldots, 11\}$ are defined by the local collision. We use a single local collision, which implies that all the other free message words are equal. That is, $\delta W_i = 0$ for $i \in \{0, 1, 2, 12, 13, 14, 15\}$.

First two steps of message expansion of SHA-2 define the message words W_{16} and W_{17} as follows:

$$W_{16} = \sigma_1(W_{14}) + W_9 + \sigma_0(W_1) + W_0$$
$$W_{17} = \sigma_1(W_{15}) + W_{10} + \sigma_0(W_2) + W_1$$

From these two equations, it is clear that if $\delta W_9 = \delta W_{10} = 0$ then the two expanded message words will be equal for Steps 17 and 18. This will result in an 18-step collision for SHA-2. Note that δW_9 and δW_{10} correspond to Steps 7 and 8 of the local collision used. Hence our target is to get differentials of the message in these two steps to vanish. The 18-step collisions as suggested above can be found with probability 1. For detailed analysis of this case and the colliding message pairs, see [9].

6   Extending a Single Local Collision to Obtain 20-Step Collisions

We follow the technique used in [6] to obtain 20-step collisions for SHA-256. This time we need to handle first 4 steps of message expansion. These steps are:

$$W_{16} = \sigma_1(W_{14}) + W_9 + \sigma_0(W_1) + W_0$$
$$W_{17} = \sigma_1(W_{15}) + W_{10} + \sigma_0(W_2) + W_1$$
$$W_{18} = \sigma_1(W_{16}) + W_{11} + \sigma_0(W_3) + W_2$$
$$W_{19} = \sigma_1(W_{17}) + W_{12} + \sigma_0(W_4) + W_3$$

If a single local collision spanning from Step 5 to Step 13 is used and all other messages outside the scope of this local collision are taken to have zero differentials, then $\delta W_i = 0$ for $i \in \{0, 1, 2, 3, 4, 14, 15\}$. This implies that if we can have $\delta W_9 = \delta W_{10} = \delta W_{11} = \delta W_{12} = 0$, then the differentials of the first 4 expanded message words will be zero. In this case the message expansion will not play a role and we will be able to extend a single local collision to 20 steps.

The local collision presented in [6] is such that the message differentials at steps $i+4$ to $i+7$ are zero for it ($i = 5$ is the starting step of the local collision). Hence it can be used to obtain 20-step collisions directly. The local collision we presented is more general but does not necessarily have 4 consecutive message differentials equal to zero. Now we find particular instances of our local collision such that we have zero differentials as desired. This time we work with sufficient conditions as in [6].

To obtain the 4 consecutive zero differentials in the local collision, we need to have differentials generated by δW_{i+4}, δW_{i+5}, δW_{i+6} and δW_{i+7} (corresponding to Steps 9, 10, 11 and 12 of the differential path) to be equal to zero. We next discuss the conditions put by these equations. We also need to control the values of y and z. As in [6], we start the local collision by choosing $x = 1$.

Condition on the value of y: This condition contains the term $\delta \Sigma_0(a_5) = \Sigma_0(a_5') - \Sigma_0(a_5)$. From the differential path we know that $\delta a_5 = a_5' - a_5 = x$. Differential behavior of the non-linear function Σ_0 is difficult to analyze. To make it tractable, we choose $\delta \Sigma_0(a_5) = x = 1$. For this case, the only solutions are $a_5 = -1 = \texttt{0xffffffff}$ and $a_5' = 0$. We also put restriction that the f_{MAJ} term doesn't propagate any difference. This condition $f_{MAJ}^5(x, 0, 0) = 0$ implies $b_5 = c_5$, i.e. $a_4 = a_3$. Conditions on a_4 and a_5 registers can be deterministically satisfied by choosing W_4 and W_5 suitably. By the choices made above, this equation gives $y = -1$.

Condition on the value of δW_{i+5}: This condition contains the term $\delta \Sigma_1(e_9) = \Sigma_1(e_9') - \Sigma_1(e_9)$. From the differential path we know that $\delta e_9 = e_9' - e_9 = x$. Differential behaviour of the non-linear function Σ_1 is difficult to analyze. Similar to the previous equation, we choose $\delta \Sigma_1(e_9) = x = 1$. Once again, the only solutions are $e_9 = -1 = \texttt{0xffffffff}$ and $e_9' = 0$. This condition can be deterministically satisfied by choosing W_9 suitably. Finally, we wish to make the following difference zero:

$$\begin{aligned}
\delta W_{10} &= -y - \delta f_{IF}^9(x, 0, z) - \delta \Sigma_1(e_9) \\
&= -(-1) - (f_{IF}(e_9 + 1, e_8, e_7 + z) - f_{IF}(e_9, e_8, e_7)) \\
&\quad - (\Sigma(e_9 + 1) - \Sigma_1(e_9)) \\
&= 1 - f_{IF}(0, e_8, e_7 + z) + f_{IF}(-1, e_8, e_7) - 1 \\
&= e_8 - e_7 - z
\end{aligned}$$

We have already chosen suitable values for x and y but z is still free. Having worked with the 18-step collisions earlier, we realize that only suitable values for z are 0, $+1$ and -1.

Condition on the value of δW_{i+7}: This condition is the easiest to satisfy. We need $\delta W_{12} = 0$. But $\delta W_{12} = \delta f_{IF}^{11}(0, 0, x)$. If the f_{IF} function chooses its middle argument then we will have the desired value. Hence we need to ensure $e_{11} = -1$. This can be done deterministically by choosing W_{11} suitably.

Condition 11 from Table 2: To get $\delta f_{MAJ}^7(0, 0, x) = 0$, it is sufficient to ensure that $a_7 = a_6$. This can be done deterministically by choosing W_7 suitably.

All the resulting conditions are summarized in Table 3.

Table 3. Conditions put on the registers and differential path along with conditions yet to be satisfied

1	$x = 1, y = -1$	5	$e_8 - z - e_7 = 0$	(Condition 7, Table 2)
2	$a_4 = a_3, a_5 = -1$	6	$\delta f_{MAJ}^6(0, x, 0) = -z$	(Condition 2, Table 2)
3	$a_7 = a_6$	7	$-x = \delta f_{IF}^8(0, z, y)$	(Condition 6, Table 2)
4	$e_9 = -1, e_{11} = -1$	8	$\delta f_{IF}^{10}(0, x, 0) = -z$	(Condition 8, Table 2)

We need to consider three choices for z: 0, 1 and -1. The middle arguments to the δf_{MAJ}^6 function are $a_5 + 1$ and a_5, both of which have already been set to specific values 0 and -1 respectively (Cf. Condition 2 in Table 3). This causes difficulty in the satisfaction of Condition 6 in Table 3 for $z = 1$. Hence we consider the other two values for z now.

6.1   When $z = 0$

This is the same 20-step differential path considered in [6]. We now attempt to satisfy conditions 5 to 8 in Table 3.

- Taking $a_6 = a_4$ satisfies condition 6. This can be done by suitably choosing W_6.
- Taking $e_8 = e_7$ satisfies condition 5. This can be done by suitably choosing W_8.
- Taking $e_{10} = 0$ satisfies condition 8. This can be done by suitably choosing W_{10}.

The only condition remaining now is Condition 7 which is $\delta f_{IF}^8(0, 0, -1) = -1$. There is no message freedom left to satisfy this condition. In [6], this condition is let to be free and is satisfied with probability $1/3$ by random choices of messages. We now show that it is possible to satisfy even this condition deterministically.

It is clear that if we have $e_8 = 0$ then f_{IF} will select its last argument which has a difference of -1. Thus the output of f_{IF} will be -1 as desired. But we have already chosen W_8 such that $e_8 = e_7$. All the earlier message words starting from W_4 have also been used to satisfy some condition or the other. We now look at the calculation of e_7:

$$e_7 = d_6 + \Sigma_1(e_6) + f_{IF}(e_6, f_6, g_6) + h_6 + K_7 + W_7$$
$$= d_6 + a_7 - \Sigma_0(a_6) - f_{MAJ}(a_6, b_6, c_6)$$
$$= a_3 + a_7 - \Sigma_0(a_6) - f_{MAJ}(a_6, a_5, a_4)$$
$$= a_4 + a_6 - \Sigma_0(a_6) - f_{MAJ}(a_6, -1, a_4)$$

If we can ensure that $a_6 = a_4 = 0$ then $e_7 = e_8 = 0$ will be deterministic, which in turn will lead to a 20-step collision with probability 1. We used W_4 to get $a_4 = a_3$ earlier. Now we choose the free word W_3 to get $a_3 = 0$. Rest of the conditions remain the same as in [6] and we get 20-step deterministic collisions for SHA-2. Examples of colliding message pairs for 20-step SHA-256 and SHA-512 are given in [9]. The set of conditions on the registers are given as Case 1 in Table 4.

Table 4. Conditions on the registers for 20-step deterministic collisions for SHA-2. Satisfaction of these conditions lead to 20-step collisions for SHA-2 with probability 1. A condition on a_i (or e_i) can be satisfied by suitable choice of W_i. The condition on e_7 in each case gets satisfied automatically when other conditions are met.

Case 1	$x = 1, y = -1,\quad z = 0$		
1	$a_3 = a_4 = 0,$	$a_5 = -1,$	$a_6 = a_7 = 0$
2	$e_7 = e_8 = 0,$	$e_{10} = 0,$	$e_9 = e_{11} = -1$
Case 2-A	$x = 1, y = -1,\quad z = -1$		
1	$a_3 = a_4 = -1,$	$a_5 = -1,$	$a_6 = a_7 = 0$
2	$e_7 = 0, e_8 = -1,$	$e_9 = -1,$	$e_{10} = e_{11} = -1$
Case 2-B	$x = 1, y = -1,\quad z = -1$		
1	$a_3 = a_4 = 0,$	$a_5 = -1,$	$a_6 = a_7 = -1$
2	$e_7 = 1, e_8 = 0,$	$e_9 = -1,$	$e_{10} = e_{11} = -1$

6.2   When $z = -1$

Similar to the case $z = 0$ above, we can determine conditions for 20-step collisions in SHA-2 and deterministically satisfy all the conditions. This time we get two sets of conditions. These are listed as Case 2-A and 2-B in Table 4. Note that this case gives rise to a new 20-step differential path for SHA-2. Colliding pairs of messages satisfying these conditions are given in Section A.

7 Extending a Single Local Collision to Obtain 21-Step Collisions

Using a single local collision to obtain 21-step collisions appears difficult because initial message words start repeating in the recursion of the message expansion this time. In [6], a single local collision spanning from Step 6 to Step 14 is used and a 21-step collision for SHA-256 is obtained probabilistically. Note that the earlier 20-step collisions had the local collision spanning from Step 5 to Step 13. This time the local collision has been slid down by one step. We first describe the method used in [6].

First 5 steps of message expansion for SHA-2 are:

$$W_{16} = \underline{\sigma_1(W_{14})} + W_9 + \sigma_0(W_1) + W_0$$
$$W_{17} = \underline{\sigma_1(W_{15})} + W_{10} + \sigma_0(W_2) + W_1$$
$$W_{18} = \underline{\sigma_1(W_{16})} + W_{11} + \sigma_0(W_3) + W_2$$
$$W_{19} = \underline{\sigma_1(W_{17})} + W_{12} + \sigma_0(W_4) + W_3$$
$$W_{20} = \underline{\sigma_1(W_{18})} + W_{13} + \sigma_0(W_5) + W_4$$

Since the chosen local collision has 4 consecutive zero message differentials within its span, we have $\delta W_i = 0$ for $i \in \{10, 11, 12, 13\}$. Further, this being the only local collision, messages outside the span of the local collision do not have any difference. Thus, we also have $\delta W_i = 0$ for $i \in \{0, 1, 2, 3, 4, 5, 15\}$. Terms which *may have* non-zero differentials in the above equations are underlined.

All these zero differentials imply that if $\delta\sigma_1(W_{14}) + \delta W_9 = 0$ then the first 5 steps of the message expansion will not produce any difference, and we will have a 21-step collision. Since both W_{14} and W_9 are random, it can be expected that they will cancel the differences in this manner. The probability for this cancellation to happen is estimated to be about $2^{-17.5}$ in [6]. Since their local collision has probability roughly $1/3$, the probability of the 21-step collision is estimated to be approximately 2^{-19}.

We use the same technique for our deterministic 20-step collisions and slide the single local collision one step to attempt a 21-step collision. We first observe that in having the 20-step collisions with probability 1, we have lost some message freedom and consequently, δW_9 is no more random for two of the three cases described in Table 4. This happens for Case 1 and Case 2-B from this table. For proof of this claim, refer to [9].

To use the 20-step collision described by Case 1 in Table 4, we need to relax some of the conditions there and obtain some randomness in δW_9. An example of such a relaxation is not to enforce $a_3 = a_4 = 0$, rather only ensure $a_3 = a_4$. This also causes relaxation on the condition on e_7, and the 20-step collision becomes probabilistic now. In fact, this is exactly the same 20-step collision described in [6]. The 21-step collision can now be found for this case as described in [6]. We describe an improvement to the search for messages satisfying $\delta\sigma_1(W_{14}) + \delta W_9 = 0$ a little later.

We note that the conditions in case 2-B of Table 4 cannot be relaxed to obtain randomness in δW_9 and consequently this case can not be used for

21-step collisions. We also note that Case 2-A introduces randomness in δW_9 by default, so we do not need to relax any condition for this case. This is a good case for obtaining 21-step collisions, since it has probability 1 for all the steps other than the cancellation of δW_9 as described above. Next we describe our improved method of searching for suitable messages such that the difference in W_{14} and W_9 cancels the difference in W_{18}.

7.1   Obtaining Messages Satisfying $\delta\sigma_1(\delta W_{14}) + \delta W_9 = 0$

We have that $\delta W_{14} = W'_{14} - W_{14} = -1$. We expect δW_9 to be random. It is stated in [6] that by random choice of message words, the condition above can be satisfied with probability $2^{-17.5}$. This expectation seems to be based on the randomness of $\delta\sigma_1(W_{14})$. We note that the difference of two σ_1 terms when their inputs differ by -1 is highly non-random.

The choices made in the local collision make the term δW_9 biased towards values which are small in magnitude. A rough idea of the distribution of δW_9 can be had from the following example: We ran the code for 21-step collisions of [6] 5×10^5 times and observed that only 174 times the value of δW_9 came out to be larger than 1000 in magnitude. Further, there were only 334 values larger than 500, 594 values larger than 300 and 1870 values larger than 100.

At the same time, $\sigma_1(W_{14} - 1) - \sigma_1(W_{14})$ is biased towards large magnitudes for random values of W_{14}. In fact, for a large number of points $p \in \{0,1\}^{32}$ there is no solution to the equation $\sigma_1(W_{14} - 1) - \sigma_1(W_{14}) = -\delta W_9 = p$. Interestingly, this equation does not have any solution for W_{14} for even values of p. The distribution of the left hand side of this equation is so non-uniform that there are only 4 values of δW_9 in $\{-300, 300\}$ for which a solution for W_{14} exists. We list these 4 values of δW_9 and corresponding values of W_{14} in Table 5.

Table 5. Some solutions to the equation $\sigma_1(W_{14}-1) - \sigma_1(W_{14}) + \delta W_9 = 0$ for SHA-256

No.	δW_9	W_{14}
1	00000041	7fc00000, 80400000
2	00000101	d5000000, 81000000, 7f000000, 2b000000
3	ffffff41	4c400000, b3c00000
4	ffffff01	19000000, 4d000000, b3000000, e7000000

This analysis suggests that a specific suitable value of δW_9 should first be selected and then we should search for corresponding W_{14}. Even if this procedure is used, the probability of being able to get the correct W_{14} is of the order of 2^{-32}. This implies that the search in [6] is not over random messages, rather a pre-computed value of W_{14} is used for a specific δW_9. From the colliding message pair given in [6], we observe that the value of δW_9 used is ffffff01 and the corresponding W_{14} is 19000000. This particular choice of δW_9 occurs with probability $2^{-17.5}$ which corresponds to the estimate given in [6].

We use a speed-up in the search for the correct W_{14}. First we create a list of pairs $(\sigma_1(p) - \sigma_1(p-1), p)$ for all $p \in \{0,1\}^{32}$. We sort this list on the first element. While running the code for 21-step collision, we compute δW_9 and do a binary search over this list. If this value matches with the first element of a pair in the list, then we use the second element to define W_{14}. With this modification, we obtain a 16 fold improvement to the probability of obtaining the correct δW_9. Since W_{14} is pre-computed, the only probability is in getting the right difference δW_9.

We have extended two types of 20-step collisions to obtain 21-step collisions for SHA-256. One of the local collisions is the Case 1 of Table 4 with some conditions relaxed. As already mentioned, this is the Nikolić-Biryukov local collision [6] having probability $1/3$. For this case our method succeeds in finding correct δW_9 with probability roughly $2^{-13.5}$. Thus the overall probability of the 21-step SHA-256 collision is about 2^{-15}.

The second 20-step collision we extend to 21 steps is described by Case 2-A of Table 4. For this case, we could find suitable δW_9 with probability roughly 2^{-17}. Since the probability of the 20-step collision is 1 in this case, we get the 21-step collision with probability roughly 2^{-17}.

8   Conclusions

In this paper we presented a generalized local collision for SHA-2. Using a single instance of this local collision, we obtained 18-step collisions with an arbitrary starting message difference. These collisions hold with probability 1. We then presented two different differential paths for 20-step collisions in SHA-2 both of which hold with probability 1. Finally, we improved on the search for 21-step collisions in SHA-256 increasing the probability of success 16 fold. Apart from the colliding message pairs for different cases and different number of steps for SHA-256, we also show colliding message pairs for up to 20-step SHA-512 for the first time in the literature.

Acknowledgements

We would like to thank anonymous reviewers for giving useful suggestions.

References

1. Chabaud, F., Joux, A.: Differential Collisions in SHA-0. In: Krawczyk, H. (ed.) CRYPTO 1998. LNCS, vol. 1462, pp. 56–71. Springer, Heidelberg (1998)
2. Gilbert, H., Handschuh, H.: Security Analysis of SHA-256 and Sisters. In: Matsui, M., Zuccherato, R.J. (eds.) Selected Areas in Cryptography, 10th Annual International Workshop, SAC 2003, Ottawa, Canada, August 14-15, 2003. LNCS, vol. 3006, pp. 175–193. Springer, Heidelberg (2003)
3. Hawkes, P., Paddon, M., Rose, G.G.: On Corrective Patterns for the SHA-2 Family. Cryptology eprint Archive (August 2004), http://eprint.iacr.org/2004/207

4. Mendel, F., Pramstaller, N., Rechberger, C., Rijmen, V.: Analysis of Step-Reduced SHA-256. In: Robshaw, M.J.B. (ed.) FSE 2006. LNCS, vol. 4047, pp. 126–143. Springer, Heidelberg (2006)
5. Mendel, F., Pramstaller, N., Rechberger, C., Rijmen, V.: Analysis of Step-Reduced SHA-256. Cryptology eprint Archive (March 2008),
   http://eprint.iacr.org/2008/130
6. Nikolić, I., Biryukov, A.: Collisions for Step-Reduced SHA-256. In: Nyberg, K. (ed.) Fast Software Encryption 2008. LNCS, pp. 1–16. Springer, Heidelberg (2008)
7. Sanadhya, S.K., Sarkar, P.: New Local Collisions for the SHA-2 Hash Family. In: Nam, K.-H., Rhee, G. (eds.) ICISC 2007. LNCS, vol. 4817, pp. 193–205. Springer, Heidelberg (2007)
8. Sanadhya, S.K., Sarkar, P.: Attacking Reduced Round SHA-256. In: Bellovin, S., Gennaro, R. (eds.) ACNS 2008. LNCS. Springer, Heidelberg (to appear, 2008)
9. Sanadhya, S.K., Sarkar, P.: Non-Linear Reduced Round Attacks Against SHA-2 Hash family. Cryptology eprint Archive (April 2008),
   http://eprint.iacr.org/2008/174
10. Shoup, V. (ed.): CRYPTO 2005. LNCS, vol. 3621. Springer, Heidelberg (2005)
11. Secure Hash Standard. Federal Information Processing Standard Publication 180-2. U.S. Department of Commerce, National Institute of Standards and Technology(NIST) (2002), http://csrc.nist.gov/publications/fips/fips180-2/fips180-2withchangenotice.pdf
12. Wang, X., Yin, Y.L., Yu, H.: Finding Collisions in the Full SHA-1. In: Shoup (ed.) [10], pp. 17–36
13. Wang, X., Yu, H.: How to Break MD5 and Other Hash Functions. In: Cramer, R.J.F. (ed.) EUROCRYPT 2005. LNCS, vol. 3494, pp. 19–35. Springer, Heidelberg (2005)
14. Wang, X., Yu, H., Yin, Y.L.: Efficient Collision Search Attacks on SHA-0. In: Shoup [10], pp. 1–16

A   Colliding Message Pairs

Table 6. Colliding message pair for 20-step SHA-256 with standard IV. These messages follow the differential path of Table 1 with $x = 1$, $y = -1$, $z = -1$. These messages satisfy Case 2-A of Table 4.

W_1	0-7	5a603c44	0f5fdd15	69e8c2a4	1754c271	60518701	feef6b5f	c7f50d13	fdc492ca
	8-15	d5d49f53	d4c9d37f	bf796ac4	aaf3823e	a24e8e62	8d8898c8	fc4456f3	8d557ae5
W_2	0-7	5a603c44	0f5fdd15	69e8c2a4	1754c271	60518701	feef6b60	d3d50e93	f9a49248
	8-15	d2326157	d4c9d37f	bf796ac4	aaf3823e	a24e8e62	8d8898c7	fc4456f3	8d557ae5

Table 7. Colliding message pair for 21-step SHA-256 with standard IV. These messages follow the differential path of Table 1 with $x = 1$, $y = -1$, $z = -1$. For these messages $\delta W_9 =$ ffffe191.

W_1	0-7	4158ecc7	3a3ffe61	ba7149f0	ed452440	4d9ab924	f016459f	22f5578c	c56333c1
	8-15	fff1941ff	19b8055b	fb2876ba	ca4d6044	8d41a28d	8194372b	7e100000	5240bb72
W_2	0-7	4158ecc7	3a3ffe61	ba7149f0	ed452440	4d9ab924	f016459f	22f5578d	c1433241
	8-15	fb39427d	19b7e6ec	fb2876ba	ca4d6044	8d41a28d	8194372b	7e0fffff	5240bb72

Table 8. Colliding message pair for 20-step SHA-512 with standard IV. These messages follow the differential path of Table 1 with $x = 1$, $y = -1$, $z = -1$. These messages satisfy Case 2-A of Table 4.

W_1	0-3	1c99041525eeeeb3	7dfc74f74bab1a89	aaca442cddb37351	21d1684a782a5b87
	4-7	3d374aed94c9d766	296c28f080eced7a	62f73e6df90ce266	d4c85286272c52c1
	8-11	e2d8e832fb623115	5c43e3fc9bee94c3	5ef6f726192a4213	aaf3823c2a004b1f
	12-15	fa18ffe92868d117	8584328bd3146ed0	c3ce87104858e6cb	6dc9cd6519344c6a
W_2	0-3	1c99041525eeeeb3	7dfc74f74bab1a89	aaca442cddb37351	21d1684a782a5b87
	4-7	3d374aed94c9d766	296c28f080eced7b	62fafe6df88ce264	d4cc928628ac52c0
	8-11	f73a261982122135	5c43e3fc9bee94c3	5ef6f726192a4213	aaf3823c2a004b1f
	12-15	fa18ffe92868d117	8584328bd3146ecf	c3ce87104858e6cb	6dc9cd6519344c6a

Collisions for Round-Reduced LAKE[*]

Florian Mendel and Martin Schläffer

Graz University of Technology,
Institute for Applied Information Processing and Communications,
Inffeldgasse 16a, A-8010 Graz, Austria
{florian.mendel,martin.schlaeffer}@iaik.tugraz.at

Abstract. LAKE is a family of cryptographic hash functions presented at FSE 2008. It is an iterated hash function and defines two main instances with a 256 bit and 512 bit hash value. In this paper, we present the first security analysis of LAKE. We show how collision attacks, exploiting the non-bijectiveness of the internal compression function of LAKE, can be mounted on reduced variants of LAKE. We show an efficient attack on the 256 bit hash function LAKE-256 reduced to 3 rounds and present an actual colliding message pair. Furthermore, we present a theoretical attack on LAKE-256 reduced to 4 rounds with a complexity of 2^{109}. By using more sophisticated message modification techniques we expect that the attack can be extended to 5 rounds. However, for the moment our approach does not appear to be applicable to the full LAKE-256 hash function (with all 8 rounds).

Keywords: cryptanalysis, hash functions, collision attack.

1   Introduction

A cryptographic hash function H maps a message M of arbitrary length to a fixed-length hash value h. A cryptographic hash function has to fulfill the following security requirements:

- *Collision resistance:* it is infeasible to find two messages M and M^*, with $M^* \neq M$, such that $H(M) = H(M^*)$.
- *Second preimage resistance:* for a given message M, it is infeasible to find a second message $M^* \neq M$ such that $H(M) = H(M^*)$.
- *Preimage resistance:* for a given hash value h, it is infeasible to find a message M such that $H(M) = h$.

The resistance of a hash function to collision and (second) preimage attacks depends on the length n of the hash value. Based on the birthday paradox the generic complexity for a collision attack is about $2^{n/2}$ hash computations, where n is the size of the hash value. For a preimage attack and a second preimage

---

[*] The work in this paper has been supported in part by the European Commission under contract IST-2002-507932 (ECRYPT) and through the Austrian Science Fund (FWF) under grant number P19863.

Y. Mu, W. Susilo, and J. Seberry (Eds.): ACISP 2008, LNCS 5107, pp. 267–281, 2008.

attack the generic complexity is about 2^n hash computations. If collisions and (second) preimages can be found with a complexity less than $2^{n/2}$ and 2^n the hash function is considered to be broken.

Recent cryptanalytic results focus on the collision resistance of hash functions. Collision attacks have been shown for many commonly used hash functions, like MD5 [13] and SHA-1 [4,12]. In the upcoming NIST competition [9] to find an alternative hash function to SHA-2, many new hash function designs will be proposed. Therefore, the cryptanalysis of new and alternative hash function designs like LAKE is of great interest. In this article, we will present a security analysis with respect to collision resistance for the hash function LAKE, proposed at FSE 2008 [2]. We are not aware of any published security analysis of this hash function until now.

The hash function LAKE is a new iterated hash function based on the HAIFA framework [3]. It is a software-oriented design and uses an internal wide-pipe strategy [7,8]. The two proposed variants of LAKE compute a 256-bit and 512-bit hash value and use an 8- and 10-round compression function, respectively. In our analysis we focus on the 256-bit variant LAKE-256 but the same attack applies to LAKE-512 as well. In the following we omit the bit size in the name if we refer to LAKE-256. We show collisions for round-reduced variants of LAKE where we exploit a structural weakness in the internal compression functions. We construct collisions in the used Boolean functions which are then extended to an attack on round-reduced variants of LAKE.

The remainder of this article is structured as follows. In the next section, we give a short description of the hash function LAKE with a focus on the relevant parts for our attacks. In Sect. 3, we explain the basic attack strategy and show a collision for a simplified variant of the full hash function. The results of the collision attacks on round-reduced variants are presented in Sect. 4. Finally, we conclude this paper with a short recommendation on how the LAKE design could be improved to withstand our attack.

2   Description of LAKE

The LAKE hash function is an iterated hash function based on the HAIFA framework [3]. It takes a salt and the message as its input. The message is padded by a specific padding rule and the initial chaining variable H_0 is computed form the initial value (IV) and parameterized by the (variable) output bit length d of the hash function. The LAKE family defines two main instances LAKE-256 and LAKE-512 which differ only in their used bit sizes, constants and rotation values. While our attack is not limited to LAKE-256 we focus on this instance of the LAKE family for the remainder of this paper.

The compression function of LAKE computes the next chaining variable H_t from the previous H_{t-1}, the current message block M_t the salt S and the current block index t. It consists of three parts which are shown in Fig. 1. The function saltstate mixes the global chaining variable H_t with the salt S, and the block index t using 8 calls to the function g. The output of saltstate is written into the

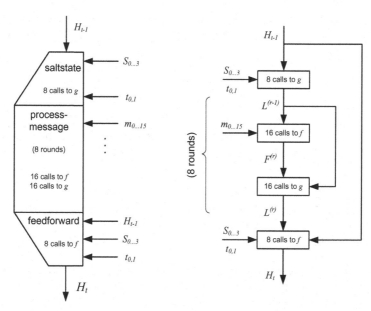

Fig. 1. The compression function of LAKE-256 consists of the three main parts salt-state, processmessage and feedforward which call two nonlinear internal compression functions f and g

internal chaining variable $L^{(r-1)}$ which is twice as large as H_{t-1}. The function processmessage is the main part of the LAKE compression function and takes the current message block M_t and the current internal chaining variable $L^{(r-1)}$ as its input. The message block is first expanded by the message permutation $\sigma_r(i)$ and then incorporated into the internal chaining variables within r rounds. Every round of processmessage uses 16 calls to two nonlinear internal compression functions f and g. The feedforward function compresses the previous global chaining variable H_{t-1}, the salt S, the block index t, and the last internal chaining variable $L^{(r)}$ by 8 calls of the function f and produces the next chaining variable H_t.

Table 1. The index $k = \sigma_r(i)$ of the message permutation of LAKE-256 for the rounds R1-R8 of **processmessage**

i	0	1	2	3	4	5	6	7	8	9	10	11	12	13	14	15
R1	0	1	2	3	4	5	6	7	8	9	10	11	12	13	14	15
R2	1	6	11	0	5	10	15	4	9	14	3	8	13	2	7	12
R3	5	8	11	14	1	4	7	10	13	0	3	6	9	12	15	2
R4	0	7	14	5	12	3	10	1	8	15	6	13	4	11	2	9
R5	0	1	2	3	4	5	6	7	8	9	10	11	12	13	14	15
R6	1	6	11	0	5	10	15	4	9	14	3	8	13	2	7	12
R7	5	8	11	14	1	4	7	10	13	0	3	6	9	12	15	2
R8	0	7	14	5	12	3	10	1	8	15	6	13	4	11	2	9

In the case of LAKE-256, the compression function uses $r = 8$ rounds and the message permutation of Table 1. The nonlinear internal compression functions f and g are defined by

$$f(a, b, c, d) = ((a + (b \vee C_0)) + (c + (a \wedge C_1))) \ggg 7) + ((b + (c \oplus d)) \ggg 13)$$
$$g(a, b, c, d) = ((a + b) \ggg 1) \oplus (c + d).$$

Depending on whether they are used in saltstate, processmessage or feedforward, these functions are parameterized by some constants $C_0, \ldots, C_{15}$, which are extracted from π:

$$
\begin{array}{llll}
C_0 = \text{452821E6} & C_4 = \text{C0AC29B7} & C_8 = \text{9216D5D9} & C_{12} = \text{2FFD72DB} \\
C_1 = \text{38D01377} & C_5 = \text{C97C50DD} & C_9 = \text{8979FB1B} & C_{13} = \text{D01ADFB7} \\
C_2 = \text{BE5466CF} & C_6 = \text{3F84D5B5} & C_{10} = \text{D1310BA6} & C_{14} = \text{B8E1AFED} \\
C_3 = \text{34E90C6C} & C_7 = \text{B5470917} & C_{11} = \text{98DFB5AC} & C_{15} = \text{6A267E96}
\end{array}
$$

In case of processmessage, the inputs of f are the previous internal chaining variables $L^{(r-1)}$, the current internal chaining variables $F^{(r)}$, the constants C_i, and the expanded message words m_k with $k = \sigma_r(i)$. The function g takes as input the current internal chaining variables $F^{(r)}$, the previous internal chaining variables $L^{(r-1)}$ using feed-forward and the new internal chaining variables $L^{(r)}$:

$$F_i^{(r)} = f(a, b, c, d) = f(F_{i-1}^{(r)}, L_i^{(r-1)}, m_k, C_i)$$
$$L_i^{(r)} = g(a, b, c, d) = g(L_{i-1}^{(r)}, F_i^{(r)}, L_i^{(r-1)}, F_{i+1}^{(r)})$$

Note that $F^{(r)}$ gets initialized by $L^{(r-1)}$ and $L^{(r)}$ gets initialized by $F^{(r)}$. We get for the sequence of chaining variables H_t and internal chaining variables $L^{(r)}$ and $F^{(r)}$:

$$H_{t-1} \rightarrow salt \rightarrow \underbrace{L^{(r-1)} \rightarrow f \rightarrow F^{(r)} \rightarrow g \rightarrow L^{(r)}}_{8\,rounds} \rightarrow feedforward \rightarrow H_t$$

3   Basic Attack Strategy

The basic observation for the attack on the compression function of LAKE is that the internal compression function f of processmessage is not bijective (not injective) regarding the chaining variables and message words. This means, that at least two message words exist, which result in the same output of f for fixed internal chaining variables. In fact, it is possible to find many different message words m_k and m_k^* which result in the same output of f. Using these inner collisions of the internal compression function f we can construct collisions for round-reduced versions of LAKE. Note that the same idea applies to both variants, LAKE-256 and LAKE-512 because the two variants differ only in the used word size, constants and rotation values.

3.1   Collisions for 1 Round of LAKE

In every round, each message word m_k is used only once by one of the 16 calls to the f function. Hence, we can construct a collision for one round of LAKE using a single inner collision in f (this has been independently observed by Stefan Lucks). By performing a collision attack on the 32-bit output of f we have been able to efficiently find many message pairs m_k and m_k^* for many internal chaining values $F_{i-1}^{(r)}$, $L_i^{(r-1)}$ and all constants C_i such that the output of f collides:

$$f(F_{i-1}^{(r)}, L_i^{(r-1)}, m_k, C_i) = f(F_{i-1}^{(r)}, L_i^{(r-1)}, m_k^*, C_i)$$

Note that the authors of LAKE have proposed to analyze a reduced variant of the hash function which uses the same constant in every round [1]. In this case we can simply use the same inner collision in f for every round of LAKE. Table 2 shows a collision for 8 rounds of LAKE using the same constant C_0 in each round which can be computed instantly on a standard PC.

Table 2. A colliding message pair for LAKE using the same constant C_0 in each round

H_0	243F6A88	85A308D3	13198A2E	03707344	A4093822	299F31D0	082EFA98	EC4E6C89
M_0	7901FB66	7120239A	75018D7B	38EFC240	04BA14F4	54B5A198	60842D9A	05CE0AF7
	1A31E11B	40B1C10C	55F91C02	559DF366	74D6D973	455E48F2	31072B72	4DB56283
M_0^*	7D11BC59	7120239A	75018D7B	38EFC240	04BA14F4	54B5A198	60842D9A	05CE0AF7
	1A31E11B	40B1C10C	55F91C02	559DF366	74D6D973	455E48F2	31072B72	4DB56283
ΔM_0	0410473F	00000000	00000000	00000000	00000000	00000000	00000000	00000000
	00000000	00000000	00000000	00000000	00000000	00000000	00000000	00000000
H_1	289B5613	0295350F	CA661380	699C892A	80CC3678	91B6F85B	FD0332EB	D89C925A
H_1^*	289B5613	0295350F	CA661380	699C892A	80CC3678	91B6F85B	FD0332EB	D89C925A

3.2   Collisions for More Than 1 Round of LAKE

The original LAKE specification defines different constants for each round and we cannot use the same inner collision for every round anymore. However, the idea of constructing collisions in f can still be extended to attack more rounds of LAKE. Then, the same message pair m_k and m_k^* has to result in an inner collision of f for each of the attacked rounds. Due to the message expansion, the message word m_k is used in a different call of f in each round. However, in each call i, the f function differs only in the used constant C_i. For instance, if we want to construct a collision for the first two rounds of LAKE, we need to find a message pair m_k and m_k^* such that we have a collision in f in both rounds.

Assume we are using message word m_0. In the first round, m_0 is used in call $i = 0$ of the function f and in the second round, m_0 is used in call $i = 3$ of f (see Table 1). Hence, we need to find a message pair m_0 and m_0^*, which results in an inner collision of f and applies to both constants C_0 and C_3 simultaneously. One method to find such a pair is to search for each constant separately and check for matching message pairs. This method might work for two constants but is insufficient for more constants. In the following we show how this can be done more efficiently.

3.3   Inner Collisions in f Using Different Constants

A better method is to analyze the differential behaviour of the f function and choose message *differences* Δm_k, which are independent of the used constants. To find a message differences which results in a collision and thus, in a zero difference of the f function, we simplify the f function to:

$$f(a, b, m_k, C_i) = c_1 + ((m_k + c_2) \ggg 7) + ((c_3 + (m_k \oplus C_i)) \ggg 13) \quad (1)$$

where the values c_1, c_2 and c_3 depend on the internal chaining variables $L_i^{(r-1)}$ and $F_{i-1}^{(r)}$. Because the majority of the remaining operations are modular additions and rotations we use signed bit differences in our attack. Note that more advanced techniques like generalized characteristics as used in the most recent attacks on SHA-1 are not needed in this case [5]. Signed bit differences have been introduced by Wang *et al.* in the analysis of the MD4-family of hash functions [11]. Using these differences, the carry expansions of the modular additions in Equation (1) can be controlled by imposing conditions on the absolute values (c_1, c_2 and c_3) and rotated without imposing further conditions. In the xor-addition $\Delta m_k \oplus C_i$ the sign of the signed bit difference Δm_k is flipped at each position where the constant C_i is one and does not change where C_i is zero. For a detailed description of signed bit differences, we refer to [6].

Before constructing a zero output difference of the f function, we define the differential representation of f regarding the message difference Δm_k by

$$\Delta f = \underbrace{(\Delta m_k \ggg 7)}_{\Delta x} + \underbrace{((\Delta m_k \oplus C_i) \ggg 13)}_{\Delta y} = 0 \quad (2)$$

where the differences Δx and Δy need to cancel each other after the rotations. For a collision over more than one round of LAKE, we need to fulfill equation 2 for different constants C_i but with the same message difference Δm_k. Therefore, we allow a signed bit difference in the message only at positions, where the values of the used constants are equal. In this case the difference Δy is independent of the used C_i. We define the equal positions of all used constants $C_{i_1}, C_{i_2}, \ldots$ by:

$$C_{eq}^{(p)} = \begin{cases} 1 & \text{if } C_{i_1}^{(p)} = C_{i_2}^{(p)} = \ldots \\ 0 & \text{otherwise} \end{cases} \quad (3)$$

where $C^{(p)}$ denotes the bit position p of the value C. Note that the difference Δx is independent of each round. To get a zero difference of f for all rounds, the differences Δy has to be the same for each round and every used constant.

The more rounds we attack, the more constants C_i are used and the less is the Hamming weight of the equal positions C_{eq} of these constants. Since at each position we can choose between a negative, a positive or no difference, the number of the allowed signed message differences is $3^{hw(C_{eq})}$. If less differences are allowed in Δm_k the probability of a collision decreases. However, the search space gets reduced as well and we can check more (or even all) signed message differences. We have implemented a search tool similar as in [10], which uses carry expansions for the differences $\Delta x = \Delta m_k$ and $\Delta y = \Delta m_k \oplus C_i$. After the rotations we check whether the resulting differences cancel each other.

Note that two signed bit differences in the MSB always cancel each other in the addition and are thus considered to be equal. Therefore, we can allow additional message differences at the MSB of each modular addition. A flip of the message difference in the MSB because of xoring it with different constants C_i results in the same difference. Since we can omit the sign of the regarding MSB in each of the 3 modular additions, we allow additional message differences at position 32, 13 and 6. A difference at position 13 in $\Delta m_k \oplus C_i$ gets rotated to the MSB in Δy and a difference at position 6 in $\Delta m_k \oplus C_i$ gets rotated to the same position as the MSB of Δm_k in Δx. By including these three cases, the search space can be increased and even includes all inner collisions of f.

4   Results of the Collision Attack

To attack more than one round of LAKE we have implemented a tool which checks for collisions in f depending on the used constants C_i. We first compute C_{eq} and determine all possible message differences Δm_k. Then, we use signed carry expansions of the message difference in Δx and Δy and check whether the differences cancel each other after the rotation. Table 3 shows which constant C_i is used for each message word m_k in each round. With our tool we are able to check all possible message differences if more than three different constants are used. In this case, the Hamming weight of C_{eq} and the search space is low enough to try all possible expanded differences. For all cases where only two constants are involved, we have limited the search to high probability differentials (with a short carry expansion) and can therefore find collisions with a high probability as well.

Table 3. For each message word m_k different constants C_i are used in every round due to the message permutation. The constants for R5-R8 are the same as for R1-R4.

	m_0	m_1	m_2	m_3	m_4	m_5	m_6	m_7	m_8	m_9	m_{10}	m_{11}	m_{12}	m_{13}	m_{14}	m_{15}
R1	C_0	C_1	C_2	C_3	C_4	C_5	C_6	C_7	C_8	C_9	C_{10}	C_{11}	C_{12}	C_{13}	C_{14}	C_{15}
R2	C_3	C_0	C_{13}	C_{10}	C_7	C_4	C_1	C_{14}	C_{11}	C_8	C_5	C_2	C_{15}	C_{12}	C_9	C_6
R3	C_9	C_4	C_{15}	C_{10}	C_5	C_0	C_{11}	C_6	C_1	C_{12}	C_7	C_2	C_{13}	C_8	C_3	C_{14}
R4	C_0	C_7	C_{14}	C_5	C_{12}	C_3	C_{10}	C_1	C_8	C_{15}	C_6	C_{13}	C_4	C_{11}	C_2	C_9

4.1   2 Rounds

For an attack on two rounds of LAKE, we need a collision in f with two different values of C_i. When attacking the first two rounds of LAKE we can choose one of the first two constants of Table 3. We have found the best result for the message word m_3. In the first round this message word is used in call 3 to f and thus, it is xored with the constant C_3. In the second round, m_3 is used in call 10 and xored with the constant C_{10}. Hence, we need to fulfill the following differential equations for f simultaneously:

$$\Delta f_3 = (\Delta m_3 \ggg 7) + ((\Delta m_3 \oplus C_3) \ggg 13) = 0 \qquad (4)$$

$$\Delta f_{10} = (\Delta m_3 \ggg 7) + ((\Delta m_3 \oplus C_{10}) \ggg 13) = 0 \qquad (5)$$

We allow signed differences in Δm_3 at all positions, where the constants C_3 and C_{10} are equal:

$$C_3 = \texttt{34E90C6C}$$
$$C_{10} = \texttt{D1310BA6}$$
$$C_{eq} = \texttt{1A27F835}$$
$$\Delta m_3 = \texttt{9A27F835}$$

The number of the equal positions in C_3 and C_{10} is 16 and by including the three MSBs we get a maximum Hamming weight for the allowed message differences of $HW(\Delta m_3) = 17$.

Using our tool we have found the following four message differences, where each of them results in a zero difference of the f function. Note that each inverted message difference results in a collision as well.

$\Delta m_3 = \texttt{8207E820}$ $\quad \Delta m_3 = [\pm 32, -26, 19, 18, 17, 16, 15, 14, 12, 6]$

$\Delta m_3 = \texttt{8207E821}$ $\quad \Delta m_3 = [\pm 32, -26, 19, 18, 17, 16, 15, 14, 12, 6, 1]$

$\Delta m_3 = \texttt{8207F820}$ $\quad \Delta m_3 = [\pm 32, -26, 19, 18, 17, 16, 15, 14, 13, -12, 6]$

$\Delta m_3 = \texttt{8207F821}$ $\quad \Delta m_3 = [\pm 32, -26, 19, 18, 17, 16, 15, 14, 13, -12, 6, 1]$

For these message difference we get many expanded differences Δx and Δy which cancel each other. For example, if we consider the message difference $\Delta m_3 = \texttt{8207E820}$, the signed differences Δx and Δy with the best probabilities are:

$$\Delta x = [-32, 26, -20, 13, 12, -8, 7, 6]$$
$$\Delta y = [-32, 26, -20, 18, 14, 12, 6]$$

where the difference Δx occurs with probability 2^{-8} and Δy with probability 2^{-7}. After rotating these difference by 7 and by 13 we get the following two differences, which cancel each other in the third modular addition:

$$\Delta x \ggg 7 = [32, 31, -25, 19, -13, 6, 5, -1]$$
$$\Delta y \ggg 13 = [31, 25, -19, 13, -7, 5, 1]$$

Therefore, we get an inner collision in f for both rounds with a probability of 2^{-15} each. Usually the expanded differences with the highest probabilities determine the complexity of the attack. However, if many expanded differences cancel each other, the actual complexity is determined by the sum of all probabilities. For the message difference $\Delta m_3 = \texttt{8207E820}$ we have found 2600 expanded signed differences Δx and 5486 expanded signed differences for Δy. By adding all possible combined probabilities of Δx and Δy we get an overall probability of $2^{-4.38}$ instead of 2^{-15}.

4.2   3 Rounds

The previous collision in f over two rounds can be easily extended to a collision over 3 rounds. To extend the attack we use a weakness in the message permutation. The message word m_3 is used in call 3 of the first round and in call 10 of the second and third round. Thus, the constant C_{10} is used twice and we can use the same collision for f as in the attack on two rounds. Note that we could do the same for message word m_{11} which uses the constant C_2 twice.

A Colliding Message for 3 Rounds of LAKE. By using the message difference $\Delta m_3 = 8207E820$ we can construct a collision for LAKE reduced to three rounds with a complexity of about $2^{3 \cdot 4.38} \approx 2^{13.2}$ round evaluations (less than 1 second on a standard PC), since we can get a collision for each round with a probability of $2^{-4.38}$. The colliding message pair is given in Table 4. Note that h_0 is the initial value and h_1 is the final hash value.

Table 4. A colliding message pair for LAKE reduced to 3 rounds

H_0	243F6A88 85A308D3 13198A2E 03707344 A4093822 299F31D0 082EFA98 EC4E6C89
M_0	2ED54018 259E7BED 6A7D12A0 12780007 57979D36 619A5DE1 2F1FA8A0 09D72979
	3428C041 1439951D 63537711 144840C4 7C75D35E 70C613E9 23DCA632 52DB6AB9
M_0^*	2ED54018 259E7BED 6A7D12A0 907FE827 57979D36 619A5DE1 2F1FA8A0 09D72979
	3428C041 1439951D 63537711 144840C4 7C75D35E 70C613E9 23DCA632 52DB6AB9
ΔM_0	00000000 00000000 00000000 8207E820 00000000 00000000 00000000 00000000
	00000000 00000000 00000000 00000000 00000000 00000000 00000000 00000000
H_1	0969AF41 101EA7CE CBF3F2FE E47832EB 60FFD511 DA156A75 150B3A20 F003BA7E
H_1^*	0969AF41 101EA7CE CBF3F2FE E47832EB 60FFD511 DA156A75 150B3A20 F003BA7E

4.3   More Than 3 Rounds

To attack more than 3 rounds we have first tried to construct a collision which uses only 3 different constants. This could be done for the message words m_0, m_3, m_8 and m_{11} (see Table 3). However, even by checking all possible message differences and carry expansions, we did not find a collision in these message words. Anyway, by trying all message words which use four different constants, we have found solutions for m_4 and m_7. The involved constants are C_4, C_7, C_5, C_{12} for m_4 and C_7, C_{14}, C_6, C_1 for m_7.

For the 4 round collision we have only found a characteristic with low probability. The possible message differences are $\Delta m_7 = \Delta m_4 = \pm 1$. Thus, we allow a difference only in the LSB of the message word. Note that the LSB of the involved constants is 1 and the xor operation flips the message difference. Therefore, the differences in Δx and Δy have a opposite sign and cancel each other if the following conditions are fulfilled ($i = 4, 7, 5, 12$):

$$F_{i-1}^{(r)} \wedge C_1 = 0 \tag{6}$$

$$L_i^{(r-1)} + C_i = \text{FFFFFFFF} \tag{7}$$

Under these conditions, the differences do not get changed by the rotations and we can get an inner collision in f for every round of LAKE.

Let us consider the case $\Delta m_4 = -1$ with $m_4 = 0$. By fulfilling the previous conditions the resulting values before the rotation are always either 00000000 or FFFFFFFF. These values do not get changed by the rotation and we get for $m_4 = 0$:

$$(0 + \underbrace{F_{i-1}^{(r)} \wedge C_1}_{F_{i-1}^{(r)} \wedge C_1 = 0}) \ggg 7 + \underbrace{(L_i^{(r-1)} + (0 \oplus C_i))}_{L_i^{(r-1)} + C_i = \text{FFFFFFFF}} \ggg 13 = \text{FFFFFFFF} \tag{8}$$

and for $m_4^* = m_4 - 1 = 0 - 1$:

$$(\underbrace{0 - 1 + F_{i-1}^{(r)} \wedge C_1}_{(F_{i-1}^{(r)} \wedge C_1) - 1 = \text{FFFFFFFF}}) \ggg 7 + (\underbrace{L_i^{(r-1)} + ((0 - 1) \oplus C_i)}_{L_i^{(r-1)} + 1 + C_i = 0}) \ggg 13 = \text{FFFFFFFF} \tag{9}$$

The two equations (6) and (7) hold in each round with a probability of $2^{-32-15} = 2^{-47}$, since the Hamming weight of C_1 is 15. Hence, we can get a collision for LAKE reduced to r rounds with a probability of $2^{-r \cdot 47}$ and for $r = 4$ rounds we get a probability of 2^{-188}.

Note that the difference $\Delta m_k = \pm 1$ works for any message word and any number of rounds, as long as the LSB of all involved constants is 1. However, due to the low probability we have only attacked 4 rounds of LAKE using message modification. By more sophisticated message modification techniques, we expect that an attack up to 5 rounds of the LAKE compression function is possible.

4.4   A Collision Attack for 4 Rounds of LAKE

The attack complexity of 2^{188} for 4 rounds of LAKE can be improved by using message modification techniques introduced by Wang et al. in the analysis of MD5 and SHA-1 [13,12]. In general, the idea of message modification is to use the degrees of freedom in the message to fulfill conditions on the state variables. This improves the probability of the attack and in the following we will show how message modification can be done for the first 2 rounds of LAKE. The sequence of internal chaining variables and calls to f and g are illustrated in App. A to comprehend the message modification steps.

Message Modification. In the first round we use basic message modification which simply adjusts the message words such that the conditions in the internal chaining variables are fulfilled. To fulfill the conditions on $F_3^{(1)} \wedge C_1 = 0$ we adjust $F_3^{(1)}$ by modifying m_3 since $F_3^{(1)} = f(F_2^{(1)}, L_3^{(0)}, m_3, C_3)$. Because of the right rotation, we can start by modifying bit 7 of the message and proceed up to bit 25 without getting any conflict due to carries. The remaining 6 bits are fulfilled by brute force which results in a complexity of 2^6. Since all further modifications change message words after call 3 of f, we perform this modification only once at the beginning. Therefore, this modification does not increase the overall complexity. Next we need to fulfill the conditions of $L_4^{(0)} + C_4 = \text{FFFFFFFF}$. Note that

$L_4^{(0)}$ depends on the *IV* or previous chaining value H_{t-1}. By using an arbitrary first message block we can construct the needed value of $L_4^{(0)}$ by brute force. This has a complexity of 2^{32} but needs do be done only once as well.

For the second round of LAKE we need to use advanced message modification techniques. Without message modification, equation $F_6^{(2)} \wedge C_1 = 0$ of the second round is fulfilled with a probability of 2^{-15} and equation $L_7^{(1)} + C_7 = \texttt{FFFFFFFF}$ is fulfilled with a probability of 2^{-32}. Note that $L_7^{(1)}$ depends on $F_8^{(1)}$ of the first round. This means that we can correct $L_7^{(1)}$ by $F_8^{(1)}$, which in turn gets modified by message word m_8. The undesired changes in the following steps ($F_9^{(1)}$ to $F_{15}^{(1)}$) can be corrected by advanced message modification using message word m_{15}. This ensures that $L_0^{(1)}$ to $L_6^{(1)}$ do not get changed as a result of the modification of m_8.

The Collision Search for 4 Rounds of LAKE. The search for a collision of LAKE reduced to 4 rounds can be summarized by the following steps:

1. We fulfill the 32 conditions on $L_4^{(0)}$ by choosing an arbitrary first message block M_0. This has a complexity of 2^{32} evaluations of the compression function and needs to be done only once at the beginning of the search.
2. Next we choose random message words $m_0, \ldots, m_3$ to compute the internal chaining variables $F_0^{(1)}, \ldots, F_3^{(1)}$.
3. The 15 conditions on $F_3^{(1)}$ can be fulfilled by adjusting m_3 using basic message modification. This step has a complexity of about 2^6 calls to $F_3^{(1)} = f(F_2^{(1)}, L_3^{(0)}, m_3, C_3)$. Since we do not change $m_0, \ldots, m_3$ later on, this step needs to be done only once as well.
4. The remaining message words $m_4, \ldots, m_{15}$ are chosen at random to compute the internal chaining variables $F_4^{(1)}, \ldots, F_{15}^{(1)}$ and $L_0^{(1)}, \ldots, L_7^{(1)}$ to check the conditions on $L_7^{(1)}$.
5. To fulfill the conditions on $L_7^{(1)}$ we compute the required value of $F_8^{(1)}$ by simply inverting the function $L_7^{(1)} = g(L_6^{(1)}, F_7^{(1)}, L_7^{(0)}, F_8^{(1)})$ and get for $F_8^{(1)} = (L_7^{(1)} \oplus ((L_6^{(1)} + F_7^{(1)}) \ggg 1)) - L_7^{(0)}$.
6. We can generate this required value of $F_8^{(1)}$ by modifying m_8 in $F_8^{(1)} = f(F_7^{(1)}, L_8^{(0)}, m_8, C_8)$ using basic message modification with a complexity of about 2^6 calls to f.
7. The modification of m_8 and $F_8^{(1)}$ leads to new values in the internal chaining variables starting from $F_9^{(1)}$. Note that $L_7^{(1)} = g(L_6^{(1)}, F_7^{(1)}, L_7^{(0)}, F_8^{(1)})$ depends only on $L_6^{(1)}$ and values prior to $F_8^{(1)}$. To guarantee that $L_7^{(1)}$ does not get changed again, it is sufficient to require that $F_{15}^{(1)}$ does not change.
8. We can ensure this by adjusting the message word m_{15} such that $F_{15}^{(1)}$ has the same value as prior to the modification of m_8. Then, the values $L_0^{(1)}, \ldots, L_7^{(1)}$ do not change and the conditions on $L_7^{(1)}$ stay fulfilled. This modification of m_{15} has again a complexity of about 2^6 calls to f.

9. The conditions on $F_6^{(2)}$ and on the internal chaining variable of round 3 and 4 can be fulfill by randomly choosing message words $m_9, \ldots, m_{14}$. We ensure the conditions on $L_7^{(1)}$ by modifying m_{15} again. Note that we have enough degrees of freedom in these 6 message words to fulfill these remaining $15 + 47 + 47 = 109$ conditions by brute-force.

These message modification techniques improve the attack complexity significantly. By performing the collision search as described above we can construct collisions for LAKE reduced to 4 rounds with an overall complexity of about 2^{109} compression function evaluations. Note that the complexity can actually be smaller if early stopping techniques are used. By applying more advanced message modification techniques we expect to be able to break up to 5 rounds of LAKE.

5   Conclusion

In this paper we have presented the first cryptanalytic results on the hash function family LAKE. We have shown how collision attacks, exploiting inner collisions in the nonlinear functions of LAKE, can be mounted on reduced variants of the hash function. We have presented an efficient attack on LAKE reduced to 3 (out of 8) rounds. Moreover, we have shown a theoretical attack on LAKE reduced to 4 rounds with a complexity of 2^{109}. We expect that our attack can also be extended to LAKE reduced to 5 rounds by using more sophisticated message modification techniques. Note that the same strategy can be used to attack LAKE-512 as well. For the moment our approach does not appear to be applicable to the full hash function.

However, this does not prove that the hash function is secure. Further analysis is required to get a good view on the security margins of LAKE. In our analysis we have shown that the security of LAKE strongly depends on the choice of the constants. Due to a weak combination of constants, attacks on round-reduced versions of LAKE are possible. Further, we note that the non-bijectiveness regarding the chaining variables can be used to cancel differences in the internal chaining variables as well. To prevent our attack we suggest to design internal compression functions which are bijective and thus, invertible regarding the message words and each chaining variable. Further, the security of these functions should not depend on the (good) choice of the used constants.

Acknowledgments

We thank the authors of LAKE for sending us a preliminary version of their paper and for helpful discussions.

References

1. Aumasson, J.-P.: The Hash Function Family LAKE. FSE talk (2008),
   http://fse2008.epfl.ch/docs/slides/day_1_sess_3/
   aumasson%20lake_slides.pdf

2. Aumasson, J.-P., Meier, W., Phan, R.C.-W.: The Hash Function Family LAKE. In: Nyberg, K. (ed.) FSE. LNCS. Springer, Heidelberg (to appear, 2008)

3. Biham, E., Dunkelman, O.: A Framework for Iterative Hash Functions - HAIFA. Cryptology ePrint Archive, Report 2007/278 (2007), http://eprint.iacr.org

4. De Cannière, C., Mendel, F., Rechberger, C.: Collisions for 70-Step SHA-1: On the Full Cost of Collision Search. In: Adams, C.M., Miri, A., Wiener, M.J. (eds.) SAC 2007. LNCS, vol. 4876, pp. 56–73. Springer, Heidelberg (2007)

5. De Cannière, C., Rechberger, C.: Finding SHA-1 Characteristics: General Results and Applications. In: Lai, X., Chen, K. (eds.) ASIACRYPT 2006. LNCS, vol. 4284, pp. 1–20. Springer, Heidelberg (2006)

6. Daum, M.: Cryptanalysis of Hash Functions of the MD4-Family. PhD thesis, Ruhr-Universität Bochum (May 2005)

7. Lucks, S.: Design Principles for Iterated Hash Functions. Cryptology ePrint Archive, Report 2004/253 (2004), http://eprint.iacr.org

8. Lucks, S.: A Failure-Friendly Design Principle for Hash Functions. In: Roy, B. (ed.) ASIACRYPT 2005. LNCS, vol. 3788, pp. 474–494. Springer, Heidelberg (2005)

9. National Institute of Standards and Technology (NIST). Cryptographic Hash Project (2007), http://www.nist.gov/hash-competition

10. Schläffer, M., Oswald, E.: Searching for Differential Paths in MD4. In: Robshaw, M.J.B. (ed.) FSE 2006. LNCS, vol. 4047, pp. 242–261. Springer, Heidelberg (2006)

11. Wang, X., Lai, X., Feng, D., Chen, H., Yu, X.: Cryptanalysis of the Hash Functions MD4 and RIPEMD. In: Cramer, R.J.F. (ed.) EUROCRYPT 2005. LNCS, vol. 3494, pp. 1–18. Springer, Heidelberg (2005)

12. Wang, X., Yin, Y.L., Yu, H.: Finding Collisions in the Full SHA-1. In: Galbraith, S.D. (ed.) Cryptography and Coding 2007. LNCS, vol. 4887, pp. 17–36. Springer, Heidelberg (2007)

13. Wang, X., Yu, H.: How to Break MD5 and Other Hash Functions. In: Cramer, R.J.F. (ed.) EUROCRYPT 2005. LNCS, vol. 3494, pp. 19–35. Springer, Heidelberg (2005)

A   Advanced Message Modification

The step update functions f and g for the first two rounds of LAKE. The internal chaining variables on which we impose conditions for the attack on 4 rounds of LAKE are underlined.

A.1   Round 1

$$F_0^{(1)} = f(L_{15}^{(0)}, L_0^{(0)}, m_0, C_0) \qquad L_0^{(1)} = g(F_{15}^{(1)}, F_0^{(1)}, L_0^{(0)}, F_1^{(1)}) \qquad (10)$$

$$F_1^{(1)} = f(F_0^{(1)}, L_1^{(0)}, m_1, C_1) \qquad L_1^{(1)} = g(L_0^{(1)}, F_1^{(1)}, L_1^{(0)}, F_2^{(1)}) \qquad (11)$$

$$F_2^{(1)} = f(F_1^{(1)}, L_2^{(0)}, m_2, C_2) \qquad L_2^{(1)} = g(L_1^{(1)}, F_2^{(1)}, L_2^{(0)}, \underline{F_3^{(1)}}) \qquad (12)$$

$$\underline{F_3^{(1)}} = f(F_2^{(1)}, L_3^{(0)}, m_3, C_3) \qquad L_3^{(1)} = g(L_2^{(1)}, \underline{F_3^{(1)}}, L_3^{(0)}, F_4^{(1)}) \qquad (13)$$

$$F_4^{(1)} = f(\underline{F_3^{(1)}}, \underline{L_4^{(0)}}, m_4, C_4) \qquad L_4^{(1)} = g(L_3^{(1)}, F_4^{(1)}, \underline{L_4^{(0)}}, F_5^{(1)}) \qquad (14)$$

$$F_5^{(1)} = f(F_4^{(1)}, L_5^{(0)}, m_5, C_5) \qquad L_5^{(1)} = g(L_4^{(1)}, F_5^{(1)}, L_5^{(0)}, F_6^{(1)}) \qquad (15)$$

$$F_6^{(1)} = f(F_5^{(1)}, L_6^{(0)}, m_6, C_6) \qquad L_6^{(1)} = g(L_5^{(1)}, F_6^{(1)}, L_6^{(0)}, F_7^{(1)}) \qquad (16)$$

$$F_7^{(1)} = f(F_6^{(1)}, L_7^{(0)}, m_7, C_7) \qquad \underline{L_7^{(1)}} = g(L_6^{(1)}, F_7^{(1)}, L_7^{(0)}, F_8^{(1)}) \qquad (17)$$

$$F_8^{(1)} = f(F_7^{(1)}, L_8^{(0)}, m_8, C_8) \qquad L_8^{(1)} = g(\underline{L_7^{(1)}}, F_8^{(1)}, L_8^{(0)}, F_9^{(1)}) \qquad (18)$$

$$F_9^{(1)} = f(F_8^{(1)}, L_9^{(0)}, m_9, C_9) \qquad L_9^{(1)} = g(L_8^{(1)}, F_9^{(1)}, L_9^{(0)}, F_{10}^{(1)}) \qquad (19)$$

$$F_{10}^{(1)} = f(F_9^{(1)}, L_{10}^{(0)}, m_{10}, C_{10}) \qquad L_{10}^{(1)} = g(L_9^{(1)}, F_{10}^{(1)}, L_{10}^{(0)}, F_{11}^{(1)}) \qquad (20)$$

$$F_{11}^{(1)} = f(F_{10}^{(1)}, L_{11}^{(0)}, m_{11}, C_{11}) \qquad L_{11}^{(1)} = g(L_{10}^{(1)}, F_{11}^{(1)}, L_{11}^{(0)}, F_{12}^{(1)}) \qquad (21)$$

$$F_{12}^{(1)} = f(F_{11}^{(1)}, L_{12}^{(0)}, m_{12}, C_{12}) \qquad L_{12}^{(1)} = g(L_{11}^{(1)}, F_{12}^{(1)}, L_{12}^{(0)}, F_{13}^{(1)}) \qquad (22)$$

$$F_{13}^{(1)} = f(F_{12}^{(1)}, L_{13}^{(0)}, m_{13}, C_{13}) \qquad L_{13}^{(1)} = g(L_{12}^{(1)}, F_{13}^{(1)}, L_{13}^{(0)}, F_{14}^{(1)}) \qquad (23)$$

$$F_{14}^{(1)} = f(F_{13}^{(1)}, L_{14}^{(0)}, m_{14}, C_{14}) \qquad L_{14}^{(1)} = g(L_{13}^{(1)}, F_{14}^{(1)}, L_{14}^{(0)}, F_{15}^{(1)}) \qquad (24)$$

$$F_{15}^{(1)} = f(F_{14}^{(1)}, L_{15}^{(0)}, m_{15}, C_{15}) \qquad L_{15}^{(1)} = g(L_{14}^{(1)}, F_{15}^{(1)}, L_{15}^{(0)}, L_0^{(1)}) \qquad (25)$$

A.2   Round 2

$$F_0^{(2)} = f(L_{15}^{(1)}, L_0^{(1)}, m_1, C_0) \qquad L_0^{(2)} = g(F_{15}^{(2)}, F_0^{(2)}, L_0^{(1)}, F_1^{(2)}) \qquad (26)$$

$$F_1^{(2)} = f(F_0^{(2)}, L_1^{(1)}, m_6, C_1) \qquad L_1^{(2)} = g(L_0^{(2)}, F_1^{(2)}, L_1^{(1)}, F_2^{(2)}) \qquad (27)$$

$$F_2^{(2)} = f(F_1^{(2)}, L_2^{(1)}, m_{11}, C_2) \qquad L_2^{(2)} = g(L_1^{(2)}, F_2^{(2)}, L_2^{(1)}, F_3^{(2)}) \qquad (28)$$

$$F_3^{(2)} = f(F_2^{(2)}, L_3^{(1)}, m_0, C_3) \qquad L_3^{(2)} = g(L_2^{(2)}, F_3^{(2)}, L_3^{(1)}, F_4^{(2)}) \qquad (29)$$

$$F_4^{(2)} = f(F_3^{(2)}, L_4^{(1)}, m_5, C_4) \qquad L_4^{(2)} = g(L_3^{(2)}, F_4^{(2)}, L_4^{(1)}, F_5^{(2)}) \qquad (30)$$

$$F_5^{(2)} = f(F_4^{(2)}, L_5^{(1)}, m_{10}, C_5) \qquad \underline{L_5^{(2)}} = g(L_4^{(2)}, F_5^{(2)}, L_5^{(1)}, \underline{F_6^{(2)}}) \qquad (31)$$

$$\underline{F_6^{(2)}} = f(F_5^{(2)}, L_6^{(1)}, m_{15}, C_6) \qquad L_6^{(2)} = g(\underline{L_5^{(2)}}, \underline{F_6^{(2)}}, L_6^{(1)}, F_7^{(2)}) \qquad (32)$$

$$F_7^{(2)} = f(\underline{F_6^{(2)}}, \underline{L_7^{(1)}}, m_4, C_7) \qquad L_7^{(2)} = g(L_6^{(2)}, F_7^{(2)}, \underline{L_7^{(1)}}, F_8^{(2)}) \qquad (33)$$

$$F_8^{(2)} = f(F_7^{(2)}, L_8^{(1)}, m_9, C_8) \qquad L_8^{(2)} = g(L_7^{(2)}, F_8^{(2)}, L_8^{(1)}, F_9^{(2)}) \qquad (34)$$

$$F_9^{(2)} = f(F_8^{(2)}, L_9^{(1)}, m_{14}, C_9) \qquad L_9^{(2)} = g(L_8^{(2)}, F_9^{(2)}, L_9^{(1)}, F_{10}^{(2)}) \qquad (35)$$

$$F_{10}^{(2)} = f(F_9^{(2)}, L_{10}^{(1)}, m_3, C_{10}) \qquad L_{10}^{(2)} = g(L_9^{(2)}, F_{10}^{(2)}, L_{10}^{(1)}, F_{11}^{(2)}) \qquad (36)$$

$$F_{11}^{(2)} = f(F_{10}^{(2)}, L_{11}^{(1)}, m_8, C_{11}) \qquad L_{11}^{(2)} = g(L_{10}^{(2)}, F_{11}^{(2)}, L_{11}^{(1)}, F_{12}^{(2)}) \qquad (37)$$

$$F_{12}^{(2)} = f(F_{11}^{(2)}, L_{12}^{(1)}, m_{13}, C_{12}) \qquad L_{12}^{(2)} = g(L_{11}^{(2)}, F_{12}^{(2)}, L_{12}^{(1)}, F_{13}^{(2)}) \qquad (38)$$

$$F_{13}^{(2)} = f(F_{12}^{(2)}, L_{13}^{(1)}, m_2, C_{13}) \qquad L_{13}^{(2)} = g(L_{12}^{(2)}, F_{13}^{(2)}, L_{13}^{(1)}, F_{14}^{(2)}) \qquad (39)$$

$$F_{14}^{(2)} = f(F_{13}^{(2)}, L_{14}^{(1)}, m_7, C_{14}) \qquad L_{14}^{(2)} = g(L_{13}^{(2)}, F_{14}^{(2)}, L_{14}^{(1)}, F_{15}^{(2)}) \qquad (40)$$

$$F_{15}^{(2)} = f(F_{14}^{(2)}, L_{15}^{(1)}, m_{12}, C_{15}) \qquad L_{15}^{(2)} = g(L_{14}^{(2)}, F_{15}^{(2)}, L_{15}^{(1)}, L_0^{(2)}) \qquad (41)$$

Preimage Attacks on Step-Reduced MD5

Yu Sasaki and Kazumaro Aoki

NTT Information Sharing Platform Laboratories,
NTT Corporation 3-9-11 Midoricho, Musashino-shi, Tokyo, 180-8585, Japan
sasaki.yu@lab.ntt.co.jp

Abstract. In this paper, we propose preimage attacks on step-reduced MD5. We show that a preimage of a 44-step MD5 can be computed to a complexity of 2^{96}. We also consider a preimage attack against variants of MD5 where the round order is modified from the real MD5. In such a case, a preimage of a 51-step round-reordered MD5 can be computed to a complexity of 2^{96}. Our attack uses "local collisions" of MD5 to create a degree of message freedom. This freedom enables us to match the two 128-bit intermediate values efficiently.

Keywords: Preimage Attack, One-Way, MD5, Hash Function, Message Expansion, Local Collision.

1 Introduction

Hash functions are cryptographic primitives that compress arbitrary length messages into n-bit hash values. Hash functions are used in many protocols, so their security is important. For hash function H, there are three important properties.

Preimage Resistance: For given y, it must be computationally hard to find x such that $H(x) = y$.
Second Preimage Resistance: For given x, it must be computationally hard to find x' such that $H(x) = H(x')$, $x \neq x'$.
Collision Resistance: It must be computationally hard to find a pair of (x, x') such that $H(x) = H(x')$, $x \neq x'$.

Because hash values are n-bit, computing a hash value of 2^n input messages should produce y. Due to this, any method to find a preimage of a given hash value faster than 2^n computations is a threat for hash functions. Such methods are called preimage attacks. More formal definitions of these properties are introduced by [17].

MD5 [16] is a hash function that is designed to be highly efficient in terms of computation time. It is used in a huge number of protocols all over the world, so a security analysis of it is interesting from both an academic and an industrial position. So far, many pseudo-collision attacks [3, 6, 7] and collision attacks [2, 9, 13, 18, 19] (the complexity of the best one being 2^{23} MD5 computations) have been proposed. However, no attack has succeeded in breaking the second preimage resistance or preimage resistance of MD5.

Y. Mu, W. Susilo, and J. Seberry (Eds.): ACISP 2008, LNCS 5107, pp. 282–296, 2008.

There are some papers in which preimage attacks are proposed. Regarding MD2, Muller proposed a preimage attack [15] and Knudsen and Mathiassen improved its result [10]. Dobbertin proposed a preimage attack against the step-reduced version of MD4 in 1998 [5]. Let a hash function that consists of round i and j of MD-x be $MDx^{(ij)}$. This attack can find a preimage of $MD4^{(12)}$. There are claims that $MD4^{(23)}$ can also be attacked by a similar approach. In 2000, Kuwakado and Tanaka proposed a preimage attack against a variant of MD4 where the round order is modified, $MD4^{(13)}$ [11]. In 2007, De et al. showed that a preimage of the first 39 steps of MD4 could be found in less than 8 hours [4]. In 2008, Leurent proposed the first preimage attack against the full MD4 [12], which has a complexity of 2^{102} MD4 computations. Regarding MD5, in 2007, De et al. also showed that the first 26 steps of MD5 were invertible [4]. To the best of our knowledge, no other preimage attack is known against MD5 or variants of MD5.

Our Contribution

In this paper, we propose preimage attacks against variants of MD5.

First, we show a preimage attack against 51 steps of round-reordered MD5 (steps 7-57 of $MD5^{(1133)}$), which has a complexity of 2^{96}. Second, we show a preimage attack against 44 steps of the real MD5 (steps 3-47 of MD5), which has a complexity of 2^{96}. A comparison of our results and previously published results is shown in Table 1[1].

Table 1. Previous preimage attacks against MD-family and our new results

Target		Attack	Number of steps	Complexity
MD4	MD4	[5]	32	2^{32}
(Total 48 steps)	$MD4^{(13)}$	[11]	32	2^{32}
	MD4	[4]	39	Not given (8 hours)
	MD4	[12]	48 (Full)	2^{102}
MD5	MD5	[4]	26	Not given
(Total 64 steps)	MD5	Our result	44	2^{96}
	$MD5^{(1133)}$	Our result	51	2^{96}

Similar to the previous preimage attacks against MD4, our attacks analyze the behaviors of intermediate chaining variables word-by-word not bit-by-bit. However, our attacks use a local-collision approach, which has been considered bit-by-bit in many collision attacks. By using local collision, we create message freedom, and this freedom enables us to match the two 128-bit intermediate values efficiently. We also analyze the message expansion and determine the implications on hash function design by analyzing the strong and weak message expansions against our attacks.

---

[1] Very recently, Aumasson et al. proposed a preimage attack against the first 47 steps of MD5 [1].

Our attacks can find preimages for any hash value, IV, and message length. By using these properties, the following attacks can be constructed.

1. For any message m and hash value h, we can find a message x such that MD5$(m||x) = h$.
2. Let a value of multi-collision be MC. (The multi-collision attacks proposed by Joux [8] or Yu and Wang [20] can generate multi-collisions.) By finding a preimage that starts from MC and ends with h, many preimages can be generated by computing one preimage.

This paper is organized as follows. Section 2 explains the specifications of MD5. In section 3, we describe the previous preimage attack against MD4 and why it is difficult to apply to MD5. In section 4, we propose a preimage attack against 51 steps of the round-reordered MD5 and determine the implications on hash function design by analyzing the strong and weak message expansion structures against our attack. In section 5, we propose a preimage attack against 44 steps of the real MD5. In section 6, we conclude this paper.

2 Description of MD5

MD5 [16] uses a Merkle-Damgård structure, which takes an arbitrary length message M as input and outputs a 128-bit hash value $H(M)$. First, M is padded to be a multiple of a 512-bit length. In the padding process, first a single bit '1' is added to M. Then, '0's are added until the message length reaches 448 mod 512. Finally, the original message length is added into the last 64 bits.

The padded message is divided into 512-bit block messages $(M_0, M_1, \cdots, M_{n-1})$. These messages go through a compression function (CF) with a 128-bit chaining variable. The initial chaining variable (H_0) is set as follows:
$a_0 = $ 0x67452301, $b_0 = $ 0xefcdab89, $c_0 = $ 0x98badcfe, $d_0 = $ 0x10325476.
The procedure of the MD5 algorithm is as follows:
$H_1 = CF(M_0, H_0)$, $H_2 = CF(M_1, H_1)$, $\cdots$, $H_n = CF(M_{n-1}, H_{n-1})$.
Finally, H_n is output as the hash value of M.

MD5 Compression Function

The compression function of MD5 takes M_i and H_i as input and outputs H_{i+1}. First, the message block M_i is divided into sixteen 32-bit length messages $(m_0, m_1, \cdots, m_{15})$. The hash value H_i is divided into four 32-bit length chaining variables $(Q_{-4}, Q_{-1}, Q_{-2}, Q_{-3})$. The compression function consists of 64 steps. Steps 0-15, steps 16-31, steps 32-47, and steps 48-63 are called the first, second, third and fourth rounds. In step j, the chaining variables Q_j are updated by the step-update expression:

$$Q_j = Q_{j-1} + (Q_{j-4} + \Phi_j(Q_{j-1}, Q_{j-2}, Q_{j-3}) + m_{\pi(j)} + k_j) \lll s_j.$$

Hereafter, '+' denotes the addition on modulo 2^{32}. Similarly, we use '−' to denote the subtraction on modulo 2^{32}. Φ_j and $\pi(j)$ are defined in Table 2. k_j is

Table 2. Boolean functions and message expansion of MD5

$0 \le j \le 15$	$\Phi_j(X, Y, Z) = (X \wedge Y) \vee (\neg X \wedge Z)$
$16 \le j \le 31$	$\Phi_j(X, Y, Z) = (X \wedge Z) \vee (Y \wedge \neg Z)$
$32 \le j \le 47$	$\Phi_j(X, Y, Z) = X \oplus Y \oplus Z$
$48 \le j \le 63$	$\Phi_j(X, Y, Z) = Y \oplus (X \vee \neg Z)$
$\pi(0) \cdots \pi(15)$	0, 1, 2, 3, 4, 5, 6, 7, 8, 9, 10, 11, 12, 13, 14, 15
$\pi(16) \cdots \pi(31)$	1, 6, 11, 0, 5, 10, 15, 4, 9, 14, 3, 8, 13, 2, 7, 12
$\pi(32) \cdots \pi(47)$	5, 8, 11, 14, 1, 4, 7, 10, 13, 0, 3, 6, 9, 12, 15, 2
$\pi(48) \cdots \pi(63)$	0, 7, 14, 5, 12, 3, 10, 1, 8, 15, 6, 13, 4, 11, 2, 9

a constant value defined in each step, and $\lll s_j$ denotes the left rotation by s_j bits. The value of s_j is defined in each step. Because our attacks work for any k_j and s_j, we omit their description. Finally, the compression function outputs the following values:

$$H_{i+1} = (h_0, h_1, h_2, h_3) = (Q_{-4} + Q_{60}, Q_{-1} + Q_{63}, Q_{-2} + Q_{62}, Q_{-3} + Q_{61}).$$

3 Related Work

In this section, we briefly describe the preimage attack against MD4 proposed by Leurent [12] and explain why this attack is difficult to apply to MD5.

3.1 Summary of Differences between MD4 and MD5

Before we explain the preimage attack against MD4, we will clarify the differences between MD4 and MD5.

- The compression function of MD4 consists of 3 rounds (48 steps).
- The step-update expression in step j is
  $$Q_j = (Q_{j-4} + \Phi_j(Q_{j-1}, Q_{j-2}, Q_{j-3}) + m_{\pi(j)} + k_j) \lll s_j.$$
  Note that Q_{j-1} is only used in Φ_j, while it is directly added in MD5. Graphs of step-update expressions of MD4 and MD5 are shown in Fig. 1. MD5 has an addition shown by the bold arrow.
- The Boolean function Φ_j and the values of $\pi(j), k_j$, and s_j are different.

3.2 Converting Pseudo-Preimage Attack to Preimage Attack

For a given hash value y, pseudo-preimage is a pair of $(M, x), x \ne IV$ such that $CF(M, x) = y$. There is a generic approach to constructing a preimage attack from a pseudo-preimage attack [14, Fact 9.99]. Assume there is an attack that finds a pseudo-preimage of a target hash value with a complexity of 2^k. If we generate $2^{(n-k)/2}$ pseudo-preimages by this attack and take hash values of $2^{(n+k)/2}$ random messages that start from the IV, we can expect that one of these hash values will be matched with high probability by the birthday paradox. The complexity is $2^{1+(n+k)/2}$. Therefore, a pseudo-preimage attack with a complexity less than 2^{n-2} can be converted to a preimage attack.

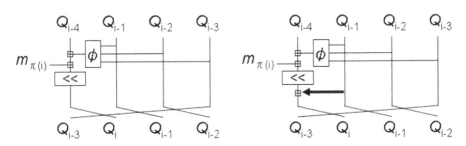

Fig. 1. Step-update expressions of MD4 (left) and MD5 (right)

3.3   Previous Preimage Attack on MD4

At FSE 2008, Leurent proposed a preimage attack against MD4 [12]. In this attack, message freedom in a late step in the third round is necessary for generating a desired hash value. However, because of the message expansion structure, modifying a message in the third round always changes the value of a message in the first and second rounds. Therefore, it is necessary to cancel these changes in the first and second rounds by constructing a differential path such that any selection of a m_i in the third round can be accepted.

The key to this preimage attack is the construction of the differential path. There are several techniques for this.

- In the first round, the change of a message is cancelled by changing the initial value to guarantee that the other chaining variables in the first round are left unchanged. Because the initial value is used only in the first 4 steps of the first round, only $m_{\pi(0)}, m_{\pi(1)}, m_{\pi(2)}$, and $m_{\pi(3)}$ can be changed.
- In the second round, a differential path has been constructed in advance so that the propagation of changes of messages in the second round corresponding to $m_{\pi(0)}, m_{\pi(1)}, m_{\pi(2)}$, and $m_{\pi(3)}$ can be controlled. To achieve such a situation, the absorption properties of Φ_j explained below, are appropriately used.

Absorption Properties of Φ_j

Φ_0 to Φ_{31} of MD4 have an absorption property, namely, the output of Φ_j can be kept unchanged even if one input element of Φ_j is changed. To check the absorption properties of MD4, please refer to [12]. We show the absorption properties of Φ_j of MD5 in Table 3. Here, **0** represents 0x00000000, **1** represents 0xffffffff, and **C** represents a constant.

Table 3. Absorption properties of Φ_j of MD5

	Absorb 1st input	Absorb 2nd input	Absorb 3rd input
$0 \leq j \leq 15$	$\Phi_j(x, \mathbf{C}, \mathbf{C}) = \mathbf{C}$	$\Phi_j(\mathbf{0}, x, \mathbf{C}) = \mathbf{C}$	$\Phi_j(\mathbf{1}, \mathbf{C}, x) = \mathbf{C}$
$16 \leq j \leq 31$	$\Phi_j(x, \mathbf{C}, \mathbf{0}) = \mathbf{C}$	$\Phi_j(\mathbf{C}, x, \mathbf{1}) = \mathbf{C}$	$\Phi_j(\mathbf{C}, \mathbf{C}, x) = \mathbf{C}$
$32 \leq j \leq 47$	-	-	-
$48 \leq j \leq 63$	$\Phi_j(x, \mathbf{C}, \mathbf{0}) = \mathbf{C}$	-	$\Phi_j(\mathbf{1}, \mathbf{C}, x) = \mathbf{C}$

3.4 Difficulties of Applying Previous Attack to MD5

MD5 consists of 64 steps, which is 16 steps longer than MD4. Therefore, finding preimage attacks on MD5 seems harder than that on MD4. However, even if we do not consider the increased number of steps, the construction of MD5 seems to be harder than that of MD4.

As explained in section 3.3, the key point of the previous preimage attack is the construction of a differential path in the second round. In the attack by Leurent, only messages corresponding to $m_{\pi(0)}, m_{\pi(1)}, m_{\pi(2)}$ and $m_{\pi(3)}$ can be changed. Fortunately, a very good differential path in the second round can be constructed by only using these four messages. However, the same strategy does not seem to be applicable to MD5 for the following reasons.

- In the step-update expression of MD5, Q_{i-1} is directly added to Q_i (Fig. 1). Therefore, to cancel the change of Q_{i-1}, we need to change a message. (In MD4, the change of Q_{i-1} can be absorbed by only the absorption property of Φ_i.) This makes the construction of a differential path harder than in MD4.
- Φ_j of MD5 in round 4, which is not used in MD4, does not have an absorption property when the second input element is changed as shown in Table 3. This makes the control of values harder than in MD4.
- The message expansion of MD5 is different from MD4. Therefore, constructing an efficient differential path in the second round by using only messages corresponding to $m_{\pi(0)}, m_{\pi(1)}, m_{\pi(2)}$, and $m_{\pi(3)}$ is hard.

4 A Preimage Attack Against 51 Steps of MD5$^{(1133)}$

As explained in section 3, the previous attack against MD4 cannot be directly applied to MD5. One reason is the structure of the MD5 message expansion. However, which message expansion is strong has not been well-analyzed. In this section, we propose an attack against modified MD5 whose message expansion is weak. Then, in the next section, we consider applying it to the real MD5.

We found that 51 steps of an MD5 variant, where the round order is modified to MD5$^{(1133)}$, does not have preimage resistance. We confirmed that this round order is the weakest as long as our strategy is used. We also show the strong round orders, and determine some implications on hash function design.

4.1 Outline of Our Attack

We considered the reduced MD5$^{(1133)}$ that starts from step 7 and ends at step 57. The outline of our attack is given below. The message expansion of MD5$^{(1133)}$ is shown in Fig. 2 and the schematic explanation in Fig. 3.

1. We focused on (m_2, m_3, m_6), which can form a local collision in the second round. We call these messages *Local-Collision Messages*, steps where the local collision is inserted *Local Collision Part*, and steps where the local-collision messages are used in the third round *Matching Part*.

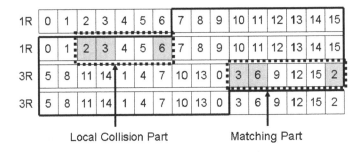

Fig. 2. Message expansion of MD5$^{(1133)}$

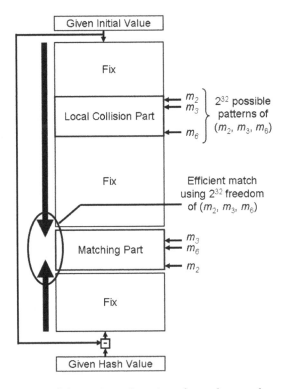

Fig. 3. Schematic explanation of attack procedure

2. Randomly determine all messages except for the local-collision messages.
3. Compute chaining variables from the initial value to the matching part.
4. From a given IV and hash value, compute chaining variables in the last step.
5. Inversely compute chaining variables from the last step to the matching part.
6. Both input and output chaining variables of the matching part (128 bits) are now fixed. In the matching part, because the local-collision messages have 2^{32} freedom, 32 bits out of 128 bits can be matched with a probability of 1. Therefore, the 128 bits are matched with a probability of 2^{-96}.

The first seven and last six steps are excluded from the attack target (Fig. 2). Therefore, m_2, m_3, and m_6 appear only twice. A local collision can be formed for any m_2, so there is 32-bit freedom in (m_2, m_3, m_6).

4.2   Detailed Procedure of Preimage Attack

First, we strictly define a modified MD5. We rewrite steps 7-57 in Fig. 2 to steps 0-50. This is shown in Fig. 4. This means $\pi(0)$ to $\pi(50)$ of the modified MD5 are shown in Fig. 4.

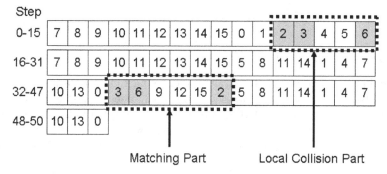

Fig. 4. Message expansion of modified MD5

We also rewrite Φ_j as follows.

$$0 \leq j \leq 8 : \Phi_j(X, Y, Z) = (X \wedge Y) \vee (\neg X \wedge Z),$$
$$9 \leq j \leq 24 : \Phi_j(X, Y, Z) = (X \wedge Y) \vee (\neg X \wedge Z),$$
$$25 \leq j \leq 40 : \Phi_j(X, Y, Z) = X \oplus Y \oplus Z,$$
$$41 \leq j \leq 50 : \Phi_j(X, Y, Z) = X \oplus Y \oplus Z.$$

s_j and $k_j, (0 \leq j \leq 50)$ of the modified MD5 are s_{j+7} and k_{j+7} of the real MD5. We use the same IV and padding rule as the real MD5. The final output is computed as follows: $H_{i+1} = (h_0, h_1, h_2, h_3) = (Q_{-4} + Q_{47}, \ Q_{-1} + Q_{50}, \ Q_{-2} + Q_{49}, \ Q_{-3} + Q_{48})$.

The attack procedure is as follows.

1. Randomly determine the values of $Q_0, \ldots, Q_5$.
2. Determine the values of $m_{13}, \ldots, m_{15}$ to satisfy MD5 message padding.
3. Compute $Q_6, \ldots, Q_8$ by the step-update expression.
4. Randomly determine the values of Q_9, Q_{10}, Q_{14}, and Q_{15}.
5. To make $\Phi_{13}(Q_{12}, Q_{11}, Q_{10})$ independent of Q_{11}, we use the absorption property of Φ_{13}. Therefore, we set Q_{12} to be 0x00000000.
6. Similarly, to make $\Phi_{14}(Q_{13}, Q_{12}, Q_{11})$ independent of Q_{11}, we set Q_{13} to be 0xffffffff.
7. For $j = 0, \ldots, 5, 9, 10, 13, 14$, compute $m_{\pi(j)}$ by the following equation:
$$m_{\pi(j)} = ((Q_j - Q_{j-1}) \ggg s_j) - Q_{j-4} - \Phi_j(Q_{j-1}, Q_{j-2}, Q_{j-3}) - k_j.$$

8. Compute $Q_{16}, \ldots, Q_{34}$ by the step-update expression.
9. Compute $Q_{47}, \ldots, Q_{50}$ by the following equations:
   $$Q_{47} = h_0 - Q_{-4}, \; Q_{50} = h_1 - Q_{-1}, \; Q_{49} = h_2 - Q_{-2}, \; Q_{48} = h_3 - Q_{-3}.$$
10. Compute $Q_{46}, \ldots, Q_{37}$ by the following equation:
   $$Q_{j-4} = ((Q_j - Q_{j-1}) \ggg s_j) - m_{\pi(j)} - \Phi_j(Q_{j-1}, Q_{j-2}, Q_{j-3}) - k_j.$$
11. Check whether the chaining variables in the matching part are matched by executing the matching method explained in section 4.3. By this method, all chaining variables are matched with a probability of 2^{-96}.
12. If all chaining variables are matched, output $m_0, \ldots, m_{15}$, then halt this algorithm. Otherwise, repeat this procedure from Step 4 or 1.

Steps 4–11 of the above procedure have the dominant complexity 2^{96}.

4.3   Matching Method

The matching method is executed in the matching part. The input is the values of $Q_{31}, \ldots, Q_{34}, Q_{37}, \ldots, Q_{40}$, and $m_{\pi(37)}, \ldots, m_{\pi(39)}$. The purpose is to determine the values of (m_2, m_3, m_6) so that 32 bits out of 128 bits of the chaining variables are matched with a probability of 1 and to check whether the other 96 bits are matched or not. Equations in the matching part are as follows. (Known fixed variables are underlined.)

$$Q_{35} = \underline{Q_{34}} + (\underline{Q_{31}} + (\underline{Q_{34}} \oplus \underline{Q_{33}} \oplus \underline{Q_{32}}) + m_3 + \underline{k_{35}}) \lll \underline{s_{35}} \qquad (1)$$

$$Q_{36} = Q_{35} + (\underline{Q_{32}} + (Q_{35} \oplus \underline{Q_{34}} \oplus \underline{Q_{33}}) + m_6 + \underline{k_{36}}) \lll \underline{s_{36}} \qquad (2)$$

$$Q_{37} = Q_{36} + (\underline{Q_{33}} + (Q_{36} \oplus Q_{35} \oplus \underline{Q_{34}}) + m_{\pi(37)} + \underline{k_{37}}) \lll \underline{s_{37}} \qquad (3)$$

$$\underline{Q_{38}} = Q_{37} + (\underline{Q_{34}} + (Q_{37} \oplus Q_{36} \oplus Q_{35}) + m_{\pi(38)} + \underline{k_{38}}) \lll \underline{s_{38}} \qquad (4)$$

$$\underline{Q_{39}} = \underline{Q_{38}} + (Q_{35} + (\underline{Q_{38}} \oplus Q_{37} \oplus Q_{36}) + m_{\pi(39)} + \underline{k_{39}}) \lll \underline{s_{39}} \qquad (5)$$

$$\underline{Q_{40}} = \underline{Q_{39}} + (Q_{36} + (\underline{Q_{39}} \oplus \underline{Q_{38}} \oplus Q_{37}) + m_2 + \underline{k_{40}}) \lll \underline{s_{40}} \qquad (6)$$

The procedure of the matching method is as follows.

1. Define X as follows:
   $$X = Q_{35} \oplus Q_{36}. \qquad (7)$$
2. From equation 4, compute the value of X:
   $$X = (((Q_{38} - Q_{37}) \ggg s_{38}) - Q_{34} - m_{\pi(38)} - k_{38}) \oplus Q_{37}. \qquad (8)$$
3. From equation 3, compute the value of Q_{36}:
   $$Q_{36} = Q_{37} - ((Q_{33} + (X \oplus Q_{34}) + m_{\pi(37)} + k_{37}) \lll s_{37}). \qquad (9)$$
4. From equation 7, compute the value of Q_{35}:
   $$Q_{35} = X \oplus Q_{36}. \qquad (10)$$
5. From equation 6, compute the value of m_2:
   $$m_2 = ((Q_{40} - Q_{39}) \ggg s_{40}) - Q_{36} - (Q_{39} \oplus Q_{38} \oplus Q_{37}) - k_{40}. \qquad (11)$$

6. From the equations for steps 11, 12, and 15 in the local collision part, compute the values of $Q_{11}, m_3,$ and m_6:

$$Q_{11} = Q_{10} + (Q_7 + \Phi_{11}(Q_{10}, Q_9, Q_8) + m_2 + k_{11}) \lll s_{11}, \qquad (12)$$

$$m_3 = ((Q_{12} - Q_{11}) \ggg s_{12}) - Q_8 - \Phi_{12}(Q_{11}, Q_{10}, Q_9) - k_{12}, \qquad (13)$$

$$m_6 = ((Q_{15} - Q_{14}) \ggg s_{15}) - Q_{11} - \Phi_{15}(Q_{14}, Q_{13}, Q_{12}) - k_{15}. \qquad (14)$$

7. Finally, check whether equations 1, 2, and 5 are correct or not. This succeeds with a probability of 2^{-96}; therefore, the matching method succeeds with a probability of 2^{-96}.

4.4   A Study of Round Orders

The message expansion structure seems to be heavily related to security. However, the strength of the message expansion is not well-analyzed. In this paper, we try all possible round orders of MD5 to detect strong and weak round orders against our attack. The outline is as follows. (Details are shown in Appendix B.)

1. For all possible round orders and selection of local-collision messages, do the followings.
2. Reduce the steps from the first and last steps until all the selected local-collision messages are excluded from the attack target in the first and fourth rounds.
3. The remaining steps are the attack target. If the attack target is long, we say such a round order is weak against our attack. If the attack target is short, the round order is strong.

We denote each round of the original MD5 as "R_1," "R_2," "R_3," and "R_4." Then, we denote each round of the modified MD5 before the step number is reduced as "first round," "second round," "third round," and "fourth round."

As a result of this analysis, we confirmed that MD5$^{(1133)}$ is the weakest round order against our attack[2]. We also found the strong round orders. We show 20 round orders that can be attacked at 35 or 36 steps at most in Table 4.

The number of steps that can be attacked depends on R_i used as the first, second, and fourth rounds. In Table 4, we denote the third round by *, which means any R_i is acceptable.

Table 4. Strong round orders against our preimage attack

Upper-bound of attackable steps	Round order			
35	1-3-*-1,			
36	1-3-*-4,	2-3-*-2,	4-3-*-1,	4-3-*-4

All the strong round orders in Table 4 use R_3 as the second round. This is because making the local collision in R_3 involves more messages than in the other R_i. We show the pattern of local-collision messages in Table 5. As we can

---

[2] Details and other weak round orders are in Appendix C.

Table 5. Local-collision messages for R_i

Round function	Local-collision messages $(0 \le j \le 11)$
R_1	$m_{\pi(j)}, m_{\pi(j+1)}, m_{\pi(j+4)}$
R_2	$m_{\pi(j)}, m_{\pi(j+1)}, m_{\pi(j+4)}$
R_3	$m_{\pi(j)}, m_{\pi(j+1)}, m_{\pi(j+2)}, m_{\pi(j+3)}, m_{\pi(j+4)}$
R_4	$m_{\pi(j)}, m_{\pi(j+1)}, m_{\pi(j+2)}, m_{\pi(j+4)}$

Why these messages form local collisions is explained in Appendix A.

see, the local-collision messages in R_3 involve five messages while the other R_i involve only three or four messages. Therefore, selecting R_3 as the second round can efficiently prevent our attack.

4.5   Implications on Hash Function Design

What we can learn from our analysis is summarized as follows.

– A local collision may damage the one-wayness of hash functions.
– As the number of messages necessary to make the local collision increases, attacking long steps by our approach becomes difficult. In the case of MD5, selecting R_3 as the second round efficiently prevents our attack.
– The number of messages necessary to make the local collision depends on the existence of the absorption property of non-linear functions. Therefore, eliminating the absorption property in the design of non-linear functions is important for preventing this kind of analysis.
– If the absorption property cannot be eliminated, a direct addition from a chaining variable to another can be a solution. In fact, MD5 is harder to analyze than MD4 because of the addition from Q_{i-1} to Q_i.

5   A Preimage Attack Against 44 Steps of MD5

5.1   Selecting Step Number

First, we select the local-collision messages in the second round. The number of steps that can be attacked is maximized (46 steps) when we select m_4, m_9 and m_8 as the local-collision messages. However, in such a case, the matching part becomes too long, and an efficient matching method cannot be constructed. As a consequence, our strategy cannot be efficiently applied to the real MD5.

The other way to construct a preimage attack is to remove the local collision part and use only the matching part. Such an attack needs a message that appears only once in the message expansion. As seen in Table 2, if we take steps 3-46 (total of 44 steps), m_2 will appear only once. By using this property, our attack succeeds with a complexity of 2^{96} reduced-MD5 computations.

5.2   Procedure of Preimage Attack

A reduced MD5 is defined similarly to the modified MD5. The attack procedure is as follows.

1. Randomly determine the values of $m_0, m_1, m_3, \ldots, m_{12}$, and determine $m_{13}, \ldots, m_{15}$ to satisfy MD5 message padding.
2. Compute $Q_0, \ldots, Q_{25}$ by the step-update expression.
3. Compute $Q_{40}, \ldots, Q_{43}$ by the following equations:
   $Q_{40} = h_0 - Q_{-4}, \ Q_{43} = h_1 - Q_{-1}, \ Q_{42} = h_2 - Q_{-2}, \ Q_{41} = h_3 - Q_{-3}.$
4. Compute $Q_{39}, \ldots, Q_{27}$ by the following equation:
   $Q_{j-4} = ((Q_j - Q_{j-1}) \ggg s_j) - m_{\pi(j)} - \Phi_j(Q_{j-1}, Q_{j-2}, Q_{j-3}) - k_j.$
5. Check that all chaining variables in the matching part can be matched by the matching method explained in section 5.3. By this method, all chaining variables are matched with a probability of 2^{-96}.
6. If all chaining variables are matched, output $m_0, \ldots, m_{15}$, then halt this algorithm. Otherwise, repeat this procedure from Step 1.

The above procedure is repeated 2^{96} times, so the complexity is 2^{96}.

5.3   Matching Method

The input of the matching method is the values of $Q_{22}, \ldots, Q_{25}, Q_{27}, \ldots, Q_{30}$ and $m_{\pi(27)}, \ldots, m_{\pi(30)}$. Equations in the matching part are as follows. (Known fixed values are underlined.)

$$Q_{26} = \underline{Q_{25}} + (\underline{Q_{22}} + \Phi_{26}(\underline{Q_{25}}, \underline{Q_{24}}, \underline{Q_{23}}) + m_2 + \underline{k_{26}}) \lll \underline{s_{26}} \tag{15}$$

$$Q_{27} = Q_{26} + (\underline{Q_{23}} + \Phi_{27}(Q_{26}, \underline{Q_{25}}, \underline{Q_{24}}) + \underline{m_{\pi(27)}} + \underline{k_{27}}) \lll \underline{s_{27}} \tag{16}$$

$$\underline{Q_{28}} = Q_{27} + (\underline{Q_{24}} + \Phi_{28}(\underline{Q_{27}}, Q_{26}, \underline{Q_{25}}) + \underline{m_{\pi(28)}} + \underline{k_{28}}) \lll \underline{s_{28}} \tag{17}$$

$$\underline{Q_{29}} = \underline{Q_{28}} + (\underline{Q_{25}} + \Phi_{29}(\underline{Q_{28}}, \underline{Q_{27}}, Q_{26}) + \underline{m_{\pi(29)}} + \underline{k_{29}}) \lll \underline{s_{29}} \tag{18}$$

$$\underline{Q_{30}} = \underline{Q_{29}} + (\underline{Q_{26}} + \Phi_{30}(\underline{Q_{29}}, \underline{Q_{28}}, \underline{Q_{27}}) + \underline{m_{\pi(30)}} + \underline{k_{30}}) \lll \underline{s_{30}} \tag{19}$$

The procedure of the matching method is as follows.

1. From equation 19, compute the value of Q_{26}.
2. From equation 15, compute the value of m_2.
3. Finally, check whether equations 16, 17, and 18 are correct or not. This succeeds with a probability of 2^{-96}.

6   Conclusion

In this paper, we considered preimage attacks against MD5. Our approach applies local collision to construct preimage attacks. As a result, we developed a preimage attack that finds a preimage of 51 steps of MD5$^{(1133)}$ with the complexity 2^{96}. We also proposed a preimage attack against 44 steps of the real MD5. The complexity of this attack is 2^{96}. Our attacks easily satisfy the message padding rule and work for any IV. Finally, we analyzed message expansion, and showed the strong and weak round orders against our attack.

Acknowledgement

We thank Jean-Philippe Aumasson, Willi Meier, and Florian Mendel for informing us of their research result.

References

1. Aumasson, J.-P., Meier, W., Mendel, F.: Preimage Attacks on 3-Pass HAVAL and Step-Reduced MD5. Cryptology ePrint Archive, Report 2008/183, http://eprint.iacr.org/2008/183.pdf
2. Black, J., Cochran, M., Highland, T.: A Study of the MD5 Attacks: Insights and Improvements. In: Robshaw, M.J.B. (ed.) FSE 2006. LNCS, vol. 4047, pp. 262–277. Springer, Heidelberg (2006)
3. den Boer, B., Bosselaers, A.: Collisions for the Compression Function of MD5. In: Helleseth, T. (ed.) EUROCRYPT 1993. LNCS, vol. 765, pp. 293–304. Springer, Heidelberg (1994)
4. De, D., Kumarasubramanian, A., Venkatesan, R.: Inversion Attacks on Secure Hash Functions Using SAT Solvers. In: Marques-Silva, J., Sakallah, K.A. (eds.) SAT 2007. LNCS, vol. 4501, pp. 377–382. Springer, Heidelberg (2007)
5. Dobbertin, H.: The First Two Rounds of MD4 are Not One-Way. In: Vaudenay, S. (ed.) FSE 1998. LNCS, vol. 1372, pp. 284–292. Springer, Heidelberg (1998)
6. Dobbertin, H.: Cryptanalysis of MD5 compress. In: Announcement at the Rump session of Eyrocrypt 1996 (1996)
7. Dobbertin, H.: The Status of MD5 After a Recent Attack. CryptoBytes The technical newsletter of RSA Laboratories, a division of RSA Data Security, Inc. 2(2), Summer 1996 (1996)
8. Joux, A.: Multicollisions in Iterated Hash Functions. Applications to Cascaded Constructions. In: Franklin, M. (ed.) CRYPTO 2004. LNCS, vol. 3152, pp. 306–316. Springer, Heidelberg (2004)
9. Klima, V.: Tunnels in Hash Functions: MD5 Collisions Within a Minute. Cryptology ePrint Archive, Report 2006/105, http://eprint.iacr.org/2006/105.pdf
10. Knudsen, L.R., Mathiassen, J.E.: Preimage and Collision Attacks on MD2. In: Gilbert, H., Handschuh, H. (eds.) FSE 2005. LNCS, vol. 3557, pp. 255–267. Springer, Heidelberg (2005)
11. Kuwakado, H., Tanaka, H.: New Algorithm for Finding Preimages in a Reduced Version of the MD4 Compression Function. IEICE TRANSACTIONS on Fundamentals of Electronics, Communications and Computer Sciences E83-A(1), 97–100 (2000)
12. Leurent, G.: MD4 is Not One-Way. In: Preproceedings of Fast Software Encryption - FSE 2008 (2008)
13. Liang, J., Lai, X.: Improved Collision Attack on Hash Function MD5. Journal of Computer Science and Technology 22(1), 79–87 (2007)
14. Menezes, A.J., van Oorschot, P.C., Vanstone, S.A.: Handbook of applied cryptography. CRC Press, Boca Raton (1997)
15. Muller, F.: The MD2 Hash Function Is Not One-Way. In: Lee, P.J. (ed.) ASIACRYPT 2004. LNCS, vol. 3329, pp. 214–229. Springer, Heidelberg (2004)
16. Rivest, R.L.: The MD5 Message Digest Algorithm. RFC 1321 (April 1992), http://www.ietf.org/rfc/rfc1321.txt

17. Rogaway, P.: Formalizing human ignorance. In: Nguyên, P.Q. (ed.) VIETCRYPT 2006. LNCS, vol. 4341, pp. 211–228. Springer, Heidelberg (2006)
18. Sasaki, Y., Naito, Y., Kunihiro, N., Ohta, K.: Improved Collision Attacks on MD4 and MD5. IEICE Transactions on Fundamentals of Electronics, Communications and Computer Sciences E90-A(1), 36–47 (2007)
19. Wang, X., Yu, H.: How to Break MD5 and Other Hash Functions. In: Cramer, R.J.F. (ed.) EUROCRYPT 2005. LNCS, vol. 3494, pp. 19–25. Springer, Heidelberg (2005)
20. Yu, H., Wang, X.: Multi-collision Attack on the Compression Functions of MD4 and 3-Pass HAVAL. In: Nam, K.-H., Rhee, G. (eds.) ICISC 2007. LNCS, vol. 4817, pp. 206–226. Springer, Heidelberg (2007)

A   Patterns of Local-Collision Messages in Each Round

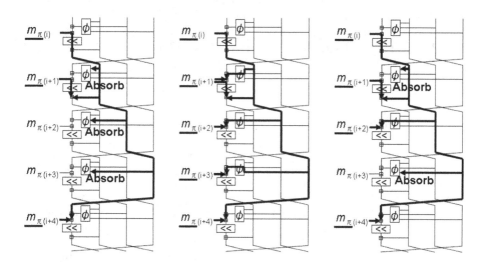

Fig. 5. Patterns of local collision in each round

$$0 \le j \le 15 : \Phi_j(X, Y, Z) = (X \wedge Y) \vee (\neg X \wedge Z),$$
$$16 \le j \le 31 : \Phi_j(X, Y, Z) = (X \wedge Z) \vee (Y \wedge \neg Z),$$
$$32 \le j \le 47 : \Phi_j(X, Y, Z) = X \oplus Y \oplus Z,$$
$$48 \le j \le 63 : \Phi_j(X, Y, Z) = Y \oplus (X \vee \neg Z).$$

The left diagram describes the local collision in the first and second rounds. The center and right describe that in the third and fourth rounds, respectively. In any round, we change $m_{\pi(i+1)}$ and $m_{\pi(i+4)}$ to offset the change of $m_{\pi(i)}$. In the third and fourth rounds, we change $m_{\pi(i+2)}$ and $m_{\pi(i+3)}$ because Φ_j cannot absorb the change. (In step $i + 1$, the change of $m_{\pi(i)}$ can be offset without the absorption properties by modifying $m_{\pi(i+1)}$.)

B   Round Order Search Algorithm

The round order search algorithm searches for strong and weak round orders against our attack. It is as follows.

1. Generate all possible round orders. Because each round has 4 options, $4^4 = 256$ round orders exist.
2. For each round order, consider all possible local-collision messages in the second round. The pattern of local-collision messages for R_i is shown in Table 5. For any R_i, there are 12 options for the local-collision messages. Therefore, consider $256 \times 12 = 3072$ patterns.
3. For each of the 3072 patterns, reduce the steps from the first and last steps until all the local-collision messages are excluded from the first and fourth rounds.
4. Finally, output the number of remaining steps for each of the 3072 patterns.

We coded the above algorithm, then we found the strong and weak round orders against our attack. Strong round orders are discussed in section 4.4. Weak round orders are shown in Table 6 of Appendix C.

C   Weak Round Orders Against Our Preimage Attack

We show weak round orders that may be attacked more than three rounds (48 steps) in Table 6.

Table 6. Weak round orders against our preimage attack

Number of steps where preimage can be found	Round order	Local-collision messages	Range of matching part
51 steps	1-1-1-3	m_2, m_3, m_6	5 steps
	1-1-2-3	m_2, m_3, m_6	13 steps
	1-1-3-3	m_2, m_3, m_6	6 steps
	1-1-4-3	m_2, m_3, m_6	10 steps
50 steps	3-1-1-1	m_{10}, m_{11}, m_{14}	5 steps
	3-1-2-1	m_{10}, m_{11}, m_{14}	8 steps
	3-1-3-1	m_{10}, m_{11}, m_{14}	6 steps
	3-1-4-1	m_{10}, m_{11}, m_{14}	12 steps
49 steps	1-2-1-2	m_3, m_7, m_8	6 steps
	1-2-2-2	m_3, m_7, m_8	5 steps
	1-2-3-2	m_3, m_7, m_8	10 steps
	1-2-4-2	m_3, m_7, m_8	8 steps
49 steps	4-2-1-2	m_3, m_7, m_8	6 steps
	4-2-2-2	m_3, m_7, m_8	5 steps
	4-2-3-2	m_3, m_7, m_8	10 steps
	4-2-4-2	m_3, m_7, m_8	8 steps

From Table 6, we can see that the weakest order may be attacked up to 51 steps. The range of the matching part is important for constructing an efficient matching method. By considering these facts, we decided to use the round order $1R - 1R - 3R - 3R$, and the local-collision messages (m_2, m_3, m_6).

Linear Distinguishing Attack on Shannon

Risto M. Hakala[1] and Kaisa Nyberg[1,2]

[1] Helsinki University of Technology, Finland
[2] Nokia Research Center, Finland
{risto.m.hakala,kaisa.nyberg}@tkk.fi

Abstract. In this paper, we present a linear distinguishing attack on the stream cipher Shannon. Our distinguisher can distinguish the output keystream of Shannon from 2^{107} keystream words while using an array of 2^{32} counters. The distinguisher makes use of a multidimensional linear transformation instead of a one-dimensional transformation, which is traditionally used in linear distinguishing attacks. This gives a clear improvement to the keystream requirement: we need approximately 2^5 times less keystream than when a one-dimensional transform is used.

Keywords: Distinguishing attacks, linear cryptanalysis, stream ciphers, Shannon.

1 Introduction

Stream ciphers are symmetric encryption primitives that are used to ensure confidentiality in digital communication. Compared to block ciphers, stream ciphers are often more efficient and allow a more compact implementation. However, their security has not been on the same level with the most secure block ciphers. Since there does not seem to be any specific reason for this, stream ciphers have started to gain more attention from the cryptographic community. To strengthen the scientific foundations of the security of stream ciphers, the ECRYPT Network of Excellence has launched the eSTREAM project [1], whose main objective is to identify new stream ciphers that might become suitable for wide-spread adoption.

The security of a stream cipher is highly dependent on how random the keystream can be made to appear. To analyze this property, statistical and algebraic distinguishing attacks have been developed. Distinguishing attacks are attacks where the attacker is able to tell whether a sequence has been generated by the keystream generator or not. In linear distinguishing attacks, the attacker tries to find statistical bias in the sequence that is obtained after a linear transform has been applied to the original sequence. In this paper, we present a linear distinguishing attack on the stream cipher Shannon [2]. Shannon is a recently proposed synchronous stream cipher designed by Hawkes et al. [2] of Qualcomm Australia. It has been designed according to PROFILE 1A of the ECRYPT call for stream cipher primitives, and it uses a secret key that may be up to 256 bits in length. In addition to keystream generation, Shannon also offers message

Y. Mu, W. Susilo, and J. Seberry (Eds.): ACISP 2008, LNCS 5107, pp. 297–305, 2008.
© Springer-Verlag Berlin Heidelberg 2008

authentication functionality. However, we consider only the keystream generator part of Shannon in this paper. To our knowledge, there are no publications with cryptographic analysis of Shannon.

Linear distinguishing attacks on stream ciphers are often based on a biased linear combination of keystream bits. In other words, these attacks employ a one-dimensional transform which is applied to the given sequence. In our attack, a multidimensional transform is used instead. We also consider the one-dimensional approach and show that the multidimensional approach significantly reduces the attack complexity. Our distinguisher can distinguish the output keystream of Shannon from approximately 2^{107} keystream words. The one-dimensional distinguishing attack requires approximately 2^{112} keystream words. Similar multidimensional distinguishing attacks have been presented previously, e.g., on SNOW 2.0 by Maximov and Johansson [3] and on Dragon by Englund and Maximov [4]. However, such attacks appear less frequently since the computational effort required for constructing a multidimensional attack is usually far too big for current techniques. In this paper, we use the Walsh-Hadamard transform for efficient computation of the probability distribution related to the multidimensional linear distinguishers. The theoretical basis for multidimensional linear distinguishing attacks has only recently started to take form. In [5], Baignères et al. present several useful results in this direction. Also relevant is the work on multiple linear approximations by Kaliski and Robshaw [6] and by Biryukov et al. [7].

The outline of the paper is as follows. In Sect. 2, we introduce those definitions and notations that are used in the paper. We give a short description of Shannon in Sect. 3. In Sect. 4, we discuss linear distinguishers on a general level. In Sect. 5, we describe our linear distinguisher for Shannon and estimate its complexity. Our conclusions are given in Sect. 6.

2   Preliminaries

Let n be a positive integer. We denote by V_n the n-dimensional binary vector space and use x to denote the n-bit vector $(x[0], \ldots, x[n-1]) \in V_n$. The vectors in V_n are identified with the integers in $\mathbb{Z}_{2^n}$ using the natural correspondence $x \leftrightarrow \sum_{i=0}^{n-1} x[i]2^i$. Addition of vectors in V_n (i.e., the bitwise exclusive-OR) is denoted by $\oplus$. For vectors $u \in V_n$ and $x \in V_n$, we let $u \cdot x$ denote the standard inner product $u \cdot x = u[0]x[0] \oplus \cdots \oplus u[n-1]x[n-1] \in V_1$. The linear function $l_u \colon V_n \to V_1$ is defined by $l_u(x) = u \cdot x$. The circular shift of x to left by a coordinates is denoted by $x \lll a$. We use $\vee$ to denote the bitwise OR of two vectors in V_n.

Let X be a random variable with the sample space V_n. We denote by $P_X(x) = \Pr[X = x]$, for all $x \in V_n$. P_X is called the probability function or the distribution of X. The n-dimensional uniform distribution P_U is a probability distribution such that $P_U(x) = 2^{-n}$, for all $x \in V_n$. For a Bernoulli distributed random variable Y, we call the value

$$\epsilon_Y = P_Y(0) - P_Y(1)$$

the bias of Y. In linear cryptanalysis [8], one commonly studies biases of expressions such as $u \cdot f(X) \oplus v \cdot X$, where $u \in V_m$, $v \in V_n$, and $f: V_n \to V_m$ is a vector-valued Boolean function. The vectors u and v are often called the linear output and input masks, respectively.

2.1 Walsh-Hadamard Transform

Given a real-valued function $f: V_n \to \mathbb{R}$ the Walsh-Hadamard transform of f is defined by

$$\mathcal{F}[f](u) = \sum_{x \in V_n} f(x)(-1)^{u \cdot x}, \quad \text{for all } u \in V_n.$$

The Walsh-Hadamard transform is easily inverted. Given the transform $F(u) = \mathcal{F}[f](u)$, for all $u \in V_n$, the values of f can be determined from the inverse transform:

$$\mathcal{F}^{-1}[F](x) = 2^{-n} \sum_{u \in V_n} F(u)(-1)^{u \cdot x}, \quad \text{for all } x \in V_n.$$

We have $f(x) = \mathcal{F}^{-1}[F](x)$, for all $x \in V_n$. Parseval's theorem for the Walsh-Hadamard transform (see, e.g., [9]) gives us the result

$$\sum_{x \in V_n} f(x)^2 = 2^{-n} \sum_{u \in V_n} F(u)^2.$$

3 Description of Shannon

The keystream generator of Shannon [2] produces a keystream of 32-bit words based on a 256-bit secret key. It is based on a single nonlinear feedback shift register and a nonlinear filter. The state of the shift register at time $t \geq 0$ consists of 16 elements s_{t+i}, $i = 0, \ldots, 15$, from V_{32}. In the specification of Shannon [2], the state update procedure is defined as

$$\begin{cases} s_{t+16} = f_1(s_{t+12} \oplus s_{t+13} \oplus K) \oplus (R_t \lll 1), \\ R_{t+1} = s_{t+1} \oplus f_2(s_{t+3} \oplus s_{t+16}), \end{cases}$$

where $f_1, f_2: V_{32} \to V_{32}$ are nonlinear Boolean functions and $K \in V_{32}$ is a 32-bit secret constant that is derived in the initialization process. The state update procedure can also be written as a single relation:

$$s_{t+16} = f_1(s_{t+12} \oplus s_{t+13} \oplus K) \oplus ((s_t \oplus f_2(s_{t+2} \oplus s_{t+15})) \lll 1). \tag{1}$$

The output z_t at time $t \geq 0$ is given by

$$z_t = s_{t+9} \oplus s_{t+13} \oplus f_2(s_{t+3} \oplus s_{t+16}).$$

The functions f_1 and f_2 are defined by

$$\begin{cases} f_1(x) = g(g(x, 5, 7), 19, 22), \\ f_2(x) = g(g(x, 7, 22), 5, 19), \end{cases}$$

with the function $g \colon V_{32} \times \mathbb{Z} \times \mathbb{Z} \to V_{32}$ defined by

$$g(x, a, b) = x \oplus ((x \lll a) \vee (x \lll b)).$$

Clearly, $g(x \lll c, a, b) = g(x, a, b) \lll c$, for all $1 \le c \le 32$. Hence, $f_i(x \lll c) = f_i(x) \lll c$, for $i = 1, 2$ and $c = 1, \ldots, 32$. The functions f_1 and f_2 are not surjective: according to [2], their ranges cover about 84.74% and 84.34% of the codomain V_{32}, respectively. For further details of Shannon, such as the initialization procedure and message authentication functionality, we refer to the specification [2].

4   Linear Distinguishers

A distinguisher is essentially an implementation of a statistical hypothesis test: a sequence $(x_t)_{t \ge 0}$ over V_n is given as input to the distinguisher and the distinguisher decides whether the input sequence is from a specific cipher or appears to be random. In other words, the distinguisher compares a sampling distribution constructed from the input to the uniform distribution P_U and the distribution P_C that sequences generated by the cipher are estimated to have. The distinguisher should be able to make the decision with high confidence level.

A linear distinguisher is a distinguisher which operates in two phases. In the first phase, a linear transformation is applied to the input sequence $(x_t)_{t \ge 0}$ to get a new sequence $(\hat{x}_t)_{t \ge 0}$ over V_m, where $m \le n$. The distribution of $(\hat{x}_t)_{t \ge 0}$ is examined in the second phase in order to make the decision. In this paper, we assume that the transformation is a linear transform $T \colon (V_n)^{|I|} \to V_m$ such that

$$\hat{x}_t = T((x_{t+i})_{i \in I}), \quad \text{for all } t \ge 0,$$

where I is an index set. To create an efficient distinguisher, the transform T should be chosen such that given a sequence produced by the keystream generator the sequence $(\hat{x}_t)_{t \ge 0}$ should deviate from the uniform distribution as much as possible with respect to the test statistic used in the distinguisher. On the other hand, $(\hat{x}_t)_{t \ge 0}$ should not be biased if the input sequence $(x_t)_{t \ge 0}$ is not from the cipher. We use P_C to denote the expected distribution of $(\hat{x}_t)_{t \ge 0}$ when a keystream sequence has been given as input.

A distinguisher uses a test statistic to perform the hypothesis test. In [5], Baignères et al. showed that the log-likelihood ratio statistic is an optimal statistic for a linear distinguisher. For a sufficiently large number N of samples $(\hat{x}_t)_{t \ge 0}$, one can perform the hypothesis test reliably. In the hypothesis test, the distribution of $(\hat{x}_t)_{t \ge 0}$ is compared to the m-dimensional distributions P_C and P_U using the log-likelihood ratio

$$\Lambda = \sum_{t=0}^{N-1} \log_2 \frac{P_C(\hat{x}_t)}{2^{-m}}. \tag{2}$$

The sample size requirement N is inversely proportional to the squared Euclidean distance between distributions P_C and P_U. More accurately, we have

$$N \propto \frac{1}{2^m \|P_C - P_U\|_2^2},$$

where $\|\cdot\|_2$ is the ℓ^2-norm. In [5], Baignères et al. call the denominator $2^m \|P_C - P_U\|_2^2 = 2^m \sum_{x \in V_m} (P_C(x) - 2^{-m})^2$ the Squared Euclidean Imbalance of P_C. Hence, to find an efficient distinguisher, one needs to find a linear transformation for the input sequence $(x_t)_{t \geq 0}$ such that the squared Euclidean distance between $(\hat{x}_t)_{t \geq 0}$ and a uniformly distributed sequence is large whenever the input sequence has been generated by the keystream generator. Note that if $m = 1$, the linear distinguisher examines linear combinations of input sequence bits. In this case, P_C is the Bernoulli distribution and we have $2^m \|P_C - P_U\|_2^2 = \epsilon_C^2$, where ϵ_C is the expected bias in $(\hat{x}_t)_{t \geq 0}$.

5   Linear Distinguishers for Shannon

To build a linear distinguisher for Shannon, we find a linear transform T which is applied to the sequence $(x_t)_{t \geq 0}$ over V_{32} given as input for the distinguisher. This transformation should be chosen such that the squared Euclidean distance between the distribution of $(\hat{x}_t)_{t \geq 0}$ and the uniform distribution is large if the input sequence $(x_t)_{t \geq 0}$ has been generated by Shannon. Since all of the nonlinearity in the keystream generator is achieved with the functions f_1 and f_2, we strive to find a transform T such that the distribution of $(\hat{x}_t)_{t \geq 0}$ is affected by f_1 and f_2 as little as possible if $(x_t)_{t \geq 0}$ is a keystream. This way, we try to make the distribution of $(\hat{x}_t)_{t \geq 0}$ as nonuniform as possible whenever a keystream is given as input. The best linear distinguisher that we found for Shannon relies on the transformation

$$T \colon (x_t, x_{t+16}) \mapsto (x_t \lll 1) \oplus x_{t+16}, \quad \text{for all } t \geq 0.$$

In the next sections, we show how this transform is constructed and how the distribution of $(\hat{x}_t)_{t \geq 0}$ can be estimated when a keystream has been given as input.

5.1   Constructing the Distinguisher

We construct the linear distinguisher for Shannon by taking a linear combination of the keystream variables z_t, $t \geq 0$, such that the combination will have a nonuniform time-invariant distribution, denoted by P_C. We use the state update function (1) to cancel out the internal state variables not given as input to f_1 or f_2. Hence, if the system was linear, this linear combination would always be equal to 0. With Shannon, however, such clear distinguishing is not possible since the functions f_1 and f_2 have nonuniform value distributions. Using a linear combination of the outputs of f_1 and f_2, deviation from the uniform distribution can still be detected. This linear combination is used as the linear transform T in the distinguisher.

The distribution P_C of $(z_t \lll 1) \oplus z_{t+16}$ can be estimated as follows. Since $f_2(x) \lll 1 = f_2(x \lll 1)$, the state update function (1) can be rewritten as

$$(s_t \lll 1) \oplus s_{t+16} = f_1(s_{t+12} \oplus s_{t+13} \oplus K) \oplus f_2((s_{t+2} \oplus s_{t+15}) \lll 1). \quad (3)$$

Recall that the output z_t is given by

$$z_t = s_{t+9} \oplus s_{t+13} \oplus f_2(s_{t+3} \oplus s_{t+16}).$$

Now, by adding the keystream variables $z_t \lll 1$ and z_{t+16} together, the relation (3) can be used twice. We get

$$\begin{aligned}
(z_t \lll 1) \oplus z_{t+16} &= ((s_{t+9} \oplus s_{t+13} \oplus f_2(s_{t+3} \oplus s_{t+16})) \lll 1) \\
&\quad \oplus s_{t+25} \oplus s_{t+29} \oplus f_2(s_{t+19} \oplus s_{t+32}) \\
&= f_1(s_{t+21} \oplus s_{t+22} \oplus K) \oplus f_2((s_{t+11} \oplus s_{t+24}) \lll 1) \quad (4) \\
&\quad \oplus f_1(s_{t+25} \oplus s_{t+26} \oplus K) \oplus f_2((s_{t+15} \oplus s_{t+28}) \lll 1) \\
&\quad \oplus f_2(s_{t+19} \oplus s_{t+32}) \oplus f_2((s_{t+3} \oplus s_{t+16}) \lll 1).
\end{aligned}$$

Here, we have again used the fact that $f_2(x) \lll 1 = f_2(x \lll 1)$. None of the state variables appear more than once in the inputs of f_1 or f_2 in (4). Hence, it is justified to assume that the inputs to f_1 and f_2 are independent uniformly distributed random variables for all $t \geq 0$. In that case, $(z_t \lll 1) \oplus z_{t+16}$ has a time-invariant distribution, which is determined from the value distributions of f_1 and f_2. Note that it is not possible to gain information about the secret constant K by using this linear transform—the distribution is independent of K when the transform is constructed this way.

A linear distinguishing attack can be performed if we know the distribution P_C of $(z_t \lll 1) \oplus z_{t+16}$. The decision is made based on the value of the log-likelihood ratio Λ given in (2): if $\Lambda \geq 0$, the distinguisher decides that the input sequence has been generated by Shannon; otherwise, the input is decided to be random.

5.2   Calculating the Distribution P_C

Let P_1 and P_2 denote the probability distributions of the outputs of f_1 and f_2, respectively. The distribution P_C of $(z_t \lll 1) \oplus z_{t+16}$ is defined as the convolution (over the exclusive-OR) of six random variables: two of them have the distribution P_1 and four of them have the distribution P_2. We make use of the Walsh-Hadamard transform for calculating P_C efficiently. Let X be a random variable with the sample space V_d and the probability distribution P_X, where $P_X(x) = \Pr[X = x]$, for all $x \in V_d$. Now, the random variable $l_u(X) = u \cdot X$ has the Bernoulli distribution $P_{u \cdot X}$. Denote by $\epsilon(u)$ the bias of $u \cdot X$. We get

$$\epsilon(u) = P_{u \cdot X}(0) - P_{u \cdot X}(1) = \sum_{x \in V_d} P_X(x)(-1)^{u \cdot x}, \quad \text{for all } u \in V_d.$$

Hence, the bias $\epsilon(u)$ is given by the transform $\mathcal{F}[P_X]$ at $u \in V_d$. Using the well-known fast Walsh-Hadamard transform, it is possible to compute $\mathcal{F}[P_X]$ in $\mathcal{O}(d2^d)$ operations. Since computation of P_X takes $\mathcal{O}(2^d)$ operations, the biases $\epsilon(u)$, $u \in V_d$, can be determined in $\mathcal{O}((d+1)2^d)$ operations. Conversely, if the biases $\epsilon(u)$, $u \in V_d$, are known, the distribution P_X can be computed by taking the inverse transform $\mathcal{F}^{-1}[\epsilon]$ (see [10, Lemma 1]). Using the fast Walsh-Hadamard transform, this takes $\mathcal{O}(d2^d)$ operations.

In order to determine the biases $\epsilon_C(u)$, $u \in V_{32}$, we first compute the distributions P_1 and P_2. Using the fast Walsh-Hadamard transform, we compute the biases $\epsilon_1(u)$ and $\epsilon_2(u)$ for the distributions P_1 and P_2 for all $u \in V_{32}$. Since we have $d = 32$, these procedures take roughly $2 \cdot (32 + 1) \cdot 2^{32} \approx 2^{38}$ operations. Next, we determine the bias $\epsilon_C(u)$ of $u \cdot ((z_t \lll 1) \oplus z_{t+16})$ for all $u \in V_{32}$. Since all six random variables in (4) are statistically independent, the biases can be computed using the Piling-Up Lemma [8]:

$$\epsilon_C(u) = \epsilon_1(u)^2 \epsilon_2(u)^4, \quad \text{for all } u \in V_{32}. \tag{5}$$

Thus, the distribution P_C can be calculated by taking the inverse transform $\mathcal{F}^{-1}[\epsilon_C]$. In the attack, the distribution P_C is used to evaluate the log-likelihood ratio Λ. Calculation of P_C and the inverse Walsh-Hadamard transform is not necessary, however, if one simply wants to determine the sample size requirement N for the distinguisher. Using Parseval's theorem, it is not hard to show that $2^m \|P_C - P_U\|_2^2 = \sum_{u \neq 0} \epsilon_C(u)^2$ [5, Proposition 11]. Hence, the sample size N can be expressed as a function of the biases $\epsilon_C(u)$, $u \in V_d$:

$$N \propto \frac{1}{\sum_{u \neq 0} \epsilon_C(u)^2}. \tag{6}$$

5.3 Results

To estimate the complexity of the distinguisher, we determined the sample size requirement N using (6). The biases $\epsilon_C(u)$, $u \in V_{32}$, were computed for all $u \in V_{32}$ using (5). We also determined the highest bias $\epsilon_C(u)$, $u \neq 0$, from these values in order to compare the complexity of one-dimensional and 32-dimensional distinguishing attacks. In the one-dimensional distinguishing attack, the distinguisher makes use of the transform $l_u \circ T$ instead of T. The highest bias $\epsilon_C(u) = 2^{-56}$ was achieved with the mask $u = \text{0x0410a4a1}$. In order to compute the log-likelihood ratio Λ, we need to store the distribution P_C to memory. For this, we need to have memory space for 2^{32} counters when the transform T is used and a single counter when the transform $l_u \circ T$ is used. The results are presented in Table 1. For completeness, we present the absolute biases $|\epsilon_1(u)|$ and $|\epsilon_2(u)|$ for $u = \text{0x0410a4a1}$ in Table 2. We also present the masks which induce the highest individual biases $|\epsilon_1(u)|$ and $|\epsilon_2(u)|$ in the same table.

The results in Table 1 show a clear advantage of using a multidimensional transform T instead of $l_u \circ T$ in the distinguisher: we need approximately 2^5 times less keystream in the former case. From (6), it is possible to see how different masks u affect the requirement N. Since $f_i(u) \lll c = f_i(u \lll c)$,

Table 1. The keystream requirement N and the memory requirement M for the distinguisher that uses the transform T and for the distinguisher that uses the transform $l_u \circ T$, where $u = \texttt{0x0410a4a1}$. In the latter case, N is simply given by $\epsilon_C(u)^{-2}$.

	T	$l_u \circ T$
N	$2^{106.996}$	2^{112}
M	2^{32}	1

Table 2. Properties of distributions of f_1 and f_2. The mask $u = \texttt{0x0410a4a1}$ gives the highest $\epsilon_C(u)$; the mask $u = \texttt{0x00021021}$ gives the highest $|\epsilon_1(u)|$; the mask $u = \texttt{0x25252525}$ gives the highest $|\epsilon_2(u)|$.

u	$|\epsilon_1(u)|$	$|\epsilon_2(u)|$
0x0410a4a1	2^{-12}	2^{-8}
0x00021021	$2^{-8.415}$	0
0x25252525	0	$2^{-7.997}$

$i = 1, 2$, we have $\epsilon_C(u) = \epsilon_C(u \lll c)$, for $c = 1, \ldots, 32$. If all nonzero masks would induce the same bias as the masks $\texttt{0x0410a4a1} \lll c$, $c = 1, \ldots, 32$, the keystream requirement N would reduce by a factor of 2^{32}. Since the reduction factor is $2^{5.004}$, all other masks have a negligible effect on the requirement: they reduce it by a factor of $2^{0.004}$. As shown in Table 2, the largest $|\epsilon_2(u)|$ is greater than the largest $|\epsilon_1(u)|$. Perhaps it is because the coverage of f_2 is slightly smaller than the coverage of f_1.

6   Conclusions

We have presented a multidimensional linear distinguishing attack on Shannon. The attack requires about 2^{107} keystream words and memory space for 2^{32} counters. The distinguisher makes use of the transform

$$T\colon (x_t, x_{t+16}) \mapsto (x_t \lll 1) \oplus x_{t+16}, \quad \text{for all } t \geq 0.$$

We have also studied the complexity of a distinguishing attack where the one-dimensional transform $l_u \circ T$, $u = \texttt{0x0410a4a1}$, is used instead. The multidimensional transform T gives a clear improvement over the transform $l_u \circ T$ in the complexity: the distinguisher needs 2^5 times less input in the former case. However, the memory requirement is larger (but still reasonable) in the multidimensional case. A crucial method in our analysis has been the fast Walsh-Hadamard transform. This has allowed handling of large probability distributions efficiently. Generally, building a multidimensional distinguisher is not possible since it requires too much computational effort to examine and handle large distributions.

In the specification for Shannon [2], the authors state that the intention of the design is to ensure that there are no distinguishing attacks on Shannon requiring less than 2^{80} keystream words and less than 2^{128} computations. The results obtained in this paper do not break these limits, and Shannon seems to be as robust against distinguishing attacks as intended. The authors also claim that Shannon should be resistant against distinguishing attacks when used subject to the condition that no key/nonce pair is ever reused, and that no more than 2^{48} words of data are processed with one key/nonce pair, and no more than 2^{80} words are processed with one key. These limitations do not affect distinguishers which work independently of the initial state of the cipher. For example, the distinguisher in this paper should work with all key/nonce pairs because the distribution of $(z_t \lll 1) \oplus z_{t+16}$ does not depend on either the key or the nonce. In theory, one could generate enough keystream for the distinguisher by rekeying the cipher repeatedly with different keys. Hence, the security requirements are not fulfilled in comparison to this claim.

References

1. ECRYPT Network of Excellence: The homepage for eSTREAM (2008), http://www.ecrypt.eu.org/stream/
2. Hawkes, P., McDonald, C., Paddon, M., Rose, G.G., Wiggers de Vries, M.: Design and primitive specification for Shannon. Technical report, Qualcomm Australia (2007), http://eprint.iacr.org/2007/044.pdf
3. Maximov, A., Johansson, T.: Fast computation of large distributions and its cryptographic applications. In: Roy, B. (ed.) ASIACRYPT 2005. LNCS, vol. 3788, pp. 313–332. Springer, Heidelberg (2005)
4. Englund, H., Maximov, A.: Attack the Dragon. In: Maitra, S., Veni Madhavan, C.E., Venkatesan, R. (eds.) INDOCRYPT 2005. LNCS, vol. 3797, pp. 130–142. Springer, Heidelberg (2005)
5. Baignères, T., Junod, P., Vaudenay, S.: How far can we go beyond linear cryptanalysis? In: Lee, P.J. (ed.) ASIACRYPT 2004. LNCS, vol. 3329, pp. 432–450. Springer, Heidelberg (2004)
6. Kaliski, B., Robshaw, M.: Linear cryptanalysis using multiple approximations. In: Desmedt, Y.G. (ed.) CRYPTO 1994. LNCS, vol. 839, pp. 26–39. Springer, Heidelberg (1994)
7. Biryukov, A., Cannière, C.D., Quisquater, M.: On multiple linear approximations. In: Franklin, M. (ed.) CRYPTO 2004. LNCS, vol. 3152, pp. 1–22. Springer, Heidelberg (2004)
8. Matsui, M.: Linear cryptanalysis method for DES cipher. In: Helleseth, T. (ed.) EUROCRYPT 1993. LNCS, vol. 765, pp. 386–397. Springer, Heidelberg (1994)
9. Beauchamp, K.G.: Applications of Walsh and Related Functions. Academic Press, London (1984)
10. Nyberg, K., Hermelin, M.: Multidimensional Walsh transform and a characterization of bent functions. In: Proceedings of the 2007 IEEE Information Theory Workshop on Information Theory for Wireless Networks, pp. 83–86. IEEE, Los Alamitos (2007)

Recovering RC4 Permutation from 2048 Keystream Bytes if j Is Stuck

Subhamoy Maitra[1] and Goutam Paul[2]

[1] Applied Statistics Unit, Indian Statistical Institute,
Kolkata 700 108, India
subho@isical.ac.in
[2] Department of Computer Science and Engineering,
Jadavpur University, Kolkata 700 032, India
goutam_paul@cse.jdvu.ac.in

Abstract. In this paper, we study the behaviour of RC4 when the index j is stuck at a certain value not known to the attacker. Though it seems quite natural that RC4 would be weak if j does not change, it has never been studied earlier in a disciplined manner. This work presents the nontrivial issues involved in the analysis, identifying how the information regarding S starts leaking with as low as 258 keystream output bytes. The leakage of information increases as more bytes are available and finally the complete S is recovered with 2^{11} bytes in around 2^{25} time complexity. The attack considers that "the deterministic index i at the point when j got stuck" and "the value at which j remains stuck" are unknown. Further, the study presents a nice combinatorial structure that is relevant to the fault analysis of RC4.

Keywords: Cryptanalysis, Fault Analysis, Keystream, Permutation, RC4, Stream Cipher.

1 Introduction

RC4 is one of the most well known stream ciphers in cryptographic literature. The cipher has been analysed for around two decades, and many weaknesses have been identified. However, none of the weaknesses could seriously affect RC4 and it can very well be used in a secure manner if certain precautions are taken. That is the reason RC4 is still being used in commercial domain.

One more motivating point behind the study of RC4 is its simplicity. The Key Scheduling Algorithm (KSA) and the Pseudo Random Generation Algorithm (PRGA) of RC4 are presented below. The data structure consists of an array S of size N (typically, 256), which contains a permutation of the integers $\{0, \ldots, N-1\}$, two indices i, j and the secret key array K. Given a secret key k of l bytes (typically 5 to 32), the array K of size N is such that $K[y] = k[y \bmod l]$ for any y, $0 \leq y \leq N-1$.

We consider a *stuck-at fault* where the value of the index j is stuck at some value x during the PRGA, $0 \leq x \leq N-1$. With this, we term the PRGA as StuckPRGA.

Y. Mu, W. Susilo, and J. Seberry (Eds.): ACISP 2008, LNCS 5107, pp. 306–320, 2008.

Algorithm KSA	Algorithm PRGA	Algorithm StuckPRGA
Initialization:	*Initialization:*	*Initialization:*
For $i = 0, \ldots, N-1$	$i = j = 0$;	$i = j = 0$;
$S[i] = i$;	*Output Keystream Generation Loop:*	*Output Keystream Generation Loop:*
$j = 0$;	$i = i + 1$;	$i = i + 1$;
Scrambling:	$j = j + S[i]$;	$j = x$;
For $i = 0, \ldots, N-1$	Swap($S[i], S[j]$);	Swap($S[i], S[j]$);
$j = (j + S[i] + K[i])$;	$t = S[i] + S[j]$;	$t = S[i] + S[j]$;
Swap($S[i], S[j]$);	Output $z = S[t]$;	Output $z = S[t]$;

The simple structure of RC4 has invited substantial attention towards its analysis. RC4 can be completely attacked if one can reconstruct the permutation S looking at the keystream output bytes. In [4, Table 2], it has been estimated that this kind of attack would require around 2^{779} to 2^{797} complexity. Later in [9, Table 7], an improved idea has been presented that estimates a complexity of 2^{731}. These results are interesting if one considers RC4 with key of size greater than 731 bits (approximately 92 bytes). However, these estimates, in no way, affect the security of RC4 if the key size of 32 bytes (256 bits) is considered. A very recent and important work [8] in this area shows that the permutation can be recovered much faster than that have been shown in [4,9] and the complexity is estimated as 2^{241}. This shows that RC4 is not secure when the key length is more than 30 bytes. Fortunately, this result does not affect RC4 for the typical secret key size of 5 to 16 bytes.

Another important kind of analysis in RC4 is to study how the keystream output bytes can be distinguished from random stream or how they are biased towards the secret key. These results can be exploited to mount certain attacks. One may refer to [5,6,7] and the references therein for more details.

Since RC4 cannot be comprehensively attacked, some easier models of RC4 have been studied in literature. In [4, Section 3], the behaviour of RC4 is studied when there is no swap or reduced number of swaps (i.e., swap would work after generation of more than one keystream output bytes during PRGA). While for no swap, it has been demonstrated that RC4 can be broken easily, in case of reduced swap, the attack requires more time complexity [4] and may not be achievable in certain cases.

The fault attacks are also an interesting area of study. Based on certain models of the fault during the execution of the cipher, the security parameters of the cipher degrade. The fault attack on RC4 has been initially studied in [3, Section 3.3]. The model in [3] is to introduce a fault on a single byte of S and then analyze the resulting stream to get back the permutation S. Empirical results show that getting certain information on S requires more than 10,000 keystream output bytes. In [1], fault is introduced in the indices i, j such that the RC4 state lands into a Finney cycle [2]. Then it becomes easier to get back the permutation S. The result of [1, Section 3] (impossible fault analysis) shows that at least 2^{16} keystream output bytes are required to mount such an attack. In [1, Table 1], it was shown that the work of [3] requires injection of 2^{16} faults and it needs 2^{26} amount of keystream bytes; whereas the work of [1, Section 4] (differential fault analysis) requires injection of 2^{10} faults and it needs 2^{16} bytes. Fault attack has also been considered in [7] where 20,000 iterations are required and 2^{14} many faults need to be injected.

In our work, we consider that the index j is stuck at a certain value during the execution of RC4 PRGA. Under this situation, the complete permutation S

can be recovered with 2048 keystream output bytes. Our strategy is to interleave the RC4 output bytes in a logical manner so that we can identify sequences of two or more consecutive elements in the permutation.

It is acceptable that the fault models always rely on optimistic assumptions and considers a weaker version of the cipher than the original one. Also it has been commented in [3, Section 1.3] that the attacker should have partial control in terms of number, location and timing of fault injections. Thus, getting a situation where j would get stuck at a certain value for some period of time is rather optimistic. However, if one accepts this model, then the attempt should be to recover the permutation with as less keystream output bytes as possible when the value of j, where it is stuck, is not known. That is what we target in this paper.

In Section 2, we build the theoretical framework considering j is stuck at 0 and it happens at the beginning of the PRGA (just after the KSA) when $i = 1$. This helps in understanding the situation clearly. In Section 3, we present the general scenario that none of i, j is known and j is stuck at an unknown value.

In [1, Page 364], a stronger fault model is mentioned where one can select the exact value of the indices i or j or one value in the permutation S. Further, it has been commented [1, Page 364] that in this case much stronger attack would exist specifically for this model. We complete the task in this paper by showing that such an attack exists by recovering the permutation S with very few (as low as 2048) keystream output bytes.

Apart from the cryptographic significance, studying RC4 with j stuck at some value reveals nice combinatorial structures. First, an internal state on any step is a restricted permutation over some fixed initial state. Secondly, if one considers consecutive outputs at steps say $r, r + 257, r + 514$ and so on, then the resulting keystream sequence (i) either consists of the same values (in very few cases), or (ii) is exactly the subarray (e.g., indices $y, y + 1, y + 2, \ldots$) of the initial permutation (in most of the cases), or (iii) the subarray (e.g., indices $y, y + 1, y + 3, y + 4, \ldots$) of the initial permutation with a jump in the initial permutation (in very few cases). These facts allow to recover the full state given only 2048 keystream bytes and this will be clear looking at Table 1.

Though the basic idea is not complicated, the formal analysis is quite involved. The complete structure of the permutation S is studied in detail in such a situation and the reconstruction of S is explained in proper theoretical framework. We show that even with 258 keystream output bytes, one can start getting information about the permutation S and increasing amount of knowledge is leaked with more bytes. The complete information on S is revealed when 2048 output bytes are known.

2 Recovering Permutation from Keystream

First we introduce a few notations and definitions and then present the theoretical analysis.

Let S_r^G be the permutation and z_r be the keystream output byte after r many rounds of the PRGA, $r \geq 1$. Also, let t_r be the index (in S_r^G) from where z_r is chosen. We also denote by S_0^G the original permutation before the PRGA starts. For the rest of the paper, we assume, without loss of generality, that $S_0^G = <a_0, a_1, a_2, \ldots, a_{N-1}>$. The subscripts in a_y's are implicitly assumed to follow arithmetic modulo N. For example, a_{-y}, a_{N-y} and in general $a_{\rho N - y}$ for any integer ρ represent the same element.

We now state a few definitions that would be needed in the subsequent analysis.

Definition 1. *A* run *of the RC4 PRGA is defined to be a set of any N consecutive rounds of keystream output byte generation during which the deterministic index i takes each value in $\{0, \ldots, N-1\}$ exactly once.*

Definition 2. *Given a permutation S, the n-th successor of an element u in S, denoted by $suc^n(u)$, is defined to be the element which appears n locations after u, if we move from left to right in S in a circular fashion. If $S = < b_0, b_1, b_2, \ldots, b_{N-1} >$, then $suc^n(b_y) = b_{y+n}$.*

Definition 3. *Given a permutation S, the n-rotated permutation, denoted by $rot^n(S)$, is defined to be the permutation obtained by circularly right-shifting S by n positions. If $S = < b_0, b_1, b_2, \ldots, b_{N-1} >$, then*

$$rot^n(S) = < b_n, b_{n+1}, \ldots, b_{N-1}, b_0, b_1, \ldots, b_{n-2}, b_{n-1} >.$$

Definition 4. *An ordered pair (u, v) is called a* candidate pair, *if u appears $N + 1$ rounds after v in the keystream and both u, v come from the same index in the respective permutations.*

Definition 5. *A set $\{(u, v_1), (u, v_2)\}$ of two candidate pairs is called a* conflict set, *if $v_1 \neq v_2$ and it is not known whether $v_1 = suc^1(u)$ or $v_2 = suc^1(u)$.*

Definition 6. *A candidate pair (u, v) is called a* resolved pair *for a permutation S, if it is known that $v = suc^1(u)$.*

Definition 7. *A permutation S of N elements is said to be* resolved, *if for each element u in S, $suc^1(u)$ is known, or in other words, if $N - 1$ many distinct candidate pairs are resolved.*

Note that since the permutation has N distinct elements, knowledge of $N - 1$ successors for any $N - 1$ elements reveals the successor of the remaining element.

Definition 8. *A permutation S of N elements is said to be* partially resolved, *if for some element u in S, $suc^1(u)$ is not known, or in other words, if less than $N - 1$ many distinct candidate pairs are resolved.*

Definition 9. *Given two partially resolved permutations S_1 and S_2 of the same N elements, we say $S_1 > S_2$ or $S_1 = S_2$ or $S_1 < S_2$, if the number of resolved pairs for S_1 is more than or equal to or less than the number of resolved pairs for S_2 respectively.*

Table 1. Evolution of the permutation during StuckPRGA with j stuck at 0

Round r	i	Bytes of the Permutation S_r^G									Output Index t_r
		0	1	2	3	4	5	...	$N-2$	$N-1$	
0		a_0	a_1	a_2	a_3	a_4	a_5	...	a_{254}	a_{255}	
1	1	a_1	a_0	a_2	a_3	a_4	a_5	...	a_{254}	a_{255}	$a_0 + a_1$
2	2	a_2	a_0	a_1	a_3	a_4	a_5	...	a_{254}	a_{255}	$a_1 + a_2$
3	3	a_3	a_0	a_1	a_2	a_4	a_5	...	a_{254}	a_{255}	$a_2 + a_3$
.	.	.	.	.	.	.	.	.	.	.	.
255	255	a_{255}	a_0	a_1	a_2	a_3	a_4	...	a_{253}	a_{254}	$a_{254} + a_{255}$
256	0	a_{255}	a_0	a_1	a_2	a_3	a_4	...	a_{253}	a_{254}	$2a_{255}$
257	1	a_0	a_{255}	a_1	a_2	a_3	a_4	...	a_{253}	a_{254}	$a_0 + a_{255}$
258	2	a_1	a_{255}	a_0	a_2	a_3	a_4	...	a_{253}	a_{254}	$a_0 + a_1$
259	3	a_2	a_{255}	a_0	a_1	a_3	a_4	...	a_{253}	a_{254}	$a_1 + a_2$
260	4	a_3	a_{255}	a_0	a_1	a_2	a_4	...	a_{253}	a_{254}	$a_2 + a_3$
.	.	.	.	.	.	.	.	.	.	.	.
511	255	a_{254}	a_{255}	a_0	a_1	a_2	a_3	...	a_{252}	a_{253}	$a_{253} + a_{254}$
512	0	a_{254}	a_{255}	a_0	a_1	a_2	a_3	...	a_{252}	a_{253}	$2a_{254}$
513	1	a_{255}	a_{254}	a_0	a_1	a_2	a_3	...	a_{252}	a_{253}	$a_{254} + a_{255}$
514	2	a_0	a_{254}	a_{255}	a_1	a_2	a_3	...	a_{252}	a_{253}	$a_0 + a_{255}$
515	3	a_1	a_{254}	a_{255}	a_0	a_2	a_3	...	a_{252}	a_{253}	$a_0 + a_1$
516	4	a_2	a_{254}	a_{255}	a_0	a_1	a_3	...	a_{252}	a_{253}	$a_1 + a_2$
.	.	.	.	.	.	.	.	.	.	.	.

Before we formally discuss our main results, let us illustrate the structure of the permutation under the above fault model at different rounds of the PRGA in Table 1. We consider $N = 256$.

Without loss of generality, throughout this section, we assume that j is stuck at $x = 0$ from round 1 onwards. Since the index i visits 0 to $N-1$ cyclically, similar results hold for $x \neq 0$ also, which will be discussed in Section 3.

Proposition 1. *Suppose the permutation after round ρN of the PRGA, $\rho \geq 0$, is $S_{\rho N}^G = < b_0, b_1, \ldots, b_{N-1} >$. Then the permutation after round $\rho N + y$ of the PRGA, $1 \leq y \leq N-1$, is given by $S_{\rho N+y}^G = < b_y, b_0, \ldots, b_{y-1}, b_{y+1}, \ldots, b_{N-1} >$.*

Proof. We prove it by induction on y.
Base Case: When $y = 1$, the deterministic index i takes the value 1. So, b_0, b_1 are swapped and $S_{\rho N+1}^G = < b_1, b_0, b_2, \ldots, b_{N-1} >$. Hence the result holds for $y = 1$.
Inductive Case: Suppose for some y, $1 \leq y \leq N-2$, the result holds, i.e.,
$S_{\rho N+y}^G = < b_y, b_0, \ldots, b_{y-1}, b_{y+1}, \ldots, b_{N-1} >$ (inductive hypothesis).
Now, in round $\rho N + y + 1$, the index i becomes $y+1$ and the other index j remains fixed at 0. Thus, the values b_y and b_{y+1} are swapped. Hence,
$S_{\rho N+y+1}^G = < b_{y+1}, b_0, \ldots, b_y, b_{y+2}, \ldots, b_{N-1} >$, i.e., the result also holds for $y + 1$. $\square$

Lemma 1
(1) *After round $\rho N + y$ of the PRGA, $\rho \geq 0$, $1 \leq y \leq N-1$, the permutation is given by $S_{\rho N+y}^G = < a_{N-\rho+y}, a_{N-\rho}, a_{N-\rho+1}, \ldots, a_{N-\rho+y-1}, a_{N-\rho+y+1}, \ldots, a_{N-\rho-2}, a_{N-\rho-1} >$ and the permutation $S_{(\rho+1)N}$ after round $\rho N + N$ is the same as the permutation $S_{\rho N+N-1}$ after round $\rho N + N - 1$.*

(2) *The index where the keystream output byte is chosen from is given by*

$$t_{\rho N+y} = \begin{cases} a_{N-\rho+y-1} + a_{N-\rho+y} & \text{if } \rho \geq 0, \ 1 \leq y \leq N-1; \\ 2a_{N-\rho} & \text{if } \rho \geq 1, \ y = 0. \end{cases}$$

Proof. The proof of item (1) will be based on induction on ρ.

Base Case: Take $\rho = 0$. We need to prove that
$S_y^G = \ <a_y, a_0, a_1, \ldots, a_{y-1}, a_{y+1}, \ldots, a_{N-2}, a_{N-1}>, \ 1 \leq y \leq N-1$. This immediately follows from Proposition 1 above, taking $\rho = 0$.

Inductive Case: Suppose the result holds for some $\rho \geq 0$, i.e., $S_{\rho N+y}^G = \ <a_{N-\rho+y}, a_{N-\rho}, a_{N-\rho+1}, \ldots, a_{N-\rho+y-1}, a_{N-\rho+y+1}, \ldots, a_{N-\rho-2}, a_{N-\rho-1}>$, for $1 \leq y \leq N-1$ (*inductive hypothesis*).

Thus, in round $\rho N + N - 1$, we have
$S_{\rho N+N-1}^G = \ <a_{N-\rho-1}, a_{N-\rho}, a_{N-\rho+1}, \ldots, a_{N-\rho-2}>$.

In the next round, i.e. in round $\rho N + N$, the deterministic index i becomes 0 which is equal to the value of j and hence no swap is involved. Thus, $S_{(\rho+1)N}^G = S_{\rho N+N-1}^G = \ <a_{N-\rho-1}, a_{N-\rho}, a_{N-\rho+1}, \ldots, a_{N-\rho-2}>$, which can be rewritten as $< b_0, b_1, \ldots, b_{N-1}>$, where $b_y = a_{N-\rho-1+y}$, $0 \leq y \leq N-1$. According to Proposition 1, $S_{(\rho+1)N+y}^G = <b_y, b_0, b_1, \ldots, b_{y-1}, b_{y+1}, \ldots, b_{N-2}, b_{N-1}> = \ <a_{N-(\rho+1)+y}, a_{N-(\rho+1)}, a_{N-(\rho+1)+1}, \ldots, a_{N-(\rho+1)+y-1}, a_{N-(\rho+1)+y+1}, \ldots, a_{N-(\rho+1)-1}>$. Hence, the result holds for the case $\rho + 1$ also.

Now we prove item (2). In round $\rho N + y$, the value of the deterministic index i is $y \ (\text{mod} N)$ and that of the index j remains fixed at 0. Hence the output is generated from the index $t_{\rho N+y} = S_{\rho N+y}^G[y] + S_{\rho N+y}^G[0]$. Writing the permutation bytes in terms of the a_y's, we get the result. $\qquad \square$

Theorem 1. *Consider the two rounds $\rho N + y$ and $(\rho+1)N + (y+1)$, $\rho \geq 0, 1 \leq y \leq N-2$. The two keystream output bytes $z_{\rho N+y}$ and $z_{(\rho+1)N+(y+1)}$ come from the same location $t = a_{N-\rho+y-1} + a_{N-\rho+y}$ in the respective permutations $S_{\rho N+y}$ and $S_{(\rho+1)N+(y+1)}$ with the following characteristics.*

1. $t = 0 \iff z_{\rho N+y} = z_{(\rho+1)N+(y+1)} = S_0^G[N - \rho + y]$.
2. $t = y+1 \iff z_{\rho N+y} = suc^2(z_{(\rho+1)N+(y+1)})$ *with respect to* S_0^G.
3. $t \in \{0, 1, \ldots, y-1, y, y+2, y+3, \ldots, N-1\}$
   $\iff z_{\rho N+y} = suc^1(z_{(\rho+1)N+(y+1)})$ *with respect to* S_0^G.

Proof. Consider $\rho \geq 0, 1 \leq y \leq N-2$. From Lemma 1, we get $t_{\rho N+y} = t_{(\rho+1)N+(y+1)} = a_{N-\rho+y-1} + a_{N-\rho+y} = t$ (say).

Again from Lemma 1, $S_{\rho N+y}$ and $S_{(\rho+1)N+(y+1)}$ are respectively given by $< a_{N-\rho+y}, a_{N-\rho}, a_{N-\rho+1}, \ldots, a_{N-\rho+y-1}, a_{N-\rho+y+1}, a_{N-\rho+y+2}, \ldots, a_{N-\rho-2}, a_{N-\rho-1}>$, and $< a_{N-\rho+y}, a_{N-\rho-1}, a_{N-\rho}, \ldots, a_{N-\rho+y-2}, a_{N-\rho+y-1}, a_{N-\rho+y+1}, \ldots, a_{N-\rho-3}, a_{N-\rho-2}>$.

Thus, $t = 0$ if and only if $z_{\rho N+y} = z_{(\rho+1)N+(y+1)} = z$ (say). And in that case, z reveals $a_{N-\rho+y}$, i.e., the value at index 0 in $S_{\rho N+y}^G$ or equivalently the value at index $N - \rho + y$ in the original permutation S_0^G. This proves item 1.

Of the $N - 1$ other possible values of t, if $t = y+1$, then $z_{\rho N+y} = a_{N-\rho+y+1}$ and $z_{(\rho+1)N+(y+1)} = a_{N-\rho+y-1}$; and vice versa. This proves item 2.

If, however, t takes any of the remaining $N-2$ values (other than 0 and $y+1$), then $z_{\rho N+y}$ appears next to $z_{(\rho+1)N+(y+1)}$ in S_0^G; and vice versa. This proves item 3. $\square$

Note that the keystream output bytes that come from the same index in two consecutive run's are always $N+1$ rounds apart.

For the sake of clarity, let us elaborate the pattern considered in the above Theorem. Consider the indices of the keystream output bytes in two consecutive run's as follows.

y	1	2	$\cdots$	$N-2$	$N-1$	N
run ρ	$a_{N-\rho}+a_{N-\rho+1}$	$a_{N-\rho+1}+a_{N-\rho+2}$	$\cdots$	$a_{N-\rho-3}+a_{N-\rho-2}$	$a_{N-\rho-2}+a_{N-\rho-1}$	$2a_{N-\rho-1}$
run $\rho+1$	$a_{N-\rho-1}+a_{N-\rho}$	$a_{N-\rho}+a_{N-\rho+1}$	$\cdots$	$a_{N-\rho-4}+a_{N-\rho-3}$	$a_{N-\rho-3}+a_{N-\rho-2}$	$2a_{N-\rho-2}$

Observe that the keystream output indices in run ρ for $y=1$ to $N-2$ exactly match with those in run $\rho+1$ for $y=2$ to $N-1$ respectively. Moreover, as discussed in the proof of Theorem 1, the permutations in run $\rho+1$ for $y=2$ to $N-1$ are right shifts of the permutations in run ρ for $y=1$ to $N-2$ respectively except at two locations.

We can exploit the above combinatorial structure identified in Theorem 1 to devise an efficient algorithm $PartResolvePerm$ for getting a $partially\ resolved$ permutation from the keystream bytes.

Algorithm PartResolvePerm

Inputs:
1. The RN many keystream output bytes from the first $R(\geq 2)$ run's of the PRGA.

Outputs:
1. A partially resolved permutation in the form of an array $Next$.
2. A set of conflict pairs in an array $Conflict$.

Steps:
1. For $u=0$ to $N-1$ do
    1.1. Set $Next[u]=-1$;
2. NumConflicts $=0$;
3. For $\rho=0$ to $R-2$ do
    3.1. For $y=1$ to $N-2$ do
        3.1.1 If $z_{\rho N+y}=z_{(\rho+1)N+(y+1)}$ then do
            3.1.1.1 Set $S_0^G[N-\rho+y]=z_{\rho N+y}$;
        3.1.2 Else do
            3.1.2.1 If $Next[z_{(\rho+1)N+(y+1)}]=-1$ then do
                3.1.2.1.1 Set $Next[z_{(\rho+1)N+(y+1)}]=z_{\rho N+y}$;
            3.1.2.2 Else if $Next[z_{(\rho+1)N+(y+1)}]\neq z_{\rho N+y}$ then do
                3.1.2.2.1 Set $NumConflicts=NumConflicts+1$;
                3.1.2.2.2 Set $Conflict[NumConflicts].value=z_{(\rho+1)N+(y+1)}$;
                3.1.2.2.3 Set $Conflict[NumConflicts].first=$
                                   $Next[z_{(\rho+1)N+(y+1)}]$;
                3.1.2.2.4 Set $Conflict[NumConflicts].second=z_{\rho N+y}$;

In the algorithm, $Next[u]$ denotes the value that comes immediately after the value u in the permutation S_0^G. If $Next[u]$ is unassigned (i.e., $Next[u]=-1$), it means that the element next to the element u in S_0^G is not yet known. Essentially, we tally two consecutive run's of the PRGA and fill in the array $Next$ by observing the $candidate\ pairs$, i.e., the keystream output bytes that come from the same index in the respective permutations. Due to $item\ 2$ of Theorem 1, for some u, one may record $suc^2(u)$ as $suc^1(u)$ resulting in some $conflict\ sets$, i.e. candidate pairs (u, v_1) and (u, v_2) such that $v_1 \neq v_2$. Then it is not known which one of v_1, v_2 is $suc^1(u)$. We keep an array $Conflict$ where each entry corresponds to a conflict set of the form $\{(u, v_1), (u, v_2)\}$ and consists of three fields, namely, (i) $value$ for storing u, (ii) $first$ for storing v_1 and (iii) $second$ for storing v_2.

Remark 1. The fact that j is stuck provides a regular structure in the secret permutation and therefore in the output bytes. At the point j gets stuck, the permutation S can be considered to be a random permutation. Thus each byte of the first run, coming out after j got stuck, can be considered to be chosen uniformly at random from $\{0, \ldots, N-1\}$. Since we are using any two consecutive run's for getting the $candidate\ pairs$, the values in each such pair can be considered uniformly random for estimating the expected numbers of distinct $candidate\ pairs$ and $conflict\ sets$. This we have also confirmed by experimentation. This uniformity assumption is followed in the technical results in the rest of this paper.

Theorem 2. *The expected number of unassigned entries in the array $Next$ after the execution of the PartResolvePerm algorithm is $N \cdot (\frac{N-1}{N})^{(R-1)(N-2)}$.*

Proof. The $candidate\ pairs$ are of the form $(z_{(\rho+1)N+(y+1)}, z_{\rho N+y}), 0 \leq \rho \leq R-2$, $1 \leq y \leq N-2$. Thus, each distinct value of $z_{\rho N+y}, 0 \leq \rho \leq R-2, 1 \leq y \leq N-2$, would give rise to a $candidate\ pair$ and hence assign exactly one entry of the array $Next$.

Let $x_u = 1$, if the value u does not occur in any of the $(R-1)(N-2)$ many keystream bytes $z_{\rho N+y}, 0 \leq \rho \leq R-2, 1 \leq y \leq N-2$; otherwise, let $x_u = 0, 0 \leq u \leq N-1$. Hence, the total number of values that did not occur in those keystream bytes is given by $X = \sum_{u=0}^{N-1} x_u$. Assuming that each keystream byte is uniformly randomly distributed in $\{0, \ldots, N-1\}$, we have $P(x_u = 1) = (\frac{N-1}{N})^{(R-1)(N-2)}$. Thus, $E(x_u) = (\frac{N-1}{N})^{(R-1)(N-2)}$ and $E(X) = \sum_{u=0}^{N-1} E(x_u) = N \cdot (\frac{N-1}{N})^{(R-1)(N-2)}$. $\square$

Corollary 1. *The expected number of distinct candidate pairs after the execution of the PartResolvePerm algorithm is $N \cdot \left(1 - (\frac{N-1}{N})^{(R-1)(N-2)}\right)$.*

Theorem 3. *The expected number of conflict sets after the execution of the PartResolvePerm algorithm is bounded by $(R-1) \cdot (\frac{N-2}{N})$.*

Proof. The $candidate\ pairs$ are of the form $(z_{(\rho+1)N+(y+1)}, z_{\rho N+y})$ and the corresponding output indices are $t_{\rho,y} = a_{N-\rho+y-1} + a_{N-\rho+y}, 0 \leq \rho \leq R-2$,

$1 \leq y \leq N - 2$. According as item 2 of Theorem 1, if $t_{\rho,y} = y + 1$, then $z_{\rho N+y} = suc^2(z_{(\rho+1)N+(y+1)})$, but due to Step 3.1.2.1.1 of the *PartResolvePerm* algorithm, $z_{\rho N+y}$ is wrongly recorded as $suc^1(z_{(\rho+1)N+(y+1)})$. For $0 \leq \rho \leq R-2$, $1 \leq y \leq N-2$, let $x_{\rho,y} = 1$ if $t_{\rho,y} = y+1$; otherwise, let $x_{\rho,y} = 0$. Hence, the total number of wrong entries in the array *Next* after the execution of the *PartResolvePerm* algorithm is given by $X = \sum_{\rho=0}^{R-2} \sum_{y=1}^{N-2} x_{\rho,y}$. Each wrong entry in *Next* is a potential contributor to one *conflict set*, i.e., $NumConflicts \leq X$. Assuming that each output index is uniformly randomly distributed, we have $P(x_{\rho,y} = 1) = \frac{1}{N}$. Thus, $E(x_y) = \frac{1}{N}$ and $E(X) = \sum_{\rho=0}^{R-2} \sum_{y=1}^{N-2} E(x_{\rho,y}) = (R - 1) \cdot (\frac{N-2}{N})$. $\square$

Given a *conflict set* $\{(u, v_1), (u, v_2)\}$, if we are able to find v_1, v_2 in a *candidate pair*, then the conflict is resolved and we know the exact order of u, v_1, v_2. Using this observation, we can devise an algorithm *ResolveConflicts* which takes as input a partially resolved permutation S_1 and a collection of conflict sets and generates as output another partially resolved permutation S_2 such that $S_2 \geq S_1$.

Algorithm ResolveConflicts
Inputs:
1. A partially resolved permutation S_1 in the form of an array *Next*.
2. A set of conflict pairs in an array *Conflict*.
Output:
1. A partially resolved permutation $S_2 \geq S_1$ in the form of the array *Next*.
Steps:
1. For $u = 1$ to *NumConflicts* do
1.1 For $\rho = 0$ to $R - 2$ do
1.1.1 For $y = 1$ to $N - 2$ do
1.1.1.1 If $Conflict[u].first = z_{(\rho+1)N+(y+1)}$ and
$Conflict[u].second = z_{\rho N+y}$ then do
1.1.1.1.1 Set $Next[Conflict[u].value] = Conflict[u].first$;
1.1.1.1.2 Set $Next[Next[Conflict[u].value]] = Conflict[u].second$;
1.1.1.2 If $Conflict[u].second = z_{(\rho+1)N+(y+1)}$ and
$Conflict[u].first = z_{\rho N+y}$ then do
1.1.1.2.1 Set $Next[Conflict[u].value] = Conflict[u].second$;
1.1.1.2.2 Set $Next[Next[Conflict[u].value]] = Conflict[u].first$;

After R many *run*'s of the PRGA, the permutation may still remain *partially resolved*. We then need to exhaustively fill in the remaining unassigned entries in the array *Next* to form possible *resolved permutations*. We run PRGA on each resolved permutation in turn, in order to determine its first element, and thereby recover the entire permutation.

Lemma 2. *If the initial permutation S_0^G becomes resolved at any stage of the RC4 PRGA, then S_0^G can be retrieved completely in $O(N)$ average time.*

Proof. Suppose one runs PRGA for M rounds starting with an arbitrary permutation S. Assuming that the keystream output bytes are uniformly randomly distributed, the probability that the set of M random keystream bytes obtained by running PRGA on S would match with the M keystream bytes in hand (obtained by running PRGA on S_0^G) is $\frac{1}{N^M}$. With $N = 256$, a small value of M such as $M = 8$ yields a negligibly small value $\frac{1}{2^{64}}$ (close to 0) of this probability. Thus, running PRGA on S for only 8 rounds, with almost certainty one would be able to determine if that permutation indeed was the original permutation S_0^G.

Now, suppose S is a resolved permutation. So for any arbitrary element in S, we know what is its successor. Starting from any element u as the first element, if we write all the elements in sequence, then we get a permutation $T = < u, suc^1(u), suc^2(u), \ldots, suc^{N-1}(u) >$ such that $S = rot^n(T)$ for some n, $0 \leq n \leq N - 1$. We run PRGA starting with the initial permutation once as T, next as $rot^1(T)$, next as $rot^2(T)$, and so on, until the first 8 keystream bytes match with the observed keystream bytes in hand. With at most N such trials, the entire permutation can be constructed. □

The above Lemma readily gives an algorithm *ConstructPerm* to construct S_0^G from a resolved permutation.

Algorithm ConstructPerm
Inputs:
1. A partially resolved permutation S in the form of an array *Next*.
Output:
1. The original permutation S_0^G before the PRGA begins.
Steps:
1. Set $m = $ the number of unassigned (i.e., -1) entries in the array *Next*;
2. For each possible assignment of those m entries do
2.1 Get the corresponding *resolved permutation* T;
2.2 For $n = 0$ to $N - 1$ do
2.2.1 Run PRGA starting with $rot^n(T)$ as the initial permutation for 8 rounds and generate the first 8 keystream bytes;
2.2.2 If the above 8 keystream bytes match with the first 8 keystream bytes obtained in the actual execution of PRGA, then do
2.2.2.1 Set $S_0^G = rot^n(T)$ and Exit.

We can combine the algorithms *PartResolvePerm*, *ResolveConflicts* and *ConstructPerm* to devise an efficient algorithm *RecoverPerm* to retrieve the original permutation S_0^G from the first few *run*'s of keystream output bytes generation.

Algorithm RecoverPerm
Inputs:
1. The RN many keystream output bytes from the first $R(\geq 2)$ *run*'s of the PRGA.
Output:
1. The original permutation S_0^G before the PRGA begins.
Steps:
1. Run *PartResolvePerm* with the given keystream bytes and generate the arrays *Next* and *Conflict*;
2. Run *ResolveConflicts* on *Next*;
3. Run *ConstructPerm* on updated *Next*;

Theorem 4. *The average case time complexity of the RecoverPerm algorithm is* $O\left((R^2 + \lceil E\rceil!)N\right)$, *where* $E = N \cdot (\frac{N-1}{N})^{(R-1)(N-2)}$.

Proof. The time complexity of Step 1 in *RecoverPerm* is $O(RN)$, since there are two nested 'for' loops in *PartResolvePerm* of $R-1$ and $N-2$ many iterations respectively and one execution of the steps inside the 'for' loops takes $O(1)$ time.

The time complexity of Step 2 in *RecoverPerm* is $O(R^2N)$, since from Theorem 3, the average value of *NumConflicts* is $O(R)$ and resolving each of them in the two nested 'for' loops in *ResolveConflicts* takes $O(RN)$ time.

According to Theorem 2, just before the execution of *ConstructPerm* in Step 3 of *RecoverPerm*, the average value of the number m of unassigned entries in the array *Next* is $E = N \cdot (\frac{N-1}{N})^{(R-1)(N-2)}$. Hence the 'for' loop in Step 2 of *ConstructPerm* is iterated $\lceil E\rceil!$ times on the average. Again, from Lemma 2, the time complexity of each iteration of the 'for' loop in Step 2 of *ConstructPerm* is $O(N)$. Hence the overall complexity of Step 3 in *RecoverPerm* is $O(\lceil E\rceil!N)$.

Thus, the time complexity of *RecoverPerm* is $O\left((R^2 + \lceil E\rceil!)N\right)$.   □

Remark 2. If $z_{\rho N+y} = z_{(\rho+1)N+(y+1)}$ for some $\rho \geq 0$ and some $y \in \{1,\ldots,N-2\}$, i.e., if the two values in a *candidate pair* turn out to be equal, then according to item 1 of Theorem 1, we would have $S_0^G[N-\rho+y] = z_{\rho N+y}$. Once the location of one entry of a resolved permutation is known, the positions of all other entries are immediately known. If one makes use of this fact in the *PartResolvePerm* algorithm, then rotating T in Step 2.2 of the *ConstructPerm* algorithm is not needed at all. After Step 2.1, one can run PRGA for 8 rounds on T itself to check whether $T = S_0^G$ or not. In that case, the average case time complexity of the *RecoverPerm* algorithm would be reduced to $O\left(R^2N + \lceil E\rceil!\right)$. However, this requires the knowledge of i. Since in general i will not be known to the attacker (see Section 3 for details), we do not make use of item 1 of Theorem 1 in our strategy.

The quantity $log_2(\lceil E\rceil!)$ can be considered as a measure of uncertainty in resolving the permutation. Considering $N = 256$, Table 2 below lists the values of E and $log_2(\lceil E\rceil!)$ for few values of R. Observe that if all the successors are unresolved (the case $R = 1$ is an example of this), then the uncertainty is $log_2(256!) = 1683.9961$.

We see that as one considers more number of *run*'s, the uncertainty in resolving the permutation decreases. In fact, the uncertainty starts decreasing when only the first 258 keystream output bytes are available, as z_1 and z_{258} come from the same index $a_0 + a_1$ (see Table 1) and constitute a *candidate pair*. Table 2 also shows that theoretically 7 *run*'s are enough to reduce the uncertainty in resolving the permutation to zero and recover the permutation in $O(R^2N)$ time. However, we empirically found that 8 *run*'s provide a conservative estimate when there is no uncertainty in resolving the permutation. In all the experiments we performed with 8 *run*'s, we could successfully recover the complete permutation. Zero uncertainty implies that the permutation obtained after *ResolveConflicts*

Table 2. Decrease in uncertainty of resolving the permutation with increasing run's

Runs R	Avg. No. of Elements with Unassigned Successors E	Uncertainty in Permutation $log_2(\lceil E \rceil!)$
1	256	1684
2	94.73	491.69
3	35.05	138.09
4	12.97	32.54
5	4.80	6.91
6	1.78	1.00
7	0.66	0.00
8	0.24	0.00

in Step 2 of *RecoverPerm* algorithm is a *resolved permutation*. In this case, the time complexity reduces to $8^2 \cdot 256 = 2^{14}$.

We can completely recover the permutation even if we have less keystream bytes at our disposal, except at the cost of increased time complexity due to exhaustive assignment of successor elements. For example, when $R = 4$, i.e., when we start with the first 1024 keystream output bytes, the average number of permutation elements whose next elements are not known is $256 \cdot (\frac{255}{256})^{3*254} = 12.97$. If we exhaustively fill in these $\lceil 12.97 \rceil = 13$ successor values, we would generate $13! \approx 2^{32}$ possible resolved permutations. The time complexity of completely recovering the permutation with 1024 keystream bytes would be around $(4^2 + 2^{32}) \cdot 256 \approx 2^{48}$.

Interestingly, if we go for $R = N$ run's, i.e. we have a total of N^2 ($= 2^{16}$ for $N = 256$) many keystream output bytes, then we can construct the permutation in $O(N)$ time. From Lemma 1, when $\rho = N$, we have $S_{\rho N} = < a_0, a_1, a_2, \ldots, a_{N-1} > \geq S_0^G$, and hence after the first N run's, the structure of the permutation, the output indices as well as the keystream output bytes start repeating in the same order. So if we consider the keystream output bytes coming from a fixed index $a_{y-1} + a_y$, i.e., the values $z_{\rho N+\rho+y}$ for a fixed y, $0 \leq \rho \leq N - 1$, then we can readily get a resolved permutation and do not need to perform exhaustive assignments.

3   Indices i, j Unknown and j Stuck

All the results above can easily be extended when j is stuck at any value $x \in \{0, \ldots, N - 1\}$. Suppose r_{st} is the round from which onwards j is stuck at x, $r_{st} \geq 1$. The value of the deterministic index i at round r_{st} is $i_{st} = r_{st} \bmod N$. Then after $d = (x - i_{st}) \bmod N$ more rounds, i.e., at round $r_{st} + d + 1$, i becomes $x + 1$ for the first time after j got stuck. One can denote the indices of the permutation and the corresponding values after the end of round $r_{st} + d$ as follows.

Permutation Index	0	1	...	$x-1$	x	$x+1$	...	$N-2$	$N-1$
Permutation Bytes	b_{N-x}	b_{N-x+1}	...	b_{N-1}	b_0	b_1	...	b_{N-2-x}	b_{N-1-x}

Thus, "the evolution of the permutation from round $r_{st} + d + 1$ onwards with j stuck at x from round r_{st}" is analogous to "the x-rotation of the permutation evolving from round 1 onwards with j stuck at 0 from round 1".

Suppose that the keystream bytes from the point when j got stuck is available to the attacker. Because of the above cyclic pattern, and because of the relative gap of $N + 1$ rounds between the values in any *candidate pair* as demonstrated in the discussion following Theorem 1 in Section 2, the attacker does not need to know r_{st} or i_{st}. If the attacker starts counting the first *run* from the point when he has the first keystream byte at his disposal, he can efficiently recover the permutation at the point when j got stuck. In the subsequent analysis, we assume that the attacker does not know

1. the round r_{st} from which j got stuck,
2. the value i_{st} of the deterministic index i when j got stuck and
3. the value x at which j is stuck.

We here like to point out the modification corresponding to Step 3.1 of the algorithm *PartResolvePerm* (and similarly Step 1.1.1 of algorithm *ResolveConflicts*), where y varies from 1 to $N - 2$. In Section 2, j was assumed to be stuck at 0 from round $r_{st} = 1$ (when i_{st} was also 1). Thus, it was known in advance that the *candidate pairs* $(z_{(\rho+1)N+(y+1)}, z_{\rho N+y})$, for $y = N - 1, N$ (i.e., when the deterministic index i takes the values $j - 1, j$), should be ignored. Here, r_{st} as well as i_{st} are both unknown. For the sake of processing the keystream bytes using the algorithms *PartResolvePerm* and *ResolveConflicts*), we initialize ρ to 0 at the point j gets stuck and from that point onwards the keystream bytes are named as $z_1, z_2, \ldots$ and so on. Given that j is stuck at an unknown value x, when the deterministic index i takes the values $x - 1$ and x, the two corresponding *candidate pairs* should be ignored. However, these two cases cannot be eliminated here as x is not known. Hence, in Step 3.1 of the algorithm *PartResolvePerm* and Step 1.1.1 of algorithm *ResolveConflicts*, we should consider that y varies from 1 to N for each value of $\rho \in \{0, 1, \ldots, R - 3\}$ and y varies from 1 to $N - 1$ for $\rho = R - 2$.

In this approach, utilizing all the RN many keystream bytes yield total $(R - 1)N - 1$ many *candidate pairs*. Following the same line of arguments as in Theorem 2, we get the expected number of unassigned entries in the array $Next$ just before the execution of Step 3 of *RecoverPerm* as $E' = N \cdot (\frac{N-1}{N})^{(R-1)N-1}$ which, for large N (such as $N = 256$), is approximately equal to $E = N \cdot (\frac{N-1}{N})^{(R-1)(N-2)}$. Since we get two extra wrong entries in each of the $R - 1$ *run*'s, the number of *conflict sets* would increase by $2(R - 1)$ from the value estimated in Theorem 3. Thus, the new bound on the expected number of *conflict sets* after the execution of the *PartResolvePerm* algorithm, when the *candidate pairs* are formed by considering all the keystream bytes in each run, is given by $(R - 1) \cdot (2 + \frac{N-2}{N})$. Observe that the bound is still $O(R)$ as in Theorem 3. However, since i_{st} and x are not known, we need to run Step 2.2 of the *ConstructPerm* Algorithm for each possible values of i_{st} and x in $\{0, \ldots, N - 1\}$, until Step 2.2.2 of *ConstructPerm* reveals the true initial permutation. Thus, we need at most N^2 executions of Step 2.2 of *ConstructPerm* for each of the $\lceil E \rceil$!

resolved permutations where $E = N \cdot (\frac{N-1}{N})^{(R-1)(N-2)}$. Thus, when i_{st} and x are unknown, the average case time complexity of *ConstructPerm* is $\lceil E \rceil ! N^3$, and following the same analysis as in Theorem 4, the average case time complexity of *RecoverPerm* is $O\left(R^2 N + \lceil E \rceil ! N^3\right)$. With $N = 256$ and $R = 8$, we have $E = 0$ and the time complexity becomes $8^2 \cdot 256 + 256^3 \approx 2^{25}$.

In the above analysis we assumed that the keystream bytes from the point when j got stuck is available to the attacker. In practical scenario, the attacker has access to the keystream output bytes only. He should be able to determine the interval during which j remains stuck at a certain value by analyzing the keystream. Then he can run the *RecoverPerm* algorithm on the keystream bytes obtained during that interval. Theoretically determining the exact point when j got stuck seems extremely tedious. However, we are going to provide a simple test which can distinguish between a sequence of normal RC4 keystream bytes when j is pseudo-randomly updated and a sequence of RC4 keystream bytes when j is stuck. We use the following theorem that shows that the number of *conflict sets* from the *PartResolvePerm* algorithm when j is pseudo-randomly updated is much more than that when j is stuck at a certain value.

Theorem 5. *Assume that the index j is pseudo-randomly updated in each round of the PRGA. Then the expected number of conflict sets after the execution of the PartResolvePerm algorithm, when the candidate pairs are formed by considering all the keystream bytes in each run, is bounded by $(R-1) \cdot (N-1) - \frac{N-1}{N}$.*

Proof. The *candidate pairs* are of the form $(z_{(\rho+1)N+(y+1)}, z_{\rho N+y})$ and the corresponding output indices are $t_{\rho,y} = a_{N-\rho+y-1} + a_{N-\rho+y}$, $1 \le y \le N$ for $0 \le \rho \le R-3$, and $1 \le y \le N-1$ for $\rho = R-2$. Let $x_{\rho,y} = 1$ if $z_{\rho N+y} \ne suc^1(z_{(\rho+1)N+(y+1)})$; otherwise, let $x_{\rho,y} = 0$. Then the total number of wrong entries in the array *Next* after the execution of the *PartResolvePerm* algorithm is given by $X = \sum_{\rho=0}^{R-3} \sum_{y=1}^{N} x_{\rho,y} + \sum_{y=1}^{N-1} x_{R-2,y}$. Each wrong entry in *Next* is a potential contributor to one *conflict set*, i.e., $NumConflicts \le X$. Assuming that the index j is pseudo-randomly updated and each output index is uniformly randomly distributed, we have $P(x_{\rho,y} = 1) = \frac{N-1}{N}$. Thus, $E(x_{\rho,y}) = \frac{N-1}{N}$ and

$$E(X) = \sum_{\rho=0}^{R-3} \sum_{y=1}^{N} E(x_{\rho,y}) + \sum_{y=1}^{N-1} E(x_{R-2,y}) = (R-1) \cdot (N-1) - \frac{N-1}{N}. \qquad \square$$

Thus, one can run the *PartResolvePerm* algorithm once on the sequence of available keystream bytes and count the number of *conflict sets*. *Numconflits* will be $O(R)$ if j is stuck during the interval when those keystream bytes were generated; otherwise, *Numconflits* will be $O(RN)$.

4   Conclusion

We theoretically show how to recover the RC4 permutation completely when the value of the pseudo-random index j is stuck at some value x from a point when $i = i_{st}$. In such a case, $8N$ keystream output bytes suffice to retrieve the permutation in around $O(N)$ time when x and i_{st} are known and in $O(N^3)$ time when they are unknown, N being the size of the permutation ($N = 256$ in standard RC4 applications). Our analysis of the evolution of the permutation and that of the output indices reveals interesting combinatorial structures.

Acknowledgments. The authors like to thank the anonymous reviewers for their comments that helped improve the editorial as well as the technical quality of the paper. Also we like to thank Prof. Palash Sarkar and Prof. Murari Mitra for discussion and valuable comments.

References

1. Biham, E., Granboulan, L., Nguyen, P.Q.: Impossible Fault Analysis of RC4 and Differential Fault Analysis of RC4. In: Gilbert, H., Handschuh, H. (eds.) FSE 2005. LNCS, vol. 3557, pp. 359–367. Springer, Heidelberg (2005)
2. Finney, H.: An RC4 cycle that can't happen (September 1994)
3. Hoch, J.J., Shamir, A.: Fault Analysis of Stream Ciphers. In: Joye, M., Quisquater, J.-J. (eds.) CHES 2004. LNCS, vol. 3156, pp. 240–253. Springer, Heidelberg (2004)
4. Knudsen, L.R., Meier, W., Preneel, B., Rijmen, V., Verdoolaege, S.: Analysis Methods for (Alleged) RCA. In: Ohta, K., Pei, D. (eds.) ASIACRYPT 1998. LNCS, vol. 1514, pp. 327–341. Springer, Heidelberg (1998)
5. Maitra, S., Paul, G.: New Form of Permutation Bias and Secret Key Leakage in Keystream Bytes of RC4. In: Workshop on Fast Software Encryption, FSE 2008 (2008)
6. Mantin, I.: Predicting and Distinguishing Attacks on RC4 Keystream Generator. In: Cramer, R. (ed.) EUROCRYPT 2005. LNCS, vol. 3494, pp. 491–506. Springer, Heidelberg (2005)
7. Mantin, I.: A Practical Attack on the Fixed RC4 in the WEP Mode. In: Roy, B. (ed.) ASIACRYPT 2005. LNCS, vol. 3788, pp. 395–411. Springer, Heidelberg (2005)
8. Maximov, A., Khovratovich, D.: New State Recovering Attack on RC4 (Full Version). IACR Eprint Server, eprint.iacr.org, number 2008/017 (January 10, 2008)
9. Tomasevic, V., Bojanic, S., Nieto-Taladriz, O.: Finding an internal state of RC4 stream cipher. Information Sciences 177, 1715–1727 (2007)

Related-Key Chosen IV Attacks
on Grain-v1 and Grain-128*

Yuseop Lee[1], Kitae Jeong[1], Jaechul Sung[2], and Seokhie Hong[1]

[1] Center for Information Security Technologies(CIST),
Korea University, Seoul, Korea
{yusubi,kite,hsh}@cist.korea.ac.kr
[2] Department of Mathematics, University of Seoul, Seoul, Korea
jcsung@uos.ac.kr

Abstract. The slide resynchronization attack on Grain was proposed in [6]. This attack finds related keys and initialization vectors of Grain that generate the 1-bit shifted keystream sequence. In this paper, we extend the attack proposed in [6] and propose related-key chosen IV attacks on Grain-v1 and Grain-128. The attack on Grain-v1 recovers the secret key with $2^{22.59}$ chosen IVs, $2^{26.29}$-bit keystream sequences and $2^{22.90}$ computational complexity. To recover the secret key of Grain-128, our attack requires $2^{26.59}$ chosen IVs, $2^{31.39}$-bit keystream sequences and $2^{27.01}$ computational complexity. These works are the first known key recovery attacks on Grain-v1 and Grain-128.

Keywords: Stream cipher, Grain-v1, Grain-128, Related-key chosen IV attack, Cryptanalysis.

1   Introduction

A bit-oriented synchronous stream cipher Grain [2] was designed by M. Hell, T. Johansson and W. Meier. Their main goal was to design an algorithm which can be implemented efficiently in hardware. Grain consists of two 80-bit shift registers, a linear feedback shift register (LFSR) and a nonlinear feedback shift register (NFSR), and a 5-input filter function. The key size is specified with 80 bits and additionally an initialization vector of 64 bits is required. But because of weakness in the filter function, a key recovery attack [1] and a distinguishing attack [5] on Grain were proposed.

In order to solve the security problem of Grain, the designers of Grain proposed the tweak versions of Grain, called Grain-v1 [3] and Grain-128 [4]. Similarly to Grain, Grain-v1 uses a 80-bit secret key and a 64-bit initialization vector to fill in an internal state of size 160 bits divided into LFSR and NFSR of length 80 bits each. The feedback function of NFSR used in Grain-v1 is not equal to

---

* This research was supported by the MKE(Ministry of Knowledge Economy), Korea, under the ITRC(Information Technology Research Center) support program supervised by the IITA(Institute of Information Technology Advancement) (IITA-2008-(C1090-0801-0025)).

Y. Mu, W. Susilo, and J. Seberry (Eds.): ACISP 2008, LNCS 5107, pp. 321–335, 2008.

that used in Grain. Grain-v1 generate a keystream bit by XORing 7-bit values from NFSR with the output value of the filter function, in contrast to XORing 1-bit value from NFSR with the output value of the filter function in Grain. The Grain-128 supports a 128-bit secret key and a 96-bit initialization vector. It consists of an 128-bit LFSR, an 128-bit NFSR and a 9-input filter function.

On the other hand, Grain, Grain-v1 and Grain-128 use the same setup mode similar to the keystream generation mode. The slide resynchronization attack (SRA) on Grain was suggested with this property [6], finds related keys and initialization vectors of Grain that generate the 1-bit shifted keystream sequence with probability 2^{-2}. In this paper, we extend the attack in [6] and propose related-key chosen IV attacks on Grain-v1 and Grain-128. To attack Grain-v1 and Grain-128, our attack uses $m + 1$ keys and does m steps repeatedly, i.e., we run the fist step by using the secret key and the first related key and then the second step by using the first related key and the second related key and so on. In each step, we apply three methods, D-Test, $*$-Change and $\dagger$-Change which will be explained in Section 3. At first, in order to construct α linear equations for the secret key, we find the initialization vector passing D-Test for the secret key and the α-bit left rotated key among chosen initialization vectors adequately. Then we apply $\dagger$-Change to recover additional α-bit key. We repeat this step m times. In case of Grain-v1 we can find $2m\alpha$-bit information of the key, the remained key bits can be recovered by the exhaustive search with computational complexity $2^{80-2m\alpha}$. The attack on Grain-128 is similar to that of Grain-v1. It decrease the computational complexity of the exhaustive search from 2^{128} to $2^{128-3m\alpha}$. Table 1 summarizes our results.

This paper is organized as follows: in Section 2, we briefly describe Grain-v1, Grain-128 and the attack proposed in [6]. We present key recovery attacks on Grain-v1 and Grain-128 in Section 3 and 4, respectively. Finally, we conclude in Section 5.

Table 1. Results on Grain-v1 and Grain-128

Stream Cipher	Related Keys	Data Complexity		Computational Complexity
		Chosen IVs	Keystream Bits	
Grain-v1	3	$2^{22.59}$	$2^{26.29}$	$2^{22.90}$ 240-clock cycles
Grain-128	3	$2^{26.59}$	$2^{31.39}$	$2^{27.01}$ 384-clock cycles

2   Preliminaries

In this section, we briefly describe Grain-v1, Grain-128 and the attack proposed in [6]. The following notations are used throughout the paper.

- S^t: the internal state of Grain-v1 and Grain-128 at time t.
- L^t: the internal state of LFSR at time t.
- N^t: the internal state of NFSR at time t.
- n^t: a feedback bit of the NFSR at time t.

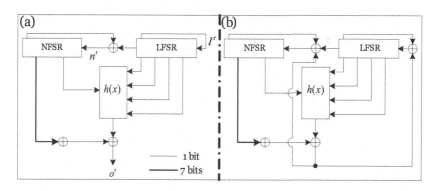

Fig. 1. (a) the keystream generation mode (b) the setup mode of Grain-v1

- l^t: a feedback bit of the LFSR at time t.
- o^t: an output bit of Grain-v1 or Grain-128 at time t.
- $Z = (z_0, z_1, \cdots)$: the keystream sequence of Grain-v1 or Grain-128.
- $Z[\alpha]$: the α-bit shifted keystream sequence of Z, i.e., $Z[\alpha] = (z_\alpha, z_{\alpha+1}, \cdots)$.

2.1 Grain-v1 and Gain-128

Grain-v1 consists of an 80-bit LFSR, an 80-bit NFSR and a 5-input filter function h. It generates the keystream sequence from an 80-bit secret key $K = (k_0, \cdots, k_{79})$ and a 64-bit initialization vector $IV = (iv_0, \cdots, iv_{63})$.

At time t, LFSR and NFSR are denoted by $L^t = (L_0^t, \cdots, L_{79}^t)$ and $N^t = (N_0^t, \cdots, N_{79}^t)$, respectively, where L_{79}^t, N_{79}^t are the most significant bits. The feedback bits of LFSR and NFSR, l^t and n^t, are computed as follows:

$$l^t = L_{62}^t \oplus L_{51}^t \oplus L_{38}^t \oplus L_{23}^t \oplus L_{13}^t \oplus L_0^t.$$

$$\begin{aligned}
n^t = {} & L_0^t \oplus N_{62}^t \oplus N_{60}^t \oplus N_{52}^t \oplus N_{45}^t \oplus N_{37}^t \oplus N_{33}^t \oplus N_{28}^t \oplus N_{21}^t \oplus N_{14}^t \oplus N_9^t \oplus N_0^t \\
& \oplus N_{63}^t N_{60}^t \oplus N_{37}^t N_{33}^t \oplus N_{15}^t N_9^t \oplus N_{60}^t N_{52}^t N_{45}^t \oplus N_{33}^t N_{28}^t N_{21}^t \oplus N_{63}^t N_{45}^t N_{28}^t N_9^t \\
& \oplus N_{60}^t N_{52}^t N_{37}^t N_{33}^t \oplus N_{63}^t N_{60}^t N_{21}^t N_{15}^t \oplus N_{63}^t N_{60}^t N_{52}^t N_{45}^t N_{37}^t \\
& \oplus N_{33}^t N_{28}^t N_{21}^t N_{15}^t N_9^t \oplus N_{52}^t N_{45}^t N_{37}^t N_{33}^t N_{28}^t N_{21}^t.
\end{aligned}$$

The filter function h takes 5-bit input values from LFSR and NFSR as follows:

$$\begin{aligned}
h(L_3^t, L_{25}^t, L_{46}^t, L_{64}^t, N_{63}^t) = {} & L_{25}^t \oplus N_{63}^t \oplus L_3^t L_{64}^t \oplus L_{46}^t L_{64}^t \oplus L_{64}^t N_{63}^t \oplus L_3^t L_{25}^t L_{46}^t \\
& \oplus L_3^t L_{46}^t L_{64}^t \oplus L_3^t L_{46}^t N_{63}^t \oplus L_{25}^t L_{46}^t N_{63}^t \oplus L_{46}^t L_{64}^t N_{63}^t.
\end{aligned}$$

At time t, the output bit o^t of Grain-v1 is generated as follows.

$$o^t = \sum_{k \in A} N_k^t \oplus h(L_3^t, L_{25}^t, L_{46}^t, L_{64}^t, N_{63}^t),$$

where $A = \{1, 2, 4, 10, 31, 43, 56\}$. Note that z_0 is equal to o^{160}, since Grain-v1 is clocked for 160 clock cycles without producing the keystream sequence.

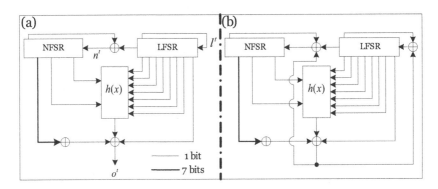

Fig. 2. (a) the keystream generation mode (b) the setup mode of Grain-128

The setup process is carried out using (K, IV) in three steps:

1. The internal state of NFSR is loaded with K as follows: $N_i^0 = k_i$ $(0 \leq i \leq 79)$.
2. The internal state of LFSR is loaded with IV as follows:

$$L_i^0 = \begin{cases} iv_i, & \text{where } 0 \leq i \leq 63 \\ 1, & \text{where } 64 \leq i \leq 80 \end{cases}.$$

3. The two registers are clocked for 160 clock cycles without producing the keystream sequence, where the output bit is fed back and XORed with the input, both to LFSR and to NFSR. See Fig. 1-(b).

Grain-128 consists of a 128-bit LFSR, a 128-bit NFSR and a 9-input filter function h. It generates keystream sequence from a 128-bit secret key $K = (k_0, \cdots, k_{127})$ and a 96-bit initialization vector $IV = (iv_0, \cdots, iv_{95})$. At time t, the feedback bits of LFSR and NFSR are computed as follows.

$$l^t = L_{96}^t \oplus L_{81}^t \oplus L_{70}^t \oplus L_{38}^t \oplus L_7^t \oplus L_0^t.$$

$$n^t = L_0^t \oplus N_{96}^t \oplus N_{91}^t \oplus N_{56}^t \oplus N_{26}^t \oplus N_0^t \oplus N_{84}^t N_{68}^t \oplus N_{65}^t N_{61}^t \oplus N_{48}^t N_{40}^t$$
$$\oplus N_{59}^t N_{27}^t \oplus N_{18}^t N_{17}^t \oplus N_{13}^t N_{11}^t \oplus N_{67}^t N_3^t.$$

The filter function h takes an input values as 7-bit values from LFSR and 2-bit values from NFSR, respectively. It is defined as follows:

$$h(L_8^t, L_{13}^t, L_{20}^t, L_{42}^t, L_{60}^t, L_{79}^t, L_{95}^t, N_{12}^t, N_{95}^t) = N_{12}^t L_8^t \oplus L_{13}^t L_{20}^t \oplus N_{95}^t L_{42}^t$$
$$\oplus L_{60}^t L_{79}^t \oplus N_{12}^t N_{95}^t L_{95}^t.$$

The output bit o^t of Grain-128 at time t is generated as follows.

$$o^t = \sum_{k \in A} N_k^t \oplus h(L_8^t, L_{13}^t, L_{20}^t, L_{42}^t, L_{60}^t, L_{79}^t, L_{95}^t, N_{12}^t, N_{95}^t) \oplus L_{93}^t,$$

where $A = \{2, 15, 36, 45, 64, 73, 89\}$ and $z_0 = o^{256}$.

The setup process of Grain-128 is similar to that of Grain-v1 except that the number of clocking without producing the keystream sequence is 256. See Fig. 2-(b).

Table 2. Conditions used in the attack on Grain

$K = (k_0, \cdots, k_{79})$, $IV = (iv_0, \cdots, iv_{79})$			$K' = (k_1, \cdots, k_{79}, n^0 \oplus o^0)$, $IV' = (iv_1, \cdots, iv_{63}, 1)$			Condition
t	N_{79}^t	L_{79}^t	t	$N_{79}'^t$	$L_{79}'^t$	
0	k_{79}	1				
1	$n^0 \oplus o^0$	$l^0 \oplus o^0$	0	$n^0 \oplus o^0$	1	$l^0 \oplus o^0 = 1$
2	$n^1 \oplus o^1$	$l^1 \oplus o^1$	1	$n'^0 \oplus o'^0$	$l'^0 \oplus o'^0$	
⋮	⋮	⋮	⋮	⋮	⋮	⋮
160	$n^{159} \oplus o^{159}$	$l^{159} \oplus o^{159}$	159	$n'^{158} \oplus o'^{158}$	$l'^{158} \oplus o'^{158}$	
161	n^{160}	l^{160}	160	$n'^{159} \oplus o'^{159}$	$l'^{159} \oplus o'^{159}$	$o'^{159} = 0$
162	n^{161}	l^{161}	161	$n'^{160} \oplus o'^{160}$	$l'^{160} \oplus o'^{160}$	
⋮	⋮	⋮	⋮	⋮	⋮	⋮

2.2 Slide Resynchronization Attack on Grain

In [6], Kücük showed that it is possible to find related keys and initialization vectors of Grain. For any pair (K, IV), slide resynchronization attack (SRA) on Grain finds the related pair $(K', IV') = ((k'_0, \cdots, k'_{79}), (iv'_0, \cdots, iv'_{63}))$ that generates the 1-bit shifted keystream sequence with probability 2^{-2}. It is based on two observations:

1. The number of updated bits for 1 clock is only 2.
2. The setup process and the keystream generation procedure are similar.

SRA is done by assuming two conditions as shown in Table 2. The relation of (K, IV) and (K', IV') is as follows:

$$K = (k_0, \cdots, k_{79}) \Rightarrow K' = (k_1, \cdots, k_{79}, b), \text{ where } b \in \{0, 1\}.$$
$$IV = (iv_0, \cdots, iv_{63}) \Rightarrow IV' = (iv_1, \cdots, iv_{63}, 1).$$

Let S^t and S'^t be internal states generated from (K, IV) and (K', IV') at time t, respectively. We assume that $S^1 = S'^0$ which is equal to $l^0 \oplus o^0 = 1$ from Table 2. Then $S^{t+1} = S'^t$ ($0 \le t \le 159$). S^{161} is updated by the keystream generation mode but S'^{160} is updated by the setup mode. If $o'^{159} = 0$, then S^{161} is equal to S'^{160}. Thus if $l^0 \oplus o^0 = 1$ and $o'^{159} = 0$, then (K', IV') generates the 1-bit shifted keystream sequence $Z[1]$ of Z generated from (K, IV). Assuming that $l^0 \oplus o^0$ and o'^{159} are uniformly distributed, we find the related pair (K', IV') with probability 2^{-2}.

3 Related-Key Chosen IV Attack on Grain-v1

In this section, we introduce a key recovery attack on Grain-v1. Firstly, we introduce some properties of Grain-v1 and propose a key recovery attack on Grain-v1 by using same properties. Let K be a secret key and IV be an initialization vector. Our attack uses $m+1$ keys $K, K_1, \cdots, K_m$. Here, we only describe the case that $((K, IV), (K_1, IV'))$ pair is used. Other cases can be done by repeating the case that $((K_i, IV)$ and $(K_{i+1}, IV'))$ is used, i.e., if we use three keys K, K_1 and K_2, we run the first attack by using K, K_1 and then second one by using K_1, K_2. The second attack procedure is almost similar to the first.

3.1   Constructing α Linear Equations for K

The related key K' and initialization vector IV' are defined as follows. Here, α is a parameter such that $1 \leq \alpha \leq 12$.

$$K = (k_0, \cdots, k_{79}) \Rightarrow K' = (k_\alpha, \cdots, k_{79}, k_0, \cdots, k_{\alpha-1}). \qquad (1)$$
$$IV = (iv_0, \cdots, iv_{63}) \Rightarrow IV' = (iv_\alpha, \cdots, iv_{63}, 1, \cdots, 1). \qquad (2)$$

Let Z and Z' be keystream sequences generated from (K, IV) and (K', IV'). Kücük assumed that S^1 is equal to S'^0 which implies S^{t+1} is equal to S'^t ($0 \leq t \leq 159$). We can get Property 1 by using this property.

Property 1. If S^α is equal to S'^0, then S^i is equal to $S'^{i-\alpha}$ for $\alpha < i \leq 160$. It means that o^i is equal to $o'^{i-\alpha}$. That is,

$$S^\alpha = S'^0 \Rightarrow S^i = S'^{i-\alpha}.$$

Proof. This property follows directly from the setup process of Grain-v1. Recall that the number of clocking without producing the keystream sequence is 160 in the setup process. □

If IV satisfies $S^\alpha = S'^0$, we say that IV is *valid*. Otherwise we say that the IV is *invalid*. In Theorem 1, we prove that we can construct total 2α equations for secret key using a valid IV and calculate the probability that a valid IV exists.

Theorem 1. *For a valid IV, we can construct 2α equations of which unknown values are K. And the valid IV exists with probability $2^{-2\alpha}$. That is,*

$$Pr\left(S^\alpha = S'^0\right) = 2^{-2\alpha}.$$

Proof. Since (K, IV) is loaded to NFSR and LFSR directly, the following holds:

$$S^\alpha = S'^0 \Leftrightarrow N^\alpha = K', L^\alpha = IV'\|(1\cdots 1).$$

For $0 \leq i < \alpha$, $N^\alpha = K'$ and $L^\alpha = IV'\|(1\cdots 1)$ imply (3) and (4).

$$n^i \oplus o^i = k_i. \qquad (3)$$
$$l^i \oplus o^i = 1. \qquad (4)$$

So, we can construct 2α equations for K using the valid IV. If n^i, o^i, l^i and k_i are assumed statically independent, (3) and (4) hold with probability 2^{-1}, respectively. Thus $S^\alpha = S'^0$ holds with probability $2^{-2\alpha}$. □

We show that how to construct α linear equations for K in Property 2 and Theorem 2.

Property 2. If h takes the input value of which some bits are fixed, then it is approximated to h' with probability 1, as follows.

Approx$_1$: If $L_{46}^t = 0, L_{64}^t = 1$ then $h' = L_3^t \oplus L_{25}^t$
Approx$_2$: If $L_3^t = L_{25}^t, L_{46}^t = 1, L_{64}^t = 1$ then $h' = N_{63}^t \oplus 1$

Using Theorem 1 and Property 2, we can induce the following theorem. This theorem shows that there exists a valid IV among $2^{2\alpha}$ IVs whose some bit positions are fixed.

Theorem 2. *For a fixed K, we choose $2^{2\alpha}$ IVs where $(iv_{45+1}, \cdots, iv_{45+\alpha}) = (0, \cdots, 0)$, $(iv_{12+1}, \cdots, iv_{12+\alpha}, iv_{24+1}, \cdots, iv_{24+\alpha})$ are all 2α-bit values and the remaining bits are fixed to b ($\in \{0,1\}$). Then there exists exactly one valid IV. Thus we can construct α linear equations for K using (6) and the IV.*

Proof. $L_{64}^0, \cdots, L_{79}^0$ are fixed to 1 in the setup mode. Thus (3) and (4) are equal to (5) and (6) respectively by Approx$_1$ of Property 2, if $iv_{45+1}, \cdots, iv_{45+\alpha}$ are fixed 0.

$$iv_i \oplus (iv_{3+i} \oplus iv_{25+i}) = (n^i \oplus iv_i) \oplus k_i \oplus \bigoplus_{s \in A} k_{s+i}, \tag{5}$$

$$(iv_i \oplus iv_{13+i} \oplus iv_{23+i} \oplus iv_{38+i} \oplus iv_{51+i} \oplus iv_{62+i}) \oplus (iv_{3+i} \oplus iv_{25+i}) = 1 \oplus \bigoplus_{s \in A} k_{s+i}, \tag{6}$$

where $0 \le i < \alpha$ and $A = \{1, 2, 4, 10, 31, 43, 56\}$. Because the right hand side of (5) and (6) are determined by K, these values are fixed for all chosen IVs. Also the remaining bits of IVs except for $(iv_{12+1}, \cdots, iv_{12+\alpha}, iv_{24+1}, \cdots, iv_{24+\alpha})$ are fixed for all chosen IVs by the assumption. Thus we can rewrite (5) as (7), where the right hand side of (7) is fixed for all chosen IVs.

$$iv_{25+i} = iv_{3+i} \oplus n^i \oplus k_i \oplus \bigoplus_{s \in A} k_{s+i}. \tag{7}$$

Since $iv_{25+i} \in \{iv_{24+1}, \cdots, iv_{24+\alpha}\}$, there exist 2^α IVs which satisfy (7) among all $2^{2\alpha}$ chosen IVs and these IVs are fixed except for $(iv_{12+1}, \cdots, iv_{12+\alpha})$. Similarly to the case of (5), we can rewrite (6) as (8), where the right hand side of (8) is fixed for all 2^α IVs.

$$iv_{13+i} = iv_i \oplus iv_{23+i} \oplus iv_{38+i} \oplus iv_{51+i} \oplus iv_{62+i} \oplus iv_{3+i} \oplus iv_{25+i} \oplus 1 \oplus \bigoplus_{s \in A} k_{s+i}. \tag{8}$$

So there exists exactly one IV satisfying (7) and (8) among all chosen $2^{2\alpha}$ IVs. By the definition of "valid IV", the IV satisfying (7) and (8) is valid. Hence there exists exactly one valid IV. Moreover, we can construct α linear equations by applying the valid IV to (6), since (6) is a linear equation for K. $\qquad\square$

Table 3. The changed bit positions of *-Change

Event	The changed bit positions	Event	The changed bit positions
*-Change$_1$	iv_{15}, iv_{40}	*-Change$_5$	$iv_{15}, iv_{40}, iv_{16}, iv_{41}$
*-Change$_2$	iv_{16}, iv_{41}	*-Change$_6$	$iv_{15}, iv_{40}, iv_{17}, iv_{42}$
*-Change$_3$	iv_{17}, iv_{42}	*-Change$_7$	$iv_{15}, iv_{40}, iv_{18}, iv_{43}$
*-Change$_4$	iv_{18}, iv_{43}	*-Change$_8$	$iv_{16}, iv_{41}, iv_{17}, iv_{42}$

Let β be the maximum value such that $z_i = 0$ ($0 \leq i < \beta$) (Note that the expected value of β is about 2, since $2 \approx 1 \cdot \frac{1}{2} + 2 \cdot \frac{1}{4} + 3 \cdot \frac{1}{8} + \cdots$). Because an updated bit affects to keystream bits after 16 clock cycles, we define $\sim_\alpha$ as follows:

$$Z \sim_\alpha Z' \Leftrightarrow z_{\alpha+i} = z'_i \ (0 \leq i < 16 - \alpha + \beta).$$

In our attack, we find a valid IV by checking that Z and Z' satisfy $Z \sim_\alpha Z'$. The following theorem enable us to distinguish a valid IV and an invalid IV.

Theorem 3. *A valid IV always satisfies $Z \sim_\alpha Z'$ but an invalid IV satisfies it with probability $2^{-(16-\alpha+\beta)}$.*

Proof. By Theorem 1, a valid IV satisfies $S^{160} = S'^{160-\alpha}$. Then o^{160} ($= z_0$) is equal to $o'^{160-\alpha}$. Since $z_i = 0$ ($0 \leq i < b$), $o'^{160-\alpha+i} = z_i = 0$ ($0 \leq i < \beta$) and $S^{160+\beta} = S'^{160-\alpha+\beta}$. After ($\alpha - \beta$) clock cycles, $L^{160+\alpha}$ and $N^{160+\alpha}$ are always equal to L'^{160} and N'^{160} except the ($\alpha - \beta$) most significant bits, respectively. Since α used in our attack is less than or equal to 12, h takes the same input values for additional ($16 - \alpha + \beta$) clock cycles in two cases. Thus (K, IV) and (K', IV') always generate the same keystream bits for additional ($16 - \alpha + \beta$) clock cycles. For an invalid IV, Z and Z' are uniformly generated. Thus the IV satisfies $Z \sim_\alpha Z'$ with $2^{-(16-\alpha+\beta)}$. ☐

If $\alpha = 12$ and $\beta = 2$, then the probability that an invalid IV satisfies $Z \sim_\alpha Z'$ is 2^{-6} (we call it D-Test) which is not small. To decrease the probability that an invalid IV passes D-Test, we use another method, *-Change. For any IV, we generate the corresponding IV^* by modifying the values of even positions in the IV. We change the bits of IV that do not affect the results of (5) and (6) as shown in Table 3. Since these bits are not used as input values of h for $1 \leq \alpha \leq 12$ and the left hand side of (6) is linear, the results of these equations do not change. Thus an IV is valid if and only if the corresponding IV^* is valid. Corollary 1 show that we can distinguish valid IVs and invalid IVs with very high probability using *-changes. In our attack, we generate ($\gamma - 1$) IV^*s for an IV where γ is the integer satisfying $2^{2\alpha - \gamma(16-\alpha+\beta)} << 1$. Hence, we can find a valid IV by Corollary 1 and construct α linear equations for K using Theorem 2 and the valid IV.

Corollary 1. *If an IV is invalid, the probability that the IV and the corresponding IV^* pass D-Test is $2^{-2(16-\alpha+\beta)}$. Further, the IV and the corresponding ($\gamma - 1$) IV^*s pass D-Test with probability $2^{-\gamma(16-\alpha+\beta)}$.*

Proof. This property follows directly from the fact that each invalid IV^* passes D-Test independently.   □

3.2   Recovering Another α-Bit Key

Up to now, we introduced the method to find a valid IV and construct α linear equations for K by using the valid IV. From this, we can get the α-bit key information. Now, we present the method, †-Change, to recover another α-bit key. For a valid IV, we will generate the corresponding $IV^\dagger$ by modifying the values of some positions in the valid IV. In case of $\alpha = 12$, Appendix A.1 presents the bit positions where †-Change modifies. The conditionally changed bit positions in †-Change$_i$ are modified only if iv_{3+i} is not equal to iv_{25+i}. Here, we focus only †-Change$_0$. Other events †-Change$_i$ ($1 \leq i \leq 11$) can be done similar to †-Change$_0$. †-Change$_0$ is done as follows:

---

1. Using Approx$_2$ of Property 2, do the followings;
   (a) Modify iv_{46} which is the third input value of h at time 0.
   (b) If iv_3 is not equal to iv_{25}, then modify iv_{25}. Here, iv_3 and iv_{25} are the first and second input values of h at time 0, respectively.
2. Modify bit positions of the IV such that the results of (5) and (6) that time is not 0 do not change.
   (a) Since iv_{46} changes the result of (6) at time 8, modify iv_{59} which is in the linear part of (6) at time 8. Note that we can change other bits which are in the linear part of (6) at time 8. But we found that the number of the additional changed bits for iv_{59} are less than for other bits.
   (b) If iv_{25} in Step 1-(b) is changed, it changes the result of (6) at time 2. Thus modify iv_{15} which is in the linear part of (6) at time 2.

Applying †-Change$_0$, the results of (5) and (6) for (K, IV) are equal to them for $(K, IV^\dagger)$ except time 0. The equations for $(K, IV^\dagger)$ at time 0 are (9) and (10). Here, $A = \{1, 2, 4, 10, 31, 43, 56\}$.

$$iv_0 \oplus (k_{63} \oplus 1) = (n^0 \oplus iv_0) \oplus k_0 \oplus \bigoplus_{s \in A} k_s. \tag{9}$$

$$(iv_0 \oplus iv_{13} \oplus iv_{23} \oplus iv_{38} \oplus iv_{51} \oplus iv_{62}) \oplus (k_{63} \oplus 1) = 1 \oplus \bigoplus_{s \in A} k_s. \tag{10}$$

If the $IV^\dagger$ is valid, (5) and (6) are equal to (9) and (10) at time 0, respectively. Thus we get (11). Otherwise we get (12). Applying other events similarly, we can recover $k_{63}, \cdots, k_{74}$.

$$iv_3 \oplus iv_{25} = k_{63} \oplus 1. \tag{11}$$

$$iv_3 \oplus iv_{25} = k_{63}. \tag{12}$$

3.3   Description of Our Attack on Grain-v1

We are ready to present our attack on Grain-v1. This attack uses $m + 1$ keys $K, K_1, \cdots, K_m$ and consists of m steps. For $0 \leq i < m$, the i-th step use K_i and K_{i+1} satisfying the following relation:

$$K_i = (k_0, \cdots, k_{79}) \Rightarrow K_{i+1} = (k_\alpha, \cdots, k_{79}, k_0, \cdots, k_{\alpha-1}).$$

Note that $K_0 = K$. In each step, we construct α linear equations for K and recover the α-bit key. Finally we find the remaining bits by the exhaustive search. Each step runs three algorithms, the FilterIV algorithm, the CheckValid algorithm and the RecoverKey algorithm. Firstly, the FilterIV algorithm finds a valid IV among $2^{2\alpha}$ IVs that satisfies Corollary 1 as follows:

---

1. Generate $2^{2\alpha}$ $(16 + \beta_i)$-bit keystream sequences Z_i by using K and IV_i $(1 \leq i < 2^{2\alpha})$ from Corollary 1. Here, β_i is the value such that the first β_i bits of Z_i are zeros.
2. Calculate the corresponding IV_i' to IV_i from (2) and generate the $(16 - \alpha + \beta_i)$-bit keystream sequence Z_i' by using K' and IV_i'.
3. Check D-test for each (Z_i, Z_i') and store all IV_i which the corresponding Z_i and Z_i' pass D-test.
4. Until only one IV remains, repeat the followings;
   (a) Set $j=1$;
   (b) Calculate IV^*s by applying *-Change$_j$ to the remaining IVs.
   (c) Calculate the $IV^{*'}$s corresponding IV^*s.
   (d) Generate keystream sequences using (K, IV^*) and $(K', IV^{*'})$.
   (e) Check D-Test for the generated keystream sequences and discard IVs that the corresponding keystream sequences do not pass D-test.
   (f) Add 1 to j.
5. Return the remaining IV.

On average, the number of IVs used in this algorithm is

$$2 \sum_{i=0}^{\gamma-1} \left(2^{2\alpha - i(16 - \alpha + \beta)} \right),$$

where α is parameter which is chosen by the attacker, β is maximum value such that $z_i = 0$ $(0 \leq i < \beta)$ and γ is the number satisfying $2^{2\alpha - \gamma(16 - \alpha + \beta)} << 1$.

From an IV, this algorithm generates the $(16 + \beta)$-bit keystream sequence for K and the $(16 - \alpha + \beta)$-bit keystream sequence for K'. Thus it requires the

$$(16 + \beta) \sum_{i=0}^{\gamma-1} \left(2^{2\alpha - i(16 - \alpha + \beta)} \right) + (16 - \alpha + \beta) \sum_{i=0}^{\gamma-1} \left(2^{2\alpha - i(16 - \alpha + \beta)} \right)$$

-bit keystream sequence on average.

The CheckValid algorithm takes an IV and checks the validity of it as follows:

---

1. Generate Z and Z' using (K, IV) and (K', IV'), respectively. Check D-test for (Z, Z'). If it does not pass D-test, then return "invalid".
2. Set $i = 1$ and if $i < \gamma$, then repeat the followings;
   (a) Calculate the IV^* by applying $*$-Change$_i$ to the IV.
   (b) Generate keystream sequences by using $(K, IV^*), (K', IV^{*\prime})$ and check D-Test for the generated keystream sequences. If they do not pass, then return "invalid".
   (c) Add 1 to i.
3. Return "valid".

This algorithm uses 2γ IVs and $((16 + \beta)\gamma + (16 - \alpha + \beta)\gamma)$-bit keystream sequence.

Finally, the RecoverKey algorithm takes a valid IV and recover the α-bit key

$$\left(k_{(62+m\alpha+1) \bmod 80}, \cdots, k_{(62+m\alpha+\alpha) \bmod 80}\right)$$

in the m-th step. Since this algorithm calls the CheckValid algorithm α times, it requires $2\alpha\gamma$ IVs and the $\alpha((16 + \beta)\gamma + (16 - \alpha + \beta)\gamma)$-bit keystream sequence. It is done as follows:

Input : a valid $IV = (iv_0, \cdots iv_{63})$
1. Set $i = 0$ and if $i < \alpha$, then repeat the followings;
   (a) Calculate the corresponding $IV_i^\dagger$ by applying $\dagger$-Change$_i$ to the IV.
   (b) Check that $IV_i^\dagger$ is valid by using the CheckValid algorithm.
   (c) If $IV_i^\dagger$ is valid, $k_{(63+m\alpha+i) \bmod 80} = iv_{3+i} \oplus iv_{25+i} \oplus 1$. Otherwise $k_{(63+m\alpha+i) \bmod 80} = iv_{3+i} \oplus iv_{25+i}$.
   (d) Add 1 to i.

We find the right secret key by the exhaustive search by using the $2m\alpha$-bit key information obtained in previous steps. We generate the 80-bit keystream sequence from each candidate key and check that it is equal to the original keystream sequence. Thus, this test requires 240-clock cycles of Grain-v1. Our attack procedure on Grain-v1 is done as follows:

---

1. Generate $2^{2\alpha}$ IVs from Theorem 2.
2. Set $i = 0$ and if $i < m$, repeat the followings;
   (a) For K_i and K_{i+1}, find an valid IV by using the FilterIV algorithm.
   (b) Construct α linear equations by using (6) and the valid IV.
   (c) Recover the α-bit key by using the RecoverKey algorithm.
3. Find the right secret key K by the exhaustive search using the $2m\alpha$-bit key information obtained in Step 2.

The number of chosen IVs used in our attack is $2m(\sum_{i=0}^{\gamma-1}(2^{2\alpha-i(16-\alpha+\beta)}) + \gamma\alpha)$ and our attack requires $m((32 - \alpha + 2\beta)(\sum_{i=0}^{\gamma-1}(2^{2\alpha-i(16-\alpha+\beta)}) + \gamma\alpha))$-bit keystream sequence. The computational complexity of Step 2 is $m(\frac{(352-\alpha+2\beta)}{240}$

Table 4. Our results on Grain-v1

m	α	γ	Data Complexity		Computational Complexity
			Chosen IVs	Keystream Bits	
1	12	6	$2^{25.02}$	$2^{28.61}$	2^{56}
2	12	6	$2^{26.02}$	$2^{29.61}$	$2^{32.02}$
3	10	4	$2^{22.59}$	$2^{26.29}$	$2^{22.90}$
3	12	6	$2^{26.61}$	$2^{30.19}$	$2^{26.70}$

Computation complexity unit: 240-clock cycles of Grain-v1

$(\sum_{i=0}^{\gamma-1}(2^{2\alpha-i(16-\alpha+\beta)})+\gamma\alpha))$ 240-clock cycles of Grain-v1. Since we get the $2m\alpha$-bit key information, the computational complexity of Step 3 is $2^{80-2m\alpha}$ 240-clock cycles of Grain-v1. Table 4 shows the complexities of our attack for parameters m, α and γ. For $m = 3$, $\alpha = 10$ and $\gamma = 4$, we recover the secret key of Grain-v1 with $2^{26.29}$ bits keystream sequence and $2^{22.90}$ computational complexity. If we use more related keys, we need less complexities to attack Grain-v1, i.e., if we use 40 related keys, then the computational complexity decrease to $2^{8.21}$ 240-clock cycles of Grain-v1 and the data complexity is as follows: $2^{8.64}$ chosen IVs and $2^{12.77}$-bit keystream sequence. The usage of 3 related keys and the computational complexity of $2^{22.90}$ is reasonable. For $m = 3$, $\alpha = 10$ and $\gamma = 4$, we practically recovered the secret key within 3 minutes on average.

4 Related-Key Chosen IV Attack on Grain-128

Since the attack on Grain-128 is similar to that on Grain-v1, we briefly present our attack on Grain-128 using one related key K'. K', IV' and $\sim_\alpha$ are defined as follows:

$$K = (k_0, \cdots, k_{127}) \Rightarrow K' = (k_\alpha, \cdots, k_{127}, k_0, \cdots, k_{\alpha-1}).$$
$$IV = (iv_0, \cdots, iv_{95}) \Rightarrow IV' = (iv_\alpha, \cdots, iv_{95}, 1, \cdots, 1).$$
$$Z \sim_\alpha Z' \Leftrightarrow z_{\alpha+i} = z'_i \ (0 \le i < 32 - \alpha + \beta).$$

In case of Grain-128, a valid IV always satisfy $Z \sim_\alpha Z'$ but an invalid IV passes D-test with probability $2^{-(32-\alpha+\beta)}$. Similarly to the attack on Grain-v1, we apply $*$-Change to decreases the probability that an invalid IV passes D-test. The changed bit positions are shown in Table 5. In the attack on Grain-v1, we change the values of even positions in IV but the positions of Table 5 do not affect all equations for $\alpha \le 15$. Thus we choose just one position in IV.

Table 5. The changed bit positions of $*$-Change on Grain-128

Event	The changed bit positions	Event	The changed bit positions
$*$-change$_1$	iv_{38}	$*$-change$_3$	iv_{40}
$*$-change$_2$	iv_{39}	$*$-change$_4$	iv_{41}

Table 6. The modification of h

Event	Fixed value	Approximated function h'
Approx$_1$	$L_8^t = 0, L_{13}^t = 0, L_{42}^t = 0, L_{60}^t = 0, L_{95}^t = 1$	$N_{12}^t N_{95}^t$
Approx$_2$	$L_8^t = 1, L_{13}^t = 0, L_{42}^t = 0, L_{60}^t = 0, L_{95}^t = 1$	$N_{12}^t \oplus N_{12}^t N_{95}^t$
Approx$_3$	$L_8^t = 0, L_{13}^t = 0, L_{42}^t = 1, L_{60}^t = 0, L_{95}^t = 1$	$N_{95}^t \oplus N_{12}^t N_{95}^t$

Table 7. Our results on Grain-128

m	α	γ	Data Complexity		Computational Complexity
			Chosen IVs	Keystream Bits	
1	15	2	2^{31}	$2^{35.73}$	2^{83}
2	15	2	2^{32}	$2^{36.73}$	$2^{38.03}$
3	12	2	$2^{26.59}$	$2^{31.39}$	2^{27}
3	15	2	$2^{32.59}$	$2^{37.31}$	$2^{32.98}$

Computation complexity unit: 384-clock cycles of Grain-128

As shown in Table 6, h is approximated to h' with probability 1. Since h takes two input value from NFSR, we can recover the 2α-bit key by applying †-Change as shown in Appendix A.2. For $0 \le i < \alpha$, the events †-Change$_i^1$ and †-Change$_i^2$ can be used to recover k_{12+i} and k_{95+i}, respectively. The conditionally changed bit positions in †-Change$_i$ are modified only if $iv_{20+i} = 0$. Note that $iv_{87}, \cdots, iv_{95}$ are fixed to 1 in order to apply †-Change.

Our attack on Grain-128 uses $2^{2\alpha}$ IVs that satisfy conditions of Approx$_1$ in Table 6. Then there exists a valid IV among these IVs. But $u^i \oplus o^i = 1$ ($0 \le i < \alpha$) is quadratic equation for K. So we construct α quadratic equations for K as follows:

$$l^i \oplus k_{12+i}k_{95+i} \oplus (k_{2+i} \oplus k_{15+i} \oplus k_{36+i} \oplus k_{45+i} \oplus k_{64+i} \oplus k_{73+i} \oplus k_{89+i}) = 1.$$

Since we can recover k_{12+i} and k_{95+i} by using the RecoverKey algorithm, we can construct α linear equations as follows:

$$l^i \oplus (k_{2+i} \oplus k_{15+i} \oplus k_{36+i} \oplus k_{45+i} \oplus k_{64+i} \oplus k_{73+i} \oplus k_{89+i}) = 1 \oplus v_i \ (v_i = k_{12+i}k_{95+i}).$$

Because the RecoverKey algorithm recovers the key bits that are quadratic part of these equations, we can construct α linear equations for K. The bit positions that are modified in †-change$_i$ is presented in Appendix A.2.

As shown in Table 7, we need $2^{26.59}$ chosen IVs, the $2^{31.39}$-bit keystream sequence and 2^{27} 384-clock cycles of Grain-128 to recover the secret key of Grain-128. If we use more related keys, we need less complexities to attack Grain-128.

5   Conclusion

In this paper, we have presented related-key chosen IV attacks on Grain-v1 and Grain-128 with the weakness that the setup mode is similar to the keystream

Table 8. Simulation results of our attack

Stream Cipher	m	α	γ	Attack Time	Success Rate (success trials/total trials)
Grain-v1	3	10	4	145 sec	1 (100/100)
Grain-128	3	12	2	95 min	1 (100/100)

generation mode. As summarized in Table 1, these results imply that Grain-v1 and Grain-128 have still the weakness, though they are designed to advance Grain which has been cryptanalyzed by a key recovery attack and a distinguishing attack by the weakness in the filter function. Our attack on Grain-v1 recovers the secret key with $2^{22.59}$ chosen IVs, $2^{26.29}$-bit keystream sequences and $2^{22.90}$ computational complexity. In case of Grain-128, our attack needs $2^{26.59}$ chosen IVs, $2^{31.39}$-bit keystream sequences and $2^{27.01}$ computational complexity. Table 8 presents simulation results that our attacks. The simulation was implemented on Pentium-4, CPU 2.4GHz, 2.0 Gb RAM, OS Windows XP Pro SP2. We could always recover the secret key of Grain-v1 and Grain-128 within 3 minutes and 100 minutes on average, respectively.

References

1. Berbain, C., Gilbert, H., Maximov, A.: Cryptanalysis of Grain. In: Robshaw, M.J.B. (ed.) FSE 2006. LNCS, vol. 4047, pp. 15–29. Springer, Heidelberg (2006)
2. Hell, M., Johansson, T., Meier, W.: Grain - A Stream Cipher for Constrained Environments, eSTREAM - ECRYPT Stream Cipher Project, Report 2005/010 (2005), http://www.ecrypt.eu.org/stream/ciphers/grain/grain.pdf
3. Hell, M., Johansson, T., Meier, W.: Grain - A Stream Cipher for Constrained Environments, eSTREAM - ECRYPT Stream Cipher Project (2007), http://www.ecrypt.eu.org/stream/p3ciphers/grain/Grain_p3.pdf
4. Hell, M., Johansson, T., Meier, W.: A Stream Cipher Proposal: Grain-128, eSTREAM - ECRYPT Stream Cipher Project (2007), http://www.ecrypt.eu.org/stream/p3ciphers/grain/Grain128_p3.pdf
5. Khazaei, S., Hassanzadeh, M., Kiaei, M.: Distinguishing Attack on Grain, eSTREAM - ECRYPT Stream Cipher Project, Report 2005/071 (2005), http://www.ecrypt.eu.org/stream/papersdir/071.pdf
6. Kücük, O.: Slide Resynchronization Attack on the Initialization of Grain 1.0, eSTREAM - ECRYPT Stream Cipher Project, Report 2006/044 (2006), http://www.ecrypt.eu.org/stream/papersdir/2006/044.ps
7. Vielhaber, M.: Breaking ONE.FIVIUM by AIDA an Algebraic IV Differential Attack, Cryptology ePrint Archive: Report 2007/413 (2007), http://eprint.iacr.org/2007/413.pdf

A   †-Change on Grain-v1 and Grain-128

A.1   The Changed Bit Positions of †-Change on Grain-v1 ($\alpha = 12$)

Event	Recovered key bit	The changed bit positions
†-Change$_0$	k_{63}	$iv_{46}, iv_{59}, iv^c_{25}, iv^c_{15}$
†-Change$_1$	k_{64}	$iv_{47}, iv_{60}, iv^c_{26}, iv^c_{16}$
†-Change$_2$	k_{65}	$iv_{48}, iv_{61}, iv^c_{27}, iv^c_{17}$
†-Change$_3$	k_{66}	$iv_{49}, iv_{62}, iv_{38}\ , iv^c_{28}, iv^c_{18}$
†-Change$_4$	k_{67}	$iv_{50}\ , iv^c_{29}, iv^c_{19}$
†-Change$_5$	k_{68}	$iv_{51}, iv_{38}, iv^c_{30}, iv^c_{20}$
†-Change$_6$	k_{69}	$iv_{52}, iv_{39}, iv^c_{31}, iv^c_{21}$
†-Change$_7$	k_{70}	$iv_{53}, iv_{40}, iv^c_{32}, iv^c_{22}$
†-Change$_8$	k_{71}	$iv_{54}, iv_{41}, iv^c_{33}, iv^c_{37}, iv^c_{61}$
†-Change$_9$	k_{72}	$iv_{55}, iv_{42}, iv^c_{34}, iv^c_{38}, iv^c_{62}$
†-Change$_{10}$	k_{73}	$iv_{56}, iv_{43}, iv^c_{35}$
†-Change$_{11}$	k_{74}	$iv_{57}, iv_{44}, iv^c_{36}$

iv^c_i: the changed bit position conditionally.

A.2   The Changed Bit Positions of †-Change on Grain-128 ($\alpha = 15$)

Event	Recovered Key bit	The changed bit positions	Event	Recovered Key bit	The changed bit positions
†-change$^1_0$	k_{12}	iv_8, iv_{68}, iv_{39}	†-change$^2_0$	k_{95}	iv_{42}, iv_{85}
†-change$^1_1$	k_{13}	iv_9, iv_{69}, iv_{40}	†-change$^2_1$	k_{96}	iv_{43}, iv_{86}
†-change$^1_2$	k_{14}	$iv_{10}, iv_{70}, iv_{41}, iv_{38}$	†-change$^2_2$	k_{97}	iv_{44}, iv_{87}
†-change$^1_3$	k_{15}	$iv_{11}, iv_{71}, iv_{85}, iv_{39}$	†-change$^2_3$	k_{98}	iv_{45}, iv_{88}
†-change$^1_4$	k_{16}	$iv_{12}, iv_{72}, iv_{86}, iv_{40}$	†-change$^2_4$	k_{99}	iv_{46}, iv_{89}
†-change$^1_5$	k_{17}	$iv_{13}, iv_{73}, iv_{87}, iv_{41}$	†-change$^2_5$	k_{100}	iv_{47}, iv_{90}
†-change$^1_6$	k_{18}	$iv_{14}, iv_{74}, iv_{77}, iv_{85}$	†-change$^2_6$	k_{101}	iv_{48}, iv_{91}
†-change$^1_7$	k_{19}	iv_{15}, iv_{78}	†-change$^2_7$	k_{102}	iv_{49}, iv_{92}
†-change$^1_8$	k_{20}	iv_{16}, iv_{79}	†-change$^2_8$	k_{103}	iv_{50}, iv_{39}
†-change$^1_9$	k_{21}	iv_{17}, iv_{80}	†-change$^2_9$	k_{104}	iv_{51}, iv_{40}
†-change$^1_{10}$	k_{22}	iv_{18}, iv_{92}	†-change$^2_{10}$	k_{105}	iv_{52}, iv_{41}
†-change$^1_{11}$	k_{23}	$iv_{19}, iv_{82}, iv_{39}$	†-change$^2_{11}$	k_{106}	iv_{53}
†-change$^1_{12}$	k_{24}	$iv_{20}, iv_{83}, iv_{40}\ , iv^c_0$	†-change$^2_{12}$	k_{107}	iv_{54}
†-change$^1_{13}$	k_{25}	$iv_{21}, iv_{84}, iv_{41}\ , iv^c_1$	†-change$^2_{13}$	k_{108}	iv_{55}
†-change$^1_{14}$	k_{26}	iv_{22}, iv^c_2	†-change$^2_{14}$	k_{109}	iv_{56}

iv^c_i: the conditional changed bit position.

Signature Generation and Detection of Malware Families

V. Sai Sathyanarayan, Pankaj Kohli, and Bezawada Bruhadeshwar

Centre for Security, Theory and Algorithmic Research (C-STAR)
International Institute of Information Technology
Hyderabad - 500032, India
{satya_vs,pankaj_kohli}@research.iiit.ac.in, bezawada@iiit.ac.in

Abstract. Malware detection and prevention is critical for the protection of computing systems across the Internet. The problem in detecting malware is that they *evolve* over a period of time and hence, traditional signature-based malware detectors fail to detect obfuscated and previously unseen malware executables. However, as malware evolves, some semantics of the original malware are preserved as these semantics are necessary for the effectiveness of the malware. Using this observation, we present a novel method for detection of malware using the correlation between the semantics of the malware and its API calls. We construct a base signature for an entire malware class rather than for a single specimen of malware. Such a signature is capable of detecting even unknown and advanced variants that belong to that class. We demonstrate our approach on some well known malware classes and show that any advanced variant of the malware class is detected from the base signature.

Keywords: Malware Detection, Signature Generation, Static Analysis.

1 Introduction

Malware or malicious code refers to the broad class of software threats to computer systems and networks. It includes any code that modifies, destroys or steals data, allows unauthorized access, exploits or damages a system, or does something that the user does not intend to do. Perhaps the most sophisticated types of threats to computer systems are presented by malicious codes that exploit vulnerabilities in applications. Pattern based signatures are the most common technique employed for malware detection. Implicit in a signature-based method is an apriori knowledge of distinctive patterns of malicious code. The advantage of such malware detectors lies in their simplicity and speed. While the signature-based approach is successful in detecting known malware, it does not work for new malware for which signatures have not yet been prepared. There is a need to train the detector often in order to detect new malware.

One of the most common reasons that the signature-based approaches fail is when the malware mutates, making signature based detection difficult. The presence of such a metamorphism has already been witnessed in the past [5, 9].

Y. Mu, W. Susilo, and J. Seberry (Eds.): ACISP 2008, LNCS 5107, pp. 336–349, 2008.

Malware authors often tend to obfuscate the executable so as to make analysis difficult and to evade detection. Four techniques [15] are commonly employed for obfuscating executables. The first approach, *insertion of dead code* involves insertion of code that does not change the malware behavior, such as a sequence of NOPs (no operation instructions). The second approach, *register reassignment* involves changing the usage of one register with another such as eax with ebx to evade detection. The third approach, *instruction substitution* replaces a sequence of instructions with an equivalent instruction sequence. Finally, the fourth approach, *code transposition* involves jumbling the sequences of instructions in such a way that the behavior of the code remains the same. We note that, although all of these approaches change the code pattern in order to evade detection, the behavior of the malware still remains the same.

Past research has focused on modeling program behavior for intrusion and malware detection. Such modeling of program behavior was first studied by Forrest et al [24]. Their approach called N-Grams used short sequences of system calls to model normal program behavior. Sekar et al [25], used system calls to construct a control flow graph of normal program behavior. Peisert et al [26], use sequence of function calls to represent program behavior. Based on such results, in our approach, we have used API calls as measure of the malware program behavior. Specifically, we use only a subset of API calls, called *critical* API calls in our analysis. These critical API calls are the ones that can possibly cause malicious behavior. API calls have been used in the past research for modeling program behavior [20, 22] and for detecting malware [19, 21, 27].

We use static analysis to extract critical API calls from known malicious programs to construct signatures for an entire malware class rather than for a single specimen of malware. In our approach, a malicious program is detected by statistical comparison of its API calls with that of a malware class. The technique presented in this paper aims to detect known and unknown malicious programs, including self-mutating malware. Also, it is capable of detecting malware that use common obfuscations. Our approach relies on the fact that the behavior of the malicious programs in a specific malware class differs considerably from programs in other malware classes and benign programs. The main contributions of this paper include:

- **Detection using API calls.** We extract critical API calls from the binary executable of a program to classify it as malicious or benign. The extracted calls are subjected to a statistical likelihood test to determine the malware class.
- **Effective against common obfuscations.** Common obfuscations such as those explained above change the code pattern but do not affect the behavior of the malware. By generating a signature that reflects the behavior of the malware, our technique is able to defeat such common obfuscations. Also, since we consider only critical API calls, such obfuscations have no effect on our signature generation approach.

- **Effective against new variants.** By constructing a signature for a malware family, our approach is automatically able to detect future variants that belong to that family.

Paper Organization. In Section 2, we present the related work done in the field of malware detection. In Section 3, we describe our approach for malware detection. In Section 4, we describe a prototype implementation of our approach, present experimental results and evaluate the effectiveness of our approach. Finally, we conclude in Section 5.

2   Related Work

Several techniques have been studied in the past for malware detection. Cohen [11] and Chess & White [12] use sandboxing to detect viruses. They proved that in general the problem of virus detection is undecidable. Christodorescu and Jha [15] use static analysis to detect malicious code in executables. Their implementation called *SAFE* handles most common types of obfuscations used by malware writers, such as insertion of NOPs between instructions, that are used to evade detection. In [4], Christodorescu et al exploited semantic heuristics to detect obfuscated malware. Although, their approach works well for obfuscated malicious programs, the time taken (over a minute to classify) by their approach makes it impractical for use in commercial antivirus scanners. Kruegel et al [16] use control flow graph information and statistical methods for disassembling obfuscated executables. Bergeron et al [18] consider critical API calls and security policies to test for presence of malicious code. Their approach does not work for obfuscated malicious executables. Zhang et al [19] use fuzzy pattern recognition to detect unknown malicious code. The approach does not handle obfuscated program binaries and gives many false positives. Martignoni et al [7] use real-time program monitoring to detect deobfuscation in memory. Their implementation *OmniUnpack* detects obfuscation for both known and unknown packers. MetaAware [27] identifies patterns of system or library functions called from a malware sample to detect its metamorphic version. Bilar [10] uses statistical structures such as opcode frequency distribution and graph structure fingerprints to detect malicious programs. The approach presented in this paper detects malicious programs including those with common obfuscations as well as previously unknown variants of malware families.

In [17], Krugel et al use dynamic analysis to detect obfuscated malicious code, using mining algorithm. Their approach works well for obfuscated malicious programs but takes several seconds to test a single program. DOME [23] uses static analysis to detect system call locations and run-time monitoring to check all system calls are made from a location identified during static analysis. Min-Sun et al [22] use dynamic monitoring to detect worms and other exploits. Their approach is limited to detection of worms and exploits that use hard-coded addresses of API calls, and does not work for other malware types such as trojans or backdoors. Also, as evident by our experimental results, our approach is much faster than all other approaches described above.

3   Our Approach for Malware Detection

In this section, first, we briefly outline our approach for malware signature generation and classification. Next, we describe our program behavior model used for signature generation and the statistical comparison technique. Then, we present our malware detection algorithm using our program behavior model. Finally, we describe our prototype implementation in detail and show a sample signature of a malware extracted using our approach.

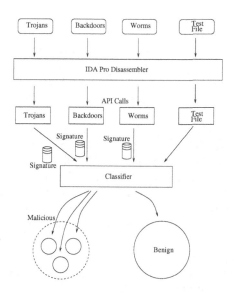

Fig. 1. Architecture of our malware detector

3.1   Malware Signature Generation and Classification Approach

We create signatures based on the characteristics of an entire malware class rather than a single sample of malware. Malware classes are defined based on similar behavior. The behavior of a malware class can be specified based on the API calls that the members of the malware calls use. For instance, a virus trying to search for executable files will typically make use of API calls such as FindFirstFileA, FindNextFileA and FindClose in KERNEL32.DLL. The behavior of searching files is captured by the use of these API calls. Rather than considering all API calls, we consider only *critical API calls* [17, 18]. Critical API calls include all API calls that can lead to security compromise such as calls that change the way the operating system behaves or those used for communication, such as Registry API, File I/O API, WinSock etc. We do not consider API calls which can be added or removed in a sample of malware without changing its malicious behavior, such as MessageBox, printf, malloc etc. For each malware class, we extract API calls and their call frequency from several malicious programs. The signature for the malware class is then computed using several samples that are known to belong to that class. From our results, we have observed that 2 or 3 samples from a malware class are adequate to create a signature. Given any test file, it is classified as malicious or benign by statistical comparison of the frequency of its critical API calls with that of the malware classes. Figure 1 shows the architecture of our malware detector. Next, we describe our strategy for malware behavior profiling and show our method is used to generate signatures and classify programs as benign or malicious. In our classification, we not only differentiate between benign and malicious programs, but also between different malware classes.

Malware Behavior Profiling. Malicious programs exhibit a behavior that can be distinguished from behavior of benign programs. The signature for a malware class is based on the frequency of *critical* API calls. Let the vector $P = (f_1, f_2, \ldots, f_n)$ be a *profile* created from a program by extracting its critical API calls, where f_i represents the frequency of ith critical API call and n being the total number of critical API calls.

We use a statistical measure to differentiate between malware and benign programs. To detect malware, we measure the difference between the proportions of the critical API calls in a signature and that of a test program using Chi-square test [6]. Chi-square test is a likelihood-ratio or maximum likelihood statistical significance test that measures the difference between proportions in two independent samples. The signature S_i for a malware class M_i specifies the frequencies of critical API calls that a sample of malware which belongs to M_i is expected to have. To test the membership of a given test file in a malware class, its API calls are extracted and compared to that in the signature. The Chi-square is then computed as:

$$\chi_i^2 = \frac{(O_i - E_i)^2}{E_i} \qquad ; 1 \leq i \leq n$$

Here, O_i is the observed frequency of the ith critical API call in the test file and E_i is its expected frequency, i.e. frequency in the signature of a malware class. Now, χ^2 is compared against a threshold value ϵ from a standard Chi-square distribution table with one degree of freedom. The degrees of freedom is associated with the number of parameters that can vary in a statistical model. A significance level of 0.05 was selected. This means that 95% of the time we expect χ^2 to be less than or equal to ϵ. For one degree of freedom and significance level 0.05, $\epsilon = 3.84$. Let $U = \{API_i \mid \chi_i^2 \leq \epsilon_i\}$. We define a *degree of membership* λ as

$$\lambda = \frac{|U|}{n}$$

Degree of membership λ is a measure of belongingness of test file to a malware class. The statistical profiling algorithm is shown in Algorithm 1.

Input: API frequency set for a file, $P = \{O_1, O_2, \ldots, O_n\}$, and another API
       frequency set $M = \{E_1, E_2, \ldots, E_n\}$
Output: Degree of membership, λ
1 **for** $i = 1$ *to* n **do**
2     $\chi_i^2 = \frac{(O_i - E_i)^2}{E_i}$;
3 **end**
4 $U = \{API_i \mid \chi_i^2 \leq 3.84\}$;
5 $\lambda = \frac{|U|}{n}$;
6 **return** λ

Algorithm 1. STAT(P, M)

Signature Generation. The signature for a malware class is then computed as follows. Let $R_i = \{P_1^i, P_2^i, \ldots, P_m^i\}$ be the set of profiles of samples in malware class M_i. The signature vector S_i for the malware class M_i is then defined as the set of the mean frequency of every critical API call occurring in M_i.

$$S_i = \frac{1}{m} \sum_{j=0}^{m} P_j^i$$

This signature vector is then tested against samples $T = \{T_1, T_2, \ldots, T_k\}$ known to belong to the same malware class M_i using the statistical analysis. We here define a threshold δ as

$$\delta_i = \frac{1}{k} \sum_{j=0}^{k} \lambda_j$$

Here λ is the outcome of a statistical analysis test. This signature S_i and threshold δ_i is computed for every malware class M_i. We note that each individual test sample shows a distinct set of frequencies, which differ noticeably from those shown by benign programs and other malware classes.

Classification Strategy. Let P be the profile obtained from a test file T. Let S_i be a signature for the malware class M_i, and δ_i be the corresponding degree of membership. Let B be the benign set and t be the total number of malware classes.

    Then, if

$$\exists \, i, \ 1 \leq i \leq t, \quad \delta_T \geq \delta_i$$
$$\Rightarrow \quad T \in M_i$$

Otherwise, if

$$\forall \, i, \ 1 \leq i \leq t, \quad \delta_T < \delta_i$$
$$\Rightarrow \quad T \in B$$

Also, if

$$\exists\, i,j,\ 1 \le i,j \le t, \qquad \delta_T \ge \delta_i \quad AND \quad \delta_T \ge \delta_j$$
$$\Rightarrow T \in M_i \cup M_j$$

Note that if $\delta_T \ge \delta_i$ and $\delta_T \ge \delta_j$, then it means the test file T contains features of both malware classes M_i and M_j.

A *false positive* occurs when a benign program is classified as malicious. A false positive for a signature S_i is defined as the probability

$$Pr\,(\delta_T \ge \delta_i \mid T \in B)$$

A *false negative* occurs when a malicious program is classified as benign. For a specific malware class M_i and signature S_i, this is defined as

$$Pr\,(\delta_T < \delta_i \mid T \in M_i)$$

This usually happens when the data in the profile is distorted and therefore M_i cannot be detected. We now formally state our malware detection algorithm. The algorithm is composed of two parts: the signature generator *SIGNATURE_GENERATE* (Algorithm 2) and the detector *DETECT* (Algorithm 3).

Input: The set of profiles $R_i = \{P_1^i, P_2^i \ldots, P_m^i\}$ for a malware class M_i
Output: Signature S_i and threshold δ_i
1 Select an arbitrary set $U \subset M_i$. Let $U = \{U_1, U_2, \ldots, U_k\}$.
2 Let $Q = M_i - U$. Let $Q = \{Q_1, Q_2, \ldots, Q_{m-k}\}$.
3 Compute signature as $S_i = \frac{1}{m-k}\sum_{j=1}^{m-k} Q_j$;
4 **for** $j = 1$ *to* k **do**
5     $\lambda_j = STAT(S_i, U_j)$;
6 **end**
7 Compute threshold as $\delta_i = \frac{1}{k}\sum_{j=1}^{k} \lambda_j$.

Algorithm 2. SIGNATURE_GENERATE(M_i)

3.2 Prototype Implementation Details

We have implemented a prototype of the technique. Our implementation is written for malware on Win32 platform and it consists of two components - API call extractor and Classifier.

API Call Extractor. The API Call Extractor component is implemented as a plugin to the IDA Pro Disassembler [8]. It begins by locating the `.idata` segment which is an `EXTERN` segment that contains list of addresses of API functions imported by the PE file. For each address in the `.idata` segment, it retrieves the corresponding API function name and its set of cross-references. The API

Input: A test file T with API frequency set $P = \{f_1, f_2, \ldots, f_n\}$, a signature S_i and corresponding threshold δ_i for a malware class M_i

Output: TRUE if $T \in M_i$, FALSE otherwise

1 $\delta_T = STAT(P, S_i);$
2 **if** $\delta_T \geq \delta_i$ **then**
3 $\quad |$ **return** *TRUE*
4 **end**
5 **return** *FALSE*

Algorithm 3. DETECT(T, M_i)

```
.idata:0040F2F0 ; int __stdcall send(SOCKET s, const char *buf, int len, int flags)
.idata:0040F2F0                    extrn __imp_send:dword   ; DATA XREF: send
```

Fig. 2. API function `send` in `.idata` segment

```
.text:004019A7 loc_4019A7:
; CODE XREF: sub_401990+31
.text:004019A7                    push    0             ; flags
.text:004019A9                    push    1             ; len
.text:004019AB                    push    esi           ; buf
.text:004019AC                    push    ebx           ; s
.text:004019AD                    call    send
....
....
....
.text:004019C3 loc_4019C3:
; CODE XREF: sub_401990+13
.text:004019C3                    push    0             ; flags
.text:004019C5                    add     edi, ebp
.text:004019C7                    push    1             ; len
.text:004019C9                    push    edi           ; buf
.text:004019CA                    push    ebx           ; s
.text:004019CB                    call    send
```

Fig. 3. Calls to API function `send` that actually transfer control to an intermediate thunk

```
.text:00401FE6
.text:00401FE6 ; Attributes: thunk
.text:00401FE6
.text:00401FE6 ; int __stdcall send(SOCKET s, const char *buf, int len, int flags)
.text:00401FE6 send           proc near
; CODE XREF: sub_401990+1D
.text:00401FE6                                          ; sub_401990+3B
.text:00401FE6                jmp     ds:__imp_send
.text:00401FE6 send           endp
```

Fig. 4. Thunk for API function `send`

call frequency is given by the number of cross-references in the code region. Note that, in many cases compiler generates code in such a way that a `call` to an API function is made through an intermediate `jmp` instruction, called a *thunk*.

```
...
...
GetWindowsDirectory 1.625000
WriteFile 9.375000
GetFileAttributes 1.125000
CopyFile 3.000000
DeleteFile 6.375000
CreateFile 9.000000
SetFileAttributes 1.125000
GetTempPath 2.375000
GetSystemDirectory 3.250000
GetModuleFileName 6.500000
...
...
```

Fig. 5. Signature for MyDoom worm family

In such a case, if a cross-reference is a thunk, it may lead to an incorrect API call frequency since several API calls will transfer control to the thunk which in turn would jump to the actual API function. Therefore, we check each cross-reference and if it is a thunk, we retrieve all cross-references for this thunk as well to get the correct API call frequency. Such a code taken from the disassembly of Borzella worm [3] is shown in Figures 2,3 and 4.

Classifier. The classifier reads the entire set of profiles produced by the API call extractor for each malware class and produces a signature. When given a file containing API call frequencies of a test file, it uses the above algorithm to classify the test file as benign or as the appropriate malware class. Figure 5 shows a sample signature created for *MyDoom* worm family.

4   Experimental Analysis

The testing environment consisted of a Windows XP Service Pack 2 machine. The hardware configuration included a Pentium 4 3.2 GHz processor and 512 MB of RAM. We used IDA Pro version 5.2.0.

4.1   Effectiveness

Testing on new variants. To test the effectiveness of our malware detector against new variants of malware families, we tested it on eight malware families. The malware families were gathered from VX Heavens [2]. For each malware family, we used two earliest possible variants to construct the signature and the rest for testing the signature. We tested our approach on the following malware families: MyDoom(30 variants), Bifrose (18 variants), Agent (14 variants), Delf (13 variants), InvictusDLL (13 variants), Netsky (10 variants), Bagle (9 variants) and Chiton (19 variants). Our approach was able to detect all variants in the above malware families except one variant in Netsky family. The detailed results are presented in Table 1 and 2.

Although, from Table 1, Netsky.r could not be detected when using the signature created from Netsky.c and Netsky.d, but it was detected when the signature was generated from Netsky.c and Netsky.p. From these results, we note that our approach is most suited for detecting many variants of a malware family. This implies that if there is a new variant that is not classified by our approach, it is probable that the malware writer has made some significant changes in its behavior. In such a case, that variant can be used for training which will be sufficient for detecting many more advanced variants of the family. We have illustrated this from the Netsky worm example.

Testing on generic malware classes. Above experiments tested specific malware families. We wanted to test our approach for detecting arbitrary and unknown malware classes by using only signatures generated from some known broad classes of malware. So, we constructed signatures for broad classes of malware such as trojans, worms, backdoors and viruses. To test the effectiveness of our detection method and to identify potential false negatives, we gathered 800 malicious programs in Portable Executable (PE) [1] format. To test the false positive rate, we gathered 200 benign programs from a fresh installation of Windows XP service pack 2. Signatures for malware classes were constructed by incrementally chosing higher number of training samples such 10, 20 and so on upto 60 samples from each malware class. 29 benign programs out of 200 were incorrectly classified as malicious. The evaluation results are presented in Table 3.

We found that several benign programs share behavior (for instance, searching files, copying files to network drives etc.) with certain malicious programs. The observed false positive rate is due to such *shared behavior*. Figure 6 shows the plot of detection rate, false negative rate and false positive rate with increasing

Table 1. Effectiveness evaluation to detect malware variants

Malware	Variants in training set	Variants Tested	Detected	Malware	Variants in training set	Variants Tested	Detected
Netsky	c d	e	✓	Chiton	a b	c	✓
		gen	✓			d	✓
		l	✓			e	✓
		m	✓			f	✓
		n	✓			h	✓
		p	✓			i	✓
		r	✗			j	✓
		x	✓			k	✓
Bagle	a bb	b	✓			l	✓
		ab	✓			m	✓
		ad	✓			n	✓
		ae	✓			o	✓
		al	✓			p	✓
		as	✓			q	✓
		bi	✓			r	✓
						t	✓
						Chiton	✓

Table 2. Effectiveness evaluation to detect malware variants (contd.)

Malware	Variants in training set	Variants Tested	Detected	Malware	Variants in training set	Variants Tested	Detected
MyDoom	a c	d	✓	Bifrose	a ab	ae	✓
		e	✓			ag	✓
		f	✓			aq	✓
		g	✓			at	✓
		h	✓			ax	✓
		l	✓			bb	✓
		o	✓			bc	✓
		q	✓			bf	✓
		r	✓			bg	✓
		u	✓			bh	✓
		v	✓			bk	✓
		y	✓			bl	✓
		aa	✓			bo	✓
		ae	✓			bs	✓
		af	✓			ca	✓
		ag	✓			cc	✓
		ai	✓	Agent	a ab	ad	✓
		aj	✓			ae	✓
		ak	✓			ah	✓
		al	✓			aj	✓
		an	✓			bc	✓
		aq	✓			bd	✓
		ar	✓			abz	✓
		as	✓			aci	✓
		at	✓			acx	✓
		av	✓			adr	✓
		ay	✓			ads	✓
		az	✓			aec	✓
Delf	62976 c	d	✓	InvictusDLL	101.a 101.b	099	✓
		f	✓			201.b	✓
		g	✓			102	✓
		h	✓			103.a	✓
		j	✓			200.b	✓
		k	✓			201.a	✓
		m	✓			200.a	✓
		n	✓			a	✓
		r	✓			b	✓
		v	✓			c	✓
		w	✓			d	✓

number of training samples. As shown in the figure, the false positive and false negative rate falls and the detection rate increases with an increase in the number of training samples. Hence, it can be inferred from the plot that the accuracy of the signature increases with an increase in the number of training samples. The results show that even in the absence of the base signature, our technique was able to detect a new malware using the signature constructed from broad malware classes with reasonable accuracy. Once the new malware is detected, its base signature can easily be constructed to detect its future variants.

Table 3. Evaluation Results

Class	Tested	Detected	False negatives
Worms	131	121	10
Trojans	362	300	62
Backdoors	161	103	58
Viruses	146	146	0

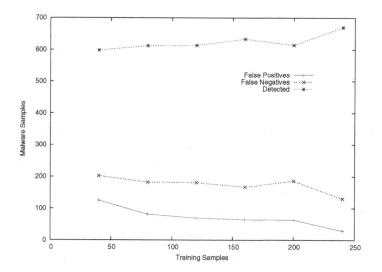

Fig. 6. Change in Detection Rate and False Negative Rate with change in number of training samples

Table 4. Time (in seconds) comparison with SAFE

Malware	Annotator/API Call Extractor		Detector	
	SAFE	**Our Approach**	**SAFE**	**Our Approach**
Chernobyl	1.444	2.172	0.535	0.0138
zombie-6.b	4.600	1.718	1.149	0.0314
f0sf0r0	4.900	1.781	0.923	0.0256
Hare	9.142	1.665	1.604	0.0282

4.2 Performance Testing

We tested the time it requires to classify a given file as malicious or benign. We consider the time taken by our approach to extract the API calls and to classify it as malicious or benign. We compare our approach to SAFE [15]. SAFE creates an abstraction pattern of the malicious code and converts it into an internal representation. Given a test program, it creates a control flow graph (CFG) of the test program, and checks whether the internal representation of malicious code is present in the CFG. SAFE has been tested only on a very few malware samples. Table 4 compares the time taken by our approach with that of SAFE for four samples of malware. Clearly, our approach is much faster than SAFE.

5   Conclusion and Future Work

We presented a method to generate signatures for malware classes to detect previously unknown malicious programs. Our malware detection approach is space efficient. Rather than creating a new signature for every variant in a malware family, it creates a single signature that reflects the behavior of the entire family. It reduces the human effort required to generate a signature for a new malware. Also, it is able to detect malicious programs with common obfuscations, a problem which the commercial antivirus scanners being used today do not address. Thus, our malware detection approach is most suitable for use in commercial antivirus scanners.

The accuracy of our signature generation method for detecting future variants of a malware family is good. Although the detection error rate for new malware in broad classes such as trojans and backdoors seems high in our experiments but the results are encouraging. Malware authors often tend to *pack* malware in order to evade detection and to make analysis difficult. Such malware use a decompression or decryption routine to extract the compressed or encrypted malicious code in memory. A limitation of our approach is that it does not work for packed malware. The future work involves incorporating a generic unpacking technique to detect even the packed malware and extending the signature generation algorithm to better utilize API calls to reduce the error rate.

References

[1] Pietrek, M.: An In-Depth Look into the Win32 Portable Executable File Format, in MSDN Magazine (March 2002)
[2] VX Heavens, http://vx.netlux.org
[3] Viruslist.com - Email-Worm.Win32.Borzella,
     http://www.viruslist.com/en/viruses/encyclopedia?virusid=21991
[4] Christodorescu, M., Jha, S., Seshia, S.A., Song, D., Bryant, R.E.: Semantics-Aware Malware Detection. In: Proceedings of the 2005 IEEE Symposium on Security and Privacy, May 08-11, 2005, pp. 32–46 (2005)
[5] Marinescu, A.: An Analysis of Simile,
     http://www.securityfocus.com/infocus/1671
[6] Sokal, R.R., Rohlf, F.J.: Biometry: The principles and practice of statistics in biological research, 3rd edn. Freeman, New York (1994)
[7] Martignoni, L., Christodorescu, M., Jha, S.: OmniUnpack: Fast, Generic, and Safe Unpacking of Malware. In: Twenty-Third Annual Computer Security Applications Conference (ACSAC), Miami Beach, FL (December 2007)
[8] Guilfanov, I.: An Advanced Interactive Multi-processor Disassembler (2000),
     http://www.datarescue.com
[9] Ferrie, P., Ször, P.: Zmist opportunities. Virus Bullettin (2001)

[10] Bilar, D.: Statistical Structures: Tolerant Fingerprinting for Classification and Analysis given at BH 2006, Las Vegas, NV. Blackhat Briefings USA (August 2006)

[11] Cohen, F.: Computer Virus: Theory and experiments. Computers and Security 6, 22–35 (1987)

[12] Chess, D.M., White, S.R.: An undetectable computer virus. In: Proceedings of Virus Bulletin Conference (2000)

[13] Landi, N.: Undecidability of static analysis. ACM Letters on Programming Language and systems (LOPLAS) 1(4), 323–337 (1992)

[14] Myres, E.M.: A precise interprocedural data flow algorithm. In: Conference Record of the 8th Annual ACM SIGPLAN-SIGACT Symp. on Principles of Programming Languages (POPL 1981), pp. 219–230. ACM Press, New York (1981)

[15] Christodorescu, M., Jha, S.: Static Anlaysis of Executables to Detect Malicious Patterns. In: Proceeding of the 12th USENIX Security Symp (Security 2003), pp. 169–186 (August 2003)

[16] Kruegel, C., Robertson, W., Valeur, F., Vigna, G.: Static disassembly of obfuscated binaries. In: Proceedings of USENIX Security, San Diego, CA, pp. 255–270 (August 2004)

[17] Christodorescu, M., Jha, S., Krugel, C.: Mining Specification of Malicious Behavior. In: Proceeding of the 6th joint meeting of the European Software Engineering Conference. ACM SIGSOFT Symp. On ESES/FSE 2007 (2007)

[18] Bergeron, J., Debbabi, M., Desharnais, J., Erhioui, M.M., Lavoie, Y., Tawbi, N.: Static Detection of Malicious Code in Executable Programs. In: Symposium on Requirements Engineering for Information Security (SREIS 2001) (2001)

[19] Zhang, B., Yin, J., Hao, J.: Using Fuzzy Pattern Recognition to Detect Unknown Malicious Executables Code. In: Wang, L., Jin, Y. (eds.) Fuzzy Systems and Knowledge Discovery. LNCS (LNAI), vol. 3613, pp. 629–634. Springer, Heidelberg (2005)

[20] Peisert, S., Bishop, M., Karin, S., Marzullo, K.: Analysis of Computer Intrusions Using Sequences of Function Calls. IEEE Transactions on Dependable and Secure Computing (TDSC) 4(2) (April-June, 2007)

[21] Bergeron, J., Debbabi, M., Erhioui, M.M., Ktari, B.: Static Analysis of Binary Code to Isolate Malicious Behaviors. In: Proceedings of the 8th Workshop on Enabling Technologies on Infrastructure for Collaborative Enterprises, June 16-18, 1999, pp. 184–189 (1999)

[22] Sun, H.-M., Lin, Y.-H., Wu, M.-F.: API Monitoring System for Defeating Worms and Exploits in MS-Windows System. In: Batten, L.M., Safavi-Naini, R. (eds.) ACISP 2006. LNCS, vol. 4058. Springer, Heidelberg (2006)

[23] Jesse, C., Rabek, R., Khazan, I., Scott, M., Robert, L., Cunningham, K.: Detection of Injected, Dynamically Generated,and Obfuscated Malicious Code. In: Proc. of 2003 ACM workshop on Rapid Malcode (October 2003)

[24] Forrest, S., Hofmeyr, S.A., Somayaji, A., Longstaff, T.A.: A Sense of Self for Unix Processes. In: IEEE Symposium on Security and Privacy 1996 (1996)

[25] Sekar, R., Bendre, M., Dhurjati, D., Bollineni, P.: A Fast Automaton-Based Method for Detecting Anomalous Program Behaviors. In: IEEE Symposium on Security and Privacy (2001)

[26] Peisert, S., Bishop, M., Karin, S., Marzullo, K.: Analysis of Computer Intrusions Using Sequences of Function Calls. IEEE Transactions On Dependable and Secure Computing 4(2) (April-June, 2007)

[27] Zhang, Q., Reeves, D.S.: MetaAware: Identifying Metamorphic Malware. In: Choi, L., Paek, Y., Cho, S. (eds.) ACSAC 2007. LNCS, vol. 4697, Springer, Heidelberg (2007)

Reducing Payload Scans for Attack Signature Matching Using Rule Classification

Sunghyun Kim and Heejo Lee[*]

Korea University, Seoul 136-713, South Korea
{afshkim,heejo}@korea.ac.kr

Abstract. Network intrusion detection systems rely on a signature-based detection engine. When under attack or during heavy traffic, the detection engines need to make fast decision whether a packet or a sequence of packets is normal or malicious. However, if packets have a heavy payload or the system has a great deal of attack patterns, the high cost of payload inspection severely diminishes the detection performance. Therefore, it would be better to avoid unnecessary payload scans by checking the protocol fields in the packet header first, before executing their heavy operations of payload inspection. Furthermore, when payload inspection is necessary, it is better to compare attack patterns as few as possible. In this paper, we propose a method which reduces payload scans by an integration of processing protocol fields and classifying payload signatures. While performance improvements are dependent on a given networking environment, the experimental results with the DARPA data set show that the proposed method outperforms the latest Snort over 6.5% for web traffic.

1 Introduction

Intrusion detection is a set of techniques and methods that are used to detect suspicious activities both at the network and host level. The process of intrusion detection aims to find data packets that contain any known intrusion-related signatures or anomalies related to the Internet protocols. Intrusion detection methods fall into two basic categories: signature-based intrusion detection and anomaly-based detection.

Signature-based detection is used to compare against activity in the network or host with predefined signatures which are produced by an analysis of an attack or malicious packets. This method relies on a database of attack signatures. Therefore, it is only as effective as its database. Most signatures have patterns to search known attacks. Anomaly-based intrusion detection, by contrast, utilizes a more generalized approach when searching for and detecting threats in a network. A rule of normal behavior is developed and when an event falls outside that norm, it is detected and logged. The behavior is a characterization of the state of the protected system, which is a reflective of the system health and is sensitive to attacks. In this context, an anomaly-based method of intrusion detection has the potential to detect new or unknown attacks. In a manner to similar to the signature-based method, anomaly-based intrusion detection relies on information that signifies what is normal and what is an anomaly.

---

[*] Corresponding author.

Y. Mu, W. Susilo, and J. Seberry (Eds.): ACISP 2008, LNCS 5107, pp. 350–360, 2008.

Network Intrusion Detection System(NIDS) captures data from the network and applies rules to that data or detects anomalies. NIDS detects malicious activities such as denial of service attacks, port scans or even attempts to hack into computers by monitoring network traffic. Based on a set of signatures and rules, after a match is found, the detection system takes some actions, such as logging the event or sending an alarm to a management console. Numerous studies about NIDS have attempted to rapidly decide which packets are malicious.

Recently, a large number of signatures are associated with well known ports, such as HTTP and SMTP. Also, because volume of multi-media data, such as video, file download services of web sites and P2P services, is increasing at an amazing rate, the cost of pattern matching in the packet payload is increasing. Therefore, to reduce the cost of payload scanning, it is reasonable to check the protocol fields before searching the payload to compare patterns. This is why we proposed the method whereby the protocol fields have a great priority than the packet payload for signature matching. The proposed method is similar to research on rule classification by protocol fields such as a decision tree [8] or an evaluation tree [9]. However, our method calculates all possible results, based on expected values of the protocol fields and makes small rule groups. Thus, the payload inspection of the packets is performed only when it is necessary. Our method has some advantages compared with previous methods, which are as follows:

- It processes the rules without considering the values of protocol fields.
- It is a flexible structure such that we can change the examining sequence of protocol fields and add or remove some of the protocol fields.
- It is more effective to handle the complex rules.

The contribution of this study is to propose a new method of rule set classification and the integrated processing of protocol signatures. In spite of additional overhead, it can yield small rule groups and provide fast detection. In the remainder of this paper, §2 briefly provides related works. §3 describes the proposed method. §4 analyzes the performance. §5 presents experimental results. In §6, we summarize our experience.

2   Related Works

Just as a network packet consists of the header and the payload, the research about signature matching can be classified into two categories. One is a pattern matching for a packet data, which consists mainly of string matching. The other is the classification of a rule set by the protocol fields. The former focuses on reducing the number of rules to be searched by grouping, in other words classification or clustering. The latter mainly focuses on the means to rapidly certain strings. We will briefly discuss some of the methods for signature matching and explore Snort's internal.

For the payload matching, several pattern matching algorithms have been proposed. Among the single pattern matching, a well-known algorithm is the Boyer and More algorithm [2]. It preprocesses the target string that is being searched for to generate a table of mismatch skip values based on the pattern position involved in the mismatch. Another well-known algorithm, Knuth-Morris-Pratt(KMP) [3] also preprocessed patterns, to generate a look-up table that indicates how many positions the pattern can be shifted to the right based on the position in the pattern where a mismatch occurs.

The multi-pattern matching method searches a text string for the occurrence of any pattern in a set of patterns, using only a single iteration. A well known algorithm is the Aho-Corasick(AC) algorithm [4] which preprocesses the set of patterns, to construct a pattern matching machine based on a deterministic finite automaton (DFA). The matching procedure works by reading successive characters from the input string, making state transitions based on each character, and producing output after a complete pattern is matched. The Wu-Manber algorithm [5], is based on the bad character heuristic, which is similar to Boyer-Moore, but uses a one or two-byte bad shift table constructed by re-processing all the patterns, instead of only one. Also it uses the hashing table to index the patterns in the actual matching phase, thus saving a great deal of time. Another method, Exclusion-based signature Matching(E^2xB) [6] is designed to provide rapid negatives, when the search string does not exist in the packet payload.

At well as this, research about the classification of rules has progressed. Kruegel and Toth proposed a decision tree method to improve signature-based intrusion detection [8]. In order to create an optimized decision tree, which is used to find malicious events, using a minimum of redundant comparisons, this method uses a well-known clustering algorithm which is applied in machine learning. The algorithm builds a decision tree from a classified set of data items with different features using the notion of information gain. Sinha et al [9] proposed an evaluation tree which determines which rule groups are maintained in memory by choosing protocol fields and values recursively. Initially, the method selects the protocol field that is most effective in rejecting the rules, and then separates those groups by values of the chosen protocol field. After forming groups for each of these values, the algorithm recursively splits the groups by other protocol fields that reject at least a threshold number of rules, producing smaller groups. By this means, it generates a hierarchy of protocol fields and values, for which groups are maintained. As discussed above, these methods are used for IDSes' detection engines.

Among several NIDSes, Snort [1,10] is an open source network intrusion prevention and detection system utilizing a rule-driven language, which combines the benefits of protocol and payload signature. Snort is commonly used to actively block or passively detect a variety of attacks and probes performing protocol analysis and content matching. Snort considers rules to be composed of 2 components, a rule header and a rule option. The rule header has predicates of the protocol fields. The rule option mainly has strings for pattern matching, and other predicates. After parsing the rules, based on the port, Snort makes 3 port groups, which consist of; a destination port group for rules having a unique destination port, a source port group for rules having a unique source port and a generic port group for rules without a unique destination port and source port. Each port in a port group has two multi-pattern matchers. One is for content, which is a keyword that searches for specific content in the packet payload. The other is for uricontent, which is a keyword that searches the normalized request URI field. Also each port has rule chains for rules without content or uricontent. A generic port group is copied to other port groups for efficiency. Snort provides the Wo-manber and the Aho-corasick pattern matching algorithm. When packets are going through, based on port number, multi-pattern matchers of the corresponding port group are called. In the worst case, a packet is scanned three times, once for the destination port group, once for the source port group and once for the generic rule group. In the best case, a packet is only scanned once for one of the three groups. Snort only uses one protocol field for grouping rules. Under the condition of a heavy payload or a large number of patterns, a great deal of time is required for inspecting the payload. Our method integrates rules' predicates into each protocol field and pre-calculates all possible results. Because we inspect the protocol fields first, we avoid unnecessary payload scanning. In what follows, Our method is discussed in detail.

3   Detection and Classification by Grouping Predicates

NIDS has been deployed behind a firewall which inspects network traffic passing through it and denies or permits passage based on policy. Thus, a large number of signatures are associated with specific ports. In table 1, based on our analysis of snort's rules[1] (VRT Certified Rules for Snort v2.7), among 6985 default rules related to TCP, 4935 (70%) rules are associated with 3 destination ports(80,445,139) and 1 source port(80).

Table 1. Top 5 lists of Snort's TCP rules classified by port

Destination Port	Rules	Source Port	Rules
80	1570	80	743
445	1359	1024	42
139	1263	23	13
1521	291	666	8
>1024	147	5050	6

Our method integrates each predicate of protocol field used in the rule set into a single data structure, we call a protocol filter, and calculates all possible results based on the values of the protocol field in advance. After pre-calculating the results, it makes small rule groups by the combination of the pre-calculated results. When a packet is moving through the system, it searches each result based on value of a packet's protocol fields. Combining these results, it identifies a single pre-calculated rule group. Only checking this rule group, our method can reduce the chance of payload scanning and alleviates the load of pattern matching. Figure 1 shows our method briefly. We shall explain this in more detail.

3.1   Formal Description

We will restrict our description to relationships of protocol fields. Let R be the set of n rules, i.e., $R = \{r_1, r_2, ...r_n\}$. Let $F = \{f_1, f_2, ..., f_m\}$ denote the set of m protocol fields present in the rule set. Let $P_{f_i} = \{p_{f_i}^1, p_{f_i}^2, ..., p_{f_i}^k\}$ denote the set of the predicates associated with a protocol field f_i in the rule set. Also let $V_{f_i} = \{v_{f_i}^1, v_{f_i}^2, ..., v_{f_i}^j\}$ denote the set of unique values which are extracted from a protocol field f_i's predicates used in R and sorted in ascending order. A rule in R can be described as the relationship of predicates of protocol fields like $r_t = p_{f_1}^j \wedge p_{f_2}^j \wedge ....p_{f_m}^k$. And a predicate

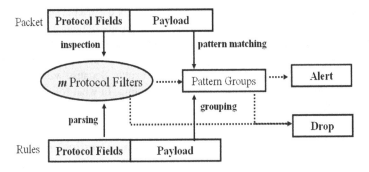

Fig. 1. Detecting and grouping by protocol filters

used in R can be presented like $p^j_{f_i} = f_i \odot v^k_{f_i}$ where $\odot$ is an operator used in the predicate($=,\leq,\geq$,etc.). Based on values of f_i, each predicate in P_{f_i} can be true or false. Likewise, based on each predicate results of P_{f_i}, each rule in R can be false or true. Therefore, Based on values of f_i, each rule in R has various result. Let $s^j_{f_i}$ denote all rules' results depending on an element of V_{f_i}. Let $dom(f_i)$ denote f_i's domain.

Like Figure 2, $dom(f_i)$ can be divided into $(2k + 1)$'s sub range or sub domain, where $k = |V_{f_i}|$. Let $s^j_{f_i}$ denote rule set's result in the jth subrange of $dom(f_i)$. And we describe $S_{f_i} = \{s^1_{f_i}, s^2_{f_i}, ...s^{2k+1}_{f_i}\}$ to present the set of all possible results which depend on all values of f_i. We can find the all results of the rule set by each value of the protocol field f_i used in the rule set in advance. Based on values of f_i, P_{f_i} is decided and then depending on P_{f_i}, which rules among $r_1, r_2, ...r_n$ is matched or not is determined. $s^{2j}_{f_i}$ of S_{f_i} has the results of $r_1, r_2, ...r_n$ regarding to $v^j_{f_i}$ of V_{f_i}. Likewise, $s^{2j+1}_{f_i}$ of S_{f_i} has the results of $r_1, r_2, ...r_n$ depending on all values between $v^j_{f_i}$ and $v^{j+1}_{f_i}$ of V_{f_i}. Because the rule set includes $v^j_{f_i}$, we can calculate $s^j_{f_i}$. Also, we can compute $s^{2j+1}_{f_i}$ if we generate any value which is included in between $v^j_{f_i}$ and $v^{j+1}_{f_i}$. The proposed method is to pre-calculate possible results, i.e., S_{f_i} and stores them for decision about rules' matching.

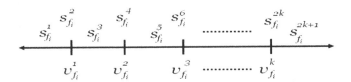

Fig. 2. Rules' results based on values of the protocol field f_i

For example, if r_1 has a predicate for destination port, like $p^1_{dport} = \{dport, >, 3\}$, r_1 obtains 3 results which is one for values of less than 3, one for a value of 3, and one for values of greater than 3. If r_2 having a predicate for destination port, like $p^2_{dport} = \{dport, =, 6\}$, is added, r_1 and r_2 can obtain 5 results which is one for values of less than 3, one for a value of 3, one for values of greater than 3 and less than 6, one for values of 6, and one for values greater than 6. The number of results of the rule set including a predicate of protocol field f_i is 5 because of $2 * n|V_{f_i}| + 1$.

3.2 Detection by Protocol Filters

As has demonstrated, we pre-calculate all the rules' results and save them into an array data structure, so called a protocol filter. Figure 3 shows the proposed method. When a packet is reached, based on the value of the packet's protocol field, we search the results of the rule set in protocol filters. Based on the combined results of the rule set, we identify whether the packet need a payload scan or not. For example, we have two rules similar to Snort's rule such as the following.

r_1: alert tcp 10.1.1.1 25 –>!$HOME_NET 80 . . . ;content:login;. . .

r_2: alert tcp 20.1.1.1 1024:2024 –>$HOME_NET !143 . . . ;content:root;. . .

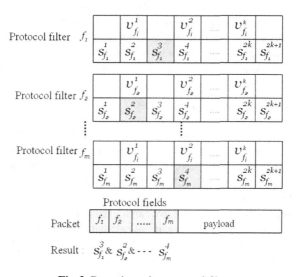

Fig. 3. Detection using protocol filters

Figure 4 shows in detail the proposed method. Let's make the protocol filter for destination port with r_1 and r_2. If a packet's destination port is less than 80, greater than 80 and less than 143, or greater than 143, only r_2 is matched. In case of the destination port 80, both rules are matched. However, for port 143, both rules are not matched. We represent the rules' result as bit strings. We call this structure "protocol filter". We made the protocol filter for the source port in the same way. In this case, we only used two protocol fields and made two protocol filters. When a packet P_1 is moving through, we search for the results of rules in protocol filter based on protocol field's value. If we obtain all corresponding result bit strings of the protocol filters, the final result is decided by 'AND' bit operation to each result bit strings. The other predicates including pattern matching are indexed by the position of bit strings. Based on value of bits, we filter out unnecessary rules.

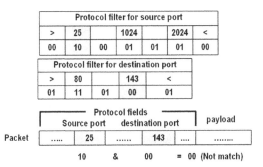

Fig. 4. Example of protocol filters

As well as reducing the cost of payload searching, the proposed method has the advantage that upon execution. It only performs search operation, irrespective of the rule set's predicates. Therefore, the greater the complexity of rules' predicates, the better the performance. Also, because protocol filters do not have a fixed order, we can change the search order. For example, if we can obtain information that a certain protocol field can drop early normal packets, we can change the checking order of protocol filters.

3.3   Grouping by Protocol Filters

As noted previously, a protocol filter for f_i provides the integrated processing of predicates and result of the rule set related to f_i. Taking this idea further, if we calculate all combinations of protocol filters for $f_1, f_2, \ldots f_m$ in advance, we obtain all possible results of the rule set, i.e., $S_{f_1}, S_{f_2}, \ldots S_{f_m}$. The maximum number of these results is 2^n if there are n rules.

In Figure 4, when we have two rules, we can make the maximum four distinct results of the rule set, because of 2^2. However, if we calculate the combination of 2 protocol filters' result bit strings, we can obtain 2 result bit strings such as '01','10'. Based on the number of result bit strings, we can classify rules into 2 small groups. We ignore result '00', which means all rules are not matched and '11', which is impossible results bit strings. The reason we do not make rule groups as much as 2^n, is that we can remove unnecessary rule groups by a combination of protocol filters. The greater the number of results, the smaller number of rules in a group. The rule grouping by protocol filters can easily tune the degree of grouping. Whereas smaller rule groups are made when many protocol filters are used, larger rule groups are made when few protocol filters are used. By contrast, the overhead of protocol fields matching is proportional to the number of protocol filters.

4   Performance Analysis

The proposed method is based on the fact that, in general, pattern matching of payload needs more processing time than protocol fields matching. In the case of TCP, while the packet header has 20 bytes without option, the packet data can have 1460 bytes, considering MTU(Maximum Transmission Unit). The size of the packet data and values of the protocol field depend on network environment. Therefore, if a packet has little or no data, checking the payload first can yield inferior results. Also the number of patterns which affects performance can be scattered in proportional to the number of protocol fields used in grouping. We analyze performance these two aspects.

We compare a single protocol field grouping with multiple protocol fields grouping. To simplify our analysis, we assume that rule set, R, has n rules and that each rule has a single predicate of $f_1, f_2, ..., f_m$. So, every rule has m predicates. As noted above, V_{f_i} is the set of unique values which are extracted from a protocol field f_i's predicates used in R and P_{f_i} is the set of the predicates associated with a protocol field f_i used in R. In addition, let D_{f_i} denote f_i's domain and let A_{f_i} denote all f_i's value ranges used in P_{f_i}. If f_i' value is within A_{f_i}, at least one among P_{f_i} satisfy the predicate. In the case of a single protocol field grouping, the average rule count of subgroups is $\frac{n}{|V_{f_i}|}$ and probability of payload scanning is $\frac{A_{f_i}}{D_{f_i}}$. However, if we make rule groups with multiple protocol fields, such as $f_1, f_2, \ldots f_m$, the average rule count of subgroups is $\frac{n}{\prod_{i=1}^{k}|V_{f_i}|}$. In a manner similar to the average rule count of subgroups, the probability of payload scanning is $\prod_{i=1}^{k}(\frac{A_{f_i}}{D_{f_i}})$. Clearly, the more protocol fields are used, the few rules are included in a subgroup and the lower the probability of payload scanning is. Small rule groups mean few patterns to search in the payload, in other words, the pattern match engines have a light work load.

For example, if rules are grouped only by the destination port, n rules can be scattered with 2^{16} because the destination port has 2 bytes. However, if rules are grouped by a combination of the destination port, source port, destination IP and source IP, which consist of 12 bytes, n rules can be scattered with 2^{96}. Also, the probability of payload scanning for subgroups is lowered in the same manner. However, the performance of the proposed method is strongly dependent on the environment of network and distribution of rules.

5   Experiments

To implement the proposed method, we have modified Snort version 2.7.0.1. The experimental platform is a personal computer with a Pentium 4 Core 2 6,400 CPU and 3 Gbytes RAM. We used the Linux operating system, Fedora 6.

The rule set used for the experiments consisted of only the TCP rules among the VRT Certified Rules for Snort version 2.7. We used well-known data sets, the DARPA Intrusion Detection Evaluation Data Set from MIT Lincoln Lab [11]. We analyzed three types of the DARPA data files and selected ports which have a large number of rules and frequently appeared in data files at the same time. Table 2 shows the average payload size and the percentage of several destination ports in data files.

We made 4 protocol filters using destination port, source port, destination IP, and source IP. Table 3 shows how the rule set can be grouped by 4 protocol fields, compare to Snort's a single protocol field grouping. In the case of the destination port 80, whereas Snort makes one port group with 2026 rules, the proposed method make 4 small groups.

Table 2. Destination port's characteristics of DARPA data set

Destination Port		1999 week1	2000 LLDOS1.0	2000 window NT
80	avg. payload bytes	261	259	409
	% of total traffic	5.7	2.47	6.02
25	avg. payload bytes	393	623	491
	% of total traffic	13.9	10.25	15.94
23	avg. payload bytes	113	114	97
	% of total traffic	0.27	0.12	0.34
139	avg. payload bytes	–	126	192
	% of total traffic	–	0.17	0.16

Table 3. Rule classification by protocol fields

Classification	80	25	23	139
	rule/group	rule/group	rule/group	rule/group
Destination port or source port (Snort)	2026/1	147/2	25/1	1263/1
4 Protocol Fields	3866/4	215/3	25/1	1263/1

Table 4. CPU times of DARPA data set

Dest Port	method	1999 week1	2000 LLDOS1.0	2000 window NT
80	Snort	26.3	12.4	29.5
	Prot. Filter	24.6	11.5	28.1
Improvement		93.6%	93.5%	93.5%
25	Snort	0.8	0.52	0.87
	Prot. Filter	0.73	0.5	0.82
Improvement		91.2%	96.1%	94.2%
23	Snort	0.038	0.026	0.035
	Prot. Filter	0.019	0.014	0.02
Improvement		50%	54%	57%
139	Snort	–	0.45	1.19
	Prot. Filter	–	0.0049	0.92
Improvement		–	1%	77%

We used the default IP address setting, consisting of only a home net and an external net. Therefore, the effect of the grouping rules was tiny.

After the method was executed 10 times, we recorded the average time of detection. We only evaluated the packets over 20 bytes which is the TCP header size, considering overhead. In Table 4, the proposed method improved the processing time to various degrees, compared with Snort. In the case of port 80 and port 25, improved performance results from the port's small rule groups, because the proportion of packets that skipped payload inspection is below 0.01%. In the other cases, improvement of port 23 and port 139 results from skipped payload inspection, because the proportion of skipped packets is between 37% and 100%. In the case of data file LLDOS1.0 and 139 port, while all packets have the external network addresses in the source IP field, all rules have the internal network addresses in the source IP field. Thus the protocol filters dropped all packets without payload inspection. Clearly, grouping by multiple protocol fields can improve performance in that the amount of pattern matching and the probability of payload scanning are reduced. Because of a packet's payload size and the distribution of the protocol fields' values, there will be a variety of results. If we use the more protocol fields to classify a rule set, we can make the smaller rule groups and avoid a great number of payload scanning. Also if the packets have a heavy payload, the performance will be much better.

6   Conclusions

In this paper, we proposed the method to reduce the cost of payload matching. The proposed method involves integrated detection of protocol fields and the separation of a large signature group into several small signature groups, by multiple protocol fields. The effect of the proposed method can be various depending on rules and packets. However, the proposed method can reduce the payload scanning for patterns matching and reduce the number of patterns for packets to check, because packets which do not match protocol fields can be dropped before payload scanning. In addition, the proposed method is independent of a predicate's operand, because of the pre-calculation of all the predicates. Also this allows a detailed rule description, which enables us to easily represent complex and complicated predicates. Unfortunately, it suffers from rule replication and bit operation overhead. However, the memory requirement can be tolerated by system, if we use only some overloaded rule groups. For a bits operation, if we adapt the proposed method to only heavy payload packets, the advantage generally more than compensates for the overhead. In the future, we intend to include some protocol fields which are frequently used in rules and can reject packet early. Also we will evaluate our method in real network environments.

Acknowledgments

This work was supported in part by the ITRC program of the Korea Ministry of Knowledge Economy. Additionally supported by a Korea University Grant.

References

1. Snort: Open source Network Intrusion Detection System, http://www.snort.org
2. Boyer, R.S., Moore, J.S.: A fast string searching algorithm. Communications of the ACM 20, 762–772 (1977)

3. Knuth, D.E., Morris, J.H., Pratt, V.R.: Fast pattern matching in strings. SIAM Journal of Computing 6, 323–350 (1977)

4. Aho, A.V., Corasick, M.J.: Fast pattern matching: an aid to bibliographic search. Communications of the ACM 18, 333–340 (1975)

5. Wu, S., Manber, U.: A Fast Algorithm for Multi-Pattern Seaching, Technical Report TR-94-17, Department of Computer Science. University of Arizona (May 1994)

6. Wang, X., Li, H.: Improvement and Implementation of Network Intrusion Detection System. Journal of Communication and Computer, 49–52 (January 2006)

7. Fisk, M., Varghese, G.: Fast Content-Based Packet Handling for Intrusion Detection, UCSD Technical Report CS2001-0670. University of California, San Diego (May 2001)

8. Kruegel, C., Toth, T.: Using Decision Trees to Improve Signature-based Intrusion Detection. In: Vigna, G., Krügel, C., Jonsson, E. (eds.) RAID 2003. LNCS, vol. 2820, pp. 173–191. Springer, Heidelberg (2003)

9. Sinha, S., Jahanian, F., Patel, J.M.: WIND:Workload-Aware INtrusion Detection Recent Advances in Intrusion Detection. In: Zamboni, D., Krügel, C. (eds.) RAID 2006. LNCS, vol. 4219, pp. 290–390. Springer, Heidelberg (2006)

10. Roesch, M.: Snort: Lightweight Intrusion Detection for Networks. In: Proc. of the USENIX LISA 1999 Conference, pp. 229–238 (November 1999)

11. McHugh, J.: Testing Intrusion Detection Systems: A Critique of the 1998 and 1999 DARPA Intrusion Detection System Evaluations as Performed by Lincoln Lab. ACM Trans. Information and Systems Security(TISSEC) 3(4), 262–294 (2000)

12. Commentz-Walter, B.: String Matching Algorithm Fast on the Average. In: Proc. of the 6th International Colloquium on Automata, Languages, and Programming, pp. 118–132 (1979)

13. Paxson, V.: Bro: A System for Detecting Network Intruders in Real-Time. Computer Networks 31(23-24), 2435–2463 (1999)

14. Sommer, R., Paxson, V.: Enhancing byte-level network intrusion detection signatures with context. In: Proc. of the 10th ACM Conference on Computer and Communication Security (CCS 2003), pp. 262–271 (October 2003)

15. Kruegel, C., Toth, T.: Automatic rule clustering for improved signature-based intrusion detection, Technical report, Distributed systems group:Technical Univ. Vienna, Austria (2002)

16. Dreger, H., Feldmann, A., Mai, M., Paxson, V., Sommer, R.: Dynamic Application-Layer Protocol Analysis for Network Intrusion Detection. In: Proc. of the 15th USENIX Security Symposium, pp. 257–272 (July 2006)

17. Allen, W.H.: Mixing Wheat with the Chaff: Creating Useful Test Data for IDS Evaluation. IEEE Security & Privacy, 65–67 (July 2007)

18. Antonatos, S., Anagnostakis, K.G., Polychronakis, M., Markatos, E.P.: Performance analysis of content matching intrusion detection systems. In: Proc. of the 4th IEEE/IPSJ SAINT (January 2004)

19. Mell, P., Hu, V., Lippmann, R.: An overview of issues in testing intrusion detection systems (June 2003),
http://csrcnist.gov/publications/nistir/nistir-7007.pdf

Implicit Detection of Hidden Processes with a Feather-Weight Hardware-Assisted Virtual Machine Monitor

Yan Wen[1], Jinjing Zhao[2], Huaimin Wang[1], and Jiannong Cao[3]

[1] School of Computer, National University of Defense Technology,
Changsha, China
wenyan@nudt.edu.cn, whm_w@163.com
[2] Beijing Institute of System Engineering, Beijing, China
misszhaojinjing@sina.com.cn
[3] Department of Computing, Hong Kong Polytechnic University,
Kowloon, Hong Kong, China
csjcao@comp.polyu.edu.hk

Abstract. Process hiding is a commonly used stealth technique which facilitates the evasion from the detection by anti-malware programs. In this paper, we propose a new approach called *Aries* to implicitly detect the hidden processes. Aries introduces a novel feather-weight hardware-assisted virtual machine monitor (VMM) to obtain the True Process List (TPL). Compared to existing VMM-based approaches, Aries offers three distinct advantages: *dynamic OS migration*, *implicit introspection of TPL* and *non-bypassable interfaces* for exposing TPL. Unlike typical VMMs, Aries can dynamically migrate a booted OS on it. By tracking the low-level interactions between the OS and the memory management structures, Aries is decoupled with the explicit OS implementation information which is subvertable for the privileged malware. Our functionality evaluation shows Aries can detect more process-hiding malware than existing detectors while the performance evaluation shows desktop-oriented workloads achieve 95.2% of native speed on average.

Keywords: Virtual machine monitor, stealth malware, hardware-assisted VMM.

1 Introduction

Over the past few years more and more desktop PC users are willing to download and execute freeware/shareware to benefit from the rich software resource on the Internet. Stealth malware programs which may be accompanied with the downloaded untrusted software are becoming a major threat to the Internet users [1]. The term "stealth malware" refers to a large class of software programs that try to hide their presence from the resource enumeration utilities commonly used by computer users and malware detectors. Hackers have proposed many stealth techniques among which *process hiding* is the most widely used one. According to statistics released by

Y. Mu, W. Susilo, and J. Seberry (Eds.): ACISP 2008, LNCS 5107, pp. 361–375, 2008.
© Springer-Verlag Berlin Heidelberg 2008

Microsoft's widely deployed *Malicious Software Removal Tool* [2], a significant fraction of the malware it encounters and removes consists of stealth rootkits with the capability of process hiding [3]. Thus, the ability to detect process-hiding malware is a clear advantage in the race to protect the computers against stealth malware.

The most effective mechanism to detect hidden processes is so-called *cross-view* validation [4]. It works by observing the process list from two perspectives and finding out the inconsistencies between them. One view is retrieved from an untrusted, high-level point. The other is obtained from within a lower layer in the system that is unlikely to have been tampered by malware. So, this information is considered trustworthy. If a process exists in the trusted view but does not appear in the untrusted view, a cross-view detector can draw a conclusion that the process has been hidden.

A significant challenge of cross-view validation is the inevitable race that develops between attackers and defenders to control the lowest reaches of a system. Obviously, cross-view validation will fail if an attacker subverts the level from which the trusted view is obtained.

From the defense point of view, building cross-view validation based on the explicit OS kernel data structures is not resistant against the attacks from the privileged malware [5-7]. Compared to these host-based methods, VMM-based mechanisms are better shielded from malicious attacks in virtue of their location in an isolated virtualization layer [8]. However, the OSes within the VMs cannot reproduce the environment of the underlying preinstalled host OSes, which are just the protecting concern on the PC platforms. In other words, they only deal with the OS deployed in the VM instead of our daily used host OS. Moreover, to retrieve the trusted view, existing VMM-based cross-view validators assume that the VMM has detailed implementation information about the OSes they observe [9; 10]. Such approaches dependent on explicit information are effective, but still susceptible to evasion by the privileged malware which has compromised the guest OS.

In this paper, we propose a new VMM-based cross-view validation approach called *Aries* for detecting hidden processes. Aries introduces a novel lightweight hardware-assisted Type I VMM [9] to deprivilege a running preinstalled OS and obtain the trusted view from deep within the VMM. Compared to previous VMM-based approaches, Aries holds three unique advantages: *dynamic OS migration, implicit introspection of TPL* and *non-bypassable interfaces for exposing TPL*.

Dynamic OS migration. The Aries VMM named with *AriesVMM* is a lightweight VMM based on the hardware-assisted virtualization technology, such as *Intel Virtualization Technology* (*Intel VT*) [10] and AMD Virtualization (AMD-V) [11]. Unlike typical VMMs which have to be started up before they construct their guest VMs, AriesVMM can migrate a running OS on it on-the-fly. The migrated OS can switch between *native mode* and *migrated mode* dynamically. In the native mode, the OS just runs above the naked computer hardware without any performance penalty. In the migrated mode, Aries will activate the hidden process detection mechanism while only imposes acceptable performance overhead. Thus, Aries provides the capability of detecting the process-hiding malware in the preinstalled OS.

Implicit introspection of TPL. Aries adopts a novel technology to facilitate the implicit introspection of TPL. By monitoring low-level interactions between OS and the memory management components, AriesVMM can accurately determine when an OS creates processes and destroys them. With this implicit introspecting technology, we decouple Aries from the subvertable explicit OS data structures. So, Aries can detect more process-hiding malware than existing anti-malware programs.

Non-bypassable interfaces for exposing TPL. Aries also provides a set of non-bypassable interfaces for providing TPL to the security services or other system tools, such as stealth malware detector and so on. The information about hidden processes will enable a more effective malware analysis.

In view of the prevalent combination of Windows and Intel on the PC platforms, Aries has been firstly implemented on Windows with VT-supported Intel x86 processors. Our experimental results with real-world rootkits which are widely applied to hide processes demonstrate Aries' unique detection capability. The performance evaluation, including *CPU, graphic 2D, graphic 3D* and *memory*, presents that Aries exacts only a reasonable performance overhead to the migrated OS, 4.8% on average.

The rest of the paper is organized as follows. Section 2 discusses the architecture of Aries. In section 3, we firstly outline the Intel VT technology, and then describe the implementation details about how Aries achieves the three advantages. Section 4 provides an evaluation for Aries, including functionalities and performance. Section 5 reviews previous related works. Section 6 discusses the potential attack against Aries and our solutions. We summarize the main features of Aries and introduce the future work in the last section.

2 Overview

Most of existing VMM-based security services are built on the Xen VMM [12], an open source Type I VMM [9]. A Type I VMM just runs above a bare computer hardware platform. It tends to be implemented as a lightweight OS with the virtualization capabilities. A Type I VMM has to be started before they create the guest VMs, viz., every OS should run above a VM. Unlike the mainframes that are configured and managed by experienced system administrators, desktop PC's are often preinstalled with a standard OS and managed by the end-user. Ignoring the difficulty of proposing a practical and seamless migration approach for the PC platforms, it will maybe take several years to migrate all of them to the Type I VMM.

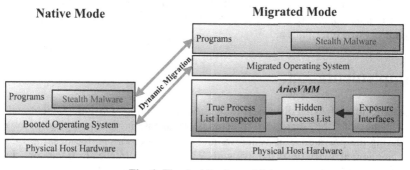

Fig. 1. The Architecture of Aries

It also might be unacceptable for a PC user to completely replace an existing OS with a Type I VMM.

In contrast, instead of introducing multiple OSes running above relevant VMs to serve as the execution environments we will introspect on, Aries switches the booted OS, the only OS in the execution model of Aries, between two states: *native mode* and *migrated mode*, as shown in Fig 1.

In the native mode, the OS runs just above the bare computer hardware, consequently it does not suffer from any performance degradation. If the users wish to detect the potential hidden processes, Aries will switch the booted OS to the migrated mode. In this mode, Aries will activate the hidden processes detecting and exposing mechanism. If a process has been hidden, it will not appear in the untrusted list but exist in a suitably obtained TPL.

Aries obtains TPL from within the AriesVMM. Aries differs from the existing VMM-based approaches, such as VMI [13], in the way how to obtain TPL. Previous approaches exploit detailed information about the location and semantics of private kernel data structures to retrieve a low-level process list. Contrarily, *True Process List Introspector* of Aries obtains its low-level information implicitly, i.e., no detailed implementation information about the OS is required. Aries uses a technology to implicitly obtain the information about process creations and exits by observing closely related events, i.e., virtual address space creation and destruction. With Intel VT enabled, such information about virtual address spaces is explicitly visible for AriesVMM by tracking CR3 register on Intel x86 processors.

Aries obtains its untrusted view of processes just like other common applications running in this OS. As a result, anti-Aries malware cannot judge accurately whether a query is invoked by Aries.

Aries obtains the untrusted process lists at short random intervals. A window of the most recent samples is preserved for use in hypothesis testing. The size of the window and the sample interval are configurable. In our implementation, samples are obtained every one second.

To reveal the *Hidden Process List* securely, Aries provides a set of *Non-bypassable Exposure Interfaces*. The communication requests are sent by issuing port I/O instructions (*in/out* on Intel processors) with Aries-specific port number. With Intel VT enabled, the execution port I/O instructions will generate traps which can be caught by AriesVMM immediately. AriesVMM responses such requests by returning the input-relative information through the specific registers. The trap/catch operations sequences cannot be intercepted with Intel VT support. Thus, AriesVMM constructs a non-bypassable communication channel with the applications which wish to get the hidden processes information.

3 Implementation

The architecture of Aries discussed in Section 2 is obvious OS-independent and also independent of the hardware-assisted virtualization technologies. However, considering the prevalence of Windows and Intel processors on the desktop PCs, we firstly implement Aries on Windows with VT-supported Intel x86 processors. In this section, we will briefly introduce the framework of the Intel VT technology, and then describe the details about how we accomplish the three key features: *dynamic migration, implicit detection of hidden processes* and *non-bypassable communication interfaces.*

3.1 Intel VT Framework Overview

Intel virtualization technology includes VT-x support for the IA-32 processor virtualization and VT-i support for the Itanium architecture [10]. AriesVMM is just built based on Intel VT-x.

VT-x augments IA-32 processors with two new forms of CPU operation: *VMX root operation* and *VMX non-root operation.* VMX root operation is intended for use by a VMM. VMX non-root operation provides an alternative IA-32 environment controlled by a VMM and designed to support a VM. Software running in VMX non-root operation is deprivileged in certain ways, regardless of privilege level. VT-x defines two new transitions: a transition from VMX root operation to VMX non-root operation—that is, from VMM to guest—called a *VM entry*, and a transition from VMX non-root operation to VMX root operation—that is, from guest to VMM—called a *VM exit*. VM entries and VM exits are managed by a new data structure called the Virtual Machine Control Structure (*VMCS*).

Processor behavior is changed substantially in VMX non-root operation. The most important change is that many instructions and events cause VM exits. Some instructions (e.g., *CPUID, INVD, MOV from/to CR3*) cause VM exits unconditionally and thus can never directly be executed in VMX non-root operation. Other instructions (e.g., *CLTS, HLT, INVLPG*) and all events can be configured to do so conditionally using *VM-execution control fields* in the VMCS.

3.2 Dynamic OS Migration with AriesVMM

There are two key issues in implementing the AriesVMM: managing the VMCS region and handling the VM exit events. Aries deals with two types of VM exit events: *modifying CR3* and *executing I/O port instructions.* Accordingly, the former indicates the virtual address space switches while the latter is used to establish the non-bypassable communication channel.

The instruction flow of dynamic migration is illustrated in Fig 2. The central functionality in AriesVMM is a loop of VMLAUNCH/VMRESUME followed by VM exits processing. AriesVMM initiates guest operation by issuing VMLAUNCH, providing the appropriate VMCS configuration. Execution of the guest continues until a conditional/unconditional VM exit occurs. The guest state, including the reason for VM exit, is placed in the guest-state area of the VMCS. AriesVMM may emulate, deny, or alter the execution of the intercepted instruction by making changes to the VMCS.

As explained in Fig 2, AriesVMM runs in VMX root operation. The migrated OS runs in VMX non-root operation, so it is more restricted, meaning that certain actions will cause a VM exit to occur. AriesVMM works out TPL and exposes the hidden processes just in the VM exit handlers.

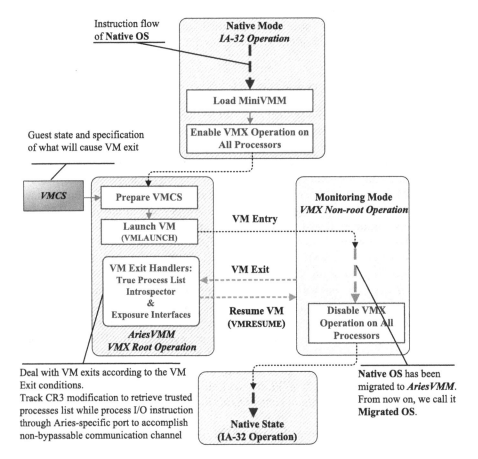

Fig. 2. Instruction Flow of Dynamic Migration

Load AriesVMM. To execute the privileged Intel VT-x instructions, AriesVMM should be implemented as a Windows kernel driver and loaded by the Windows driver management APIs.

Enable VMX Operation on All Processors. For IA-32 processors, Intel adds a part to the CR4 control register to enable VMX or not. Therefore, we must set this bit to enable VMX on the processor. Then we create a VMXON region in a non-pageable memory block and align it to a 4-byte boundary. The VMXON region must be hosted in cache-coherent memory. Finally, we issue VMXON with the physical address of the VMXON region to enable VMX operation. This process must be repeatedly executed on all the logical processors.

Prepare VMCS. After calling VMXON, the processor is now in VMX root operation. We then create a VMCS region in non-pageable memory pages and initialize the version identifier in the VMCS. The next operations are to initialize the VMCS properly for CR3 register tracking and communicating through reading/writing Aries-specific I/O port.

Referring to the Intel VT-x specification, the instruction of reading CR3 will cause VM exit unconditionally while writing CR3 triggers VM exit event conditionally via setting *CR3-target count* in VMCS to 0. The I/O bitmap in VMCS defines the port numbers through which the I/O operations will incur VM exits. In fact, there are two 4KB I/O bitmaps, A and B, which control I/O instructions on various ports. Respectively, bitmap A manages the ports from 0000 to 7FFF while bitmap B is in charge of the ports in the range of 8000-FFFF. We only set the bits for the Aries-specific port (0x7981 in our prototype) through which the covert communication channels of Aries is constructed.

Then, we call VMWRITE to initialize various guest-state area fields in the working VMCS. This sets up the context and entry-point for guest execution upon VM entry. Finally, we set stack point (ESP), instruction pointer (EIP) for both host and guest execution context.

Launch VM. After the above complex preparations, we can now launch VM just by invoking the instruction of VMLAUNCH.

VM Exit Handlers. After setting the relevant fields in VMCS, the instructions writing CR3 or the I/O instructions accessing Aries-specific port will incur VM exits. AriesVMM will catch these exit events to track CR3 modification and transfer data through specific I/O port. The implementation details of these two types of exiting handlers will be described in Section 3.3 and 3.4.

Disable VMX Operation on All Processors. If the users desire to switch back to the native mode, AriesVMM will release all allocated memory resource and invoke VMXOFF on all processors.

3.3 Implicit Detection of Hidden Process

The detailed description about how we implement the implicit detection of hidden process has been presented in our previous work [14]. This section only presents the framework of this technology.

The key to figure out TPL is being aware of the process creation and destruction. Intel x86 processors use a two-level, in-memory, architecturally-defined page table. The page table is organized as a tree with a single fixed-sized, commonly 4KB, memory page called the *page directory* at its root. Each 4-byte entry in the page directory can point to a 4KB page of the *page table* for a process. A page directory serves as the root of the page table tree that describes each address space. A single address space is active per processor at any given time. The address of the page directory is therefore characteristic of a single address space.

Examining existing community OSes supporting x86 processors, they informs the processor's memory management unit (MMU) that a new address space should become active by writing the physical address of the page directory for the new address space into a specific control register - *CR3 register* for x86 processors. This mechanism facilitates the implicit awareness of the process activating behavior. With Intel VT enabled, accessing to CR3 register will trigger a VM exit event to enter into the VMX root operation. AriesVMM will catch such events and retrieve the new CR3 value. Based on tracking the process activating/deactivating indicated via the CR3 changes,

---

Input: *AriesVMM State, New CR3 Value*
Output: None
Method:
1. **if** *New CR3 Value* refers to the *System* process
2.   **for** all existing processes in TPL
3.   Remap the *EPROCESS* address of the process;
4.   **if** the remapped mapped page is set un-present
5.   Remove this process from TPL;
6.   **break;**
7.   **end if**
8.   **end for**
9. **else**
10.   **if** *New CR3 Value* is not present in TPL
11.   Create a new tree node to contain the information for this new process;
12.   Insert this node into TPL;
13.   Retrieve the OS-level semantic information of this process;
14.   **else**
15.   Update the schedule count of this process;
16.   **if** the OS-level semantic information of this process has not been initialized
17.   Retrieve the OS-level semantic information of this process;
18.   **end if**
19.   **end if**
20. **end if**
21. **End Algorithm** Introspecting True Process List

Fig. 3. Introspecting True Process List

Aries works out TPL. An outlined description of TPL introspection algorithm is listed in Fig 3.

In addition, Aries should map a PUID to an OS-understandable process ID for the malware detectors which use it to get the detailed process information. We select the process Id which is widely used by Windows API as the OS-understandable process ID. When detecting a process creation, we call the kernel function *PsGetCurrentProcessId* and *PsGetCurrentProcess* to retrieve the *process Id* and *EPROCESS* (the kernel data structure containing the process information). Then we create a list entry for them and their key (PUID) in TPL.

Thus, with the accurate trace of process creation and destruction, AriesVMM implements the capability of retrieving TPL at virtualization-layer.

To construct the untrusted process view, we call a Windows native API, namely *ZwSetSystemInformation,* with a process information related parameter termed of *SystemProcessesAndThreadsInformation* to enumerate all the processes. This is the most common API to list the running processes. In Aries implementation, untrusted process view is sampled every one second and then subtracted from TPL to generate the hidden process list.

From the security point of view, anti-Aries malware cannot ascertain whether an API call is issued by AriesVMM because AriesVMM invokes this function just in the process contexts of other common applications. So this is infeasible to bypass AriesVMM by hooking the APIs used by AriesVMM.

3.4 TPL Exposure Interfaces

To reveal the hidden process list to the applications, Aries provides a set of non-bypassable interfaces. This mechanism enables a more effective post-mortem malware analysis. These interfaces are implemented by issuing I/O instructions (*in/out* in Intel processors) with Aries-specific port number. As discussed in Section 3.2, the execution of I/O port instructions will be caught by AriesVMM. AriesVMM returns the input-relative information through specific registers. The basic communication framework can be described with the following assembly code.

```
// for the application retains information
MOV EAX, 0x79068104; // set magic number
MOV ECX, Command Number;
MOV DX, 0x7981;        // Aries-specific port
IN EAX, DX;

// For the AriesVMM VM exit handler for I/O port
MOV  Register, ReturnResult // function-specific
```

In the above snippet, the program first loads the hexadecimal value 0x79068104, acting rather like a fixed password for the channel, into register EAX. Next, it loads the value into register ECX, which will tell the Aries communications channel what the application wants to do. We then load into register EDX a value of 0x7981, a specialized I/O port for Aries. Finally, the program is ready to retrieve the information of the hidden processes from Aries by using the IN instruction.

Aries has provided two functions through these interfaces.

Enumerating the process IDs of hidden processes. Process ID is the OS-wide unique identifier for a process. With process ID, user-mode programs can open a process and obtain the process-related information. The applications should input the address of a page-aligned memory area, which is to contain the snapshot of the hidden process IDs, through EBX. Then Aries will copy the ID list to this memory area directly through physical memory page access, and then set ECX the count of the IDs. If this memory region is not enough for the current ID list, Aries will also set ECX the count of the IDs but set EBX 0xFFFFFFFF and return. In this case, the application should allocate more memory pages and try again. It's maybe easier to transfer hidden process IDs by returning them through a register one by one, but it will likely fail to achieve the state consistency of a running OS because of the frequent processes creation and destruction.

Retrieving the indicated process information. Although the Aries has exposed the hidden process IDs to the user-mode applications, these applications perhaps still cannot get the relevant process information because some malware may have intercepted the process-related APIs. So, Aries also provides an API-independent way to obtain the process information. All the process-related information indeed can be obtained from kernel mode, such as EPROCESS on Windows. Aries implements an interface to copy these contents to the use-mode applications. They can be easily dissected according to the detailed definitions in Windows Driver Development Kit. The information transferring is accomplished similar with previous function.

4 Evaluation

Our testbed host is a notebook PC, containing Intel Core 2 Duo CPU T7300 2.0GHz with VT-x enabled, and 2G bytes memory. The host OS are Windows XP SP2.

Hidden Processes Detection. We also evaluate Aries with five popular process-hiding rootkits. *Aphex* [15] modifies the Import Address Table entry for the *ZwQuerySystemInformation* API to intercept the process list queries . *Hacker Defender* [16] also hijacks the queries with another technique: tempering the first few machine codes of *NtQuerySystemInformation* with a "jmp" instruction. *FU* [17] hides a process by using so-called *Direct Kernel Object Manipulation* (*DKOM*) technique to remove its corresponding entry from the *Active Process List* (a kernel data structure in Windows). *FUTo* [5] (an improved version of the *FU* rootkit) has the added ability to manipulate the *PspCidTable* without using any function calls. The *PspCidTable* is a "handle table for process and thread client IDs". Every process's Id corresponds to its location in the *PspCidTable*, i.e., the job of the PspCidTable is to keep track of all the processes and threads. *PE386* proposed another powerful DKOM-based process-hiding rootkit called *phide_ex* [18] which have bypassed several existing hidden process detectors.

We compare Aries to the anti-rootkit programs recommended by Anti Rootkit Group [19], including *F-Secure BlackLight* 2.2 [20], *DarkSpy* 1.0.5 (normal and super mode) [21], *IceSword* 1.20 [22], *RkUnhooker* 3.7.3 [23], *UnHackMe* 4.6 [24], *GMER* 1.0 [25], *KProcCheck* 0.2 [26], *Process Hunter* 1.1 [27] and *TaskInfo* 6.2 [28].

The first two rootkits, *Aphex, Hacker Defender*, can be found out by using the *Active Process List* as the truth. *FU* can be detected by all the above anti-rootkit programs while *Icesword* and *F-Secure Blacklight* fail to find the FUTo-hiding processes. Aries can detect all the processes hidden by the above five rootkits. Evaluation results show that Aries is the only detector which can identify the hidden process of *phide_ex* (*phide_ex.exe*).

Performance Overhead. To measure the time discrepancies due to the operation of tracking CR3 modification, we use the familiar UNIX kernel microbenchmark *forkwait* and port it to Windows, which stresses the virtualization overhead by process creation and destruction. This program repeats the operation of creating a process and waiting until the process exits. In our evaluation, the iteration count is 10000. The program is perhaps most concisely described by its ported source:

```
if (argc > 1) return 0;
PROCESS_INFORMATION ProcessInfo; STARTUPINFO StartupInfo;
memset (&StartupInfo, 0, sizeof (StartupInfo));
for (int i = 0; i < 10000; i++) {
    CreateProcess (NULL, "ForkWait.exe child", NULL,
        NULL, FALSE, 0, NULL, NULL, &StartupInfo, &ProcessInfo);
    WaitForSingleObject (ProcessInfo.hProcess, INFINITE);
    CloseHandle (ProcessInfo.hProcess);
    CloseHandle (ProcessInfo.hThread);  }
```

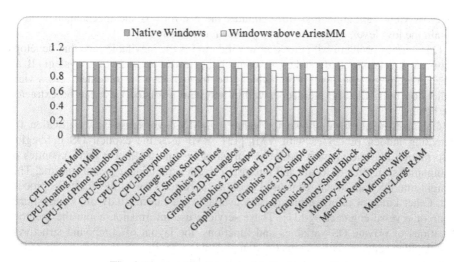

Fig. 4. Benchmark of Aries using *PerformanceTest*

forkwait focuses intensely on virtualization-sensitive operations, resulting in low performance relative to native execution. Measuring *forkwait*, our host required 35.926 seconds to create and destroy 10000 processes, while AriesVMM consumed 41.324 seconds, only incurring 15.0% overhead. The overhead of VMware Workstation 6.0, VirtualPC 2007 and Parallels Workstation 2.2 is respectively 19.6%, 20.2% and 23.4%. Of course, comparing a lightweight VMM to a heavyweight VMM is unfair. Our evaluation only illustrates the low performance overhead incurred by AriesVMM.

For a desktop-oriented workload, we run *Passmark PerformanceTest 6.1* both in the native mode and in the migrated mode. *PerformanceTest* is a synthetic suite of microbenchmarks intended to isolate various aspects of workstation performance. Since user-level computation is almost not taxing for VMMs, we expect that the migrated Windows above AriesVMM should run to score close to native. The CPU microbenchmarks in Fig 4 confirm this expectation, showing a slowdown over native of 0-18.28%. Exploring all the test results, including *CPU, graphic 2D, graphic 3D* and *memory*, the migrated Windows achieves 95.2% of native performance on average. The results show that the graphic system suffers the most significant performance penalty. This is because the graphics workloads issues much more VMX exits events than the computing-sensitive workloads. However, such performance penalty is definitely much less than the performance overhead exacted by a heavyweight VMM, such as Xen, VMware ESX Server and so on [29].

5 Related Work

Cross-view validation for hiding detection has been studied and variously implemented in user applications [30], within the OS kernel [4], inside a virtual machine monitor [13], and using dedicated coprocessor hardware [30]. The key aspect of cross-view validation that differentiates these efforts is the mechanism used to obtain the low-level, trusted view of the resource of interest.

One serious problem with cross-view validation is the inevitable race that develops between attackers and defenders to control the lowest reaches of a system. If an attacker subverts the level from which the trusted view is obtained, cross-view validation fails. Clearly, the deeper within a system a trusted view can be extracted the better.

Garfinkel et al., have shown the value of VMM-level cross-view validation for detecting hidden processes with VMI [13]. VMI uses the explicit OS debugging information like the memory addresses of variables and the layout and semantics of compound structures to locate and interpret private kernel data types at runtime. This insight into OS data structures is used to obtain a trusted view of the guest OS process list. Other kinds of information are only available via careful study of system source code or reverse engineering [31]. These services use information about the memory locations of private OS variables and functions, the layout of compound structures, and detailed semantics of various OS components to perform their work. Some of this information can be obtained automatically from debugging symbols [13].

VMM-level services based on explicit implementation information are effective, but there are drawbacks. One drawback is that they may be just as susceptible to evasion by an attacker that has subverted the guest OS as if they were located within the guest itself. In spite of their location at the VMM-layer, these services depend on guest-level information which is still open to simple guest-level manipulation. For example, if a service depends on the correctness of the guest OS process list, a kernel-resident attacker can modify the list to hide its presence. If a security system depends on monitoring the location of a function like fork to be informed of process creation, it may be thwarted by an attacker that re-directs invocations of the system call to their own implementation.

From the usability point of view, constructing an environment above a heavyweight VMM will suffer remarkable performance overhead, especially for the virtualized devices [29]. In addition, unlike mainframes that are configured and managed by experienced system administrators, desktop and workstation PC's are often preinstalled with a standard OS and managed by the end-user. Existing VMM-based solutions cannot provide the capability of introspecting on the preinstalled running OS.

Our previous work called Libra [14] makes use of the local-booted virtual machine [32] to reproduce the execution environment of the preinstalled OS and detect the hidden processes within this local-booted OS. But Libra can only find out the process-hiding malware which starts up with the OS. In contrast, Aries provides the unique advantage of catching the hidden processes in a running OS no matter whether they are launched with the OS or not.

6 Further Discussion

From a security point of view, Aries is less vulnerable to evasion by guest software than previously presented VMM-based security services. Demonstrating that one system is more secure than another in general is notoriously difficult (or impossible).

In this section we describe our rationale for the claim and why we believe implicit techniques can represent a net benefit for VMM-level system defense.

If a VMM-based security service depends on the correctness of any guest-level component, it is vulnerable to malicious corruption of that component [33]. Aries is based on implicitly obtained process information. Aries obtains its process information by observing how an OS manages its virtual address spaces. To evade Aries, an attacker must modify how the OS implements a fundamental feature (virtual memory) and must do so in a way that remains consistent with its desired user-level view of processes.

In summary, Aries is perhaps best described as "differently" subject to gaming and evasion on the part of compromised guests. We believe the effort required to deceive Aries about ongoing process hiding while still maintaining a fully consistent outward appearance exceeds that of earlier VMM-based detectors. This is a feature of VMM-based security services based on implicitly obtained information and raises the bar against malicious process hiding.

Aries depends on an untrusted process view. One way to attack Aries is to manipulate this view. In this attack, an adversary hides the presence of a malicious process from a defender, but doesn't hide it from Aries. In this way Aries fails to detect hiding because, from its perspective, no hiding takes place.

But in fact, this style of attack is infeasible, as well as impractical from an engineering standpoint. An adversary must be able to reliably identify the enumeration requests made on behalf of Aries. In the general case, this task will be difficult because Aries uses the same standard APIs to enumerate processes as any other process introspection tool like *ps* or the *Windows task manager*.

7 Conclusions and Future Work

Stealth malware are a current and alarming security issue. In this paper, we have described, implemented, and evaluated a novel VMM-based approach called Aries to detect hidden process implicitly. Like previous VMM-based security services, Aries is resilient to kernel-mode malware attack by virtue of its location within a VMM.

Unlike prior VMM-layer process hiding detectors, Aries achieves coexisting with preinstalled OS by introducing a lightweight hardware-assisted VMM called AriesVMM. Besides, Aries adopts a new implicit processes introspection technique which is independent on the subvertable OS implementation information. By decoupling Aries with a specific OS version and patch-level, the service can be deployed in diverse environments without the burden of maintaining version-specific implementation information. Aries also provides a set of non-bypassable interfaces for providing the hidden process list to other security services. This information will enable a more effective malware analysis.

In our evaluation, Aries correctly detects process hiding in each of hundreds of trials. The evaluation results show that Aries has more powerful detection ability than existing detectors. The performance evaluation, exploring *CPU, graphic 2D, graphic 3D* and *memory*, presents that Aries only exacts an average performance overhead of 4.8% to the migrated OS.

Aries is likely less susceptible to evasion attacks on the part of a compromised OS. Aries also implements a non-bypassable mechanism to protect the Aries-related memory pages.

To make Aries a more complete anti-malware solution, we are to integrate more stealth malware detection techniques into Aries, such as hidden modules, hidden files and other hidden resources.

Acknowledgements

This research is supported by National Basic Research Program of China (Grant No. 2005CB321801), National Natural Science Foundation of China (Grant No. 60673169), and National Science Fund for Outstanding Youths under Grant No. 60625203.

References

1. Zombie PCs: Silent, Growing Threat. PC World (July 2004),
   `http://www.pcworld.com/news/article/0,aid,116841,00.asp`
2. Microsoft: Windows Malicious Software Removal Tool,
   `http://www.microsoft.com/security/malwareremove/`
3. Naraine, R.: Microsoft: Stealth Rootkits Are Bombarding XP SP2 Boxes (December 2005), `http://www.eweek.com/article2/0,1895,1896605,00.asp`
4. Wang, Y.-M., Beck, D., Vo, B., Roussev, R., Verbowski, C.: Detecting Stealth Software with Strider GhostBuster. In: Proceedings of 35th Annual IEEE/IFIP International Conference on Dependable Systems and Networks (DSN 2005), pp. 368–377 (2005)
5. Silberman, P., C.H.A.O.S. : FUTo: Bypassing Blacklight and IceSword (2007),
   `https://www.rootkit.com/newsread.php?newsid=433`
6. Effective file hiding : Bypassing Raw File System I/O Rootkit Detector,
   `http://www.rootkit.com/newsread.php?newsid=690`
7. Bypassing Klister 0.4 with No Hooks or Running a Controlled Thread Scheduler,
   `http://hi-tech.nsys.by/33/`
8. Jung, J., Paxson, V., Berger, A.W., Balakrishnan, H.: Fast Portscan Detection Using Sequential Hypothesis Testing. In: IEEE Symposium on Security and Privacy (2004)
9. Goldberg, R.P.: Architectural Principles for Virtual Computer Systems, Ph.D. Thesis. Harvard University, Cambridge, MA (1972)
10. Uhlig, R., Neiger, G., Rodgers, D., Santoni, A.L., Martins, F.C.M., Anderson, A.V., Bennett, S.M., Kägi, A., Leung, F.H., Smith, L.: Intel Virtualization Technology. IEEE Computer 38, 48–56 (2005)
11. AMD: AMD64 Vrtualization Codenamed pacifica Technology: Secure Virtual Machine Architecture Reference Manual (May 2005)
12. Barham, P., Dragovic, B., Fraser, K., Hand, S., Harris, T., Ho, A., Neugebauery, R., Pratt, I., Warfield, A.: Xen and the Art of Virtualization. In: Proceedings of the 19th ACM Symposium on Operating Systems Principles (SOSP 2003), pp. 164–177 (2003)
13. Garfinkel, T., Rosenblum, M.: A Virtual Machine Introspection Based Architecture for Intrusion Detection. In: Proceedings of Network and Distributed System Security Symposium (NDSS 2003) (2003)
14. Wen, Y., Zhao, J., Wang, H.: Implicit Detection of Hidden Processes with a Local-Booted Virtual Machine. In: Proceedings of 2th International Conference on Information Security and Assurance (ISA 2008), pp. 150–155 (2008)

15. Aphex: AFX Windows Rootkit (2003), http://www.iamaphex.cjb.net
16. Hacker Defender, http://hxdef.org/
17. fuzen_op: FU Rootkit, http://www.rootkit.com/project.php?id=12
18. PE386: phide_ex -untimate process hiding example,
    http://forum.sysinternals.com/
    printer_friendly_posts.asp?TID=8527
19. Anti Rootkit Group, http://www.antirootkit.com/blog/
20. F-Secure Blacklight, http://www.f-secure.com/blacklight/
21. DarkSpy, http://www.fyyre.net/~cardmagic/index_en.html
22. Icesword, http://pjf.blogcn.com/index.shtml
23. RootKit Unhooker,
    http://www.antirootkit.com/software/RootKit-Unhooker.htm
24. UnHackMe, http://www.greatis.com/unhackme/
25. Gmer, http://www.gmer.net/index.php
26. Kernel Hidden Process/Module Checker,
    http://www.security.org.sg/code/kproccheck.html
27. Process Hunter, http://ms-rem.dot-link.net/
28. TaskInfo, http://www.iarsn.com/taskinfo.html
29. Adams, K., Agesen, O.: A Comparison of Software and Hardware Techniques for x86 Virtualization. In: Proceedings of The 12th International Conference on Architectural Support for Programming Languages and Operating Systems (ASPLOS 2006), pp. 2–13 (2006)
30. Petroni, N.L., Fraser, T., Molina, J., Arbaugh, W.A.: Copilot - a Coprocessor-based Kernel Runtime Integrity Monitor. In: Proceedings of the 13th USENIX Security Symposium, pp. 179–194 (2004)
31. Joshi, A., King, S.T., Dunlap, G.W., Chen, P.M.: Detecting Past and Present Intrusions through Vulnerability-Specific Predicates. In: Proceedings of the 20th ACM Symposium on Operating Systems Principles (SOSP 2005), Brighton, United Kingdom, pp. 91–104 (2005)
32. Wen, Y., Wang, H.: A Secure Virtual Execution Environment for Untrusted Code. In: Nam, K.-H., Rhee, G. (eds.) ICISC 2007. LNCS, vol. 4817, pp. 156–167. Springer, Heidelberg (2007)
33. Dunlap, G.W., King, S.T., Cinar, S., Basrai, M.A., Chen, P.M.: ReVirt: Enabling Intrusion Analysis through Virtual-Machine Logging and Replay. In: Proceedings of the 5th Symposium on Operating Systems Design and Implementation (OSDI 2002), pp. 211–224 (2002)

FormatShield: A Binary Rewriting Defense against Format String Attacks

Pankaj Kohli and Bezawada Bruhadeshwar

Centre for Security, Theory and Algorithmic Research (C-STAR)
International Institute of Information Technology
Hyderabad - 500032, India
pankaj_kohli@research.iiit.ac.in, bezawada@iiit.ac.in

Abstract. Format string attacks allow an attacker to read or write anywhere in the memory of a process. Previous solutions designed to detect format string attacks either require source code and recompilation of the program, or aim to defend only against write attempts to security critical control information. They do not protect against arbitrary memory read attempts and non-control data attacks. This paper presents FormatShield, a comprehensive defense against format string attacks. FormatShield identifies potentially vulnerable call sites in a running process and dumps the corresponding context information in the program binary. Attacks are detected when malicious input is found at vulnerable call sites with an exploitable context. It does not require source code or recompilation of the program and can defend against arbitrary memory read and write attempts, including non-control data attacks. Also, our experiments show that FormatShield incurs minimal performance overheads and is better than existing solutions.

Keywords: Format String Attacks, Binary Rewriting, Intrusion Detection, System Security.

1 Introduction

Format string vulnerabilities are a result of the flexible features in the C programming language in the representation of data and the use of pointers. These features have made C the language of choice for system programming. Unfortunately, this flexibility comes at a cost of lack of type safety and function argument checking. The format string vulnerability applies to all format string functions in the C library, and exists in several popular software and server programs [4, 6, 9, 14, 16, 28]. Attackers have exploited format string vulnerabilities on a large scale [12, 36], gaining root access on vulnerable systems. As of January 2008, Mitre's CVE project [3] lists more than 400 entries containing the term "format string".

Format string vulnerabilities occur when programmers pass user supplied input to a format function, such as `printf`, as the format string argument i.e., using code constructs such as `printf(str)` instead of `printf("%s", str)`. This

Y. Mu, W. Susilo, and J. Seberry (Eds.): ACISP 2008, LNCS 5107, pp. 376–390, 2008.

```
int main(int argc, char **argv) {
    char string[8] = "DATA";
    if (argc > 1)
        printf(argv[1]);
    return 0;
}
```

Fig. 1. A program vulnerable to format string attack

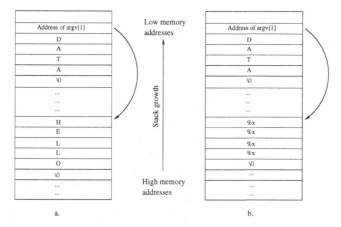

a.   b.

Fig. 2. Stack layout for the program given in Figure 1 when `printf` is called. **a.** On giving a legitimate input, the program prints HELLO. **b.** On giving a malicious input ("%x%x%x%x"), the program prints 44415441 (hex equivalent of "DATA").

input is interpreted by the format function as a format string, and is scanned for the presence of format specifiers such as %x, %s, %n etc. For each format specifier, corresponding value or address is picked from the stack and is read or written, depending on the format specifier. For example, the format specifier %d specifies an integer value to be read from the stack, while the format specifier %n specifies a value to be written to the address picked from the stack. An attacker can use this to perform reads or writes to arbitrary memory locations. Vulnerable functions in libc include printf family, warn and err family, syslog, vsyslog and several others.

In Figure 1, we show an example of a program vulnerable to a format string attack that passes the user input to printf. Here a malicious user could insert format specifiers in the input to cause the program to misbehave. Figure 2 shows the stack for this program when a legitimate and a malicious input in given. The malicious user gives as input %x%x%x%x, which causes printf to pick and display the next few bytes from the stack (44415441 - hex representation of "DATA" in this case), allowing him to read the stack. Similarly, use of %s format specifier makes the format function interpret the four bytes on the stack as the address of the string to be displayed. Using direct parameter access, i.e. %N$d, allows an attacker to access the Nth argument on the stack without accessing the previous $N - 1$ arguments. The value of N is so specified by the attacker such that the corresponding address is picked from the format string itself and hence can be controlled by the attacker. This allows an attacker to read any memory location within the address space of the process. The common form of the attack uses %n format specifier, which takes an address to an integer as an argument, and writes the number of bytes printed so far to the location specified by the address. The number of bytes printed so far can easily be controlled by printing an integer with large amount of padding such as %656d. Using %n format specifier, an attacker can overwrite the stored return address on the stack with the address of his own code, taking control of the program when the function returns. Other targets include address of destructor functions in DTORS table, address of library functions in Global Offset Table (GOT), function pointers and other security critical data. Also, an attacker can crash the process using several %s format specifiers, when an illegal address is picked from the stack, the program terminates with a segmentation fault.

Many techniques have been devised to defend against format string attacks [18, 15, 13, 10, 8, 30, 25, 19, 7]. All these approaches are valuable and defend against arbitrary code execution attacks. However, each of them suffers from at least one of the two drawbacks: either they require source code and recompilation of the program to be protected, or they aim to defend only against write attempts to security critical control information, such as return address, GOT and DTORS entries, etc. They do not guard against arbitrary memory read attempts, which can lead to critical information disclosure leading to further attacks. Also, none of the previously proposed solutions protects against non-control data attacks, in which an attacker targets a program specific security critical data, such as a variable storing user privileges, instead of control information. Such attacks have been studied in the past [20].

In this paper, we present FormatShield, a comprehensive solution to format string attacks. FormatShield does not require source code and recompilation, and can be used to protect legacy or proprietary programs for which source code may not be available. It does not take into consideration the presence of any specific format specifier such as %n in the format string, and thus, it can defend against both types of format string attacks, i.e. arbitrary memory read attempts and arbitrary memory write attempts. Also, FormatShield is capable of defending against non-control data attacks. It does not rely on the target of the format specifiers, and thus can protect against both, attacks that target control information such as return address on the stack, and those which target program specific security sensitive non-control information.

Organization of the Paper. The rest of the paper is organized as follows. Section 2 presents the technical description of the approach used by FormatShield. Section 3 describes the design and implementation of FormatShield. Section 4 presents experimental results on the effectiveness and performance evaluation. Limitations are discussed in section 5, followed by related work in section 6. Finally, section 7 concludes the paper.

2   Overview of Our Approach

FormatShield works by identifying call sites in a running process that are potentially vulnerable to format string attacks. A potentially vulnerable call site is identified when a format function is called with a probable legitimate user input as a format string argument. Further, a probable legitimate user input can be identified by checking whether the format string is writable and without any format specifiers. The format string argument of a non-vulnerable call site, such as in printf("%s", argv[1]), would lie in a non-writable memory segment, while that of a vulnerable call site, such as in printf(argv[1]), would lie in a writable memory segment. The key idea here is to augment the program binary with the program context information at the vulnerable call sites. A program context represents an execution path within a program and is specified by the set of return addresses on the stack. Since all execution paths to the vulnerable call site may not lead to an attack, FormatShield considers only those with an exploitable program context. For e.g., Figure 3 shows a vulnerable code fragment. Here the vulnerability lies in the function output(), which passes its argument as the format string to printf. Although output() has been called from three different call sites in main(), note that only one of these three, i.e. output(argv[1]), is exploitable. Here, the contexts, i.e. the set of return addresses on the stack, corresponding to all the three calls will be different, and thus the context corresponding to output(argv[1]) can easily be differentiated from those of other two calls to output(). As the process executes, the exploitable program contexts are identified. The next time, if the vulnerable call site is called with an exploitable program context with format specifiers in the format string, a violation is raised. When the process exits, the entire list of exploitable program contexts is dumped into the binary as a new loadable read-only section, which is made available at runtime for subsequent runs of the program. If the section already exists, the list of exploitable program contexts is updated in the section. The program binary is updated with context information over use and becomes immune to format string attacks.

```
void output(char *str) {
    printf(str);
}

int main(int argc, char **argv) {
    output("alpha");
    .....
    output("beta");
    .....
    output(argv[1]);
    .....
}
```

Fig. 3. Only the third call to output() is exploitable

3   Implementation

FormatShield is implemented as a shared library that intercepts calls to the vulnerable functions in `libc`, preloaded using `LD_PRELOAD` environment variable. This section explains the design and implementation of FormatShield. First we explain how FormatShield identifies vulnerable call sites in a running process. Then we describe the binary rewriting approach used to augment the binary with the context information.

3.1   Identifying Vulnerable Call Sites

During process startup, FormatShield checks if the new section (named `fsprotect`) is present in the binary of the process. This is done by resolving the symbol `fsprotect`. If present, the list of exploitable program contexts is loaded. During process execution, whenever the control is transferred to a vulnerable function intercepted by FormatShield, it checks if the format string is writable. This is done by looking at the process memory map in `/proc/pid/maps`. If the format string is non-writable, corresponding equivalent function (such as `vprintf` for `printf`) in `libc` is called since a non-writable format string cannot be user input and hence cannot lead to an attack. However, if the format string is writable, FormatShield identifies the current context of the program, and checks if this context is in the list of exploitable program contexts. The current context of the program, i.e. the set of return addresses on the stack, is retrieved by following the chain of stored frame pointers on the stack. Instead of storing the entire set of return addresses on the stack, FormatShield computes a lightweight hash of the return addresses. If the current context is not present in the list of exploitable contexts, FormatShield checks if the format string is without any format specifiers. If the format string does not contain any format specifiers, it is identified as a legitimate user input, and the current context is added to the list of exploitable contexts. Any future occurrences of format specifiers in the format string of such a call with an exploitable context is flagged as an attack. Otherwise, if the format string contains format specifiers, it is not added to the list of exploitable contexts. In either case, FormatShield calls the equivalent function in `libc`. However, if the current context is already in the list of exploitable contexts, FormatShield checks if there are any format specifiers in the format string. If the format string does not contains any format specifiers, FormatShield calls the equivalent function in `libc`. Otherwise, if the format string contains format specifiers, FormatShield raises a violation. On detecting an attack, the victim process is killed, and a log is written to `syslog`.

Note that, if the format string is writable and contains format specifiers, it could be a case when an exploitable context is not yet identified by FormatShield and is being exploited by an attacker. However, FormatShield takes a safer step of not identifying it as an attack, since dynamically created format strings with format specifiers are commonly encountered and identifying such cases as attacks would terminate an innocent process which is not under attack. Also, the default

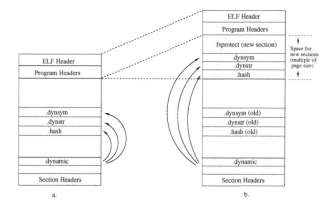

Fig. 4. ELF binary **a.** before rewriting **b.** after rewriting

```
. . . .
[003]  0x08048148  a------  .hash      sz:00000040  link:04
[004]  0x08048170  a------  .dynsym    sz:00000080  link:05
[005]  0x080481C0  a------  .dynstr    sz:00000076  link:00
. . . .
```

Fig. 5. Sections before rewriting the binary

```
. . . .
[003]  0x080480E8  a------  .hash      sz:00000044  link:04
[004]  0x08048030  a------  .dynsym    sz:00000096  link:05
[005]  0x08048090  a------  .dynstr    sz:00000088  link:00
. . . .
[026]  0x08047114  a------  fsprotect  sz:00003868  link:00
[027]  0x08048170  a------             sz:00000080  link:00
[028]  0x080481C0  a------             sz:00000076  link:00
[029]  0x08048148  a------             sz:00000040  link:00
```

Fig. 6. Sections after rewriting the binary. A new loadable read-only section named **fsprotect** is added which holds the context information. The **.dynsym**, **.dynstr** and **.hash** sections shown are extended copies of the original ones. The original **.dynsym**, **.dynstr** and **.hash** are still loaded at their original load addresses.

action to terminate the process can be used as a basis to launch denial of service (DoS) attack against the victim process by an attacker. However, silently returning from the vulnerable function without terminating the process may lead to an application specific error. For e.g., if the vulnerability lies in a call to **vfprintf**, skipping the call may lead to no output being printed to terminal if the string is being printed to **stdout**, which may not be fatal. However, if the string is being printed to a file, skipping the **vfprintf** call may lead to a corrupted file. Terminating the victim process would create "noise" that a conventional host-based intrusion detection system can detect the intrusion attempt.

```
DYNAMIC SYMBOL TABLE:
00000000      DF  *UND*      000000e7    __libc_start_main
00000000      DF  *UND*      00000039    printf
080484a4   g  DO  .rodata    00000004    _IO_stdin_used
00000000   w  D   *UND*      00000000    __gmon_start__
```

Fig. 7. Dynamic symbol table before rewriting the binary

```
DYNAMIC SYMBOL TABLE:
00000000      DF  *UND*      000000e7    __libc_start_main
00000000      DF  *UND*      00000039    printf
080484a4   g  DO  .rodata    00000004    _IO_stdin_used
00000000   w  D   *UND*      00000000    __gmon_start__
08047114   g  DO  fsprotect  0000000a    fsprotect
```

Fig. 8. Dynamic symbol table after rewriting the binary. A new dynamic symbol named **fsprotect** is added while rewriting the binary which points to the new section at address 0x08047114.

3.2 Binary Rewriting

FormatShield uses an approach (Figure 4) similar to that used by TIED [22] to insert context information in the program binary. FormatShield currently supports only ELF [11] executables. In the ELF binary format, .dynsym section of binary contains symbols needed for dynamic linking, .dynstr section contains the corresponding symbol names, and .hash section holds a hash look up table to quickly resolve symbols. .dynamic section holds the addresses of these three sections. The information to be inserted is a list of hashes of stored return addresses corresponding to exploitable contexts at different vulnerable call sites in the program. During process exit, the entire list is dumped into the executable as a new read-only loadable section. If the section is already present, the context information in the section is updated. A typical ELF binary loads at virtual address 0x08048000. To add a new section (Figures 5,6), FormatShield extends the binary towards lower addresses, i.e. lower than address 0x08048000. This is done to ensure that the addresses of existing code and data do not change. To make the context information available at run time, a new dynamic symbol (Figures 7,8) is added to the .dynsym section and the corresponding address is set to that of the new section. Since this requires extending .dynsym, .dynstr and .hash sections which cannot be done without changing the addresses of other sections, FormatShield creates an extended copy of these sections, i.e. .dynsym, .dynstr and .hash, and changes their addresses in .dynamic section. The address of the new section is so chosen such that the sum of the sizes of the four new sections is a multiple of page size[1]. The space overhead is of the order of few kilobytes (less than 10 KB for most binaries).

---

[1] As per ELF specification [11], loadable process segments must have congruent values of the load address, modulo the page size.

3.3 Implementation Issues

One of the issues with FormatShield is when the program uses some kind of Address Space Randomization (ASR) [2, 21, 23]. ASR involves randomizing base addresses of various segments so as to make it difficult for an attacker to guess an address. Since the base addresses of various code segments are randomized, the absolute memory locations associated with the set of return addresses will change from one execution of the program to the next. To compensate for this, we decompose each return address into a pair {name, offset}, where name identifies the executable or the shared library, and offset identifies the relative distance from the base of the executable or shared library.

4 Evaluation

We conducted a series of experiments to evaluate the effectiveness and performance of FormatShield. All tests were run in single user mode on a Pentium-4 3.2 GHz machine with 512 MB RAM running Linux kernel 2.6.18. All programs were compiled with gcc 4.1.2 with default options and linked with glibc 2.3.6.

4.1 Effectiveness

We tested FormatShield on five programs with known format string vulnerabilities:

- wuftpd version 2.6.0 and earlier suffer from a format string vulnerability [6] in the "SITE EXEC" implementation. A remote user can gain a root shell by exploiting this vulnerability.
- tcpflow 0.2.0 suffers from a format string vulnerability [28], that can be exploited by injecting format specifiers in command line arguments. A local user can gain a root shell by exploiting this vulnerability.
- xlock 4.16 suffers from a format string vulnerability [29] when using command line argument -d, that can be used by a local user to gain root privileges.
- rpc.statd (nfs-utils versions 0.1.9.1 and earlier) suffers from a format string vulnerability [9], which allows a remote user to execute arbitrary code as root.
- splitvt version 1.6.5 and earlier suffer from a format string vulnerability when handling the command line argument -rcfile. A local user can gain a root shell[2] by exploiting this vulnerability.

The above programs were trained "synthetically" with legitimate inputs before launching the attacks so as to identify the vulnerable call sites and the corresponding exploitable contexts. FormatShield successfully detected all the above attacks, and terminated the programs to prevent execution of malicious code. The results are presented in Table 1.

---

[2] The attack gives a root shell if the program is installed suid root, otherwise it gives a user shell.

Table 1. Results of effectiveness evaluation

Vulnerable program	CVE #	Results without FormatShield	Results with FormatShield
wuftpd	CVE-2000-0573	Root Shell acquired	Process Killed
tcpflow	CAN-2003-0671	Root Shell acquired	Process Killed
xlock	CVE-2000-0763	Root Shell acquired	Process Killed
rpc.statd	CVE-2000-0666	Root Shell acquired	Process Killed
splitvt	CAN-2001-0112	Root Shell acquired [2]	Process Killed

Table 2. Comparison with previous approaches

Feature	LibFormat	Format-Guard	Libsafe	White-Listing	Format-Shield
Works without source code	✓	✗	✓	✗	✓
Supports vprintf like functions	✓	✗	✓	✓	✓
Supports wrapper functions	✗	✗	✓	✓	✓
Prevents read attacks	✗	✓ [3]	✗	✗	✓
Prevents write attacks	✓	✓	✓ [4]	✓	✓
Prevents non control data attacks	✗	✓ [3]	✗	✗	✓
Not format string specific	✓	✓	✓	✗	✓

To check the effectiveness of FormatShield on non-control data attacks, we modified the publicly available exploit for the wuftpd 2.6.0 format string vulnerability [6] to overwrite the cached copy of user ID pw->pw_uid with 0 so as to to disable the server's ability to drop privileges. FormatShield successfully detected the write attempt to the user ID field and terminated the child process. Table 2 shows a detailed comparison of FormatShield and the previous approaches to detection of format string attacks.

4.2   Performance Testing

To test the performance overhead of FormatShield, we performed micro benchmarks to measure the overhead at function call level, and then macro benchmarks to measure the overhead at application level.

Micro benchmarks. To measure the overhead per function call, we ran a set of simple benchmarks consisting of a single loop containing a single sprintf

---

[3] FormatGuard protects by counting arguments and number of format specifiers, and thus can protect against arbitrary memory reads and non-control data attacks. However, it does not work for format functions called from within a wrapper function and those with variable argument lists such as vprintf.

[4] Libsafe defends against writes to stored return address and frame pointer, but does not protect against writes to GOT and DTORS entries.

Table 3. Micro benchmarks

Benchmark	FormatGuard	White-Listing	FormatShield
sprintf, no format specifiers	7.5%	10.2%	12.2%
sprintf, 2 %d format specifiers	20.9%	28.6%	4.6%
sprintf, 2 %n format specifiers	38.1%	60.0%	3.3%
vsprintf, no format specifiers	No protection	26.4%	15.5%
vsprintf, 2 %d format specifiers	No protection	39.8%	1.9%
vsprintf, 2 %n format specifiers	No protection	74.7%	3.4%

call. A six character writable string was used as the format string. With no format specifiers, FormatShield added an overhead of 12.2%. With two %d format specifiers, overhead was found to be 4.6%, while with two %n format specifiers the overhead was 3.3%. We also tested vsprintf using the same loop. The overheads were found to be 15.5%, 1.9% and 3.4% for no format specifiers, two %d format specifiers, and two %n format specifiers respectively. The overheads were found to be much less than those with the previous approaches. Table 3 compares micro benchmarks of FormatShield with those of FormatGuard and White-Listing.

Macro benchmarks. To test the overhead at the application level, we used man2html since it uses printf extensively to write HTML-formatted man pages to standard output. The test was to translate 4.6 MB of man pages. The test was performed multiple times. It took man2html 0.468 seconds to convert without FormatShield, and 0.484 seconds with FormatShield. Thus, FormatShield imposed 3.42% run-time overhead.

5   Discussion

In this section, we discuss the false positives and false negatives of FormatShield, and its limitations when applied to the software protection.

5.1   False Positives and False Negatives

FormatShield can give false positives or false negatives in certain cases. It is when a format string is dynamically constructed as a result of a conditional statement and then passed to a format function. A false positive can be there if one outcome of the condition creates a format string with format specifiers and the other outcome creates one without format specifiers. Similarly, a false negative can be there when one outcome of the condition reads user input into the format string and the other outcome creates a format string with format specifiers. Also, there can be a false negative when format specifiers are present at the vulnerable call site but the corresponding context is not yet identified.

5.2   Limitations

FormatShield requires frame pointers to obtain the set of stored return addresses on the stack, which are available in most cases. However, it may not be able to

protect programs compiled without frame pointers, such as those compiled with
-fomit-frame-pointer flag of gcc. Also, FormatShield requires that exploitable
contexts of the vulnerable call sites are identified before it can detect attacks.
This may require the program to be trained, either by deploying or by exercising
"synthetically". Another limitation of FormatShield is that it requires programs
to be dynamically linked (since library call interpositioning works only with dynamic linked programs). However, this is not a problem if we consider Xiao's
study [31] according to which 99.78% applications on Unix platform are dynamically linked. Also, since FormatShield keeps updating the context information
in the program binary till it becomes immune to format string attacks, it may
interfere with some integrity checkers.

6   Related Work

Several techniques have been proposed to defend against format string attacks.
These can be divided into three categories: compile-time approaches, run-time
approaches, and combined compile-time and run-time approaches.

6.1   Compile-Time Approaches

PScan [7] works by looking for printf-style functions where the last parameter
is a non-static format string. Similar to PScan's functionality, gcc itself provides
flags such as "-Wformat=2" to statically check the format string and issue warnings for dangerous or suspect formats. Both PScan and gcc work at the lexical
level. They require source code, are subject to missing format string vulnerabilities and even issue warnings about safe code. Another compile-time technique
for detecting format string attacks is presented by Shankar et al [8]. In their
approach, all untrusted inputs are marked as tainted, and the propagation of
tainted data is tracked throughout the program operation. Any data derived
from tainted data is itself marked as tainted. If at some point in the program,
the tainted data is used as a format string, an error is raised. This approach does
not work for already compiled code. Moreover, it requires programmers' efforts
to specify which objects are tainted.

6.2   Run-Time Approaches

LibFormat [10] works by intercepting calls to printf family of functions, and
aborts any process if the format string is writable and contains %n format specifier. This technique is quite effective in defending against real format string
attacks, but in most cases writable format strings containing %n format specifier
are legal, and consequently it generates many false alarms. Libsafe [13] implements a safe subset of format functions that will abort the running process if the
address corresponding to a %n format specifier points to a return address or a
frame pointer. However, it still allows writes to GOT and DTORS entries, and therefore is subject to missing many attack attempts. Lin et al [15] use dynamic taint

and validation to detect format string attacks. In their approach, if the format string is non-static and contains %n format specifier, and if the corresponding address points to the return address, frame pointer, or GOT or DTORS entries, an attack is detected and the process is aborted. The approach is effective in preventing arbitrary memory write attempts to control sensitive addresses, but does not defends against arbitrary memory read attempts and non-control data attacks. Kimchi [25] is another binary rewriting defense technique, that inserts code in the binary which prevents a format string to access memory beyond the stack frame of its parent function. However, it is subject to missing many attack attempts when the format string itself is declared in the parent function, and therefore lies in the parent function's stack frame. Lisbon [30] identifies the input argument list, and places a canary word immediately after the list's end. A violation is raised if the program attempts to access the canary word. This approach works for attacks that aim to probe the underlying stack using a series of %x%x%x... format specifiers. However, the approach will miss all the read and write attempts where the attacker uses a format specifiers with direct parameter access. For example, the input %18$x will read the 18th argument without accessing the canary. All the above approaches detect write attempts using %n format specifiers but fail to detect arbitrary memory read attempts.

Address Space Randomization (ASR) [2, 21, 23, 34] is a generic technique to defend against any kind of memory corruption attack. The idea behind ASR is that the successful exploitation of such an attack requires an attacker to have knowledge of the addresses where the critical information is stored and/or where the attacker specified code is present. By randomizing the locations of various memory segments and other security critical structures, ASR makes it hard for an attacker to guess the correct address. For the Intel x86 architecture, PaX ASLR [1, 2] provides 16, 16 and 24 bits of randomness for the executable, mapped and stack areas respectively. However, many successful derandomization attacks against PaX have been studied in the past. Durden [32] uses a format string attack to deduce the value of delta_mmap. Another brute force derandomization attack has been presented by Shacham et al [17], which defeats PaX ASLR in less than 4 minutes. Instruction Set Randomization (ISR) [24, 27] is another generic defense technique that defends against code injection attacks by randomizing the underlying instruction set. Since the attacker does not know the randomizing key, his injected code will be invalid for the injected process, causing a runtime exception. However, overheads associated with ISR make it an impractical approach to defend against attacks. Also, attacks have been published [33] capable of defeating ISR in about 6 minutes. Moreover, both kinds of randomizations still allow information disclosure attacks.

6.3   Combined Compile-Time and Run-Time Approaches

FormatGuard [18] provides argument number checking for printf-like functions using GNU C compiler. Programs need to be recompiled without any modification. It provides protection against only a subset of functions and does not work for functions that expect variable argument lists such as vprintf. White-listing

[19] uses source code transformation to automatically insert code and maintains checks against the whitelist containing safe %n writable address ranges via knowledge gained from static analysis. Both FormatGuard and White-Listing require source code and recompilation of the program.

7   Conclusion and Future Work

Format string vulnerabilities are one of the few truly threats to software security. This paper described the design, implementation and evaluation of Format-Shield, a tool that protects vulnerable programs by inserting context information in program binaries. Although the current implementation is designed to work on Linux platform, the same approach can be made to work on Win32 platform as well, using the Detours [35] framework. We have shown that FormatShield is effective in stopping format string attacks, and incurs a very nominal performance penalty of less than 4%. However, FormatShield requires the process to be trained using synthetic data or by deploying in order to identify vulnerable call sites. We believe static analysis can be used to identify such vulnerable call sites. Hence, the future work involves covering this limitation of FormatShield to make it much more effective in defending against format string attacks.

References

[1] PaX. Published on World-Wide Web (2001), http://pax.grsecurity.net
[2] PaX Team. PaX address space layout randomization (ASLR),
    http://pax.grsecurity.net/docs/aslr.txt
[3] CVE - Common Vulnerabilities and Exposures, http://www.cve.mitre.org
[4] Kaempf, M.: Splitvt Format String Vulnerability,
    http://www.securityfocus.com/bid/2210/
[5] CWE - Vulnerability Type Distributions in CVE,
    http://cve.mitre.org/docs/vuln-trends/index.html
[6] tf8.: Wu-Ftpd Remote Format String Stack Overwrite Vulnerability,
    http://www.securityfocus.com/bid/1387
[7] De Kok, A.: PScan: A limited problem scanner for C source files,
    http://www.striker.ottawa.on.ca/~aland/pscan/
[8] Shankar, U., Talwar, K., Foster, J.S., Wagner, D.: Detecting format string vulnerabilities with type qualifiers. In: Proceedings of the 10th USENIX Security Symposium (Security 2001), Washington, DC (2001)
[9] Jacobowitz, D.: Multiple Linux Vendor rpc.statd Remote Format String Vulnerability, http://www.securityfocus.com/bid/1480
[10] Robbins, T.: Libformat,
    http://www.wiretapped.net/~fyre/software/libformat.html
[11] Tool Interface Standard (TIS) Committee: Executable and linking format (ELF) specification, version 1.2 (1995)
[12] CERT Incident Note IN-2000-10, Widespread Exploitation of rpc.statd and wu-ftpd Vulnerabilities (September 15, 2000)
[13] Tsai, T., Singh, N.: Libsafe 2.0: Detection of Format String Vulnerability Exploits, http://www.research.avayalabs.com/project/libsafe/doc/
    whitepaper-20.pdf

[14] Pelat, G.: PFinger Format String Vulnerability,
http://www.securityfocus.com/bid/3725

[15] Lin, Z., Xia, N., Li, G., Mao, B., Xie, L.: Transparent Run-Time Prevention of
Format-String Attacks Via Dynamic Taint and Flexible Validation. In: De Meuter,
W. (ed.) ISC 2006. LNCS, vol. 4406, Springer, Heidelberg (2007)

[16] NSI Rwhoisd Remote Format String Vulnerability,
http://www.securityfocus.com/bid/3474

[17] Shacham, H., Page, M., Pfaff, B., Goh, E.-J., Modadugu, N., Boneh, D.: On the
effectiveness of address-space randomization. In: Proceedings of the 11th ACM
conference on Computer and communications security, Washington DC, USA,
October 25-29 (2004)

[18] Cowan, C., Barringer, M., Beattie, S., Kroah-Hartman, G.: FormatGuard: Automatic protection from printf format string vulnerabilities. In: Proceedings of the
10th USENIX Security Symposium (Security 2001), Washington, DC (2001)

[19] Ringenburg, M., Grossman, D.: Preventing Format-String Attacks via Automatic
and Efficient Dynamic Checking. In: Proceedings of the 12th ACM Conference on
Computer and Communications Security (CCS 2005), Alexandria, Virginia (2005)

[20] Chen, S., Xu, J., Sezer, E.C., Gauriar, P., Iyer, R.K.: Non-control-data attacks
are realistic threats. In: Proceedings of the 14th conference on USENIX Security
Symposium, Baltimore, MD (2005)

[21] Bhatkar, S., DuVarney, D.C., Sekar, R.: Address obfuscation: An efficient approach to combat a broad range of memory error exploits. In: USENIX Security
Symposium, Washington, DC (August 2003)

[22] Avijit, K., Gupta, P., Gupta, D.: TIED, LibsafePlus: Tools for Runtime Buffer
Overflow Protection. In: Proceedings of the 13th USENIX Security Symposium,
San Diego, CA (2004)

[23] Bhatkar, S., Sekar, R., DuVarney, D.C.: Efficient Techniques for Comprehensive
Protection from Memory Error Exploits. In: Proceedings of the 14th USENIX
Security Symposium, July 31-August 05, p. 17 (2005)

[24] Barrantes, E.G., Ackley, D.H., Palmer, T.S., Stefanovic, D., Zovi, D.D.: Randomized Instruction Set Emulation to Disrupt Binary Code Injection Attacks.
In: Proceedings of the 10th ACM conference on Computer and communications
security, Washington D.C, USA (October 27-30, 2003)

[25] You, J.H., Seo, S.C., Kim, Y.D., Choi, J.Y., Lee, S.J., Kim, B.K.: Kimchi: A
Binary Rewriting Defense Against Format String Attacks. In: WISA 2005 (2005)

[26] Cowan, C., Pu, C., Maier, D., Hinton, H., Walpole, J., Bakke, P., Beattie, S.,
Grier, A., Wagle, P., Zhang, Q.: Stackguard: Automatic adaptive detection and
prevention of buffer-overflow attacks. In: Proceedings of the 7th USENIX Security
Symposium, San Antonio, TX, pp. 63–78 (January 1998)

[27] Kc, G.S., Keromytis, A.D., Prevelakis, V.: Countering Code-Injection Attacks
with Instruction-Set Randomization. In: Proceedings of the 10th ACM conference
on Computer and Communications Security, Washington D.C, USA, October 27-
30 (2003)

[28] @stake, Inc. tcpflow 0.2.0 format string vulnerability (August 2003),
http://www.securityfocus.com/advisories/5686

[29] bind: xlockmore User Supplied Format String Vulnerability,
http://www.securityfocus.com/bid/1585

[30] Li, W., Chiueh, T.-c.: Automated Format String Attack Prevention for
Win32/X86 Binaries. In: Proceedings of 23rd Annual Computer Security Applications Conference, Florida (December 2007)

[31] Xiao, Z.: An Automated Approach to Software Reliability and Security. Invited Talk, Department of Computer Science. University of California at Berkeley (2003)

[32] Durden, T.: Bypassing PaX ASLR protection. Phrack Magazine 59(9) (June 2002), http://www.phrack.org/phrack/59/p59-0x09

[33] Sovarel, N., Evans, D., Paul, N.: Where's the FEEB? The Effectiveness of Instruction Set Randomization. In: 14th USENIX Security Symposium (August 2005)

[34] Xu, J., Kalbarczyk, Z., Iyer, R.: Transparent Runtime Randomization for Security. In: Fantechi, A. (ed.) Proc. 22nd Symp. on Reliable Distributed Systems –SRDS 2003, pp. 260–269. IEEE Computer Society, Los Alamitos (2003)

[35] Hunt, G., Brubacher, D.: Detours: Binary interception of Win32 functions. In: Proceedings of the 3rd USENIX Windows NT Symposium, Seattle, WA, pp. 135–143 (1999)

[36] Lemos, R.: Internet worm squirms into Linux servers. Special to CNET News.com (January 17, 2001), http://news.cnet.com/news/0-1003-200-4508359.html

Advanced Permission-Role Relationship in Role-Based Access Control*

Min Li[1], Hua Wang[1], Ashley Plank[1], and Jianming Yong[2]

[1] Department of Mathematics & Computing
University of Southern Queensland, Australia
{limin,wang,plank}@usq.edu.au
[2] School of Information Systems, Faculty of Business
University of Southern Queensland, Australia
yongj@usq.edu.au

Abstract. Permission-role assignment is an important issue in role-based access control (RBAC). There are two types of problems that may arise in permission-role assignment. One is related to authorization granting process. Conflicting permissions may be granted to a role, and as a result, users with the role may have or derive a high level of authority. The other is related to authorization revocation. When a permission is revoked from a role, the role may still have the permission from other roles. In this paper, we discuss granting and revocation models related to mobile and immobile memberships between permissions and roles, then provide proposed authorization granting algorithm to check conflicts and help allocate the permissions without compromising the security. To our best knowledge, the new revocation models, local and global revocation, have not been studied before. The local and global revocation algorithms based on relational algebra and operations provide a rich variety. We also apply the new algorithms to an anonymity scalable payment scheme.

1 Introduction

Role-based access control (RBAC) is a flexible and policy-neutral access control technology and is a promising access control technology for the modern computing environment [1,3,6,16]. In RBAC, permissions(each permission is a pair of objects and operations) are associated with roles and users are assigned to appropriate roles thereby acquiring the roles' permissions. As such, a user in RBAC is a human being. It can be easily reassigned from one role to another. A role is a job function or job title and created for various job functions in an organization and users are assigned roles based on responsibilities and qualifications. A permission is an approval of a particular mode of access to one or more objects. The user-role and permission-role assignment relations are many-to-many between users and roles, and between roles and permissions as depicted in Fig. 1. Roles can be granted new permissions as new applications come on

---

* The research is support by an ARC Discovery Grant DP0663414.

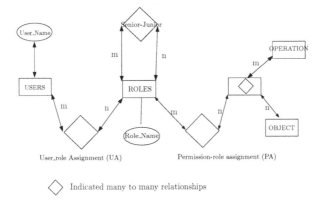

Fig. 1. RBAC relationship

line and permissions can be revoked from roles as needed. Within RBAC, users are not granted permission to perform operations on an individual object, but permissions are associated with roles.

Significant developments have been made within RBAC. The NIST model of RBAC [2] and Web implementation of RBAC incorporates an administrative tool that provides rudimentary support for an RBAC database that stores information about user and permission role assignments and role hierarchies [4]. Nyanchama and Osborn [7] define a role graph model that rigorously specifies operational semantics for manipulating role relations in the contexts of a role hierarchy. ARBAC97 builds on these previous attempts to construct administrative models [10] over all aspects of the RBAC model. Sandhu and Munawer [11] extends the ARBAC97 model by adding the concept of mobile and immobile permissions for the first time in this area. In [11], the authors distinguished two kinds of membership in a role. Immobile membership grants the role to have the permission, but does not make that permission eligible for further role assignment. Mobile membership on the other hand, covers both aspects.

However, there is a consistency problem when using RBAC management. For instance, if there are hundreds of permissions and thousands of roles in a system, it is very difficult to maintain consistency because it may change the authorization level, or imply high-level confidential information when more then one permission is requested and granted. Specifically, [11] does not mention conflicts when assigning permissions to roles. Therefore, there is no support to deal administrative role with regular roles, especially mobile and immobile members.

In this paper, we develop formal approaches to check the conflicts and therefore help allocate the permissions without compromising the security. We analyze authorization granting and revocation models with the mobility of permission-role relationship. Our main contribution in this paper is the relational algebra-based authorization granting and local, global revocation algorithms. Furthermore, we include an applicable example to illustrate our algorithms. Another contribution is that our algorithms could check conflicts when granting

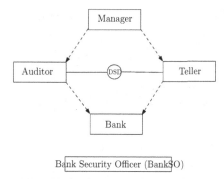

Fig. 2. Administrative role and role relationships in a bank

more than one permission as mobile or immobile member to a role in the system. As far as we know, there is no previous work addressing these issues for permission allocation and conflict detection concerning on mobile memberships.

The organization of the paper is as follows. In section 2, we consider the mobility of permission-role relationship and problems related to permission assignment and revocation. The relational algebra-based authorization granting and revocation algorithms are given in section 3. In section 4, we review an anonymity scalable electronic commerce payment scheme and apply algorithms to this scheme. Comparisons with previous work are discussed in section 5. Finally, we conclude the paper in section 6.

2   Motivation and Problem Definitions

There are two kinds of membership between permissions and roles, namely mobile and immobile [11]. Immobile membership grants the role the permission but does not make that permission eligible for further role assignments. Mobile membership on the other hand covers both aspects which means the role has the permission and the permission also becomes eligible for assignment to other roles by appropriate administrative roles.

The distinction between mobile and immobile membership can be very important in practice. Fig. 2 shows the administrative and regular roles that exist in a bank department. The permission-role assignment allows us to give BankSo the authority to take a permission assigned to Manager and grant it to roles Teller, Auditor, and Bank. The idea is that each administrative role can delegate permissions of the senior role to more junior roles. While this may be acceptable for most permissions of a senior role, it is likely that some permissions are not suitable for such delegation. For instance in Fig. 2, suppose 'approving a loan' is a permission of the role Manger, which should only be executed by the Manger. Consider the two kinds of membership between permissions and roles, if this permission is assigned to the role Manger as a mobile member, it is possible that all the roles junior to the Manger can hold this permission through permission-

Table 1. Example of the relation PERM

PermName	Oper	Object	ConfPerm
Approval	approve	cash / check	Funding
Funding	invest	cash	Approval
Audit	audit	record	Teller
Teller	transfer	cash	Audit

role assignment, which leads to security breach. So this permission can only be assigned to Manager as immobile while the others can be assigned as mobile.

This example demonstrates that the situations with mobile and immobile relationship between permissions and roles can be very useful in practice to avoid the security breach. Throughout the paper, we consider the following two problems that may arise in permission-role assignment.

Authorization granting problem: Is a permission in conflict with the permissions of a role when granting the permission to the role as a mobile or immobile member?

Authorization revocation problem: Has a permission with mobile or immobile membership of a role been revoked from the role?

Conflicting permissions may be granted to a role in permission-role assignment. For example, the permission for approving a loan in a bank and that of funding a loan are conflicting. These two permissions can not be assigned to a role at the same time. It is easy to find conflicts between permissions when assigning permissions to a role in a small database but it is hard to find them when there are thousands of permissions in a system. Moreover, it is even more complicated if taking mobile and immobile permissions into account. Our aim is to provide relational algebra algorithms to solve these problems and then automatically check conflicts when assigning and revoking.

For convenience, we recall some basic definitions in paper [15] with no further explanation. Let D be a database with a set of relations REL and a set of attributes Attri. REL includes PERM, ROLE-PERM and SEN-JUN etc. Attri includes attributes such as Role-Name, PermName, Senior and Junior, etc.

PERM is a relation of PermName, Oper, Object and ConfPerm. Perm-Name is the primary key for the table and is the name of the permission in the system. Oper is the name of the operation granted. It contains information about the object to which the operation is granted. Object is the item that can be accessed by the operation, which may be a database, a table, a view, an index or a database package. ConfPerm is a set of permissions that is conflicting with the PermName in the relation. For example, a staff in a bank cannot have permissions of approval and funding at the same time (as well as permissions of audit and teller). The relation of PERM is expressed in Table 1.

SEN-JUN is a relation of roles in a system. SEN and JUN are the senior and junior of the two roles, senior roles are shown at the top of the role hierarchies. Senior roles inherit permissions from junior roles. For example, in Fig. 2 role 'Manager' is the senior role of role 'Teller' and inherit all permissions of 'Teller'.

Table 2. Example of *can-assignp-M* in Fig. 2

Admin.role	Prereq.condition	Role Range
BankSO	Manager$\wedge\overline{Teller}$	[Auditor, Auditor]
BankSO	Manager$\wedge\overline{Auditor}$	[Teller, Teller]

Table 3. Example of *can-assignp-IM* in Fig. 2

Admin.role	Prereq.condition	Role Range
BankSO	Manager	[Auditor, Audior]
BankSO	Manager	[Teller, Teller]

ROLE-PERM is a relation between the roles and the permissions, listing what permissions are granted to what roles. For example, permission 'Approval' is assigned to role 'Teller' and the permission 'Funding' to role 'Manager'.

3   Authorization Granting and Revocation Algorithms Based on Relational Algebra

In this section, we provide granting and revocation algorithms based on relational algebra. As discussed before, a permission's membership in a role can be mobile or immobile, so each role x is separated into two sub-roles Mx and IMx. Note that membership in Mx is mobile whereas membership in IMx is immobile.

A role x' has all permissions of a role x when $x' > x$ [1]. A permission p is an explicit member of a role x if $(p, x) \in PA$ and p is an implicit member of a role x if for some role $x' < x, (p, x') \in PA$. Combining mobile and immobile membership with the notion of explicit and implicit membership gives us four distinct kinds of role membership:

(1) Explicit mobile member $EMx = \{p | (p, Mx) \in PA\}$
(2) Explicit immobile member $EIMx = \{p | (p, IMx) \in PA\}$
(3) Implicit mobile member $ImMx = \{p | \exists x' < x, (p, Mx') \in PA\}$
(4) Implicit immobile member $ImIMx = \{p | \exists x' < x, (p, IMx') \in PA\}$

It is possible for a permission to have more than one kind of membership in a role at the same time. Hence there is strict precedence among these four kinds of membership [2].

$$EMx > EIMx > ImMx > ImIMx$$

A prerequisite condition is evaluated for a permission p by interpreting role x to be true if $p \in EMx \vee (p \in ImMx \wedge p \notin EIMx)$ and $\overline{x}$ to be true if $p \notin EMx \wedge p \notin EIMx \wedge p \notin ImMx \wedge p \notin ImIMx$.

---

[1] $x' > x$ means role x' is senior than x; $x' < x$ means role x' is junior than x.

[2] Even though a role can have multiple kinds of membership in a permission, at any time only one of those is actually in effect.

Table 4. *can-revokep-M* in Fig. 2

Admin.role	Prereq.condition	Role Range
BankSO	Bank	[Bank, Manager]

Table 5. *can-revokep-IM* in Fig. 2

Admin.role	Prereq.condition	Role Range
BankSO	Bank	[Bank, Bank]

For a given set of roles R, let AR be a set of administrative roles and CR denote all possible prerequisite conditions that can be formed using the roles in R. Not every administrator can assign a permission to a role. The following relations provide what permissions an administrator can assign mobile members or immobile members with prerequisite conditions.

Can-assignp-M, used to assign the permission as mobile members, is a relation in $AR \times CR \times 2^R$. While *can-assignp-IM* assigns the permission as immobile members. Table 2 and 3 show the example of these two relations. The meaning of $(BankSO, Manager \land \overline{Teller}, [Auditor, Auditor]) \subseteq$ *can-assignp-M* is that $BankSO$ can assign a permission whose current membership satisfies the prerequisite condition $Manager \land \overline{Teller}$ to role $Auditor$ as a mobile member. $(BankSO, Manager, [Teller, Teller]) \subseteq$ *can-assignp-IM* means that $BankSO$ can assign a permission whose current membership satisfies the prerequisite condition $Manager$ to role $Teller$ as an immobile member. To identify a role range within the role hierarchy, the following closed and open interval notation is used:

$$[x,y]=\{r \in R | x \geq r \land r \geq y\}, \ (x,y]=\{r \in R | x > r \land r \geq y\}$$

$$[x,y)=\{r \in R | x \geq r \land r > y\}, \ (x,y) = \{r \in R | x > r \land r > y\}$$

Suppose an administrator role (ADrole) wants to assign a permission p_j to a role r with a set of permissions P which may include mobile and immobile members. The permission p_j may be assigned as a mobile and immobile member if there is no conflict between p_j and the permissions in P. We analyze both mobile and immobile members in the following algorithm, which deals with whether the ADrole can assign the permission p_j to r with no conflicts. In algorithm 1, P^* is the extension of P, which includes the explicit and implicit members of P; i. e. $P^* = \{p | p \in P\} \cup \{p | \forall r' < r, (p, r') \in PA\}$.

Algorithm 1 provides a way to check whether or not a permission can be assigned as mobile or immobile member to a role. It can prevent conflicts when assign a permission to a role with mobile or immobile memberships as well. After considering the authorization, we consider the revocation of permission-role membership.

In the revocation model, a prerequisite condition is evaluated for a permission p by interpreting role x to be true if $p \in EMx \lor p \in EIMx \lor p \in ImMx \lor p \in ImIMx$ and $\overline{x}$ to be true if $p \notin EMx \land p \notin EIMx \land x \notin ImMx \land p \notin ImIMx$). Permission-role revocation of mobile and immobile memberships are authorized by the relations *can-revokep-M* $\subseteq AR \times CR \times 2^R$ and *can-revokep-IM* $\subseteq AR \times CR \times 2^R$ respectively.

$(BankSO, Manager, [Bank, Manager)) \subseteq$ *can-revokep-M* in Table 4 means that $BankSO$ can revoke the mobile membership of a permission from any role in

Algorithm 1. Authorization granting algorithm; *Grantp(ADrole, r, p_j)*

Input: ADrole, role r and a permission p_j

Output: true if ADrole can assign p_j to r with no conflicts; false otherwise

---

*Step 1. /*whether the ADrole can assign the permission p_j to r or not*/*

  Let $S_{M1} = \pi_{prereq.condition}(\sigma_{admin.role=ADrole}(can\text{-}assignp\text{-}M))$,

  $\quad S_{IM1} = \pi_{prereq.condition}(\sigma_{admin.role=ADrole}(can\text{-}assignp\text{-}IM))$,

  and $R = \pi_{Rolename}(\sigma_{Permname=p_j}(ROLE\text{-}PERM))$

  Suppose p_j is a mobile member of the role r.

  If $S_1 = S_{M1} \cap R \neq \emptyset$, there exists a role $r_1 \in S_1$, such that $(p_j, r_1) \in PA$ and

  $\quad r_1 \in \pi_{prereq.condition}(\sigma_{admin.role=ADrole}(can\text{-}assignp\text{-}M))$

  Go to *Step 2*;

  Suppose p_j is a immobile member of the role r.

  If $S_2 = S_{IM1} \cap R \neq \emptyset$, there exists a role $r_2 \in S_2$, such that $(p_j, r_2) \in PA$ and

  $\quad r_2 \in \pi_{prereq.condition}(\sigma_{admin.role=ADrole}(can\text{-}assignp\text{-}IM))$

  Go to *Step 2*;

  else

  return false and stop

Step 2. / whether the permission p_j is conflicting with permissions of r or not*/*

  Let $ConfPermS = \pi_{ConfPerm}(\sigma_{PermName=p_j}(PERM))$

  If $ConfPermS \cap P^* \neq \emptyset$, then p_j is a conflicting permission with role r

  return false;

  else

  return true;

[*Bank, Manager*) which satisfies the revoke prerequisite condition *Bank*. Similarly, the *can-revokep-IM* in Table 5 refers to revoking the immobile membership.

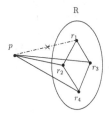

Fig. 3. Local revocation

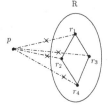

Fig. 4. Global revocation

Before giving out our revocation algorithms, first we introduce the concept of local and global revocation [12]. Local revocation only happens to the explicit relationship between permissions and roles, while global revocation effects all other roles which are junior to the role with the revoked permission. For local revocation, the permission is revoked only if the permission is an explicit member of the role. For example in Fig. 3, the role r_1 still has the permission p which has been locally revoked since the role is senior to role r_2 and r_3 which are associated

Algorithm 2. Local Revocation Algorithm; *Local-revoke(ADrole, r, p_j)*

Input: ADrole, role r and a permission p_j
Output: true if ADrole can locally revoke p_j from r; false otherwise

---

Step 1. If $p_j \notin \{p | (p, r) \in PA\}$
      return false and stop.
      /*there is no effect with the operation of the local revocation since the permission P_j is not an explicit member of the role r*/
      else Go to *Step 2. /*p_j is an explicit member of r*/*
Step 2. /*whether the ADrole can revoke the permission p_j from r or not*/
      Let $RoleRange1 = \pi_{RoleRange}(\sigma_{admin.role=ADrole}(can\text{-}revokep\text{-}M))$,
          $RoleRange2 = \pi_{RoleRange}(\sigma_{admin.role=ADrole}(can\text{-}revokep\text{-}IM))$
      and $Roles_{withp_j} = \pi_{RoleName}(\sigma_{PerName=p_j}(ROLE\text{-}PERM))$.
      Suppose $r \in EMp_j$
      If $r \in RoleRange1 \cap Roles_{withp_j} \neq \emptyset$; /*$r$ is in the role range to be revoked
      by ADrole in can-revokep-M and the mobile membership with P_j*/
      return true;
      Suppose $r \in EIMp_j$
      If $r \in RoleRange2 \cap Roles_{withp_j} \neq \emptyset$; /*$r$ is in the role range to be revoked
      by ADrole in can-revokep-IM and the immobile membership with P_j*/
      return true;
      else
      return false and stop. /*ADrole has no right to revoke the permission P_j
      from the role r*/

---

with the permission p. Therefore, local revocation from a role has no effect when a permission is an implicit member of the role. However, global revocation requires revocation of both explicit memberships and implicit memberships. If we globally revoke permission p from the role r_1, all the relationships between the permission p and roles junior to r_1 are revoked (see Fig. 4). Global revocation therefore has a cascading effect downwards in the role hierarchy. Global revocation of a permission's mobile and immobile membership from role r requires that the permission be removed not only from the explicit mobile and immobile membership in r, but also from explicit and implicit mobile and immobile membership in all roles junior to r.

Algorithms 2 and 3 are used to revoke permission $p_j \in P$ from a role r by ADrole, where P is the set of permissions which have been assigned to the role r. Algorithm 2 can be used revoke explicit mobile and immobile memberships, while Algorithm 3 can revoke explicit and implicit mobile and immobile members. It should be noted that the global revocation algorithm does not work if ADrole has no right to revoke p_j from any role in *Jun*.

4   Applying the Relational Algebra Algorithms

In this section, we apply the new relational algebra algorithms to a consumer anonymity scalable payment scheme. We first briefly introduce the payment

Algorithm 3. Global Revocation Algorithm; *Global-revoke(ADrole, r, p_j)*

Input: ADrole, role r and a permission p_j
Output: true if ADrole can globally revoke p_j from r; false otherwise

---

Begin. If $p_j \notin P^*$
return false; /*there is no effect with the operation of the local revocation
since p_j is not an explicit and implicit member of r*/
else
(1) If $p_j \in P$ is a mobile member of the role and $r \in EMp_j$,
Local-revoke(ADrole, r, p_j); /*p_j is locally revoked as a mobile member*/
If $p_j \in P$ is an immobile member of the role and $r \in EIMp_j$,
Local-revoke(ADrole, r, p_j); /*p_j is locally revoked as an immobile member*/
(2) Suppose $Jun = \pi_{junior}(\sigma_{Senior=r}(SEN\text{-}JUN))$
For all $y \in Jun$ with mobile membership with the permission
Local-revoke(ADrole, y, p_j) as $y \in EMp_j$;
For all $y \in Jun$ with immobile membership with the permission
Local-revoke(ADrole, y, p_j) as $y \in EIMp_j$;
/*P_j is locally revoked from all such $y \in Jun$*/
If all local revocations are successful,
return true;
otherwise
return false.

---

scheme and consider the relationships of the roles in the scheme, and then analyze applications of our relational algebra algorithms.

4.1   The Anonymity Scalable Electronic Payment Scheme

The payment scheme provides different degrees of anonymity for consumers. Consumers can decide the levels of anonymity. They can have a low level of anonymity if they want to spend coins directly after withdrawing them from the bank. Consumers can achieve a high level of anonymity through an anonymity provider (AP) agent without revealing their private information and are secure in relation to the bank because the new certificate of a coin comes from the AP agent who is not involved in the payment process.

Electronic cash has sparked wide interest among cryptographers [5,8,9]. In its simplest form, an e-cash system consists of three parts (a bank, a consumer and

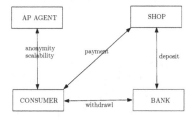

Fig. 5. Electronic cash model

Table 6. ROLE-PERM relation

RoleName	PermName
Director(DIR)	Funding
Director(DIR)	Approval
Director(DIR)	Teller
TELLER	Approval
FPS	Approval
Bank	Teller

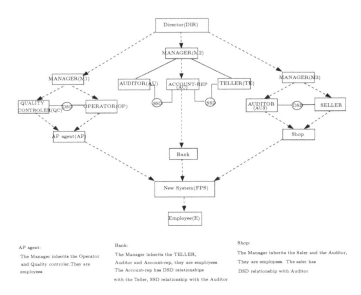

Fig. 6. User-role assignment in the payment scheme

a shop) and three main procedures (withdrawal, payment and deposit). Besides the basic participants, a third party named anonymity provider (AP) agent is involved in the scheme. The AP agent helps the consumer to get the required anonymity but is not involved in the purchase process. The model is shown in Fig. 5. The AP agent gives a certificate to the consumer when he/she needs a high level of anonymity.

From the viewpoint of banks, consumers can improve anonymity if they are worried about disclosure of their identities. This is a practical payment scheme for internet purchases because it has provided a solution with different anonymity requirements for consumers. However, consumers cannot get the required level of anonymity if the role BANK and AP are assigned to one user. It shows the management importance of the payment scheme. To simplify the management, we analyze its management with the relational algebra algorithms.

4.2   Applying the Authorization Granting Algorithm

Due to the length limit, we only include an application of the authorization granting algorithm. A hierarchy of roles and a hierarchy of administrative roles are show in Fig. 6 and 7 respectively, we define the *can-assignp-M* in Table 7. Here, we only show the process of assigning a permission to a role as a mobile member.

Here, we only analyze NSSO tuples in Table 7 (the analysis for APSO, BankSO and ShopSO are similar). The first tuple authorizes NSSO to assign permissions whose current membership satisfies the prerequisite condition role DIR to role M1 in the AP agent as mobile members. The second and third tuples authorize NSSO to assign permissions whose current membership satisfies the prerequisite

Fig. 7. Administrative role assignment in the scheme

Table 7. *Can-assignp-M* of Fig. 6

Admin.role	Prereq.condition	Role Range
NSSO	DIR	[M1, M1]
NSSO	DIR	[M2, M2]
NSSO	DIR	[M3, M3]
APSO	M1 $\wedge \overline{OP}$	[QC, QC]
APSO	M1 $\wedge \overline{QC}$	[OP, OP]
BankSO	M1 $\wedge \overline{TE} \wedge \overline{AU}$	[AC, AC]
BankSO	M1 $\wedge \overline{TE} \wedge \overline{AC}$	[AU, AU]
BankSO	M1 $\wedge \overline{AU} \wedge \overline{AC}$	[TE, TE]
ShopSO	M1 $\wedge \overline{SALER}$	[AUDITOR, AUDITOR]
ShopSO	M1 $\wedge \overline{AUDITOR}$	[SALER, SALER]

condition role DIR to role M2 and M3 respectively as mobile members. Table 6 shows parts of the relations between permissions and roles in the scheme. Assume the role FPS with permission set $P = \{Approval\}$ and $P^* = P = \{Approval\}$. The administrative role NSSO wants to assign the permission *Teller* to the role FPS as a mobile member. Using the first step of the granting algorithm *Grantp(NSSO, FPS, Teller)*, we could get:

$S = \pi_{prereq.condition}(\sigma_{admin.role=NSSO}(can\text{-}assignp\text{-}M)) = \{DIR\}$ and $R = \pi_{Rolename}(\sigma_{Permname=Teller}(ROLE\text{-}PERM)) = \{DIR, Bank\}$;

Since $R \cap S = \{DIR\} \neq \emptyset$, NSSO can assign permission *Teller* to the role FPS as a mobile member. Applying the second step based on Table 1, we could get: $ConfPermS = \pi_{ConfPerm}(\sigma_{PermName=Teller}(PERM)) = \{Audit\}$ and $ConfPermS \cap P^* = \emptyset$. Hence there are no conflicts when assigning permission *Teller* to the role FPS as a mobile member.

5   Comparisons

Our work substantially differs from [11] in two aspects. First, the paper [11] only introduce the definition of mobility of permission-role membership in permission-role assignment. By contrast, we discuss various cases in detail and focus on possible problems with mobility of permission-role relationship. Second, the authors only described the management of permission-role assignment with mobility in [11], but do not mention conflicts when assigning permissions to roles. Therefore, there is no support to deal administrative roles with regular roles in the proposal, especially mobile and immobile members. In this paper, we present a number of special authorization algorithms for access control, especially the local and global revocation algorithms which have not been studied before. These algorithms provide a rich variety of options that can handle the document of administrative roles with permissions as mobile and immobile members. In our earlier work [14], we developed authorization approaches for permission-role assignment. This paper is an extension of that study. Actually, if all membership is restricted to being mobile, our algorithms can imply the algorithms described in [14]. Moreover, compared with [14], mobile, immobile memberships and prerequisite conditions are discussed in this paper.

6   Conclusion

In this paper, we provide new authorization allocation algorithms for RBAC along with mobility that is based on relational algebra operations. The authorization granting algorithm, local and global revocation algorithm defined in this paper can automatically check conflicts when granting more than one permission as mobile or immobile member to a role in the system. We have also discussed how to use the algorithms for an electronic payment scheme.

References

1. Bertino, E., Ferrari, E., Atluri, V.: Specification and enforcement of authorization constraints in workflow management systems. ACM Transactions on Information and System Security 2(1) (February 1999)
2. Feinstein, H.L., et al.: Small Business Innovation Research (SBIR): Role-Based Access Control: Phase 1, McLean, VA, SETA Corporation (January 20, 1995)
3. Ferraiolo, D.F., Barkley, J.F., Richard Kuhn, D.: A role based access control model and reference implementation within a corporate intranet. ACM Transactions on Information and System Security 2(1) (February 1999)
4. Ferraiolo, D.F., Barkley, J.F.: Specifying and Managing Role-Based Access Control Within a Corporate Intranet. In: Proc.of the 2ed ACM Workshop on Role-Based Access Control, pp. 77–82 (1997)
5. Frankel, Y., Tsiounis, Y., Yung, M.: Fair off-line e-cash made Easy. in Advance in Cryptology. In: Proc. of Asiacrypt 1998. LNCS, vol. 1294, pp. 257–270. Springer, Heidelberg (1998)
6. Gligor, V.D., Gavrila, S.T., Ferraiolo, D.: On the formal denition of separation-of-duty policies and their composition. In: Proceedings of IEEE Symposium on Research in Security and Privacy, Oakland, CA, pp. 172–183 (May 1998)
7. Nyanchama, M., Osborn, S.: The Role Graph Model and Conflict of Internet. ACM Transaction on Information and System Security 2(1), 3–33 (1999)

8. Okamoto.: On efficient divisible electronic cash scheme. In: Advances in Cryptology-CRYPTO 1995. LNCS, vol. 963, pp. 438–451. Springer, Heidelberg (1995)

9. Rivest, R.: The MD5 Message-Digest Algorithm. RFC 1321. MIT Laboratory for Computer Science and RSA DATA Security Inc. (April 1992)

10. Sandhu, R., Bhamidipati, V., Munawer, Q.: The ARBAC97 model for role-based administration of roles. ACM Transaction on Information and System Security 1(2), 105–135 (1999)

11. Sandhu, R., Munawer, Q.: The ARBAC99 Model for Administration of Roles. In: The Annual Computer Security Applications Conference, pp. 229–238. ACM Press, New York (1999)

12. Wang, H., Cao, J.: Delegating revocations and authorizations. In: 1st International Workshop on Collaborative Business Processes, Brisbane, Australia (2007)

13. Wang, H., Cao, J., Kambayashi, Y.: Building a Consumer Anonymity Scalable Payment Protocol for the Internet Purchases. In: The 12th International Workshop on Research Issues on Data Engineering: Engineering E-Commerce/E-Business Systems, San Jose, USA, February 25-26, 2002, pp. 159–168 (2002)

14. Wang, H., Cao, J., Zhang, Y.: Formal authorization approaches for permission-role assignment using relational algebra operations. In: Proceedings of the 14th Australasian Database Conference, Adelaide, Australia, February 2-7, 2003, vol. 25(1), pp. 125–134 (2003)

15. Wang, H., Cao, J., Zhang, Y.: Formal Authorization Allocation Approaches for Role-Based Access Control Based on Relational Algebra Operations. In: The 3rd International Conference on Web Information Systems Engineering (WISE 2002), Singapore, December 3-6, 2002, pp. 301–310 (2002)

16. Zurko, M., Simon, R., Sanlippo, T.: A user-centered modular authorization service built on an rbac foundation. In: Proceedings of IEEE Symposium on Research in Security and Privacy, Oak-land, CA, pp. 57–71 (May 1999)

Enhancing Micro-Aggregation Technique by Utilizing Dependence-Based Information in Secure Statistical Databases

B. John Oommen* and Ebaa Fayyoumi

School of Computer Science, Carleton University, Ottawa, Canada: K1S 5B6
oommen@scs.carleton.ca, efayyoum@scs.carleton.ca

Abstract. We consider the Micro-Aggregation Problem (MAP) in secure statistical databases which involves partitioning a set of individual records in a micro-data file into a number of mutually exclusive and exhaustive groups. This problem, which seeks for the best partition of the micro-data file, is known to be NP-hard, and has been tackled using many heuristic solutions. In this paper, we would like to demonstrate that in the process of developing Micro-Aggregation Techniques ($MATs$), it is expedient to incorporate information about the dependence between the random variables in the micro-data file. This can be achieved by pre-processing the micro-data *before* invoking any MAT, in order to extract the useful dependence information[1] from the joint probability distribution of the variables in the micro-data file, and then accomplishing the micro-aggregation on the "maximally independent" variables. Our results, on real life data sets, show that including such information will enhance the process of determining how many variables are to be used, and which of them should be used in the micro-aggregation process.

1   Introduction

A lot of attention has recently been dedicated to the problem of maintaining the confidentiality of statistical databases through the application of statistical tools, so as to limit the identification of information on individuals and enterprises. Statistical Disclosure Control (SDC) seeks a balance between the confidentiality and the data utility criteria. For example, federal agencies and their contractors who release statistical tables or micro-data files are often required by law or by established policies to protect the confidentiality of released information. However, this restriction should not affect public policy decisions which are made by accessing only non-confidential summary statistics [1, 2]. Therefore, optimizing the Information Loss (IL) and the Disclosure Risk (DR) so as to reach an equilibrium point between them is not an easy task [1].

---

* This author is also an Adjunct Professor with the University of Agder in Grimstad, Norway.
[1] To the best of our knowledge, the inference of dependence information has not been used in enhancing the MAT in secure statistical databases.

Y. Mu, W. Susilo, and J. Seberry (Eds.): ACISP 2008, LNCS 5107, pp. 404–418, 2008.
© Springer-Verlag Berlin Heidelberg 2008

Micro-aggregation is one of the most recent techniques that has been used to mask micro-data files with the intention of protecting them against re-identification in secure statistical databases [3, 4, 5, 6, 7, 8]. Moreover, it can be modeled as a clustering mechanism with group size constraints, where the primitive goal is to group a set of records into clusters of size at least k, based on a proximity measure involving the variables of interest [8, 9, 10, 11, 12, 13, 14].

The Micro-Aggregation Problem (MAP), as formulated in [5, 7, 9, 12, 13], can be stated as follows: A micro-data set $\mathcal{U} = \{U_1, U_2, \ldots, U_n\}$ is specified in terms of the n "micro-records", namely the $U_i's$, each representing a data vector whose components are d continuous variables. Each data vector can be viewed as $U_i = [u_{i1}, u_{i2}, \ldots, u_{id}]^T$, where u_{ij} specifies the value of the jth variable in the ith data vector. Micro-aggregation involves partitioning the n data vectors into, say, m, mutually exclusive and exhaustive groups so as to obtain a k-partition $\mathbb{P}_k = \{G_i \mid 1 \leq i \leq m\}$, such that each group, G_i, of size, n_i, contains either k data vectors or between k and $2k - 1$ data vectors.

The optimal k-partition, $\mathbb{P}_k^*$, is defined to be the one that maximizes the within-group similarity, which is defined as the *Sum of Squares Error, SSE* $= \sum_{i=1}^{m} \sum_{j=1}^{n_i} (X_{ij} - \bar{X}_i)^T (X_{ij} - \bar{X}_i)$. This quantity is computed on the basis of the Euclidean distance of each data vector X_{ij} to the centroid $\bar{X}_i$ of the group to which it belongs. The *Information Loss* is measured as $IL = \frac{SSE}{SST}$, where SST is the squared error that would result if all records were included in a single group, and is given as $SST = \sum_{i=1}^{m} \sum_{j=1}^{n_i} (X_{ij} - \bar{X})^T (X_{ij} - \bar{X})$, where $\bar{X} = \frac{1}{n} \sum_{i=1}^{n} X_i$.

Understanding the presence and structure of dependency between a set of random variables is a fundamental problem in the design and analysis of many types of systems including filtering, pattern recognition etc. As far as we know its application in SDC has been minimal. Utilizing this information is the goal of this paper. Typically, in modern day systems, the data protector has been able to choose the technique and set its parameters without a thorough understanding of the characteristics of the micro-data file, and the stochastic dependence of the variables. Although gleaning this information could be particularly difficult and even time-consuming, our hypothesis is that this information is central to the micro-data file, especially when working in a high dimensional space.

In general, the result of the multi-variate $MATs$ depends on the number of variables used in the micro-aggregation process. In other words, deciding on the number of variables to be taken into account, and on the *identity* of the variables to be micro-aggregated, is far from trivial. The authors of [11] have reported that multi-variate micro-aggregation on unprojected data taking two or three variables at a time (rather than incorporating the information in all the variables) offers the best trade-off between IL and DR. The unanswered question is that of inferring which variables should be used in this process. We believe that a solution to this puzzle lies in the inter-variable "dependence" information.

The authors of [15] have emphasized that the decision about which variables are to be chosen has to be gleaned from *a priori* "knowledge about the characteristics of each variable from the experts". While this is a feasible approach, we argue that it is subjective, and that a formal objective method is desirable.

Indeed, what will happen if the researcher encounters a new project for which there is no prior knowledge? Or how we will proceed if an expert for a specific data domain is not available? Our aim is to minimize the necessity to depend on a human expert, but rather to have the ability to study the characteristics of each variable objectively. Thus, we seek a systematic process by which we can choose the desired variables automatically and micro-aggregate the file.

This paper involves $MATs$, but rather from a different perspective. We propose a scheme by which we can avoid using the information in *all* the dimensions. Furthermore, neither will we resort to projecting the micro-data file onto a single axis, nor will we attempt to micro-aggregate it using any specific sorting method [7, 8, 16, 17, 18, 19, 20, 21]. The main contribution of this paper is to extract useful information from the joint probability distribution of the variables in the file to be micro-aggregated. Then, rather than use *all* the variables in the micro-data file, we propose to only process the "maximally independent" variables in the subsequent multi-variate micro-aggregation. Indeed, we propose to use such a method as a pre-processing step before *any* MAT is invoked, and to test the effect of using such a dependency analysis on the micro-aggregation process so as to reduce the computational time, and IL.

The structure of this paper is as follows: In Section 2 we summarize the background about the most recent $MATs$. In Section 3 we present a brief description of the Maximum Distance Average Vector ($MDAV$) method. In Section 4 the enhanced micro-aggregation dependence is presented informally and algorithmically. Then, in Section 5, we present the results of experiments we have carried out for real data sets. The paper finishes in Section 6 with some conclusions.

2   Micro-Aggregation

As mentioned in Section 1, the MAP has been tackled using different techniques, which can be further classified as below.

- *Uni-variate vs. Multi-variate*
  The difference between the uni-variate and the multi-variate $MATs$ depends on the number of random variables used in the micro-aggregation process. Uni-variate $MATs$ deal with multi-variate data sets by micro-aggregating one variable at a time such as Individual ranking [17, 18, 19]. Multi-variate $MATs$ either rank multi-variate data by projecting them onto a single axis[2], or dealing directly with the unprojected data. Examples of unprojected multi-variate $MATs$ are the Maximum Distance to Average Vector ($MDAV$)[5, 22], the Minimum Spanning Tree (MST) [13], the Object Migrating Micro-aggregated Automaton ($OMMA$) [23], and Interactive-Associative Micro-Aggregation Technique ($IAMAT$) [24].

---

[2] The multi-variate data is projected onto a single axis by using either a particular variable, the sum-z-scores or a principle component analysis prior to micro-aggregation [7, 21].

— *Fixed-size vs. Data-oriented*

The difference between the fixed-size and the data-oriented $MATs$ depends on the number of records in each group. Fixed-size $MATs$ require all groups to be of size k except for a single group whose cardinality is greater than k when the total number of records, n, is not a multiple of k. Data-oriented $MATs$ allow groups to be of size greater than k and less than $2k - 1$ depending on the structure of the data. These methods yield more homogenous groups which help to further minimize the IL [4, 5, 7]. Examples of data-oriented $MATs$ are those which use a genetic algorithm [5, 7, 21], the k-Ward MAT [5, 7, 21, 25] and the Variable-size Maximum Distance to Average Vector scheme $(V - MDAV)$ [26].

— *Optimal vs. Heuristic*

The first reported optimal uni-variate MAT with a polynomial complexity is given in [12], which solves the MAP as a shortest path problem on a graph. Unfortunately, the optimal MAP for multi-variate micro-aggregation is an NP-hard problem [27]. Therefore, researchers seek heuristic $MATs$ that provide a good solution - close to the optimal.

3   Maximum Distance Average Vector ($MDAV$)

The first algorithm to accomplish micro-aggregation without projecting the multi-variate data onto a single axis was proposed in [5], and is known as the Maximum Distance to Average Vector ($MDAV$). It micro-aggregates the multi-variate micro-data file based on the concept of the diameter distance of the data set. In 2005, an enhanced version of $MDAV$ appeared in [22] is based on utilizing the centroid concept in the micro-aggregation. In a nutshell, the process is as follows: First of all, the algorithm computes the centroid of the data. After this, a quick search for the most distant record from the centroid, say X_r, is done. Subsequently, a new search for the most distant record from the record X_r, say X_s, is accomplished. The next step consists of creating two clusters, the first one comprising of X_r and *its* $k - 1$ nearest records, while the second comprises of X_s with *its* nearest $k - 1$ records. At the end of this stage, the two clusters are micro-aggregated and removed from the original data set. The latter steps are iteratively repeated until there are no more records remaining in the original data set. The advantages of this new modified version of the $MDAV$ are the increased speed of the micro-aggregation, and the reduction in the IL.

4   Enhancing Micro-Aggregation with Dependence

It is well-known that the result of the multi-variate $MATs$ depends on the number and the *identity* of the variables used in the micro-aggregation process. Since multi-variate micro-aggregation using two or three variables at a time offers the best trade-off between the IL and the DR [11], the question we intend to resolve involves understanding why we have to use vast dimension-dependent resources in the clustering phase in order to compute the distance between the micro-records. We shall also study how we can minimize the computation time needed to evaluate the distance between a single micro-data record and the mean of the group it belongs to. This computation involves evaluating

$$D(X,Y) = \sqrt{\sum_{i=1}^{d}(x_i - y_i)^2}. \qquad (1)$$

where X and Y are two multi-variate data vectors with their components being $\{x_i\}$ and $\{y_i\}$ respectively, and d represents the dimension of the space.

We consider the problem of determining the dependencies between the different variables within a micro-data file, and then combining the latter with the MAT in such a way as to reduce the overall required computational time, and/or reduce the corresponding IL.

The primary goal of any MAT is to reduce the loss in the data utility by choosing the most suitable sub-set of variables with size equal to three [11] prior to invoking the multi-variate micro-aggregate. Theoretically, to know the best sub-set of variables that has to be used in order to obtain the minimum value of the IL, we have to consider all different possibilities of combinations, namely the $\binom{S}{C} = \frac{S!}{C!(S-C)!}$ combinations, where S is the number of variables in the original micro-data file, and C is the number of chosen variables which are used in projecting and micro-aggregating the data file.

We propose that the key idea in choosing a sub-set of the variables by avoiding the combinatorial solution, should be based on the dependence model of the micro-data file. If the variables are highly-correlated, then using any one of them will somehow reflect the stochastic nature of the others. If we, thus, incorporate this logic into our consideration, we believe that we can reduce the number of variables which will be used to measure either the distance between the micro-unit and the mean of the group it belongs to, or the distance between the micro-units themselves. Thus, in turn, this will reduce the dimensionality of the space to $d' < d$. The new distance that will thus be computed will be:

$$D'(X,Y) = \sqrt{\sum_{i=1}^{d'}(x_i - y_i)^2} \qquad \text{where } d' < d. \qquad (2)$$

The reader should observe that our goal is quite distinct from the reported methods of projecting the multi-dimensional space onto a single axis using a particular variable, the sum z-scores scheme, or a principle component analysis. The reduction in the dimensionality is not done randomly. Rather it is to be done based on a formal criterion. Our aim is to micro-aggregate the multi-dimensional vector by maximally using the information in the almost independent variables, and we plan to do this by finding the best dependence tree. We believe that we can achieve this by evaluating the dependence between the variables in the micro-data file by using either the method due to Chow and Liu [28] or the method due to Valiveti and Oommen [29, 30].

We formalize these concepts. The joint probability distribution of the random vector $\mathbf{V} = [V_1, V_2, \ldots, V_d]^T$ in terms of conditional probabilities is given as

$$P(\mathbf{V}) = P(V_1)P(V_2|V_1)P(V_3|V_1, V_2)\ldots P(V_d|V_1, V_2, \ldots, V_{d-1}). \qquad (3)$$

where each V_i is a random variable.

It is obvious, from the above expression, that each variable is conditioned on an increasing number of other variables. Therefore, estimating the kth term of this equation requires maintaining the estimates of all the kth order marginals. Clearly, it is impractical to gather the estimates for the joint density function $P(\mathbf{V})$ for all the different values which V could assume. We, therefore, simplify the dependency model by restricting ourselves to the lower-order marginals, using the approximation which ignores the conditioning on multiple variables, and retaining only dependencies on at most a single variable at a time. This leads us to the following [29]:

$$P_a(\mathbf{V}) = \prod_{i=1}^{d} Pr(V_i|V_{j(i)}). \qquad (4)$$

where $P_a(\mathbf{V})$ is the approximated form of $P(\mathbf{V})$, and V_i is conditioned on $V_{j(i)}$ for $0 \leq j(i) < i$.

The dependence of the variables can be represented as a graph $\mathbf{G} = (\mathbf{V}, \mathbf{E}, \mathbf{W})$ where $\mathbf{V} = \{V_1, V_2, \ldots, V_d\}$ is a finite set of vertices, which represents the set of random variables in the micro-data file with d dimensions, $\mathbf{E}$ is a finite set of edges $\{\langle V_i, V_j \rangle\}$, where $\langle V_i, V_j \rangle$ represents an edge between the vertices V_i and V_j. Finally, $\mathbf{W} = \{w_{i,j}\}$ is a finite set of weights, where $w_{i,j}$ is the weight assigned to the edge $\langle V_i, V_j \rangle$ in the graph. The values of these weights can be calculated based on a number of measures, as will be explained presently.

In $\mathbf{G}$, the edge between any two nodes represents the fact that these variables are statistically dependent [28]. In such a case, the weight, $w_{i,j}$, can be assigned to the edge as being equal to the Expected Mutual Information Measure ($EMIM$) metric between them. In general, the $EMIM$ metric between two variables, given by $I^*(V_i, Vj)$ for discrete distributions, has the form:

$$I^*(V_i, V_j) = \sum_{v_i, v_j} Pr(v_i, v_j) \log \frac{Pr(v_i, v_j)}{Pr(v_i)Pr(v_j)}. \qquad (5)$$

where the summation above is done over all values of v_i and v_j which V_i and V_j can assume.

We observed that any edge, say $\langle V_i, V_j \rangle$ with the edge weight $I^*(V_i, V_j)$ represents the fact that V_i is stochastically dependent on V_j, or that V_j is stochastically dependent on V_i. Although, in the worst case, any variable pair could be dependent, the model expressed by Eq.(4) imposes a tree-like dependence. It is easy to see that this graph includes a large number of trees (actually, an $\bigcirc(d^{(d-2)})$ of such spanning trees). Each of these trees represents a unique approximated form for the density function $P(\mathbf{V})$. Chow and Liu proved that searching for

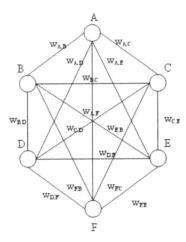

Fig. 1. The fully-connected undirected graph represents the dependence between six random variables

the best "dependence tree" is exactly equivalent to searching for the Maximum Spanning Tree[3](MST) of the graph [28]. Further, since the probabilities that are required for computing the edge weights are not known *a priori*, Valiveti and Oommen showed that this could be achieved by estimating them in a maximum likelihood manner [29, 30]. They showed that the maximum likelihood estimate (ML) for the best dependence tree, can be obtained by computing the MST of the graph, where the edge weights are computed using the $EMIM$ of the estimated probabilities.

By way of example, consider a micro-data file which incorporates 6 variables (as in Figure 1) and thousands of records. Let us assume that we intend to micro-aggregate this file using any MAT, for example, the $MDAV$ method. In such a case, the prior art will process all the six variables to quantify the relevant distances during the clustering stage. We could choose a sub-set of size three to be used in the micro-aggregation process. In general, we will have to go through the 20 different combinations of size three in order to attain the minimum value of the IL. However, if we are able to discover any existing inter-variable dependencies, this could render the problem simpler. Let us assume that we compute the $EMIM$-based edge weights for all pairs of nodes, and create the fully-connected undirected graph G, as in Figure 1. By using the strategy alluded to above, we obtain a tree as in Figure 2.a, which shows the case when the MST leads to the ML condition that the variables B, C, and D depend on the variable A, and that variables E and F depend on variable D. Since these dependent variables are maximally-correlated to the variable that they depend

---

[3] Two generic greedy algorithms can be used to solve the Minimum Spanning Tree problem, namely, the so-called Kruskal and the so-called Prim algorithms [31].We have used the Kruskal algorithm in our experiments.

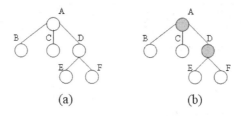

(a)   (b)

Fig. 2. An example of a dependence tree used to micro-aggregate the data file containing 6 variables

on, we propose to use the vertices that have the maximum number of In/Out edges in the graph to micro-aggregate the micro-file. We believe that the nodes which possess this property are the best candidates to reflect the characteristics of the entire multi-variate data set because they connect to the maximum number of nodes that statistically depend on it, as argued in Conjecture 1. The rationale for Conjecture is omitted here in the interest of brevity.

Conjecture 1. Micro-aggregating the micro-data file can be best achieved if the nodes which possess the maximum number of In/Out edges in the tree obtained as the MST of the underlying graph **G**, are used as an input to solve the MAT.

In order to involve this property, we first rank the nodes of the graph based on the number of In/Out edges in a descending order and choose the first d' variables, where d' is usually determined by the data protector and is usually equal to 3 or 4. Thus, for example, the data represented by the variables of Figure 2, based on the above discussion, the micro-aggregation process will be invoked by using two variables instead of using the entire set of six variables in the micro-data file. Figure 2.b. shows that the selected sub-set of the variables is $\{A, D\}$, since both of them connect to 3 variables while the other variables in the micro-data file connect to only a single variable. The outline process has been formalized in Algorithm 1, which gives an automated way to select a sub-set of the variables to be used in the micro-aggregation process.

5   Experimental Results

5.1   Data Sets

In order to verify the validity of our methodology in projecting the multi-variate data set into a subset of random variables to be used in the micro-aggregation process. Two benchmark real data sets have been used as benchmarks in previous studies: (i)**Tarragona Data Set** contains 834 records with 13 variables [5]. (ii)**Census Data Set** contains 1,080 records with 13 variables [32].

Algorithm 1. Enhanced Micro-Aggregation Dependence

Input: $\mathcal{U}$: the micro-data file, and C: the number of variables that will be used in the micro-aggregation process.

Output: d': the sub-set of the variables that will be used in the multi-variate MAT.

Method:

1: Estimate the first and second order marginals of the random variables from the various micro-records.

2: Create a fully-connected undirected graph, where the

   Nodes: Represent the random variables in the micro-data file.

   Edges: Represent the statistically dependent variables.

   Weights of the edges are computed either by using:

$$EMIM \Rightarrow I^*(V_i, V_j) = \sum_{v_i, v_j} Pr(v_i, v_j) \log \frac{Pr(v_i, v_j)}{Pr(v_i)Pr(v_j)}, \text{ OR}$$

$$\chi^2 \Rightarrow I_\chi(V_i, V_j) = \sum_{v_i, v_j} \frac{(Pr(v_i, v_j) - P(v_i)P(v_j))^2}{P(v_i)P(v_j)}.$$

3: Invoke Kruskal's algorithm to compute the Maximum Spanning Tree of the graph.

4: Rank the nodes of the graph based on the number of In/Out edges in a decreasing order, and add the first C variables to the d' sub-set.

5: **Return** the sub-set of variables which will be used in the micro-aggregation process before invoking the MAT

6: **End Algorithm** Enhanced Micro-Aggregation Dependence.

5.2   Results

The experiments conducted were of two categories: In the first set of experiments the intention was primarily focused on testing whether the best dependence tree can be learned (or rather, inferred) from the continuous micro-data file, and if it sufficiently reflected the dependence model. In the second set of experiments, the goal was primarily to validate our strategy of determining the subset of variables (from the entire set of variables) to micro-aggregate the micro-data file, and to study its effect on the value of the IL.

Experiment Sets 1

The first set of experiments was done on the real data sets which possess an unknown dependence model between the variables. It is worth mentioning that we could not approximate the dependence information of the multi-variate data set in its current form due to the inaccurate estimation for the joint and marginal probability distributions for continuous variables. This is a consequence of having a large domain space with only few records (sometimes only one or two) for each value in the random variable. Consequently, most of the *estimated* marginal and joint probability values were close to zero. Clearly, in these cases, the *estimated* probabilities will not reflect the actual dependence relationship between any corresponding variables.

In order to overcome this challenging problem that prevents us from utilizing the dependence information, we were forced to reduce the domain space by categorizing the micro-data file as follows: We first scanned the micro-data file to specify the domain space of each variable in the file, and then divided it into a number of sub-interval sharing the same width. After that, we achieved a categorization phase by replacing the values belonging to a certain sub-interval in each variable by the corresponding category/code. The above procedure was repeated for all the variables so as to generate the categorical micro-data file.

From the above discussion, it is clearly shown that "width" parameter plays a predominant role in controlling the degree of smoothing and estimating the best dependence tree. Our experiments indicated that assigning a suitable value to the width parameter guaranteed the convergence of the MST to the true underlying (unknown) structure of the best dependence tree. The most important point that one has to be aware of in a practical scenario is that a larger value for the width parameter implies a lower variance and a higher bias, because we are essentially assuming a constant value within the sub-interval. Generally speaking, the value of the width parameter should be large enough to generate a sufficient number of sub-intervals from the defined domain space to guarantee a satisfactory level of smoothing. The actual value used is specified in the experimental results.

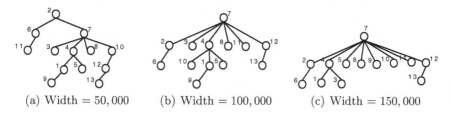

(a) Width = 50, 000   (b) Width = 100, 000   (c) Width = 150, 000

Fig. 3. The best dependence tree for the Tarragona data Set obtained by using the $EMIM$ metric with various values of the width parameter

Approximating the dependence information for the real data sets was tricky, because of the unknown structure for the best dependence tree. Changing the value of the width parameter has an effect on the structure of the best dependence tree to which the algorithm converged. Figures 3 and 4 clearly show different structures for the best dependence tree by changing the value of the width parameter for the Tarragona and Census data sets, respectively.

Experiment Sets 2

The second set of experiments verified our conjecture that using the sub-set of the variables obtained (from the best dependence tree) by projecting the micro-data file into 3, 4 or 5 variables before invoking the micro-aggregation process.

Since a MAT seeks to reduce the loss in the data utility, it must be pointed out here that the value of the IL depends on the sub-set of variables used to micro-aggregate the multi-variate data file. As mentioned earlier, to infer the

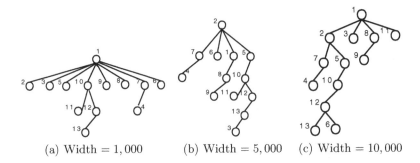

(a) Width = 1,000   (b) Width = 5,000   (c) Width = 10,000

Fig. 4. The best dependence tree for the Census data set obtained by using the $EMIM$ metric with various values of the width parameter

Table 1. The value of the IL using the $MDAV$ multi-variate MAT after projecting various data sets into the specific number of variables

Data Set	No. of projected variables	No. of possible combin.	Indices of the variables used to obtained the min. value of IL	The min. value of IL	Indices of the variables used to obtained the max. value of IL	The max. value of IL	The ave. value of IL
	1	13	10	37.6374	8	48.1006	43.1017
	2	78	11,13	24.7415	5,8	45.6925	31.6609
$Tarragona$	3	286	2,3,10	20.7141	5,6,11	34.1569	25.1587
	4	715	2,3,10,11	20.7141	5,6,11,12	34.1569	25.4997
	5	1287	2,3,10,11,12	20.7141	5,6,11,12,13	34.1569	25.6141
	1	13	10	38.2133	1	62.9093	45.79787
	2	78	4,13	22.5795	1,8	55.634	31.618
$Census$	3	286	7,8,10	15.6043	1,8,9	45.815	21.2046
	4	715	7,8,10,11	15.6043	1,8,9,10	45.815	22.0308
	5	1287	7,8,10,11,12	15.6043	1,8,9,10,11	45.815	22.8299

best sub-set of variables to be used in the micro-aggregation, we have to go through all the different projection possibilities. The results (Table 1) show that the estimation of the percentage value of the IL for real data sets obtained by projecting the entire data set into specified number of variables prior to invoking the $MDAV$ method. The value of the IL was bounded between the minimum value (in the fourth column) that was obtained by using the variable indices addressed in the third column, and the maximum value (in the sixth column) that was obtained by using the indices addressed in the fifth column. The last column in Table 1 represents the average value of the IL over all the different combinations of projected variables in the micro-data file.

The most interesting observation was that the minimum value of the IL obtained by using 3, 4 or 5 projected variables in the Tarragona and Census data sets were exactly the same. This implies using the same "most independent variables", which in turn, preserve the same high a mount of the variance. Therefore, we recommend projecting the entire micro-data file using 3 variables, since using a larger number of variables to project the micro-data file requires more time without leading to significant reduction in the IL value.

Practically, due to the exponential number of combinations, we could not cover the entire solution space so as to reach to the best sub-set of the variables to be used in the micro-aggregation[4]. As opposed to this, by involving only the vertices that have the maximum number of I/O edges in the connected undirected graph to micro-aggregate the micro-data file, we were able to obtain an acceptable value of the IL close to its lower bound, and always remains below the average value in all the cases. Thus, such an automated strategy for projecting the multi-variate data sets will reduce the solution space to be searched which, in turn, reduces the computation time required to test the candidate variables, and to choose the best sub-set from them.

Tables 2 shows the percentage value of the IL obtained by using our strategy in projecting the micro-data file into sub-sets of size 3, prior to invoking the $MDAV$ method. The minimum values of the IL for Census data set when the width value was set to $1,000$, $5,000$ and $10,000$ were equal to 17.47%, 16.23% and 18.29%, respectively. It is worth mentioning that the values obtained were quite close to the lower bound of the IL, *i.e.*, 15.60%, as shown in Table 1, besides being superior to the average values over all the different combinations (*i.e.*, 21.20%). In Tarragona data set, the minimum values of the IL when the width value was set to $50,000$, $100,000$ and $150,000$ were equal to 24.13%, 24.13% and 25.04%, respectively. The values obtained were quite close to the lower bound of the IL, *i.e.*, 20.71%, as shown in Table 1, besides being superior to the average values over all the different combinations (*i.e.*, 25.16%).

Table 2. The value of the IL using the $MDAV$ multi-variate MAT after projecting various data sets using 3 variables by using the $EMIM$ metric to calculate the edge weights in the connected undirected graph

Data set	Width value	No. of possibilities	Variable indices	IL
Tarragona	50,000	5	7,4,1	24.1333
			7,4,10	24.1881
			7,4,2	25.0465
			7,4,12	25.6574
			7,4,6	25.6826
	100,000	3	7,4,1	24.1333
			7,4,2	25.0465
			7,4,12	25.6574
	150,000	2	7,4,2	25.0465
			7,4,12	25.6574
Census	1,000	2	1,10,7	17.4700
			1,10,12	25.3632
	5,000	6	2,10,8	16.2332
			2,10,5	17.3421
			2,10,1	17.7012
			2,10,13	21.0694
			2,10,7	21.1128
			2,10,12	21.5828
	10,000	1	1,2,12	18.2996

---

[4] On our processor, it took up to a few hours depending on the dimensionality and cardinality of the data set, to exhaustively search the entire space.

6 Conclusions

In this paper, we have shown how the information about the structure of the dependence between the variables in the micro-data file can be used as a fundamental indicator before invoking any MAT. By using this information, we have proposed a new automated scheme as a pre-processing phase to determine the number and the identity of the variables that are to be used to micro-aggregate the micro-data file for minimizing the IL in secure statistical databases. This is achieved by constructing a connected undirected graph whose nodes represent the random variables in the micro-data file, edges represent the statistically dependencies, and the edges weights are computed by using the $EMIM$ metric. The experimental results show that such a methodology involving projecting the multi-variate data sets reduces the solution space, which further directly reduces the computation time required to search the entire space combinatorially. In spite of this, this methodology leads to a solution whose IL values are close to the minimum value of the IL that can be obtained by exhaustively searching over the entire search space.

In conclusion, our work has demonstrated the intractability of the MAP and presented a promising tool for enhancing the data utility. We are looking to extend this work by studying the effect of using the χ^2 metric and the correlation matrix (assuming Normality) on calculating the edges weight of the connected dependence graph with respect to the computation time required to search the entire space and the accuracy for estimating the dependence model.

References

1. Adam, N., Wortmann, J.: Security-Control Methods for Statistical Databases: A Comparative Study. ACM Computing Surveys 21(4), 515–556 (1989)
2. Kim, J., Winkler, W.: Masking Microdata Files. In: Proceedings of the Section on Survey Research Methods, pp. 114–119 (1995)
3. Baeyens, Y., Defays, D.: Estimation of Variance Loss Following Microaggregation by the Individual Ranking Method. In: Proceedings of Statistical Data Protection 1998, Luxembourg: Office for Official Publications of the European Communities, pp. 101–108 (1999)
4. Cuppen, M.: Secure Data Perturbation in Statistical Disclosure Control. PhD thesis, Statistics Netherlands (2000)
5. Domingo-Ferrer, J., Mateo-Sanz, J.: Practical Data-Oriented Microaggregation for Statistical Disclosure Control. IEEE Transactions on Knowledge and Data Engineering 14(1), 189–201 (2002)
6. Hundepool, A., Domingo-Ferrer, J., Franconi, L., Giessing, S., Lenz, R., Longhurst, J., Nordholt, E., Seri, G., Wolf, P.: Handbook on Statistical Disclosure Control. A CENtre of EXcellence for Statistical Disclosure Control CENEX SDC (2006)
7. Mateo-Sanz, J., Domingo-Ferrer, J.: A Method for Data-Oriented Multivariate Microaggregation. In: Proceedings of Statistical Data Protection 1998, Luxembourg: Office for Official Publications of the European Communities, pp. 89–99 (1999)
8. Panaretos, J., Tzividis, N.: Aspects of Estimation Procedures at Eurostat with Some Emphasis on Over-Space Harmonisation. In: HERCMA 2001 Conference (2001)

9. Crises, G.: Microaggregation for Privacy Protection in Statistical Databases. Technical report (2004)
10. Domingo-Ferrer, J.: Statistical Disclosure Control in Catalonia and the CRISES Group. Technical report (1999)
11. Domingo-Ferrer, J., Torra, V.: Aggregation Techniques for Statistical confidentiality. In: Aggregation operators: new trends and applications, pp. 260–271. Physica-Verlag GmbH, Heidelberg (2002)
12. Hansen, S., Mukherjee, S.: A Polynomial Algorithm for Univariate Optimal Microaggregation. IEEE Transactions on Knowledge and Data Engineering 15(4), 1043–1044 (2003)
13. Laszlo, M., Mukherjee, S.: Minimum Spanning Tree Partitioning Algorithm for Microaggregation. IEEE Transactions on Knowledge and Data Engineering 17(7), 902–911 (2005)
14. Torra, V.: Microaggregation for Categorical Variables: A Median Based Approach. In: Domingo-Ferrer, J., Torra, V. (eds.) Privacy in Statistical Databases: CASC Project International Workshop, PSD 2004 Proceedings, pp. 162–174. Springer, Berlin (2004)
15. Sanchez, J., Urrutia, J., Ripoll, E.: Trade-Off between Disclosure Risk and Information Loss Using Multivariate Microaggregation: A Case Study on Business Data. In: Domingo-Ferrer, J., Torra, V. (eds.) Privacy in Statistical Databases: CASC Project International Workshop, PSD 2004 Proceedings, pp. 307–322. Springer, Berlin (2004)
16. Defays, D.: Protecting Microdata by Microaggregation: the Experience in Eurostat. Questiio 21, 221–231 (1997)
17. Defays, D., Anwar, M.: Masking Micro-data Using Micro-Aggregation. Journal of Official Statistics 14(4), 449–461 (1998)
18. Defays, D., Anwar, N.: Micro-Aggregation: A Generic Method. In: Proceedings of the 2nd International Symposium on Statistical Confidentiality, Luxembourg: Office for Official Publications of the European Communities, pp. 69–78 (1995)
19. Defays, D., Nanopoulos, P.: Panels of Enterprises and Confidentiality: the Small Aggregates Method. In: Proceedings of 1992 Symposium on Design and Analysis of Longitudinal Surveys, pp. 195–204. Statistics Canada, Ottawa (1993)
20. Mas, M.: Statistical Data Protection Techniques. Technical report, Eustat: Euskal Estatistika Erakundea,Instituto Vasco De Estadistica (2006)
21. Mateo-Sanz, J., Domingo-Ferrer, J.: A Comparative Study of Microaggregation Methods. Questiio 22(3), 511–526 (1998)
22. Domingo-Ferrer, J., Torra, V.: Ordinal, Continuous and Heterogeneous k-Anonymity Through Microaggregation. Data Mining and Knowledge Discovery 11(2), 195–212 (2005)
23. Fayyoumi, E., Oommen, B.: A Fixed Structure Learning Automaton Micro-Aggregation Technique for Secure Statistical Databases. In: Privacy Statistical Databases, Rome, Italy, pp. 114–128 (2006)
24. Oommen, B., Fayyoumi, E.: A Novel Method for Micro-Aggregation in Secure Statistical Databases Using Association and Interaction. In: Information and Communications Security, 9th International Conference on Information and Communications Security. LNCS, vol. 4861, pp. 126–140. Springer, Heidelberg (2007)
25. Fayyoumi, E., Oommen, B.: On Optimizing the k-Ward Micro-Aggregation Technique for Secure Statistical Databases. In: 11th Austratasian Conference on Information Security and Privacy Proceeding, Australia, Melbourne, pp. 324–335 (2006)

26. Solanas, A., Martìnez-Ballestè, A.: V-MDAV: A Multivariate Microaggregation With Variable Group Size. In: 17th COMPSTAT Symposium of the IASC, Rome (2006)
27. Oganian, A., Domingo-Ferrer, J.: On The Complexity of Optimal Microaggregation for Statistical Disclosure Control. Statistical Journal of the United Nations Economic Comission for Europe 18(4), 345–354 (2001)
28. Chow, C., Liu, C.: Approximating Discrete Probability Distributions with Dependence Trees. IEEE Trans. Information Theory 14(11), 462–467 (1968)
29. Valiveti, R., Oommen, B.: On Using the Chi-Squared Metric for Determining Stochastic Dependence. Pattern Recognition 25(11), 1389–1400 (1992)
30. Valiveti, R., Oommen, B.: Determining Stochastic Dependence for Normally Distributed Vectors Using the Chi-squared Metric. Pattern Recognition 26(6), 975–987 (1993)
31. Cormen, T., Leiserson, C., Rivest, R.: Introduction to Algorithms. MIT Press, McGraw-Hill (1990)
32. Domingo-Ferrer, J., Torra, V.: A Quantitative Comparison of Disclosure Control Methods for Microdata. In: Confidentiality, Disclosure and Data Access: Theory and Practical Applications for Statistical Agencies, pp. 113–134. North-Holland, Springer (2002)

Montgomery Residue Representation Fault-Tolerant Computation in $GF(2^k)$

Silvana Medoš* and Serdar Boztaş

School of Mathematical and Geospatial Sciences,
RMIT University, GPO Box 2476V, Melbourne 3001, Australia
{silvana.medos,serdar.boztas}@ems.rmit.edu.au

Abstract. In this paper, we are concerned with protecting elliptic curve computation in a tamper proof device by protecting finite field computation against active side channel attacks, i.e., fault attacks. We propose residue representation of the field elements for *fault tolerant Montgomery residue representation multiplication algorithm*, by providing fault models for fault attacks, and countermeasures to some fault inducing attacks.

Keywords: finite field, fault tolerant computation, fault attacks.

1 Introduction

Finite field arithmetic is fundamental for *Elliptic Curve Cryptography (ECC)* which was proposed independently by Koblitz [13] and Miller [20] in 1985. ECC has received commercial acceptance and has been included in numerous standards. Its computation relies on a very large finite field (with more than 2^{160} elements). Security of ECC is based on the difficulty of the *discrete logarithm problem (DLP)*, but it is proven that security of cryptosystems does not only depend on the mathematical properties. *Side channel attacks* provide information which reveals important and compromising details about secret data. Some of these details can be used as a new trapdoor to invert a trapdoor one-way function without the secret key. This allows an adversary to break a cryptographic protocol, even if it proved to be secure in the mathematical sense. Specifically, in case of *fault attacks* which are active attacks, an adversary has to tamper with an attacked device in order to create faults. E.g. if an adversary can inflict some physical stress on the smartcard, he can induce faults into circuitry or memory, as a result these faults are manifested in computation as a errors. Therefore, faulty final result is computed. Moreover, if computation depends on some secret key, facts about secret key can be concluded. For further references please see [4], [7], [10], [12].

In this paper we are concerned with protecting elliptic curve computation in a tamper proof device by protecting finite field computation against active side channel attacks, i.e., fault attacks where an adversary induces faults into a device, while it executes the correct program. Our paper is organized as follows.

---

* The first author was supported by ARC Linkage grant LP0455324.

Y. Mu, W. Susilo, and J. Seberry (Eds.): ACISP 2008, LNCS 5107, pp. 419–432, 2008.

After outlining the background in the section 1, fault attacks in section 2, and *Montgomery multiplication algorithm* in section 3, we present fault tolerant Montgomery Residue Representation (RR) multiplication algorithm in section 4. In section 5 we provide possible fault models, while in section 6 is described possible Euclid's Algorithm which is used for decoding of *redundant residue polynomial codes [27]*. Also in this section we discuss computation efficiency, and demonstrate our idea through an example. Paper is concluded by section 7.

2   Fault Attacks

An elliptic curve (non-supersingular) over field $GF(2^k)$ is given by simplified *Weierstrass equation*:

$$E/\mathbb{F}_{2^k} : y^2 + xy = x^3 + a_2x^2 + a_6, \tag{1}$$

along with a point at infinity O. Given two points $P = (x_1, y_1) \in E(\mathbb{F}_{2^k})$, and $Q = (x_2, y_2) \in E(\mathbb{F}_{2^k})$ where $P \neq \pm Q$ then $P + Q = (x_3, y_3)$, where

$$x_3 = \lambda^2 + \lambda + x_1 + x_2 + a_2 \quad \text{and} \quad y_3 = \lambda(x_1 + x_3) + x_3 + y_1 \tag{2}$$

with $\lambda = (y_1 + y_2)/(x_1 + x_2)$. Also, if $P = Q$ then $2P = (x_3, y_3)$ where

$$x_3 = \lambda^2 + \lambda + a_2 \quad \text{and} \quad y_3 = x_1^2 + \lambda x_3 + x_3, \tag{3}$$

with $\lambda = (x_1 + y_1)/x_1$.

Security of *elliptic curve cryptosystem* relies on the hardness of solving the *elliptic curve discrete logarithm problem (ECDLP)*, i.e., given P and $Q = dP$ on an elliptic curve, one has to recover the scalar d. In many practical applications of *ECC* the *secret key* is stored inside a *tamper-resistant* device, i.e., smartcard. Since cryptographic algorithms are public, an adversary can determine what variables are used and what values they have. This makes it easy to determine what kind of error will cause a certain reaction which may be observable by an adversary. In [6] Biehl, Meyer and Müller considered an elliptic curve (1), and they have noticed that parameter a_6 is not involved in the addition. Therefore, if a cryptographic device (e.g. smartcard) receives on input a point $\widetilde{P} = (\widetilde{x}, \widetilde{y}) \in \mathbb{F}_{2^k} \times \mathbb{F}_{2^k}$, but $\widetilde{P} \notin E$ then scalar multiplication $d\widetilde{P}$ will take place over the curve $\widetilde{E}/\mathbb{F}_{2^k} : Y^2 + XY = X^3 + a_2X^2 + \widetilde{a_6}$, with $\widetilde{a_6} = \widetilde{y}^2 + \widetilde{x}\widetilde{y} + \widetilde{x}^3 + a_2\widetilde{x}^2$ instead over the original curve E.

Case1. Assume that point $\widetilde{P}$ is chosen such that $\widetilde{E}(a_2, \widetilde{a_6})$ is an elliptic curve whose order has a small factor h and $ord_{\widetilde{E}}\left(\widetilde{P}\right) = h$. Then the value $d(mod\, h)$ can be recovered given the subgroup $< \widetilde{P} >$ of order h. With sufficiently many different chosen points $\widetilde{P}_i$ we get $d\,mod\,h$ from $d\widetilde{P}_i$, and by *Chinese Remainder Theorem* whole value of d.

Case 2. Let the point $P = (x, y)$ be a system parameter that is stored in the non-volatile memory of the cryptographic device. It is read from that memory for computation of dP. Assume that only the x coordinate of point P is corrupted (or only y is corrupted). The cryptographic device then computes $\widetilde{Q} = d\widetilde{P}$, where $\widetilde{P} = (\widetilde{x}, y)$ is unknown, but fixed, (see [8]). It is easy to recover value of $\widetilde{P}$ from output value $\widetilde{Q} = d(\widetilde{x}, y) = (\widetilde{x}_d, \widetilde{y}_d)$. Point $\widetilde{Q}$ defines a curve $\widetilde{E}(a_2, \widetilde{a}_6)$ with

$$\widetilde{a}_6 = \widetilde{y}_d^{\,2} + \widetilde{x}_d\widetilde{y}_d + \widetilde{x}_d^{\,3} + a_2\widetilde{x}_d^{\,2}. \tag{4}$$

Since $\widetilde{P} = (\widetilde{x}, y)$, $\widetilde{x}$ is a root in $GF(2^k)$ of the polynomial

$$X^3 + a_2X^2 + yX + \widetilde{a}_6 + y^2. \tag{5}$$

By assuming that (5) has a unique root $\widetilde{x}$, where $h = ord_{\widetilde{E}}(\widetilde{P})$ is small enough so that *discrete logarithm* of $\widetilde{Q}$ is computable then value of $d \bmod h$ can be recovered. Otherwise, there are 2, or 3 candidates for $\widetilde{x}$, since $\widetilde{x}$ is a root of (5). In permanent-fault model it is assumed that only portion of x is corrupted, so the candidate having the most bits matching those of x is likely to be $\widetilde{x}$. In transient fault model, the whole value of x is likely to be corrupted.

Case 3. Assume that both coordinates x, y are corrupted, such that $\widetilde{P} = (\widetilde{x}, \widetilde{y})$ is the corresponding point. Output value $\widetilde{Q} = d\widetilde{P} = d(\widetilde{x}_d, \widetilde{y}_d)$ yields the value $\widetilde{a}_6$ as in (4). We only know that point $\widetilde{P}$ lies on the curve $\widetilde{E}(a_2, \widetilde{a}_6)$. Further assumptions are needed to completely recover $\widetilde{P}$.

The authors of [6], [8] claim that if the smartcard checks if the final result is a valid point on the original curve then the faulty point is captured with overwhelming probability. By this, any attack that yields faulty result which is a *valid point* on the original curve, would be undetectable by standard countermeasures. Therefore, those undetectable points can be used for a new attacks. E.g., fault induced into the addition or doubling formulas for elliptic curve points might be useful to recover secret data. Assume faut attack on y_3 in (2), and that fault is induced into λ, i.e. $\lambda \mapsto \lambda + e$, $e \in GF(2^k)$, then computed faulty value is: $\widetilde{y}_3 = y_3 + e(x_1 + x_3)$. Faulty point $\widetilde{P}_3 = (x_3, \widetilde{y}_3)$ is a valid faulty point only if $y^2 + xy + x^3 + a_2x^2 + a_6 = 0$ over $GF(2^k)$. Therefore, $\widetilde{y}_3^2 + x_3\widetilde{y}_3 + x_3^3 + a_2x_3^2 + a_6 = e(x_3(x_1 + x_3) + e(x_1 + x_3)^2) + T = 0$, where $T = \widetilde{y}_3 + x_3^3 + a_2x_3^2 + a_6 = 0$. Therefore, valid faulty point happens if $e = \frac{x_3}{x_1+x_3}$, $x_1 \neq x_3$. Similarly, if fault is induced into x_1 of y_3 in (2), i.e., $x_1 \mapsto x_1 + e$, $e \in GF(2^k)$, then valid faulty point will occur if $e = \frac{x_3}{\lambda}$, $\lambda \neq 0$.

3 Montgomery Multiplication in $GF(2^k)$

In [14] is given finite field $GF(2^k)$ analogue of the Montgomery multiplication for modular multiplication of integers [21]. Elements of the finite field are considered as a polynomials of degree $< k$, while $p(x) = x^k$ is used as a *Montgomery factor*, since reduction modulo x^k, and division modulo x^k consist in ignoring the terms of order larger then k for the remainder operation, and shifting the polynomial to the right by k places for the division. Instead of computing $a(x)b(x) \in GF(2^k)$ for $a(x), b(x) \in GF(2^k)$ it computes $a(x)b(x)p^{-1}(x) \bmod f(x)$, where $f(x)$ is a irreducible polynomial of degree k with coefficients in $GF(2)$, and $p^{-1}(x)$ is inverse of $p(x)$ modulo $f(x)$. The *Montgomery multiplication method* requires that $p(x)$ and $f(x)$ are relatively prime, i.e., $gcd(p(x), f(x)) = 1$, such that by an *Extended Euclidean Algorithm* $p(x)p^{-1}(x) + f(x)f'(x) = 1$. Bajard et al. [2] extended the same idea to any extension field $GF(p^k)$ and to any polynomial of degree k as a *Montgomery factor* such that $gcd(p(x), f(x)) = 1$. Also, instead of division by $p(x)$ in Step 2 of Algorithm 1, it is used multiplication by $p^{-1}(x) \, (mod \, p'(x))$. Therefore, Algorithm 1 computes $a(x)b(x)p^{-1}(x) mod \, f(x)$ such that $gcd \, (p(x), p'(x)) = (p(x), f(x)) = 1$, and $deg \, (p(x)) = deg \, (p'(x)) \geq k$. Bajard et al. [3] have proposed first general Montgomery multiplication

---

Algorithm 1. Montgomery Multiplication in $GF(2^k)$

Inputs: $a(x), b(x) \in GF(p)[x] / < f(x) >$, irreducible polynomial $f(x)$, $deg(f(x)) = k$, $deg(a(x)), deg(b(x)) \leq k - 1$, $p(x) = p'(x) \geq k$, s.t. $gcd(p(x), f(x)) = gcd(p(x), p'(x)) = 1$

Output: $a(x)b(x)p^{-1}(x) mod \, f(x)$

1. $q(x) \leftarrow -a(x)b(x)f'(x) mod \, p(x)$
2. $r(x) \leftarrow (a(x) \, b(x) + q(x) \, f(x)) \, p^{-1}(x) mod \, p'(x)$

---

algorithm based on the trinomial residue arithmetic. We consider that algorithm, i.e., Algorithm 2 to the residues in *Mersenne form*, or *pseudo-Mersenne form* and extend its use to the fault tolerant computation in the field $GF(2^k)$ by use of redundancy. Here, finite field $GF(2^k)$ is considered as a the set of polynomials

---

Algorithm 2. Residue Representation Modular Multiplication

Inputs: $a_i(x), b_i(x), a_{v+j}(x), b_{v+j}(x), f_{v+j}(x), \; i, j = 1, \ldots, v$. *Precomputed:* $f_i'(x)$, $p_{v+j}^{-1}(x), k_{v+j}(x), k_i(x), i, j = 1, \ldots, v, \; v \times v$ matrices ω, ω'.
Output: $(r_1(x), \ldots, r_v(x))$.

1. $(t_1(x), \ldots, t_v(x)) \leftarrow (a_1(x), \ldots, a_v(x)) \otimes (b_1(x), \ldots, b_v(x))$
2. $(q_1(x), \ldots, q_v(x)) \leftarrow (t_1(x), \ldots, t_v(x)) \otimes (f_1'(x), \ldots, f_v'(x))$
3. Change of RR: $(q_1(x), \ldots, q_v(x)) \rightarrow (q_{v+1}(x), \ldots, q_{2v}(x))$
4. $(r_{v+1}(x), \ldots, r_{2v}(x)) \leftarrow [(t_{v+1}(x), \ldots, t_{2v}(x)) \oplus (q_{v+1}(x), \ldots, q_{2v}(x))]$
   $\otimes (f_{v+1}(x), \ldots, f_{2v}(x)) \otimes (p_{v+1}^{-1}(x), \ldots, p_{2v}^{-1}(x))$
5. Change of RR: $(r_{v+1}(x), \ldots, r_{2v}(x)) \rightarrow (r_1(x), \ldots, r_v(x))$.

---

modulo a irreducible polynomial $f(x)$, $deg(f(x)) = k$, i.e., $GF(2)[x] / < f(x) >= \{a_0 + \ldots + a_{k-1}x^{k-1} | a_i \in GF(2)\}$, and $\{m_1(x), \ldots, m_v(x)\}$ is set of v relatively prime polynomials from polynomial ring $GF(2)[x]$, such that

$$n = deg \, (m_1 \, (x)) + \ldots + deg \, (m_v \, (x)) \geq k,$$

where $m(x) = \prod_{i=1}^{v} m_i(x)$, $m(x) \in GF(2)[x]$. Then by *Chinese Remainder Theorem (CRT)* there exist ring isomorphism, i.e.,

$$GF(2)[x]/ < m(x) > \cong GF(2)[x]/ < m_1(x) > \times \ldots \times GF(2)[x]/ < m_v(x) > .$$

Therefore, all $a(x) \in GF(2^k)$ have corresponding *residue representation*, i.e.,

$$a(x) \leftrightarrow a = (a_1(x), \ldots, a_v(x)),$$

where $a_i(x) = a(x)(mod\, m_i(x))$ for $i = 1 \ldots v$. *Montgomery factor* is $p(x) = \prod_{i=1}^{v} m_i(x)$ such that $gcd(p(x), f(x)) = 1$, and $p'(x) = \prod_{i=v+1}^{2v} m_i(x)$ where $gcd(p(x), p'(x)) = 1$, such that $gcd(m_i(x), m_j(x)) = 1$ for $i \neq j$, $i, j = 1 \ldots 2v$. Also, in Algorithm 2, $\otimes$ is componentwise multiplication, $\oplus$ is componentwise addition. More details follows in next section.

Algorithm 3. Fault Tolerant RR Modular Multiplication

Inputs: $a_i(x), b_i(x), a_{c+j}(x), b_{c+j}(x), f_{c+j}(x)$, $i, j = 1, \ldots, c$, $c > v$. *Precomputed:* $f'_i(x), p'^{-1}_{c+j}(x), k_{c+j}(x), k_i(x)$, $i, j = 1, \ldots, c$, $c \times c$ matrices ω, ω', $c > v$.
Output: $r(x) \in GF(2)[x]/ < m_1(x) > \times \ldots \times GF(2)[x]/ < m_c(x) >.$

1. $(t_1(x), \ldots, t_c(x)) \leftarrow (a_1(x), \ldots, a_c(x)) \otimes (b_1(x), \ldots, b_c(x))$
2. $(q_1(x), \ldots, q_c(x)) \leftarrow (t_1(x), \ldots, t_c(x)) \otimes (f'_1(x), \ldots, f'_c(x))$
3. Change of RR: $(q_1(x), \ldots, q_c(x)) \rightarrow (q_{c+1}(x), \ldots, q_{2c}(x))$
4. $(r_{c+1}(x), \ldots, r_{2c}(x)) \leftarrow [(t_{c+1}(x), \ldots, t_{2c}(x)) \oplus (q_{c+1}(x), \ldots, q_{2c}(x)) \otimes (f_{c+1}(x), \ldots, f_{2c}(x)) \otimes (p'^{-1}_{c+1}(x), \ldots, p'^{-1}_{2c}(x))$
5. Change of RR: $(r_{c+1}(x), \ldots, r_{2c}(x)) \rightarrow (r_1(x), \ldots, r_c(x))$.
6. CRT interpolation: $r(x) \leftarrow (r_1(x), \ldots, r_c(x))$.

---

4   Fault Tolerant Residue Representation Multiplication

Depending on the security required, to protect computation in the finite field we add redundancy by adding more $(c > v)$ parallel, modular channels than what is required by minimum, i.e., see Fig. 1. Added redundant modular channels $m_{v+1}(x), \ldots, m_c(x) \in GF(2)[x]$ have to be relatively prime to each other and to the non-redundant modular channels $m_1(x), \ldots, m_v(x)$. Therefore, now computation happens in the larger direct product ring R''

$$GF(2)[x]/<m_1(x)>\times \ldots \times GF(2)[x]/ < m_v(x) > \times \ldots \times GF(2)[x]/ < m_c(x) >,$$

where

$$m'(x) = m_1(x) \cdot \ldots \cdot m_v(x) \cdot \ldots \cdot m_c(x), \quad m'(x) \in GF(2)[x], \quad deg\,(m'(x)) > n,$$

such that $R'' \cong GF(2)[x]/ < m'(x) >$. The redundant polynomial modulus have to be of degree larger then the largest degree of the non-redundant moduli, i.e.,

$$deg(m_{v+j}(x)) > max\{deg\{m_1(x), \ldots, m_v(x)\}\}$$

and

$$deg\left\{\frac{m'(x)}{max\{m_{j_1}(x)\cdot\ldots\cdot m_{j_{c-v}}(x)\}}\right\} \geq n \geq k \qquad (6)$$

where $c - v$ is added redundancy. Therefore, all $a(x) \in GF(2^k)$ have corresponding *redundant residue representation*, i.e.,

$$a(x) \leftrightarrow a = (a_1(x), \ldots, a_v(x), \ldots, a_c(x)),$$

where $a_i(x) = a(x)(mod\, m_i(x))$ for $i = 1 \ldots c$. Now, $p(x) = \prod_{i=1}^{c} m_i(x)$, $i = 1, \ldots, c$ is *Montgomery factor*, such that $gcd(p(x), f(x)) = 1$, and computation is done in parallel, i.e. $q_i(x) = a_i(x)b_i(x)f_i'(x)$, $i = 1 \ldots c$, where $f'(x) \equiv f^{-1}(x)(mod\, p(x))$. Since, inverse modulo $p(x)$ of $p(x)$ does not exist, $r(x) = (a(x)b(x) + q(x)f(x))\,p^{-1}(x)$ is evaluated by choosing polynomial $p'(x) = \prod_{i=c+1}^{2c} m_i(x)$, where $gcd(p(x), p'(x)) = 1$, and $gcd(m_i(x), m_j(x)) = 1$ for $i \neq j$, $i, j = 1 \ldots 2c$. Therefore, change of the residue representation $(q_1(x), \ldots, q_c(x))$ to $(q_{c+1}(x), \ldots, q_{2c}(x))$ is done by:

$$\begin{pmatrix} q_{c+1}(x) \\ q_{c+2}(x) \\ \vdots \\ q_{2c}(x) \end{pmatrix} = \begin{pmatrix} w_{1,c+1}(x)\, w_{2,c+1}(x)\, \ldots\, w_{c,c+1}(x) \\ w_{1,c+2}(x)\, w_{2,c+2}(x)\, \ldots\, w_{c,c+2}(x) \\ \vdots \quad \vdots \quad \vdots \quad \vdots \\ w_{1,2c}(x) \quad w_{2,2c}(x) \quad \ldots\, w_{c,2c}(x) \end{pmatrix} \begin{pmatrix} k_1(x) \\ \vdots \\ k_{c-1}(x) \\ k_c(x) \end{pmatrix},$$

where

$$w_{i,c+j}(x) = \left(\frac{p(x)}{m_i(x)}\right)(mod\, m_{c+j}(x)), \quad i, j = 1, \ldots, c, \quad \text{and}$$

$$k_i(x) = \left(q_i(x)\left(\frac{p(x)}{m_i(x)}\right)^{-1} mod\, m_i(x)\right) mod\, m_i(x),$$

$i = 1, \ldots, c$. Now, computation of step 4 of Algorithm 3 happens in the following ring:

$$GF(2)[x]/ < m_{c+1}(x) > \times \ldots \times GF(2)[x]/ < m_{2c}(x) >$$

Change of the residue representation $(r_{c+1}(x), \ldots, r_{2c}(x))$ to $(r_1(x), \ldots, r_c(x))$ is done by:

$$\begin{pmatrix} r_1(x) \\ r_2(x) \\ \vdots \\ r_c(x) \end{pmatrix} = \begin{pmatrix} w'_{c+1,1}(x)\, w'_{c+2,1}(x)\, \ldots\, w'_{2c,1}(x) \\ w'_{c+1,2}(x)\, w'_{c+2,2}(x)\, \ldots\, w'_{2c,2}(x) \\ \vdots \quad \vdots \quad \vdots \quad \vdots \\ w'_{c+1,c}(x)\, w'_{c+2,c}(x)\, \ldots\, w'_{2c,c}(x) \end{pmatrix} \begin{pmatrix} k_{c+1}(x) \\ k_{c+2}(x) \\ \vdots \\ k_{2c}(x) \end{pmatrix},$$

where

$$w'_{c+i,j}(x) = \left(\frac{p'(x)}{m_{c+i}(x)}\right)(mod\, m_j(x)), \quad i, j = 1, \ldots, c, \quad \text{and}$$

$$k_{c+j} = \left(r_{c+j}(x)\left(\frac{p'(x)}{m_{c+j}(x)}\right)^{-1} mod\, m_{c+j}(x)\right) mod\, m_{c+j}(x), \quad j = 1 \ldots c.$$

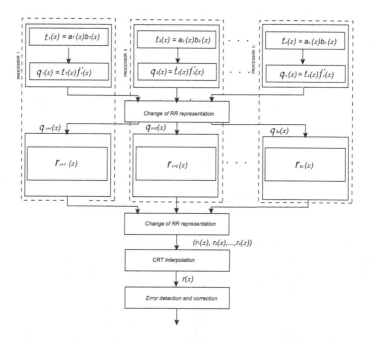

Fig. 1. Fault tolerant computation of the finite field $GF(2^k)$

By *Chinese Remainder Algorithm (CRA)* [9], if there are no fault effects, c output components will determine a unique polynomial of degree $< n \geq k$ with coefficients $a_i \in GF(2)$, otherwise, it will be of degree $\geq n \geq k$.

Definition 1. *The set of correct results of computation is*

$$C = \{r(x) \in GF(2)[x]/ < m'(x) > |deg(r(x)) < n \geq k\}.$$

4.1 Complexity

Chinese Remainder Algorithm([9]) is only applied at the end of the computation, and its complexity is:

Theorem 1 ([9]). *Let $GF(2)[x]$ be polynomial ring over a field $GF(2)$, $m_1(x)$, ..., $m_c(x) \in GF(2)[x]$, $d_i = deg(m_i(x))$ for $1 \leq i \leq c$, $l = deg(m'(x)) = \sum_{1 \leq i \leq c} d_i$, and $r_i(x) \in GF(2)[x]$ with $deg(r_i(x)) < d_i$. Then the unique solution $r'(x) \in GF(2)[x]$ with $deg(r'(x)) < l$ of the Chinese Remainder Problem $r'(x) \equiv r_i(x)(mod\, m_i(x))$ for $1 \leq i \leq c$ for polynomials can be computed using $O(l^2)$ operations in $GF(2)$.*

Theorem 2. *Computation complexity of the Algorithm 3 is $O(l^2)$.*

Proof. Let $deg(m_1(x)) = d_1, \ldots, deg(m_c(x)) = d_c$, and $d_1 + \ldots + d_c = l$. Then complexity of step 1 is $\sum_{i=1}^{c} O(d_i^2) < O((\sum_{i=1}^{c} d_i)^2) = O(l^2)$, same as of step 2. In step 3, matrix and vector are precomputed, and their multiplication has complexity $O(sc^2) + \sum_{i=1}^{c} O(d_{i+c}) < O(l^2)$, where s is degree of two polynomials multiplied such that $s \leq \max_{i}(2d_i)$, $i = 1, \ldots, c$. Complexity of computing step 4 is $4 \sum_{i=1}^{c} O(d_{i+c}^2) + \sum_{i=1}^{c} O(d_{i+c}) < O(l^2)$. In step 5, $O(s'(c^2)) + \sum_{i=1}^{c} O(d_i) < O(l^2)$, where s' is degree of two polynomials multiplied such that $s' \leq \max_{i}(2d_i)$, $i = c + 1, \ldots 2c$. Step 6 has complexity $O(l^2)$. Therefore, complexity of the algorithm 3 is $O(l^2)$. $\square$

5   Error Detection and Correction

Assume that here is one processor per independent channel as in Fig. 1. Let us assume that we have c processors, where each processor computes i -th polynomial residue and i -th residue operations. Also, we assume that *Chinese Remainder Algorithm* [9] on the end of the computation is error free.

As fault attacks, we consider methods, approaches and algorithms which when applied to the attacked processor return the effect desired by an attacker, e.g., by applying cosmic rays, heat/infrared radiation, power spikes, clock glitches, etc. An adversary can run the processor several times until the desired effects occur. As a reaction attacked processor malfunctions, and its output is erroneous such that computation assigned to the faulty processor is disturbed, and its channel is affected. The fault manifests itself in a modified data, or a modified program execution. We identify memory cells with their values, and we say that faults are induced into variables, or bits. Note that any fault induced in a variable x can be described by means of an additive error term $x \mapsto x' = x + e(x)$ but the error term $e(x)$ can itself take on quite different characteristics, depending on the type of the fault:

Stuck-at Faults. Let b be an arbitrary bit stored in memory. Assume that b is modified by a stuck-at fault. Then $b \mapsto b' = c$, where the constant $c = 1$ or $c = 0$. The value of the affected bit is not changed any more, even if a variable x, which uses these bits, is overwritten. Clearly stuck-at faults will have a noticeable effect only if the variable is overwritten at some point.

Bitflip Faults. Let b be an arbitrary bit stored in memory. Assume that b is modified by a bitflip fault. Then $b \mapsto b' = b + 1 \pmod{2}$. The effect may be transient, permanent or destructive. A bitflip fault is easy to visualize, and always results in a fault on a variable using the bit which is faulty.

Random Faults. Let b be an arbitrary bit stored in memory. Assume that b is modified by a random fault. Then $b \mapsto b'$ where b' is a random variable taking on the values 0 or 1. The effect may be transient, permanent or destructive. Since several physical methods of fault induction are difficult to control precisely, random faults are considered to be the most realistic fault type. The random variable which models the fault may be uniform or non-uniform. Note that the above faults can be considered for an arbitrary but unknown set of bits B, where assumptions about how the adversary controls the choice of B can also model different attack scenarios. Therefore, following fault models (inspired by [22]) are assumed which appear in [18], but are necessary for completeness of presentation:

Random Fault Model (RFM). Assume that an adversary does not know much about his induced faults to know its effect, but he knows the affected variable at specific channel. Therefore, we assume that affected variable $r_j \in GF(2)[x]/ < m_j(x) >$ at specific channel j is changed to some random value from the $GF(2)[x]/ < m_j(x) >$, where all values can occur with the same probability. This model is used if attacker knows that an induced fault at j-th channel will set affected variable to a random uniformly distributed value from $GF(2)[x]/ < m_j(x) >$, or if his fault attack does not depend on some special values that have to appear at some time. This fault model relies on the *random fault type*.

Arbitrary Fault Model (AFM). An adversary can target specific line of code at specific channel, but no specific variable in that line, i.e., adversary has limited control over induced faults, does not know much about his induced faults to know its type, or error distribution. In *AFM*, transient faults on any variable, or operation in the affected line of code at specific channel is the same as if the result of the targeted line of code is changed by some fault at specific channel. In the situation of permanent fault, we assume that all variables used in the targeted line of code are hit with the same uniform probability. This attack is successful if attacker does not need the assumptions about distribution of the error value, or does not need to be able to guess the error term to get information. Also, we can assume that an adversary can not target specific line of code, but will hit any line with known probability.

Mathematically, the effect of an attack using these fault models can be modeled as an addition of an unknown error $e_i \in GF(2)[x]/ < m_i(x) >$. In case of RFM we assume that a variable r_j at specific channel j is changed to some random value $r_j + e_j$, where $e_j \in GF(2)[x]/ < m_j(x) >$ with the same uniform probability, i.e., fault may result in any faulty value, while for AFM if we let r_i be component to which is assigned the result of the affected line of code, then the faulty value is $r_i + e_i$, where $e_i \in GF(2)[x]/ < m_i(x) >$, and whose probability distribution is arbitrary and unknown.

Since computation is decomposed into parallel, mutually independent channels, the adversary can use either RFM, or AFM per channel. Assume that at most $c - v$ channels have faults. Let $r' \in R''$ be computed vector with c components, where $e_j \in GF(2)[x]/ < m_j(x) >$ is the error polynomial at j-th position; then the computed component at the j-th positions is $b_j = r(x)(mod\, m_j(x)) + e_j(x)(mod\, m_j(x))$, and each processor will have as an output component

$$b_j = \begin{cases} (r(x) + e_j(x))(mod\, m_j(x)), \ j \in \{j_1, \ldots, j_\lambda\}, \\ r(x)(mod\, m_j(x)), \qquad\qquad\quad \text{else.} \end{cases}$$

Here, we have assumed that the set of error positions are $\{j_1, \ldots, j_\lambda\}$. By CRA the computed vector $r' \in R''$ with corresponding set of c modulus $m_i(x)$, gives as a output polynomial $r'(x) \in GF(2)[x]/ < m'(x) >$,

$$
\begin{aligned}
r'(x) &\equiv \left(\sum_{1 \le i \le c} r_i(x) T_i(x) M_i(x) \right) (mod\, m'(x)) \\
&= \left(\sum_{1 \le i \le c} r_i(x) T_i(x) M_i(x) + \sum_{1 \le i \le \lambda} e_{j_i}(x) T_{j_i}(x) M_{j_i}(x) \right) (mod\, m'(x)) \\
&= (r(x) + e(x))\,(mod\, m'(x)),
\end{aligned} \tag{7}
$$

where $M_i(x) = \frac{m'(x)}{m_i(x)}$, polynomials $T_i(x)$ are computed by solving congruences $T_i(x) M_i(x) \equiv 1 (mod\, m_i(x))$, $M_{j_i}(x) = \frac{m'(x)}{m_{j_i}(x)}$. Moreover, $r(x)\,(mod\, m'(x))$ is *correct polynomial* of degree $< n$ and $e(x)\,(mod\, m'(x)) \in GF(2)[x]/ < m'(x) >$ is *the error polynomial* such that

Theorem 1. *Let $e_{j_i} \in GF(2)[x]/ < m_{j_i}(x) >$ be error polynomial at positions j_i, $i \in \{1, \ldots, \lambda\}$, $\lambda \le c - v$ then $deg(e(x)) \ge n \ge k$.*

Proof. We have that

$$
\begin{aligned}
e(x) &= \left(\sum_{1 \le i \le \lambda} e_{j_i}(x) T_{j_i}(x) M_{j_i}(x) \right) (mod\, m'(x)) \\
&= e_{j_1}(x) T_{j_1}(x) M_{j_1}(x) + \ldots + e_{j_\lambda}(x) T_{j_\lambda}(x) M_{j_\lambda}(x) \\
&= \frac{m'(x)}{m_{j_1}(x) \cdot \ldots \cdot m_{j_\lambda}(x)} \sum_{i=1}^{\lambda} \frac{m_{j_1}(x) \cdot \ldots \cdot m_{j_\lambda}(x)}{m_{j_i}(x)} T_{j_i}(x) e_{j_i}(x).
\end{aligned} \tag{8}
$$

Since, $deg \left(\sum_{i=1}^{\lambda} \frac{\prod_{l=1}^{\lambda} m_{j_l}}{m_{j_i}(x)} T_{j_i}(x) e_{j_i}(x) \right) < deg \left(\frac{m'(x)}{\prod_{l=1}^{\lambda} m_{j_l}(x)} \right)$, and by (6), $deg \left(\frac{m'(x)}{\prod_{l=1}^{\lambda} m_{j_l}} \right) \ge n \ge k$, we have that $deg(e(x)) \ge n \ge k$. $\qquad \square$

Therefore, faulty processors affect the result in an additive manner.

Lemma 1. *The error is masked iff $deg(e(x)) < n \ge k$.*

Proof. Let $deg\,(e\,(x)) < n$, $n \ge k$ in (7), then $deg(r'(x)) < n$, i.e., $r'(x) \in C$. $\quad \square$

Lemma 2. *Let the degree of the ring modulus $m'(x)$ be greater then $n \ge k$, and let $c > v$ be the number of parallel, independent, modular channels (or number of processors). Then if up to $c - v$ channels fail, the output polynomial $r'(x) \notin C$.*

Proof. By referring to (7), since if $deg(e(x)) \ge n$, the output polynomial $r'(x)$ has to be such that $deg(r'(x)) \ge n$. By Definition 1, $r'(x) \notin C$. $\qquad \square$

Lemma 3. *Let the degree of the ring modulus $m'(x)$ be greater then $n \geq k$, and let $c > v$ be number of parallel, independent, modular channels (or number of processors). If there is no faulty processors then $r'(x) \in GF(2)[x]/ < f(x) >$.*

Proof. If there are no faulty processors, then clearly no errors occurred, and $deg(r'(x)) < n$, $n \geq k$ so that $r'(x) = r(x)$, $r'(x) \in C$. Therefore, $r'(x) \in GF(2)[x]/ < f(x) >$.   □

Theorem 2. *(i) If the number of parallel, mutually independent, modular, re-dundant channels is $d + t \leq c - k$ $(d \geq t)$, then up to t faulty processors can be corrected, and up to d simultaneously detected. (ii) By adding $2t$ redundant independent channels at most t faulty processors can be corrected.*

6   Decoding Based on the Euclidean Algorithm

Extended Euclid's algorithm yields two polynomials $s(x)$, $t(x)$ such that $s(x)m'(x) + t(x)r'(x) = gcd(m'(x), r'(x)) = d(x)$, where we set $s_1(x) = 1$, $s_2(x) = 0$, $t_2(x) = 0$, $t_2(x) = 1$. Let $m^+(x) = \prod_{i=1}^{\lambda} m_{j_i}(x)$, $\nu = \sum_{i=1}^{v} deg(m_i(x)) + \sum_{i=1}^{\lambda} deg(m_{j_i}(x)) - 1$, $u = \sum_{i=1}^{\lambda} deg(m_{j_i}(x))$, then

Lemma 3 ([27]). *If $\nu \geq deg(gcd(m'(x), r'(x)))$, $u + \nu = deg(m'(x)) - 1$, then there is unique index j in the algorithm such that $deg(t_j) \leq u$, $deg(d_j) \leq \nu$.*

Theorem 4 ([27]). *If $t(x)$, $d(x)$ are nonzero and $t(x)r'(x) \equiv d(x) \pmod{m'(x)}$, $deg(t(x)) + deg(d(x)) < deg(m'(x))$, then there exist a unique index j and a polynomial $\zeta(x)$ such that $t(x) = \zeta(x)t_j(x)$, $d(x) = \zeta(x)d_j(x)$.*

By (7) and (8) we have $r'(x) = r(x) + \frac{m'(x)}{m^+(x)} \sum_{i=1}^{\lambda} \frac{m^+(x)}{m_{j_i}(x)} T_{j_i}(x)e_{j_i}(x)$,   i.e.,

$$r'(x)m^+(x) - m'(x) \sum_{i=1}^{\lambda} \frac{m^+(x)}{m_{j_i}(x)} T_{j_i}(x)e_{j_i}(x) = r(x)m^+(x) \qquad (9)$$

Using (9) we applay Theorem (4) with $t(x) = m^+(x)$, and $d(x) = r(x)m^+(x)$, then correct output residue is $r(x) = \frac{r(x)m^+(x)}{m^+(x)} = \frac{d(x)}{t(x)} = \frac{d_j(x)}{t_j(x)}$ where j is the first index for which $deg(d_j(x)) < \sum_{i=1}^{v} deg(m_i(x)) + \sum_{i=1}^{\lambda} deg(m_{j_i}(x))$. If $deg(d_j(x)) - deg(t_j(x)) \geq \sum_{i=1}^{v} deg(m_i(x))$, or $t_j(x) \nmid d_j(x)$, then more then λ errors occurred.

6.1   Computational Efficiency

To have efficient reduction in the smaller polynomial rings $GF(2)[x]/ < m_i(x) >$, $i = 1, \ldots, c$, modulus $m'(x)$ have to be chosen as a product of the pairwise rela-tively prime polynomials which are of the special low Hamming weight, leading to efficient modular reduction. Therefore, smaller ring modulus can be chosen to be in the *Mersenne form* $x^n - 1$, or *pseudo-Mersenne form* $x^n + u(x)$, where polynomial $u(x)$ is of low weight. In $GF(2^k)$, the reduction is relatively inexpensive if the field is constructed by choosing the reduction polynomial to be a *trinomial*, i.e., $x^k + x^m + 1$ with $m < k/2$, or a *pentanomial* (if no trinomial available) $x^k + x^m + x^n + x^h + 1$ with $h < n < m < k/2$.

Example 1. *Assume that we want to protect computation in the finite binary field $GF(2^3) \cong GF(2)[x]/ < x^3 + x + 1 >$. Let the inputs to the computation be the following finite field elements: $a(x) = x$, $b(x) = x + 1$. We want to compute following expression $(a(x)b(x)) \bmod f(x)$, where $f(x) = x^3 + x + 1$. Let $R[x] = GF(2)[x]/ < m'(x) >$, where $m'(x) = x^2 \left(x^2 + x + 1\right)\left(x^3 + x^2 + 1\right)\left(x^4 + x + 1\right)$. Now, $v = 2$, $c - v = 2$ and error correction capability is $t = 1$. Therefore, computation will happen with encoded field elements in the following direct product ring: $GF(2)[x]/ < m_1(x) > \times \ldots \times GF(2)[x]/ < m_4(x) >$, where $a(x) \leftrightarrow a = (x, x, x, x)$, $b(x) \leftrightarrow b = (x + 1, x + 1, x + 1, x + 1)$, $f'(x) \leftrightarrow f' = (x + 1, x + 1, x, x^2 + 1)$, such that $a \otimes b = \left(x, 1, x^2 + x, x^2 + x\right)$, $q = \left(x, x + 1, 1, x^3 + x^2 + 1\right)$, where $\otimes$ is componentwise multiplication and $\oplus$ is componentwise addition. Let $\{m_5(x), m_6(x), m_7(x), m_8(x)\}$ be new set of residues, such that $\gcd(m_i(x), m_j(x)) = 1$, $i, j = 1, \ldots, 8$, and $p'(x) = \prod_{i=5}^{8} m_i(x)$, $\gcd(m'(x), p'(x)) = 1$, i.e., $p'(x) = (x^4 + x^3 + 1)(x^5 + x^3 + x^2 + x + 1)\left(x^6 + x^5 + x^2 + x + 1\right)\left(x^7 + x + 1\right)$. Therefore, change of residue representation of q is done by:*

$$\omega = \begin{pmatrix} x^2 + x & x^3 + x^2 + x & x^3 + 1 & x^3 + x + 1 \\ x^4 + x^3 + 1 & x^2 + x + 1 & x^3 + x^2 + x + 1 & x^4 + x^3 + x^2 + x + 1 \\ \sum_{i=0}^{5} x^i & x^5 + x^2 & x^4 + x^3 + x^2 + x + 1 & x^5 + x^2 + 1 \\ x^6 + x^4 + x^3 + 1 & x^4 + x^2 + x & x^6 + x^5 + 1 & x^3 + x^2 + x + 1 \end{pmatrix}$$

$$k = \begin{pmatrix} x \\ x \\ x^2 + x \\ x^3 \end{pmatrix},$$

such that $q' = \omega k = \left(x + 1, x^2, x^3 + x^2 + x, x^5 + x^2 + 1\right)$. Now, computatin happens in the new ring: $GF(2)[x]/ < m_5(x) > \times \ldots \times GF(2)[x]/ < m_8(x) >$, with, $a(x) \leftrightarrow a' = (x, x, x, x)$, $b(x) \leftrightarrow b' = (x + 1, x + 1, x + 1, x + 1)$, $f(x) \leftrightarrow f = \left(x^3 + x + 1, x^3 + x + 1, x^3 + x + 1, x^3 + x + 1\right)$, $p^{-1}(x) \leftrightarrow p^{-1} = (1, x^3 + 1, x^5 + x + 1, x^5 + x^4 + x^3 + x)$, such that $a' \otimes b' = \left(x^2 + x, x^2 + x, x^2 + x, x^2 + x\right)$, $q' \otimes f = \left(x^2, x + 1, x^2 + 1, x^6 + 1\right)$, $a' \otimes b' \oplus q' \otimes f = \left(x, x^2 + 1, x + 1, x^6 + x^2 + x + 1\right)$, i.e., result of computation is $r' = (a' \otimes b' \oplus q' \otimes f) \otimes p^{-1} = (x, x, x, x)$. Now, we do change of residue representation by:

$$\begin{pmatrix} r_1(x) \\ r_2(x) \\ r_3(x) \\ r_4(x) \end{pmatrix} = \begin{pmatrix} x + 1 & 1 & 1 & 1 \\ x + 1 & x + 1 & x + 1 & 1 \\ x^2 & 1 & x^2 + x & x^2 + x \\ 1 & x^2 + x + 1 & x^3 + x^2 + x & x^3 + x^2 \end{pmatrix} \begin{pmatrix} 1 \\ x^2 + x + 1 \\ x^5 + x^3 + x + 1 \\ x^6 + x^5 + x^4 + x^2 + 1 \end{pmatrix},$$

so that final result of computation is:

$$r = (x, x, x, x). \tag{10}$$

By applaying CRA on (10) we get $r(x) = x$. Since, $deg(r(x)) < 4$, $r(x) \in C$, i.e., $r(x) \in GF(2)[x]/ < f(x) >$. Now assume that an adversary induces faults into point $P \in E/\mathbb{F}_{2^k}$ by inducing faults into one of 8 processors by some physical set up, causing attacked processor to be faulty, such that erroneous output of the computation is

$$r'(x) = (\underline{x+1}, x, x, x) \tag{11}$$

By applying CRA on (11) we get

$$r'(x) = x^9 + x^6 + x^4 + x^2 + x + 1. \tag{12}$$

Since $deg(r'(x)) > 4$ we detect error, and by extended Euclid's algorithm for $gcd(r'(x), m'(x))$ we have that at $j = 1$ $d(x) = x^3$, and $t(x) = x^2$. Therefore, correct residue output is $r(x) = d(x)/t(x) = x$.

7   Conclusion

We have presented protection of the elliptic curve computation in a tamper proof device by protection of the finite field computation against active side channel attacks, i.e., fault attacks. Our method where field elements are represented by *the redundant residue representation* enables us to overcome the problem if one, or both coordinates $x, y \in GF(2^k)$ of the point $P \in E/\mathbb{F}_{2^k}$ are corrupted. We decompose computation of the field elements into parallel, mutually independent, modular channels, so that in case of fault at one channel, errors will not distribute to others. Since computation happens over modular channels for efficiency, we suggest smaller ring modulus to be of the special low Hamming weight. Arbitrarily powerful adversaries can create faults in enough channels and overwhelm the system proposed here, but it is part of the design process to decide on how much security is enough, since all security (i.e. extra channels) has a cost.

References

1. Anderson, R., Kuhn, M.: Tamper Resistance - a Cautionary Note. In: Proceedings of the Second Usenix Workshop on Electronic Commerce, vol. 2, pp. 1–11 (1996)
2. Bajard, J.C.B., Imbert, L., Negre, C., Plantard, T.: Efficient Multiplication $GF(p^k)$ for Elliptic Curve Cryptography. In: Proceedings of the 16th IEEE Symposium on Computer Arithmetic (ARITH 2003), p. 182 (2003)
3. Bajard, J.C., Imbert, L., Jullien, A.G.: Parallel Montgomery Multiplication in $GF(2^k)$ using Trinomial Residue Arithmetic. In: Proceedings of the 17th IEEE Symposium on Computer Arithmetic(ARITH 2005), pp. 164–171 (2005)
4. Bao, F., Deng, R.H., Han, Y., Jeng, A.B., Narasimhalu, A.D., Ngair, T.-H.: Breaking Public Key Cryptosystems on Tamper Resistant Devices in the Presence of Transient Faults. In: Christianson, B., Lomas, M. (eds.) Security Protocols 1997. LNCS, vol. 1361, pp. 115–124. Springer, Heidelberg (1998)
5. Beckmann, P.E., Musicus, B.R.: Fast Fault-Tolerant Digital Convolution Using a Polynomial Residue Number System. IEEE Transactions on Signal Processing 41(7), 2300–2313 (1993)

6. Biehl, I., Meyer, B., Muller, V.: Differential fault attacks on elliptic curve cryptosystems. In: Proceedings of the 20th Annual International Cryptology Conference on Advances in Cryptology, vol. 1880, pp. 131–146 (2000)
7. Boneh, D., DeMilo, R.A., Lipton, R.J.: On the Importance of Eliminating Errors in Cryptographic Computations. Journal of Cryptology 14, 101–119 (2001)
8. Ciet, M., Joye, M.: Elliptic Curve Cryptosystems in the Presence of Permanent and Transient Faults. Designs, Codes and Cryptography 36 (July 2005)
9. Gathen, J., Gerhard, J.: Modern Computer Algebra. Cambridge University Press, UK (1999)
10. Gaubatz, G., Sunar, B.: Robust Finite Field Arithmetic for Fault-Tolerant Public-Key Cryptography. In: Workshop on Fault Diagnosis and Tolerance in Cryptography, Edinburgh, Scotland (September 2005)
11. Halbutoğullari, A., Koç, Ç.: Mastrovito Multiplier for General Irreducible Polynomials. IEEE Transactions on Computers 49(5), 503–518 (2000)
12. Imbert, L., Dimitrov, L.S., Jullien, G.A.: Fault-Tolerant Computation Over Replicated Finite Rings. IEEE Transaction on the Circuits Systems-I: Fundamental Theory and Applications 50(7) (July 2003)
13. Koblitz, N.: Elliptic Curve Cryptosystems. Mathematics of Computation 48(177), 203–209 (1987)
14. Koç, C.K., Acar, T.: Montgomery Multiplication in $GF(2^k)$. Design, Codes and Cryptography 14(1), 57–69 (1998)
15. Kocher, P.C., Jaffe, J., Jun, B.: Differential Power Analysis. In: CRYPTO 1999. LNCS, vol. 1966, pp. 388–397. Springer, Heidelberg (1999)
16. Lidl, R., Niederreiter, H.: Introduction to Finite Fields and Their Applications. Cambridge University Press, London (1986)
17. VLSI Designs for Multiplication over Finite Fields $GF(2^m)$. In: Proceedings of the 6th International Conference on Applied Algebra, Algebraic Algorithms and Error-Correcting Codes, vol. 357, pp. 297–309 (1988)
18. Medoš, S., Boztaş, S.: Fault-Tolerant Finite Field Computation in the Public Key Cryptosystems. In: Boztaş, S., Lu, H.-F(F.) (eds.) AAECC 2007. LNCS, vol. 4851, pp. 120–129. Springer, Heidelberg (2007)
19. Medo, S., Boztaş, S.: Fault-Tolerant Lagrange Representation Multiplication in the Finite Field $GF(2^k)$. In: Proceedings of Information Security and Cryptology Conference, December 2007, pp. 90–95 (2007)
20. Miller, V.S.: Use of Elliptic Curves in Cryptography. In: Williams, H.C. (ed.) CRYPTO 1985. LNCS, vol. 218, pp. 417–426. Springer, Heidelberg (1986)
21. Montgomery, P.L.: Modular multiplication without trial division. Mathematics of Computation 44(170), 519–521 (1985)
22. Otto, M.: Fault Attacks and Countermeasures, PhD Thesis (December 2004)
23. Reed, I.S., Solomon, G.: Polynomial Codes over Certain Finite Fields. Journal of the Society for Industrial and Applied Mathematics 8(2), 300–304 (1960)
24. Reyhani-Masoleh, A., Hasan, M.A.: Towards Fault-Tolerant Cryptographic Computations over Finite Field. ACM Transaction on Embedded Computing Systems 3(3), 593–613 (2004)
25. Welch, L., Berlekamp, E.R.: Error corrections for algebraic block codes, U.S. Patent 4 633, 470 (September 1983)
26. Wicker, S.B., Bhargava, V.K.: Reed-Solomon Codes and Their Applications. IEEE Press, New York (1994)
27. Shiozaki, A.: Decoding of Redundant Residue Polynomial Codes Using Euclid's Algorithm. IEEE Transactions on Information Theory 34(5), 1351–1354 (1988)

A Tree-Based Approach for Computing Double-Base Chains

Christophe Doche[1,*] and Laurent Habsieger[2]

[1] Department of Computing
Macquarie University, Australia
doche@ics.mq.edu.au
[2] Institut Camille Jordan, CNRS UMR 5208
Université Lyon 1, 69622 Villeurbanne Cedex, France
Laurent.Habsieger@math.univ-lyon1.fr

Abstract. We introduce a tree-based method to find short Double-Base chains. As compared to the classical greedy approach, this new method is not only simpler to implement and faster, experimentally it also returns shorter chains on average. The complexity analysis shows that the average length of a chain returned by this tree-based approach is $\frac{\log_2 n}{4.6419}$. This tends to suggest that the average length of DB-chains generated by the greedy approach is not $O(\log n / \log \log n)$. We also discuss generalizations of this method, namely to compute Step Multi-Base Representation chains involving more than 2 bases and extended DB-chains having nontrivial coefficients.

Keywords: Double-base number system, scalar multiplication, elliptic curve cryptography.

1 Introduction

In the context of public-key cryptography, elliptic curves have attracted more and more attention since their introduction about twenty years ago by Miller and Koblitz [19, 21]. The main reason is that the only known algorithms to solve the discrete logarithm problem on a well-chosen elliptic curve all have an exponential-time complexity. This is in contrast with the existence of subexponential time algorithms to factor integers or to solve discrete logarithm problems in finite fields.

For a general presentation of elliptic curves, we recommend [22]. We refer to the following books [1, 7, 8, 18] for a discussion of elliptic curves in the context of cryptography.

Given a point P on a curve E and a integer n, the operation to compute the point $[n]P$ is called a *scalar multiplication*. It is the most time-consuming operation in many curve-based cryptographic protocols. Not surprisingly, this operation has been the subject of intense research, as indicated by the abundant

---

* This work was partially supported by ARC Discovery grant DP0881473.

Y. Mu, W. Susilo, and J. Seberry (Eds.): ACISP 2008, LNCS 5107, pp. 433–446, 2008.

literature on this particular topic. The standard method to efficiently compute such a scalar multiplication is the *double and add*, also known as the *left-to-right* since it scans the bits of n from the left to the right and performs a doubling for each bit, followed by an addition in case the current bit of n is 1. The number of doublings is therefore equal to $\log_2 n$ whereas the number of additions depends on the *density* of the binary representation of n, which is equal to $\frac{1}{2} \log_2 n$, on average. Scalar multiplications being similar to exponentiations, all the techniques used to speed up the computation of x^n can be used to obtain $[n]P$. See [17] for an exhaustive presentation of exponentiation techniques. For instance, we can consider *windowing methods*, which rely on the representation of the scalar in a larger basis. The expansion is then shorter and it includes nontrivial coefficients. As a result, less additions are necessary to compute $[n]P$ but precomputations must be used to take advantage of this approach.

Also, since computing the negative of a point P can be done virtually at no cost, a further gain can be obtained by considering *signed digit representations* of the scalar n, involving negative coefficients and giving a smaller density. This is the principle of the NAF whose density is $\frac{1}{3}$. Using signed coefficients greater than one leads to window NAF methods having an even smaller density.

Another possibility to accelerate the computation of $[n]P$ is to make use of special *endomorphisms*. An endomorphism of E is a rational map which sends the point at infinity onto itself. Examples of such endomorphisms include $[k]$, the multiplication by k map, for any integer k. We have seen that the double and add method relies on doublings and additions to compute $[n]P$. Other endomorphisms, potentially faster than doublings, could be used to compute scalar multiplications more efficiently. For instance, on Koblitz curves, *cf.* [16], the Frobenius endomorphism ϕ defined by $\phi(x, y) = (x^2, y^2)$ is trivial to compute and for any integer n, the map $[n]$ can always be expressed as $\sum_i d_i \phi^i$, for some d_i's in $\{-1, 0, 1\}$. From this observation, it is possible to devise a very efficient *Frobenius and add* scalar multiplication algorithm which does not require any doubling.

Tripling that sends P on $[3]P$, is also a very natural endomorphism to consider. Using triplings to compute scalar multiplications can be traced back to 2003, *cf.* [9]. For elliptic curves defined over a finite field of large characteristic, Ciet *et al.*, managed to eliminate an inversion to obtain a tripling in affine coordinates with 1 field inversion, 7 multiplications, and 4 squarings, which we abbreviate by $1I + 7M + 4S$. Note that the naïve computation of $[3]P$ as $[2]P + P$ requires $2I + 4M + 3S$. Later Dimitrov *et al.* [14], showed how to compute $[3]P$ with $10M + 6S$. Then Doche *et al.* considered a special family of curves for which a tripling can be obtained with as little as $6M + 6S$, *cf.* [5, 13]. Recently, Bernstein *et al.* [6] described a tripling on well chosen Edwards curves that needs only $9M + 4S$.

New representations are needed to fully take advantage of these efficient tripling maps.

2   Double-Base Number System

In [9], Ciet *et al.* propose a *binary/ternary method* to perform a scalar multiplication by means of doublings, triplings, and additions. Let $v_p(m)$ denotes the *p-adic valuation* of the integer m, then the principle of this method is as follows. Starting from some integer n and a point P, divide n by $2^{v_2(n)}$ and perform $v_2(n)$ doublings, then divide the result by $3^{v_3(n)}$ and perform $v_3(n)$ triplings. At this point, we have some integer m that is coprime to 6. This implies that $m \bmod 6$ must be equal to 1 or 5. Setting $m = m - 1$ or $m = m + 1$ allows to repeat the process at the cost of a subtraction or an addition.

In fact, the binary/ternary method computes an expansion that is a particular case of a more general type of representation, called the *Double-Base Number System*, *DBNS* for short. It was initially introduced by Dimitrov and Cooklev [11] and later used in the context of elliptic curve cryptography [14]. With this system, an integer n is represented as

$$n = \sum_{i=1}^{\ell} d_i 2^{a_i} 3^{b_i}, \text{ with } d_i \in \{-1, 1\}. \tag{1}$$

It is not hard to see that there is no unique DBNS representation of n. In fact, this system is highly redundant and among all the possibilities, it seems always possible to find an expansion involving very few terms. Let us be more precise. A greedy approach is used to find such an expansion. Its principle is to find at each step the best approximation of a certain integer (n initially) in terms of a $\{2, 3\}$-*integer*, *i.e.* an integer of the form $2^a 3^b$. Then compute the difference and reapply the process.

Example 1. *Take the integer $n = 841232$. We have the sequence of approximations*

$$841232 = 2^7 3^8 + 1424,$$
$$1424 = 2^1 3^6 - 34,$$
$$34 = 2^2 3^2 - 2.$$

As a consequence, $841232 = 2^7 3^8 + 2^1 3^6 - 2^2 3^2 + 2^1$.

In [15], Dimitrov *et al.* showed that for any integer n, this greedy approach returns a DBNS expansion of n involving at most $O(\frac{\log n}{\log \log n})$ signed $\{2, 3\}$-integers.

Even if this class of DBNS is very sparse, it is in general not suitable to compute scalar multiplications. Indeed, we need *at least* $\max a_i$ doublings and $\max b_i$ triplings to compute $[n]P$ using (1). It is easy to perform only $\max a_i$ doublings *or* $\max b_i$ triplings. For that simply order the terms with respect to the powers of 2 *or* to the powers of 3. However, the challenge with this type of DBNS is to attain these two lower bounds *simultaneously*. Now, if by chance the sequences of exponents are simultaneously decreasing, *i.e.* $a_1 \geqslant a_2 \geqslant \cdots \geqslant a_\ell$ and $b_1 \geqslant b_2 \geqslant \cdots \geqslant b_\ell$, it becomes trivial to compute $[n]P$ with $\max a_i$ doublings *and* $\max b_i$ triplings.

This remark leads to the concept of *Double-Base chain, DB-chain* for short, introduced in [14], where we explicitly look for expansions having this property. In fact, the binary/ternary method discussed in [9] implicitly produces a DB-chain. Another way to obtain a DB-chain is to modify the greedy algorithm. At each step, simply restrain the search of the best exponents (a_{j+1}, b_{j+1}) to the interval $[0, a_j] \times [0, b_j]$.

Example 2. *A DB-chain for n can be derived from the following sequence of equalities*

$$841232 = 2^7 3^8 + 1424,$$
$$1424 = 2^1 3^6 - 34,$$
$$34 = 3^3 + 7,$$
$$7 = 3^2 - 2,$$
$$2 = 3^1 - 1.$$

As a consequence, $841232 = 2^7 3^8 + 2^1 3^6 - 3^3 - 3^2 + 3^1 - 1$ and $[841232]P$ can be obtained by the following Horner-like computation

$$[841232]P = [3]\big([3]\big([3]\big([2^1 3^3]\big([2^6 3^2]P + P\big) - P\big) - P\big) + P\big) - P.$$

We can see that this DB-chain is strictly longer than the DBNS expansion given in Example 1. Experiments show that this is true in general as well but it is not known whether the bound $O\big(\frac{\log n}{\log \log n}\big)$ on the number of terms is still valid for DB-chains. Another concern for DB-chains, which also affects DBNS expansions, is the time required to actually find such an expansion. In particular, the search of the closest approximation of an integer in terms of a $\{2,3\}$-integer can be relatively long. See [4, 12] for a review of different methods to find such an approximation.

Remark 3. *The DBNS has still some merit in cryptography, for instance on supersingular curves defined over $\mathbb{F}_3$. In this case, a tripling is virtually free, so that $[n]P$ can be computed with $\max a_i$ doublings, $O\big(\frac{\log n}{\log \log n}\big)$ additions, and the necessary number of triplings [10]. The same holds for a generalization of the DBNS in the context of Koblitz curves [2].*

Recent developments regarding DB-chains include the use of new endomorphisms, such as optimized quintupling [20]. This leads to a new type of representation, called *Step Multi-Base Representation*, SMBR for short, where an integer n is represented as

$$n = \sum_{i=1}^{\ell} d_i 2^{a_i} 3^{b_i} 5^{c_i} \quad \text{with } d_i \in \{-1, 1\} \tag{2}$$

and the exponents $(a_i), (b_i), (c_i)$ form three separate monotonic decreasing sequences. Again, a variant of the greedy algorithm is used to derive such an expansion. However, finding the best approximation of an integer in terms of a

$\{2, 3, 5\}$-integer is not easy and thus finding a short SMBR of an integer on the fly can be a problem, at least for certain devices.

Also, the concept of *extended DBNS* has been proposed in [12]. The idea is to introduce nontrivial coefficients in DBNS expansions, namely represent an integer by

$$n = \sum_{i=1}^{\ell} d_i 2^{a_i} 3^{b_i} \text{ with } |d_i| \in \mathcal{S}, \tag{3}$$

where $\mathcal{S}$ is a set of predefined coefficients. The computation of $[n]P$ then relies on the set of precomputed values $[d]P$ for all d in $\mathcal{S}$.

3   A New Approach

The proposed method to compute DB-chains can be seen as a generalization of the binary/ternary approach. First, let us assume that n is coprime to 6. We can start building a tree by considering two leaves corresponding to $n - 1$ and $n + 1$. After removing the powers of 2 and 3 from $n - 1$ and $n + 1$, we can reapply the process and for each node, add and subtract 1. Repeating this will create a binary tree. Eventually, one of its branch will reach 1 leading to a DB-chain expansion. Obviously, this approach is too costly for integers in the cryptographic range, say those of length 160 bits and above. However, we can eliminate certain branches and hope that the overall length of the DB-chain will not be affected too much. Fixing a bound B at the beginning, we can keep only the B smallest nodes before creating the next level of the tree. Note that it is very important that the nodes that are kept are all different. The algorithm is as follows.

Algorithm 1. Tree-based DB-chain search

INPUT: An integer n and a bound B.

OUTPUT: A binary tree containing a DB-chain computing n.

1.   Set $t \leftarrow f(n)$ $[f(n) = n/(2^{v_2(n)} 3^{v_3(n)})]$

2.   Initialize a binary tree $\mathcal{T}$ with root node t

3.   **repeat**

4.   **for** each leaf node m in $\mathcal{T}$ insert 2 children

5.   Left child $\leftarrow f(m - 1)$

6.   Right child $\leftarrow f(m + 1)$

7.   Discard any redundant leaf node

8.   Discard all but the B smallest leaf nodes

9.   **until** a leaf node is equal to 1

10. **return** $\mathcal{T}$

Example 4. *Let us compute a DB-chain for* $n = 841232$ *using Algorithm 1. First, set* $B = 2$. *We obtain the chain*

$$841232 = 2^{18}3^1 + 2^{14}3^1 - 2^{11}3^1 + 2^9 + 2^4.$$

Then setting $B = 4$, *we obtain the even shorter chain*

$$841232 = 2^7 3^8 + 2^6 3^3 - 2^5 3^2 - 2^4.$$

See the appendix for details, including the trees returned by Algorithm 1 in each case.

Remark 5. *As sketched in the previous example and as we will see in Section 6, the size of the bound* B *has a great impact on the length of the DB-chain. Experimentally,* $B = 4$ *is a good compromise between the size of the tree and the quality of the expansion found. With these settings, the computation of the DB-chain is very fast since every operation in Algorithm 1 is totally elementary.*

4   Complexity Analysis

First, let us analyze the binary/ternary method. We show that the average length of the DB-chain of an integer n returned by the binary/ternary method has the upper bound $\frac{\log_2 n}{4.3774}$. For that, we investigate the average number of bits gained at each step. Take an integer $m > 1$ coprime to 6. Setting $m' = m-1$ or $m' = m+1$ so that 6 is a divisor of m', it is not hard to see that the probability for $\alpha \geqslant 1$ to be $v_2(m')$ and for $\beta \geqslant 1$ to be $v_3(m')$ is

$$\frac{1}{2^{\alpha-1}}\left(1 - \frac{1}{2}\right)\frac{1}{3^{\beta-1}}\left(1 - \frac{1}{3}\right).$$

The corresponding gain in that case is $\alpha + \beta \log_2 3$. So, the average number of bits gained is

$$\sum_{\alpha=1}^{\infty}\sum_{\beta=1}^{\infty}\frac{\alpha + \beta \log_2 3}{2^{\alpha-1}3^{\beta}} = 2 + \frac{3}{2}\log_2 3 = 4.3774\ldots$$

Since each step is independent of the other ones, we deduce that the average number of iterations, and therefore the average length of the DB-chain returned by the binary/ternary method, is bounded above by $\frac{\log_2 n}{4.3774}$. Also, the average values for α and β at each step are respectively 2 and $\frac{3}{2}$, which implies that on average

$$a_1 = \frac{\log_2 n}{1 + \frac{3}{4}\log_2 3} \approx 0.4569\log_2 n \quad \text{and} \quad b_1 = \frac{\log_2 n}{\frac{4}{3} + \log_2 3} \approx 0.3427\log_2 n$$

in the DB-chain computed by the binary/ternary method. Since $a_1 = \max a_i$, $b_1 = \max b_i$ and the sequences of exponents are simultaneously decreasing, we need a_1 doublings and b_1 triplings, on top of $\frac{\log_2 n}{4.3774}$ additions to compute $[n]P$ on average.

We use a similar probabilistic argument to analyze Algorithm 1 and obtain the following result.

Theorem 1. *The average number of bits gained at each step in Algorithm 1 is 4.6419.... It follows that the average length of a DB-chain returned by Algorithm 1 is approximately equal to $\frac{\log_2 n}{4.6419}$. Also the average values for a_1 and b_1 are approximately equal to $0.5569 \log_2 n$ and $0.2795 \log_2 n$, respectively.*

Proof. Let us fix $B = 1$. This means that of the two leaf nodes created at each step, only the smallest is kept before reapplying the process. Now imagine that $m > 1$ is an integer coprime to 6. Let $\alpha_1 = v_2(m - 1)$ and $\beta_1 = v_3(m - 1)$. Similarly, let $\alpha_2 = v_2(m+1)$ and $\beta_2 = v_3(m+1)$. Set $\alpha = \alpha_1 + \alpha_2$ and $\beta = \beta_1 + \beta_2$. Then it is easy to show that $\alpha \geqslant 3$ and $\beta \geqslant 1$. Furthermore, we can show that there are four possibilities for (α_1, β_1) and (α_2, β_2), namely

$$
\begin{array}{ll}
(\alpha - 1, \beta), & (1, 0) \\
(1, 0), & (\alpha - 1, \beta) \\
(\alpha - 1, 0), & (1, \beta) \\
(1, \beta), & (\alpha - 1, 0).
\end{array}
$$

Considering residues modulo $2^{\alpha+1}3^{\beta+1}$, we see that all the cases occur with the same probability $\frac{1}{2^{\alpha-1}3^{\beta}}$.

The maximal gain for the first two cases is $\alpha - 1 + \beta \log_2 3$, whereas it is $\max(\alpha - 1, 1 + \beta \log_2 3)$, for the last two. It follows that on average, the gain at each step is

$$
\sum_{\alpha=3}^{\infty} \sum_{\beta=1}^{\infty} \frac{2(\alpha - 1) + 2\beta \log_2 3 + 2\max(\alpha - 1, 1 + \beta \log_2 3)}{2^{\alpha-1}3^{\beta}}. \tag{4}
$$

Computing only the first few terms in this sum, we find that the gain is equal to 4.6419... This shows that Algorithm 1 performs better than the binary/ternary approach whose average gain is 4.3774...

When $B > 1$, we cannot precisely compute the average gain at each step for we do not know which branch will be selected in the end to compute a DB-chain for n. However, it is clear that on average the gain at each step will be larger than or equal to the gain when $B = 1$. In fact, tests show that even for very small $B > 1$, Algorithm 1 finds strictly shorter chains than when $B = 1$. For instance, the average gain at each step when $B = 4$ is close to 4.90, cf. Section 6, especially Table 1. Note that for very particular integers, a larger B can increase the length of the chain. The smallest example of this unexpected phenomenon is 31363, for which Algorithm 1 returns a DB-chain of length 5 when $B = 1$ and of length 6 when $B = 2$.

Concerning the average value of a_1 and b_1, a similar computation to (4) shows that we divide on average by $2^{2.5851}$ and $3^{1.2976}$ at each step. Multiplying by the average length of the chain, we deduce the quantities claimed in Theorem 1.   □

To close this section, let us investigate the worst case for Algorithm 1 when $B = 1$. It corresponds to a minimal gain at each step. Based on the proof of Theorem 1, we see that this occurs when $(\alpha_1, \beta_1) = (2, 0)$ and $(\alpha_2, \beta_2) = (1, 1)$ or the converse. Given an integer ℓ, let us consider the DB-chain of length ℓ

$$2^{\ell-1}3^{\ell-1} - \sum_{i=0}^{\ell-2} 2^i 3^i$$

and let us denote by m_ℓ the actual integer corresponding to this chain. Then it is easy to see that m_ℓ is the smallest integer for which Algorithm 1 returns a DB-chain having at least ℓ terms. Indeed, it is clear that $m_\ell - 1$ is congruent to 4 mod 8 and to 1 mod 3. In the same way, $m_\ell + 1$ is congruent to 6 mod 36. Applying Algorithm 1 to m_ℓ, it follows that $(\alpha_1, \beta_1) = (2, 0)$ and $(\alpha_2, \beta_2) = (1, 1)$. So, the next nodes in the tree are $(m_\ell - 1)/4$ and $(m_\ell + 1)/6$. The smallest that is kept, $i.e.$ $(m_\ell + 1)/6$ is in fact $m_{\ell-1}$.

The case $(\alpha_1, \beta_1) = (1, 1)$ and $(\alpha_2, \beta_2) = (2, 0)$, corresponds to the slightly larger integer $\sum_{i=0}^{\ell-1} 2^i 3^i$.

5   Generalizations

We can generalize the tree-based search in order to obtain other kinds of DB-chains. The first variant is to produce extended DB-chains, $i.e.$ including non-trivial coefficients as in (3). This approach has been successfully exploited in [12] to compute very short DB-chains and to perform scalar multiplications using precomputations. In our case, given a set of coefficients $\mathcal{S}$, it is enough to slightly modify Algorithm 1, namely Lines 4, 5, and 6, to return extended DB-chains. Given a leave node in the tree, the only change is to insert $2|\mathcal{S}|$ children instead of just 2. More precisely, for each integer $d \in \mathcal{S}$, create 2 leave nodes corresponding to $f(m - d)$ and $f(m + d)$. The rest of the algorithm remains unchanged.

Another DB-chain variant is the SMBR. Again a simple change in Algorithm 1 allows to easily find short SMBRs. For instance, to find expansions as in (2), set the function $f(n)$ to return $n/(2^{v_2(n)}3^{v_3(n)}5^{v_5(n)})$. The number of nodes created at each step is the same as for regular DB-chains so that the computation of SMBRs is very fast. Note that it is also possible to mix the two ideas, $i.e.$ return a SMBR with coefficients. For the bases 2, 3, and 5, the set of coefficients $\mathcal{S} = \{1, 7, 11, 13\}$ is a particularly effective choice. Indeed, after applying f to a certain node, we obtain an integer congruent to $\pm 1, \pm 7, \pm 11$, or ± 13 modulo 30. This implies that one of the eight children created for this node is divisible by 30. So, the gain at each step is larger than $\log_2 30$, giving rise to a very short chain.

6   Experiments

In this part, we analyze results of computations performed on random integers of various sizes. The first observation is that even when $B = 1$, the length of the DB-chain returned by Algorithm 1 is in general less than what is obtained from the greedy approach. The impact of B on the average length of the chains has also been particularly tested. For each size, we ran Algorithm 1 on a thousand random integers with different choices of B, namely $B = 1, 2, 4, 8, 16, 32, 64$, and 128. As expected, the length of the DB-chains tends to decrease when we increase B. However, experiments show that this decrease is quite slow, cf. Figure 1. As a result, there is little benefit in choosing a large B, especially since the time complexity to compute a chain linearly depends on B. That is why for subsequent DB-chain computations, B was set to 4, as it is a good compromise between the length of the chain and the time necessary to find it.

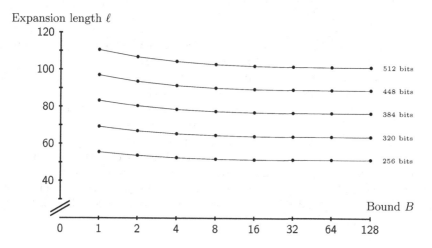

Fig. 1. Impact of B on the average length of DB-chains returned by Algorithm 1

Next, we compare the lengths of DB-chains obtained with various methods: binary/ternary, more importantly the greedy algorithm, and our new tree-based approach. We include the NAF for the record. In each case, ten thousand integers were tested. The average length of tree-based DB-chains is approximately 10% shorter than the length of chains returned by the greedy method, cf. Table 1. Note also that Algorithm 1 is somewhat easier to implement and faster in practice than the greedy approach.

Finally, we investigate the cost of a scalar multiplication on an elliptic curve in Edwards form

$$x^2 + y^2 = (1 + dx^2y^2)$$

using inverted Edwards coordinates [6]. Furthermore, we assume that multiplications by d can be neglected, so that the complexities of addition, doubling,

Table 1. Parameters of DB-chains obtained by various methods

Size	256 bits			320 bits			384 bits			448 bits			512 bits		
Method	ℓ	a_1	b_1	ℓ	a_1	b_1	ℓ	a_1	b_1	ℓ	a_1	b_1	ℓ	a_1	b_1
NAF	85.3	256	0	106.7	320	0	128.0	384	0	149.3	448	0	170.7	512	0
Bin./tern.	58.0	116.5	87.1	72.5	145.7	109.0	87.2	175.1	130.9	101.8	204.3	152.9	116.5	233.5	174.9
Greedy	58.0	150.7	65.5	72.5	189.1	81.6	87.0	228.5	97.2	101.5	266.7	113.4	116.2	305.1	129.6
Tree	52.5	145.7	68.6	65.5	182.0	86.2	78.4	218.4	103.5	91.4	255.2	120.7	104.3	291.3	138.3

Table 2. Complexity of various scalar multiplication methods for different sizes

Size	256 bits		320 bits		384 bits		448 bits		512 bits	
Method	N_M	Gain	N_M	Gain	N_M	Gain	N_M	Gain	N_M	Gain
NAF	1817.60	—	2423.47	—	3029.33	—	3635.20	—	4241.06	—
Bin./tern.	1761.19	3.10%	2353.59	2.88%	2944.94	2.79%	3537.21	2.70%	4129.57	2.63%
Greedy	1725.45	5.07%	2301.96	5.01%	2879.12	4.96%	3455.23	4.95%	4032.41	4.92%
Tree	1691.31	6.95%	2255.80	6.92%	2820.99	6.88%	3385.97	6.86%	3950.26	6.86%

and tripling are respectively 9M + S, 3M + 4S, and 9M + 4S, *cf.* [5]. To simplify comparisons between the different methods used to produce DB-chains, we make the usual assumption S = 0.8M. We these settings, N_M is the number of field multiplications necessary to compute $[n]P$ with each method, *cf.* Table 2. Note that the speed-up is expressed with respect to the NAF representation.

In case the device performing the computations allows some precomputations, it is possible to build DB-chains having nontrivial coefficients, *cf.* Section 5. In this case as well, tests show that the tree-based approach returns chains 10% shorter than the greedy algorithm. However, in this situation it is probably best to express the scalar multiple in some window-NAF representation and to take advantage of the very fast doublings provided by inverted Edwards coordinates, as pointed out in [3].

7   Conclusion

In this work, we describe a new method to find short DB-chains. So far DB-chains have been exclusively obtained with a greedy approach, relying on the search of the closest $\{2,3\}$-integer to a given number. However to accommodate the main proprerty of DB-chains, that is simultaneously decreasing sequences of exponents, this search is done under constraints that tends to increase the length of the chain. Our new method, called tree-based search, only produces DB-chains. Given a parameter B, it consists in building a binary tree and eliminating all but the smallest B nodes at each step. Quite surprisingly, even for very small B, the algorithm performs extremely well. In fact, the tree-based approach outclasses the greedy algorithm for every choice of B we tested. As a side effect of its simplicity, this method is very easy to implement, *cf.* Algorithm 1. It is also straightforward to analyze. As shown in Section 4, the average length of a DB-chain returned by the tree-based method is approximately equal to $\frac{\log_2 n}{4.6419}$ when

$B = 1$. This is interesting because the complexity of the greedy algorithm is not well understood, when it comes to compute DB-chains. For instance, it is an open question to decide if the average length of DB-chains returned the greedy approach is $O\left(\frac{\log n}{\log \log n}\right)$ or not. This work suggests that it is not the case. Note however that for scalar multiples n routinely used in elliptic curve cryptography, typically in the range 192 to 320 bits, $\log \log n$ is between 4.8910 and 5.4018, so not too far away from 4.6419. Regarding scalar multiplications, our method suits devices where the use of precomputations is limited, if not impossible. In this situation, the tree-based approach induces an overall speed-up close to 7% over the NAF that is still widely used in practice.

References

1. Avanzi, R.M., Cohen, H., Doche, C., Frey, G., Nguyen, K., Lange, T., Vercauteren, F.: Handbook of Elliptic and Hyperelliptic Curve Cryptography. In: Discrete Mathematics and its Applications, Chapman & Hall/CRC, Boca Raton (2005)
2. Avanzi, R.M., Dimitrov, V.S., Doche, C., Sica, F.: Extending Scalar Multiplication Using Double Bases. In: Lai, X., Chen, K. (eds.) ASIACRYPT 2006. LNCS, vol. 4284, pp. 130–144. Springer, Heidelberg (2006)
3. Bernstein, D.J., Birkner, P., Lange, T., Peters, C.: Optimizing double-base elliptic-curve single-scalar multiplication. In: Srinathan, K., Rangan, C.P., Yung, M. (eds.) INDOCRYPT 2007. LNCS, vol. 4859, pp. 167–182. Springer, Heidelberg (2007)
4. Berthé, V., Imbert, L.: On Converting Numbers to the Double-Base Number System. In: Luk, F.T. (ed.) Advanced Signal Processing Algorithms, Architecture and Implementations XIV. Proceedings of SPIE, vol. 5559, pp. 70–78 (2004)
5. Bernstein, D.J., Lange, T.: Explicit-formulas database,
   http://www.hyperelliptic.org/EFD/
6. Bernstein, D.J., Lange, T.: Inverted Edwards Coordinates. In: Boztaş, S., Lu, H.-F(F.) (eds.) AAECC 2007. LNCS, vol. 4851, pp. 20–27. Springer, Heidelberg (2007)
7. Blake, I.F., Seroussi, G., Smart, N.P.: Elliptic Curves in Cryptography. London Mathematical Society Lecture Note Series, vol. 265. Cambridge University Press, Cambridge (1999)
8. Blake, I.F., Seroussi, G., Smart, N.P.: Advances in Elliptic Curve Cryptography. London Mathematical Society Lecture Note Series, vol. 317. Cambridge University Press, Cambridge (2005)
9. Ciet, M., Joye, M., Lauter, K., Montgomery, P.L.: Trading Inversions for Multiplications in Elliptic Curve Cryptography. Des. Codes Cryptogr. 39(2), 189–206 (2006)
10. Ciet, M., Sica, F.: An Analysis of Double Base Number Systems and a Sublinear Scalar Multiplication Algorithm. In: Dawson, E., Vaudenay, S. (eds.) Mycrypt 2005. LNCS, vol. 3715, pp. 171–182. Springer, Heidelberg (2005)
11. Dimitrov, V.S., Cooklev, T.: Hybrid Algorithm for the Computation of the Matrix Polynomial $I+A+\cdots+A^{N-1}$. IEEE Trans. on Circuits and Systems 42(7), 377–380 (1995)
12. Doche, C., Imbert, L.: Extended Double-Base Number System with Applications to Elliptic Curve Cryptography. In: Barua, R., Lange, T. (eds.) INDOCRYPT 2006. LNCS, vol. 4329, pp. 335–348. Springer, Heidelberg (2006)

13. Doche, C., Icart, T., Kohel, D.R.: Efficient Scalar Multiplication by Isogeny Decompositions. In: Yung, M., Dodis, Y., Kiayias, A., Malkin, T.G. (eds.) PKC 2006. LNCS, vol. 3958, pp. 191–206. Springer, Heidelberg (2006)

14. Dimitrov, V.S., Imbert, L., Mishra, P.K.: Efficient and Secure Elliptic Curve Point Multiplication Using Double-Base Chains. In: Roy, B. (ed.) ASIACRYPT 2005. LNCS, vol. 3788, pp. 59–78. Springer, Heidelberg (2005)

15. Dimitrov, V.S., Jullien, G.A., Miller, W.C.: An Algorithm for Modular Exponentiation. Information Processing Letters 66(3), 155–159 (1998)

16. Doche, C., Lange, T.: Arithmetic of Special Curves. In: [1], pp. 355–388

17. Doche, C.: Exponentiation. In: [1], pp. 145–168

18. Hankerson, D., Menezes, A.J., Vanstone, S.A.: Guide to Elliptic Curve Cryptography. Springer, Heidelberg (2003)

19. Koblitz, N.: Elliptic Curve Cryptosystems. Math. Comp. 48(177), 203–209 (1987)

20. Mishra, P.K., Dimitrov, V.S.: Efficient Quintuple Formulas for Elliptic Curves and Efficient Scalar Multiplication Using Multibase Number Representation. In: Garay, J.A., Lenstra, A.K., Mambo, M., Peralta, R. (eds.) ISC 2007. LNCS, vol. 4779, pp. 390–406. Springer, Heidelberg (2007)

21. Miller, V.S.: Use of Elliptic Curves in Cryptography. In: Williams, H.C. (ed.) CRYPTO 1985. LNCS, vol. 218, pp. 417–426. Springer, Heidelberg (1986)

22. Washington, L.C.: Elliptic Curves. In: Discrete Mathematics and its Applications. Number theory and cryptography, Chapman and Hall, Boca Raton (2003)

Appendix: Detailed Examples

Let us build a binary tree and find a DB-chain for $n = 841232$. First, set $B = 2$. Some extra information has been added to the tree returned by Algorithm 1 in order to facilitate the computation of the DB-chain. The branch that is actually used to compute the DB-chain appears in dashed line.

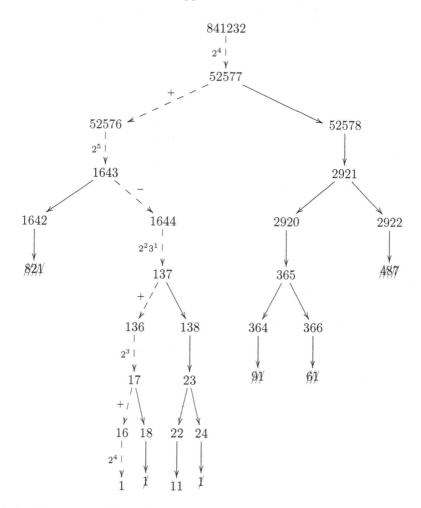

From this tree we deduce that

$$841232 = 2^4\big(2^5\big(2^23^1\big(2^3(2^4 + 1) + 1\big) - 1\big) + 1\big)$$

which implies that

$$841232 = 2^{18}3^1 + 2^{14}3^1 - 2^{11}3^1 + 2^9 + 2^4.$$

That is one term less than for the chain obtained with the greedy algorithm, *cf.* Example 2.

If we execute the algorithm again with $B = 4$, we obtain the following tree

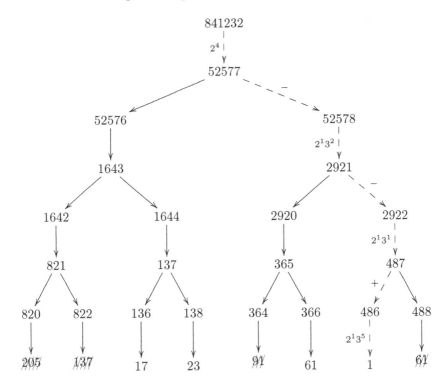

from which we derive the expansion

$$841232 = 2^4\left(2^13^2\left(2^13^1(2^13^5 + 1) - 1\right) - 1\right)$$

that leads to the even shorter DB-chain

$$841232 = 2^73^8 + 2^63^3 - 2^53^2 - 2^4.$$

Extractors for Jacobians
of Binary Genus-2 Hyperelliptic Curves

Reza Rezaeian Farashahi[1,2]

[1] Dept. of Mathematics and Computer Science, TU Eindhoven,
P.O. Box 513, 5600 MB Eindhoven, The Netherlands
[2] Dept. of Mathematical Sciences, Isfahan University of Technology,
P.O. Box 85145 Isfahan, Iran

Abstract. Extractors are an important ingredient in designing key exchange protocols and secure pseudorandom sequences in the standard model. Elliptic and hyperelliptic curves are gaining more and more interest due to their fast arithmetic and the fact that no subexponential attacks against the discrete logarithm problem are known.

In this paper we propose two simple and efficient deterministic extractors for $J(\mathbb{F}_q)$, the Jacobian of a genus 2 hyperelliptic curve H defined over $\mathbb{F}_q$, where $q = 2^n$, called the *sum* and *product* extractors.

For non-supersingular hyperelliptic curves having a Jacobian with group order $2m$, where m is odd, we propose the modified *sum* and *product* extractors for the main subgroup of $J(\mathbb{F}_q)$. We show that, if $D \in J(\mathbb{F}_q)$ is chosen uniformly at random, the bits extracted from D are indistinguishable from a uniformly random bit-string of length n.

Keywords: Jacobian, Hyperelliptic curve, Deterministic extractor.

1 Introduction

The problem of converting random points of a group into random bits has several cryptographic applications. Examples are key derivation functions, key exchange protocols and the design of cryptographically secure pseudorandom number generators. For instance, at the end of the Diffie-Hellman key exchange protocol (e.g. the well-known (hyper)elliptic curve Diffie-Hellman protocol), the parties agree on a common secret element of the group. This element is indistinguishable from a uniformly random group element under the decisional Diffie-Hellman assumption (denoted by DDH). However, the binary representation of the common secret element is *distinguishable* from a uniformly random bit-string of the same length. Therefore one has to convert this group element into a bit string statistically close to uniformly random. The classical solution is to use a hash function. Then the indistinguishability cannot be proved in the standard model but only in the random oracle model. A deterministic extractor for a group G is a function that converts a random group element to a fixed length bit-string that is statistically close to uniformly random. The security of extractors is based on standard assumptions and so they allow us to avoid the random oracle model for key exchange protocols.

Y. Mu, W. Susilo, and J. Seberry (Eds.): ACISP 2008, LNCS 5107, pp. 447–462, 2008.

The DLP in a group can always be solved in time $O(\sqrt{\#G})$ and for suitably chosen groups there are no faster attacks known. To match security levels, the key for a symmetric cipher with n bits key should be derived from a group element of a group of size $2n$ bits, i.e. the extractor should reduce the bit-length by at least a factor of 2.

Koblitz, [14], was the first to suggest using the discrete logarithm problem in the Jacobian of a hyperelliptic curve over a finite field in public key cryptography. Hyperelliptic curves of genus 2 are undergoing intensive study (e.g. see [3]) and have been shown to be competitive with elliptic curves in speed and security and for suitably chosen curves the best attacks run in $O(\sqrt{\#G})$. Many researchers have optimized genus 2 arithmetic so that in several families of curves they are faster than elliptic curves [8,9,17]. The security of genus 2 hyperelliptic curves is in general assumed to be similar to that of elliptic curves of the same group size [7].

In this paper, we suggest the *sum* and *product* extractors for $J(\mathbb{F}_q)$, the Jacobian of a hyperelliptic curve H defined over a finite field $\mathbb{F}_q$, with $q = 2^n$. Binary fields offer particularly good performance for hardware implementations (see, e.g., [11]) and genus 2 curves over binary fields were the first ones to beat elliptic curves in speed. Then we propose the modified *sum* and *product* extractors for the main subgroup of $J(\mathbb{F}_q)$, where H is a non-supersingular hyperelliptic curve having a Jacobian group order $2m$, for odd integer m. We analyse these extractors and show that if the point D is chosen uniformly at random, the bits extracted from the point D are indistinguishable from a uniformly random bit-string of length n.

Sequences of the abscissas of pseudorandom points on elliptic curves have been studied in [12,15,16,21]. So far, several deterministic randomness extractors for elliptic curves are known. The TAU technique, [2], allows to extract almost all the bits of the abscissa of a point of the union of an elliptic curve and its quadratic twist. This technique uses the idea in [13], that if a point is taken uniformly at random from the union of an elliptic curve and its quadratic twist then the abscissa of this point is uniformly distributed in the finite field. The proposed extractors in [5,6,10] do extract almost half of the bits of the abscissa of a point on particular families of curves. The proof techniques used in [6] required to work with elliptic curves defined over a binary field of the form $\mathbb{F}_{2^{2m}}$ in order to find a geometric description of the points having fixed bits in their representation. For the genus 2 curves studied in this paper no such restriction is necessary, in particular, the extractors can be applied to curves defined over fields $\mathbb{F}_{2^n}$, where n is a prime. This is the most common choice in cryptographic applications to avoid Weil descent attacks. So the results presented in this paper are more practical than earlier ones. It is possible to extend the results to curves of larger genus but then the statements get more involved and the curves are less useful for cryptography. Recently in [4], the *sum* and *product* extractors have been proposed for the Jacobian of a genus 2 hyperelliptic curve defined over a finite field of odd characteristic. Furthermore, the modified version of the *sum* and *product* extractors are suggested for the associated Kummer surface. This paper fills the gap by providing an extractor for genus 2 curves over binary fields.

2   Preliminaries

In this section we give some important notations and recall the basic definitions that are used throughout the paper.

Notation. The finite field with q elements is denoted by $\mathbb{F}_q$, and its algebraic closure by $\overline{\mathbb{F}}_q$. Denote by $\mathbb{F}_q^*$ the set of nonzero elements of $\mathbb{F}_q$. Let C be a curve defined over $\mathbb{F}_q$. Then the set of $\mathbb{F}_q$-rational points on C is denoted by $C(\mathbb{F}_q)$. The x-coordinate of a point P on a curve is denoted by x_P. The cardinality of a finite set S is denoted by $\#S$. We make a distinction between a variable $\mathbf{x}$ and a specific value x in $\mathbb{F}$.

2.1   Binary Genus 2 Hyperelliptic Curve H

An imaginary hyperelliptic curve H of genus 2 over $\mathbb{F}_q$, with $q = 2^n$, is defined by an equation of the form

$$\mathbf{y}^2 + h(\mathbf{x})\mathbf{y} = f(\mathbf{x}),$$

where $h = h_2\mathbf{x}^2 + h_1\mathbf{x} + h_0$ and $f = \mathbf{x}^5 + f_4\mathbf{x}^4 + f_3\mathbf{x}^3 + f_2\mathbf{x}^2 + f_1\mathbf{x} + f_0$. For any subfield $\mathbb{K}$ of $\overline{\mathbb{F}}_q$ containing $\mathbb{F}_q$, the set

$$H(\mathbb{K}) = \{(x, y) \in \mathbb{K} \times \mathbb{K} : y^2 + h(x)y = f(x)\} \cup \{P_\infty\},$$

is called the set of $\mathbb{K}$-*rational points* on H. The point P_∞ is called the *point at infinity* for H. A point P on H, also written $P \in H$, is a point $P \in H(\overline{\mathbb{F}}_q)$. The negative of a point $P = (x, y)$ on H is defined as $-P = (x, y + h(x))$ and $-P_\infty = P_\infty$.

2.2   On the Jacobian of H

For elliptic curves one can take the set of points together with a point at infinity as a group. This is no longer possible for hyperelliptic curves: Instead a group law is defined via the Jacobian of H over $\mathbb{F}_q$, denoted by $J(\mathbb{F}_q)$. One can efficiently compute the sum of two points in the Jacobian of H over $\mathbb{F}_q$, using the algorithms described in [3,14]. There are two isomorphic representations of the Jacobian of an imaginary hyperelliptic curve H, namely as the divisor class group of H and as the ideal class group of the maximal order in the function field of H. The latter representation is often called Mumford representation.

For each nontrivial point on the Jacobian of H over $\mathbb{F}_q$ there exist a unique divisor D on H defined over $\mathbb{F}_q$ of the form

$$D = \sum_{i=1}^{r} P_i - rP_\infty,$$

where $P_i = (x_i, y_i) \in H(\overline{\mathbb{F}}_q)$, $P_i \neq P_\infty$ and $P_i \neq -P_j$, for $i \neq j$, $r \leq 2$. By means of Mumford's representation [19], each nontrivial point on $J(\mathbb{F}_q)$ can be uniquely represented by a pair of polynomials $[u(\mathbf{x}), v(\mathbf{x})]$, $u, v \in \mathbb{F}_q[x]$, where u is monic, $\deg(v) < \deg(u) \leq 2$ and u divides $(v^2 + hv + f)$. The neutral element of $J(\mathbb{F}_q)$, denoted by $\mathcal{O}$, is represented by $[1, 0]$.

2.3   Deterministic Extractor

In our analysis we use the notion of a *deterministic extractor* and a quality measure called *statistical distance*, so we recall them briefly. For general definition of extractors we refer to [20,22].

Definition 1. *Let A and B be S-valued random variables, where S is a finite set. Then the* statistical distance $\Delta(A, B)$ *of A and B is*

$$\Delta(A, B) = \tfrac{1}{2} \sum_{s \in S} |\Pr[A = s] - \Pr[B = s]|.$$

Let U_S denote a random variable uniformly distributed on S. We say that a random variable A on S is δ-uniform, if $\Delta(A, U_S) \leq \delta$.

Note that if the random variable A is δ-*uniform*, then no algorithm can distinguish A from U_S with advantage larger than δ, that is, for all algorithms $D : S \longrightarrow \{0, 1\}$

$$|\Pr[D(A) = 1] - \Pr[D(U_S) = 1]| \leq \delta.$$

See [18].

Definition 2. *Let S, T be finite sets. Consider the function $\mathtt{ext} : S \longrightarrow T$. We say that $\mathtt{ext}$ is a* deterministic (T, δ)-extractor *for S if $\mathtt{ext}(U_S)$ is δ-uniform on T. That means*

$$\Delta(\mathtt{ext}(U_S), U_T) \leq \delta.$$

If $T = \{0, 1\}^k$, we say $\mathtt{ext}$ is a δ-deterministic extractor for S.

3   The Extractors for the Jacobian

The *sum* and *product* extractors have been proposed, [4], for the Jacobian of a genus-2 hyperelliptic curve defined over a finite field of odd characteristic. In this section we define the *sum* and *product* extractors for the Jacobian of a genus-2 hyperelliptic curve defied over a binary finite field.

3.1   The Sum Extractor

We shall now define the *sum extractor* for $J(\mathbb{F}_q)$ using the notation of divisor classes to explain the name. Then we translate the definition to the Mumford representation.

Definition 3. *The sum extractor* SE *for the Jacobian of* H *over* $\mathbb{F}_q$ *is defined as the function* $\text{SE} : J(\mathbb{F}_q) \longrightarrow \mathbb{F}_q$, *by*

$$\text{SE}(D) = \begin{cases} \sum_{i=1}^{r} x_{P_i}, & \text{if } D = \sum_{i=1}^{r} P_i - rP_{\infty}, \ 1 \leq r \leq 2, \\ 0, & \text{if } D = \mathcal{O}. \end{cases}$$

By means of Mumford's representation for the points of $J(\mathbb{F}_q)$, the function SE can alternatively be defined by

$$\text{SE}(D) = \begin{cases} u_1, & \text{if } D = [\mathbf{x}^2 + u_1\mathbf{x} + u_0, v(\mathbf{x})], \\ u_0, & \text{if } D = [\mathbf{x} + u_0, v(\mathbf{x})], \\ 0, & \text{if } D = [1, 0]. \end{cases}$$

To analyse the extractor SE, we need to examine the distribution of the random variable $\text{SE}(D)$, for D chosen uniformly at random in $J(\mathbb{F}_q)$. So we need to obtain estimates for the cardinalities of preimages of $\text{SE}(D)$. We note that by the Hasse-Weil bound $\#J(\mathbb{F}_q) \approx q^2$ and that $J(\mathbb{F}_q) = \bigcup_{a \in \mathbb{F}_q} \text{SE}^{-1}(a)$. For a uniformly distributed sequence we expect $\#\text{SE}^{-1}(a) \approx q$, for $a \in \mathbb{F}_q$. The following theorem shows that the expected cardinality of each fiber essentially equals q. It also gives a precise bound on the deviation. Furthermore an exceptional case is discussed, which rarely occurs. To state the number of preimages, we first need a rather technical definition. We refer to Subsection 5.1 for an explanation of the case distinction.

Definition 4. *We define the set* $I_{\text{SE}} \subset \mathbb{F}_q^*$, *corresponding to the hyperelliptic curve* H, *as*

$$I_{\text{SE}} = \begin{cases} \{\frac{h_1}{h_2}\}, & \text{if } h_2 \neq 0 \text{ and } d_1 = 0, \\ \{z \in \mathbb{F}_q^* : z^5 + zf_3^2 + h_0^2 = 0\}, & \text{if } h_2 = h_1 = 0, \\ \{\}, & \text{otherwise,} \end{cases}$$

where $d_1 = h_2^4 h_1^3 f_4 + h_2^4 h_1 f_3^2 + h_2^5 (h_2 h_0 + h_1^2) f_3 + h_2^6 h_1 f_2 + h_2^7 f_1 + h_2^5 h_0^2 + h_2^4 h_1^2 h_0 + h_2^3 h_1^4 + h_1^5$.

We will show later that for $a \in I_{\text{SE}}$ we can only give a trivial estimate for $\#\text{SE}^{-1}(a) - q$. However, we note that $\#I_{\text{SE}} \leq 1$ unless the curve has $h_2 = h_1 = 0$. Curves of the latter type are supersingular. They are interesting for pairing based protocols but should be avoided if only the DL setting is needed. Even in this case, the cardinality of I_{SE} is easily bounded by 5.

Theorem 1. *For all* $a \in \mathbb{F}_q^*$, *we have*

$$|\#\text{SE}^{-1}(a) - (q+1)| \leq \begin{cases} 6\sqrt{q} + 2, & \text{if } h_2 \neq 0 \text{ and } a \notin I_{\text{SE}}, \\ 6\sqrt{q} + 1, & \text{if } h_2 = 0 \text{ and } h_1 \neq 0, \\ 4\sqrt{q} + 1, & \text{if } h_2 = h_1 = 0 \text{ and } a \notin I_{\text{SE}}, \\ q + 4\sqrt{q} + 1, & \text{if } a \in I_{\text{SE}}. \end{cases}$$

We also have

$$\left|\#\text{SE}^{-1}(0) - (q+1)\right| \leq 4\sqrt{q} + 2.$$

We give a proof of this theorem in Section 5.

3.2   The Product Extractor

In a similar way we propose the *product extractor* for $J(\mathbb{F}_q)$.

Definition 5. *The product extractor* PE *for the Jacobian of H over $\mathbb{F}_q$ is defined as the function* $\text{PE} : J(\mathbb{F}_q) \longrightarrow \mathbb{F}_q$, *by*

$$\text{PE}(D) = \begin{cases} \prod_{i=1}^{r} x_{P_i}, & \text{if } D = \sum_{i=1}^{r} P_i - rP_\infty, \ 1 \leq r \leq 2, \\ 0, & \text{if } D = \mathcal{O}. \end{cases}$$

Using Mumford's representation for the points of $J(\mathbb{F}_q)$, we can alternatively define the extractor PE by

$$\text{PE}(D) = \begin{cases} u(0), & \text{if } D = [u(\mathbf{x}), v(\mathbf{x})], \\ 0, & \text{if } D = [1, 0]. \end{cases}$$

In the next theorem we give the estimates for the number of points on the fibers of PE. The proof of this theorem is similar to the proof of Theorem 1.

Definition 6. *We define the set $I_{\text{PE}} \subset \mathbb{F}_q^*$, corresponding to the hyperelliptic curve H, as*

$$I_{\text{PE}} = \begin{cases} \{(\frac{h_1}{h_2})^2\}, & \text{if } h_2 \neq 0, h_0 = 0 \text{ and } d = 0, \\ \emptyset, & \text{otherwise,} \end{cases}$$

where $d = h_2^4(f_1 + h_1\sqrt{f_0}) + h_1^4$.

Theorem 2. *For all $b \in \mathbb{F}_q^*$, we have*

$$\left|\#\text{PE}^{-1}(b) - q\right| \leq \begin{cases} 8\sqrt{q} + 2, & \text{if } h_0 \neq 0, \\ 6\sqrt{q} + 2, & \text{if } h_0 = 0 \text{ and } b \notin I_{\text{PE}}, \\ q + 4\sqrt{q} + 2, & \text{if } b \in I_{\text{PE}}. \end{cases}$$

We also have

$$\left|\#\text{PE}^{-1}(0) - (eq + 1)\right| \leq 4e\sqrt{q},$$

where $e = \#\{(x, y) \in H(\mathbb{F}_q) : x = 0\}$.

We note that $0 \leq e \leq 2$.

3.3   Analysis of the Extractors

In this subsection we show that, provided the divisor D is chosen uniformly at random in $J(\mathbb{F}_q)$, the bits extracted from the divisor D by the extractors SE or PE are indistinguishable from a uniformly random bit-string of length n.

Let $U_{\mathbb{F}_q}$ be a uniform random variable. Let A be a $\mathbb{F}_q$-valued random variable that is defined as $A = \text{SE}(D)$, for $D \in_R J(\mathbb{F}_q)$.

Proposition 1. *The random variable A is statistically close to uniform.*

$$\Delta(A, U_{\mathbb{F}_q}) = O\left(\frac{1}{\sqrt{q}}\right).$$

Proof. Let $a \in \mathbb{F}_q$. For $U_{\mathbb{F}_q}$ as uniform random variable we have $\Pr[U_{\mathbb{F}_q} = a] = 1/q$. For the $\mathbb{F}_q$-valued random variable A we have $\Pr[A = a] = \frac{\#\text{SE}^{-1}(a)}{\#J(\mathbb{F}_q)}$. The genus of the curves we consider is 2 and so the Hasse-Weil theorem bounds the number of points as follows.

$$(\sqrt{q} - 1)^4 \le \#J(\mathbb{F}_q) \le (\sqrt{q} + 1)^4.$$

Theorem 1 gives the bound for $\#\text{SE}^{-1}(a)$, for all $a \in \mathbb{F}_q$. Hence

$$\Delta(A, U_{\mathbb{F}_q}) = \frac{1}{2} \sum_{a \in \mathbb{F}_q} \left|\Pr[A = a] - \Pr[U_{\mathbb{F}_q} = a]\right| = \frac{1}{2} \sum_{a \in \mathbb{F}_q} \left|\frac{\#\text{SE}^{-1}(a)}{\#J(\mathbb{F}_q)} - \frac{1}{q}\right|$$

$$= \sum_{a \in I_{SE}} \frac{|q\#\text{SE}^{-1}(a) - \#J(\mathbb{F}_q)|}{2q\#J(\mathbb{F}_q)} + \sum_{a \in \mathbb{F}_q \setminus I_{SE}} \frac{|q\#\text{SE}^{-1}(a) - \#J(\mathbb{F}_q)|}{2q\#J(\mathbb{F}_q)}.$$

Let $w = \#I_{SE}$. Then

$$\Delta(A, U_{\mathbb{F}_q}) \le \frac{(q^2 + 8q\sqrt{q} - 4q + 4\sqrt{q} - 1)w + (10q\sqrt{q} - 3q + 4\sqrt{q} - 1)(q - w)}{2q(\sqrt{q} - 1)^4}$$

$$= \frac{(q - 2\sqrt{q} - 1)w + 10q\sqrt{q} - 3q + 4\sqrt{q} - 1}{2(\sqrt{q} - 1)^4} = \frac{5 + \epsilon(q)}{\sqrt{q}},$$

where $\epsilon(q) = \frac{\sqrt{q}(q - 2\sqrt{q} - 1)w + 37q\sqrt{q} - 56q + 39\sqrt{q} - 10}{2(\sqrt{q} - 1)^4}$. In general w equals 0. Then, $\epsilon(q) < 1$ for $n \ge 9$. In case that w equals 5, $\epsilon(q) < 1$ for $n \ge 10$.   □

Corollary 1. SE *is a deterministic $\frac{6}{\sqrt{q}}$-extractor for $J(\mathbb{F}_q)$, for $n \ge 10$.*

Similarly, by the result of Theorem 2, we obtain the following analysis for the *product extractor*.

Corollary 2. PE *is a deterministic $\frac{7}{\sqrt{q}}$-extractor for $J(\mathbb{F}_q)$, for $n \ge 10$.*

4   Extractor for a Subgroup

We note that the number of points of the Jacobian of any genus 2 non-supersingular binary hyperelliptic curve is even. Therefore, the DDH problem in the full group is easy. Then the main subgroup G of $J(\mathbb{F}_q)$ is suggested for cryptographic applications. In particular, the order of G can be chosen to be prime, so the DDH problem in G can be assumed to be intractable.

Let H be an imaginary hyperelliptic curve of genus 2 defined over $\mathbb{F}_q$, such that the order of $J(\mathbb{F}_q)$ is even. In particular let $\#J(\mathbb{F}_q) = 2m$, where m is odd. In this section we propose a new extractor for the main subgroup of $J(\mathbb{F}_q)$ by means of an extractor for $J(\mathbb{F}_q)$, where the main order subgroup is the group of m-torsion points.

Let G be the main subgroup of $J(\mathbb{F}_q)$ of order m. Assume T is the point of order 2 in $J(\mathbb{F}_q)$. Let β be a bit distinguishing D from $-D$ satisfying

$$\beta : J(\mathbb{F}_q) \to \{0,1\},$$
$$\beta(D) = 0, \text{ if } D = -D,$$
$$\beta(D) + \beta(-D) = 1, \text{ if } D \neq -D.$$

Assume Ext is an extractor for $J(\mathbb{F}_q)$ such that $\texttt{Ext}(D) = \texttt{Ext}(-D)$ for all $D \in J(\mathbb{F}_q)$. Examples are the *sum* and *product* extractors. Furthermore, assume $\texttt{Ext}(\mathcal{O}) = \texttt{Ext}(T)$. We propose an extractor ext for G as a modified version of Ext. The extractor ext is defined as the function

$$\texttt{ext} : G \to \mathbb{F}_q,$$
$$\texttt{ext}(D) = \texttt{Ext}(D + \beta(D)T).$$

Proposition 2. *Let $z \in \mathbb{F}_q$. Then*

$$\#\texttt{Ext}^{-1}(z) = 2\#\texttt{ext}^{-1}(z).$$

Proof. We consider the map $\xi : \texttt{Ext}^{-1}(z) \longrightarrow \texttt{ext}^{-1}(z)$ defined by

$$\xi(D) = \begin{cases} D & \text{if } D \in G, \, \beta(D) = 0, \\ -D & \text{if } D \in G, \, \beta(D) = 1, \\ -D + T & \text{if } D \notin G, \, \beta(D + T) = 0, \\ D + T & \text{if } D \notin G, \, \beta(D + T) = 1. \end{cases}$$

The map ξ is surjective. Indeed it is a $2 : 1$ map, since $\texttt{Ext}(D) = \texttt{Ext}(-D)$ for all $D \in J(\mathbb{F}_q)$ and $\texttt{Ext}(\mathcal{O}) = \texttt{Ext}(T)$. $\square$

Proposition 3. *Ext is an $(\mathbb{F}_q, \delta)$-deterministic extractor for $J(\mathbb{F}_q)$ if and only if ext is an $(\mathbb{F}_q, \delta)$-deterministic extractor for G.*

Proof. Proposition 2 concludes the proof of this proposition.

Example 1. Let H_1 be a hyperelliptic curve defined over $\mathbb{F}_{2^{113}}$ by the equation $y^2 + xy = x^5 + x^2 + 1$. Then $\#J(\mathbb{F}_{2^{113}}) = 2p$, where $p = 5391989333430127871582$ $3297673841230760642802715019043549764193368381$ is a prime number. Let G_1 be the main subgroup of $J(\mathbb{F}_{2^{113}})$ of order p. Let $\texttt{se}_1$ be a modified version of the *sum* extractor for G_1. Then $\texttt{se}_1$ is a deterministic $\frac{3.83}{\sqrt{2^{113}}}$-extractor for G_1.

Example 2. Let H_2 be a hyperelliptic curve defined over $\mathbb{F}_{2^{167}}$ by the equation $\mathbf{y}^2 + \mathbf{xy} = \mathbf{x}^5 + \mathbf{x}^2 + 1$. Then $\#J(\mathbb{F}_{2^{167}}) = 2p$, where $p = 174980057982640953949800201801707026200539332079716076013980390634220813519478186543669247174978887493$ is a prime number. Let G_2 be the main subgroup of $J(\mathbb{F}_{2^{167}})$ of order p. Let se_2 be a modified version of the *sum extractor* for G_2. Then se_2 is a deterministic $\frac{2.08}{\sqrt{2^{167}}}$-extractor for G_2.

5 Proofs of Theorems

In this section we give a proof of Theorem 1. The proof of Theorem 2 can be followed in a similar approach. First we discuss the background of the case distinction in Theorems 1 and 2, then we recall some properties of hyperelliptic curves which will be used in the proofs.

5.1 Relation between Discriminant and the Case Distinction

In the following remark we discuss about the nonsingularity of the hyperelliptic curve H. The description of the extractors required stating some special cases. The parameter d_1 in the definition of the *sum extractor* is intimately related to the discriminant of H. Indeed the description of the discriminant of H is needed to explain the nonsingularity of the fibers of the extractors.

Remark 1. We note that a genus 2 hyperelliptic curve is nonsingular by definition. So for $H : \mathbf{y}^2 + h(\mathbf{x})\mathbf{y} = f(\mathbf{x})$ the following system of equations has no solution in $\overline{\mathbb{F}}_q \times \overline{\mathbb{F}}_q$.

$$\begin{cases} \mathbf{y}^2 + h(\mathbf{x})\mathbf{y} = f(\mathbf{x}) \\ h'(\mathbf{x})\mathbf{y} = f'(\mathbf{x}) \\ h(\mathbf{x}) = 0, \end{cases} \tag{1}$$

where h' and f' are respectively the derivatives of h and f. System (1) has a solution in $\overline{\mathbb{F}}_q \times \overline{\mathbb{F}}_q$ if and only if the following equations have a common root in $\overline{\mathbb{F}}_q$.

$$\begin{cases} \zeta(\mathbf{x}) = h'^2(\mathbf{x})f(\mathbf{x}) + f'^2(\mathbf{x}) = 0, \\ h(\mathbf{x}) = 0. \end{cases} \tag{2}$$

Let $\mathcal{D} = \mathbf{Res}(h, \zeta)$. System (2) has a solution in $\overline{\mathbb{F}}_q$ if and only if $\mathcal{D} = 0$. That means $\mathcal{D} \neq 0$, since the curve H is nonsingular. We consider the following types for H.

1. If $h_2 \neq 0$, then

$$\mathcal{D} = \frac{h_0 h_1^4 d_1^2 + h_1^3 d_1 d_0 + h_2 d_0^2}{h_2^7},$$

where

$$\begin{aligned} d_1 ={}& h_2^4 h_1^3 f_4 + h_2^4 h_1 f_3^2 + h_2^5 (h_2 h_0 + h_1^2) f_3 + h_2^6 h_1 f_2 + h_2^7 f_1 + h_2^5 h_0^2 \\ &+ h_2^4 h_1^2 h_0 + h_2^3 h_1^4 + h_1^5, \\ d_0 ={}& h_2^4 h_1^2 h_0 (h_2 h_0 + h_1^2) f_4 + h_2^4 h_0 (h_2 h_0 + h_1^2) f_3^2 + h_2^5 h_1^3 h_0 f_3 + h_2^6 h_1^2 h_0 f_2 \\ &+ h_2^7 f_1^2 + h_2^7 h_1^2 f_0 + h_2^3 h_1^5 h_0 + h_2^3 h_0^4 + h_2 h_1^4 h_0^2 + h_1^6 h_0. \end{aligned}$$

2. If $h_2 = 0$ and $h_1 \neq 0$, then

$$\mathcal{D} = h_1^6 h_0^4 f_4 + h_1^4 h_0^4 f_3^2 + h_1^7 h_0^3 f_3 + h_1^8 h_0^2 f_2 + h_1^8 f_1^2 + h_1^9 h_0 f_1 + h_1^{10} f_0 + h_1^5 h_0^5 + h_0^8.$$

3. If $h_2 = h_1 = 0$ and $h_0 \neq 0$, then $\mathcal{D} = h_0^8$.

5.2   Details of the Divisor Class Group Representation

We defined SE and PE both in terms of divisor classes and of ideal classes. While for the definition via the Mumford representation it is instantly clear that the values are in $\mathbb{F}_q$ it is not completely obvious for the divisor class group setting. Here we explain what it means for the points constituting the reduced divisor class that the class is defined over $\mathbb{F}_q$.

Let $\phi : \overline{\mathbb{F}}_q \longrightarrow \overline{\mathbb{F}}_q$ be the Frobenius map defined by $\phi(\mathbf{x}) = \mathbf{x}^q$. This map is extended to the Jacobian of H as follows. For a divisor $D = \sum_{i=1}^r P_i - r P_\infty$ in the Jacobian of H, $\phi(D) = \sum_{i=1}^r \phi(P_i) - r\phi(P_\infty)$, where $\phi(P_i) = (x_i^q, y_i^q)$ for $P_i = (x_i, y_i)$ and $\phi(P_\infty) = P_\infty$. Furthermore $\phi(D) = D$, for all $D \in J(\mathbb{F}_q)$.

We partition $J(\mathbb{F}_q)$ as $J(\mathbb{F}_q) = J_0 \cup J_1 \cup J_2$, where $J_0 = \{\mathcal{O}\}$ and J_r, for $r = 1, 2$, is defined as

$$J_r = \{D \in J(\mathbb{F}_q) : D = \sum_{i=1}^r P_i - r P_\infty\}.$$

If $D \in J_1$, then $D = P - P_\infty$, where $P \neq P_\infty$ and $P = (x_P, y_P) \in H(\mathbb{F}_q)$. Furthermore, D is represented by $[\mathbf{x} - x_P, y_P]$. If $D \in J_2$, then $D = P + Q - 2P_\infty$ for some points P, Q, where $P, Q \neq P_\infty$ and $P \neq -Q$. Then D is represented by $[u(\mathbf{x}), v(\mathbf{x})]$, where $u(\mathbf{x}) = (\mathbf{x} - x_P)(\mathbf{x} - x_Q)$, $v(x_P) = y_P$ and $v(x_Q) = y_Q$.

Remark 2. We partition J_2 as follows. Let $D \in J_2$.

1. Suppose $\phi(P) = P$. Since $\phi(D) = D$, then $\phi(Q) = Q$. Thus $P, Q \in H(\mathbb{F}_q)$. Hence $x_P, x_Q \in \mathbb{F}_q$. That means u is a reducible polynomial over $\mathbb{F}_q$.
2. Suppose $\phi(P) \neq P$. Since $\phi(D) = D$, so $\phi(P) = Q$ and $\phi(Q) = P$. Then $\phi(\phi(P)) = P$ and $\phi(P) \neq \pm P$. Hence $P \in H(\mathbb{F}_{q^2})$. Furthermore, u is an irreducible polynomial over $\mathbb{F}_q$.

Let

$$\mathcal{J} = \{(P, Q) : P, Q \in H(\mathbb{F}_q), P, Q \neq P_\infty, Q \neq -P\},$$
$$\mathcal{J}^\phi = \{(P, \phi(P)) : P \in H(\mathbb{F}_{q^2}), P \neq P_\infty, \phi(P) \neq -P\}.$$

Remark 3. Let $\sigma : \mathcal{J} \longrightarrow J_2$ be the map defined by $\sigma(P, Q) = P + Q - 2P_\infty$ and let $\sigma_\phi : \mathcal{J}^\phi \longrightarrow J_2$ be the map defined by $\sigma_\phi(P, \phi(P)) = P + \phi(P) - 2P_\infty$. Then $\#\sigma^{-1}(D) + \#\sigma_\phi^{-1}(D) = 2$, for all $D \in J_2$.

5.3   Proof of Theorem 1

For the proof of Theorem 1, we need several lemmas and propositions. First we modify the problem to a corresponding problem via Proposition 4. The new problem is to find estimates for the sum of the cardinalities of two related sets.

These sets are defined by Definition 7. Second, by Proposition 5, we give a formula for this sum in terms of the numbers of $\mathbb{F}_q$-rational points on H and a particular curve. Finally we obtain tight estimates for all fibers of SE, by means of Proposition 8 and the Hasse-Weil theorem.

Definition 7. *Let $a \in \mathbb{F}_q$. Let*

$$\Sigma_a = \{(P,Q) : P,Q \in H(\mathbb{F}_q), P,Q \neq P_\infty, x_P + x_Q = a\},$$

$$\Sigma_a^\phi = \{(P,\phi(P)) : P \in H(\mathbb{F}_{q^2}), P \neq P_\infty, x_P + x_{\phi(P)} = a\}.$$

Proposition 4. *For all $a \in \mathbb{F}_q^*$,*

$$\#(\mathrm{SE}^{-1}(a) \cap J_2) = \frac{\#\Sigma_a + \#\Sigma_a^\phi}{2}.$$

Proof. Let $a \in \mathbb{F}_q^*$. Let $\mathcal{S}_a = \sigma^{-1}(\mathrm{SE}^{-1}(a) \cap J_2)$ and $\mathcal{S}_a^\phi = \sigma_\phi^{-1}(\mathrm{SE}^{-1}(a) \cap J_2)$ (see Remark 3). It is easy to see that $\Sigma_a = \mathcal{S}_a$ and $\Sigma_a^\phi = \mathcal{S}_a^\phi$, since $a \neq 0$. Remark 3 implies that $\#\mathcal{S}_a + \#\mathcal{S}_a^\phi = 2\#(\mathrm{SE}^{-1}(a) \cap J_2)$. That concludes the proof of this proposition. □

Let ν and ω be the polynomials in $\mathbb{F}_q[x_1, x_2]$ defined as

$$\nu(x_1, x_2) = h(x_1)h(x_2),$$

$$\omega(x_1, x_2) = f(x_1)h^2(x_2) + f(x_2)h^2(x_1).$$

Clearly ν and ω are symmetric polynomials. Consider the two-variable polynomials $\theta, \psi \in \mathbb{F}_q[a, b]$ such that

$$\theta(x_1 + x_2, x_1 x_2) = \nu(x_1, x_2), \quad \psi(x_1 + x_2, x_1 x_2) = \omega(x_1, x_2).$$

One can show that

$$\theta(a, b) = h_2 h_0 a^2 + h_2 h_1 ab + h_1 h_0 a + h_2^2 b^2 + h_1^2 b + h_0^2,$$

$$\psi(a, b) = h_0^2 a^5 + (h_2^2 f_0 + h_0^2 f_4)a^4 + h_1^2 a^3 b^2 + (h_2^2 f_1 + h_0^2)a^3 b + h_0^2 f_3 a^3 +$$
$$(h_2^2 f_2 + h_1^2 f_4)a^2 b^2 + (h_1^2 f_0 + h_0^2 f_2)a^2 + h_2^2 ab^4 + (h_2^2 f_3 + h_1^2)ab^3 +$$
$$(h_2^2 f_1 + h_1^2 f_3 + h_0^2)ab^2 + (h_1^2 f_1 + h_0^2 f_3)ab + h_0^2 f_1 a.$$

Let $\mathcal{X}$ be the algebraic set defined over $\mathbb{F}_q$, by the equation

$$F(a, b, z) = z^2 + \theta(a, b)z + \psi(a, b) = 0.$$

Let $a \in \mathbb{F}_q$. Let $\mathcal{X}_a$ be the affine curve defined by the equation

$$F_a(b, z) = z^2 + \theta_a(b)z + \psi_a(b) = 0, \tag{3}$$

where $\theta_a(b) = \theta(a, b)$ and $\psi_a(b) = \psi(a, b)$.

Proposition 5. *Let $a \in \mathbb{F}_q$. Then*

$$\#\Sigma_a + \#\Sigma_a^\phi = 2(\#H(\mathbb{F}_q) + \#\mathcal{X}_a(\mathbb{F}_q) - q - 1).$$

The proof of Proposition 5 can be followed in a similar way to the proof of Proposition 12 in [4].

For almost all $a \in \mathbb{F}_q^*$ the affine curve $\mathcal{X}_a$ is absolutely irreducible and non-singular. We will now show that in fact the curve $\mathcal{X}_a$ is reducible if and only if $a \in I_{SE}$. Provided that the curve $\mathcal{X}_a$ is absolutely irreducible, the genus of the nonsingular model of $\mathcal{X}_a$ is at most 1. We give conditions for $\mathcal{X}_a$ to be non-singular. For a nonsingular curve we can use the Hasse-Weil theorem to bound $\#\mathcal{X}_a(\mathbb{F}_q)$ which leads to a proof of Theorem 1.

Proposition 6. *The affine curve $\mathcal{X}_a$, for $a \in \mathbb{F}_q^*$, is absolutely irreducible if and only if $a \notin I_{SE}$.*

Proof. The affine curve $\mathcal{X}_a$, for $a \in \mathbb{F}_q^*$, is defined by Equation (3). So we consider the polynomial

$$F_a(\mathbf{b}, \mathbf{z}) = \mathbf{z}^2 + \theta_a(\mathbf{b})\mathbf{z} + \psi_a(\mathbf{b}).$$

First, we assume $h_2 \neq 0$. Then the leading terms of θ_a and ψ_a are respectively $h_2^2 \mathbf{b}^2$ and $h_2^2 a \mathbf{b}^4$. Suppose F_a is reducible. So there exists a bivariate polynomial M in $\overline{\mathbb{F}}_q[\mathbf{b}, \mathbf{z}]$, which is a nontrivial factor of F_a and thus has degree 1. We can put

$$M(\mathbf{b}, \mathbf{z}) = \mathbf{z} + e(\mathbf{b}) = \mathbf{z} + \mathbf{e}_2\mathbf{b}^2 + \mathbf{e}_1\mathbf{b} + \mathbf{e}_0,$$

where $\mathbf{e}_2$, $\mathbf{e}_1$ and $\mathbf{e}_0$ are unknowns in $\overline{\mathbb{F}}_q$. Since M is a factor of F_a, the substitution of $e(\mathbf{b})$ for $\mathbf{z}$ in F_a must lead to $F_a(\mathbf{b}, e(\mathbf{b})) = 0$. The remainder is

$$r(\mathbf{b}) = r_4\mathbf{b}^4 + r_3\mathbf{b}^3 + r_2\mathbf{b}^2 + r_1\mathbf{b} + r_0 \overset{!}{=} 0.$$

We obtain the following set of equations:

$$\begin{cases} r_4 = \mathbf{e}_2^2 + h_2^2\mathbf{e}_2 + h_2^2 a = 0 \\ r_3 = te_2 + h_2^2\mathbf{e}_1 + (h_2^2 f_3 + h_1^2)a = 0 \\ r_2 = se_2 + \mathbf{e}_1^2 + te_1 + h_2^2\mathbf{e}_0 + h_1^2 a^3 + (h_2^2 f_2 + h_1^2 f_4)a^2 \\ \qquad + (h_2^2 f_1 + h_1^2 f_3 + h_0^2)a = 0 \\ r_1 = se_1 + te_0 + (h_2^2 f_1 + h_0^2)a^3 + (h_1^2 f_1 + h_0^2 f_3)a = 0 \\ r_0 = \mathbf{e}_0^2 + se_0 + h_0^2 a^5 + (h_2^2 f_0 + h_0^2 f_4)a^4 + h_0^2 f_3 a^3 \\ \qquad + (h_1^2 f_0 + h_0^2 f_2)a^2 + h_0^2 f_1 a = 0, \end{cases} \quad (4)$$

where $s = h_0(h_2 a^2 + h_1 a + h_0)$ and $t = h_1(h_2 a + h_1)$. We compute $\mathbf{e}_1$ from the equation of r_3 and substitute in equations r_2 and r_1. Then from the new equation of r_2, we compute $\mathbf{e}_0$ and substitute in equations r_1 and r_0. Then

$$\begin{cases} r_4 = \mathbf{e}_2^2 + h_2^2\mathbf{e}_2 + h_2^2 a = 0, \\ h_2^6 r_1 = t^3 r_4 + a^2(h_2 a + h_1)d_1 = 0, \\ h_2^{12}h_1^2 r_0 = t^4 r_4^2 + h_2^6 h_1^2(h_2^2 s^2 + st^2)r_4 \\ \qquad + a^2(a^2 d_1^2 + h_2^5(h_2 a + h_1)^2 d_0 + h_2^5 h_1^2 h_0(h_2 a + h_1)d_1) = 0. \end{cases}$$

From the first and second equations of above, we have $(h_2a + h_1)d_1 = 0$, since $a \neq 0$. If $h_2a + h_1 = 0$, by the third equation, $d_1 = 0$. And if $d_1 = 0$, then $h_2a + h_1 = 0$, since $d_0 \neq 0$ (see Remark 1). So $a \in I_{SE}$.

Now, for the inverse direction, suppose $a \in I_{SE}$. Hence $(h_2a+h_1) = d_1 = 0$. We note that $h_1 \neq 0$, since $a \neq 0$. The above shows that System (4) has a solution. So F_a is reducible.

Second we assume $h_2 = 0$ and $h_1 \neq 0$. Then the leading terms of θ_a and ψ_a are respectively $h_1^2 \mathbf{b}$ and $h_1^2 ab^3$. Clearly F_a, for all $a \in \mathbb{F}_q$, is absolutely irreducible. Indeed in this case $I_{SE} = \emptyset$.

Finally we assume $h_2 = h_1 = 0$ and $h_0 \neq 0$. The leading terms of θ_a and ψ_a are respectively h_0^2 and $h_0^2 ab^2$. Suppose the polynomial $\mathbf{z} + e(\mathbf{b})$ in $\overline{\mathbb{F}}_q[\mathbf{b}, \mathbf{z}]$, where $e(\mathbf{b}) = e_1\mathbf{b} + e_0$, is a factor of F_a. We substitute $\mathbf{z}$ by e in the equation of F_a. Then we have a reminder $r_2\mathbf{b}^2 + r_1\mathbf{b} + r_0$. Then

$$\begin{cases} r_2 = & e_1^2 + h_0^2 a = 0, \\ r_1 = & h_0^2 e_1 + h_0^2 a(a^2 + f_3) = 0, \\ r_0 = & e_0^2 + h_0^2 e_0 + h_0^2(a^5 + f_4a^4 + f_3a^3 + f_2a^2 + f_1a) = 0. \end{cases}$$

We compute e_1 from the second equation and substitute in the first one. We obtain $a(a^5 + f_3^2 a + h_0^2) = 0$. So F_a is reducible if and only if $a^5 + f_3^2 a + h_0^2$, since $a \neq 0$. $\qquad \square$

Proposition 7. *The affine curve $\mathcal{X}_a$, for $a \in \mathbb{F}_q^*$, is singular if and only if $h_2 \neq 0$ and $ah_2 + h_1 = 0$.*

Proof. Suppose the affine curve $\mathcal{X}_a$, for $a \in \mathbb{F}_q^*$, is singular. Then the following system of equations has a solution in $\overline{\mathbb{F}}_q \times \overline{\mathbb{F}}_q$.

$$\begin{cases} F_a(\mathbf{b}, \mathbf{z}) = \mathbf{z}^2 + \theta_a(\mathbf{b})\mathbf{z} + \psi_a(\mathbf{b}) = 0 \\ \dfrac{\partial F_a}{\partial \mathbf{b}}(\mathbf{b}, \mathbf{z}) = \theta_a'(\mathbf{b})\mathbf{z} + \psi_a'(\mathbf{b}) = 0 \\ \dfrac{\partial F_a}{\partial \mathbf{z}}(\mathbf{b}, \mathbf{z}) = \theta_a(\mathbf{b}) = 0, \end{cases} \tag{5}$$

where θ_a' and ψ_a' are respectively the derivatives of θ_a and ψ_a with respect to $\mathbf{b}$. Then, from System (5), the following equations have a common root in $\overline{\mathbb{F}}_q$.

$$\begin{cases} \zeta_a(\mathbf{b}) = \theta_a'^2(\mathbf{b})\psi_a(\mathbf{b}) + \psi_a'^2(\mathbf{b}) = 0 \\ \theta_a(\mathbf{b}) = 0. \end{cases}$$

So the resultant of ζ_a and θ_a equals 0. Let $\mathcal{R} = \mathbf{Res}(\zeta_a, \theta_a)$. First assume $h_2 \neq 0$. Then $\mathcal{R} = a^4(ah_2 + h_1)^8 \mathcal{D}$. So $ah_2 + h_1 = 0$, since $\mathcal{D} \neq 0$. Now assume $h_2 = 0$. If $h_1 \neq 0$, then $\mathcal{R} = a^2 h_1^4 \mathcal{D}$. Hence $\mathcal{R} \neq 0$, which is a contradiction. If $h_1 = 0$ and $h_0 \neq 0$, then $\theta_a(\mathbf{b}) = h_0^2 \neq 0$. $\qquad \square$

Proposition 8. *For all* $a \in \mathbb{F}_q^*$, *we have*

$$
\left| \#\mathcal{X}_a(\mathbb{F}_q) - q \right| \leq
\begin{cases}
2\sqrt{q} + 1, & \text{if } h_2 \neq 0 \text{ and } a \notin I_{\mathrm{SE}}, \\
2\sqrt{q}, & \text{if } h_2 = 0 \text{ and } h_1 \neq 0, \\
0, & \text{if } h_2 = h_1 = 0 \text{ and } a \notin I_{\mathrm{SE}}, \\
q, & \text{if } a \in I_{\mathrm{SE}}.
\end{cases}
$$

Proof. Let $a \in \mathbb{F}_q^*$. Let $\widetilde{\mathcal{X}}_a$ be the nonsingular projective model of $\mathcal{X}_a$. First assume $h_2 \neq 0$. Suppose $a \notin I_{\mathrm{SE}}$. From Proposition 6, the affine curve $\mathcal{X}_a$ is absolutely irreducible. The projective model of $\mathcal{X}_a$ has one point at infinity which is a singular point. By means of the Newton polygon of F_a, one can see that the genus of $\widetilde{\mathcal{X}}_a$ is at most 1. If $a \neq \frac{h_1}{h_2}$, by Proposition 7, the affine curve $\mathcal{X}_a$ is nonsingular. If $a = \frac{h_1}{h_2}$, the curve $\mathcal{X}_a$ has a singular point, so the genus of $\widetilde{\mathcal{X}}_a$ equals 0. The number of $\mathbb{F}_q$-rational points on $\widetilde{\mathcal{X}}_a$, which are lying over this singular point in the resolution map, equals 1 (see e.g. see [1], Remark 3.16 and 3.18). The number of $\mathbb{F}_q$-rational points on $\widetilde{\mathcal{X}}_a$, which are lying over the point at infinity, is at most 2. Hence $\left| \#\mathcal{X}_a(\mathbb{F}_q) - \#\widetilde{\mathcal{X}}_a(\mathbb{F}_q) + 1 \right| \leq 1$. By means of Hasse-Weil's Theorem for $\widetilde{\mathcal{X}}_a$, we obtain an estimate for $\#\mathcal{X}_a(\mathbb{F}_q)$.

Second assume $h_2 = 0$ and $h_1 \neq 0$. From Propositions 6 and 7, $\mathcal{X}_a$ is an absolutely irreducible nonsingular curve. Indeed the projective model of $\mathcal{X}_a$ is an elliptic curve. Hence $|\#\mathcal{X}_a(\mathbb{F}_q) - q| \leq 2\sqrt{q}$.

Now assume $h_2 = h_1 = 0$ and $h_0 \neq 0$. Suppose $a \notin I_{\mathrm{SE}}$. Then $\mathcal{X}_a$ is an absolutely irreducible nonsingular curve (see Propositions 6 and 7). The projective model of $\mathcal{X}_a$ is a nonsingular curve of genus 0. It has one point at infinity. Hence $\#\mathcal{X}_a(\mathbb{F}_q) = q$.

If $a \in I_{\mathrm{SE}}$ the curve $\mathcal{X}_a$ is reducible. So, we just obtain a trivial bound for $\#\mathcal{X}_a(\mathbb{F}_q)$. $\qquad\square$

Proof of Theorem 1. Let $a \in \mathbb{F}_q^*$. From Propositions 4 and 5 we have

$$
\#(\mathrm{SE}^{-1}(a) \cap J_2) = \frac{\#\Sigma_a + \#\Sigma_a^\phi}{2} = \#H(\mathbb{F}_q) + \#\mathcal{X}_a(\mathbb{F}_q) - q - 1.
$$

Since $\mathrm{SE}^{-1}(a) \subset J(\mathbb{F}_q)$ and $J(\mathbb{F}_q) = J_0 \cup J_1 \cup J_2$ we can bound $\#\mathrm{SE}^{-1}(a)$ from bounds on $\#(\mathrm{SE}^{-1}(a) \cap J_1)$ and $\#(\mathrm{SE}^{-1}(a) \cap J_0)$. The latter is 0 since $a \neq 0$ while the former equals $0, 1$ or 2. Hence

$$
\left| \#\mathrm{SE}^{-1}(a) - \#H(\mathbb{F}_q) - \#\mathcal{X}_a(\mathbb{F}_q) + q \right| \leq 1.
$$

By Hasse-Weil's Theorem, we have $|\#H(\mathbb{F}_q) - q - 1| \leq 4\sqrt{q}$. Then Proposition 8 concludes the proof of Theorem 1, for all $a \in \mathbb{F}_q^*$.

If $a = 0$, then it is easy to show that $\#\mathrm{SE}^{-1}(0) = \#H(\mathbb{F}_q) + e - s$, where $e = \#\{(x, y) \in H(\mathbb{F}_q) : x = 0\}$ and $s = \#\{(x, y) \in H(\mathbb{F}_q) : h(x) = 0\}$. Hence, the proof of this theorem is completed. $\qquad\square$

6   Conclusion

In this paper we proposed the first extractors for binary hyperelliptic curves of genus 2. We gave bounds on the number of preimages for the two generators and showed that the resulting bit strings are close to uniform. We also proposed a way to construct an extractor for the main subgroup based on an extractor of the full group in order to use only the subgroup of cryptographic interest.

Acknowledgment. The author would like to thank T. Lange for her fruitful suggestions and valuable remarks on this paper. The author also thanks anonymous referees for their helpful comments.

References

1. Beelen, P., Pellikaan, R.: The Newton Polygon of Plane Curves with Many Rational Points. Designs Codes and Cryptography 21, 41–67 (2000)
2. Chevassut, O., Fouque, P., Gaudry, P., Pointcheval, D.: The Twist-AUgmented Technique for Key Exchange. In: Yung, M., Dodis, Y., Kiayias, A., Malkin, T.G. (eds.) PKC 2006. LNCS, vol. 3958, pp. 410–426. Springer, Heidelberg (2006)
3. Cohen, H., Frey, G.: Handbook of Elliptic and Hyperelliptic Curve Cryptography. Chapman & Hall/CRC, New York (2006)
4. Farashahi, R.R.: Extractors for Jacobian of Hyperelliptic Curves of Genus 2 in Odd Characteristic. In: Galbraith, S.D. (ed.) Cryptography and Coding 2007. LNCS, vol. 4887, pp. 313–335. Springer, Heidelberg (2007)
5. Farashahi, R.R., Pellikaan, R.: The Quadratic Extension Extractor for (Hyper)Elliptic Curves in Odd Characteristic. In: Carlet, C., Sunar, B. (eds.) WAIFI 2007. LNCS, vol. 4547, pp. 219–236. Springer, Heidelberg (2007)
6. Farashahi, R.R., Pellikaan, R., Sidorenko, A.: Extractors for Binary Elliptic Curves. In: Workshop on Coding and Cryptography–WCC 2007. Designs, Codes and Cryptography, pp. 127–136. Codes and Cryptography, Open access (2007), http://www.springerlink.com/content/lm35kv103x34j754
7. Gaudry, P.: An Algorithm for Solving the Discrete Log Problem on Hyperelliptic Curves. In: Preneel, B. (ed.) EUROCRYPT 2000. LNCS, vol. 1807, pp. 3419–3448. Springer, Heidelberg (2000)
8. Gaudry, P.: Fast genus 2 arithmetic based on Theta functions. J. Math. Crypt. 1, 243–265 (2007)
9. Gaudry, P., Lubicz, D.: The arithmetic of characteristic 2 Kummer surfaces (2008), http://www.loria.fr/~gaudry/tmp/c2.pdf
10. Gürel, N.: Extracting bits from coordinates of a point of an elliptic curve, Cryptology ePrint Archive, Report 2005/324 (2005), http://eprint.iacr.org/
11. Hankerson, D., Menezes, A., Vanstone, S.: Guide to Elliptic Curve Cryptography. Springer, New York (2004)
12. Hess, F., Shparlinski, I.E.: On the Linear Complexity and Multidimensional Distribution of Congruential Generators over Elliptic Curves. Designs, Codes and Cryptography 35(1), 111–117 (2005)
13. Kaliski, J.B.S.: A Pseudo-random Bit Generator Based on Elliptic Logarithms. In: Odlyzko, A.M. (ed.) CRYPTO 1986. LNCS, vol. 263, pp. 84–103. Springer, Heidelberg (1987)

14. Koblitz, N.: Hyperelliptic Cryptosystem. J. of Cryptology 1, 139–150 (1989)
15. Lange, T., Shparlinski, I.E.: Certain Exponential Sums and Random Walks on Elliptic Curves. Canad. J. Math. 57(2), 338–350 (2005)
16. Lange, T., Shparlinski, I.E.: Distribution of Some Sequences of Points on Elliptic Curves. J. Math. Crypt. 1, 1–11 (2007)
17. Lange, T., Stevens, M.: Efficient Doubling on Genus Two Curves over Binary Fields. In: Handschuh, H., Hasan, M.A. (eds.) SAC 2004. LNCS, vol. 3357, pp. 170–181. Springer, Heidelberg (2004)
18. Luby, M.: Pseudorandomness and Cryptographic Applications. Princeton University Press, USA (1994)
19. Mumford, D.: Tata Lectures on Theta II. Progress in Mathematics 43 (1984)
20. Shaltiel, R.: Recent Developments in Explicit Constructions of Extractors. Bulletin of the EATCS 77, 67–95 (2002)
21. Shparlinski, I.E.: On the Naor-Reingold Pseudo-Random Function from Elliptic Curves. Applicable Algebra in Engineering, Communication and Computing—AAECC 11(1), 27–34 (2000)
22. Trevisan, L., Vadhan, S.: Extracting Randomness from Samplable Distributions. In: IEEE Symposium on Foundations of Computer Science, pp. 32–42 (2000)

Efficient Modular Arithmetic in Adapted Modular Number System Using Lagrange Representation

Christophe Negre[1] and Thomas Plantard[2]

[1] Team DALI, University of Perpignan, France
[2] Centre for Information Security Research
School of Computer Science and Software Engineering
University of Wollongong, Australia

Abstract. In 2004, Bajard, Imbert and Plantard introduced a new system of representation to perform arithmetic modulo a prime integer p, the Adapted Modular Number System (AMNS). In this system, the elements are seen as polynomial of degree $n - 1$ with the coefficients of size $p^{1/n}$. The best method for multiplication in AMNS works only for some specific moduli p. In this paper, we propose a novel algorithm to perform the modular multiplication in the AMNS. This method works for any AMNS, and does not use a special form of the modulo p. We also present a version of this algorithm in *Lagrange Representation* which performs the polynomial multiplication part of the first algorithm efficiently using Fast Fourier Transform.

Keywords: Prime Field, Modular Multiplication, Modular Number System, Lagrange Representation.

1   Introduction

Several cryptographic applications like the Diffie-Hellman key exchange protocol [12], ECC [16,14], RSA [19] or pairing based protocol require efficient modular integer arithmetic. Specifically, for Diffie-Hellman key exchange the main operation is an exponentiation modulo a prime integer p: this operation is generally done using a chain of squaring and multiplication modulo p. For ECC, the main operation is the scalar multiplication which requires also a chain of additions and multiplications modulo a prime integer p.

The multiplication modulo p consists to multiply two integers A and B and after that to compute the remainder modulo p. The methods to perform this operation differ if the integer p has a special form or not. If p is arbitrary, the most used methods are the method of Montgomery [18] and the method of Barrett [9]. But the cost of these two methods is roughly equal to the cost of three integer multiplications.

When the integer p has a sparse binary representation [23] the reduction modulo p can be done really efficiently. This last case is, for now, the most efficient, consequently standards recommends these types of prime integer [1].

Y. Mu, W. Susilo, and J. Seberry (Eds.): ACISP 2008, LNCS 5107, pp. 463–477, 2008.

On the other hand these types of prime are rare, and it thus interesting have efficient modular arithmetic modulo any prime.

Recently Bajard, Imbert and Plantard [6] proposed a new method to perform modular arithmetic by using a new representation of the elements. An integer A modulo p is expressed as $A = \sum_{i=0}^{n-1} a_i \gamma^i$ with $\gamma^n \equiv \lambda \mod p$ with λ a very small constant. The coefficients a_i are small relatively to p and γ (roughly $|a_i| \leq \rho \cong p^{1/n}$ and $\gamma \cong p$).

In this representation the multiplication of A and B is done in two steps: the first step consists to multiply the polynomials A and B in γ modulo $\gamma^n - \lambda$, the second step consists to reduce the coefficients.

In this paper, we will present a modified version of the multiplier of [6]. The initial proposition in [6] use lookup table which can't be used for big size modulus. Our approach is similar to Montgomery's [18,3] to perform the reduction of the coefficients. We add a multiple of the moduli p to kill the lower part of the coefficients of the polynomial product $C = A \times B \mod (\gamma^n - \lambda)$.

To use Fast Fourier Transform, to perform the polynomial multiplication, we slightly modify the first algorithm, and use a Lagrange approach to perform arithmetic modulo $(\gamma^n - \lambda)$. We then obtain an algorithm with a sub-quadratic complexity.

This article is organized as follows: in the first section we will briefly recall the AMNS representation, we will present our new multiplication in AMNS representation, and we will study the construction of the *shortest polynomial* which is required in the multiplication. After that, we will recall the Lagrange representation (LR) approach [5,4] to perform polynomial modular arithmetic, and present the Lagrange form of our algorithm. We conclude by a study of its cost and by a presentation of an implementation.

2   Modular Number System

2.1   Definition

Efficient arithmetic modulo a prime integer p is generally deeply related to the system of representation used to represent the elements. Generally integers are expressed as a sum $A = \sum_{i=0}^{n} a_i \beta^i$ where $0 \leq a_i < \beta$ (in practice β is often chosen as a power of 2). Here we are interested in integer multiplication modulo a prime integer p, and specifically for p of cryptographic size $2^{160} \leq p$.

We will use a modified version of this classical representation: the *Modular Number System* [6] to represent the elements modulo p.

Definition 1 (MNS [6]). *A Modular Number System (MNS) $\mathcal{B}$, is a quadruple (p, n, γ, ρ), such that for all positive integers $0 \leq a < p$ there exists a polynomial $A(X) = \sum_{i=0}^{n-1} a_i X^i$ such that*

$$
\begin{aligned}
&A(\gamma) = a \mod p, \\
&\deg(A(X)) < n, \\
&\|A\|_\infty < \rho.
\end{aligned}
\tag{1}
$$

The polynomial $A(X)$ is a representation of a in $\mathcal{B}$.

The Modular Number System is a system of representation which includes the modulo p used in the modular arithmetic. Generally the MNS have a basis $\gamma \cong p$ and small coefficients $|a_i| < \rho \cong p^{1/n}$.

Example 1. In the table 1, we prove that the quadruplet $(17, 3, 7, 2)$ is a MNS.

Table 1. The elements of $\mathbb{Z}_{17}$ in $\mathcal{B} = MNS(17, 3, 7, 2)$

0	1	2	3	4	5
0	1	$-X^2$	$1 - X^2$	$-1 + X + X^2$	$X + X^2$

6	7	8	9	10	11
$-1 + X$	X	$1 + X$	$-X - 1$	$-X$	$-X + 1$

12	13	14	15	16
$-X - X^2$	$1 - X - X^2$	$-1 + X^2$	X^2	-1

In particular, we can verify that if we evaluate $(-1 + X + X^2)$ in γ, we have $-1 + \gamma + \gamma^2 = -1 + 7 + 49 = 55 \equiv 4 \bmod 17$. We have also $\deg(-1 + X + X^2) = 2 < 3$ and $\| -1 + X + X^2 \|_\infty = 1 < 2$.

The second definition of this section corresponds to a sub-family of the Modular Number System. We use the possibility to choose freely the basis γ to have advantageous properties for the modular arithmetic. That's why Bajard *et al.* said that these systems are adapted to the modular arithmetic: this is the *Adapted Modular Number System*.

Definition 2 (AMNS [6]). *A Modular Number System* $\mathcal{B} = (p, n, \gamma, \rho)$ *is called Adapted (AMNS) if there exists a small integer* λ *such that* $\gamma^n = \lambda \bmod p$. *We call E the polynomial* $X^n - \lambda$. *γ is a root of the polynomial E in* $\mathbb{Z}/p\mathbb{Z}$: $E(\gamma) \equiv 0 \pmod{p}$. *We also note* $(p, n, \gamma, \rho)_E$ *the Modular Number System* (p, n, γ, ρ) *which is adapted to the polynomial E.*

The difficulty in the construction of AMNS is to find an n-th roots of a fixed element λ in $\mathbb{Z}/p\mathbb{Z}$. Since p is prime the problem can be easily solved [11] (when such root exists) and in this paper we will focus on AMNS associated to p prime. If p were a composite number, for example an RSA number, the problem could be solved using the factorization of p. This means that the method presented in this paper, could be extended to multiply two integers modulo an RSA number which admits such n-th roots.

2.2 Multiplication in AMNS

As described in [6] the multiplication of two elements A and B in AMNS is done through the three following steps

1. Polynomial multiplication $C(X) = A(X) \times B(X)$.
2. Polynomial reduction $C'(X) = C(X) \mod E(X)$.
3. Coefficient reduction $R = CoeffRed(C')$: the coefficients of C' lie in the interval $]-n\rho^2\lambda, n\rho^2\lambda[$, they must be reduced such that they have absolute value smaller than ρ.

The first step can be done using usual methods: polynomial school-book, Karatsuba, or FFT methods. The second step is quite easy because of the form of E: we have only to add the lower part of C with λ times the high part of C to get C'. The last part, is for now the most complicated: in [7] Bajard, Imbert and Plantard proposed a method using look up table, the performance of such algorithm is not easy to evaluate, it depends on the size of the table, and the memory access delay.

Consequently some improvements need to be done to have efficient coefficient reduction and thus efficient multiplication in AMNS.

3   Novel AMNS Multiplication

In this section, we will present a new AMNS-multiplication algorithm. Let us fix an AMNS (p, n, γ, ρ) and $M(X)$ a polynomial such that $M(\gamma) = 0 \mod p$ and $\gcd(M, E) = 1$. As we will see later, M must be chosen in practice with small coefficients.

To perform the multiplication in the AMNS, we use a trick similar to Montgomery's method [18]. We will use the polynomial M to kill the lower part of the coefficients of the product $C = A \times B \mod E$. This method work as follows.

Algorithm 1. AMNS Multiplication (Polynomial version)

Input   : $A, B \in \mathcal{B} = AMNS(p, n, \gamma, \rho)_E$ with $E = X^n - \lambda$
Data   : M such that $M(\gamma) \equiv 0 \pmod{p}$
            an integer m and $M' = -M^{-1} \mod (E, m)$
Output: R such that $R(\gamma) = A(\gamma)B(\gamma)m^{-1} \mod p$
begin
  $\quad C \leftarrow A \times B \mod E$;
  $\quad Q \leftarrow C \times M' \mod (E, m)$;
  $\quad R \leftarrow (C + Q \times M \mod E)/m$;
end

We remark that if we take $m = 2^k$, in the third step we add some multiple of the modulo p (i.e. $Q \times M$ is a multiple of p since $Q(\gamma)M(\gamma) \equiv 0 \mod p$) to annihilate the lest significant bit of the coefficients of C in the same way as in classical Montgomery Multiplication.

Let us check that Algorithm 3 is exact: we have to verify that $R(\gamma) = A(\gamma)B(\gamma)m^{-1} \mod p$. We know that $E(\gamma) \equiv 0 \pmod{p}$ (See Definition 2), thus we have $C(\gamma) \equiv A(\gamma)B(\gamma) \mod p$. We know also that $M(\gamma) \equiv 0 \pmod{p}$ thus we have

$$C(\gamma) + Q(\gamma)M(\gamma) \equiv C(\gamma) \equiv A(\gamma)B(\gamma) \mod p$$

We now prove that the division by m is exact. This is equivalent to prove that $(C + Q \times M \bmod E) \equiv 0 \bmod m$. We have by definition that $Q \equiv Q \bmod m$ and also that $Q = C \times P \bmod E$ and that $P = -M^{-1} \bmod E$. We obtain that

$$C + Q \times M \bmod E \equiv (C + C \times (-M^{-1} \times M) \bmod E) \bmod m$$
$$\equiv (C - C \bmod E) \bmod m$$
$$\equiv 0 \bmod m$$

as required. At the end, we have $R(\gamma) \equiv A(\gamma)B(\gamma)m^{-1} \bmod p$ since an exact division (the division by m) is equal to the multiplication by an inverse modulo p. $\qquad\square$

At this step we know that the resulting polynomial R of the previous algorithm satisfies $R(\gamma) = A(\gamma)B(\gamma)m^{-1} \bmod p$, but we do not know whether it is expressed in the AMNS, i.e., when the coefficients of R are smaller than ρ. This is the goal of the following theorem.

Theorem 1. *Let $\mathcal{B} = AMNS(p, n, \gamma, \rho)_E$ an Adapted Modular Number System, M a polynomial of $\mathcal{B}$ such that $M(\gamma) \equiv 0 \pmod{p}$ and $\sigma = \|M\|_\infty$, and A, B two elements of $\mathcal{B}$, if we have ρ and an integer m such that $\rho > 2|\lambda|n\sigma$ and $m > 2|\lambda|n\rho$ then the polynomial R output by the Algorithm 3 with input $\mathcal{B}, M, m, A$ and B is in the Adapted Modular Number System $\mathcal{B}$.*

Proof. From the Definition 1, the polynomial R is in the Modular Number System $\mathcal{B} = (p, n, \gamma, \rho)_E$, if $\deg R < n$ and if $\|R\|_\infty < \rho$. The fact that $\deg R < n$ is easy to see since all the computation in the Algorithm 3 are done modulo $E = X^n - \lambda$.

Thus we have only to prove that $\|R\|_\infty < \rho$. We first have the following inequalities

$$\|R\|_\infty = \|A \times B + Q \times M \bmod E\|_\infty / m$$
$$\leq |\lambda|n(\|A\|_\infty\|B\|_\infty + \|Q\|_\infty\|M\|_\infty)/m$$
$$\leq |\lambda|n(\rho^2 + m\sigma)/m = |\lambda|n(\tfrac{\rho^2}{m} + \sigma)$$

using that $\|A\|_\infty, \|B\|_\infty \leq \rho$.

But, by hypothesis, we have $\rho > 2|\lambda|n\sigma$, $\quad m > 2|\lambda|n\rho$. Thus if we use the fact that $m > 2|\lambda|n\rho$, we obtain:

$$\|R\|_\infty < |\lambda|n(\tfrac{\rho^2}{2|\lambda|n\rho} + \sigma) \leq \tfrac{\rho}{2} + |\lambda|n\sigma.$$

And with $\rho > 2|\lambda|n\sigma$, i.e., $\sigma < \tfrac{\rho}{2|\lambda|n}$, we get the required result

$$\|R\|_\infty < \frac{\rho}{2} + |\lambda|n\frac{\rho}{2|\lambda|n} \leq \frac{\rho}{2} + \frac{\rho}{2} = \rho.$$

An important remark on the Theorem 1 is that the length of the coefficients of the representation depends on the length $\|M\|_\infty$ of the polynomial M, specifically if σ is small then ρ can be also taken small. So now we will focus on the construction of such *short polynomial M*.

3.1   The Shortest Polynomial

To construct such polynomial we will use technique provided by lattice theory. Indeed the Modular Number System has an interesting link with lattice theory. We recall the definition of Lattice.

Definition 3 (Lattice)
A lattice $\mathcal{L}$ is a discrete sub-group of $\mathbb{R}^n$, or equivalently the set of all the integral combinations of $d \leq n$ linearly independent vectors over $\mathbb{R}$.

$$\mathcal{L} = \mathbb{Z}\, \boldsymbol{b}_1 + \cdots + \mathbb{Z}\, \boldsymbol{b}_d = \{\lambda_1 \boldsymbol{b}_1 + \cdots + \lambda_d \boldsymbol{b}_d \; : \; \lambda_i \in \mathbb{Z}\}.$$

The set of vector $\boldsymbol{B} = (\boldsymbol{b}_1, \ldots, \boldsymbol{b}_d)$ is called a basis *of $\mathcal{L}$.*

The lattice associated to an MNS is a subset of the polynomials $\mathbb{Z}[X]$ of degree $n - 1$

$$\mathcal{L} = \{A \in \mathbb{Z}[X] \text{ such that } \deg A \leq n - 1 \text{ and } A(\gamma) \equiv 0 \mod p\}.$$

It is easy to check that such set form a subgroup of $\mathbb{Z}_n[X] = \{Q \in \mathbb{Z}[X] \text{ with } \deg Q \leq n - 1\} \cong \mathbb{Z}^n$. Indeed let $A, B \in \mathcal{L}$, then $A \pm B \in \mathcal{L}$ since $(A \pm B)(\gamma) \equiv A(\gamma) \pm B(\gamma) \equiv 0 \mod p$.

If we associate each polynomial in $\mathbb{Z}_n[X]$ a vector with entries in $\mathbb{Z}$, we get the following set vectors of the lattice $\mathcal{L}$

$$\boldsymbol{B} = \begin{pmatrix} p & 0\;0\;0\;\ldots 0 \\ -\gamma & 1\;0\;0\;\ldots 0 \\ -\gamma^2 & 0\;1\;0\;\ldots 0 \\ \vdots & \ddots \quad \vdots \\ -\gamma^{n-2} & 0\;0\;\ldots\;1\;0 \\ -\gamma^{n-1} & 0\;0\;\ldots\;0\;1 \end{pmatrix} \begin{array}{l} \leftarrow p \\ \leftarrow X - \gamma \\ \leftarrow X^2 - \gamma^2 \\ \vdots \\ \leftarrow X^{n-2} - \gamma^{n-2} \\ \leftarrow X^{n-1} - \gamma^{n-1} \end{array}.$$

If we define by $\mathcal{L}'$ the lattice spanned by these n vectors, we can easily note that the vectors $\boldsymbol{b} \in \boldsymbol{B}$ are clearly linearly independent and thus the dimension of $\mathcal{L}'$ (and thus of $\mathcal{L}$) is equal to n: $\mathcal{L}$ and $\mathcal{L}'$ are full dimensional lattices.

In Algorithm 3 we need a polynomial M such that $M(\gamma) \equiv 0 \mod p$ and $\|M\|_\infty$ is small. This is related to the classical problem in lattice to find the shortest vector since, $M \in \mathcal{L}'$: the best choice for M is the shortest polynomial in $\mathcal{L}'$.

Definition 4 (Shortest Polynomial). *A polynomial M is called Shortest Polynomial of a MNS $\mathcal{B} = (p, n, \gamma, \rho)$ if we have*

$$\left. \begin{array}{l} M \neq 0 \\ M(\gamma){=}0 \bmod p \\ \deg(M) < n \end{array} \right\} and \; \forall A \in \mathbb{Z}[X], \; if \; \left\{ \begin{array}{l} A \neq 0 \\ A(\gamma){=}0 \bmod p \\ \deg(A) < n \end{array} \right\} \; then \; \|M\|_\infty \leq \|A\|_\infty$$

$$(2)$$

We note σ the length of M: $\sigma = \|M\|_\infty$.

In 1896 [17], Minkowski gave a bound for the length of the shortest vector of a lattice $\mathcal{L}$ for all norm, precisely in the case of the norm $\| \cdot \|_\infty$ the shortest vector v satisfies $\|v\|_\infty \leq |\det \mathcal{L}'|^{1/d}$ if $d = \dim \mathcal{L}$.

A straightforward consequence of the Theorem of Minkowski is the following corollary which gives an upper bound on $\sigma = \|M\|_\infty$ the length of the shortest polynomial.

Corollary 1. *If the polynomial M is the Shortest Polynomial of the MNS $\mathcal{B} = (p, n, \gamma, \rho)$, we have $\|M\|_\infty \leq p^{1/n}$.*

Proof. This is trivial if we note that $\det(\mathcal{L}') = p$.

For practical application we will need to compute efficiently an approximation of the shortest polynomial M of a given AMNS (only an approximation is sufficient since we only need an M with small $\|M\|_\infty$). There is several algorithm to compute such M (cf. [20,21,13,8]), but LLL [15] might be the most efficient in our case.

In practice, in actual computers, LLL could not compute an LLL basis (and thus the M) for lattices of dimension bigger than 250. This restrict the use of AMNS to small range of n, we will discuss the consequences of this fact in Section 6.

4   Improved AMNS Multiplication

The AMNS multiplication (Algorithm 3) requires several polynomial multiplications modulo $E = X^n - \lambda$. There is different strategies to perform this operation efficiently: the polynomial multiplication can be done with classical methods (schoolbook method, Karatsuba, Toom-Cook or FFT algorithm), followed by a reduction modulo E.

Here we will study a modified version of Algorithm 3 by using a Lagrange representation of the polynomials. Our method performs the polynomial multiplication and the reduction modulo E at the same time. We begin by a brief review on Lagrange representation [5].

4.1   Lagrange Representation

The Lagrange representation represents a polynomial by its values at n points, the roots of $E = \prod_{i=1}^{n}(X - \alpha_i)$ modulo an integer m. In an arithmetic point of view, this is related to the Chinese Remainder Theorem which asserts that the following application is an isomorphism.

$$\mathbb{Z}/m\mathbb{Z}[X]/(E) \longrightarrow \mathbb{Z}/m\mathbb{Z}[X]/(X - \alpha_1) \times \cdots \times \mathbb{Z}/m\mathbb{Z}[X]/(X - \alpha_n)$$
$$A \longmapsto (A \bmod (X - \alpha_1), \ldots, A \bmod (X - \alpha_n)). \tag{3}$$

We remark that the computation of $A \bmod (X - \alpha_i)$ is simply the computation of $A(\alpha_i)$. In other words the image of $A(X)$ by the isomorphism (3) is nothing other than the multi-points evaluation of A at the roots of E.

Definition 5 (Lagrange representation). *Let $A \in \mathbb{Z}[X]$ with $\deg A < n$, and $\alpha_1, \ldots, \alpha_n$ be the n distinct roots modulo m of $E(X)$.*

$$E(X) = \prod_{i=1}^{r}(X - \alpha_i) \quad \mathrm{mod} \ m$$

If $a_i = A(\alpha_i) \mod m$ for $1 \leq i \leq k$, the Lagrange representation (LR) of $A(X)$ modulo m is defined by $\mathrm{LR}(A(X), m) = (a_1, \ldots, a_n)$.

The advantage of the LR representation to perform operations modulo E is a consequence of the Chinese Remainder Theorem. Specifically the arithmetic modulo E in classical polynomial representation can be costly if E has a high degree, in LR representation this arithmetic is decomposed into n independent arithmetic units, each does arithmetic modulo a very simple polynomial $(X - \alpha_i)$. But arithmetic modulo $(X - \alpha_i)$ is the arithmetic modulo m since the product of two degree zero polynomials is just the product modulo m of the two constant coefficients.

4.2   Improved AMNS Algorithm Using Lagrange Representation

Let us go back to the Algorithm 3 and let us see how to use Lagrange representation to perform polynomial arithmetic in each step of the algorithm.

In view to use Lagrange representation, we select two integers m_1 and m_2 such that the polynomial $E = (X^n - \lambda)$ splits in $\mathbb{Z}/m_i\mathbb{Z}[X]$

$$E = \prod_{i=1}^{n}(X - \alpha_i) \quad \mathrm{mod} \ m_1, \quad E = \prod_{i=1}^{n}(X - \alpha_i') \quad \mathrm{mod} \ m_2.$$

We can then represent the polynomials A and B in Algorithm 3 in Lagrange representation modulo m_1 and m_2.

Notation 1. *We will use in the sequel the following notation : for a polynomial A of degree $n - 1$ we will denote $\overline{A}$ the Lagrange representation in α_i modulo m_1 and $\overline{\overline{A}}$ the Lagrange representation in α_i' modulo m_2.*

In this situation we can do the following modification in the Algorithm 3:

- the computation of C in the Algorithm 3 can be done in Lagrange representation modulo m_1;
- the last step of the Algorithm 3 can be done in Lagrange representation modulo m_2, providing that $m_2 \geq 2\rho$.

We have to deal with some troubleshooting provided by this strategy. Indeed, at the end of the first step we only know $\overline{Q}$, but we do not know $\overline{\overline{Q}}$ which is required in the modified step 3 of the AMNS multiplication. So we must perform a *change of Lagrange representation* to compute $\overline{\overline{Q}}$ from $\overline{Q}$. Similarly, to get a complete multiplication algorithm, we need to know the $\overline{R}$ at the end of the AMNS multiplication to get the Lagrange representation of R modulo m_1 and m_2.

Let us call $ChangeLR$ the routine which performs the change between two Lagrange representations. We will show later how this $ChangeLR$ works. For now we can set the Lagrange version of the Algorithm 3.

Algorithm 2. Lagrange-AMNS Multiplication

Input : $\overline{A}, \overline{\overline{A}}, \overline{B}, \overline{\overline{B}}$ the Lagrange representation modulo m_1 and m_2 of A
and B

Data : $\overline{M}$ the LR representation of the shortest polynomial M,
$\overline{M'}$ the LR representation of $M' = -M^{-1} \mod E$.

Output: $\overline{R}, \overline{\overline{R}}$ such that $R \in \mathcal{B}$ and $R(\gamma) = A(\gamma)B(\gamma)m_1^{-1} \mod p$

begin

$\quad \overline{Q} \leftarrow \overline{A} \times \overline{B} \times \overline{M'}$;

$\quad \overline{\overline{Q}} \leftarrow ChangeLR_{m_1 \to m_2}(\overline{Q}))$;

$\quad \overline{\overline{R}} \leftarrow (\overline{\overline{A}} \times \overline{\overline{B}}) + \overline{\overline{Q}} \times \overline{\overline{M}}) \times m_1^{-1}$;

$\quad \overline{R} \leftarrow ChangeLR_{m_2 \to m_1}(\overline{\overline{R}})$;

end

4.3   The Change of Lagrange Representation

Let us fix A a polynomial of degree $(n-1)$ and $\overline{A}, \overline{\overline{A}}$ its Lagrange representations modulo m_1 and m_2. The basic method to perform the change of representation from $\overline{A}$ to $\overline{\overline{A}}$ consists

1. to first reconstruct the polynomial form $A(X)$ from its Lagrange representation $\overline{A}$
2. secondly, to evaluate the polynomial $A(X)$ at the root of E modulo m_2.

- We first deal with the problem to compute the Lagrange representation $\overline{A}$ from the polynomial representation of A. Recall that $E = X^n - \lambda$ split totally modulo m, thus the roots α_j of E modulo m are of the form $\alpha_j = \mu\omega^j$ where μ is an arbitrary roots of E modulo m and ω is a primitive n-th roots. To compute $A(\mu\omega^j)$ for $j = 1, \ldots, n$ we first determine

$$\widetilde{A}(X) = A(\mu X) = \sum_{i=0}^{n-1} a_i \mu^i X^i.$$

After that we get $\overline{A} = (\widetilde{A}(1), \widetilde{A}(\omega), \ldots, \widetilde{A}(\omega^{n-1})) = DFT(m, n, \widetilde{A}, \omega)$.
- For the reverse problem which consists to reconstruct the polynomial $A(X)$ from its Lagrange representation $\overline{A}$ we simply reverse the previous process:
  1. we first compute $\widetilde{A} = DFT^{-1}(m, n, \overline{A}, \omega)$,
  2. and after that $A(X) = \widetilde{A}(\mu^{-1}X) = \sum_{i=0}^{n-1} \widetilde{a}_i \mu^{-i} X^i$.

So now, by joining these two methods we get the overall algorithm to perform the change of Lagrange representation $\overline{A} \to \overline{\overline{A}}$.

Algorithm 3. ChangeLR

Input : $\overline{A}$
Output: $\overline{\overline{A}}$
$\widetilde{A} \leftarrow DFT^{-1}(m_1, n, \omega_1, \overline{A})$;
$A(X) \leftarrow A(\mu_1^{-1}X) \mod m_1$;
$\widetilde{A}(X) \leftarrow A(\mu_2 X) \mod m_2$;
$\overline{\overline{A}} \leftarrow DFT(m_2, n, \omega_2, \widetilde{A}(X))$;

Finally the change of the representation is mainly reduced to the computation of one DFT and one DFT^{-1}. This is really interesting when the integer n is a power of 2 since is in this case we can use the so-called Fast Fourier Transform which performs this efficiently. This algorithm compute the DFT using $\frac{n}{2}\log_2(n)$ multiplications modulo m and $n\log_2(n)$ additions modulo m. (see [24] for a complete presentation of this algorithm).

Example 2. In the table 2, we present an example of the Lagrange-AMNS multiplication for the prime $p = 247649$ and for the two elements A and B expressed in the AMNS

$$A = 236 + 176X - 66X^2 - 248X^3, \quad B = -199 + 122X + 73X^2 - 148X^3.$$

Table 2. Example of AMNS Multiplication

AMNS/Lagrange System
$\mathcal{B} = (p = 247649, n = 4, \gamma = 106581, \rho = 2^8)$,
$m_2 = 2^8 + 1, m_1 = 2^{12} + 1$,
$E = X^4 + 1$
$E = \prod_{i=0}^3 (X - \mu_1\omega_1^i) \mod m_2$,
$E = \prod_{i=0}^3 (X - \mu_2\omega_2^i) \mod m_1$.
$M = -8 - 5X - 17X^2 + 11X^3$
$M' \mod m_1 = 497 + 3175X + 338X^2 + 895X^3$

Entries		
	Lag.E, m_1	LagE, m_2
A	$(1548, 2454, 2767, 2369)$	$(203, 256, 213, 15)$
B	$(3419, 3148, 1430, 3498)$	$(209, 195, 187, 155)$
M		$(147, 245, 64, 26)$
M'	$(1838, 1504, 1450, 1293)$	

AMNS Multiplication
Step 1. $Q = \overline{ABM'} = (2384, 2371, 1252, 1591)$
Step 2. $\overline{\overline{Q}} = ChangeLR_{m_1 \to m_2}(\overline{Q}) = (23, 176, 248, 182)$
Step 3. $\overline{R} = (\overline{AB} + \overline{QM})m_1^{-1} = (13, 51, 210, 232)$
Step 4. $\overline{\overline{Q}} = ChangeLR_{m_2 \to m_1}(\overline{R}) = (3454, 1159, 2560, 1013)$

To verify that the result is exact, we have to build the polynomial form $R = -2 - 8X - 17X^2 + 9X^3$ and then we can easily check that $R(\gamma) = ABm_1^{-1}$ mod $p = 114760$.

See [7], for other needed operations in a AMNS.

5   Complexity Evaluation and Comparison

Let us now evaluate the cost of AMNS multiplication in Lagrange Representation. We evaluate the cost of the algorithm in term of the number of additions and multiplications modulo m_1 and m_2. We assume that that m_1 and m_2 have the same size (generally m_1 is bigger since $m_1 \geq 2\lambda\rho$ and $m_2 \geq 2\rho$). Consequently an operation modulo m_1 and m_2 is assumed to have the same cost. In the table below we give the cost of each step of the Lagrange AMNS multiplication and the cost of the overall algorithm, in the case n is a power of 2 and FFT is used in the $ChangeLR$ routine.

Table 3. Complexity of basic operations

Computation	# Multiplications	# Additions
$\overline{ABM'}$	n	0
$ChangeLR_{m_1 \to m_2}(\overline{Q})$	$n\log_2(n) + 2(n-1)$	$2n\log_2(n)$
$(\overline{AB} + \overline{QM})m_1^{-1}$	$3n$	n
$ChangeLR_{m_2 \to m_1}(\overline{Q})$	$n\log_2(n) + 2(n-1)$	$2n\log_2(n)$
Total	$2n\log_2(n) + 6n - 2$	$4n\log_2(n) + n$

Let us briefly compare our scheme with a strategy *Montgomery Multiplication using Schönage-Strassen for integer multiplication*, which seems to be the best strategy for large integer arithmetic. Recall that Montgomery algorithm has a cost of 3 integer multiplications of size $\cong p$.

In Schönage-Strassen [22] integer a are expressed in the first step of the recursive algorithm as $a = \sum_{i=0}^{n-1} a_i X^i$ where $n \cong \log_2(p)/2$ and $a_i \leq p^{1/n}$.

Interpolation using FFT modulo an integer $m \cong p^{2/n}$ is done to compute ab mod $X^{2n} - 1$. Thus each integer multiplication requires $3FFT$ (counting only the first step of the recursion) at $2n$ points with a modulo m with size $p^{2/n}$.

Consequently: we have $9FFT$ in $2n$ points computations at for the overall Montgomery algorithm, with coefficients size $p^{2/n}$ in FFT compared to $4FFT$ in n points with coefficient size $p^{1/n}$ for AMNS.

We must mention that in Schönage-Strassen products with roots of unity in the FFT has a cost of one addition because of the choice of m, but such strategy could also be also applied in AMNS.

6   Practical Aspects and Implementation

Let us discuss some troubleshouting which can appear in the implementation of AMNS-Lagrange multiplication.

First of all, due to the discussion on the construction of M in Section 2, and the fact that n must be a power of 2 to have efficient *ChangeRep*, n must be taken be taken in the set $\{2, 4, 8, 16, 32, 64, 128\}$.

For these special values of n, we prove that we can always find for any prime p a integer γ which is a root of a polynomial $X^n - \lambda$ modulo p with λ not too big (see Lemma 1)

Lemma 1. *Let m be an odd integer, and n an integer such that there exits an integer $k > 0$ with $n = 2^k$, there exists a polynomial $X^n - \lambda$ such that:*

i) $X^n - \lambda$ *is irreducible in $\mathbb{Z}$*
ii) there exist a root γ of $X^n - \lambda$ in $\mathbb{Z}/m\mathbb{Z}$
iii) $|\lambda| \leq 2^{\frac{n}{2}}$

Proof. Let be g a generator of the group of the invertible of $\mathbb{Z}/p\mathbb{Z}$ and $\phi(p)$ be the length of this group.

We decompose $\phi(p)$ with a positive integer k_1 and an odd integer p_1 such that $\phi(p) = 2^{k_1} p_1$.

2 is invertible in $\mathbb{Z}/p\mathbb{Z}$, so there exist an integer i such that $g^{i \bmod \phi(p)} = 2 \bmod p$. We decompose i with an positive integer k_2 and an odd integer p_2 such that $i = 2^{k_2} p_2$.

p is odd, so we have $\phi(p)$ even ($k_1 \geq 1$). We also know that $g^{2^{k_1-1} p_1} = -1 \bmod p$.

We have now four case:

1. If $k < k_1$, we choose $\lambda = -1$ and $\gamma = g^x$ with $x = 2^{k_1-1-k} p_1$ and we have
   i) $X^n + 1$ is irreducible in $\mathbb{Z}$
   ii) $\gamma^n = g^{xn} = g^{2^{k_1-1-k} p_1 2^k} = g^{2^{k_1-1} p_1} = -1 \bmod p$
   iii) $|\lambda| = 1 < 2^{\frac{n}{2}}$
   We can easily verify that x is an integer.

2. If $k \leq k_2$, we choose $\lambda = 2$ and $\gamma = g^x$ $x = 2^{k_2-k} p_2$, then we have
   i) $X^n - 2$ is irreducible in $\mathbb{Z}$
   ii) $\gamma^n = g^{xn} = g^{2^{k_2-k} p_2 2^k} = g^{2^{k_2} p_2} = \lambda \bmod p$
   iii) $|\lambda| = 2 \leq 2^{\frac{n}{2}}$
   We can easily verify that x is an integer.

3. If $k > k_2 \geq k_1$, we choose $\lambda = 2$ and $\gamma = g^x$ with $x = \frac{2^{k_2-k_1} p_2 + y p_1}{2^{k_1-k}}$ with $y = -2^{k_2-k_1} p_2 p_1^{-1} \bmod 2^{k-k_1}$
   i) $X^n - 2$ is irreducible in $\mathbb{Z}$
   ii) $\gamma^n = g^{xn} = g^{(2^{k_2-k_1} p_2 + y p_1) 2^{k_1-k} 2^k} = g^{2^{k_2} p_2 + y p_1 2^{k_1}} = 2$
   iii) $|\lambda| = 2 \leq 2^{\frac{n}{2}}$

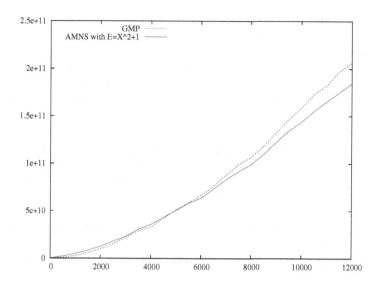

Fig. 1. Comparison between GMP's modular multiplication and Algorithm 2 with $E = X^2 + 1$

We verify that x is an integer, that s the case if $2^{k_2-k}p_2 + yp_1 2^{k_1-k}$ can be divide by 2^{k-k_1}.

$$2^{k_2-k}p_2 + yp_1 2^{k_1-k} \equiv (2^{k_2-k_1}p_2 + (-2^{k_2-k_1}p_2 p_1^{-1} \bmod 2^{k-k_1})p_1) \bmod 2^{k-k_1}$$
$$\equiv 2^{k_2-k_1}p_2 - 2^{k_2-k_1}p_2 p_1^{-1}p_1) \bmod 2^{k-k_1}$$
$$\equiv 2^{k_2-k_1}p_2 - 2^{k_2-k_1}p_2) \bmod 2^{k-k_1}$$
$$\equiv 0 \bmod 2^{k-k_1}$$

4. If $k \geq k_1 > k_2$ then we choose $\lambda = -2^{2^{k_1-k_2-1}}$ and $\gamma = g^x$ with $x = \frac{\frac{p_1+p_2}{2}+yp_1}{2^{k_1-k}}$ with $y = -\frac{p_1+p_2}{2}p_1^{-1} \bmod 2^{k-k_1}$

  i) $X^n + 2^{2^{k_1-k_2}}$ is irreducible in $\mathbb{Z}$

  ii) $\gamma^n = g^{xn} = g^{(\frac{p_1+p_2}{2}+yp_1)2^{k_1-k}2^k} = g^{(p_1+p_2)2^{k_1-1}+yp_1 2^k_1}$
  $= g^{(p_1 2^{k_1-1}+p_2 2^{k_1-1}+y\phi(p))} = -g^{p_2 2^{k_1-1}} = -g^{p_2 2^{k_2+k_1-k_2-1}} = -2^{2^{k_1-k_2-1}}$

  iii) $|\lambda| = 2^{2^{k_1-k_2-1}} \leq 2^{2^{k-1}} \leq 2^{\frac{n}{2}}$

We verify that x is an integer, that's the case if $\frac{p_1+p_2}{2} + yp_1$ is divisible by 2^{k-k_1}

$$\frac{p_1+p_2}{2} + yp_1 \equiv \frac{p_1+p_2}{2} + yp_1 \bmod 2^{k-k_1}$$
$$\equiv \frac{p_1+p_2}{2} + (-\frac{p_1+p_2}{2}p_1^{-1})p_1 \bmod 2^{k-k_1}$$
$$\equiv \frac{p_1+p_2}{2} - \frac{p_1+p_2}{2} \bmod 2^{k-k_1}$$
$$\equiv 0 \bmod 2^{k-k_1} \qquad\qquad \square$$

So, we can construct AMNS for all prime with good conditions on n and λ.

There is an alternative strategy on the drawback due to the restriction of the size of n : in AMNS-Lagrange multiplication if m_1 and m_2 are Fermat number, we can use Schönage-Strassen [10] method to perform arithmetic modulo m_1 and m_2, and keep the advantageous of the method.

Let us now present a result on the implementation of AMNS-LR multiplication. Figure 1 give the time in function of the modulus size of an implementation of Algorithm 2 in the special case $n = 2$ and $\lambda = -1$ on a Pentium 4, 2 GHz. The case $n = 2$ and $\lambda = -1$ is an interesting case, since AMNS can be constructed for prime p when $p - 1$ is divisible by 4 (this is the case for 50% of prime p).

We compare this implementation of Algorithm 2 with GMP 4.2.1 [2] modular multiplication. For GMP, we use the modular multiplication of the modular exponentiation, to have its best one. Our implementation use also GMP [2] tools to construct AMNS-Lagrange system, and to perform the multiplication itself. Our code, could be highly optimized, for example, by using astuciously the fact that m_1 and m_2 are Fermat numbers.

We can see that even if we don't use the advantageous form of Fermat moduli, Algorithm 2 begin to be faster when p have a size around 5000 bits. We expect that we could get better result with bigger n, since the complexity decrease with n.

7   Conclusion

In this paper we have presented a novel algorithm to perform integer modular arithmetic. Primarily, we gave a polynomial formulation of our algorithm which uses the AMNS [6] representation of integer and a Montgomery-like method to reduce the coefficients. Secondly we modify this algorithm in view to use a Lagrange representation to speed-up the polynomial multiplication part of the algorithm. From practical implementation, we expect that it should improve classical algorithm (Montgomery, Barrett) to perform modular multiplication modulo arbitrary for prime p of size several thousand bits.

References

1. FIPS PUB 197: Advanced Encryption Standard (AES). FIPS PUB. NIST (2001)
2. The GNU Multiple Precision arithmetic librairy (May 2006)
3. Bajard, J.-C., Didier, L.-S., Kornerup, P.: An RNS Montgomery modular multiplication algorithm. IEEE Transactions on Computers 47, 766–776 (1998)
4. Bajard, J.-C., Imbert, L., Nègre, C.: Arithmetic operations in finite fields of medium prime characteristic using the lagrange representation. IEEE Trans. Computers 55(9), 1167–1177 (2006)
5. Bajard, J.-C., Imbert, L., Negre, C., Plantard, T.: Efficient multiplication in gf(p^k) for elliptic curve cryptography. In: ARITH'16: IEEE Symposium on Computer Arithmetic, June 2003, pp. 181–187 (2003)
6. Bajard, J.-C., Imbert, L., Plantard, T.: Modular Number Systems: Beyond the Mersenne Family. In: Handschuh, H., Hasan, M.A. (eds.) SAC 2004. LNCS, vol. 3357, pp. 159–169. Springer, Heidelberg (2004)
7. Bajard, J.-C., Imbert, L., Plantard, T.: Arithmetic operations in the polynomial modular number system. In: ARITH'17: IEEE Symposium on Computer Arithmetic (June 2005)

8. Banihashemi, A.H., Khandani, A.K.: On the complexity of decoding lattices using the Korkin-Zolotarev reduced basis. IEEE Transactions on Information Theory 44(1), 162–171 (1998)
9. Barrett, P.: Implementing the Rivest Shamir and Adleman Public Key Encryption Algorithm on a Standard Digital Signal Processor. In: Odlyzko, A.M. (ed.) CRYPTO 1986. LNCS, vol. 263, pp. 311–323. Springer, Heidelberg (1987)
10. Brassard, G., Monet, S., Zuffellato, D.: Algorithms for very large integer arithmetic. Tech. Sci. Inf. 5(2), 89–102 (1986)
11. Cohen, H.: A course in computational algebraic number theory. In: Grad. Texts Math, vol. 138, Springer, Heidelberg (1993)
12. Diffie, W., Hellman, M.E.: New directions in cryptography. IEEE Trans. on Inf. Theory IT-22(6), 644–654 (1976)
13. Kannan, R.: Minkowski's convex body theorem and integer programming. Math. Oper. Res. 12(3), 415–440 (1987)
14. Koblitz, N.: Elliptic curve cryptosystems. Mathematics of Computation 48(177), 203–209 (1987)
15. Lenstra, A.K., Lenstra, H.W., Lovász, L.: Factoring polynomials with rational coefficients. In: Mathematische Annalen, vol. 261, pp. 513–534. Springer, Heidelberg (1982)
16. Miller, V.: Use of Elliptic Curves in Cryptography. In: Williams, H.C. (ed.) CRYPTO 1985. LNCS, vol. 218, pp. 417–426. Springer, Heidelberg (1986)
17. Minkowski, H.: Geometrie der Zahlen. In: Teubner, B.G. (ed.) Leipzig (1896)
18. Montgomery, P.L.: Modular multiplication without trial division. Mathematics of Computation 44(170), 519–521 (1985)
19. Rivest, R., Shamir, A., Adleman, L.: A method for obtaining digital signatures and public-key cryptosystems. Com. of the ACM 21(2), 120–126 (1978)
20. Schnorr, C.-P.: Block Korkin-Zolotarev bases and successive minima (1996)
21. Schnorr, C.-P.: Fast LLL-type lattice reduction. Information and Computation 204(1), 1–25 (2006)
22. Schonhage, A., Strassen, V.: Schnelle multiplikation grosser zahlen. Computing 7, 281–292 (1971)
23. Solinas, J.: Generalized Mersenne numbers. Research Report CORR-99-39, Center for Applied Cryptographic Research, University of Waterloo, Canada (1999)
24. von zur Gathen, J., Gerhard, J.: Modern Computer Algebra. Cambridge University Press, Cambridge (2003)

Author Index